Lecture Notes in Computer Science   8868

Commenced Publication in 1973
Founding and Former Series Editors:
Gerhard Goos, Juris Hartmanis, and Jan van Leeuwen

T0212745

Leandro Pecchia   Liming Luke Chen
Chris Nugent   José Bravo (Eds.)

Ambient Assisted Living and Daily Activities

6th International Work-Conference, IWAAL 2014
Belfast, UK, December 2-5, 2014
Proceedings

 Springer

Volume Editors

Leandro Pecchia
University of Warwick, School of Engineering
Coventry CV4 7AL, UK
E-mail: l.pecchia@warwick.ac.uk

Liming Luke Chen
De Montfort University, School of Computer Science and Informatics
The Gateway, Leicester LE1 9BH, UK
E-mail: liming.chen@dmu.ac.uk

Chris Nugent
University of Ulster, Computer Science Research Institute
School of Computing and Mathematics, Jordanstown Campus
Shore Road, Newtownabbey BT37 0QB, UK
E-mail: cd.nugent@ulster.ac.uk

José Bravo
Castilla-La Mancha University, Escuela Superior de Informática
Paseo de la Universidad 4, 13071 Ciudad Real, Spain
E-mail: jose.bravo@uclm.es

ISSN 0302-9743   e-ISSN 1611-3349
ISBN 978-3-319-13104-7   e-ISBN 978-3-319-13105-4
DOI 10.1007/978-3-319-13105-4
Springer Cham Heidelberg New York Dordrecht London

Library of Congress Control Number: 2014953277

LNCS Sublibrary: SL 3 – Information Systems and Application, incl. Internet/Web
and HCI

Typesetting: Camera-ready by author, data conversion by Scientific Publishing Services, Chennai, India

Printed on acid-free paper

Springer is part of Springer Science+Business Media (www.springer.com)

Preface

This volume contains the works presented at the 6th International Work-Conference on Ambient Assisted Living (IWAAL 2014) held in Belfast during December 2–5, 2014. This event was established in 2009, inspired by the European Union's Ambient Assisted Living Joint Program (AAL JP). The ageing of the population has immense impact on national healthcare systems throughout all developed countries in relation to the increasing burdens being placed on the provision of health and social care. Predictions have estimated that by 2020 around one quarter of the European population will be over 65. This will make healthcare systems almost unable to sustain adequate delivery of care provision unless new models of care, prevention, and social integration are introduced. The AAL JP has a core strategy to support the development of solutions to improve the delivery of care and increase levels of independence for an ageing population.

Information and communication technologies provide a way toward a new paradigm of advanced systems aimed at both preventing and managing long-term healthcare conditions in addition to de-hospitalizing care provision. The interest of healthcare stakeholders is continuously growing around such technological solutions that help address the impact of the ageing of the population. As a result, Ambient Assisted Living (AAL) is becoming a well-recognized domain. AAL relates to the use of ICT technologies and services in both daily living and working environments aiming to help inhabitants by preventing health conditions and improving wellness, in addition to assisting with daily activities, promotion of staying active, remaining socially connected and of living independently.

The theme of this year's event was "Ambient Assisted Living and Daily Activities." This year, once again, IWAAL collected a remarkable set of scientific works reporting new methods, methodologies, algorithms, and tools specifically devised to address AAL research challenges. In addition, a variety of assistive applications that harness the benefits of sensing technologies, human–computer interaction, and ambient intelligence were included.

Moreover, some valuable case studies and trials in which healthcare technologies for AAL have been tested to prove their cost-effectiveness were collected. This reflects the growing awareness that one of the problems blocking the adoption of AAL in every-day practice is the lack of well-designed Health Technology Assessment (HTA) studies capable of assessing the real impact of AAL on healthcare systems and society as a whole. Taking this into consideration, for the first time, a special session on "HTA of Healthcare Telematics" was organized during IWAAL in collaboration with the HTA Division of the International Federation of Medical and Biological Engineering (IFMBE). These contributions are also included in these proceedings.

The review process of the material submitted was supported by over 70 members from an international Program Committee. This included members from the following countries in Europe: Czech Republic, the UK, Spain, Italy, Austria, Belgium, England, Germany, The Netherlands, France, and Cyprus; it was further supported by members from the USA, Canada, Mexico, Chile, Panama, and Costa Rica. Each paper was allocated up to three reviewers and the final decision was made in consultation with the workshop co-chairs.

In the present edition, 62 papers were submitted with an acceptance rate of 51%. The final set of papers represents a truly international perspective of research with authors from countries including: Argentina, Australia, Austria, Canada, Chile, Costa Rica, Croatia, Cyprus, Finland, Germany, Greece, Iran, Italy, Japan, Korea, Mexico, The Netherlands, Norway, Panama, Portugal, Spain, Sweden, UK, and USA.

To conclude, we wish to thank all authors for their contributions and the members of the Program Committee for their time and effort for reviewing and for helping us to realize a top-quality conference and to produce this volume.

December 2014

Leandro Pecchia
Liming Luke Chen
Chris Nugent
José Bravo

Organization

General Chairs

José Bravo   Castilla-La Mancha University, Spain
Chris Nugent   University of Ulster, UK

IWAAL PC Chairs

Leandro Pecchia   University of Warwick, UK
Luke Chen   De Montfort University, UK

HTA PC Chairs

Nicolas Pallikarakis   University of Patras, Greece
Ratko Magjarevic   University of Zagreb, Croatia
Fabio De Felice   University of Cassino, Italy
Leandro Pecchia   University of Warwick, UK

WAGER PC Chairs

Antonio Fernández-Caballero   Castilla-La Mancha University, Spain
Pascual González   Castilla-La Mancha University, Spain
Elena Navarro   Castilla-La Mancha University, Spain

Publicity Chairs

Vladimir Villarreal   Technological University of Panama, Panama
Jesús Fontecha Diezma   Castilla-La Mancha University, Spain

Local Organizing Chair

Ian Cleland   University of Ulster, UK

Organizing Committee

Jesús Fontecha, Spain   Mark Beattie, UK
Tania Mondéjar, Spain   Colin Shewell, UK
Vladimir Villarreal, Panama   Joseph Rafferty, UK
Gabriel Urzáiz, Mexico   Philip Hartin, UK
Iván González, Spain   Andrew Ennis, UK

Web Masters

Kyle Boyd	University of Ulster, UK
Mark Beattie	University of Ulster, UK

Program Committee

Bessam Abdulrazak	Université de Sherbrooke, Canada
Xavier Alamán	Autonomous University of Madrid, Spain
Mariano Alcañiz	UPV - i3bh/LabHuman, Spain
Rosa Arriaga	Georgia Institute of Technology, USA
Danilo Avola	Sapienza University of Roma
Emilia I. Barakova	Technical University of Eindhoven, The Netherlands
José Barbosa	Universidad Particular de Loja, Ecuador
Nadia Bianchi-Berthouze	University College London, UK
José Bravo	Castilla-La Mancha University, Spain
Giorgio Carpino	DIBET University of Naples Federico II, Italy
Luis Carriço	University of Lisbon, Portugal
José Carlos Castillo	Universidad Carlos III de Madrid, Spain
Álvaro Castro González	Universidad Carlos III de Madrid, Spain
Filippo Cavallo	Scuola Superiore Sant' Anna, Italy
Marco Ceccarelli	University of Cassino, Italy
Liming Luke Chen	De Montfort University, UK
Ian Cleland	University of Ulster, UK
Antonio Coronato	ICAR-CNR, Italy
Michael Craven	NHS, USA
Fabio De Felice	Università degli Studi di Cassino, Italy
Félix de La Paz	UNED, Spain
Fernando De La Torre	Carnegie Mellon University, USA
Clarence W. de Silva	The University of British Columbia, Canada
Giuseppe Depietro	ICAR - CNR (Italian National Council of Research), Italy
Julie Doyle	Dundalk Institute of Technology
Rachael Dutton	Accord Group, UK
Jesus Favela	CICESE, Mexico
Antonio Fernández-Caballero	Castilla-La Mancha University, Spain
Giuseppe Fico	Polytechnic University of Madrid, Spain
Antonio Fratini	Aston University, UK
Pascual González	Castilla-La Mancha University, Spain
Terje Grimstad	Karde AS, Norway
Luis Guerrero	Universidad de Chile, Chile

Sylvie Ratté	École de Technologie Supérieure, Canada
Marcela Rodriguez	UABC, Mexico
Albert Ali Salah	Boğaziçi University, Turkey
Miguel Angel Salichs	Universidad Carlos III de Madrid, Spain
Enzo Pasquale Scilingo	University of Pisa, Italy
François Siewe	De Monfort University, UK
S. Shyam Sundar	The Pennsylvania State University, USA
Jonathan Synnott	University of Ulster, UK
Monica Tentori	CICESE, USA
Gabriel Urzaiz	Universidad Anahuac Mayab, Mexico
Carmela Vanzanella	Italian National Research Council, CNR, Italy
Vladimir Villarreal	Technological University of Panama, Panama
Andreas Voss	University of Applied Sciences Jena, Germany
José Ramón Álvarez	UNED, Spain

Additional Reviewers

Jonathan Synnott (UK)	Michael Craven (UK)
Timothy Patterson (UK)	Giuseppe Fico, (Spain)
Alberto Calzada (UK)	Giorgio Carpino (Italy)
Ian Cleland (UK)	Jseús Fontecha (Spain)
Phillip Hartin (UK)	Iván González (Spain)

Table of Contents

ADL Detection, Recognition, Classification

Behavioural Changes, Coaching and Education

AAL Design and Technical Evaluation

Expression, Mood and Speech Recognition

Health Monitoring, Risk Prediction and Assessment

Localization

User Preferences, Usability, AAL Acceptance and Adoption

Workshop on User and Ambient Adaptive Gerontechnologies (WAGER)

Special Session: Health Technology Assessment (HTA) of Healthcare Telematics

X-Factor HMMs for Detecting Falls
in the Absence of Fall-Specific Training Data

Shehroz S. Khan[1], Michelle E. Karg[1,2,3], Dana Kulić[1,2,3], and Jesse Hoey[1,3]

[1] David R. Cheriton School of Computer Science
[2] Department of Electrical and Computer Engineering,
University of Waterloo, Canada
[3] Toronto Rehabilitation Institute, Canada
{s255khan,mekarg,dkulic,jhoey}@uwaterloo.ca

Abstract. Detection of falls is very important from a health and safety perspective. However, falls occur rarely and infrequently, which leads to either limited or no training data and thus can severely impair the performance of supervised activity recognition algorithms. In this paper, we address the problem of identification of falls in the absence of training data for falls, but with abundant training data for normal activities. We propose two 'X-Factor' Hidden Markov Model (XHMMs) approaches that are like normal HMMs, but have "inflated" output covariances (observation models), which can be estimated using cross-validation on the set of 'outliers' in the normal data that serve as proxies for the (unseen) fall data. This allows the XHMMs to be learned from only normal activity data. We tested the proposed XHMM approaches on two real activity recognition datasets that show high detection rates for falls in the absence of training data.

Keywords: Fall Detection, Hidden Markov Models, X-Factor, Outlier Detection.

1 Introduction

Detection of falls is important because it can have direct implications on the health and safety of an individual. However, falls occurs rarely, infrequently and unexpectedly w.r.t. other normal Activities of Daily Living (ADL) and this leads to either little or no training data [9], which makes it very difficult to learn generalized fall detection classifiers due to the skewed class distributions. A typical supervised activity recognition system may not be very useful as a fall may not have occurred earlier. An alternative strategy is to build fall detection specific classifiers [5] that assume sufficient training data for falls, which is hard to obtain in practice. Another challenge is the data collection for falls, as it may require a person to actually undergo falling which may be harmful, ethically questionable, and cumbersome. The research question we address in this paper is: *Can we recognise falls by observing only normal ADL with no training data for the falls in a person independent manner?* To tackle this problem, we present two Hidden Markov model (HMM) based sequence classification approaches for detecting short-term fall events. The first method models individual activities by separate HMMs and an alternative HMM is constructed whose model parameters are averages of normal activity models, while the averaged covariance matrix is artificially "inflated"

L. Pecchia et al. (Eds.): IWAAL 2014, LNCS 8868, pp. 1–9, 2014.

to model falls. In the second method, all the normal activities are grouped together and modelled with a common HMM and an alternative HMM is constructed to model falls with a covariance matrix "inflated" w.r.t the normal model. The inflation parameters of the proposed approaches are estimated using a novel cross-validation approach in which the outliers in the normal data are used as proxies for the (unseen) fall data.

In Section 2, we discuss the related research work, and the proposed HMM based approaches for fall detection in Section 3 and 4. Experimental results are presented in Section 5, followed by conclusions in Section 6.

2   Related Work

Several research works in fall detection are based on thresholding techniques [2], wherein raw or transformed sensor data is compared against a single or multiple pre-defined thresholds. A two-layer HMM approach, *SensFall* [13], is used to identify falls from other normal activities. In the first layer, the HMM classifies an unknown activity as normal vertical activity or "other", while in second stage the "other" activity is classified as either normal horizontal activity or as a fall. Chen et al. [4] present a fall detection algorithm that uses accelerometer data from a smartphone. A HMM is employed to filter out noisy data, One-class Support Vector Machines (OSVM) is applied to reduce false positives, followed by a posture analysis to reduce false negatives. Honda et al. [8] present an approach detecting nearly fall incidents of pedestrians in outdoor situations. They use Wii and Wii motion plus sensors and collected data for both normal activities and nearly fall incidents and use a SVM classifier for their identification. Zhang et al. [25] trained an OSVM from positive samples (falls) and outliers (non-fall ADL) and show that falls can be detected effectively. Yu et al. [24] propose to train Fuzzy OSVM on fall activity captured using video cameras and tuned parameters using both fall and non-fall activities. Their method assigns fuzzy membership to different training samples to reflect their importance during classification and is shown to perform better than OSVM. Shi et al. [19] use standard HMMs to model several normal activities including falls and perform classification with high accuracy from inertial sensors. Tong et al. [22] uses the accelerometer time series from human fall sequences and a HMM is trained on events just before the collision for early fall prediction. They also compute two thresholds for fall prediction and detection to tune the accuracy. Thome et al. [20] present a Hierarchical HMM (HHMM) approach for fall detection in video sequences. The HHMM's first layer has two states, an upright standing pose and lying. They study the relationship between angles in the 3D world and their projection onto the image plane and derive an error angle introduced by the image formation process for a standing posture. Based on this information, they differentiate other poses as 'non-standing' and thus falls can be identified from other motions.

The research works mentioned above assume that sufficient 'fall' data is available for training, which is hard to obtain in practice. Learning with few 'fall' samples has the disadvantage that it can underfit the results and may not produce generalized classifiers that work across people. To overcome the need for a sufficient set of representative 'fall' samples while learning, we propose two 'X-Factor' HMM based approaches that can identify falls across different people while learning only on data from normal activities.

3   Proposed Fall Detection Approaches

3.1   Threshold Based Detection – $HMM1_{out}$ and $HMM2_{out}$

The traditional way to detect unseen abnormal activities is to model each normal activity using an HMM, compare the likelihood of a test sequence with each of the trained models and if it is below a pre-defined threshold then identify it as an anomalous activity (we call this method as $HMM1_{out}$) [12, 21]. In respect to fall detection, this method can be described as follows: Each normal activity i is independently modelled by an ergodic HMM which evolves through a number of k states. The observations $o_j(t)$ in state j are modelled by a single Gaussian distribution. Each model i is described by the set of parameters, $\lambda_i = \{\pi_i, A_i, (\mu_{ij}, \Sigma_{ij})\}$, where π_i is the prior, A_i is the transition matrix, and μ_{ij} and Σ_{ij} are the mean and covariance matrix, respectively, of a single Gaussian distribution, $\mathcal{N}(\mu_{ij}, \Sigma_{ij})$, giving the observation probability $P(o_j|j)$ for the jth HMM state. The parameters, λ_i, of a given HMM are trained by the Baum-Welch (BW) algorithm [18]. This method estimates the probability that an observed sequence has been generated by each of the n_i models of normal activities. If this probability falls below a (pre-defined) threshold T_i for each HMM, a fall is detected ($HMM1_{out}$).

Another common method to detect anomalous activities is to model all the normal activities by a common HMM instead of modelling them separately. The idea is to learn the 'normal concept' from the labelled data itself. The parameters of this combined HMM are $\lambda_{normal} = \{\pi, A, (\mu_j, \Sigma_j)\}$. This method estimates the probability that the observed sequence has been generated by this common model and if this probability falls below a (pre-defined) threshold T, a fall is detected ($HMM2_{out}$) [10].

3.2   Approach I - (XHMM1)

The 'X-factor' approach [17] deals with unmodelled variation from the normal events that may not have been seen previously by inflating the system noise covariance of the normal dynamics to determine the regions with highest likelihood which are far away from normality based on which events can be classified as 'not normal'. We extend this idea by constructing an alternate HMM to model unseen fall activity, which has the same number of states as the other n_i models for normal activities (each normal activity is modelled with same number of states). The parameters of this alternate HMM is obtained by averaging the parameters of n_i HMMs and increasing the averaged covariances by a factor of ξ such that each state's covariance matrix is expanded. Thus, the parameters of the X-Factor HMM will be $\lambda_{XHMM1} = \{\bar{\pi}, \bar{A}, \bar{\mu}, \xi\bar{\Sigma})\}$, where $\bar{\pi}, \bar{A}, \bar{\mu}$, and $\bar{\Sigma}$ are the average of the parameters π_i, A_i, μ_i and Σ_i of each n_i HMMs. The value of ξ is computed using cross validation.

3.3   Approach II - (XHMM2)

Similar to $XHMM1$, an alternative HMM is constructed to model the unseen 'fall' activities ($XHMM2$) whose parameters remain the same as the HMM to model normal activities (λ_{normal}) except for the inflated covariance, and is given by, $\lambda_{XHMM2} = \{\pi, A, (\mu_j, \xi\Sigma_j)\}$. The parameter ξ is computed using cross validation.

4   Threshold Selection and Proxy Outliers

Our goal is to train both the XHMMs and threshold based HMMs using only "normal" data (activity sequences that are not falls, see Figure 2). Typically, this is done by setting a threshold on the likelihood of the data given an HMM trained on this "normal" data. This threshold is normally chosen as the maximum of negative log-likelihood [10], and can be interpreted as a slider between raising false alarms or risking miss alarms [21]. However, any abnormal sensor reading or mislabelling of training data can alter this threshold and adversely effect the classification performance.

We propose to use outliers from the "normal" data to set thresholds. The idea is that, even though the "normal" data may not contain any falls, it will contain sensor readings that are spurious, incorrectly labelled or significantly different. These outliers can be used to set the thresholds that are required for fall detection, thereby serving as a proxy for the fall data in order to learn the parameters of the (X)HMMs. To find the outliers, we use the concept of quartiles from descriptive statistics. The quartiles of a ranked set of data values are the three points that divide the data set into four equal groups, where each group comprises of a quarter of the data. Given the log-likelihoods of sequences of training data for a HMM and the lower quartile (Q_1), the upper quartile (Q_3) and the inter-quartile range ($IQR = Q_3 - Q_1$), a point P is qualified as an outlier if

$$P > Q_3 + w \times IQR \quad || \quad P < Q_1 - w \times IQR \tag{1}$$

where w represents the percentage of data points that are within the non-extreme limits. Figure 1 (a) shows the log-likelihood $\log P(O|\lambda_{running})$ for 1262 equal length (1.28s) running activity sequences. Figure 1 (b) is a box plot showing the quartiles for this dataset, and the outliers (shown as +) for $w = 1.5$ (representing 99.3% coverage). Figure 1 (c) shows the same data as in (a) but with the outliers removed.

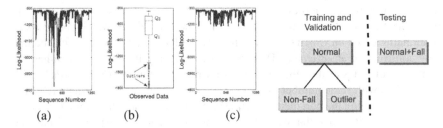

Fig. 1. Outlier removal using IQR on likelihoods   **Fig. 2.** Cross Validation Scheme

To train both the XHMMs/HMMs using only normal data, we first split the normal data into two sets: "non-fall" data and "outlier" data (see Figure 2). We do this using Equation 1 with a parameter $w = w_{CV}$ that is manually set and only used for this initial split. We train the HMMs on the "non-fall" data and then set the thresholds (w (which is defined as T_i for $HMM1_{out}$ and T for $HMM2_{out}$) and ξ for $XHMM1$ and $XHMM2$) by evaluating performance on the "outlier" data. We use a 3-fold cross validation: the HMMs are trained on $2/3^{rd}$ of the 'non-fall' data, and tested on $1/3^{rd}$ of the 'non-fall' data and on all the "outlier" data. This is repeated for different values of w and ξ. The value of parameters that give the best averaged $gmean$ (see Table 4) over 3-folds are chosen as the best parameters. Then, each classifier is re-trained with these values on 'non-fall' activities.

5 Experimental Analysis

5.1 Dataset

The proposed fall detection approaches are evaluated on the following two datasets:

1. German Aerospace Center (DLR) [15]: This dataset is collected using an Inertial Measurement Unit with integrated accelerometer, gyroscope and 3D magnetometers with sampling frequency of 100 Hz. The dataset contains samples taken from 19 people under semi-natural conditions. The sensor was placed on the belt either on the right/left side of the body or in the right pocket in different orientations. The dataset contains 7 activities: standing, sitting, lying, walking (up/downstairs, horizontal), running/jogging, jumping and falling.

2. MobiFall [23]: This dataset is collected using a Samsung Galaxy S3 device equipped with 3D accelerometer and gyroscope. The mobile device was placed in a trouser pocket in random orientations. Mean sampling of 87Hz is reported for accelerometer and 200Hz for the gyroscope. The dataset is collected from 11 subjects; eight normal activities are recorded in this dataset: step-in car, step-out car, jogging, jumping, sitting, standing, stairs (up and down joined together) and walking. Four different types of falls are recorded – forward lying, front knees lying, sideward lying and back sitting chair. Different types of falls are joined together for testing.

5.2 Data Pre-Processing

For the DLR dataset, accelerometer and gyroscope sensor readings are tilt compensated with the calibration matrix provided with the dataset. For MobiFall dataset, due to the difference in sampling rates, readings from the gyroscope were not used. Sensor noise is removed by using a Buttersworth low-pass filter with a cutoff frequency of 20Hz. The dataset is segmented with 50% overlapping windows, where each window size is 1.28 seconds to simulate a real-time scenario with fast response. To extract temporal dynamics for the XHHMs and HMMs, each window is sub-divided into 16ms frames and features are computed for each frame. Each activity in the XHHMs and HMMs is modelled with 4 states, and 5 representative sequences per activity are manually chosen to initialize the parameters. Initialization is done by segmenting a single sequence into 4 equal parts and computing μ_{ij} and Σ_{ij} for each part and further smoothing by BW with 3 iterations. The transition Matrix A_i is chosen such that transition probabilities from one state to another are 0.025, self-transitions are set accordingly. Four signals were extracted from the dataset (see Table 1) and 19 time and frequency-domain features are computed from them (see Table 2).

Table 1. Different signals extracted from sensor readings

Name of Signal	Description
Norm of acceleration	$a_{norm} = \sqrt{x^2 + y^2 + z^2}$
Horizontal acceleration	$a_{horiz} = \sqrt{x^2 + y^2}$
Vertical acceleration	$a_{vert} = z$
Horizontal Angular velocity	$\omega_{horiz} = \sqrt{\omega_x^2 + \omega_y^2}$

Table 2. Number of computed features

#features	Type of feature
3	Mean of a_{norm}, a_{horiz}, a_{vert}
3	Max of absolute values of a_{norm}, a_{horiz}, a_{vert}
3	Standard Deviation of of a_{norm}, a_{horiz}, a_{vert}
4	IQR of a_{norm}, a_{horiz}, a_{vert}, ω_{horiz}
1	Normalized Average PSD of a_{norm}
1	Spectral Entropy of a_{norm} [6]
1	DC component after FFT of a_{norm} [1]
1	Normalized Information Entropy of the Discrete FFT component magnitudes of a_{norm} [1]
1	Energy i.e. sum of the squared discrete FFT component magnitudes of a_{norm} [1]
1	Correlation between a_{norm} and a_{vert}

To estimate the performance of the proposed approaches for fall detection, we perform leave-one-subject-out cross validation (LOOCV) [7], where *only* normal activities from $(N-1)$ subjects are used to train the classifiers and the Nth subject's normal activities and fall events are used for testing. This process is repeated N times and the average performance metric is reported. This evaluation is person independent and demonstrates the generalization capabilities as the subject who is being tested is not included in training the classifiers. For the DLR dataset, one person did not have falls data and for the MobiFall dataset, two subjects only performed falls activity; hence these subjects are removed from the analysis. The different values of w tested for $HMM1_{out}$ and $HMM2_{out}$ are $[1.5, 1.7239, 3, \infty]$ and ξ for $XHMM1, XHMM2$ are $[1.5, 5, 10, 100]$. The value of w_{CV} for rejecting outliers from the normal activities is set to 1.5. Table 3 and Table 4 shows the performance metrics used in the paper.

Table 3. Confusion Matrix

		Predicted Labels	
		Normal	Falls
Actual Labels	Normal	True Positive (TP)	False Negative (FN)
	Falls	False Positive (FP)	True Negative (TN)

Table 4. Performance Metric

Metric	Formula
Geometric Mean ($gmean$) [11]	$\sqrt{\frac{TP}{(TP+FN)} * \frac{TN}{(TN+FP)}}$
Fall Detection Rate (FDR)	$\frac{TN}{TN+FP}$
False Alarm Rate (FAR)	$\frac{FN}{(TP+FN)}$

Table 5. Performance of Fall Detection methods

Method	DLR			MobiFall		
	$gmean$	FDR	FAR	$gmean$	FDR	FAR
$HMM1_{full}$	0	0	0.0001	0	0	0
$HMM2_{full}$	0	0	0.0001	0	0	0.0001
$HMM1_{out}$	0.068	0.029	0.008	0.030	0.003	0.022
$HMM2_{out}$	0.831	0.859	0.175	**0.793**	0.755	0.159
$XHMM1$	**0.883**	0.882	0.102	0.413	0.222	0.224
$XHMM2$	0.581	0.974	0.640	0.752	0.938	0.390

5.3 Results

For comparison purpose, we implemented two threshold based HMMs similar to $HMM1_{out}$ and $HMM2_{out}$ with the difference that they are trained on full 'normal' data and the threshold is set as maximum of negative of log-likelihood. We call them as $HMM1_{full}$ and $HMM2_{full}$. Table 5 shows the performance of the $XHMM$ methods along with threshold based HMMs on both the datasets. When the fall data is not present during the training phase, for the DLR dataset, $XHMM1$ has the highest $gmean$ in comparison to other X-factor and threshold based methods. $XHMM2$ has the highest FDR but at the cost of high FAR. The reason for poor performance of $HMM1_{out}$ is that most of the falls are misclassified as jumping/running. For Mobi-Fall dataset, $HMM2_{out}$ and $XHMM2$ show higher value of $gmean$ in comparison to other X-factor and threshold based methods, with $XHMM2$ having the highest FDR, whereas $XHMM1$ and $HMM1_{out}$ classify most falls as sitting and step in car, thus their performance is greatly reduced. We also observe that $HMM1_{full}$ and $HMM2_{full}$ that are trained on full 'normal' data performed worst and are unable to detect falls due to setting of large negative of log-likelohood threshold due to the presence of outliers in the training data for normal activities.

We also implemented two supervised versions of XHMMs ($HMM1_{Sup}$ and $HMM2_{Sup}$): a) when only 1 fall is used (chosen randomly 10 times and average metric reported), and b) where all the falls data are used, during the training phase. This experiment demonstrates a practical scenario when we have very little falls data and compares it with an optimistic view on collection of data for falls. Table 6 shows that the supervised versions with very small falls data did not show consistent performance for both the datasets, however when all the falls data present is used for training, performance is improved both in terms of higher $gmean$ and FDR and lower FAR, except for $HMM1_{sup}$ where most of the falls are misclassified as sitting or step in/out car. Our results show that when there is no fall data available during training time, the supervised methods cannot be used and the performance of these methods is not consistent if very few training data is available.

Table 6. Supervised Fall Detection

#Falls data	Method	DLR			MobiFall		
		$gmean$	FDR	FAR	$gmean$	FDR	FAR
1	$HMM1_{Sup}$	0.247	0.172	0.013	0.173	0.067	0.003
	$HMM2_{Sup}$	0.442	0.480	0.326	0.552	0.406	0.038
All	$HMM1_{Sup}$	0.660	0.525	0.022	0.249	0.066	0.005
	$HMM2_{Sup}$	0.729	0.709	0.174	0.875	0.837	0.083

6 Conclusions

Falling is the most common cause of both fatal and nonfatal injuries among older adults [3]. Recent advancements in ambient assistive living have led to the development of several commercial devices (e.g. Philips Lifeline [16]), MobileHelp Fall Button™ [14] etc). However, these products may fail to identify diverse types of falls, can produce lot of false alarms and require manual intervention. The reason is that the performance of fall detection algorithms is hampered by the lack of training data for falls because they occur rarely and infrequently. With little or no training data for falls, supervised classification algorithms may underperform as they may either underfit or not-model falls correctly. In this paper, we presented two 'X-factor' HMM based fall detection approaches that learn only from the normal activities captured from a body-worn sensor. To tackle the issue of no training data for falls, we introduced a new cross-validation method based on the IQR of log-likelihoods that rejects spurious data from normal activities to help in optimizing the model parameters. The XHMM methods show high detection rates for fall. We also showed that the traditional method of thresholding with HMMs trained on full normal data to identify falls is ill-posed for this problem.

References

1. Bao, L., Intille, S.S.: Activity recognition from user-annotated acceleration data. In: Ferscha, A., Mattern, F. (eds.) PERVASIVE 2004. LNCS, vol. 3001, pp. 1–17. Springer, Heidelberg (2004)
2. Bourke, A.K., Lyons, G.M.: A threshold-based fall-detection algorithm using a bi-axial gyroscope sensor. Medical Engineering and Physics 30(1), 84 (2008)
3. CDC: Falls in nursing homes (2014),
   http://www.cdc.gov/HomeandRecreationalSafety/Falls/nursing.
   html (accessed on January 19, 2014)
4. Cheng, H., Haiyong, L., Zhao, F.: A fall detection algorithm based on pattern recognition and human posture analysis. In: IET International Conference on Communication Technology and Application. pp. 853–857 (2011)
5. Dai, J., Bai, X., Yang, Z., Shen, Z., Xuan, D.: Perfalld: A pervasive fall detection system using mobile phones. In: Pervasive Computing and Communications Workshops, pp. 292–297. IEEE (2010)
6. Ermes, M., Parkka, J., Cluitmans, L.: Advancing from offline to online activity recognition with wearable sensors. In: 2008 30th Annual International Conference EMBS. pp. 4451–4454 (2008)
7. He, Z., Jin, L.: Activity recognition from acceleration data based on discrete consine transform and svm. In: SMC, pp. 5041–5044. IEEE (2009)
8. Honda, D., Sakata, N., Nishida, S.: Activity recognition for risk management with installed sensor in smart and cell phone. In: HCI (3), pp. 230–239 (2011)
9. Igual, R., Medrano, C., Plaza, I.: Challenges, issues and trends in fall detection systems. BioMedical Engineering OnLine 12(1), 1–24 (2013)
10. Khan, S.S., Karg, M.E., Hoey, J., Kulic, D.: Towards the detection of unusual temporal events during activities using hmms. In: SAGAWARE - Proceedings of the 2012 ACM Conference on Ubiquitous Computing, UbiComp 2012, pp. 1075–1084. ACM (2012)
11. Kubat, M., Matwin, S.: Addressing the curse of imbalanced training sets: one-sided selection. In: ICML, vol. 97, pp. 179–186 (1997)
12. Lühr, S., Venkatesh, S., West, G.A.W., Bui, H.H.: Explicit state duration HMM for abnormality detection in sequences of human activity. In: Zhang, C., Guesgen, H.W., Yeap, W.-K. (eds.) PRICAI 2004. LNCS (LNAI), vol. 3157, pp. 983–984. Springer, Heidelberg (2004)
13. Luo, X., Liu, T., Liu, J., Guo, X., Wang, G.: Design and implementation of a distributed fall detection system based on wireless sensor networks. EURASIP Journal on Wireless Communications and Networking 2012, 1–13 (2012)

14. MobileHelp: Fall button (2014), `http://www.mobilehelpnow.com/products.php` (accessed on September 12, 2014)
15. Nadales, M.J.V.: Recognition of Human Motion Related Activities from Sensors. Master's thesis, University of Malaga and German Aerospace Cener (2010)
16. Philips: Lifeline (2014), `http://www.lifelinesys.com/content/lifeline-products/auto-alert` (accessed on September 12, 2014)
17. Quinn, J.A., Williams, C.K., McIntosh, N.: Factorial switching linear dynamical systems applied to physiological condition monitoring. IEEE Transactions on PAMI 31(9), 1537–1551 (2009)
18. Rabiner, L.: A tutorial on hidden markov models and selected applications in speech recognition. Proceedings of the IEEE 77(2), 257–286 (1989)
19. Shi, G., Zou, Y., Jin, Y., Cui, X., Li, W.J.: Towards hmm based human motion recognition using mems inertial sensors. In: ROBIO, pp. 1762–1766. IEEE (2008)
20. Thome, N., Miguet, S.: A hhmm-based approach for robust fall detection. In: ICARCV, pp. 1–8. IEEE (2006)
21. Tokumitsu, M., Murakami, M., Ishida, Y.: An adaptive sensor network for home intrusion detection by human activity profiling. Artificial Life and Robotics 16(1), 36–39 (2011)
22. Tong, L., Song, Q., Ge, Y., Liu, M.: Hmm-based human fall detection and prediction method using tri-axial accelerometer. IEEE Sensors Journal 13(5), 1849–1856 (2013)
23. Vavoulas, G., Pediaditis, M., Spanakis, E., Tsiknakis, M.: The mobifall dataset: An initial evaluation of fall detection algorithms using smartphones. In: 2013 IEEE 13th International Conference on Bioinformatics and Bioengineering (BIBE), pp. 1–4 (November 2013)
24. Yu, M., Naqvi, S., Rhuma, A., Chambers, J.: Fall detection in a smart room by using a fuzzy one class support vector machine and imperfect training data. In: ICASSP, pp. 1833–1836 (2011)
25. Zhang, T., Wang, J., Xu, L., Liu, P.: Fall detection by wearable sensor and one-class svm algorithm. In: Intelligent Computing in Signal Processing and Pattern Recognition, vol. 345, pp. 858–863. Springer, Heidelberg (2006)

A Thermal Data Simulation Tool for the Testing of Novel Approaches to Activity Recognition

Jonathan Synnott[1], Chris D. Nugent[1], and Paul Jeffers[2]

[1] School of Computing and Mathematics, University of Ulster,
Jordanstown, UK
{j.synnott,cd.nugent}@ulster.ac.uk
[2] IoT Tech Ltd., Lisburn, UK
care@iottech.co.uk

Abstract. Researchers require access to sensor datasets for the development of novel data driven activity recognition approaches. Access to such datasets is limited due to issues including sensor cost, availability and deployment time. The use of simulated environments may facilitate rapid generation of comprehensive datasets with minimal cost. This paper introduces an approach to the simulation of thermal sensor data for activity detection and recognition. The approach utilizes multi-touch interfaces to facilitate intuitive recordings of a range of scenarios and supports deployment to a range of mobile platforms. Functional testing has considered the ability of the approach to record activities including: normal room navigation, falling, hypothermia and multiple occupant navigation.

Keywords: Simulation, Computer Vision, Activity Detection, Thermal Sensor.

1 Introduction

Access to sensor datasets is required for the development and testing of data driven activity recognition approaches [1]. Nevertheless, access to such datasets is limited for several reasons. The implementation of Intelligent Environments (IEs) containing sensors is both expensive [2] and time consuming, and the technology to be used may be difficult to obtain or may not yet be available [2, 3]. Additionally, annotations of existing datasets may be of limited detail and accuracy. The issues with the collection of such datasets may slow advances in the development of novel activity recognition approaches [4]. The use of simulated datasets may accelerate research by facilitating production of verifiable, highly realistic activities with the ability to fine tune activity and simulator performance [4]. Existing work in the simulation of datasets includes parameterized [1] and simulated environment approaches [5]. These approaches rely on the creation of activity or environment models to generate datasets. This paper describes a novel approach to thermal sensor simulation, facilitating the intuitive simulation of activities within a scene using a multi-platform, multi-touch interface. The following Sections describe the approach, its implementation and functional testing.

L. Pecchia et al. (Eds.): IWAAL 2014, LNCS 8868, pp. 10–13, 2014.

2   Approach

The simulator was designed to represent a thermal sensor capable of producing an *n*-by-*m* array of temperature values detected within a scene. The solution was designed to model a sensor placed in an overhead position with a bird's-eye view of a scene. To facilitate the testing of a range of sensor configurations, the design facilitates adjustment of several parameters including: sensor resolution (Pixels), noise amplitude (Celsius), noise frequency (Hz), and sample rate (Hz). Other parameters relate to the scene and heat sources, including background temperature (Celsius), heat source temperature increase and decrease rate (Degrees Celsius per second), heat source maximum temperature, minimum temperature (Celsius) and size (Pixels).

The approach was designed to support provision of input through the use of touch screen devices with multi-touch support. This was chosen given that these devices are capable of facilitating intuitive, yet complex interaction, providing control over the speed and direction of movement of multiple heat sources simultaneously within a scene. Multi-touch support also facilitates the use of gestures to control the size and shape of heat sources. Heat sources are positioned at any location touched by the user, affecting the recorded temperature at the corresponding location according to the specified parameters.

3   Implementation

The simulation tool was implemented using Unity v4.3 [6]. Unity was chosen as the development platform as it supports multi-platform deployment to desktop, web, and mobile platforms including Android, iOS and Windows Phone.

The sensor is represented in the simulation tool by a two-dimensional array of cells, each with an associated temperature value. The grid dimensions are defined by the user and the size of each cell is scaled to fit the device screen. The temperature value of each cell defaults to the *background temperature*. Upon receiving a touch event, all cells within a radius of 0.5 x *heat source size* are increased in temperature at *heat source temperature increase rate* until the *heat source maximum temperature* value is reached. Cells unaffected by touch events either return to *background temperature* or *heat source minimum temperature* at a rate defined by *heat source temperature decrease rate*. Manipulation of these parameters allows the user to manipulate a scene by moving multiple heat sources simultaneously throughout the scene using a multi-touch interface. Additionally, users can place fixed heat sources within a scene with a variety of sizes and temperatures. A Gaussian noise filter with adjustable amplitude and frequency provides increased realism and facilitates testing of the robustness of novel algorithms in handling noisy data.

A grayscale color gradient is used to represent the temperature value of each cell, where black represents the *minimum scene temperature* and white represents the *maximum scene temperature*. Data samples are saved at a rate defined by the *sample rate* property and are saved to a time stamped plaintext file.

4   Functional Testing

For the purposes of testing, the simulator was deployed to 2 mobile platforms - Android (on a Nexus 7 tablet) and Windows Phone (on a Windows Surface 2). Additionally, the simulator was deployed as a Windows desktop application and was also embedded into a web page for internal testing, demonstration and distribution. Functional testing of the simulation tool was performed through the recording of 4 scenarios. These were: Single occupancy – a person entering the scene and following a fixed path; a fall – a person entering the scene and following a fixed path before briefly falling over; hypothermia – a person entering a scene, remaining stationary and slowly reducing in body temperature; multiple occupancy – two persons moving within a scene simultaneously. These scenarios were chosen to provide examples of the types of interactions that can be recorded using a multi-touch interface, and were recorded using a Nexus 7 tablet. A sensor resolution of 16x16 pixels was chosen as the authors are currently involved in research into the use of low-cost, low-resolution thermal sensors, currently being developed by IoT Tech Ltd [7].

The data collected during the performance of each of the scenarios was used to test the performance of an object tracking function written in Matlab. The data values were converted to grayscale images, and then background subtraction was performed to create a binary mask containing heat sources within a scene. An assignment-cost algorithm based on Euclidean distance was implemented and used to assign blob detections to continuous tracks for scenes with multiple heat sources. Fig. 1 (a) provides an example of the simulated data converted to a grayscale image. The data represents two people moving within a scene. Fig. 1 (b) is the resulting binary mask with blob labels after background subtraction and blob detection was performed. Fig. 1 (c) provides an example of a grayscale representation of the simulated data generated during the recording of a fall, and Fig. 1 (d) provides an example representing a stationary individual emitting a low amount of heat, which may be indicative of hypothermia.

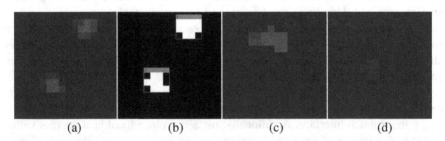

(a)   (b)   (c)   (d)

Fig. 1. An example of the simulated thermal sensor data representing multiple scenarios. (a) Simulated data demonstrating multiple occupancy, represented as a grayscale image. Darker areas are colder, lighter areas are warmer. (b) The binary mask and blob annotations resulting from background subtraction and blob detection. (c) A subject who has fallen and (d) A subject with a reduced temperature (hypothermia).

The simulator has received positive feedback from industrial partners who are currently developing a low resolution thermal sensor for activity monitoring, and has proven successful in facilitating the development of activity monitoring solutions prior to the completion of sensor development.

5   Conclusion

The use of simulated sensor datasets has the potential to address the difficulties associated with the collection of data from IEs. This paper has introduced a thermal sensor simulation tool which provides researchers with the ability to generate temperature data describing a range of scenarios using a multi-touch interface with adjustable sensor and scene parameters. Four scenarios have been considered in this paper. The ability to input the generated data into an object tracking algorithm has also been demonstrated. Future work with the simulator will focus on the modelling of more complex background and foreground heat sources with characteristic heat patterns. For example, the ability to include heat patterns representative of common household objects such as televisions and refrigerators, or heat patterns associated with activities such as opening a window. Other future work will involve a comparison study investigating the similarity between data generated by the simulator and real sensor implementations.

Acknowledgements. Invest Northern Ireland is acknowledged for supporting this project under the Competence Centre Program Grant RD0513853 - Connected Health Innovation Centre.

References

1. Helal, S., Lee, J.W., Hossain, S., Kim, E., Hagras, H., Cook, D.: Persim-Simulator for Human Activities in Pervasive Spaces. In: 7th International Conference on Intelligent Environments, pp. 192–199 (2011)
2. Mendez-Vazquez, A., Helal, A., Cook, D.: Simulating Events to Generate Synthetic Data for Pervasive Spaces. In: Workshop on Developing Shared Home Behavior Datasets to Advance HCI and Ubiquitous Computing Research (2009)
3. Poland, M.P., Nugent, C.D., Wang, G., Chen, L.: Development of a Smart Home Simulator for use as a Heuristic Tool for Management of Sensor Distribution. Technology and Health Care 17(3), 171–182 (2009)
4. Helal, S., Kim, E., Hossain, S.: Scalable Approaches to Activity Recognition Research. In: 8th International Conference on Pervasive Computing (2010)
5. Synnott, J., Nugent, C.D., Chen, L., Moore, G.: The Creation of Simulated Activity Datasets using a Graphical Intelligent Environment Simulation Tool. In: 36th Annual International Conference of the IEEE Engineering in Medicine and Biology Society (accepted for publication, 2014)
6. Unity – Game Engine, http://unity3d.com/
7. IoT Tech Ltd, http://iottech.co.uk/

Consolidation of Results amongst Undergraduate Occupational Therapist Students in Scoring of the Barthel ADL

Elizabeth Sarah Martin[1], Chris D. Nugent[1], Raymond Bond[1], and Suzanne Martin[2]

[1] School of Computing and Mathematics
[2] School of Health Sciences
University of Ulster, Jordanstown, UK
{martin-e17}@email.ulster.ac.uk,
{cd.nugent,rb.bond,s.martin}@ulster.ac.uk

Abstract. Within the medical domain, paper based and electronic approaches are the two main methods of collecting and sharing various types of medical information. Through the continual development of technology, healthcare services and industries are engaging more and more with online resources in an effort to become part of the digital age. This paper presents a study involving 26 participants who were familiar in using the paper based Barthel Index assessment for the assessment of Activities of Daily Living (ADLs). The experiment conducted considered the subjects completing the assessment using both a digital variant of the assessment technique deployed through the World Wide Web, in addition to a traditional paper based version. Results from post-evaluation assessment indicated that 22 participants found that the digital variant of the ADL assessment tool was more effective than, if not the same, as the test if it where conducted on paper.

Keywords: Activity of Daily Living, digital healthcare provision.

1 Introduction

Within the medical domain, paper based and electronic approaches are the two main methods of collecting and sharing various types of medical information. Nevertheless, most hospital records, medicine charts, health and wellness charts in addition to patient records are still predominantly paper based and are therefore prone to "human error" [1, 2]. In relation to investigating the design for reducing the amount of human error, analysis will occur between paper based data and the same data reproduced digitally.

The Barthel Index Activity of Daily Living (ADL) affectively processes the functional disability of an individual by scoring their performance in 10 activities of daily living [3]. These activities are; mobility indoors, transfers, stairs, toilet use, bladder, bowels, bathing, grooming, dressing and feeding [4]. A therapist would score each activity based on assessing the individual. The total calculation is presented as a score out of 20. The higher the score, the more independent the individual can be considered to

L. Pecchia et al. (Eds.): IWAAL 2014, LNCS 8868, pp. 14–17, 2014.

be in undertaking various aspects of daily living [2]. The therapist would use the totalled score to recommend the best action plan that would be individually suited to the user; for example, recommending the installation of a stair lift in the home or providing the person being assessed with an aid such as a walking frame etc. This study aims to evaluate results from participants completing the Barthel ADL on paper, as well as the Barthel ADL reproduced digitally.

2   Methods

The digital version of the ADL assessment was designed in accordance with the paper version of the Barthel Index of Activities of Daily Living. This approach was chosen as it has been considered the 'gold standard' for measuring ADLs [5]. With this technique there are 10 ADLs to be assessed and each assessor must select only one option for each, based on the scenarios provided. The digital ADL was created as a web-based solution. This allows data from a large group of users to be collected simultaneously during evaluations [6]. A comparison of both the digital and paper based ADL assessment was performed on a class of 26 undergraduate students (25 female, one male with an average age of 22) studying in their final year for the degree of BSc (Hons) Occupational Therapy at the University of Ulster. The participants were provided with three scenarios, one to be completed using the web-based assessment tool and a further two to be completed using the conventional paper based assessment approach. The study was granted ethical approval by the University of Ulster ethics committee and participants gave their written consent prior to the start of the study. The scenarios were prepared as vignettes and would not be used in any session that would affect real life patient treatment. Once the participant submitted their selections, using the various scenarios, a score was displayed along with a recommendation for further assistance if required. The recommendation is based on the score of the digital ADL and differs between 0-5, 6-10, 11-15 and 16-20. The higher the score, the more independent the individual is deemed capable [2].

3   Results

Overall results from the study illustrate that there was a degree of subjectivity and variation between participants in all of the three scenarios. Scenario 1: Male with a recent back injury relies on his wheelchair to move about his home. He is unable to use the stairs as his legs are too weak. He is doubly incontinent and has a catheter fitted. He requires help with showering, dressing and grooming. He is able to make and prepare meals, although this is done from his wheelchair. The first scenario was completed online and had as its highest calculation a score of 8/20, however, at the lower end of a scale there was a calculation of 2/20 (range = 6). The mean score was 4.7, the standard deviation (SD) was 1.4 and the variance was 2.02. Scenario 2: Male with a head trauma can move with an aid around his home. There is no issue with stairs and he is doubly continent. Bathing can sometimes be a struggle and he also needs help with dressing, especially clothing that requires to be put on/taken off over his head. He is able to partly prepare meals, however can sometimes get confused as to 'what comes next' in the recipe. With the second scenario (completed online as well) the maximum score calculation was 19/20 and the lowest score was 10/20 (range = 9) [2]. The mean was 15.7, the SD was 2.6 and the variance was 6.76. Scenario 3: Female with multiple sclerosis, finds it difficult to get around her home even with the use of an aid. Stairs are a challenge and sometimes can't be climbed at all. She is doubly continent and can shower unaided. She is able to dress herself without any help and can still prepare meals. The third and final scenario was completed by all participants on paper. This was the method that all participants were familiar with and had previously used in the assessment of real patients. In this instance, the maximum score was 19/20 and the lowest was 13/20 (range=6), the mean for is 17, the SD is 1.58 and the variance is 2.5.

Throughout the study, results varied from scenario to scenario and activity to activity. Fig.1 illustrates results showing the subjective variance amongst participants in scenario 3 in relation to assessing the ability of transferring around the home.

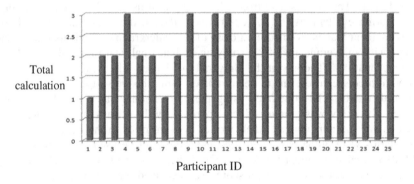

Participant ID

Fig. 1. The activity of transfers for scenario 3 that was completed on paper. Two participants answered with a score of one, indicating they agreed that the fictitious character from the scenario required major help. 12 others were in agreement that the character needed minor help and scored a 2, whilst 11 agreed a score of three illustrating the character was completely independent. In this instance, the mean is 2.36 and the SD is 0.63 and the variance is 0.40.

All users were provided with the same three scenarios to assess and complete online and on paper. The variance in results could be explained as being down to difference in opinion. What one participant may assess as "needs help" others may view as being "independent with use of an aid." Additionally, analysis of the paper based Barthel ADL indicated that a 10/25 participants had either crossed a number out, or had miscalculated the total figure. In relation to results from the online tool, each total score was 100% accurate based on the participant's selections. Additionally, 22 of the 26 participants liked the online version more than the paper version based on its ability to calculate the final score automatically. Also participants indicated that they favoured the online version given that any errors made during assessment were easily changed in comparison to the paper based Barthel ADL where mistakes and handwriting eligibility could look untidy and unprofessional when presented to a carer or the person receiving the care.

4   Conclusion

To conclude, within the medical domain, paper based and electronic approaches are the two main methods of collecting and sharing various types of medical information. In relation to investigating the reduction in errors, an analysis was undertaken between paper based data and the same data reproduced digitally. This study evaluated results from participants completing the Barthel ADL on paper, in addition to the Barthel ADL reproduced digitally. Overall, there was the same inter-rater reliability and variance in results with the Barthel ADL completed on paper, and with the Barthel ADL completed online. Future developments would involve the same study being carried out by healthcare professionals who work with various forms of ADLs on a daily basis, as well as an increase in scenarios from the initial three to ten with different levels of severity. This would offer an improved comparison in relation to results and would prove valuable in terms of further developments based upon their scores and recommendations.

References

1. McDowell, S.E., Ferner, H.S., Ferner, R.E.: The pathophysiology of medication errors: how and where they arise. Br. J. Clin. Pharmacol. 67, 605–613 (2009)
2. Martin, E., Nugent, C., Bond, R.R., Finlay, D., Martin, S.: Evaluation of the barthel index presented on paper and developed digitally. In: International Conference on Smart Homes and Health Telematics (ICOST), June 25-27 (2014)
3. Mahoney, F.I., Barthel, D.W.: Functional Evaluation: The Barthel Index. Md. State Med. J. 14, 61–65 (1965)
4. Roley, S.E., DeLany, J.V., Barrows, C.J., et al.: Occupational therapy practice framework: Domain & practices (2nd edn). Am. J. Occup. Ther. 62, 625–683 (2008)
5. Kwakkel, G., Veerbek, J.M., Harmeling-vanderWel, B.C., Vanwegen, E., Kollen, B.J.: Diagnostic Accuracy of the Barthel Index for Measuring Activities of Daily Living Outcome After Ischemic Hemispheric Stroke, Stroke, American Heart Association (2011)
6. Martin, E.S., Finlay, D.D., Nugent, C.D., Bond, R.R., Breen, C.J.: An interactive tool for the evaluation of ECG visualisation formats. In: Computing in Cardiology Conference (CinC), September 22-25, pp. 779–782 (2013)

KNX-Based Sensor Monitoring
for User Activity Detection in AAL-environments

Marcus Märker, Sebastian Wolf, Oliver Scharf, and Daniel Plorin, and Tobias Teich

University of Applied Sciences Zwickau, Dr.-Friedrichs-Ring 2A, 08056 Zwickau, Germany
{marcus.maercer,sebastian.wolf,oliver.scharf,
tobias.teich}@fh-zwickau.de,
daniel.plorin@mb.tu-chemnitz.de

Abstract. We present an approach to monitor user activity by utilizing commercially and readily available home automation technology. Varying user constitutions demand an adaptive system that involves components from several device-families, which are not particularly designed to work together as an entity. We introduce the concept of a modular gateway architecture to meet these challenges. To evaluate our research with field studies, a prototype apartment, that uses largely but not exclusively KNX-based components has been implemented. Within the scope of this paper we focus on the integration of those devices into a larger OSGi-based framework.

Keywords: KNX, ambient intelligence, home gateway, activity monitoring.

1   Introduction

Against the background of demographic change in industrialized countries, new strategies for the health care systems and the support of older people have to be developed. Due to the increasing aging society, the disparity between service users and providers keeps on growing. Therefore, there are not enough resources for inpatient or outpatient care of the relevant age groups in the near future. Older people in need of care should be able to live as long as possible and independent in their familiar home environment. To meet the requirements resulting from an aging society and the growing number of people in need of care the living environment hat to adapt itself to the prevailing conditions of it residents. A contribution to this adaptation is provided through modular equipment with innovative, modular ubiquitous home automation technology. The installed technology should act as inconspicuously as possible to be accepted by the residents [1].

2   Classification

The research project A²LICE – Ambient Assisted Living in Intelligent Controlled Environments - deals with practical approaches for technically supported housing for the elderly. In 2012 we successfully concluded the research project Low Energy

L. Pecchia et al. (Eds.): IWAAL 2014, LNCS 8868, pp. 18–25, 2014.

Living [2]. The building automation infrastructure designed in the context of this project represents the base for the A²LICE project. The involved practice partners pursue sustainable use of the existing technical building equipment (TBE) and aspire an expansion into other aspects of living. For example sensor data derived from home automation can be used for the detection of activities of daily living (ADL), which has been discussed in several publications [3,4,5,6]. For our project related field studies, a prototype apartment has been equipped with TBE and is used to evaluate different technologies for ADL recognition. A further goal is to enhance certain residential aspects with additional equipment. To increase acceptance, the needs of the inhabitants were taken into account. Especially for the target group of elderly people, the interaction with the TBE was reduced to a minimum [7]. After testing the TBE on a test setup, the devices were installed in prototype apartment.

3   Technology Used

For the major part of the TBE installed in the prototype apartment we chose KNX [8] devices. This decision is based on several reasons: As already mentioned, we were able to draw on the experience with KNX-devices gained in previous projects. In addition, KNX is a widespread bus standard and its acceptance range will be expanded in the coming years. The installed KNX-devices are listed in the following table.

Table 1. KNX-devices and useage

KNX device	Useage
IP Router Gateway	Communication and programming of KNX devices
Switch actuators	Switching of the lighting and sockets, power consumption measurement
Heating actuator	Heating valve control
Room temperature controller	Temperature control, humidity measurement
Air quality sensor	CO_2 measurement
Presence detector	Presence detection
Smoke detector	Smoke detector
Button interface	Input for binary contacts
Switch / push button	Diverse uses
LED indicators	Display status main function

Because KNX-devices do not cover all areas of living and do not offer enough programming freedom, we installed equipment using various other standards. The WAGO [9] components serve as an interface between different standards and offer the possibility to use the advanced Codesys IDE for Programmable Logic Controller (PLC). The connection of the modular arranged components was realized by using a Wago controller. Furthermore, various wireless solutions (EnOcean, Z-Wave),

Dali-controlled LED technology, binary contacts on drawers, beds, doors and windows and sensors for vital data acquisition and safety of the residents were installed in the prototype apartment.

The collected data is used to detect inactivity and ADLs. In addition, LEDs and audio transducer indicate events and dangers for the resident via aural and visual signals. We partially installed redundant technology to verify the practicability and profitability of each solution. One example is the sensor arrangement of the bed. Strain gauge elements as well as force-resistive sensor strips were attached to the slatted frame. In the field test the most cost effective and reliable solution will be determined.

For programming of the KNX devices we used the ETS-program [10]. For more complex scenarios, 'Codesys' IDE [11] and the automation software 'IP-Symcon' [12] were used. 'IP-Symcon' in particular is characterized by the versatility and was additionally used for visualization and data storage.

In some residential areas we have installed in-house developments in order to reflect specific processes. For access management, an RFID reader was attached invisibly behind the doorbell push. A further in-house development is the stove distance sensor, which measures presence close to the stove.

4   Home Gateway

One of the biggest challanges to overcome is the lack of a scalable system to incorparate a heterogenous collection of devices. The intrinsic characteristics of the various device-families make it difficult to unify them under a common framework. Using the WAGO-System as a gateway would be a less-than-ideal solution due to its overall costs and limited options for advanced programming. To solve this we have been designing custom hard- and software components that allow us to connect those systems on a physical and logical layer. By applying the OSGi [13] concepts for modular software we are able to abstract the complexity of the different standards and create a unified front-end for developing applications and interacting with the TBE. Building a first prototype gateway we focused on incorparating KNX into our system because the installed KNX-devices cover the majority of the functionality. Beyond that, the gateway is designed to be highly modular, so that expansions and modifications can be made at any point later in the project.

The different software layers for such a system include the operational system (OS) with kernel and device drivers, as well as the application software itself. The KNX bus access is realized by using the 'Calimero'-API [14]. Since both OSGi and Calimero are Java-based we had to consider appropriate hardware to run the OS and Java environment. The gateway is going to be rail-mounted in an electric cabinet within the prototype appartment, therefore a quiet and subtle operation is desirable. At the same time it has to offer enough processing power and memory to support a scaled-down Linux system with Java Virtual Machine and Run Time Environment. To meet all the requirements the Beagleboard-xM [15] – an open source ARM-based GNU/Linux computer - was chosen as a prototyping platform. It runs with Ångström-Linux and OpenJDK as a base for Java development. A custom add-on board was

Fig. 1. Gateway prototype with Beagleboard (red) and add-on board (green)

designed to service as a rigid interface between the Beagleboard and KNX. This add-on board makes use of the KNX-Bus-Interface-Module (BIM) made by Opternus [16]. The BIM provides access to the KNX bus line via serial interface. The board incorparates a circuitry to connect the BIM with one of the Beagleboards native UART[1] ports and is galvanically isolated to avoid safety issues between the Beagleboard logic and the 30 Volt potential of the KNX bus line. Opternus provides a development kit for developing and configuring BIM-applications. This includes pre-compiled demos and source code to programm the BIM. For our purpose the BIM was configured in 'transparent mode'. This means that every KNX frame that appears on the link-layer is forwarded to the UART without additional packet filtering. The Calimero-based software binding then polls the UART for newly arrived KNX frames and processes them.

5   KNX Binding

In addition to our self-developed hardware platform we also implemented our own software environment to monitor and control the devices connected to the KNX bus system. The main reason for that was that we wanted to become more independent of commercial logging software such as 'IP-Symcon' or 'ETS' and to enable our external software components to access and work with KNX devices as well as the KNX bus system and thus to allow us to be more flexible in our software development processes. To achieve this we have been designing and implementing a simple software service through which other components can access the KNX bus system. That brings the advantage that not every service that wants to use KNX devices for its work needs to implement the entire communication infrastructure by itself, but can instead call service methods on a server-side component which then delivers the information requested. An example for this could be a simple logging service that frequently checks the state of a device and writes its values to a database. This service does not need to implement its own communication logic to access the KNX bus system, but instead calls a service that returns the requested data back to it. The main

---

[1]   Universal Asynchronous Receiver Transmitter.

objective of such a service is to provide a solid programming interface and to improve the compatibility between subsystems by using a standardized data exchange format to deliver data point values back to its callers.

5.1   KNX Bus Access

Because the KNX standard definition is very complex and an implementation of the standard itself would be a non-trivial project, we decided to look for open source software or libraries that provide us with a basic communication infrastructure. This includes reading and writing device data, but also reacting to bus events that can be emitted by KNX devices at any time. The coverage of these three main aspects would allow the user to efficiently monitor and control a KNX network and react to occurring events.

Since most of our software development work is based on the Java platform and technology stack, we were primarily focussing our search on software, libraries and frameworks that were developed using Java technologies and thus are easy to integrate into already existing Java software and components. Our investigations have shown, that there is only one library that really suits our needs, called 'Calimero' [17] library. As far as we can tell, this library is the only Java library of its kind and that there are thus no alternatives to it. Also this library has already been successfully used by a handful of other projects that were working with KNX networks, which encouraged our decision towards 'Calimero'.

5.2   KNX Service Design and Implementation

After covering the basic technological requirement of accessing the KNX bus system, the necessity for a device and network management arose. This included defining data structures for storing device information such as group addresses, data types and device names, as well as managing access to the bus system by providing an interface that can be accessed by other systems or components.

As a first step we defined the database structure, followed by a REST interface that makes the database accessible for other applications and software components, using the HTTP[2] protocol. A major advantage of a REST interface over other technologies is that it is well supported by a lot of programming languages.

The last step to finishing our communication component was to define a simple data exchange format. Just like before, we wanted to go with a platform independent solution, which led us to use JSON. This allowed us to define a human readable data format. Figure 1 shows the schematic structure of the KNX access service. As can be seen, it consists of a service interface, which handles the communication with the caller, and a second layer that holds the internal services for accessing the data point database and a communication component that can read and write data point values.

---

[2] HTTP, Hypertext Transfer Protocol.

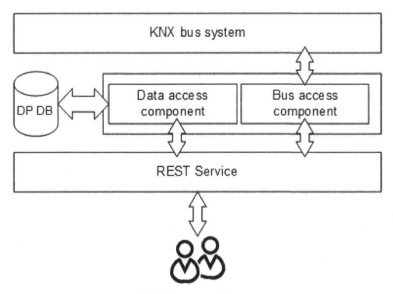

Fig. 2. System architecture

5.3   Database and Service Structure

Since data points are complex objects which are defined by extra information like data point types and group addresses it was necessary to store them. To accomplish this we developed a very slim data model using basic object rational mapping (ORM) technologies, i.e. Java Persistence API (JPA), Hibernate, as well as data access capabilities delivered by the 'Spring' framework [18]. As can be derived, this data model is kept really simple. The data point entity is the main part of this model and will later be accessed by a RESTful[3] service. This service will provide access methods to cover all CRUD[4] mechanisms needed by using the appropriate HTTP verbs.

The service architecture is the main part of this bus access component. Not only does it provide access to data point information over a REST interface, but also internally manages KNX connections and data transmission. It wraps basic 'Calimero' operations in a service-oriented environment and reports read values or error messages back to the caller of its service methods. These services were implemented using the 'Spring' framework.

As outlined in Figure 1, the service layer consists of two components, the data access component and the bus access component. Internally the bus controller component is defined as a REST controller, which means that it is responsible for serving REST requests. The data access component on the other hand provides internal services that allow other components to access the database. This capability is used by the REST controller to read certain data points. For example if a user wants to read the value of a data point, the bus access component reads the data point information

---

[3] REST, Representational State Transfer.
[4] CRUD, Create Read Update Delete.

using the data access component and then accesses the KNX bus to read the current value. This value then can be interpreted with respect to its data point type.

5.4 Data Exchange and Representation

As already mentioned we wanted to keep the data exchange free from platform or programming language specific technologies. That is, why we decided to use JSON[5] as a data exchange format. JSON allows us to easily define a data representation that fits our needs. It is also well supported by 'Spring', so that we can simply create JSON representations of plain Java objects (POJO's [6]). In our current implementation we defined two data types, of which one represents a data point value and the other an error information data type.

If, for example, a user calls the GET method of the REST interface, the bus access components reads the value of the data point with a given identification number. Depending whether or not the call was successful, the user gets a JSON representation of the current value or an error object back. This can look like in the following code snippet:

```
{
    "dataPointId": 1,
    "dataPointNme": "Temperature data point",
    "value": "26.48 °C",
    "timeStamp": 1400502780575
}
```

6   Conclusion

Within the scope of this paper we were outlining the design and implementation of a platform for accessing a home automation system through non-proprietary hard- and software components. The major advantages of this approach are the increased scalability and flexibility it provides to our work within the context of ambient assisted living (AAL) projects.

To further showcase the usage of those platforms we were initially describing a current scenario in which KNX devices play a major role to control home automation devices inside a prototype apartment environment. We then introduced our hardware platform, which allows us to integrate our own devices within a KNX network. It provides the capabilities of running Java applications and thus builds the foundation for more complex software components. An example for a software component like this was then introduced in the last part of the paper, which handled the KNX binding within a Java context. We showed that it is useful to further abstract the KNX device access logic, to enable other applications to comfortably control, i.e. read and write device data such as temperature sensors and switches. To achieve this we choose to

---

[5] JSON, Java Script Object Notation.
[6] POJO, Plain Old Java Object.

implement a simple REST-based service with a separate device database, which uses JSON as its data exchange format, since this approach gave us the most benefits regarding system interoperability.

Acknowledgements. The work reported on in this publication has been financially supported by the European Science Foundation (ESF), in the framework of the Research Networking Programme, the project A²LICE (Ambient Assisted Living in Intelligent Controlled Environments).

References

1. Randow, A., Golubski, W., Heinze, M., Leonhardt, S., Herting-Thomasius, R.: Akzeptanzforschung zu ausgewählten Assistenzfunktionen im Kontext von Ambient Assisted Living, Mobilität im Wandel, Zwickau (2012)
2. Szendrei, D., Franke, S.: Smarthome im Geschosswohnungsbau - Low Energy Living in Forschung und Praxis. In: 21st International Scientific Conference Mittweida, Scientific Reports - Energieeffizienz, pp. 34–37 (2011)
3. Clement, J., Ploennigs, J., Kabitzsch, K.: Intelligente Zähler: ADLs erkennen und individualisieren. In: Deutscher AAL-Kongress 2012. VDE Verlag GmbH, Berlin – Offenbach (2012)
4. Clement, J., Ploennigs, J., Kabitzsch, K.: Erkennung verschachtelter ADLs durch Smartmeter. In: Deutscher AAL-Kongress 2013. VDE Verlag GmbH, Berlin – Offenbach (2013)
5. Bieber, S., Fernholz, G.: Ambiente Umgebungen und mobile Aktivitätserkennung als neue Kommunikationsgrundlage. In: 3. Deutscher AAL-Kongress, ch. 3. VDE Verlag GmbH, Berlin (2010)
6. Wilken, Hein, Gietzelt, Reichertz, Spehr: Ein Ansatz zur Fusion von Aktivitätswahrscheinlichkeiten zur robusten Identifikation von Aktivitäten des täglichen Lebens (ADL). In: Deutscher AAL-Kongress, ch. 4, VDE Verlag GmbH, Berlin (2011)
7. Gast, R.: Der unsichtbare Pfleger. In: Die Zeit, Nr.2 (2013)
8. KNX, http://www.knx.org/knx-en/index.php
9. WAGO, http://global.wago.com/en/overview/index.jsp
10. ETS, http://www.knx.org/de/knx-tools/ets4/description/
11. Codesys, http://www.codesys.com/
12. IP-Symcon, http://www.ip-symcon.de/en/
13. OSGi, http://www.osgi.org/Main/HomePage
14. Calimero, http://sourceforge.net/p/calimero/wiki/Home/
15. Beagleboard-xM, http://beagleboard.org/Products/BeagleBoard-xM
16. Opternus BIM M13x, http://www.opternus.com/de/siemens/knx-bus-interface-odule/bim-m130-135.html
17. Malinowsky, B., Neugschwandtner, G., Kastner, W.: Calimero: Next Generation. Automation Systems Group. Institute of Automation, Vienna University of Technology (2007)
18. Spring framework, http://spring.io/docs

A Multiple Kernel Learning Based Fusion Framework for Real-Time Multi-View Action Recognition

Feng Gu, Francisco Flórez-Revuelta, Dorothy Monekosso, and Paolo Remagnino

Digital Imaging Research Centre, Kingston University, London, UK

Abstract. Due to the increasing demand of multi-camera setup and long-term monitoring in vision applications, real-time multi-view action recognition has gain a great interest in recent years. In this paper, we propose a multiple kernel learning based fusion framework that employs a motion-based person detector for finding regions of interest and local descriptors with bag-of-words quantisation for feature representation. The experimental results on a multi-view action dataset suggest that the proposed framework significantly outperforms simple fusion techniques and state-of-the-art methods.

1 Introduction

Multi-view action recognition has gain a great interest in video surveillance, human computer interaction, and multimedia retrieval, where multiple cameras of different types are deployed to provide complementary field of views (FOVs). Data fusion of multiple camera views leads to more robust decisions on both tracking multiple targets and analysing complex human activities, especially where there are occlusions. Weinland *et al.* [12] introduced motion history volumes (MHV) as a free-viewpoint representation for human actions in the case of multiple calibrated, and background subtracted, video cameras. Cilla *et al.* [3] proposed a probabilistic distributed system that fuses the posterior distribution corresponding to each camera view into a single distribution for the final decision making. Later on they applied a feature fusion approach to efficiently combine 2D observations extracted from different camera viewpoints in [4]. Holte *et al.* [6] demonstrated an approach that detects 4D spatio-temporal interest points and local description of 3D motion features in multi-view images, using 3D reconstructions of the actors and pixel-to-vertex correspondences of the multi-camera setup. However, the above methods are computationally expensive and thus the recognition can only be performed in an offline manner. Researchers have therefore shifted their focus onto real-time multi-view action recognition. Weinland *et al.* [11] proposed an approach to provide robustness to both occlusions and viewpoint changes, which is capable of processing over 500 frames per second while maintaining a reasonable recognition performance. Chaaraoui *et al.* [1] presented a method, where pose representation is based on the contour points of the human silhouette and actions are learned by making use of sequences of multi-view key poses. Their method is able to process 26 frames per second, and the recognition accuracy and speed are then further improved in [2].

In this paper, we propose a multiple kernel learning (MKL) based fusion framework, for real-time multi-view action recognition. We evaluate the proposed framework on a

L. Pecchia et al. (Eds.): IWAAL 2014, LNCS 8868, pp. 26–33, 2014.

multi-view action dataset, by comparing it with some simple fusion techniques, as well as the state-of-the-art methods in the literature.

2   Framework Overview

The proposed framework consists of two major components, namely 'motion-based person detector' and 'multi-view action recognition system'. The former localises the region of interest (ROI), e.g. a person constituted by moving pixels, in the image plane at every frame. The latter extracts low-level local descriptors of appearance and motion as visual features, which are then classified by discriminative models.

2.1   Motion-Based Person Detector

There exist a number of challenges in detecting the person of interest under the multi-camera setting: for some views only the top part (e.g. head and shoulders) and bottom part (e.g. feet) of a person is visible in most frames, in addition to drastic and frequent changes of subject shapes and appearances. We choose the background subtraction based detector, due to the difficulty in modelling the subject's shapes and appearances

Here we adopt the motion-based detector by Stauffer and Grimson [7], which employs a segmentation algorithm based on an adaptive background subtraction method that models each pixel as a mixture of Gaussians and uses an online approximation to update the model. Each pixel of an upcoming frame is then evaluated against the background to determine its corresponding Gaussian distribution of colour in the background model. Any pixels that do not match the background model are consider foreground, until sufficient and consistent evidence is presented to suggest the creation of a new Gaussian distribution, and the background mixture is then updated. The foreground pixels are connected to form the ROI of the person of interest.

2.2   Multi-View Action Recognition

We use local descriptors of Space-Time Interest Points (STIP) and improved dense trajectories (IDT) [10], to represent appearances and motions of actions. The STIP descriptor employs Harris 3D to detect local interest points that define particular spatio-temporal regions in a video. The histograms of gradient (HOG) and histograms of optical flow (HOF) are extracted for each interest point along with its regional spatio-temporal attributes, to represent as the local feature for that particular spatio-temporal region. The IDT descriptor employs dense sampling to extract video blocks at regular positions and scales in space and time. Those video blocks are then tracked using a state-of-the-art dense optical flow algorithm to detected trajectories that potentially corresponds to the actions of interest. The HOG, HOF and motion boundary histograms (MBH) are extracted along the detected trajectories to represent visual features.

For both descriptors, the Bag-of-Words (BoW) approach is used to generate a codebook from the training set through K-Means clustering. Descriptor features inside a spatio-temporal cuboid are then matched to the generated codebook to compute a high dimensional histogram feature vector potentially corresponding to an action. STIP descriptor uses the entire image plane, while IDT descriptor requires person detections for find the spatial location of the cuboid. A learned action model is then used to classify the cuboid into one of the predefined action classes. Although the IDT descriptor [10] has shown the best performance up to date on a range of action recognition datasets, the STIP descriptor has the advantage of computational efficiency due to the sparse nature of its features and not requiring the precomputed person detections. As a result, both descriptors are considered in this paper. The classification stage uses discriminative models to learn the appearance and motion patterns of each action class, while employing various fusion techniques to combine either the visual features or the classification scores of multiple camera views for an aggregated decision making.

Simple Fusion Strategies. Let $\mathbf{x}_i^k \in \mathbb{R}^D$, where $i \in \{1, 2, \ldots, N\}$ is the index of a feature vector and $k \in \{1, 2, \ldots, K\}$ is the index of a camera view. We define a number of simple fusion techniques that combine either the input histogram feature vectors or the output classification scores as follows:

– *Concantenation of Features:* a simple solution is to concatenate the histogram feature vectors of multiple views of a spatio-temporal cuboid that is potentially associated with an action, into one single feature vector $\tilde{\mathbf{x}}_i = [\mathbf{x}_i^1, \ldots, \mathbf{x}_i^K]$. The concatenated feature vectors are then used to train a SVM model per action class as

$$f(\mathbf{x}) = \sum_{i=1}^{N} \alpha_i y_i \mathbf{k}(\mathbf{x}_i, \mathbf{x}) + b \tag{1}$$

where α_i is the dual-form weight, $y_i \in \{-1, +1\}$ is the label with respect to the action class, $\mathbf{k}(\cdot)$ is the non-linear kernel function, and b is the bias. Thus we can compute a classification score in terms of the probability of an instance $\mathbf{x}$ being positive via a sigmoid function as

$$p(y = 1|\mathbf{x}) = \frac{1}{1 + \exp(-f(\mathbf{x}))} \tag{2}$$

– *Sum of Classification Scores:* we can also train a SVM model and compute a classification score for each camera view with respect to an action class, i.e. $p(y = 1|\mathbf{x})$ as in 2, and then average them across all the camera views as $\frac{1}{K} \sum_{k=1}^{K} p(y = 1|\mathbf{x}^k)$

– *Product of Classification Scores:* alternatively if we assume that a camera view is independent of another, we can apply the product rule as $\prod_{k=1}^{K} p(y = 1|\mathbf{x}^k)$

Multiple Kernel Learning. Multiple kernel learning (MKL) algorithms have been shown to be flexible and effective for learning complex problems involving multiple, heterogeneous data sources [5]. They consider multiple kernels that correspond to the multiple data sources, and combine them via a convex function such as

$$\mathcal{K}(\mathbf{x}_i, \mathbf{x}_j) = \sum_{k=1}^{K} \beta_k \mathbf{k}_k(\mathbf{x}_i, \mathbf{x}_j) \tag{3}$$

where $\beta_k \geq 0$ and $\sum_{k=1}^{K} \beta_k = 1$ and each kernel $\mathbf{k}_k$ only uses a distinct set of features. We can rewrite 1 with respect to a kernel $\mathbf{k}_k$ as $f(\mathbf{x}^k) = \sum_{i=1}^{N} \alpha_i^k y_i \mathbf{k}_k(\mathbf{x}_i^k, \mathbf{x}^k) + b^k$. As a result, in addition to learning the α^k weights and b^k bias of a standard SVM model, the system also needs to learn the parameters β_k in the combination function 3. Such an optimisation problem involves two set of continuous parameters, namely 'kernel parameters' (α^k, b^k) and 'combination parameters' (β_k). A popular solution is to employ a two-step optimisation as suggested in [5], where the first step finds the optimum of the kernel parameters (α^k, b^k), e.g. via quadratic programming, while fixing the combination parameters (β_k), and the second step searches for the optimum of the combination parameters, e.g. via line search based gradient decent, while fixing the kernel parameters. The system keeps alternating between these two steps, until it converges to an optimal solution of both sets of parameters.

In [9], the authors employ a generalised MKL algorithm [8] for object detection, where each kernel corresponds to a particular type of visual features. We adopt a similar idea, however each kernel in our framework corresponds to a particular camera view. The intuition behind this is that the optimal combination of parameters enables a weighted sum of all the camera views while ensuring the optimality of the kernel parameters. Such a system should be advantageous over methods merely using weighted sum of classification scores. We therefore hypothesise that it should outperform the methods using the simple fusion techniques, due to the inherited advantage of MKL algorithms for coping with the heterogeneous nature of multiple camera views.

2.3   Real-Time Capacity of The Framework

Assuming the codebook of BoW and action models are learned through training, the system executes the following steps at testing: an *image per frame* (1) and *local descriptors* (2) are simultaneously extracted, where the image is compared with the learned background models to derive *foreground detection of a person of interest* (3) at each frame. The derived person detections and local descriptors are used to compute the *histogram feature of an instance* that is potentially associated with one of the action classes (4). The histogram features are then classified by the action models to produce the *recognition results* (5). Empirically we find the actual bottleneck of the above pipeline is step (2). The STIP descriptor can be extracted at about 48 frames per second, while the IDT descriptor can be extracted at around 25 frames per second. As a result, the framework satisfies the requirement of real-time action recognition, if the testing videos have a frame rate less than 25 or 48.

3   Experimental Conditions

In order to validate our hypothesis that MKL (SVM-MKL) outperforms other simple fusion techniques, e.g. concatenation (SVM-COM), sum (SVM-SUM) and product (SVM-PRD) rules, for multi-view action recognition, we conduct a series of experiments on the INRIA Xmas Motion Acquisition Sequences (IXMAS) dataset [11], and evaluate the recognition rates of all the compared methods.

3.1 IXMAS Multi-View Datasets

IXMAS is a multi-view dataset created for view-invariant human action recognition [11]. The dataset captured 13 daily actions, each of which was performed 3 times by 12 actors. Original views of 5 cameras produce video sequences at 23 frames per second and 390×291 resolution. Each actor was free to choose the location and the direction to which they face while performing the actions. As a result, the view of each camera may vary from one actor to another for different runs. We use all 12 actors and 5 cameras, and evaluate 11 actions classes as in [11]. A subject-wise leave-one-out cross validation is applied, and the reported recognition rate will be the mean of all the folds.

3.2 Implementation Details

We use the default parameters of the motion-based person detector, STIP and IDT descriptors. A codebook sized 4000 is quantised from 100000 randomly selected descriptor features of the training set. The codebook is then used to compute the histogram feature vectors. As described in the previous section, the STIP descriptor uses the entire image plane and the frame span of an action given in the ground truth to define a spatio-temporal cuboid, while the IDT descriptor relies on the person detections in addition to the frame span. All the SVM models use ℓ_1 normalisation and employ the χ^2 kernel as

$$\chi^2(\mathbf{x}_i, \mathbf{x}_j) = 2 \sum_{l=1}^{D} \frac{\mathbf{x}_{il}\mathbf{x}_{jl}}{\mathbf{x}_{il} + \mathbf{x}_{jl}} \tag{4}$$

where l is the dimension index of feature vectors. All the cost parameters of SVM models are set to 100, which is found to give the overall best performance on a validation set randomly selected from the training set. Preprocessing steps of the proposed framework are implemented in OpenCV and C++, while the classification stage is implemented in MATLAB. All the experiments are run on a machine with Intel i7 Quad-Core CPU, 32GB RAM and Ubuntu 14.04 LTS installed.

4 Results and Analysis

In this section, we firstly provide an internal comparison among the methods described in Section 3, while using the STIP descriptor and BoW or the IDT descriptor and BoW. This is mainly to test whether the MKL method is indeed advantageous over the other methods for multi-view action recognition. We then give an external comparison between our proposed framework and the state-of-the-art methods applied to the IXMAS dataset in the literature under similar experimental conditions.

Fig.1 lists the person detection results of all the camera views, produced by our motion-based person detector for the subject 'Alba'. As all the camera views are temporally synchronised, we randomly select a frame number and plot the corresponding bounding boxes generated from the foreground detections. We have also quantitatively evaluated our person detections against the silhouette ground truth, by considering detections that satisfy the following inequality $\mathbf{b}_d \cap \mathbf{b}_g / \mathbf{b}_d \cup \mathbf{b}_g \geq 0.5$ (a commonly used

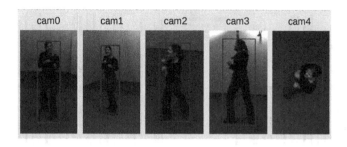

Fig. 1. Detections of our motion-based person detector of the first run of the subject 'Alba', for all the camera views, at a randomly selected frame

threshold in the object detection literature) as true positives, where b_d and b_g are the boxing box of a person detection and that of the ground truth respectively. The overall detection rate is 100%, which indicates our motion-based person detector is capable of localising the person of interest with a great accuracy.

4.1   Comparison Between MKL and Simple Strategies

Fig.2 (a) plots the recognition rates of all the compared methods using the STIP descriptor and BoW. The MKL method shows overall superior performance over the other methods and gives significantly better results of certain actions, e.g. 'scratch head' and 'punch'. Similarly Fig.2 (b) displays the recognition rates of the compared method using the IDT descriptor and BoW. The results of the all methods have been drastically improved, compared those using STIP descriptor and BoW. The MKL method also produces overall better performance than the other methods.

First of all, the combination of IDT descriptor and BoW appears to be a better choice than that of STIP descriptor and BoW for feature representation. This is mostly due to the fact the IDT descriptor uses dense sampling and additional MBH features, which leads to more expressive visual features in terms of appearance and motion. In addition, it is facilitated by the use of person detections to have more accurate ROIs of a person in the image plane. However visual features of the STIP and BoW approach are much faster to compute and do not require the extra computation of person detections. As a result, for scenarios where person detections are easy to obtain and the ROIs are reliable, the IDT and BoW approach should be applied, while for those where recognition speed is more important than recognition accuracy or limited computational resource is available, the STIP and BoW approach could be applicable. Nevertheless, for both combinations, the MKL method shows superior performance over all the other methods, which confirms our hypothesis. The guaranteed optimality of both the kernel parameters and combination parameters significantly contributes to not only the classification of each camera view but also the fusion of all camera views.

4.2   Comparison with The State-of-The-Art

Based on the results demonstrated in the previous section, the proposed MKL framework using the IDT descriptor and BoW significantly outperforms all the other compared

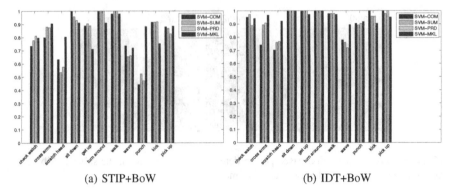

(a) STIP+BoW   (b) IDT+BoW

Fig. 2. Class-wise mean recognition rates of all the folds of the compared methods using STIP descriptor and BoW, where $\mu_{SVM-COM} = 0.819$, $\mu_{SVM-SUM} = 0.820$, $\mu_{SVM-PRD} = 0.815$, and $\mu_{SVM-MKL} = 0.842$, and those using IDT descriptor and BoW, where $\mu_{SVM-COM} = 0.915$, $\mu_{SVM-SUM} = 0.927$, $\mu_{SVM-PRD} = 0.921$, and $\mu_{SVM-MKL} = 0.950$

Table 1. Comparison of the proposed MKL method using improved trajectory descriptor and BoW, where the methods with 'N/A' in the FPS column are offline systems

Method	Actions	Actors	Views	Rate	FPS
Cilla et al. [3]	11	12	5	0.913	N/A
Weiland et al. [12]	11	10	5	0.933	N/A
Cilla et al. [4]	11	10	5	0.940	N/A
Holte et al. [6]	13	12	5	1.000	N/A
Weinland et al. [11]	11	10	5	0.835	500
Chaaraoui et al. [1]	11	12	5	0.859	26
Chaaraoui et al. [2]	11	12	5	0.914	207
SVM-MKL (IDT+BoW)	11	12	5	**0.950**	25

methods. As a result, we here compare it with state-of-the-art methods (both offline and real-time) in the literature.

Table 1 lists the experimental conditions and recognition rates of the proposed MKL framework and the state-of-the-art methods. Top half of the table includes methods that can only perform action recognition offline, and the bottom half details the real-time methods. Our framework is comparable with the offline methods while outperforming all the real-time methods. It is capable of processing 25 frames per second, which is more than enough for the IXMAS dataset, captured at 23 frames per second. As a result, our framework is sufficiently fast to process streamed videos with a similar frame rate in real-time, and to produce good performance for multi-view action recognition.

5   Conclusions and Future Work

According to the internal and external comparisons on multi-view action recognition, the proposed multiple kernel learning based framework outperforms not only the simple fusion techniques but also the state-of-the-art methods, on the IXMAS dataset. It is also capable of performing real-time action recognition at 25 frames per second. As a result, we have introduced a practical framework that is easy to implement and produces great performance in terms of both recognition accuracy and speed. For future work, we want to apply our framework to other vision problems with a similar setup. In addition, it would also be beneficial to study alternative feature representation and fusion techniques, to further improve the recognition performance.

Acknowledgments. This work has been supported by the Ambient Assisted Living Joint Programme and the Technology Strategy Board under project 'BREATHE Platform for self-assessment and efficient management for informal caregivers' (AAL-JP-2012-5-045). The funders had no role in study design, data collection and analysis, decision to publish, or preparation of the manuscript.

References

1. Chaaraoui, A.A., Climent-Perez, P., Florez-Revuelta, F.: Silhouette-based human action recognition using sequences of key poses. Pattern Recognition Letters 34, 1799–1807 (2013)
2. Chaaraoui, A.A., Padilla-Lopez, J.R., Ferrandez-Pastor, F.J., Nieto-Hidalgo, M., Florez-Revuelta, F.: A vision-based system for intelligent monitoring: human behaviour analysis and privacy by context. Sensors 14, 8895–8925 (2014)
3. Cilla, R., Patricio, M.A., Berlanga, A.: A probabilistic, discriminative and distributed system for the recognition of human actions from multiple views. Neurocomputing 75, 78–87 (2012)
4. Cilla, R., Patricio, M.A., Berlanga, A., Molina, J.M.: Human action recognition with sparse classification and multiple-view learning. Expert Systems (2013), doi:10.1111/exsy.12040
5. Gonen, M., Alpaydm, E.: Multiple kernel learning algorithms. Journal of Machine Learning Research (JMLR) 12, 2211–2268 (2011)
6. Holte, M., Chakraborty, B., Gonzalez, J., Moeslund, T.: A local 3-D motion descriptor for mult-view human action recognition from 4-D spatio-temporal interest points. IEEE Journal of Selected Topics in Signal Processing 6, 553–565 (2012)
7. Stauffer, C., Grimson, W.: Learning patterns of activity using real time tracking. IEEE Transactions on Pattern Analysis and Machine Intelligence (PAMI) 22(8), 747–767 (2000)
8. Varma, M., Babu, B.R.: More generality in efficient multiple kernel learning. In: International Conference on Machine Learning, ICML (2009)
9. Vedaldi, A., Gulshan, V., Varma, M., Zisserman, A.: Multiple kernels for object detection. In: International Conference on Computer Vision, ICCV (2009)
10. Wang, H., Schmid, C.: Action recognition with improved trajectories. In: IEEE International Conference on Computer Vision, ICCV (2013)
11. Weinland, D., Özuysal, M., Fua, P.: Making action recognition robust to occlusions and viewpoint changes. In: Daniilidis, K., Maragos, P., Paragios, N. (eds.) ECCV 2010, Part III. LNCS, vol. 6313, pp. 635–648. Springer, Heidelberg (2010)
12. Weinland, D., Ronfard, R., Boyer, E.: Free viewpoint action recognition using motion history volumes. Computer Vision and Image Understanding 104(2-3), 249–257 (2006)

PAM-Based Behavior Modelling

Thien Huynh-The[1], Ba-Vui Le[1], Muhammad Fahim[1], Sungyoung Lee[1],
Yongik Yoon[2], and Byeong Ho Kang[3]

[1] Department of Computer Engineering,
Kyung Hee University, Gyeonggi-do, 446-701, Korea
{thienht,lebavui,fahim,sylee}@oslab.khu.ac.kr
[2] Department of Multimedia Science,
Sookmyung Women University, Korea
yiyoon@sookmyung.ac.kr
[3] Department of Computing and Information Systems,
University of Tasmania, Australia
byeong.kang@utas.edu.au

Abstract. A novel approach for human behavior modelling is represented in this paper based on the Pachinko Allocation Model (PAM) algorithm for the video-based road surveillance. In particular, the authors focus on the behavior analysis and modelling for learning and training as the main distribution of this research. Sparse object features in sequence of frames are modelled into activities and behaviors with full topic correlations to avoid omissions of small activities.

Keywords: human behavior modelling, CCTV system, pachinko allocation model, video-based road surveillance.

1 Introduction

In recent years, Human Behavior Analysis via the CCTV systems has become an interesting field, however, achieving high performance of recognition is not an easy task, especially in the real-time environment. The recognition performance by classifying the new behavior based on existing models depends on the modelling. Therefore, the correlation of a behavior and its class would be described via a probabilistic model. As a simple Dynamic Bayesian Network (DBN) [1], [2], the Hidden Markov Models (HMMs) [3], [4], have become the powerful tool for activity modelling. However, they are usually sensitive to noise or input errors which are the reasons for low recognition rate. Therefore, these shortcomings have motivated recent approaches to apply topic models as the effective and novel solution. These approaches such as Latent Dirichlet Allocation (LDA) [5], Dual Hierarchical Dirichlet Process (DHDP) [6], can define the relationship between each atomic activity with its corresponding behavior through the probabilistic model. However, they can not represent relationships fully, especially topic-topic and topic-word, thus missing or incorrect classification can occur in both the modelling and recognition stage. In this paper, the authors propose a modelling approach using the Pachinko Allocation Model [7] to solve existing problem of previous approaches.

L. Pecchia et al. (Eds.): IWAAL 2014, LNCS 8868, pp. 34–37, 2014.

2   A PAM-Based Behavior Modelling

After achieving the object features as position and direction, they need to be modelled into sparse activities. The behavior is the collection of atomic activities which are considered in the sequence of frames. In this paper, PAM is proposed to capture not only correlations among activities but also correlations among behaviors themselves. As a special structure, a four-level hierarchy PAM consists one root behavior, s_1 behaviors at the second level $T = \{t_1, t_2, \ldots, t_{s_1}\}$, s_2 activity groups at the third level $T' = \{t'_1, t'_2, \ldots, t'_{s_2}\}$ and N features at the bottom. In PAM, behaviors are fully associated to activity groups which are then connected to features. The Fig. 1 shows the hierarchical topic model (a) and the graphic model (b) of PAM for behavior modelling. The multinomial of the root θ_r^d and behaviors $\theta_{t_i}^d$ are sampled from the Dirichlet distribution $g_r(\alpha_r)$ and $g_i(\alpha_i)|_{i=1}^{s_1}$, respectively, where d is a matrix containing features of a number of frames. A long clip D presenting for a certain behavior will be divided into n small clips $D = \{d_1, d_2, \ldots, d_n\}$. Meanwhile the activity group is modelled with fixed multinomial distributions $\phi_{t'_j}|_{j=1}^{s_2}$ and $\psi_{t'_j}|_{j=1}^{s_2}$ which are sampled from Dirichlet distributions $g(\beta)$ and $g(\gamma)$, respectively. For each small clip:

1. Derive a multinomial distributions θ_r from α_r.
2. For each behavior, derive s_1 multinomial distributions θ_{t_i} from α_i.
3. Derive s_2 multinomial distributions $\phi_{z'}$ from β and $\psi_{z'}$ from γ for each activity group z'. For kth feature with location p_k and direction q_k in d:
   (a) Derive a behavior z_k and a activity group z'_k from θ_r and θ_z
   (b) Derive a location p_k and direction feature q_k from $\phi_{z'}$ and $\psi_{z'}$.

The hyper-parameters as Dirichlet priors α, β, and γ can be estimated via the Gibbs sampling [7]. The marginal probability of a small clip as:

$$P(d|\alpha, \beta, \gamma) = \int P(\theta_r|\alpha_r) \prod_{i=1}^{s_1} P(\theta_{t_1}|\alpha_i)$$

$$\prod_k \sum_{z_k, z'_k} (P(z_k|\theta_r) P(z'_k|\theta_z) P(f_k|\phi_{z'}, \psi_{z'})) d\theta^{(d)} \quad (1)$$

Finally, the probability of generating D is computed as:

$$P(D|\alpha, \beta, \gamma) = \int \prod_{j=1}^{s_2} (P(\phi_{t'_j}|\beta) + P(\psi_{t'_j}|\gamma)) \prod_d P(d|\alpha, \beta, \gamma) \, d\phi d\psi \quad (2)$$

In order to recognize, the Support Vector Machines (SVMs) is chosen to train the model derived from the behaviors and activity groups with labels.

3   Experimental Results

The QMUL data set [8] was used for evaluation with non-overlapping clips which run at 30fps in frame rate and 360×288 in frame resolution. The QMUL dataset

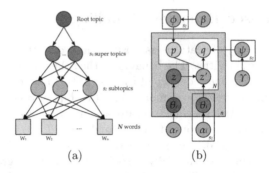

Fig. 1. Pachinko Allocation Model: (a) Hierarchical topic model (b) Graphic model

contains 108 clips (72 for training and 36 for testing) presenting 2 behaviors: vertical and horizontal traffic. The 4-second clips will be generated from a long clip for assessment. The Fig. 2 represents the detected activities in some samples as small clips which will be modelled for different probabilistic models. Some activities can appear in clips of both behaviors, therefore, the decision of class is employed based on a trained structure of SVM with the highest correlation. Moreover, the evaluation is performed though recall and precision value and compared with an approach using the LDA. The detail results have been shown in the Table. 1. In both recall and precision results, PAM is better than LDA due to subtopic as activity group layer. However, taking more computation time in learning and recognition is the trade-off of this approach. Thus, this limitation can be reduced by discarding reduplicated models for the training stage to ensure the real-time results.

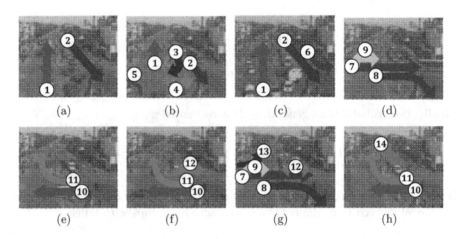

Fig. 2. Activities have been detected in PAM-modelling for training. (a)-(c): 3 models of the vertical traffic behavior. (d)-(h): 5 models of the horizontal traffic behavior.

Table 1. Confusion matrix of the SVM classifier

	PAM			LDA		
Behavior	Vertical	Horizontal	Recall	Vertical	Horizonta	Recall
Vertical	53	7	0.883	49	11	0.817
Horizontal	7	48	0.873	8	47	0.855
Precision	0.883	0.873		0.860	0.810	

4 Conclusion

In this paper, we proposed the human behavior modelling based on the four-level hierarchy PAM, in which, the probabilistic data presenting the relationship of features and behaviors will be generated for training stage. The PAM captures correlations among words as features and among topics as activities or behaviors, thus the errors in modelling will be limited to improve the recognition rate. The model was also evaluated and compared with the LDA approach. In the future, we need to improve the recognition performance by filtering highest characteristic features for training and optimizing the SVM classifier.

Acknowledgments. This research was support by the MSIP (Ministry of Science, ICT&Future Planning), Korea, under the ITRC (Information Technology Research Center) support program supervised by the NIPA (National IT Industry Promotion Agency) (NIPA-2014-(H0301-14-1003)).

References

1. Oliver, N., Rosario, B., Pentland, A.: A bayesian computer vision system for modeling human interactions. IEEE Trans. Pattern Anal. Mach. Intell. 22(8), 831–843 (2000)
2. Xiang, T., Gong, S.: Video behavior profiling for anomaly detection. IEEE Trans. Pattern Anal. Mach. Intell. 30(5), 893–908 (2008)
3. Brand, M., Kettnaker, V.: Discovery and segmentation of activities in video. IEEE Trans. Pattern Anal. Mach. Intell. 22(8), 844–851 (2008)
4. Xiang, T., Gong, S.: Beyond tracking: Modelling activity and understanding behaviour. Int J. Comput. Vis. 67(1), 21–51 (2006)
5. Zhao, L., Shang, L., Gao, Y., Yang, Y., Jia, X.: Video behavior analysis using topic models and rough sets [applications notes]. IEEE Comput. Intell. Mag. 8(1), 56–67 (2013)
6. Wang, X., Ma, X., Grimson, W.: Unsupervised activity perception in crowded and complicated scenes using hierarchical bayesian models. IEEE Trans. Pattern Anal. Mach. Intell. 31(3), 539–555 (2009)
7. Li, W., McCallum, A.: Pachinko allocation dag-structured mixture models of topic correlations. In: 23th International Conference on Machine Learning, pp. 557–584. ACM Press, New York (2006)
8. QMUL Junction Dataset, http://www.eecs.qmul.ac.uk/~ccloy/downloads_qmul_junction.html

Energy Expenditure Analysis: A Comparative Research of Based on Mobile Accelerometers

Ángel Ruiz-Zafra[1], Eva Orantes Gonzalez[2], Manuel Noguera[1], Kawtar Benghazi[1], and José María Heredia Jiménez[2]

[1] Departamento de Lenguajes y Sistemas Informáticos, Granada, Spain
{angelr,mnoguera,benghazi}@ugr.es
[2] Departamento de Educación Física y Deportiva, Granada, Spain
{maevor,herediaj}@ugr.es

Abstract. Nowadays, the Metabolic Equivalent Task (MET) is the most often used indicator for energy expenditure (EE) calculation of physical activity (PA). The use of novel devices based on inertial movements (e.g. accelerometers) enable the measurement of the PA using "counts":, where each count is an aggregated value that can be used to determine the number of METs. For some kind of users, such as elderly people or patients in AAL environments, the MET is an important indicator in order to maintain a good health. At present, there exist several types of inertial devices that enable different forms of count calculation and types of exercise monitoring. From the point of view of process analysis and infrastructure needed, they differ in several aspects, such as extra devices required and out-of-device processing. This paper presents a survey analysis about the possibilities of different types of accelerometers to measure EE in AAL contexts. To achieve this objective, we have conducted several experiments based on the performing of different exercises with different accelerometers placed in different body parts.

Keywords: Energy expenditure, elderly people, ambient assisted living, accelerometers.

1 Introduction

The special attention given to health and wellness is a main concern nowadays. Several organizations around the world are targeting at healthy activities promotion, emphasizing on changeable health risk factors such as unhealthy habits [1], where physical activity (PA) has proven to be an important factor related to a number of positive health outcomes [2].

Although for most people the performance of a self and informally managed PA is enough [3], for other kinds of users, such as elderly people or dependent people -for whom Ambient Assisted Living (AAL) technology is required-, accurate awareness and assessment of their PA (how energy is expended) is crucial to ensure health and wellbeing [4].

To measure the energy expenditure (EE), the most commonly used unit of measure is the Metabolic Equivalent Task (MET), where many research about the equivalence

L. Pecchia et al. (Eds.): IWAAL 2014, LNCS 8868, pp. 38–45, 2014.

between a specific physical activity and the number of calories burned have been carried out so far [5][6].

For the intermediate user, the use of these equivalence are enough, because although the EE of each user is not totally accurate, the margins of error do not cause a problem to their health. However, for other kinds of users, e.g., elderly people or dependent people at home, the EE spent in the performance of a PA must be bounded according to professional advice in order to prevent a worsening of health.

The use of accelerometers to measure the PA is one of the most often used approaches for this aim since they make it possible to define the intensity of the PA [7] and represent an alternative out-of-lab method to estimate EE, enabling to take measures in indoor and outdoor conditions [8].

To measure the amount of PA detected by an accelerometer, the concept of "count" [9] is used in this research. Unlike MET, where a MET has equivalence in calories [6], there is no consensus or standard calculation (in calories or METS) about how counts are computed and in which time unit (e.g. per minute). In this way, the number of counts of a PA is dependent of the device and the calculation process used.

In this paper we analyzed different types of accelerometers for EE measurement, in order to provide further insights and comparisons about the kinds of data they provide, how the collection process is, the exercises for which they can be used and if they need additional hardware to interact with them. We have conducted several experiments where different exercises have been carried out and supported by three different accelerometers placed on three different parts of the body or clothing: legs, chest and pocket.

With the results obtained, we discuss which sensor should be used depending on the PA to be performed and the kind of user with special focused on AAL domain.

This paper is organized as follows. Section 2 presents the related work. Section 3 introduces EE methods. The research study carried out in this work is presented in Section 4. The results of this research are presented in Section 5 and discussed in Section 6. Finally, Section 7 summarizes the conclusions and future work.

2   Related Work

The calculation of the EE is not an easy challenge, and several researches have appeared in the last decades intending to provide a good method to estimate it.

Before the use of novel technologies, the calculation of the EE was done on the basis of medical features such as Basal Metabolic Rates (BMR), obtaining a close approximation, but generalizing the results [10]. Other, and more recent, methods such as the use of indirect calorimetry or bioelectrical impedance are also used to provide an approximation of the real EE [11].

Recent proposals intend to measure the PA using accelerometers, showing the effectiveness and powerful of these devices in the inertial measurement [12].

Many projects applied with elderly people, which could be also apply in AAL, have shown the importance of the measurement of the EE in these kind of users [13].

For example, the research presented in [14-15] show the evolution of the EE in elderly people during a period of time, determining the importance of measuring EE to enhance, or at least maintain, health and wellbeing of users. However, these proposals are focused on the EE of a particular PA or are based on the use of a single accelerometer. This entails that the results obtained are fully conditioned by the technology used or by the PA performed, so in some cases the EE has a high margin of error. In this paper, we address this issue. We have conducted several activities with different accelerometers to study how they behave depending on the activities to monitor.

3   Energy Expenditure Assessment

EE is a key indicator that can be used to determine the intensity and duration of a PA. In some contexts (e.g., rehabilitation and AAL) and for different types of users, such as elderly people, this indicator can be useful to define which activities (intensity, duration) are suitable to be performed [4].

Furthermore, the recent advances in the integration of sensors and wireless devices are given rise to the proliferation of accelerometer devices which can be placed on different body members: accelerometers of smartphones (which are usually taken in the pocket), a chest and waist sensor with accelerometers, etc.

The EE calculation process of a PA is not a single and closed process. Several methodologies have been proposed based on different approaches to calculate the EE [11]. Nowadays, one of the most common approaches to measure the PA is based on the use of accelerometers [12]. Using these devices, the researchers can estimate the EE in a precise manner, using the concept of count [9] as PA indicator.

Several processes to calculate the counts from the raw accelerometer information (x, y and z axis) have been proposed, being the most used the following three approaches [9].

1.   Use a digital counter to accrue the number of times the signal crosses a preset threshold.
2.   Use an algorithm that can determine the maximum value for a selected time period (epoch).
3.   Use the area under the curve (integration) algorithm.

According to the literature [9], the third one is the most used approach and the one chosen for this research work.

4   Experiment

There exist different correlated factors to determine the EE: the type of user, the type of physical activity to be performed and the type of accelerometer. In this research we have analyzed three different types of accelerometers (two open stand-alone sensors and one smartphone accelerometer) applied in three activities, studying the process to collect data and infrastructure required in terms of additional devices and software. In this study we address the following objectives:

- Perform different kind of activities using three different accelerometers with different features and placed in different body member to determinate which is the one that get a better approximation to the EE real cost.
- According to the results obtained from the previous study discuss about the results, in order to determine in which situations/contexts is appropriate to use each accelerometer, depending on the PA and the user.

4.1   Energy Expenditure Calculation Process

The number of METs can be calculated according to the number of counts obtained from the accelerometers and other characteristics of the user, such as weight, height or gender.

Figure 1 shows the complete process to obtain the number of METs. The calculation process of the counts from the accelerometer sensors is a static process, regardless of the kind of user or sensor, unlike the final calculation of METS, which depends on the user information. To calculate the counts, we have applied the following algorithm:

1. Obtain the X, Y, Z axis values from the accelerometer(s) for a period of time (the duration of the physical activity).
2. There are many accelerometers from different vendors whose values range from +-2g, +-4g or +-8g in standby, so is needed to filter the data obtained from each accelerometer. We applied a Low-pass filter to isolate the force of gravity and a High-pass filter to remove the gravity, obtaining the linear acceleration:

```
alpha = 0.8;
//Low-pass filter
gravity_x = alpha + gravity_x + (1 - alpha) * x_value
gravity_y = alpha + gravity_y + (1 - alpha) * y_value;
gravity_z = alpha + gravity_z + (1 - alpha) * z_value
//High-pass filter
linear_x = x_value - gravity_x;
linear_y = y_value - gravity_y;
linear_z = z_value - gravity_z;
```

3. Using the linear acceleration values from the previous step, and since these values range from negative to positive values, the values are normalized to obtain a representative positive value for each accelerometer captured data:

$$\sqrt{(linear\_x)^2 + (linear\_y)^2 + (linear\_z)^2}$$

4. We apply an integration process to calculate the area under the curve (AUC) to determine the value for every two different values of the array. We have decide to use the Trapezoidal rule [16]:

$$\int_a^b f(x)\, dx = (b-a) * \frac{f(a) - f(b)}{2}$$

The sums of these areas (raw counts) equal the total number of counts obtained by the accelerometer in the PA performed.

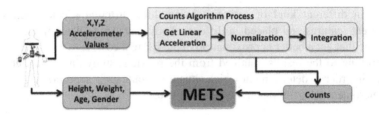

Fig. 1. Energy expenditure calculation process

5   Results

We have applied the algorithm shown in Section 4 to different PAs (walk at 4Km/h, sweep the floor and watch TV) and with different accelerometers, in order to compare the results provided by each type of accelerometer in the different activities performed.

Two of the three accelerometers are commercial devices and the third one is the internal accelerometer of a smartphone (Nexus 5). These devices have been selected because they are designed to be placed on different parts of the body: chest (Sensor 1), pocket (Smartphone) and legs (Sensor 2).

In order to compare the effectiveness and the importance of the accelerometer used, as well as the place to use it, we have performed each activity with the three different sensors in the three different possible locations.

All the PAs have been done for the same interval of time, 60 seconds, and in the same conditions. The number of counts for each sensor and activity is represented in the Table 1 (C = Chest; P=Pocket; L=Leg).

Table 1. Numbers of counts obtained from the accelerometers in the different PA

	Sensor 1			Sensor 2			Smartphone		
	C	P	L	C	P	L	C	P	L
Walk at 4Km/h	121	200	342	16	22	30	1351	2433	3250
Sweep the floor	65	88	86	18	15	11	1660	1324	1191
Watch TV	25	21	17	2	8	4	175	206	117

To calculate the number of METs we have used the formulas of the research work presented in [17], which are defined for different group of users. We selected medium and standard values for the different groups: youth (180 cm, 80Kg, male), adult (180cm, 80kg, male) and elderly (180cm, 80kg, male). Table 2 shows the METs obtained of the Sensor 1, Table 3 of the Sensor 2 and Table 4 of the Smartphone.

Table 2. Number of METs of Sensor 1

Group	Walk at 4KM/h			Sweep the floor			Watch TV		
	C	P	L	C	P	L	C	P	L
All groups	1.02	1.06	1.14	0.98	1.00	1.00	0.96	0.96	0.96
Youth	1.62	1.67	1.77	1.58	1.60	1.60	1.56	1.56	1.55
Adults	1.04	1.09	1.69	1.01	1.03	1.03	0.99	0.99	0.99
Elderly	1.35	1.39	1.45	1.32	1.33	1.33	1.30	1.30	1.30

Table 3. Number of MET of Sensor 2

Group	Walk at 4KM/h			Sweep the floor			Watch TV		
	C	P	L	C	P	L	C	P	L
All groups	0.96	0.96	0.97	0.96	0.96	0.95	0.95	0.95	0.95
Youth	1.55	1.56	1.56	1.55	1.55	1.55	1.54	1.55	1.54
Adults	0.99	0.99	1.00	0.99	0.99	0.99	0.98	0.98	0.98
Elderly	1.30	1.30	1.31	1.30	1.30	1.30	1.29	1.30	1.29

Table 4. Number of METs of Smartphone

Group	Walk at 4KM/h			Sweep the floor			Watch TV		
	C	P	L	C	P	L	C	P	L
All groups	1.70	2.31	2.77	1.88	1.69	1.62	1.05	1.06	1.01
Youth	2.43	3.14	3.68	2.63	2.41	2.33	1.66	1.68	1.62
Adults	1.71	2.29	2.73	1.88	1.69	1.62	1.07	1.09	1.04
Elderly	1.93	2.44	2.82	2.07	1.91	1.85	1.37	1.39	1.35

6   Discussion

The different results obtained in the section 4 show that each accelerometer differs in the number of counts it allows to be reckoned for each PA and such differences are not linear, i.e., they vary depending on the type of activity.

In order to compare the results with a reliable source, we compare the results with the study presented in [18], which is one of the most referenced papers in the literature. This paper provides results of several activities from different contexts. To compare the results we selected the elderly people sample presented in the tables above.

The EE of walking at 4KM/h (2.5 mph) is 3 METs per minute, sweeping the floor is 3.3 METs and watching TV is 1 MET [18]. According to Table 4, the best approximation to the counts of walking at 4Km/h is obtained with the smartphone accelerometer placed in the leg (2.82 Mets). In the same way, in the floor sweeping experiment, the best result is also obtained with the smartphone placed in the chest, but with a greater margin of error: from 2.07 to 2.7.

Instead, the results obtained with the three sensors in the last exercise (watch TV) are very similar, around 1.30. So in this case any of them could be used for measurement of this kind of activities.

Focusing in a specific group, such as elderly people in AAL, we can conclude, according to the results and the interpretation of them, that the appropriate choice would be the use of the smartphone (pocket) as accelerometer to measure the PA, but placed in different parts of the body, depending on the activity to perform. In two of the three exercises, walk and watch television, the result obtained with the smartphone has been conclusively: 3 as reference value and 2.82 as value obtained; 1 as real value and 1.30 as value obtained.

In the other activity (sweep the floor), the error has been around 1.4 METS. Even in this case, the margin of error is the smallest compared to the other two accelerometers (2 METs –Sensor 1- and 1.9 METs – Sensor 2-).Besides, although Sensor 1 is considerably more expensive than Sensor 2, they obtained practically the same results.

Finally, the results presented in this paper have been obtained in a set of experiments performed by a single case study with the same interval time (60 seconds). In this manner, this research work is not intended to be conclusive, but the first stage of a broader study.

7   Conclusions and Future Work

Nowadays the attention about health and wellness is a main concern in order to enhance the quality of life. The EE of PAs (METs) is crucial in some contexts, such as elderly people and dependent people monitoring at home (AAL), where the supervision of the EE is mandatory to be aware of a good health condition.

This research presents 27 experiments where three accelerometers have been used in three different body parts, in order to perform different real activities and determine which accelerometer provides a better approximation.

The results have concluded that the closest approximation of EE obtained is using the internal accelerometer of the smartphone (placed in different body members, depending on the PA to perform). Focusing in AAL environment, such as monitoring of elderly people, the success rate has been highly enlightening. The use of smartphone accelerometer has obtained better results. Smartphones have additional benefits, such as the use of only one device to monitor all the process and the avoiding of manual transfer of data to second devices, which results more convenient to users and supervisors. In addition, the smartphone is more and more an affordable and natural device for the age group studied. However, ergonomics is also an aspect to be considered and smartphones are not naturally (and even used) taken in the chest or certain body limbs, so that special straps are needed.

As for future work, we will try to carry out several studies with different kinds of users and using different accelerometers with others characteristics, in order to broaden and validate the research proposed in this paper.

References

1. World Health Organization. Milestones in health promotion: Statements from Global Conferences (2009)
2. U.S. Department of Health and Human Services. Physical Activity and Health: A Report of the Surgeon General. Atlanta, GA: U.S. Department of Health and Human Services, Centers for Disease Control and Prevention, National Center for Chronic Disease Prevention and Health Promotion (1996)
3. Sallis, J.F., Saelens, B.E.: Assessment of physical activity by self-report: status, limitations, and future directions. Research quarterly for exercise and sport 71(2 Suppl), S1–S14 (2000)
4. Goran, M.I., Poehlman, E.T.: Total energy expenditure and energy requirements in healthy elderly persons. Metabolism 41(7), 744–753 (1992)
5. Ainsworth, B.E., et al.: Compendium of physical activities: an update of activity codes and MET intensities. Medicine and Science in Sports and Exercise 32(9, Suppl1), S498–S504 (2000)
6. Byrne, N.M., et al.: Metabolic equivalent: one size does not fit all. Journal of Applied Physiology 99(3), 1112–1119 (2005)
7. Freedson, P.S., et al.: Evaluation of artificial neural network algorithms for predicting METs and activity type from accelerometer data: validation on an independent sample. Journal of Applied Physiology 111(6), 1804–1812 (2011)
8. Yang, C.-C., Hsu, Y.-L.: A review of accelerometry-based wearable motion detectors for physical activity monitoring. Sensors 10(8), 7772–7788 (2010)
9. Chen, K.Y., Bassett, D.R.: The technology of accelerometry-based activity monitors: current and future. Medicine and Science in Sports and Exercise 37(11), S490 (2005)
10. Calloway, D.H.: Zanni, Eleni. Energy requirements and energy expenditure of elderly men. The American Journal of Clinical Nutrition 33(10), 2088–2092 (1980)
11. Pinheiro Volp, A.C., et al.: Energy expenditure: components and evaluation methods. Nutr. Hosp. 26(3), 430–440 (2011)
12. Garatachea, N., Torres Luque, G., Gonzalez Gallego, J.: Physical activity and energy expenditure measurements using accelerometers in older adults. Nutr. Hosp. 25(2), 224–230 (2010)
13. Bourke, A.K., et al.: Embedded fall and activity monitoring for a wearable ambient assisted living solution for older adults. In: Engineering in Medicine and Biology Society (EMBC), 2012 Annual International Conference of the IEEE, pp. 248–251. IEEE (2012)
14. Goran, M.I., Poehlman, E.T.: Endurance training does not enhance total energy expenditure in healthy elderly persons. American Journal of Physiology 263, E950-E950 (1992)
15. Clegg, A., et al.: Frailty in elderly people. The Lancet 381(9868), 752–762 (2013)
16. Tallarida, R.J., Murray, R.B.: Area under a Curve: Trapezoidal and Simpson's Rules. In: Manual of Pharmacologic Calculations, pp. 77–81. Springer, New York (1987)
17. Santos-Lozano, A., et al.: Actigraph GT3X: Validation and Determination of Physical Activity Intensity Cut Points. International Journal of Sports Medicine 34(11), 975–982 (2013)
18. Ainsworth, B.E., et al.: Compendium of physical activities: an update of activity codes and MET intensities. Medicine and Science in Sports and Exercise 32(9 Suppl1), S498–S504 (2000)

Doorstep Security; Using a Technology Based Solution for the Prevention of Doorstep Crime

Ian Cleland[1], Timothy Patterson[1], Chris D. Nugent[1], Federico Cruciani[2], Norman Black[1], and Cristiano Paggetti[2]

[1]Computer Science Research Institute and School of Computing and Mathematics, University of Ulster, Newtownabbey, Co. Antrim, BT37 0QB, UK
`{i.cleland,t.patterson,cd.nugent,nd.black}@ulster.ac.uk`
[2] I+ SRL, 50144 Florence, Italy
`{f.cruciani,c.paggetti}@i-piu.it`

Abstract. Safety and security rank highly in the priorities of older people on both an individual and policy level. Older people are commonly targeted as victims of doorstep crime, as they can be perceived as being vulnerable. As a result, this can have a major effect on the victim's health and wellbeing. There have been numerous prevention strategies implemented in an attempt to combat and reduce the number of doorstep crimes. There is, however, little information available detailing the effectiveness of these strategies and how they impact on the fear of crime, particularly with repeat victims. There is clear merit in the creation and piloting of a technology based solution to combat doorstep crime. This paper presents a solution which utilizes everyday technology to provide increased security for older people within their home whilst simultaneously reinforcing doorstep etiquette through educational material.

Keywords: Independent living, Doorstep crime, Security.

1 Introduction

The term doorstep crime covers a number of offences including, distraction burglary, rogue traders and pressure sales. This includes cases where the offender first enters the premises and subsequently uses distraction burglary tactics in order to remain on the premises in order to commit burglary [1]. Indeed, doorstep crime has been highlighted as a priority within the Consumer Protection Partnership (CPP) Priorities Report 2013/2014 as an area, which is currently or has the potential to cause, the greatest detriment to consumers [2]. In 2010/2011 5,480 distraction burglaries were recorded in England and Wales [3]. Not all offences, however, are reported. Distraction burglary is often cited as one of the most under reported crimes. Some studies have estimated the actual number of cases to be between 15,344-17,294 [4]. It has been further estimated that the social and economic cost of distraction burglary in the UK is £35 million [4]. This paper considers the nature and prevalence of doorstep crime, in addition to prevention strategies and describes an information and communication technology (ICT) based solution to aid in its prevention.

L. Pecchia et al. (Eds.): IWAAL 2014, LNCS 8868, pp. 46–50, 2014.

2   Background

Research has shown that victims of doorstep crime are predominantly older, female and white [1]. Data from Operation Liberal, which focused on combating doorstep crime, indicated that the average age of doorstep crime victims was 81 and over two thirds (69%) were female [5]. Worryingly, it is estimated that 63% of victims of distraction burglary experience repeat victimization [6]. Specific targeting of a victim is characteristic of doorstep crime, with criminals assessing the potential risks and rewards. Older people are perceived as 'suitable targets' as they are commonly associated with increased vulnerability. The stereotype of an older person can include: living alone; keeping amounts of cash within the home; less likely to remember stolen items; less likely to make good identification of perpetrator and less likely to report the incident [7].

A number of prevention strategies have previously been employed in an attempt to prevent doorstep crime. These can broadly be broken into 3 categories; Enforcement, Situational and Educational. The aims of these strategies along with examples are presented in Table 1.

Table 1. The aim of the three categories of prevention strategies for doorstep crime; enforcement, situational and educational, including examples

Prevention Strategy	Aim	Example
Enforcement	Improve detection rates so more offenders are brought to justice and increase local knowledge.	Specialist distraction burglary detectives/task force and specialist forensics to gather evidence.
Situational	Manipulation of the environment with the aim of reducing susceptibility to crime.	The use of locks and chains to prevent forced entry or intercoms, and security camera as deterrents.
Educational	Raise awareness of the risk of doorstep crime and what steps can be taken to minimize the risk.	Educational events, Television adverts, Trusted Trader register, doorstep etiquette to improve safety.

The use of situational security devices has increased over time. For example the use of double locks has increased by 13% since 1995 [8]. Security enhancements can range from simple physical solutions, such as door chains and peepholes, to audio and video intercoms and more complicated solutions such as remote video and access devices. The effectiveness of these solutions is, however, yet to be fully evaluated and understood [5]. One study found that installation of a voice intercom system provided a reduction of 21.5% in distraction related burglaries [9]. Installing these features does not, however, address the issues as the victim may still be persuaded to grant access to the perpetrator. Therefore, education and reinforcement of proper doorstep etiquette is essential in lessening the risk of falling victim to doorstep crime [10]. The Cambridgeshire Distraction Burglary and Rogue Trader Taskforce organized awareness days which included an introduction of the 'Stop, Chain, Check' message, a video on doorstep crime and multiple advertisements highlighting the issue [10]. While such events may receive positive feedback, it is difficult to assess if these approaches actually prevent attendees from becoming victims of doorstep crime.

3   Implemented Solution to Reduce Doorstep Crime

The solution, described within this paper, combines situational ICT prevention strategies with educational approaches allowing the user to seek assistance in deciding if it is safe to grant access to a person visiting their house. In Figure 1, an overview of the implemented solution is presented. A key component is a low-cost ($\approx$€40) wireless IP camera (Fig. 1a) which provides a video stream input of the area outside a user's door. The introduction of a person at the user's door (a caller) to this image scene results in motion. A motion detection algorithm [11] is used to identify frames potentially containing the caller. A face detection algorithm, based on the Viola-Jones method [12], is then executed on each of these frames. Should a face be identified within a frame the user is alerted via a sound and web browser notification (Fig. 1b). The person may then either request help through the system or indicate that they are familiar with the caller. In future iterations the option to capture photos from the press of a door bell will also be included. Upon requesting help, alert details containing the user's id, alert time and the caller's image are transmitted and stored in a remotely hosted SQL database. A Google Cloud Message (GCM) is subsequently pushed to all carers who are registered for the relevant user. GCM is utilized as it provides an off-the-shelf solution for pushing light-weight notifications (<=4Kb) to multiple devices. Additionally, in the event of a carer's device being offline the GCM architecture includes message persistency whereby messages are stored on the GCM servers and retransmitted when the device regains connectivity. When the carer clicks the GCM notification on their mobile device an Android based application is launched (Fig. 1c) which retrieves and displays an image of the caller. In addition to the image of the caller being displayed the following options are relayed to the user, e)'let in' or f)'keep out'. Once the carer chooses an option the recommended action is transmitted to the SQL database and a GCM message is pushed to the remaining

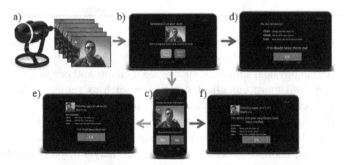

Fig. 1. ICT solution incorporating both situational and educational approaches, a) low cost camera and captured images, b) user interface showing caller image and choices, c) carer app showing captured image, d)doorstep etiquette educational information, e) carer response to allow entry and f) carer response to deny entry.

carers informing them that the alert has been answered. The recommended action is subsequently fetched by the user-side device which continuously polls the database until a carer response has been inserted or a timeout value (10 minutes) is reached. In all end cases (Fig. 1 d, e, f) educational content relating to doorstep etiquette is displayed to the user thus helping to reinforce safe doorstep behavior.

4   Conclusion

This paper describes the issues around doorstep crime and the effects it can have on health and economy. In order to address this, an ICT solution which can combat these issues has been developed. This technology solution is targeted at older people (70-80) who may suffer from a limiting cognitive, functional, mobility, visual or hearing impairment, that can give the impression that the person is vulnerable to becoming a victim of doorstep crime. The solution within this paper combines situational and educational prevention methods to provide piece of mind for the user whilst reaffirming doorstep etiquette. By keeping the installed technology to a minimum and as unobtrusive and familiar as possible the system will avoid heightening the user's fear of crime. Future work shall seek to evaluate the system with a cohort of older adults who have been previously targeted by doorstep crime in the past.

Acknowledgments. Invest Northern Ireland is acknowledged for partially supporting this project under the R and D grant RD0513844.The authors would also like to thank members of the Police Service of Northern Ireland (PSNI), the Good Morning Network and the Connected Health Innovation Centre (CHIC) for their input to this work.

References

1. Lister, S., Wall, D.: Deconstructing distraction burglary: an ageist offence? In: Wahidin, A., Cain, M. (eds.) Ageing, Crime and Society, pp. 107–123 (2008)
2. Consumer Protection Partnership, Consumer Protection Partnership; Priorities Report 2013-14 (2014)
3. Office of National Statistics, Crime statistics 2011/12, Statistical Bulliten (2013)
4. Mills, H., Skodbo, S., Blyth, P.: Understanding organised crime: estimating the scale and the social and economic costs (2013)
5. Gorden, C., Buchanan, J.: A Systematic Literature Review of Doorstep Crime: Are the Crime Prevention Strategies More Harmful than the Crime? The Howard Journal of Criminal Justice 52, 498–515 (2013)
6. Bertie, A.: Doorstep crime and rogue trader activity. Age UK (2010)
7. Lister, S., Wall, D.: Deconstructing distraction burglary: an ageist offence? In: Wahidin, A., Cain, M. (eds.) Ageing, Society and Crime, pp. 107–123 (2008)
8. Office for National Statistics, Crime Statistics, Focus on Property Crime, 2012/13 Release (2013)
9. Leicestershire Constabulary.: Protection and Reassurance Initiative to Defend the Elderly, Reducing Burglary, reducing the fear of crime (2001)

10. Collomb-Roberts, N., Williams, S., Moore, L., Tortoriello, M.: Cambridgeshire Distraction Burglary and Rouge Trade Taskforce: an evaluation (2004)
11. Cruciani, F., Donnelly, M.P., Nugent, C.D., Parente, G., Paggetti, C., Burns, W.: DANTE: A video based annotation tool for smart environments. In: Par, G., Morrow, P. (eds.) S-CUBE 2010. LNICST, vol. 57, pp. 179–188. Springer, Heidelberg (2011)
12. Viola, P., Jones, M.J.: Robust real-time face detection. International Journal of Computer Vision 57, 137–154 (2004),
http://dx.doi.org/10.1023/B:VISI.0000013087.49260.fb

Encouraging Behavioral Change via Everyday Technologies to Reduce Risk of Developing Alzheimer's Disease

Phillip J. Hartin[1], Chris D. Nugent[1], Sally I. McClean[2], Ian Cleland[1], JoAnn T. Tschanz[3], Christine Clark[4], and Maria C. Norton[3, 4]

[1] School of Computing and Mathematics, University of Ulster,
Jordanstown Campus, BT370QB, UK
{pj.hartin,cd.nugent,i.cleland}@ulster.ac.uk
[2] School of Computing and Information Engineering, University of Ulster,
Coleraine Campus, BT521SA, UK
si.mclean@ulster.ac.uk
[3] Department of Psychology, Utah State University, Logan, UT 84322-4440, USA
joann.tschanz@usu.edu
[4] Department of Family, Consumer, and Human Development,
Utah State University, Logan, UT 84322-2915, USA
christine.clark@aggiemail.usu.edu, maria.norton@usu.edu

Abstract. Alzheimer's Disease is a global health concern, with no known cure. There is evidence, however, that certain risk factors can be targeted to prevent the development of the disease. Most of these risk factors are non-genetic and can be modified by behavioral change. In this paper, we present a smartphone app with a gamification element designed to encourage and track this behavior change as part of a 6-month randomized control trial with 146 participants. Initial results from the first 9 weeks of the study have been promising; 98% (n=102) of participants in the treatment group (n=104) are using the app on a daily basis to check their self-reported behaviors against recommended values, predominantly at the end of each day (9pm-12am). Additionally, based on session duration data, users appear to become familiar with the app following 1 week of use.

Keywords: behavior change, preventative healthcare, gamification, mobile computing, Alzheimer's disease.

1 Introduction

Alzheimer's disease (AD) is a recognized global health concern. It is the most common cause of dementia and the sixth leading cause of death in the United States [1]. Currently, a new AD case develops every 68 seconds, which is projected to surge to every 33 seconds by 2050 [1]. There is, however, currently no cure for AD. Current research is now focusing on the risk factors and prevention methods associated with the condition. International experts agree that AD may be preventable and have called

L. Pecchia et al. (Eds.): IWAAL 2014, LNCS 8868, pp. 51–58, 2014.
© Springer International Publishing Switzerland 2014

for a concentrated effort to study modifiable risk factors related to dementias [2]. All genetic factors discovered to date that are associated with AD account for approximately one third of the risk of developing the disease, leaving the majority of risk due to lifestyle and environmental factors and their effects on genetic function [3].

1.1   Non-genetic Risk Factors

To date efforts to create a preventive vaccine for dementia have proven unsuccessful. Nonetheless, findings from epidemiological and clinical studies, have suggested that biological, behavioural, social and environmental factors may delay or prevent the onset of dementia [4, 5]. These studies have investigated the possibility of inducing longitudinal behavioural change across multiple lifestyle domains. Multi-domain preventative interventions, targeting several risk factors simultaneously, have been suggested to have the highest likelihood of being effective [4]. Additionally, as each of the domains are addressed, additional unintended benefits are also observed, such as lowering the risk of other chronic diseases (diabetes, heart disease and stroke), accompanied with a 10% reduction in body mass index in those who are overweight [6]. It was noted that adherence to a healthy lifestyle that addresses these risk factors throughout life may be more important than after disease treatment, especially if the person has a genetic predisposition to AD [7].

1.2   Behavior Change

Health education programs have demonstrated the effectiveness of empowering individuals with health-related knowledge of factors affecting risk for various diseases, for example, breast cancer [8] and coronary heart disease [9]. A limited number of studies have, however, been conducted with a focus on AD risk reduction via lifestyle behavioral change. Nevertheless, positive results from health education interventions targeting other health conditions suggest that a similar effort targeting AD prevention would be likely to result in favorable rates of adoption of healthy behaviors, given that AD shares many of the same risk factors [10]. Cardiovascular factors (heart failure, hypertension, high cholesterol and sedentary lifestyle), psychosocial factors (education, higher work complexity, social participation and intellectual activities) [11] diabetes and dietary factors (endocrine disorders, high body mass index and eating a balanced diet) [12], have all been linked to cognitive decline and the onset of AD. Importantly, these factors are modifiable and could, therefore, be useful targets for the prevention of cognitive decline and dementia through behavioural change programs. It is therefore hypothesized that, health education programs that provide evidence-based knowledge about ways to reduce risk for AD may have the additional benefit of reducing risk for these other health conditions.

It is becoming more widely accepted that the neuropathological processes involved in AD may begin decades before symptoms emerge, thereby justifying preventative interventions in mid-life. Motivation for positive lifestyle changes may be enhanced for AD risk reduction given that there is no known cure and many middle-aged persons have experienced first-hand substantial dementia caregiving burden. Rather than targeting just one health-related behavior, there has been a recent movement to test risk-reduction efforts that target multiple behavioral domains, in recognition that a disease such as AD may have multiple etiologies [13].

Behavior change can be positively reinforced with a sense of achievement. In the gaming world, this sense of achievement is provided through in-game rewards or via a points system. Gamification utilizes game design techniques and mechanics to engage and motivate individuals through incentives and a sense of achievement, specifically for non-gaming domains [14]. Gamification to encourage behavior change in healthcare is a recent concept, however, has been successfully applied in health care promotions to maximize engagement [14].

None of the aforementioned longitudinal studies relating to AD have, however, investigated multi-domain interventions within a middle aged population (40-64 years), focusing instead on an older population (65-80 years). The current Gray Matters project, a collaborative project between Utah State University and the University of Ulster, aims to assess the effect of behavioral changes on the risk of developing AD, through the use of everyday technologies, with a gamification element, as a platform to deliver lifestyle recommendations.

2   Methods

The Gray Matters Project has recruited 146 participants (age 40-64) for a 6-month pilot study from the state of Utah, USA. This state has the quickest projected growth rate of AD cases in the US [15]. Participants have been randomized to control (n=42) or treatment group (n=104), with a full health assessment conducted prior to the study and a further assessment scheduled for the end of the study. The treatment group is involved in a comprehensive health education campaign focused on evidence-based methods for lowering their risk of developing AD. As part of this campaign, they have been provided access to the Gray Matters smartphone app, developed by the Smart Environments Research Group at the University of Ulster.

2.1   App Design

An interdisciplinary team of computer scientists, biomedical engineers, mathematicians, psychologists, gerontologists, epidemiologists and statisticians designed the functionality of the Gray Matters app. Initially the app was developed for the iOS 7.x platform due to initial screening of the cohort and the prevalence of iOS device ownership amongst those recruited. As recruitment progressed, Android handset owners expressed the desire to also be involved in the study, which required a version to be developed for the Android 4.x platform. The functionality of both versions of the Gray Matters app are identical. The app has been designed to provide the user with 3 core functions:

1. Presenting a fact and behavior suggestion pair relating to AD prevention.
2. Facilitating behavior self-reporting.
3. Calculating and presenting personalized performance feedback.

Each feature is contained within its own tab in the app. From each tab the user can perform a number of bespoke functions which are detailed in the following Sections.

Fact and Suggestion Pairs (Tips tab). The knowledgebase for the app is based upon 6 domains: Food, Physical, Cognitive, Social, Sleep and Stress. For each domain, fact and suggestion pairs (n=164) have been generated from peer-reviewed literature, to provide information about AD and preventative strategies. An example pair is as follows: "Consuming high amounts of processed foods is related to cognitive decline."; "Try a fresh salad for dinner instead of something from a box". The fact and suggestion pairs are displayed in their own 'tips' tab, accompanied by a sports coach avatar; to aid visual delivery and personification of the knowledge source. These motivating fact and suggestion pairs are refreshed daily and can be accessed by the user at any time. The user may tap the fact text to display the reference and URL of the literature source, to gain further detailed information if required.

Self-Report Behavior (Log tab). The Log tab enables the user to self-report their behavior via the app. This is performed by asking the user 12 questions daily. Each question relates to a specific domain and has a recommended answer value. For example, in the physical domain the following question: "How many minutes of moderate physical activity did you do today?" has a recommended value of 30 minutes, based on the Center for Disease Control and Prevention's (CDC) minimum daily target [16]. The user, if unsure, can tap the question to receive information as to what constitutes 'moderate' physical activity (walking, heavy gardening, yoga). By answering all 12 questions the user can longitudinally track and report their behavior across the 6 core domains. A 7th domain, named NikeFuel, has been included to track physical activity points which are calculated by a wrist worn activity monitor developed by Nike. Data entry for the answers is facilitated by a bespoke list view that uses a draggable slider to allow a quick entry of data (refer to Fig. 1). Using a fixed width slider, with a fixed upper limit, enables the user to have an immediate understanding of their progress. The fixed upper limit, however, is typically double the recommended value. This is to facilitate the users who exceed the recommended values and wish to log precise values.

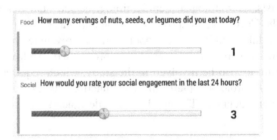

Fig. 1. Custom sliders (android) for user data entry in the log tab view. The length of the bar provides visual feedback to the user on their progress.

Performance Feedback (Performance tab). The performance tab accumulates and summarizes the data gathered from the log tab and presents it to the user in the form of a star rating. Utilizing the concepts of gamification, a user can achieve a maximum of 5 stars in each domain, for their efforts in reaching the recommended values. As such all log values are normalized to a range of 0-5, for the purpose of plotting onto stars, using the following equation:

$$f(x) = \begin{cases} \dfrac{(x - Q_L) \times (R_U - R_L)}{Q_G - Q_L} + R_L, & Q_L \leq x < Q_G \\ \\ R_U, & x \geq Q_G \end{cases} \quad (1)$$

where x is the user's answer value to a particular question, Q_G is the goal value for the question, Q_L is the lowest possible value for that question, R_U is the upper boundary of the normalized result and R_L is the lowest boundary. The resulting star ratings produced from this equation are presented in Fig. 2a.

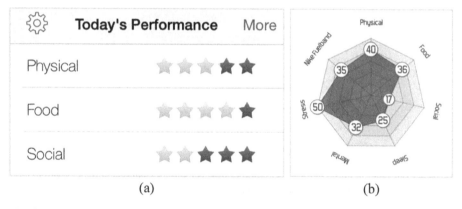

(a)   (b)

Fig. 2. (a) A snippet of the performance screen on iOS showing the current day's performance in the form of a 5 star rating. (b) A radar chart typically displayed to the user, showing their performance across all domains for the past 7 days.

The stars are designed to encourage and reinforce the user's effort to change their behavior. Additionally, the user may wish to view their overall performance over the past 7 days. To facilitate this the app makes a call to a graphing service on the server, which collates the data for that specific user, renders a radar chart and pushes the chart image to the handset, as presented in Fig. 2b.

The user is reminded via notifications, that they have a new fact/suggestion pair and a log to complete each day. They are also reminded once a week that they can view a summary of their weekly effort. Combined, these 3 core features of the app allow the user to become informed about AD and preventative measures whilst highlighting, at a glance, which domains they can make the most impact by changing their lifestyle or behavior.

3   Results

Following in-house beta testing, the app was initially released for the iOS platform and subsequently for the Android platform in week 3 of the study. Of the 104 participants in the treatment group who were permitted to use the app, currently 102 have installed the app. As of week 9 in the study, based on installation figures, there are 119 total installations of the app with 100 (84.03%) on the iOS platform and 19 (15.97%) on the Android platform. There are more installations of the app than participants in the treatment group due to participants opting to install the app on both a smartphone and a tablet. Smartphone installs account for 82 (68.91%) installs and tablets 37 (31.09%) installs. With regard to operating system versions, 90.26% of iOS devices and 52.63% of Android devices are running the latest releases of their respective platform. Additionally, all in-app behavior, including session time, time of day, day of week, number of times each tab is checked and preferences for notifications is all anonymously tracked. An example of such data has been presented in Fig. 3 showing a summary of the time of day that participants have been using the app.

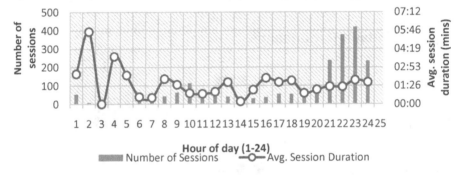

Fig. 3. A combination graph showing the total number of sessions generated by all participants and their average duration against the 24 hours in a day

Additionally, from the analysis of the weekly usage data (refer to Fig. 4) we can observe that the participant's average session time has steadily reduced over time.

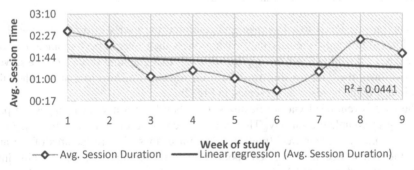

Fig. 4. A graph of the average session time of all participants within the first 9 weeks of the study. A linear regression line shows the average session time declining over the period.

4   Discussion

Supplementary to observing user data relating to behavioral change for AD prevention, the study is also monitoring and analyzing typical usage patterns of the app. Analytic data may be used to identify if participants require encouragement, by setting a threshold to detect a drop in their session data. In addition to targeting individuals for support, analytic data enables the investigators to examine the profile of the average user, providing insight into how the app is currently used, or can be improved. From Fig. 3 we can find that there is a peak of activity in the morning around 9-10am, which correlates to the default reminder time for the daily fact. Conversely, the notification for the log reminder is defaulted for 6pm, however, usage data reveals that most user's sessions peak around the hours of 9pm to 12pm, a significant time after the reminder has been issued. This has been highlighted for future releases to alter the default reminder time to the late evening. The average session duration of the app during these times (9pm-12pm) is 1 minute 49 seconds, which is representative of the global session average across all devices (1 minute 29 seconds). Nevertheless, at 2am, 3am and 5am there are abnormal session duration times that peak at over 5 minutes. 2 participants have been identified as the origin of these anomalies. On average, during each session users typically look at 2.62 screens. Further analysis of screen flow behavior explains this observation, as users typically check the performance tab, then update their log, and then finally re-check their performance. This supports the theory that gamification elements encourage continual engagement with the app, however, the long term effects of this are yet to be fully examined in this study. From the analysis of the weekly usage data (refer to Fig. 4) we can observe that the participant's average session time has steadily reduced over time. It is believed this is indicative that the users are becoming more comfortable and efficient using the features of the app. Spikes in session time averages in week 3 and 8 coincide with new app version releases, for iOS and Android respectively.

5   Conclusion

We have developed an app to encourage positive behavioral change for a middle aged cohort, aiming to reduce the risk of developing AD in later life by targeting individual risk factors. For that purpose, we have chosen to develop a multi-platform app to allow for maximal adoption from the target cohort. Additionally, we have added a gamification element to the logging aspect of the app, with the aim of improving and maintaining frequent engagement with the app, to ultimately induce behavior change.

Initial results from the first 9 weeks of usage data have been promising. The adoption rate of the app amongst the treatment group is very high with 98% running the app on their smartphone or tablet. Future development work will include continual improvement and support for the platform, with additional lower level behavioral tracking implemented to assess the utility of individual components. Ultimately the Gray Matters study would like to observe the clinical impact of the app assessed against the control group in 4 months.

Acknowledgements. This research was supported by the Office of the Vice President for Research and Graduate Studies and the Emma Eccles Jones College of Education and Human Services, Utah State University, the Intermountain Logan Regional Hospital Foundation and the Department of Education and Learning Northern Ireland.

References

1. Thies, W., Bleiler, L.: Alzheimer's disease facts and figures. Alzheimers. Dement. 9(2013), 208–245 (2013)
2. Smith, A.D., Yaffe, K.: Dementia (including Alzheimer's disease) can be prevented: statement supported by international experts. J. Alzheimers. Dis. 38, 699–703 (2014)
3. Ridge, P.G., Mukherjee, S., Crane, P.K., Kauwe, J.S.K.: Alzheimer's disease: analyzing the missing heritability. PLoS One 8, e79771 (2013)
4. Solomon, A., Mangialasche, F., Richard, E., Andrieu, S., Bennett, D.A., Breteler, M., Fratiglioni, L., Hooshmand, B., Khachaturian, A.S., Kivipelto, M.: Advances in the prevention of Alzheimer's disease and dementia. J. Intern. Med. 275, 229–250 (2014)
5. Lövdén, M., Xu, W., Wang, H.-X.: Lifestyle change and the prevention of cognitive decline and dementia: what is the evidence? Curr. Opin. Psychiatry. 26, 239–243 (2013)
6. Lin, P.-J., Yang, Z., Fillit, H.M., Cohen, J.T., Neumann, P.J.: Unintended benefits: the potential economic impact of addressing risk factors to prevent Alzheimer's disease. Health Aff. (Millwood) 33, 547–554 (2014)
7. Pope, S.K., Shue, V.M., Beck, C.: Will a healthy lifestyle help prevent Alzheimer's disease? Annu. Rev. Public Health. 24, 111–132 (2003)
8. Mason, T.A., Thompson, W.W., Allen, D., Rogers, D., Gabram-Mendola, S., Arriola, K.R.J.: Evaluation of the Avon Foundation community education and outreach initiative Community Patient Navigation Program. Health Promot. Pract. 14, 105–112 (2013)
9. Krantz, M.J., Coronel, S.M., Whitley, E.M., Dale, R., Yost, J., Estacio, R.O.: Effectiveness of a community health worker cardiovascular risk reduction program in public health and health care settings. Am. J. Public Health. 103, e19–e27 (2013)
10. Lorig, K., Ritter, P.L., Plant, K., Laurent, D.D., Kelly, P., Rowe, S.: The South Australia health chronic disease self-management Internet trial. Health Educ. Behav. 40, 67–77 (2013)
11. Wang, H.-X., Jin, Y., Hendrie, H.C., Liang, C., Yang, L., Cheng, Y., Unverzagt, F.W., Ma, F., Hall, K.S., Murrell, J.R., Li, P., Bian, J., Pei, J.-J., Gao, S.: Late life leisure activities and risk of cognitive decline. J. Gerontol. A. Biol. Sci. Med. Sci. 68, 205–213 (2013)
12. Morris, M.C.: Nutritional determinants of cognitive aging and dementia. Proc. Nutr. Soc. 71, 1–13 (2012)
13. Anstey, K.J., Bahar-Fuchs, A., Herath, P., Rebok, G.W., Cherbuin, N.: A 12-week multidomain intervention versus active control to reduce risk of Alzheimer's disease: study protocol for a randomized controlled trial. Trials 14, 60 (2013)
14. Schoech, D., Boyas, J.F., Black, B.M., Elias-Lambert, N.: Gamification for Behavior Change: Lessons from Developing a Social, Multiuser, Web-Tablet Based Prevention Game for Youths. J. Technol. Hum. Serv. 31, 197–217 (2013)
15. Hebert, L.E., Scherr, P.A., Bienias, J.L., Bennett, D.A., Evans, D.A.: State-specific projections through 2025 of Alzheimer disease prevalence. Neurology 62, 1645 (2004)
16. Pate, R.R., Pratt, M., Blair, S., et al.: Physical activity and public health: A recommendation from the centers for disease control and prevention and the american college of sports medicine. JAMA 273, 402–407 (1995)

A Virtual Coach for Active Ageing
Based on Sentient Computing and m-health

Zoraida Callejas[1], David Griol[2],
Michael F. McTear[3], and Ramón López-Cózar[1]

[1] Dept. Languages and Computer Systems, Univ. of Granada, CITIC-UGR, Spain
{zoraida,rlopezc}@ugr.es
[2] Dept. Computer Science, Univ. Carlos III of Madrid, Spain
dgriol@inf.uc3m.es
[3] School of Computing and Mathematics, Univ. of Ulster, UK
mf.mctear@ulster.ac.uk

Abstract. As life expectancy increases it has become more necessary to find ways to support healthy ageing. A number of active ageing initiatives are being developed nowadays to foster healthy habits in the population. This paper presents our contribution to these initiatives in the form of a conversational agent that acts as a coach for physical activities. The agent can be developed as an Android app running on smartphones and coupled with cheap widely available sport sensors in order to provide meaningful coaching. It can be employed to prepare exercise sessions, provide feedback during the sessions, and to discuss the results after the exercise. It incorporates an affective component that informs dynamic user models to produce adaptive interaction strategies.

Keywords: Sentient computing, m-health, wearable technologies, active ageing, mobile interfaces, conversational interfaces, multimodal interacion.

1 Introduction

Although life expectancy has increased due to advances in medicine and health-care, it is important to ensure that this longevity is coupled with a good quality of life. Active ageing is concerned with extending healthy life expectancy in several different ways. The World Health Foundation in a report from 2012[1] indicated different guidelines to make active ageing possible, the first being the promotion of "good health and healthy behaviours at all ages to prevent or delay the development of chronic disease". These include being physically active, eating a healthy diet, and avoiding alcohol and tobacco. Also they highlighted the need that the strategies developed should take into account the constraints of low- and middle-income health systems.

We are particularly interested in the guideline of promoting physical activity. Currently there are different technologies being developed to help users achieve

---

[1] http://whqlibdoc.who.int/hq/2012/WHO_DCO_WHD_2012.2_eng.pdf

L. Pecchia et al. (Eds.): IWAAL 2014, LNCS 8868, pp. 59–66, 2014.

this goal. For example, there exist many commercial applications, especially for runners, which rely on sensors that offer feedback about the user's achievements after the exercise sessions. Most of these applications are rather static in the sense that they offer the information after the sessions, mainly in the form of statistics and graphics. Also, they follow a traditional HCI approach in which the interaction with the user is limited.

As will be discussed in Section 2, research systems offer more natural interaction through the use of conversational agents that allow speech-based interaction. However, in this case there is a lack of dynamic feedback while the exercise is being performed, as most agents do not incorporate sentient computing.

The proposal in this paper is an architecture to build conversational coaches to encourage healthy habits, monitoring the user's health during the exercises, planning appropriate exercise routines, and supporting users to achieve their goals. The system employs easily accessible and widely available sensors that can be used together with mobile speech technologies in order to foster and control regular exercising at an appropriate pace for each user. Our proposal adapts the interaction metaphor to the different conditions in which the system can be used, and includes an affective component that allows the user about how they felt during the sessions, which helps to build a complex user model for a more intelligent system behaviour.

2   Related Work

Traditionally, healthcare applications have been designed for in-home use in the context of assisted living, where users can, for example, communicate some vital signs to a system that logs them, provides feedback and/or forwards them to a doctor [1], or obtain advice [2]. However, advances in the development of smartphones and their spread among the population provide interesting opportunities to migrate such functionality to m-health apps that offer the possibility to make more meaningful and dynamic interventions [3].

Conversational interfaces have been used in recent years to provide services such as interviews [4], counselling [2], chronic symptoms monitoring [5,6], medication adherence [7,8], and the adoption of healthy behaviours [9].

However, we often find a dichotomy between mobile and home applications which rarely combine to provide more dynamic services in different contexts. Also we can differentiate between applications that are focused on monitoring, for example blood pressure for diabetes [10], and others that are more focused on counselling [11,12], or planning, e.g. plan and remind medication intake [13].

Sophisticated industrial sport coaches (e.g. by Adidas™, Garmin™, or Nike™) include personalised workouts and performance tracking. However, they are not aimed at older populations, and the interaction modes are restricted. While exercising, some of such applications provide voice messages, but there are no conversational features and the user's affect is not considered in the design of the training plans.

We propose a single framework to develop a virtual coach that operates in two modes that combine the benefits of mobile and in home applications and that fulfil the objectives of monitoring, planning and coaching. The first mode is active while the user is engaged in exercise, for example, going for a walk. In this mode the system monitors and provides multimodal feedback to the user, while it updates the user model with their achievements. The second mode corresponds to a more relaxed situation in which the user can talk to the agent to plan new activities or discuss their progress; an affective component makes it possible for the system to support the user appropriately.

3   The Proposed Architecture

In the following sections we describe the main aspects of our proposal, including the sensors and mobile technology required for its implementation, the models defined, how the interaction is controlled and the operation modes of the agent (see Figure 1).

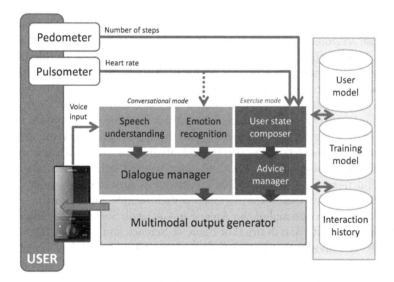

Fig. 1. Architecture of the virtual coach

3.1   Sensors and Mobile Technology

The sensors employed in our architecture belong to two types. The first type involves sensors that are already incorporated in the smartphone running the coach. These include the microphone and GPS.

The second type involves sensors that are external to the smartphone, such as the pulsometer and pedometer. These sensors measure biosignals: pulsometers offer information about heart rate and skin conductivity, whereas pedometers count the number of steps during walking. They are widely available and can be found in sport shops with prices under 30 euros, in the form of easily wearable devices, such as watches and bands. One of the key points of our proposal is that the user can choose the brand and type of sensors they prefer, so it is not necessary to buy any special or expensive equipment for the app.

With respect to mobile technology, there are several novel possibilities offered by Android. In particular, the Google speech APIs enable the user to communicate with the app using speech. Text-to-speech (TTS) is provided as standard on Android devices and offline speech recognition is also available on more recent devices in addition to cloud-based speech recognition services. We augment the speech interface with multimodal facilities and a dialogue capability is provided using the Pandorabots chatbot technology (http://www.pandorabots.com/). In [14] we provide several tutorials on how to use the Google speech APIs and how to enhance them with multimodal capabilities and chatbot technologies.

3.2   User, Training and History of Interaction Models

In our proposal there are three main knowledge sources: the user model, training model, and interaction model. The user model contains "static" information (name, age, and gender), as well as information that is updated according to the exercise sessions and interactions. This dynamic part deals mainly with the user's progress in the exercises and the user's affect in relation to this progress. Currently, for the user progress we consider the frequency of use of the app, the frequency of exercise sessions, and for each session the extent to which the objective of the session is achieved (e.g. if the user had to cover a certain distance, what is the percentage covered), heart rate register (percentage), distance register (kms), time register (minutes), and rhythm register (km/minute).

The training model codifies the best strategies for the coach according to the physical condition of the user, and the expected behaviour of the user in positive and negative scenarios. This knowledge is provided by expert trainers and codified as rules which are augmented with suggestions from the scientific literature (e.g. from Journal of the American Geriatric Society, Journal of Aging and Physical Activity and Journal of Exercise Science and Fitness. With respect to the affective model, currently we consider a simple model of polarity and arousal (positive vs. negative affect and intensity level specified as a percentage), which is coupled with the information of the exercise session to which it relates. All this information is codified as tuples *(session id, expected results, observed results, expected affect, observed affect)*.

The history of the interaction is saved as logs including the date, interaction mode (see Section 4), log of sensor information, and log of sensor communication errors. Moreover, when there is a conversation with the agent we trace interaction parameters (duration of the dialogue, number of user turns, number of system turns, information about the speech recognizer performance, speech understanding success rates), and emotion recognition results.

3.3   Interaction Management

By interaction management we refer to both setting the global goals of the agent and managing the conversation between the user and the agent.

The goals are related to choosing the most appropriate exercises and scheduling them, as well as to avoiding negative affect and fostering positive attitudes. The common goal for all users is to keep them practising regularly and to try to make them be positive about their results.

These objectives are achieved by choosing appropriate training for each individual user and providing supporting dialogues, which are based on the user, training and interaction models described in the previous section. This is finally translated into the scheduled training sessions, which are expressed as time goals (e.g. to walk for 20 minutes), rhythm (e.g. to walk at a certain pace), and/or distance (e.g. to walk to a certain spot for a number of kms).

The exercises included in the app are walking, running, doing aerobic exercises and playing petanque. In Spain there is special equipment in public spaces with infrastructure specially designed for elderly people, so sessions in these spaces are also included (e.g. exercises to strengthen their joints).

With respect to the dialogue, there are planning/explanatory and motivational interactions. Planning/explanatory interactions are modelled like a form-filling task in which the system prompts the user for some pieces of information (e.g. the time they have for exercising or their preferences for certain types of exercises), agrees a schedule with the user, and explains how they should perform the sessions (e.g. how to use certain equipment or what are the main objectives). To do this we use a dialogue management technique based on a simplified VXML, using an enhanced version of the interpreter that we presented in [14].

Motivational interactions are centred on the emotion conveyed by the user. Currently for these dialogues we propose a very basic speech understanding method based on a database of relevant keywords. The idea is to be able to assess and respond to the user's affect. For recognizing the user's emotions we use the acoustic information as in our previous work [15], and optionally the information conveyed by the pulsometer. To respond to the user's affect the system employs the strategies encoded in the training model, a user state composer approach [16], as well as a rapport building mechanism based on [17][18].

4   Agent Operation Modes

The virtual coach has two operation modes: *exercise* and *conversation*. The first mode is used during exercise, and the second before and after the exercise in order to prepare and discuss the sessions.

4.1   *Exercise* Mode

The first mode corresponds to the training sessions. During exercise, the user wears the sensors, which communicate with the smartphone via bluetooth. The system collects the biosignals at run time and updates the user state. When a significant change occurs either because there is an important change in the user state, or because they have reached a target in the training session, the system provides feedback to the user.

Systems that provide feedback based on biosignals, for example, smart watches for runners, usually present just statistics and graphics, and often once the session is finished and not during the training session. In our case, the system is able to provide feedback to the user which, on the one hand, is tailored to the user's needs whilst on the other provides reinforcement for the exercise, giving advice and support to the user, for example, how to continue or when to stop.

As can be observed in Figure 1, in the first stage the *user state composer* takes the biosignals and the user model as input and constructs the user state which is forwarded to the *advice manager*. This manager is a specialised dialogue manager that does not require any user input and that computes the best coaching advice taking into account the the user and training models. For example, walking for 40 minutes at a high speed may be good for some users, but too exhausting for others. Thus, the advice depends on the type of exercise, the dynamic user state, and the user characteristics.

Finally, once the output is decided, the *multimodal output generator* produces an appropriate feedback to the user which is visual (through graphics and texts in the smartphone screen), spoken (through synthesised messaged) and tactile (through vibrations). The user is able to configure the multimodal output so that it adapts to their preferences and needs.

4.2   *Conversational* Mode

The second mode corresponds to the interaction with the system when it plays the role of a coach before and after each exercise session. In this case, the system follows an architecture which is similar to traditional multimodal dialogue systems (see Figure 1), enhanced by an emotion recognition module.

Wearing a pulsometer is not mandatory in this mode. Thus, the user can talk to the agent through the smartphone and can also wear the heart rate sensor so that the system can check how their heart rate changes when preparing or remembering the exercise sessions.

In a setting before the exercise, the agent and the user can discuss the schedule for the next set of exercises, and the agent can provide appropriate support depending on the user state. For example, if the agent finds that the user is very stressed, it may try to provide some comfort and try to relieve the stress by planning a schedule with smaller challenges so that the user can experience some progress more easily.

At any time after doing exercise, the user can switch the system to *conversational* mode and describe how they felt. This information is then used to update the user model and the training schedule.

5   Conclusions and Future Work

As life expectancy increases, there is a need to find ways to support healthy ageing. This is the purpose of active ageing initiatives that aim to foster healthy behaviours in the population. In this paper we present a coaching conversational agent that helps users to keep exercising at an appropriate level.

In this paper we presented a proposal to build a coaching conversational agent based on m-health and sentient computing. This agent is developed in Android and supports two modes. On the one hand, an *exercise* mode that processes information from sensors dynamically producing run-time advice based on the user state, the characteristics of the user, the knowledge about the exercise, the history of the interaction and the user's achievements. On the other hand, the agent features a *conversational* mode that offers coaching dialogues between the user and the system, before and after the exercise sessions, with emotion recognition from voice and optionally from the biosignal captured by sensors.

The sensors are widely available in general sport shops at a cheap price, and do not pose special requirements to be used with the app. Also, the *conversational* mode can be used without sensors, so that the coaching agent can be used with just a smartphone.

For future work we plan to implement an Android app based on the architecture proposed and carry out an evaluation of the system with elderly users with different fitness conditions. This will allow us not only to assess user satisfaction with the system, but also to obtain a rich knowledge base for the training sessions with feedback from expert personal trainers.

References

1. Grönvall, E., Verdezoto, N.: Beyond self-monitoring: Understanding non-functional aspects of home-based healthcare technology. In: UbiComp 2013 - Proceedings of the 2013 ACM International Joint Conference on Pervasive and Ubiquitous Computing., pp. 587–596 (2013)
2. Hudlicka, E.: Virtual training and coaching of health behavior: Example from mindfulness meditation training. Patient Education and Counseling 92(2), 160–166 (2013)
3. Poole, E.: HCI and mobile health interventions: How human-computer interaction can contribute to successful mobile health interventions. Translational Behavioral Medicine 3(4), 402–405 (2013)
4. Pfeifer, L., Bickmore, T.: Designing Embodied Conversational Agents to Conduct Longitudinal Health Interviews. In: Proc. Intelligent Virtual Agents 2010, pp. 4698–4703 (2010)
5. Giorgino, T., Azzini, I., Rognoni, C., Quaglini, S., Stefanelli, M., Gretter, R., Falavigna, D.: Automated spoken dialogue system for hypertensive patient home management. Journal of Medical Informatics 74, 159–167 (2004)
6. Mooney, K., Beck, S., Dudley, W., Farzanfar, R., Friedman, R.: A computer-based telecommunication system to improve symptom care for women with breast cancer. Annals of Behavioral Medicine Annual Meeting Supplement 27, 152–161 (2004)
7. Allen, J., Ferguson, G., Blaylock, N., Byron, D., Chambers, N., Dzikovska, M., Galescu, L., Swift, M.: Chester: towards a personal medication advisor. Journal of Biomedical Informatics 39(5), 500–513 (2006)
8. Bickmore, T., Puskar, K., Schlenk, E., Pfeifer, L., Sereika, S.: Maintaining reality: Relational agents for antipsychotic medication adherence. Interacting with Computers 22, 276–288 (2010)

9. Farzanfar, R., Frishkopf, S., Migneault, J., Friedman, R.: Telephone-linked care for physical activity: A qualitative evaluation of the use patterns of an information technology program for patients. Journal of Biomedical Informatics 38, 220–228 (2005)
10. Harper, R., Nicholl, P., McTear, M.F., Wallace, J.G., Black, L.A., Kearney, P.: Automated phone capture of diabetes patients readings with consultant monitoring via the web. In: Proc. ECBS 2008, pp. 219–226 (2008)
11. Bickmore, T.W., Schulman, D., Sidner, C.L.: A reusable framework for health counseling dialogue systems based on a behavioral medicine ontology. Journal of Biomedical Informatics 44(2), 183–197 (2011)
12. Bickmore, T.W., Schulman, D., Sidner, C.: Automated interventions for multiple health behaviors using conversational agents. Patient Education and Counseling 92(2), 142–148 (2013)
13. Dalgaard, L., Gronvall, E., Verdezoto, N.: Mediframe: A tablet application to plan, inform, remind and sustain older adults' medication intake. In: Proc. ICHI 2013, pp. 36–45 (2013)
14. McTear, M.F., Callejas, Z.: Voice Application Development for Android. Packt Publishing Ltd (2013)
15. Callejas, Z., López-Cózar, R.: Influence of contextual information in emotion annotation for spoken dialogue systems. Speech Communication 50(5), 416–433 (2008)
16. Callejas, Z., Griol, D., López-Cózar, R.: Predicting user mental states in spoken dialogue systems. EURASIP Journal on Advances in Signal Processing 2011(1), 6 (2011)
17. Acosta, J.C., Ward, N.G.: Achieving rapport with turn-by-turn, user-responsive emotional coloring. Speech Communication 53(9-10), 1137–1148 (2011)
18. Kang, S.-H., Gratch, J.: Exploring users' social responses to computer counseling interviewers' behavior. Computers in Human Behavior 34, 120–130 (2014)

An Ontology Based Approach to the Provision of Personalized Patient Education

Susan Quinn, Raymond Bond, and Chris D. Nugent

School of Computing and Mathematics, University of Ulster, UK
Quinn-S47@email.ulster.ac.uk,
{rb.bond,cd.nugent}@ulster.ac.uk

Abstract. Current approaches to patient education provide standardized materials to all patients regardless of their demographics and abilities. Nevertheless, the effectiveness of this approach may suffer from a patient's motivation to fully engage with the material. To alleviate these concerns this study proposes a personalized approach to patient education that is tailored to the individual characteristics and health objectives of the patient. Personalized features will enhance the comprehensibility and usability of the process of medical education. Taking this into consideration, this paper introduces a conceptual framework to create web based personalized patient education. A central component of this architecture comprises ontological models of the patient, medical conditions and the educational components. Use case scenarios are also provided to highlight the effectiveness of personalized education provision.

Keywords: personalization, patient education, ontology, context.

1   Introduction

Patient education is an essential component of healthcare services as it can equip patients with the knowledge and skills they require to manage their condition and make informed decisions about subsequent treatment and daily care [1]. Sources of education can include medical websites and printed pamphlets [1-3]. Pamphlets can provide standardized, medically certified information that can be revisited at varying stages of treatment [1, 2]. Nevertheless, the effectiveness of this educational approach may be hampered due to a patient's inability or motivation to engage with the material. A patient may have difficulty understanding the medical terminology and images used or may feel overwhelmed or confused by the volume of information introduced [2]. These factors may result in a patient finding it difficult to identify important points or misinterpreting fundamental information [4, 5]. Personalization presents a means to overcome these concerns by enabling the provision of education that focuses on the particular needs and health objectives tailored for each patient. Personalization has been used in health communication to motivate patients to process health messages and improve their health behaviors [6]. Personalized education may be more accessible, usable and engaging for the patient by providing advice that is more relevant to their lifestyle when compared to standardized pamphlets.

L. Pecchia et al. (Eds.): IWAAL 2014, LNCS 8868, pp. 67–74, 2014.

Decreasing levels of physical activity and increases in unhealthy dietary habits have contributed to a worldwide increase in non-communicable conditions such as diabetes and obesity [7]. This paper proposes a web based framework for providing personalized education to patients that have been diagnosed with diabetes or obesity. Successful management of these conditions includes an increase in physical activity and following a healthy diet [7], activities which typically must be incorporated into a patient's lifestyle. This framework addresses the limitations of standardized education for diabetic and obese patients through the provision of education that is adapted to the characteristics, health objectives and lifestyle of each patient.

The remainder of this paper is structured as follows. Section 2 discusses related work in the field of patient education. Section 3 describes a framework for personalized patient education and introduces the ontological models within the framework. Section 4 provides two use case scenarios describing typical usage and Section 5 describes the conclusions drawn from the research.

2   Related Work

A recent focus in health informatics research has been the concept of health literacy, which is the ability to obtain, understand and apply health information [8-11]. Health literacy is considered a prominent factor in a patient's ability to make health decisions and to carry out self-management and medication practices [10]. A patient's comprehension of written health information can be affected by the readability level of the information. The readability of a piece of text refers to the reading comprehension level that a person must have to understand it [3]. There is, however, a clear association between low levels of literacy and poor health outcomes [8, 10], which highlights the need for educational materials that are suited to a range of readability levels. The readability of online and printed patient education material has been widely investigated. In many cases the materials examined are found to be at a higher readability level than the national recommendation. Examples of this include an evaluation of hearing and paediatric hearing loss pamphlets in which 95% were above the expected level [9] and an analysis of websites targeted at adolescents diagnosed with the cancer osteosarcoma in which 86% exceeded the recommended grade level [12]. In cases where the readability level of materials is high there is a concern that the engagement of patients with low levels of literacy or limited patience may be reduced [11, 12]. In addition to the words and grammar used, many other features can limit a patient's ability to understand and use medical information. This may include the introduction of excessive information, a poor flow of information and descriptions that are overly complex [9, 11]. For many patients and caregivers the preference is for simple and understandable language [9]. It is being increasingly recognized that health literacy can be affected by contextual factors. For example a patient with a sufficient level of literacy may find it difficult to interpret information that contains unfamiliar terms and diagrams [9] or they may find it more demanding to understand information at different stages of their treatment or at times of stress [8]. For this reason some patients have expressed a desire to be able to choose between different levels of complexity and detail in the information supplied [8].

Other research directions have focused on the effectiveness of patient participation in the design of educational material. Such participatory approaches can help to identify complexities in the material, and can enhance the comprehensibility of the materials for a range of literacy levels [11, 13]. The authors of [13] evaluated the effect of patient participation in the design of an Internet-based education system for patients affected by Fibromyalgia Syndrome. The developers used online user forum discussions to add tools that correlated to user suggestions. Appraisal of the system usage and user feedback found that many of the sections that were designed in collaboration with the end users were frequently used. The developers proposed that this approach should be further developed so that functionality derived from patient requirements could be mapped to specific outcomes such as increased learning.

Much of the research in this area has focused on the factors that can limit the effectiveness of patient education. The composition, readability and format of materials are prominent factors, and a patient's level of health literacy can also affect their ability to use health information. The involvement of patients in the design of educational materials has been one approach to improving usability. Prominent goals in this field include the design of materials that fulfill the informational needs and objectives of patients whilst also facilitating learning.

3   A Conceptual Framework for Personalized Patient Education

This paper proposes a novel framework for creating personalized patient education. A conceptual model for the framework is illustrated in Fig. 1. In this framework information is captured about 3 main entities; the patient, the educational content and the medical conditions. This information is modeled as an ontology in the Modelling and Management layer. An ontology has been defined as "a shared understanding of some domain of interest" [14]. It reflects a particular world view of a domain by representing domain knowledge as an organization of concepts, definitions and relationships [14]. Modeling data in an ontology ensures that the meaning of the data is unambiguous and is therefore suitable for processing by reasoning technologies [15]. The information modeled in the Modelling and Management layer includes characteristics of the patient, aspects of diabetes and obesity such as symptoms, health risks and treatments, and formatting features of the educational content. A patient's demographic characteristics may be populated from their electronic medical record, with further health and activity specifications entered by a physician.

The Personalisation and Contextualisation layer contains a set of personalization rules and a reasoning engine. The reasoning component can utilize the ontology and rules to make inferences about associations in the data [15]. For example a rule could be specified to determine an association between a set of symptoms exhibited by the patient and a particular health complication. The educational content is maintained in the Educational Repository which includes text and graphical components. Personalization mechanisms determine the combination of components that are selected for each patient. The educational content will be formatted as a web page and presented to the patient through a web browser.

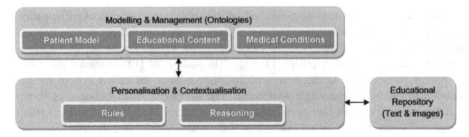

Fig. 1. Proposed framework to provide personalized patient education

3.1 Ontological Modeling of Patients, Medical Conditions and Education

In order to generate personalized education we need to design a comprehensive set of data about the user. User modeling is the process of determining which user characteristics are relevant to a service and designing a structure that will capture these attributes. User modeling results in the definition of a User Model, a uniform template of the attributes that should be included for each user. A User Profile is an instance of the user model that retains the unique attribute values for an individual user. In this framework the user model and models of the health conditions and educational content are encoded as an ontology. The ontology was developed using Protégé, an ontology editor and has been represented using the Web Ontology Language (OWL).

Fig. 2. An excerpt of the user model (within Protégé) illustrating (a) classes, (b) object properties and (c) datatype properties

Within an ontology, the concepts of a domain are defined as classes and are arranged in a hierarchy of superclass-subclass relationships. A class will contain properties to represent features and restrictions [16]. Object properties denote relationships between classes whilst datatype properties denote attributes or data values of a class [16]. Fig. 2 provides an illustration of the classes and properties that are included in the user model.

Fig. 3 indicates how associations can be inferred between classes represented in the user model and the educational content model. These associations are then utilized to adapt the composition and presentation of the education to the preferences and needs of each patient. Associations are normally derived from the properties of each class. The data captured in the user model is categorized in three strands that are represented by the classes, *PersonalProfile*, *HealthProfile* and *EducationProfile*. *PersonalProfile* captures personal characteristics of a patient such as their age, gender, ethnicity and language preference. *HealthProfile* captures aspects of the patient's health status and activity objectives. *EducationProfile* captures data that is used to derive a patient's readability level. During the design of the ontology a number of sources were reviewed to determine which characteristics should be captured for the user and health conditions models. These sources included academic publications, Diabetes UK, the American Diabetes Association and the UK National Health Service.

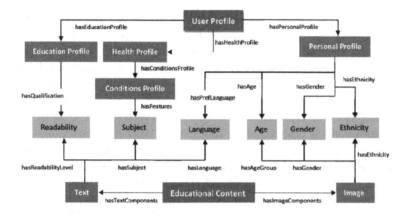

Fig. 3. Association characteristics of the user model and educational content model

The educational content comprises text and graphical components such as illustrations and diagrams. The educational content model contains 3 classes, *Educational-Content*, *Text* and *Image*. The attributes and relationships modeled can be used to infer associations with characteristics and preferences that are captured in the user profile. In order to enhance a patient's identification with the education it will contain images that are personalized to their age group, gender and ethnicity. *Image* properties including *hasAgeGroup*, *hasGender* and *hasEthnicity* provide a means to infer associations with similar characteristics captured about the patient. This will ensure that images that correspond most with the patient's profile are selected from the education repository. Class *Text* represents text information that pertains to aspects of diabetes and obesity. For example a paragraph of text could describe a particular symptom of diabetes. Text components are categorized by several properties including *hasLanguage*, *hasSubject* and *hasReadabilityLevel*. These properties can be associated with aspects of the patient's *EducationProfile* and *PersonalProfile* to ensure that the text information matches the readability needs and language preferences of the patient.

One further aspect of providing personalized education is to consider how the patient's needs are affected by contextual factors. A person's context comprises of entities and factors that can affect their behavior and their use of a service [14]. As discussed earlier, variations in the patient's level of anxiety or medical condition can affect health literacy. This framework provides a means to adapt to contextual changes by dynamically correlating a patient's readability level with textual information. The *EducationProfile* contains the patient's highest qualification and this information can be used to deduce their readability level. Furthermore the *HealthProfile* indicates whether the patient is experiencing stress. This characteristic can be modified at different stages of the patient's treatment and can be used to adapt their readability level accordingly. Deriving associations between the readability level of the user and the text ensures that the education is comprehensible and useful for the user in their current situation.

A Conditions model captures the characteristics of diabetes and obesity. The characteristics modeled include symptoms and health risks, specific treatments such as medications and health checks, and more generic treatments such as lifestyle changes. Although aspects of diabetes and obesity are common to many patients it is likely that not all patients will have the same combination of symptoms, health concerns and treatments. Personalization can ensure that the education provided focuses on the particular aspects of the condition that are relevant to each patient. Data regarding a patient's health status is captured in the user model class *ConditionsProfile*. The patient's combination of symptoms, health risks and treatments are represented through relationships with instances of the conditions model. This information can be utilized to ensure that the education components selected correlate with the pertinent aspects of the condition. For example, for a patient with type 2 diabetes, the information provided could relate to treatments such as cholesterol checks and weight management, while for another patient with the same condition the education may concentrate more on diabetic medications. Tailoring the education in this way ensures that the education is focused on the needs of the patient and can change dynamically in response to changes in their medical status. Moreover the patient is not overwhelmed by information that is not directly applicable to their needs.

One aspect of treatment for diabetes and obesity relates to increased physical activity. An activity model has been designed to model various aspects of physical activity. Class *Activity* captures various sporting activities which are categorized in the subclasses *AerobicExercise* and *ResistanceExercise*. Activities are also characterized by properties including *hasEnvironment* which specifies whether the activity takes place indoors or outdoors and *hasLocation*. Each patient has an activity profile which denotes their preferred physical activities, preferred activity environments and current physical activity level. Associations between these two models can be utilized to ensure that activity suggestions are focused on the patient's preferred activities and are suitable to their current physical capability. Nevertheless, while it is favorable to provide information that is personalized to the preferences of the patient it must also be contextualized to their lifestyle. One means by which to achieve this is to consider whether it is convenient for the patient to take part in this activity. Location information is captured for activities and can be used to determine whether this activity takes place within a specified distance of the home or workplace of the patient. This ensures that the activity advice provided is relevant to the patient's lifestyle and is applicable to the different environments in which they reside.

4   Use Scenarios for Personalized Patient Education

The following vignettes are presented to illustrate how personalized education can adapt to the particular health objectives of two patients that have been diagnosed with type 2 diabetes. Fig. 4 presents illustrations of the personalized education.

Peter is a 26 year old man who has just been diagnosed with type 2 diabetes. His physical activity level is quite low and he is eager to increase this to help him manage his condition. He has identified cycling as an activity that he is interested in and this preference is added to his activity profile. His personal profile also holds his home address. Information from Peter's profile is then used to identify places where he could go cycling. His home is very close to a bike trail so this is suggested for bicycles trips. The information provided to Peter includes a description of the trail, and directions and a map are also provided.

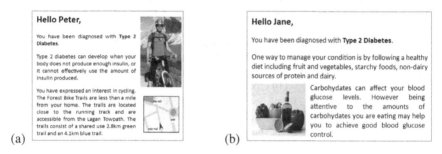

(a)   (b)

Fig. 4. Screen shots of web based personalized education delivered to (a) Peter, (b) Jane

Jane is a 55 year old woman who has just been diagnosed with type 2 diabetes. She is worried about this diagnosis, however, her physician explains that one way to manage her condition is by maintaining good blood glucose control. The education provided to Jane focuses on her worries about managing her blood glucose level by describing how a balanced healthy diet can help, and she finds that the information uses vocabulary that she can understand. Jane's profile also indicates that she has a mild sight impairment therefore the text is presented in a suitable size.

5   Conclusion

This paper introduces a novel approach to providing personalized patient education. An analysis of related literature highlighted the limitations of the current approach of providing standardized education for all patients regardless of background, educational capability and health status. The proposed approach overcomes these weaknesses by tailoring the education to the changing needs and goals of each patient under variable contexts. Ontological models of user characteristics, health conditions and educational content were presented. Associations between these models can be utilized to create educational content that is focused on the particular health concerns of the patient and supports their understanding of the material. Two use case scenarios were also provided to describe potential educational provision. The future development of the framework includes implementation of the personalization mechanisms, population of the educational repository and evaluation.

References

1. Hong, J., Nguyen, T.V., Prose, N.S.: Compassionate Care: Enhancing physician–patient Communication and Education in Dermatology: Part II: Patient Education. J. Am. Acad. Dermatol. 68, 364.e1–364.e10 (2013)
2. Cawsey, A., Grasso, F., Paris, C.: Adaptive Information for Consumers of Healthcare. In: Brusilovsky, P., Kobsa, A., Nejdl, W. (eds.) Adaptive Web 2007. LNCS, vol. 4321, pp. 465–484. Springer, Heidelberg (2007)
3. Schmitt, P.J., Prestigiacomo, C.J.: Readability of Neurosurgery-Related Patient Education Materials Provided by the American Association of Neurological Surgeons and the National Library of Medicine and National Institutes of Health. World Neurosurgery 80, e33-e39 (2013)
4. Davis, T.C., Wolf, M.S., Bass, P.F., et al.: Literacy and Misunderstanding Prescription Drug Labels. Ann. Intern. Med. 145, 887–894 (2006)
5. Pander Maat, H., Lentz, L.: Improving the Usability of Patient Information Leaflets. Patient Educ. Couns. 80, 113–119 (2010)
6. Hawkins, R.P., Kreuter, M., Resnicow, K., et al.: Understanding Tailoring in Communicating about Health. Health Educ. Res. 23, 454–466 (2008)
7. International Diabetes Federation, Diabetes Atlas, 6th ed., http://www.idf.org/diabetesatlas
8. Smith, F., Carlsson, E., Kokkinakis, D., et al.: Readability, Suitability and Comprehensibility in Patient Education Materials for Swedish Patients with Colorectal Cancer Undergoing Elective Surgery: A Mixed Method Design. Patient Educ. Couns. 94, 202–209 (2014)
9. Joubert, K., Githinji, E.: Quality and Readability of Information Pamphlets on Hearing and Paediatric Hearing Loss in the Gauteng Province, South Africa. Int. J. Pediatr. Otorhinolaryngol. 78, 354–358 (2014)
10. Nutbeam, D.: The Evolving Concept of Health Literacy. Soc. Sci. Med. 67, 2072–2078 (2008)
11. Kandula, N.R., Nsiah-Kumi, P.A., Makoul, G., et al.: The Relationship between Health Literacy and Knowledge Improvement After a Multimedia Type 2 Diabetes Education Program. Patient Educ. Couns. 75, 321–327 (2009)
12. Lam, C.G., Roter, D.L., Cohen, K.J.: Survey of Quality, Readability, and Social Reach of Websites on Osteosarcoma in Adolescents. Patient Educ. Couns. 90, 82–87 (2013)
13. Camerini, L., Camerini, A., Schulz, P.J.: Do Participation and Personalization Matter? A Model-Driven Evaluation of an Internet-Based Patient Education Intervention for Fibromyalgia Patients. Patient Educ. Couns. 92, 229–234 (2013)
14. Uschold, M., Gruninger, M.: Ontologies: Principles, Methods and Applications. The Knowledge Engineering Review 11, 93–136 (1996)
15. Ye, J., Coyle, L., Dobson, S., et al.: Ontology-Based Models in Pervasive Computing Systems. The Knowledge Engineering Review 22, 315–347 (2007)
16. A Practical Guide To Building OWL Ontologies Using Protégé 4 and CO-ODE Tools Edition Edition 1.3, http://130.88.198.11/tutorials/protegeowltutorial/

Technical Validation of COPD Activity Support Monitor- Towards COPD Self-management

Mark Paul Beattie, Huiru Zheng, Chris D. Nugent, and Paul McCullagh

University of Ulster, Shore Road, Newtownabbey, Co Antrim, UK
{mp.beattie,h.zheng,cd.nugent,pj.mccullagh}@ulster.ac.uk

Abstract. By 2030 it has been predicted that Chronic Obstructive Pulmonary Disease (COPD) will affect, on a global scale, over 64 million people and will be the third leading cause of death worldwide. This work discusses the development of a self-management system that records physiological and contextual information via a smartphone, a wrist worn accelerometer for measuring activity and a chest worn device for monitoring patterns of respiration. The data recorded through this system facilitates analysis to identify changes in the patterns of the bio-signals and may pave the way for advice to be offered regarding the self-management of this long-term condition. Feedback relating to specific activity goals that can be set and monitored will be provided to the user as part of the self-management solution

Keywords: COPD, Self-management, Activity recognition, Chronic disease, wearable Sensors.

1   Introduction

A significant shift in population ageing is currently taking place. The median age for European citizens has been projected to increase from 41 years in 2013 to 46 years in 2050 [1]. This dramatic shift will impact upon the provision of healthcare, given that increased life expectancy will increase the number of people at risk of developing long term conditions. Chronic Obstructive Pulmonary Disease (COPD) is set to have an increased prevalence. It is one of the most common chronic diseases affecting the older age groups [2]. It has been projected that over three million people in the UK are afflicted with COPD, however, just over 900,000 have been clinically diagnosed and are receiving treatment [3]. In addition, COPD has been reported as consuming 50% of the European Union Health Care budget allowance for respiratory disease [4] This is set to increase as COPD becomes more prevalent.

Symptoms, which are indicative of COPD, include shortness of breath known as dyspnoea, chronic cough and the production of excess sputum. It is common for those with COPD to suffer from exacerbations, an acute increase in previously mentioned symptoms alongside increased levels of nocturnal awakening, breathlessness and wheeze [5]. Research has shown that delayed treatment following an exacerbation correlates directly with a lower Health Related Quality Of Life (HRQoL), delayed recovery time and a dramatically increased risk of hospitalisation [6]. Self-management has been

L. Pecchia et al. (Eds.): IWAAL 2014, LNCS 8868, pp. 75–82, 2014.
© Springer International Publishing Switzerland 2014

defined as: "any formalized patient education programme aimed at teaching skills needed to carry out medical regimens specific to the disease, guide health behavior change, and provide emotional support for patients to control their disease and live functional lives" [11]. Self-management solutions availing of technological advances may therefore offer benefit to those suffering from COPD by offering relevant and timely information relating to their condition. This information and its interpretation could facilitate self-management, which in turn could lead to behaviour change by facilitating goal setting and ensuring relevant and timely feedback is presented to the user[7] and may even reduce symptomatic conditions. This could reduce the burden on the healthcare system. In addition, such an approach empowers the patient with an increased level of control over their healthcare [8].

It is conceived that the detection of sudden or gradual declines in physical activity could lead to earlier non-pharmaceutical interventions. This would enable levels of activity to recover to an appropriate level before a decline impacts upon the person's daily life, in the hope that this could lead to a reduction in disease progression and further complications. Section 2 presents a background review into the management of COPD and technology based self-management techniques. A self-management monitor currently under development referred to as CAS (COPD Activity Support) is discussed in Section 3. Section 4 discusses implementation and initial testing of CAS with section 5 discussing future work.

2   Background

The management of a chronic condition such as COPD is expensive and time consuming placing a burden on National Health Services, those with COPD and their immediate family. Self-management alleviates an aspect of this burden by enabling the person with COPD to manage their own condition [9][10].

The American Thoracic Society stated that "pulmonary rehabilitation will lead to a reduction in symptomatic features of COPD, improve functional status and will lead to a reduction in health care costs by either reversing or stabilising the condition"[14]. Pulmonary rehabilitation has been defined as: "an evidence based, multidisciplinary and comprehensive intervention for patients with chronic respiratory diseases which are symptomatic and often have decreased daily life activities" [13]. A typical pulmonary rehabilitation course includes: a physical exercise programme, carefully designed for each individual; advice on lung health and coping with breathlessness; and a friendly, supportive atmosphere. In such a programme physical activity is focused on the exercise programme, not monitoring. This ensures that the participant is provided with a core set of skills enabling them to self-manage their condition more effectively. Pulmonary rehabilitation has been determined to provide significant short term levels of improvement for those with moderate to severe COPD, such as the ability to carry out physical activities, however, improvements may not last[15][16]. Research in this area has found that benefits gained from pulmonary rehabilitation return to levels witnessed prior to the intervention within 1 – 2 years [17] [16]. With this information, it is therefore important to determine how benefits gained can be maintained over a longer period of time. Several research studies have discovered that providing activity related feedback to the end users can be of benefit. Studies have investigated the use of a pedometer as a motivational feedback tool [18][19][20] and found that levels of physical activity in participants increased when presented with feedback on activity [18]. Positive results were also presented by Verwey et. al. [20], however, a number of technical problems relating to the system architecture resulted in 90% of participants not always retrieving activity feedback. The authors in [20] also queried how sustainable the positive results would be with less human support.

Changes in levels of physical activity over a period of 6 months in those who had previously completed a pulmonary rehabilitation course were monitored by Dwyer et. al. [21] using an Activpal accelerometer. A trend in decline was identifiable at 6 weeks in participants who would subsequently continue to deteriorate after rehabilitation with no identifiable cause over those that did not. The authors, however, postulated that this could be due to lower levels of self efficacy [21].

This Section has highlighted the benefits and difficulties associated with the self-management of COPD and how supporting this with technology can offer improvements, however, also lead to difficulties. The current work will contribute to COPD self-management by creating a system that will be self-contained, enabling consistent provision of feedback to the participant whilst also recording comprehensive physiological and contextual data enabling post trial analysis to determine which factors and their combination correlate with changes in activity levels. This information can e used to inform future work in the area.

3   CAS (COPD Activity Support) Monitor

A self-management tool, COPD Activity Support or CAS monitor, was designed and developed to achieve the aim of physiological monitoring and the provision of feedback on levels of daily physical activity for those with COPD. An iterative design process was followed complimented with utilisation of current medical guidelines and knowledge to ensure the system design was relevant and appropriate for those with COPD. It is anticipated that this CAS monitor may regulate levels of activity whilst simultaneously empowering participants with more knowledge and information concerning their own condition therefore touching upon the subject of self-efficacy. It will also provide a tool which has the facility to collect a dataset providing an insight into how physiological and contextual information contribute to symptoms and behavior in those with COPD.

The self-management monitor requires participants to use a smart mobile phone and two 'off-the-shelf' sensor(s), a wrist worn Fitbit bracelet (http://www.fitbit.com/uk/flex) and a chest worn bio-harness strap (http://zephyranywhere.com/). The former records activity information, specifically, steps taken, distance traveled (estimated), number of active minutes per day, total number of hours asleep, number of times awoken during the night and information related to sleep quality (the number of awakenings throughout the night). The latter records physiological information from the participant, specifically heart rate, respiration rate, levels of activity and electrocardiogram R-R intervals. Sensors within the smartphone (GPS, Microphone) record contextual information from the participant, specifically ambient noise to determine if a noisy sleeping environment is the cause of disturbed sleep and location specific weather/atmospheric information. Participants will also self-report qualitative information on how they feel each day.

3.1   Architectural Framework of the CAS Monitor

The architecture for the CAS monitor, detailing system interaction is presented in Figure 1.

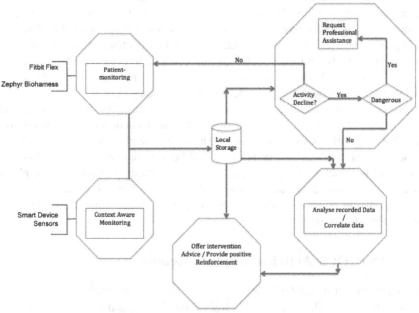

Fig. 1. CAS monitor archtecture, detailing how data are recoreded, analysed and when feeback is presented to the particpant

Participant monitoring and context (location / environment) aware monitoring are two vital aspects of the CAS monitor and take place continuously. Data recorded within these two aspects of the system are stored within an SQLite database on the mobile device and uploaded to a remote server for access by a clinician for further review if necessary. As the data are recorded, each feature is analysed to determine if it is within pre-determined ranges set from clinical guidelines by a COPD specialist within the research team. If not an alert is immediately generated and sent to a member of the research team. If recorded features are not dangerous but are considered to be in decline, analysis will occur to determine the most relevant advice to be provided to the participant. Advice to be provided will adhere to medical guidelines. Data collection will occur in three different ways; firstly information will be recorded from the participant manually through the mobile device. This will collect answers to pre-set questions on how the participant is feeling that day; the color of sputum produced, how tired they felt and other relevant information to be gathered. Questions will be answered using a traffic light metaphor, 'green' indicating good, 'orange' indicating moderate, and 'red' indicating bad. This will provide a subjective overview that can then be correlated against recorded contextual and physiological data. Secondly weather information will be retrieved from a weather API using GPS coordinates to specify location. Ambient noise levels will be recorded at night. The microphone within the smartphone will be utilised from 10pm to 8am or set for normal sleeping time. Real time audio processing is carried out on data retrieved from the microphone to generate ambient decibel levels (dB), which are stored. This ensures that background or conversational data are not stored addressing possible privacy issues. Finally the bioharness and accelerometer sensors provide a live data stream of heart rate, respiration rate and activity levels.

Table 1. Data to be recorded from the end user throughout the trial period

Features to Record	Method	Unit	Example
Cough	Manual input (Subjective)	Text	*Increased Cough*
Sputum Levels & Color	Manual input (Subjective)	Text	*Sputum Yellow*
Wheeze	Manual input (Subjective)	Text	*Decreased Wheeze*
Fatigue	Manual input (Subjective)	Text	*Increased Fatigue*
Diet	Manual Entry	Text	*1 Chicken fillet*
Weight	Digital Scales	Kilogram	*74kg*
Activity (Steps)	Fitbit (sensor)	Daily Steps	*3421 Steps*
Sleep Efficiency	Fitbit (sensor)	Percentage	*98%*
Total time asleep	Fitbit (sensor)	Hours & Min	*7h 32m*
# times awakened	Fitbit (sensor)	Integer	*6 times*
Heart rate	Zephyr	Beats per Minute	*66*
Respiration rate	Zephyr	Breaths per Minute	*22*
Activity Level	Zephyr	g	*16 - 16*
R-R interval	Zephyr	Milliseconds	*780*
Location	Smartphone GPS	Lat - Long	*(54.686 -5.882)*
Ambient Night Noise	Smartphone microphone	dB	*120*

Recorded symptomatic and contextual information is presented to the participant visually on the smart mobile device. This enables current and historical information to be reviewed and potentially empowers the participant with greater knowledge regarding their health. The CAS monitor automatically presents the participant with relevant information daily, for example, current weather conditions and outside temperature. Feedback on how close the participant is to achieving a specific number of steps for that day is also presented. Participants can also set a heart rate limit. If the heart rate limit is reached an audible and visual alarm will sound on the mobile alerting the user of their condition. The alarm will then delay for 30 seconds at which point it will sound again if the participant's heart rate is still at or above the set limit. This is useful for a participant to monitor how their heart rate fluctuates depending on the activity carried out. The participant can also review recorded information, total number of steps achieved, number of active minutes completed that day, total hours slept the night before and the quality of sleep rating for the previous night.

Conditional rules will be determined empirically enabling a traffic light system indicating that everything is either within a personalised pre-set range. Green will indicate that everything is ok, orange will indicate readings are just outside predetermined safe ranges and red indicating readings are outside the guideline limit.

4   Implementation and Testing

The CAS monitor has been developed in Android Studio and deployed for testing on a Google Nexus 4 smart device and Nexus 7 tablet. Both devices have differing form factors and future work will determine the most appropriate user interface for use with this system. Figure 2 presents the visual interface of the CAS monitor as displayed on a Nexus 4 and also the Fitbit and Zephyr Bioharness peripheral devices.

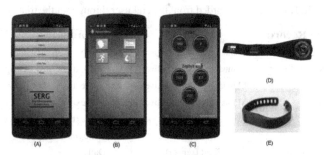

Fig. 2. Participant interface of the CAS monitor, (A) presents the main menu, (B) the manual recording selection screen and (C) the method of displaying live data from the sensors to participants. (D) Presents Zephyr Bioharness chest strap (http://zephyranywhere.com/) and (E) presents the Fitbit Flex wrist strap (http://www.fitbit.com/uk/flex).

4.1   Hardware and System Integration Testing

An initial test of the CAS monitor in the laboratory has found the system functioned as expected and a distinction could be made amongst differing physical activities based on a number of recorded readings.. One such reading was taken over a period of 5 minutes and the CAS monitor was able to simultaneously communicate with the FitBit sensor and Zephyr bioharness; data from each sensor was streamed successfully to the mobile device where it was then displayed to the end user The data was also stored on the device and subsequently uploaded to a remote server for backup. An algorithm implemented to compute and inform participants how much more activity they had to complete that day and the number of steps required to reach their daily goal functioned correctly. Figure 3 presents an exemplar dataset recorded from the CAS monitor.

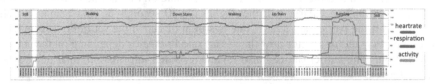

Fig. 3. Two minutes of recorded data from the CAS monitor while the user (member of the development team) is performing a range of daily living activities. Blue trace represents heart rate, red trace represents respiration and the green trace represents activity.

A distinction can be found between each activity, specifically fluctuations in activity levels. No significant increase in respiration rate can be detected due to the brief recording period; however, it can be found that the heart rate gradually increases over the recording period. A technology validation will be carried out to ensure that sensor readings are correct, specifically respiration rate as little deviation occurred during the initial test.

5 Conclusions and Future Work

Future work will involve further system validation and a usability study with 10 normal participants using the system for a period of 5-10 days. Participants will have a background in computing or nursing therefore offering distinct perspectives on the system. It is anticipated that 10 participants will provide sufficient feedback for further system refinement. Following this, generation of an initial dataset on levels of activity with an expert patient performing pulmonary rehabilitation will occur. This will provide baseline data, which can be used to determine if activity levels are in decline over a set period of time and to what degree. Daily activity analysis will also be carried out to determine if prompts on the mobile device encourage increased levels of activity or a quieter sleeping environment can effect levels of daily activity.

This CAS monitoring tool, when further validated, could provide a method of detecting the early onset of activity or health decline and may lead to earlier implementation of relevant interventions. It is important that future trials be carried out over a longer period of time allowing for the creation of a large dataset with the goal of testing a cohort of users with COPD.

Acknowledgement. Invest Northern Ireland is acknowledged for partially supporting this project under the R and D grant RD0513844. The Authors also wish to acknowledge the funding support from the Department of Education and Learning, Northern Ireland.

References

1. United Nations Department of Economic and Social Affairs/Population Division. World Population Prospects: The 2012 Revision, Key Findings and Advance Tables (2013)
2. Kamel Boulos, M.N., Lou, R.C., Anastasiou, A., et al.: Connectivity for healthcare and well-being management: examples from six European projects. International Journal of Environmental Research and Public Health 6(7), 1947–1971 (2009)
3. NHS Choices. Chronic Obstructive Pulmonary Disease (2011),
   http://www.nhs.uk/conditions/chronic-obstructive-pulmonary-disease/Pages/Introduction.aspx
4. Rabe, K.F., Hurd, S., Anzueto, A., et al.: Global strategy for the diagnosis, management, and prevention of chronic obstructive pulmonary disease: GOLD executive summary. American Journal of Respiratory and Critical Care Medicine 176(6), 532–555 (2007)
5. Van den Berge, M., Hop, W.C.J., van der Molen, T., et al.: Prediction and course of symptoms and lung function around an exacerbation in chronic obstructive pulmonary disease. Respiratory Research 13, 44 (2012)

6. Wilkinson, T.M.A., Donaldson, G.C., Hurst, J.R., Seemungal, T.A.R., Wedzicha, J.A.: Early therapy improves outcomes of exacerbations of chronic obstructive pulmonary disease. American Journal of Respiratory and Critical Care Medicine 169(12), 1298–1303 (2004)
7. Van der Weegen, S., Verwey, R., Spreeuwenberg, M., Tange, H., van der Weijden, T., de Witte, L.: The Development of a Mobile Monitoring and Feedback Tool to Stimulate Physical Activity of People With a Chronic Disease in Primary Care: A User-Centered Design. JMIR mhealth and uhealth 1(2), e8 (2013)
8. Health and Social Care. Transforming Your Care, A Review of Health and Social Care in Northern Ireland (2011)
9. Gallefoss, F., Bakke, P.S.: Cost–benefit and cost-effectiveness analysis of self-management in patients with COPD—a 1-year follow-up randomized, controlled trial. Respiratory Medicine 96(6), 424–431 (2002)
10. Van der Heijden, M., Lucas, P.J.F., Lijnse, B., Heijdra, Y.F., Schermer, T.R.J.: An autonomous mobile system for the management of COPD. Journal of Biomedical Informatics 46(3), 458–469 (2013)
11. Monninkhof, E., van der Valk, P., van der Palen, J., van Herwaarden, C., Partridge, M.R., Zielhuis, G.: Self-management education for patients with chronic obstructive pulmonary disease: a systematic review. Thorax 58(5), 394–398 (2003)
12. Aires, B.: CHRONIOUS: An open, ubiquitous and adaptive chronic disease management platform for Chronic Obstructive Pulmonary Disease (COPD), Chronic Kidney Disease (CKD) and renal insufficiency. IEEE Engineering in Medicine and Biology Society, 6850–6853 (2010)
13. Jácome, C., Marques, A.: Pulmonary rehabilitation for mild COPD: a systematic review. Respiratory care 59(4), 588–594 (2014)
14. Nici, L., Donner, C., Wouters, E., et al.: American Thoracic Society/European Respiratory Society statement on pulmonary rehabilitation. American Journal of Respiratory and Critical Care Medicine 173(12), 1390–1413 (2006)
15. Lacasse, Y., Martin, S.: Meta-analysis of respiratory rehabilitation in chronic obstructive pulmonary disease. A Cochrane Systematic Review. Europa ... 43(4), 475–485 (2007)
16. Bestall, J.C., Paul, E.A., Garrod, R., Garnham, R., Jones, R.W., Wedzicha, A.J.: Longitudinal trends in exercise capacity and health status after pulmonary rehabilitation in patients with COPD. Respiratory Medicine 97(2), 173–180 (2003)
17. Ries, A.L., Kaplan, R.M., Myers, R., Prewitt, L.M.: Maintenance after Pulmonary Rehabilitation in Chronic Lung Disease 167, 880–888 (2003)
18. De Blok, B.M.J., de Greef, M.H.G., ten Hacken, N.H.T., Sprenger, S.R., Postema, K., Wempe, J.B.: The effects of a lifestyle physical activity counseling program with feedback of a pedometer during pulmonary rehabilitation in patients with COPD: a pilot study. Patient Education and Counseling 61(1), 48–55 (2006)
19. Van der Weegen, S., Verwey, R., Spreeuwenberg, M., Tange, H., van der Weijden, T., de Witte, L.: The Development of a Mobile Monitoring and Feedback Tool to Stimulate Physical Activity of People With a Chronic Disease in Primary Care: A User-Centered Design. JMIR mhealth and uhealth 1(2), e8 (2013)
20. Verwey, R., van der Weegen, S., Spreeuwenberg, M., Tange, H., van der Weijden, T., de Witte, L.: A pilot study of a tool to stimulate physical activity in patients with COPD or type 2 diabetes in primary care. Journal of Telemedicine and Telecare 20(1), 29–34 (2014)
21. Dyer, C.A E., Harris, N.D., Jenkin, E., et al.: Activity levels after pulmonary rehabilitation - what really happens? Physiotherapy 99(3), 228–232 (2013)

Lessons Learned from a Long-Running Assistive System for Geriatric Care

Valeria Soto-Mendoza and J. Antonio Garcia-Macias

CICESE Research Center, Ensenada, Baja California, Mexico
vsoto@cicese.edu.mx, jagm@cicese.mx

Abstract. Pervasive healthcare aims for a decentralized, preventive, and assistive approach to healthcare. Recognizing their merits, many authors have proposed systems based on this approach; some include theoretical proposals and architectural designs, while others have implemented real working systems. Most systems are tested in controlled laboratory conditions, and just a few of them in real-setting scenarios.

For three years now, we have been using a system that assists caregivers in performing their duties at a geriatric residence. In this paper, we report the lessons learned with this system, during a period spanning the requirements gathering, design, implementation, maintenance, update and continuous running phases. This report tries to fill a void in the literature for real-life experiences that can be taken into account when designing and implementing pervasive healthcare systems to be installed in real settings.

Keywords: pervasive healthcare, AAL, elders, caregivers, in-situ evaluations.

1 Introduction

Many Ambient Assisted Living (AAL) systems and environments have been proposed to improve care assistance services to elders [1]. Several overviews of research challenges and systems issues can be found in the literature [2,3,4]. The majority of them describe multi-layer system architectures that support care processes and involve the participation of elders, caregivers, nurses, doctors and external healthcare services (hospitals, emergency services, etc.).

Figure 1 depicts a general and usual scheme of the AAL systems for elders. The first layer (level 1) is usually formed with a Body Area Network (BAN) with medical sensors and smart devices embedded in the environment around the elder. The data generated through the BAN are stored in local devices or sent to a collector or server for further analysis. The wireless communication is guaranteed by a Wireless Sensor Network (WSN) which connects all the sensors and actuators. The combined infrastructure of sensing and wireless communication enable continuous monitoring of the elders, and data about elders' life styles are collected and stored. The second layer (level 2) provides intelligent capabilities to recognize activities, or to infer risky and unusual situations.

L. Pecchia et al. (Eds.): IWAAL 2014, LNCS 8868, pp. 83–90, 2014.

In the third level layer are all notifications systems to support formal and informal caregivers, and other medical services. Depending on the elder's behaviours, the system triggers notifications and alarms which are sent to caregivers, family, physician, and emergency services. The last layer (level 3) is in charge of managing these notifications.

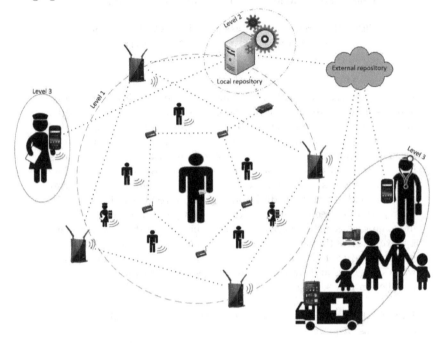

Fig. 1. Generic scheme of AAL systems

Our Approach

In the past three years we have worked with geriatric residences in Baja California, Mexico, where elders suffering different conditions live. Alzheimer, Parkinson, dementia, cognitive impairment are the most common illnesses there. One phase of our methodology [5] involved a qualitative study with staff members(n=6), nurses(n=7), caregivers(n=12), physician(n=1), family members(n=2) and older adults(n=72). Then we designed a system with a three-level architecture, similar to other works found in the literature [6]; we called our system SMAMI (Sistema de Monitoreo de Adultos Mayores Institucionalizados, spanish acronym for Monitoring System for Residents [7]), and it contains the following modules:
- Sensing module. For the first level of our system, a WSN was deployed in the residence to support real-time communication, recording the tracking of elders inside the residence. Each resident wore a wireless sensor [8]. The data generated by three-axis accelerometer and signal strength were stored.
- Activity analyser module. This module is part of level 2 of SMAMI. It analysed accelerometer's data, motion activities (walking, sitting down, standing up and

lying down); and events like falling down were recognized. Also, signal strength was used to determine the location of each elder. Location and time were used and combined to recognize elders' daily activities (feeding, resting, hygiene, medical and recreation).

- Behaviour register module. This module complements level 2 of SMAMI. It considered the temporal events and activities, deviations from the usual behaviours were detected based on activities and locations' logs using decision trees.

- Notifications module. Level 3 of SMAMI included an Android application developed for caregivers and nurses. The application showed the location of the residents in real-time, and alerted caregivers when a dangerous situation occurred. For example, in an emergency when a fall occurs.

The development of all these subsystems is not an easy task. Moreover, if the research demands a real implementation, the *in-situ* deployment of the technology could imply some changes in the prototypes. Controlled laboratory environments are not enough for feedback, and there is a gap in the literature discussing the challenges faced in this kind of research.

The objective in this work is not to present with great detail our pervasive system approach or give a list of technical issues presented during evaluations. Instead we present the socio-technical issues found during the design and implementation of our system under real conditions. This work complements the technical-oriented experiences reported by others researchers about field studies. We aim at helping researchers with non-technical advices when conducting *in-situ* studies or evaluations.

2 Realities vs Expectations

The initial thrill of designing a system full of features, with sleek design, unobtrusive, useful and neat, drive the expectations at very high levels. The daily experiences wear out the initial expectations, and the researcher has to be prepared for unexpected challenges. We share our practical experiences obtained all along the process, since the initial gathering of contextual understanding, through deployment and continuous use of the system.

2.1 Designing for People

Before proposing an application or solution for a specific community and environment, a qualitative field study is useful to acquire all the initial knowledge about the problem. Understanding and modelling the problem and its peculiarities enables researchers to design and develop *ad-hoc* technology for users.

Through a field study researchers collect information using qualitative and quantitative techniques, such as interviews, focus groups, questionnaires, shadowing, and many others. The objective is working with people's comments and perceptions, and at the same time capturing the big picture about what they do and how they do it, what issues users face and how they solve them. Ideally, the researcher expects full commitment and collaboration from the stakeholders, but in reality this is not always true.

For our particular problem we conducted a field study to know how the elders' care process took place inside a geriatric center, and to find design insights useful to guide the development of the system. We describe below the problems we faced in this stage.

Time. Setting up meetings with the stakeholders is inevitable. In the process of matching agendas of the participants we noticed that, on the part of the researchers, possessing social skills, empathy, and patience is fundamental. Perhaps the only time stakeholders can participate would be within their own working hours, when they are immersed in their duties and distractions are not welcome.

Moods and personalities. Each participant is different, some are shy and others are extroverted. This situation could be a problem when a focus group is conducted because the extroverts can overshadow the participation of others. Sometimes participants had a bad workday and they would not have a good mood to participate or share their experiences.

Individual and group discussions. Researchers need to balance the number of participants per session. In small groups interactions are minimal, and the process is not as rich as with a large group. One consequence is a large number of versions of the same topic, which implies more hours devoted to further off-line analysis. Larger groups encourage controversy, more vivid discussions but also lead to dispersion; participants tend to start unrelated topics. Also, having as many people as possible in a focus group would be optimal to maximize the resources, but in reality getting as few as two people per focus group can be a complicated task.

Explanations needed. Participants need explanations. The study goals should be shared with elders and caregivers. The explanations offered should be simple enough without being misleading. Some of the elders may have Alzheimer or some kind of cognitive impairment which causes them to not understand technical aspects or why the study is conducted. Sometimes researchers need to play a game with elders as if they were actors performing. With caregivers the fine point to understand is the wide array of educational levels, some of them may need extra help to understand complex concepts or even to write and to express themselves.

2.2 Continuous Monitoring

Figure 1 shows the BAN sensing infrastructure to continuously monitor elders. We expected the elders to wear the sensing devices at all times, we also expected batteries to last for a fair amount of time. The expectations came from pre-deployment trials done in the laboratory, by students and staff performing as elders. However, some things did not go according to expectations because participants are real people living in real conditions. Even if we tried to depict and anticipate all possible situations in a constrained environment, unexpected behaviours and situations emerged.

People using technology. Pervasive healthcare involves people and technology. Therefore when *in-situ* studies are conducted, researchers should find ways to engage users, as not all may enjoy wearing gadgets. We found that sometimes older adults feel that having a lot of devices is a sign of illness, while others think that the device will help them, for instance, to lose weight. In this respect, researchers should use subtle and non-obtrusive sensors [9]. Elders could frighten when a lot of devices are set around them. Sometimes elders would take off the wearable sensor and they would hide it too, because they used to change clothes frequently. Some older adults are used to save things, the sensors are not the exception. Finding them could be an exhaustive task, our suggestion is over provisioning of devices considering they could be lost, hidden or damaged.

Batteries. Portable devices for continuous monitoring should have a continuous source of energy; we expected, of course, battery power to be exhausted. We also anticipated that elders cannot be asked to recharge the batteries. The only other alternative was asking caregivers to do that, however adding this task to the list of other activities results in perceiving the technology as a burden. Hence, a third-party was needed to monitor the sensors' energy and recharge the battery when necessary.

Real workers. *In-situ* studies have the advantages of getting first-hand information and acquiring the most real characteristics from a process, because participants are immersed into their real environment. This is a double-edged sword because surely they would provide the know how, but it would depend on their work load and the commitment to participate into the study. Since the initial observations and interviews, it is advisable to identify the most experienced staff.

2.3   Real-Time Wireless Communication

When enhancing an environment with intelligent technology, it is an almost obvious choice to install wireless nodes, as they are less intrusive, require no wiring, and thus incur less cost and set-up time. However, there are some inherent problems with wireless technologies, as they are prone to interference, noise, and other physical phenomena that adversely affect communications.

Physical infrastructure. Care institutions were not planned having in mind the installation of small wireless nodes at all places. They lack infrastructure for base nodes (not even wall plugs where they were needed). Sometimes a simple piece of furniture or wall may interfere with the signals, and finding the failure could take a considerable amount of time. Since the transmitted data may be critical, it is paramount to allocate time for designing a robust communication system, performing tests for signal strength, identifying sources of interference, and devising strategies for recovering from data lost.

Energy sources. As previously stated, deploying battery-operated nodes is too burdening, as somebody should monitor and recharge the batteries. Choosing the alternative of connecting nodes to the electrical plugs carry a set of problems, as most times the electrical plugs were placed in low locations (to connect vacuum cleaners, for instance), or in odd places such as near the water sinks. Hence, connecting the nodes blocks the plugs and either the nodes are disconnected by the staff when needed for their intended purposes (or even by accident), or else many cumbersome, multi-plug power strips were connected. In any case, the placement of the plugs is not ideal for wireless transmitting nodes. We also observed that there were periods of power supply outages, leading to servers, sensors and communications to be down. As suggested by [10] alternative and sustainable energy sources can be considered to support continuous information infrastructure operation.

2.4   Intelligent Module

The second level of our prototype was the data analysis module. The server processed the received data and recognized the activities processing the accelerometer data using well-known decision tree algorithms [11]. Furthermore, the recognized activities and location were combined in the server to detect risky situations, and immediately send notifications to caregivers; for example, when residents entered restricted areas (e.g. the kitchen or the infirmary) or in case they suffered a fall. The notifications module (third level) was built considering mobility, places, duration and the hour of the day. Also, a decision tree [12] was used to decide when to send notifications and inform caregivers about the risk situations.

Synchronization. Sometimes it is difficult to synchronize data packets traveling through the WSN with the server. Timestamps do not match, affecting the real time system. For further analysis of the collected data it is necessary to devise a timestamp synchronization method to allow all stored data to be processed to find correlations and time-based patterns.

Support for easy maintenance. At the application level, procedures should be devised to backtrack to a previous state in case some failures occur (due for instance to a power outage). These procedures should allow to identify when the failures occur and immediately notify the system administrators.

2.5   Withdrawal of the Technology

In long term studies it is usual to propose new versions of the original system, after various design iterations and evaluations. Sometimes the technology should be reclaimed to deploy new versions [13]. The next version release may take sizable time, disturbing the participants in the waiting. Moreover, the participants could be reticent to restart the study due to the protracted wait.

Obsolescence

Due to the constant technological advances in devices and platforms, technology expires. The initial gadget used could not be compatible with some of the improvements and facets of the new version. The researcher needs to allocate time to adapt and update software and hardware, and for retraining participants.

Adoption of Technology

Once the benefits and advantages are experienced by the participants, the managers and administrative staff could adopt the ideas proposed. Besides, they could start to develop their own systems and technology. This development may seem to benefit the research. However, if requirements are not perfectly understood by a generic IT developing company the work already done is regressed. This fact could cause that caregivers become sceptical about the technology advantages and decline participation when starting a new study. There is a gap to be filled because neither the generic IT developer, the researcher or the caregiver are to blame. The goal of research is not to have a product, but to test new ideas and produce pre competitive prototypes. To ensure a continued cooperation with an institution, managers should be convinced to provide sizeable funds to develop a competitive prototype by a third party.

3   Summary of Lessons Learned

1. Participants include working people, so researchers should be flexible to match schedules (even if this implies working during the night shifts).
2. From the research team, the person with the most social skills, empathy and patience should be the one participating in meetings with stakeholders (qualitative study).
3. If possible, try to disguise as part of the staff, this will make it easier to blend in and collect the information needed.
4. Promote good relationships with participants, as this could lead to increased engagement in the project.
5. Explanations about the study should be as simple as possible; this could involve providing the information in the form of a play.
6. Buildings were rarely built having "smart spaces" in mind, therefore the conditions may not be ideal for wireless communications, nodes placement, finding electrical plugs in the right amount and at the right place.
7. Devices running on batteries have the advantage of easier placement (not necessarily where the plugs are) but need more attention in order to monitor power and replace batteries; consider who will do that.
8. For long term studies, it should be kept in mind that technology expires and upgrades will be surely needed. This involves allocating time not only for upgrades, but also for retraining participants.

4 Conclusion

In this paper, we described some socio-technical issues we have faced during three years of *in-situ* study within geriatric centers. We presented a list of recommendations regarding the technical aspects as well as social aspects when conducting studies in realistic environments. We consider these evidences are useful for researchers to save time when *in-situ* studies are addressed.

References

1. Rashidi, P., Mihailidis, A.: A survey on ambient-assisted living tools for older adults. IEEE Journal of Biomedical and Health Informatics 17(3)
2. Varshney, U.: Pervasive healthcare. Computer 36(12), 138–140 (2003)
3. Bardram, J.E.: Pervasive Healthcare as a Scientific Discipline. Methods of Information in Medicine 47(3), 178–185 (2008)
4. Arnrich, B., Mayora, O., Bardram, J., Tröster, G.: Pervasive Healthcare Paving the Way for a Pervasive, User-Centered and Preventive Healthcare Model. Methods of Information in Medicine 47(1), 67–73 (2010)
5. Soto-Mendoza, V., Garcia-Macias, J.A., Chavez, E., Martinez-Garcia, A., Favela, J., Serrano-Alvarado, P., Zuiga, M.R.: Design of a Predictive Scheduling System to Improve Assisted Living Services for Elders (Unpublished manuscript under review)
6. Viswanathan, H., Chen, B., Pompili, D.: Research challenges in computation, communication, and context awareness for ubiquitous healthcare. IEEE Communications Magazine 50(5), 92–99 (May 2012)
7. Soto Mendoza, V.: Detección de situaciones de cuidado en adultos mayores institucionalizados (Risk Detection Situations for Institutionalized Older Adults). Master thesis. CICESE (2012)
8. Shimmer: http://www.shimmersensing.com/
9. Kropf, J., Roedl, L., Hochgatterer, A.: A modular and flexible system for activity recognition and smart home control based on nonobtrusive sensors. In: Proceedings of the 6th International Conference on Pervasive Computing Technologies for Healthcare (2012)
10. Cohn, G., Gupta, S., Lee, T.J., Morris, D., Smith, J.R., Reynolds, M.S., Tan, D.S., Patel, S.N.: An ultra-low-power human body motion sensor using static electric field sensing. In: UbiComp 2012, p. 99 (2012)
11. Jeong, D.U., Kim, S.J., Chung, W.Y.: Classification of Posture and Movement Using a 3-axis Accelerometer. In: 2007 International Conference on Convergence Information Technology (ICCIT 2007), pp. 837–844 (November 2007)
12. Rokach, L., Maimon, O.: Data mining with decision trees: theory and applications. World Scientific Pub. Co. Inc. (2008)
13. Hayes, G.R.: The relationship of action research to human-computer interaction. ACM Transactions on Computer-Human Interaction 18(3), 1–20 (July 2011)

mHealthDroid: A Novel Framework for Agile Development of Mobile Health Applications

Oresti Banos, Rafael Garcia, Juan A. Holgado-Terriza, Miguel Damas,
Hector Pomares, Ignacio Rojas, Alejandro Saez, and Claudia Villalonga

Research Center for Information and Communications Technologies of the University
of Granada (CITIC-UGR), C/Periodista Rafael Gomez Montero 2, Granada, Spain
oresti@ugr.es

Abstract. Mobile health is an emerging field which is attracting much
attention. Nevertheless, tools for the development of mobile health applications are lacking. This work presents mHealthDroid, an open source Android implementation of a mHealth Framework designed to facilitate the
rapid and easy development of biomedical apps. The framework is devised
to leverage the potential of mobile devices like smartphones or tablets,
wearable sensors and portable biomedical devices. The framework provides functionalities for resource and communication abstraction, biomedical data acquisition, health knowledge extraction, persistent data storage,
adaptive visualization, system management and value-added services such
as intelligent alerts, recommendations and guidelines.

Keywords: mHealth framework, mobile health, digital health, portable
sensors, wearable sensors, biomedical sensors, health devices.

1 Introduction

The way healthcare services are delivered has radically changed during the last
years. Recent surveys show a growing tendency in physician mobile health adoption. Mainstream medical applications are mostly devoted to learning and informative purposes [13]. Physicians increasingly recommend the use of health
apps to patients [1]. While most apps require users to actively report about
their health conditions, e.g., through annotating dietary habits [9] or daily routines [12], new technological trends seek to benefit from the information collected
through wearable biomedical devices. For example, built-in smartphone sensors
[10,14] or external wearable devices [11,8,6] may be used to detect abnormal
conditions.

Mobile health (mHealth) is far from mature. Scientists still need to build and
assess the complete spectrum of mHealth technologies. Powerful frameworks and
tools that support the development and validation of multidisciplinary mHealth
applications are required. Various attempts exist to this respect. For example,
[7] provides an open source code for electrocardiogram signal processing. In
[3] a mobile phone platform to collect users psychological, physiological, and
activity information is presented. A mHealth middleware framework integrating

L. Pecchia et al. (Eds.): IWAAL 2014, LNCS 8868, pp. 91–98, 2014.

multiple interfaces and multiparameter monitoring of physiological measurement is proposed in [5]. Tools to analyze the provenance of mHealth data have also been suggested in [4]. These solutions focus on a specific domain or lack essential features for health applications. Therefore, this work proposes a novel mHealth Framework for the development of safe, scalable and effective applications.

2 Requirements of a mHealth Framework

The main goal of mHealth frameworks is to foster the research and development in health and medical domains as well as to accelerate the market of mobile health technologies and applications. The essential requirements needed in the design of a mHealth framework are outlined next. A certain level of abstraction from heterogeneous resources should be ensured to make hardware and its communication transparent to the developer. For the sake of interoperability, the framework should define a unified model for multimodal health data. Secure local and remote storage of health data is required to ensure persistence. The framework should provide techniques to extract health knowledge from raw medical and physiological data. Mechanisms to visualize medical and health information in a user-friendly fashion must be also provided for both average users and specialists. Another major requirement refers to the provision of healthcare services such as health delivery, personalized guidelines and intelligent recommendations. Finally, the framework should be modular and extensible to future sensor technologies and application needs.

3 Architecture of the mHealth Framework

In the light of the requirements defined in Section 2, a novel framework devised to enable the easy and agile development of mHealth applications leveraging on heterogeneous wearable biomedical devices is proposed. This mHealth Framework implements functionalities to support resource and communication abstraction, biomedical data acquisition, health knowledge extraction, persistent data storage, adaptive visualization, system management and value-added services.

Figure 1 shows the architecture that implement the functionalities and the components of the mHealth Framework. mHealth data delivered by mobile and biomedical sensors is collected and structured by the Communication Manager. This raw data can be stored in the Storage Manager, further processed by the Data Processing Manager, graphically represented by the Visualization Manager or directly used by the applications built on the mHeath Framework. Moreover, the medical knowledge derived by the Data Processing Manager can also be stored in the Storage Manager, input to advanced functionalities provided by the Service Enablers or used by the mHealth applications. Since the Storage Manager offers persistence, stored data can be offline processed by the Data Processing Manager, graphically represented by the Visualization Manager or accessed by the mHealth applications. Finally, the mHealth Framework offers, by means of the System Manager, functionalities to manage general resources of the mobile device.

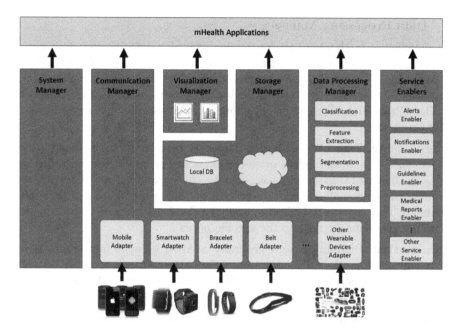

Fig. 1. mHealth Framework architecture

3.1 Communication Manager

mHealth applications may operate on multiple heterogeneous mobile and biomedical devices. The Communication Manager provides the abstraction level required to enable the functioning of applications independently of the underlying health technologies. This manager makes the communication transparent and serves as interpreter of the multimodal health data. In order to procure transparent communication and data retrieval, the Communication Manager incorporates Adapters, which are standalone modules devised to support the use of an specific mobile or biomedical device. The Adapter manages the connection with the device, interprets the received data and maps it to the unified data model (Section 3.7). The modularity of the Adapters makes the Communication Manager extensible and evolvable to future devices and technologies.

3.2 Storage Manager

The Storage Manager provides data persistence both locally and remotely. It enables the easy retrieval of stored data, abstracting the queries from the underlying storage system. This manager is also responsible for the efficient synchronization of the data and its secure transmission to the remote store, either in the cloud or remote server.

3.3 Data Processing Manager

This manager is in charge of the processing of health data by providing signal processing, data mining and machine learning techniques. These functionalities can run either on-the-fly by processing the data collected at runtime by the Communication Manager, or offline by retrieving the data from the Storage Manager. The Data Processing Manager includes four independent modules typically used in data processing.

Preprocessing. The collected health data may be affected by diverse type of artifacts such as spurious spikes or electronic noise, or be loosely controlled resulting in abnormal values and inconsistencies. Accordingly, it may be necessary to remove these anomalies from the raw data, e.g., by using filtering or screening techniques. This module is devised to apply mechanisms to clean, transform and ultimately adequate the data to the specific needs.

Segmentation. Biodata streams generally need to be split into segments or pieces. For example, sliding window approaches are commonly used for the partitioning of body-motion data. This module provides diverse techniques to split the data.

Feature Extraction. To provide a more tractable representation of the signals general or domain-specific features are extracted. Examples of features are statistical functions such as the mean or median, time/frequency transformations, heuristics, etc. This module permits to transform the input data into a reduced representation set of features or feature vector.

Classification. Artificial intelligence algorithms are widely used to gain knowledge from the collected health data. The features extracted by the Feature Extraction module are input to this type of algorithms provided by the Classification module to eventually categorize the data.

3.4 Visualization Manager

The data representation is a fundamental element of any mHealth app. Since applications may have different objectives and target users, developers require a wide sort of graphical representation tools. This manager is in charge of providing diverse modes and ways to display data. An online mode is identified for the depiction of the data provided by the Communication Manager, which corresponds to the information collected by the health sensors at runtime. On the other hand, an offline operation mode is defined for the visualization of data saved by the Storage Manager. Not only raw signals may be represented but also the information obtained after the data processing.

3.5 System Manager

The System Manager provides developers with functionalities to manage general resources of the mobile device. Examples of these resources are wireless connections (WiFi, 3G connection, Bluetooth), geopositioning technologies (GPS), screen configuration or battery management.

3.6   Service Enablers

An important characteristic of several mHealth applications is the intervention on health states. Health data may be profited to influence elements of the intervention and yield new information from which to act. This information is here devised to be provided to the users through a set of Service Enablers, which support advanced functionalities for alerts, notifications, guidelines and reports.

Alerts Enabler. This enabler provides mechanisms to trigger alerts and emergency procedures when abnormalities or risk situations are detected. Examples of these mechanisms are automatic phone calls and messages that may be delivered to the patients' family, carers and emergency services in the event of a critical situation (fall detection, cardiac event, etc.).

Notifications Enabler. Users may need to be timely or occasionally informed about important facts of their healthcare and wellbeing process. Health remainders (medication, workout, etc.) are essential mechanisms to engage users in the care process, to procure their organization and to empower them to meet the treatment goals. This enabler is devised to support prescheduled or event-based user-friendly notifications that may also trigger additional services.

Guidelines Enabler. Instructions, encouragements and educational information from specialists are of high value to promote healthy lifestyles and to support the patient self-care. This enabler provides multimedia tools for displaying guidelines that may be personalized and adapted to the user's needs and conditions.

Medical Reports Enabler. This enabler is devised to facilitate the structuring of the medical knowledge in an expert-oriented format. It may help clinicians and care professionals to interpret health trends and to support medical decisions.

3.7   Data Model

A unified Data Model enables the representation of heterogeneous health data and guarantees interoperability among the mHealth Framework components and applications. A generic, flexible and extensible model is of utmost importance due to the variety of available and future sensing modalities. The mHealth Data Model comprises five elements. The Session object is the main element and represents a recording session including its metadata. The Session is composed of several Sample objects which refer to each sample from the data stream collected during the session. Each Sample links to multiple Device objects which represent the devices streaming during the session. Since a device offers different sensor modalities, the Device links to the Sensor objects. The Sensor contains the data collected by a given sensor in a specific moment. Metadata is required to interpret the data collected by the multimodal sensors and the different devices. To reduce the model overhead and since the metadata does not vary during a session, the Metadata object is associated to the Session. The Metadata defines the types of sensors, the units of the measurements, the start and end time of the recorded session and the sampling rate.

4   mHealthDroid: mHealth Framework Implementation

mHealthDroid is the Android implementation of the proposed mHealth Framework, released open source[1] under the GNU General Public License version 3. mHealthDroid is devised to operate on the Android operating system 4.2 ("Jelly Bean"), although it provides backwards compatibility to version 2.3.3 ("Gingerbread").

The mHealthDroid Communication Manager has been implemented to facilitate the incorporation of new Adapters. To do so, it provides a generic Adapter skeleton. The current implementation of mHealthDroid provides the Adapter for Android mobile devices and the Adapter for the Shimmer3 wearable device [2]. The Android Mobile Adapter abstracts the sensors embedded into the mobile device, e.g., GPS, temperature or humidity. Likewise, the Shimmer Adapter provides the means to communicate the wearable device with the mobile device and map the data to the proprietary format. The Shimmer3 device provides multiple sensing modalities that span from inertial sensing via accelerometer, gyroscope, magnetometer, and altimeter, to physiological signs measurement such as electrocardiogram or electromyogram among others.

The Storage Manager incorporates a SQLite[2] database to implement the local persistence functionality. SQLite is a popular database engine on memory constrained systems, like mobile devices, since it runs in minimal stack space and very little heap. The Storage Manager also offers an interface to easily retrieve, based on diverse identifiers (session, device identifier, date, time interval), the data stored in the SQLite database. Database consistency check procedures are implemented by the Storage Manager to ensure integrity in the synchronization between the remote and local storage. The transmission to the remote storage is implemented using a HTTP POST request method which encloses in the request message's body the JSON[3] representation of the data. mHealthDroid also offers a server side implementation for remote persistence. This implementation builds on a MySQL[4] database and provides PHP scripts that use the MySQLi[5] API to manage the remote database.

The mHealthDroid Data Processing Manager provides an essential set of functionalities typically used in the data processing chain. The Preprocessing module implements two techniques: upsampling to increase the sampling rate and downsampling to reduce the sampling rate. A sliding window approach, widely-used in signal processing problems, is implemented by the Segmentation module. The Feature Extraction module implements some generic statistical features such as mean, variance, standard deviation, zero crossing rate, mean crossing rate, maximum and minimum. The Classification module builds on an open source stripped version of Weka[6]. It provides functionalities to train and validate

---

[1] Available at https://github.com/mHealthDroid/mHealthDroid

[2] http://www.sqlite.org/

[3] http://json.org/

[4] http://www.mysql.com/

[5] http://www.php.net/manual/en/book.mysqli.php

[6] https://github.com/rjmarsan/Weka-for-Android

machine learning models, that can be used for classification purposes. mHealth-Droid currently implements Naive Bayes, Adaboost, Decision Trees, Linear Regression and ZeroR classification techniques.

The Visualization Manager builds on the open source library Graphview[7], which has been adapted to fulfill the particular needs of mHealth data representation. The manager allows multiplot visualization, multisignal representation and customization for diverse graph types.

The System Manager offers simple interfaces to access common mobile devices resources (WiFi, 3G, Bluetooth and screen) and builds on the standard Android API.

mHealthDroid implements three Service Enablers. The Alerts Enabler provides interfaces to trigger phone calls and text messages. The Notifications Enabler implements text remainders that can be scheduled in a simple way. Moreover, this enabler also provides advanced notifications that can trigger external functionalities or applications. Both Alerts and Notifications Enablers build on the standard Android API. Finally, the Guidelines Enabler provides interfaces to reproduce multimedia content, both locally and remotely stored. The Media Player Android[8] API is used in mHealthDroid to control playback of audio and video files for the local content. For the reproduction of remote multimedia content, the Guidelines Enabler implements a set of functions that build on the YouTube Android Player[9] API. This is particularly practical to access a huge variety of medical and wellbeing content.

An exemplary app[10] (see Figure 2) has been developed to illustrate the potential of the mHealthDroid implementation and to validate it.

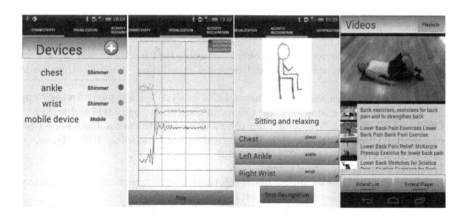

Fig. 2. Exemplary mHealth app developed using mHealthDroid

---

[7] http://android-graphview.org/

[8] http://developer.android.com/reference/android/media/MediaPlayer.html

[9] https://developers.google.com/youtube/android/player/

[10] Available in Google Play at https://play.google.com/store/apps/details?id=com.mHealthDroid.activitydetector&hl=es_419

5   Conclusions

This paper presents a novel framework devised to facilitate the development of mobile health applications in a simple and agile fashion. The framework has been designed taking into account the essential requirements of mHealth technologies and applications. Moreover, this work introduces mHealthDroid, an open source implementation of the proposed mHealth Framework that operates on the Android OS. The mHealthDroid initiative aims at bringing developers, healthcare professionals, academics and health enthusiasts together to exchange ideas and cooperate in the definition of valuable tools for a healthier world. Accordingly, the authors encourage the community to contribute to this innovative platform by supporting the use of the latest sensors, incorporating new behavioral algorithms or simply making use of it for the development of mobile health applications.

Acknowledgments. Work supported by the CICYT SAF2010-20558 and UGR Plan Propio PP2012-PI11 projects and the FPU Spanish grant AP2009-2244.

References

1. Taking the Pulse®(US). Technical report, Manhattan Research (2014)
2. Burns, A., et al.: SHIMMER. A Wireless Sensor Platform for Noninvasive Biomedical Research. IEEE Sensors Journal 10(9), 1527–1534 (2010)
3. Gaggioli, A., et al.: A Mobile Data Collection Platform for Mental Health Research. Pers. Ubi. Comp. 17(2), 241–251 (2013)
4. Prasad, A., et al.: Provenance framework for mHealth. In: 5th Int. Conf. on Comm. Syst. and Net, pp. 1–6 (2013)
5. Chen, P.H., Chen, H.M.: Framework design-integrating an android open platform with multi-interface biomedical modules for physiological measurement. Journal of Conv. Infor. Tech. 7(12), 310–319 (2012)
6. Banos, O., et al.: Physiodroid: combining wearable health sensors and mobile devices for a pervasive, continuous and personal monitoring. The Scientific World Journal (2014)
7. Oster, J., et al.: Open source Java-based ECG analysis software and Android app for Atrial Fibrillation screening. In: Comp. in Cardiology, pp. 731–734 (2013)
8. Oresko, J.J., et al.: A Wearable Smartphone-Based Platform for Real-Time Cardiovascular Disease Detection Via Electrocardiogram Processing. IEEE Trans. on Inf. Tech. in Biomed. 14(3), 734–740 (2010)
9. LoseIt®, http://www.loseit.com/
10. Habib, M.A., et al.: Smartphone-based solutions for fall detection and prevention: challenges and open issues. Sensors 14(4), 7181–7208 (2014)
11. Bsoul, M., et al.: Apnea MedAssist: Real-time Sleep Apnea Monitor Using Single-Lead ECG. IEEE Trans. on Inf. Tech. in Biomed. 15(3), 416–427 (2011)
12. MyFitnessPal®, http://www.myfitnesspal.com/
13. Khalifian, S., et al.: Medical student appraisal: searching on smartphones. Appl. Clinical Inf. 4(1), 53–60 (2012)
14. Mazilu, S., et al.: Online detection of freezing of gait with smartphones and machine learning techniques. In: 6th Int. Conf. on Perv. Comp. Tech. for Healthcare, pp. 123–130 (2012)

A Framework for Situation Awareness Based upon Dynamic Situation Modeling

Ryan Pearson, Mark Donnelly, Jun Liu, and Leo Galway

School of Computing and Mathematics, University of Ulster, Jordanstown, UK
pearson-r2@email.ulster.ac.uk,
{mp.donnelly,j.liu,l.galway}@ulster.ac.uk

Abstract. This paper proposes a framework to model dynamically changing situations in real world environments. In the real world, situations naturally vary in how they occur. Understanding these variations is essential to establish accurate knowledge of the environment and provide situation aware services. Current approaches to situation modeling may benefit from the inclusion of a dedicated method of adapting to changes in how situations occur over time. The proposed framework is introduced and a description of its components and their relations is provided. The proposed implementation of the framework is described in a smart office based scenario.

Keywords: Situation Awareness, Knowledge Representation, Sensor Data Fusion.

1 Introduction

The conventional approach to modelling situations has focused on modeling static concepts with fixed methods of interpretation for the purpose of conducting research into decision-making applications of situation awareness [1,2,3]. In real-world environments situations have complex dynamic characteristics that evolve in response to changes in the environment [4]. Issues with and approaches to adaptive situation modelling have been investigated by the following [5,6,7]. The work by Chen et al. defines a method of adapting an activity specification for situation awareness [8]. They develop a three-step approach consisting of knowledge based activity modeling, activity recognition and activity specification learning. They describe how a probabilistic learning algorithm can incrementally discover changes in activity specifications over time. The work provides a theoretical basis for investigating methods of learning complex situation models that reflect changes in how situations occur in real world environments.

The data produced by the range of sensor devices are deployed in smart environments is characteristically complex and heterogeneous [9]. This prevents the knowledge required to interpret situations from being easily extracted from sensor data [10]. The framework proposed in this paper aims to address this issue through the use of a novel platform for collecting, managing and storing generic sensor data from multiple sources.

L. Pecchia et al. (Eds.): IWAAL 2014, LNCS 8868, pp. 99–102, 2014.

2   Description of the Framework

The proposed framework is presented in Figure 1. The framework is designed to be domain independent in respect to application orientated use. Specifically, it will provide a platform to capture and fuse generic multisensor data and leverage its full value. This platform will provide a representation of the fused sensor data from which knowledge of the temporal, spatial and domain specific attributes of a situation can be interpreted. It will also extend existing research into domain independent methods of modelling and interpreting context in real world dynamic environments [8] by investigating situation interpretation under similar conditions. The following sections provide a description of the architecture.

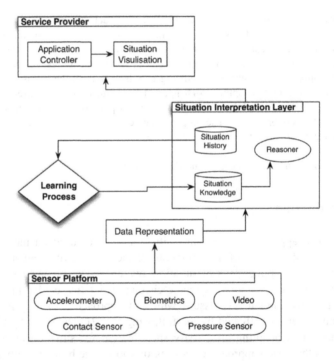

Fig. 1. Proposed situation awareness framework depicting how data driven situation interpretation can be achieved in a dynamically changing environment

2.1   Sensor Data Representation and Situation Interpretation

Multisensor data is typically impaired by a lack of uniformity and structure [10]. Specifically, multisensor data is characteristically uncertain, multimodal and heterogeneous [4]. Being able to effectively use multisensor data to create situation awareness requires these challenges to be addressed [10]. Comparatively little research has addressed a generic method of fusing non-specific sensor data to form a representation of that information which can be used in situation awareness [12]. A technique is required that can leverage generic multisensor data, as the sensor platform in Figure 1 depicts, to form a consistent and reasonable representation of the situations represented within sensor data. By using such a representation higher level fusion processes can reliably interpret situations. Lee et al. define a platform for sensor data management that allows non-specific or generic sensor data input [12]. Their approach utilizes a schema-less data storage architecture allowing the flexibility that multisensor data management requires. Their work provides a theoretical backing to generic sensor data management, fusion and representation for situation awareness. Such an approach should allow the information outputs of low-level fusion to satisfy the requirements of higher-level fusion and situation interpretation.

An ontology can serve as an adaptable model of situations [8]. An ontology-based specification of domain knowledge will act as the primary situation specification and reasoning method in the framework. It will contain expert knowledge on specific situations within a particular domain. However, interpretation of these situations is not sensor specific but simply requires an appropriate information input representation as described above. The work by Ye and Dobson [11] demonstrated a method of activity recognition and situation awareness using a context lattice. We believe this approach is adaptable to the demands of dynamic situation modeling in an ontology-based specification, as depicted in Figure 1. It should also be capable of driving potential intelligent services, such as decision support, depicted as the service provider in Figure 1. It is envisioned that wireless smartphone technologies utilizing a graphical user interface would provide these services to users. Similar services have been proposed by [9]. The knowledge representation, adapted from [11] will maintain its capability of rich semantic reasoning in the framework, to drive application-orientated behavior. The situation history component will contain semantically enriched sensor data from previous instantiations of the situation knowledge model.

3   Planned Proof of Concept

To validate the proposed framework a case study using an intelligent office based scenario is planned. Specifically a person's current situation will be categorized to assess their availability for interaction with another person in the office. Initial situation models will be constructed and refined over time using knowledge derived via the framework. A variety of sensor devices including proximity, contact and motion and camera based sensors will be utilized in the experiment.

4   Conclusion

In this paper, a framework to model dynamically changing situations was proposed. It focuses on a method of learning the evolving characteristics of situations in a dynamic environment and using this knowledge to update and refine existing situation specification. A protocol for sensor data representation is proposed to allow situation inference from generic multisource sensor data.

Future work aims to develop a situation aware application in a smart environment based upon the user scenario described in Section 3. It will also investigate the approaches to sensor data representation, situation specification, learning and interpretation presented here.

References

1. Nwiabu, N., Allison, I., Holt, P., Lowit, P., Oyeneyin, B.: Case-Based Situation Awareness. In: IEEE International Multi-Disciplinary Conference on Cognitive Methods in Situation Awareness and Decision Support, pp. 22–29 (2012)
2. Li, Z.Y., Park, J.C., Lee, B., Youn, H.Y.: Situation Awareness Based on Dempster-Shafer Theory and Semantic Similarity. In: IEEE 16th International Conference on Computational Science and Engineering, pp. 545–552 (2013)
3. Pereira, I., Costa, P.D., Almeida, J.P.: A Rule-Based Platform for Situation Management. In: IEEE International Multi-Disciplinary Conference on Cognitive Methods in Situation Awareness and Decision Support (CogSIMA), pp. 83–90 (2013)
4. Leida, M., Gusmini, A., Davies, J.: Semantics-Aware Data Integration for Heterogeneous Data Sources. Journal of Ambient Intelligence and Humanized Computing 4(4), 471–491 (2012)
5. Fischer, Y., Beyerer, J.: Defining Dynamic Bayesian Networks for Probabilistic Situation Assessment. In: IEEE 15th Conference on Information Fusion (FUSION), pp. 888–895 (2012)
6. Baumgartner, N., Gottesheim, W., Mitsch, S., Retschitzegger, W., Schwinger, W.: BeAware!— Situation Awareness, the Ontology-Driven way. Data & Knowledge Engineering 69(11), 1181–1193 (2010)
7. Roy, N., Gu, T., Das, S.K.: Supporting Pervasive Computing Applications with Active Context Fusion and Semantic Context Delivery. Pervasive and Mobile Computing 6(1), 21–42 (2010)
8. Chen, L., Nugent, C., Okeyo, G.: An Ontology-Based Hybrid Approach to Activity Modeling for Smart Homes. IEEE Transactions on Human-Machine Systems 44(1), 92–105 (2014)
9. Moradi-Pari, E., Tahmasbi-Sarvestani, A.F., Yaser, P.: Wireless Architectures for Heterogeneous Sensing in Smart Home Applications: Concepts and Real Implementation. Proceedings of the IEEE 8(1), 1–10 (2014)
10. Luo, R.C., Chang, C.C., Lai, C.C.: Multisensor Fusion and Integration: Theories, Applications, and its Perspectives. IEEE Sensors Journal 11(12), 3122–3138 (2011)
11. Ye, J., Dobson, S.: Exploring Semantics in Activity Recognition using Context Lattices. Journal of Ambient Intelligence and Smart Environments 2(4), 1–18 (2010)
12. Lee, C.H., Birch, D., Wu, C., Silva, D., Tsinalis, O., Li, Y., Yan, S., Ghanem, M., Guo, Y.: Building a Generic Platform for Big Sensor Data Application. In: IEEE International Conference on Big Data Building, pp. 94–102 (2013)

Context-Aware and User-Centered Evaluation of Assistive Systems. Methodology and Web Analysis Tool

Jesús Fontecha[1], Ramón Hervás[1], Tania Mondéjar[1],
José Bravo[1], and Gabriel Urzaiz[2]

[1] MAmI Research Lab, University of Castilla-La Mancha, Ciudad Real, Spain
{jesus.fontecha,ramon.hlucas,jose.bravo}@uclm.es,
tania.mondejar@esmile.es
[2] Division of Engineering and Exact Sciences, Anáhuac Mayab University, Mexico
gabriel.urzaiz@anahuac.mx

Abstract. One of the main challenges on Ambient Assisted Living (AAL) is to reach the massive use and acceptance of the promising assistive systems that are being developed. This challenge entails the appropriate evaluation of these systems following a user-centered perspective. We propose a framework to deal with this issue that consists of a methodology and a web-based analysis tool developed based on methodology. The basis of this software tool is to gather information of the user from two different sources: adapted psychological questionnaires and naturalistic observation of their own context in a transparent way. The aim is to enable an in-deep analysis focused on improving the life quality of end users.

Keywords: Ambient Intelligence, Ambient Assisted Living, Evaluation, User-centered Methodology, Context-awareness, Psychological Assessment.

1 Introduction

Ambient Assisted Living (AAL) is an initiative that promotes technological solutions to enhance the quality of life (QoL) of elderly people. There are an increasing number of solutions because of the evolution of assistive technologies and the public support in this area. However, it seems that there is a big gap between the promising results from those solutions and end users and market.

In last years, an important number of assistive systems applies user-centered participatory approaches that involve end-users during the whole project lifecycle [1]. The application of user-centered methods (scenarios, mock-ups, focus groups, interviews, real tests, naturalistic observation, etc.) enhances the requirement acquisition, the effective evaluation and, theatrically, ensures the final product aceptation.

In general, the problem of these user-centered methods is that they require a huge human effort and interdisciplinary groups of work. Additionally, the user-centered evaluation tests are typically developed into a lab environment. Even

L. Pecchia et al. (Eds.): IWAAL 2014, LNCS 8868, pp. 103–110, 2014.

those tests conducted in the real user environment usually require that experts observing the evaluation activities.

The present work deals with the problems described above. We propose a mechanism to evaluate assistive systems consisted of two artifacts (a) a conceptual methodology to determine the specifications and guidelines to analyse the user experience and the achieved assistive benefits; and (b) a software infrastructure that includes an adaptable web application to easily create, distribute and hand out psychological assessments, and several web services to monitor and acquire information from user interactions in a transparent way. Additionally, the web application makes easier the analysis of data through information visualization techniques. In this work, the data analysis provide us an input mechanism to develop decision-support systems, although we need to consider colateral issues related to ethical aspects of monitored users.

Section 2 describes briefly some relevant works on the same line of this paper. Section 3 describes the proposed methodology for analysis of assistive systems. Section 4 shows a particular scenario in which the methodology and the analysis tools are being used and tested. Finally, Section 5 includes the conclusions obtained from this work.

2   Related Work

The use of automatic or semi-automatic tools to evaluate software systems is not new. There are tools for analyzing accessibility of web sites [2], for remote analysis of usability [3], for evaluation of user experience of user interfaces (UI) [4], etc. However, the analysis of assistive systems is a more complex scenario that involves different roles of users using different devices in real environments and needing a transversal evaluation (health, psychology, usability, etc). Curcin et al. [5] propose a model-driven approach software to evaluate the feasibility of healthcare systems based on data gathering and reports visualization. Other works such as [6] present the advantages of information service systems to provide valuable results for doctors and patients in hospital environments.

On the other hand, the assessment of users, in healthcare contexts, is another field to be taken into account by our system. The completion of questionnaires by using electronic devices, to facilitate the gathering of information and the analysis of results, is usual today. There are many applications which offer this kind of services, however these applications are not focused on paticular domains. An example of these is SurveyMonkey engine [1]. It allows the creation of surveys to collect information about users. This tool provides a solution to study users and markets, but it is limited when the questionnaires must be more specific and we need to have available all collected data. In healthcare domain, there are companies which provide mobile solutions to convert traditional questionnaires into electronic ones[2]. However, there are important drawbacks when the own users need to manage these tools. Besides, the work presented takes into account

---

[1] https://www.surveymonkey.com/
[2] http://www.totalmobile.co.uk/healthcare

other sources of information, not only those relating to tests. Interactions with elements of the environment are used as a part of the result assessment.

3 Methodological Specifications

3.1 General View

This proposal is based on different areas and knowledge fields. Since we are finding a methodology for an assistive and interactive system, it is necessary to study both Human-Computer Interaction (HCI) and social sciences methodologies. Moreover, this methodology can be considered a development methodology because it lays the foundations to deploy software tools for analysis, and also this is an evaluation methodology due to the included procedures and tests to evaluate assistive systems. In general, this methodology is a set of guidelines and specifications of good practices to integrate analytics user-centered tools into assistive systems. The user-centered activities can be grouped in two types:

- **Questionnaires-Based Survey**: many user-centered activities are based on questionnaires such as interviews, focus groups, psychological assessments, and user experience evaluations. The methodology establishes the guidelines to conduct these activities through an integrated web application. It is possible to prepare personalized questionnaires to different roles of users, hand out them, and collect and analyze the results.
- **Naturalistic Observation (Awareness)**: Naturalistic observation involves recording subject behavior in their natural environment. This type of research is very useful because the observation of users in a controlled environment (lab) would be unrealistic and could affect the subject's behavior. The methodology helps to settle down the requirements to monitor the user interactions with the assistive system and analyze that information.

3.2 Methodology Sub-models and Stages

Inspired in the sub-model organization of interactive system development process proposed by Peter Warren [7], we have defined 5 sub-models:

- **Psychological and Sociological Model**: this model is concerned with the relevant backgrounds on psychological analysis of use on assistive systems, e.g how they can improve the quality of life and well being [8] of users and their families and caregivers.
- **Conceptual Model**: this model will characterize parts of the reality, or more precisely, it will represent the context as an information source.
- **Task Model**: this model embraces all activities related to users. The task model describes the logical activities that have to be carried out in order to reach users goals. It does not necessary involve interactions with the system.
- **Interaction Model**: it defines how users manipulate elements of the system and receive feedback from it. The interaction model is hardly linked to the user's task and to the conceptual elements associated to those tasks.

– **Developers Model**: this model defines what the system has to do to achieve the user requirements. The developers model obtains information from the conceptual model and the interaction model.

This methodology also determines how the life cycle is, i.e., the description of the set of phases to achieve the goal of analyses and evaluate assistive systems. The **observation phase** to identify and quantify the problems that users face and how assistive systems help on them. **Planing phase**, consisting of a problem definition and description of end results in solving the problem, and the knowledge about the background of the problem. **Design phase**, in which the sub-models will be developed. **Development phase**, which corresponds to the web tools production. **Base-line phase**, to gather initial information about health and psychological status from the particular users (e.g., by using scales such as [9] to assess depression items and [10] regarding functional measurements). It will be compared with data obtained after using the assistive system. **Execution phase**, which corresponds to the running of the system at the environment. Evaluation phase, to obtain the needed conclusions and evaluate the suitability of the particular assistive system.

4   Scenario: The Analysis Tool in an Elderly Context

Since the generic perspective of the methodology and web tools, this proposal has been developed in the context of the Personal IADL Assistant (PIA) EU AAL project[3], being IADL, Instrumental Activities of Daily Living [11]. Using the methodological specifications defined in section 3, we have developed a web analysis tool, which plays as back-end application, for supporting the evaluation carried out by AAL systems. Thus, three types of users have been identified: elders as primary users, carers as secondary users (who take care of primary ones) and researchers as third-party users (who perform the analysis of primary and secondary users).

The developed analysis platform provides researchers a tool for managing questionnaires and users, and also for analyzing the state of such users (carers and elders) based on results of the own questionnaires, and collection of external interactions at elder's home regarding IADL, carer stress, and QoL measures. Similarly, a front-end web application has been developed to receive the convenient feedback from carers. Carers can know their state (related to QoL and stress level) and the IADL actions taken by the associated elders. This application also shows recommendations to secondary users for improving the eldercare.

4.1   Researcher's Side. Back-End Web Application

User Management. The community of users can be created and managed from the web tool. Each user has a role to determine the access privileges in the assistive system. Carers are associated with researchers and elders are associated

---

[3] http://pia-project.org

with carers. Note that the user can access to the AAL system from different locations (e.g., mobile, web or desktop application); for that reason, read-only tokens can be considered to know the source of user login and facilitate user retrieving from/to external applications.

Action Management. The actions have been modeled following the methodological specification in the interaction model.

Every action carried out by the users of the assistive system can be defined in the analysis tool. The action consists of the following attributes: an action code or identifier, name, brief description and the source of the action. Sources are also defined in the analysis tool.

Actions are used as part of inputs in the assistive system which show the activities performed by users of this system as it is mentioned in section 4.2.

Questionnaires Management. Third-party users with privileges, researchers in our scenario, can create and edit test templates to know the state of primary or secondary users based on considered measures. Measures are determined in the analysis tool before test creation, and each measure is identified by a name and a brief description.

We have identified two kind of tests or questionnaires, standard and interactive. The first ones, consists of several common fields and a set of blocks of questions, and each question can have one or more possible answers. Three types of responses have been defined: exclusive, multiple or text.

Meanwhile, an interactive test consists of a set of blocks with only one question per block (with multiple or exclusive choices), such as, next questions depend on the responses to that questions. Fig 1 shows a fragment of flow diagram which represents a part of interactive test. These tests have a final score which determines one or more recommendations to be provided to the secondary users, depending the own score and the path followed along the test.

The created tests are stored in the system and they are filled by primary and secondary users in the developed assistive system to evaluate that users taking into account the measure related to the test. The analysis tool allows the management of every test of the assistive system.

4.2   Results Management

The analysis tool also comprises the management and visualization of results by researchers. These results come from the interaction between users and applications of the AAL system. In this sense, we consider the results from the main activities (see section 3.1). **Inputs** corresponds to events caused by external applications of the assistive system, and they are associated with a specific user and action (see section 4.1). All the inputs generated by the external applications are listed and monitored in the analysis tool (in both, front-end and back-end). Figure 2 shows an screenshot with an example of AAL inputs. In this case, input information regarding elders are displayed in the web application for carers to

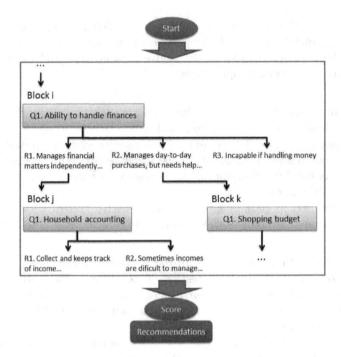

Fig. 1. Example of flow of an interactive questionnaire

know the tasks performed at the elderly home. And **test assignments** which indicates the assignation of a created test to a specific carer. Thus, the analysis tool can monitor the activity of test assignments and third-party users can also modify the assignment properties. The tests are shown in the web application for carers according their publication dates.

The results of tests already completed by primary and secondary users are stored and managed in the analysis tool. A *Results* entity is responsible for saving the results of the responses from all questions of the completed and assigned

	Action	Target user	Device	Performed on				
✔	[AC1] Edit account	Jonas Taylor	mobile0001	20/05/2014 16:54	ℹ	↻		
✔	[AC1] Edit account	Jonas Taylor	mobile0001	24/02/2014 16:51	ℹ	↻		
✔	[AC12] Play video tablet	Jonas Taylor	mobile0001	21/02/2014 09:51	ℹ	↻		

Fig. 2. Example of inputs in the carer web application

tests, setting up a log for statistical and analysis purposes. Results are also used to provide feedback to carers as recommendations.

4.3 Carer's Side. Front-End Web Application

Analysis tool also comprises a web tool to provide secondary users (carers) information about their own activities and the actions related to primary users (elders) those who take care. The main functionalities of this application include management of user profile, notifications and reminders, visualization of carer tasks (pending and completed), visualization of IADL inputs and completion of questionnaires. In this sense, questionnaires proposed by researchers from the analysis tool are shown in the carer web application to assess different aspects related to IADL, stress level and QoL. Interactive questionnaires provide users an instant feedback, proposed by researchers in the back-end application, once the test is completed. Results are useful for analysis and statistical tasks.

5 Conclusions and Future Work

This paper aims to settle down basics for the evaluation of assistive systems from a user-centered point of view. We propose a methodology to appropriately analyse psychological aspect of assistive systems as a success measure. For that, we have proposed several models and procedures to conduct that analysis through questionnaires and monitoring of the user interactions with an assistive system.

From this methodology, we have developed a common back-end known as analysis tool to be integrated in assistive systems. The main aim of this software is to collect relevant information about primary and secondary users to perform different assessments focused on improving life quality levels, for example, of people who live alone at home and their closest caregivers. Besides, a front-end web application has been developed to allow secondary users the completion of tests and a simple monitoring activities on related elders.

Although the analysis tool has been developed for generic purposes inside assistive perspective, this is being deployed in an elderly context to support elderly people to manage the instrumental activities of daily living, as well as to know stress aspects of the carers applying tests and questionnaires created by the own tool, following the principles of the methodology.

The future work includes the application of the analysis tool to evaluate a group of elders and caregivers in a real environment, providing us a validation of the tools and a more detailed user-system feedback. The results provided by this system could be used by other applications to create detailed reports and charts, both valuable for healthcare professionals and researchers in AAL scopes.

Acknowledgment. This work is conducted in the context of the EU AAL PIA project (AAL-2012-4-033). The authors gratefully acknowledge the contributions from all members of the PIA consortium. Also, we appreciate the support of UBIHEALTH project under International Research Staff Exchange Schema (MC-IRSES 316337).

References

1. Hellman, R.: Usable user interfaces for persons with memory impairments. In: Wichert, R., Ebehardt, B. (eds.) Ambient Assisted Living. 5. AAL-Kongress 2012, pp. 167–176. Springer (2012)
2. W3C, Accesibility evalaution resources. W3C (March 2014), http://www.w3.org/WAI/eval/
3. Hartson, H., Castillo, J., Kelso, J., Neale, W.: Remote evaluation: The network as an extension of the usability laboratory. In: The Computer Human Interaction Conference (CHI 1996), pp. 228–235 (1996)
4. Vaananen-Vainio-Mattila, K., Waljas, M.: Developing an expert evaluation method for user experience of cross-platform web services. In: Mindtrek 2009. ACM (2009)
5. Curcin, V., Woodcock, T., Poots, A.J., Majeed, A., Bell, D.: Model-driven approach to data collection and reporting for quality improvement. Journal of Biomedical Informatics (in press, 2014)
6. Xing, L., Pin, W., Yi, L.: Research and development on health care information service system. Advance Journal of Food Science and Technology 5(11), 1510–1513 (2013)
7. Warren, P.: Understanding hci methodologies (unpublished work)
8. Joseph, S., Becker, S., Elwick, H., Silburn, R.: Adult carers quality of life questionnaire (ac-qol): development of an evidence-based tool. Mental Health Review Journal 17(2), 57–69 (2012)
9. Alexopoulos, G.S., Abrams, R.C., Young, R.C., Shamoian, C.: Cornell scale for depression in dementia. Biological Psychiatry 23, 271–284 (1988)
10. Functional status measurements in primary care, WONCA. Springer, New York (1990)
11. Lawton, M., Brody, E.: Assessment of older people: self-maintaining and instrumental activities of daily living. Geronthology 9, 179–186 (1969)

A Clinically Assisted Collaborative System Architecture for Preventing Falls in Elderly People

Javier Orozco[1], Rodrigo Santos[1], Sergio Ochoa[2], Leo Ordinez[1],
Roc Messeguer[3], and Nelson Baloian[2]

[1] Dep. Electrical Engineering and Computers, IIIE, UNS-CONICET, Argentina
[2] Computer Science Department, Universidad de Chile, Chile
[3] Computer Science Department, Universidad Politecnica de Catalunya, Spain

Abstract. Falls in older adults are not only frequent but also potentially disabling for them. Detecting and preventing these falls have an important impact in the life of the elderly people. This paper presents the architecture of a pervasive system designed to perform early detection of older adults in risk of falling or fell down. The system notifies the appropriate people or healthcare organizations in case of detecting a fall of the monitored person. This monitoring process produces minimum disruption in the life style of the elderly.

Keywords: Falls Prevention and Detection, Pervasive Healthcare.

1 Introduction

Advances in embedded systems and new communication technologies have opened many opportunities to address healthcare procedures, treatments and strategies to deal with several illnesses. For instance, wireless sensing technology has shown to be successful in monitoring elderly people suffering chronic diseases or living alone.

Falls in older adults represent one of the main causes of hospitalization, and they are also responsible not only of causing disabling fractures and other physical injuries, but also psychological traumas that reduce their independence and confidence [1]. Detecting falls using sensors is not a simple task, particularly if the solution should be pervasive, keep the privacy of the monitored persons and accurately recognize their current condition [2]. Detecting people in risk of falling is still more useful, but complex.

This paper presents the architecture of a pervasive system that helps prevent falls of older adults, by doing early detection of people in risk of falling. The system involves a combination of wearable sensors connected through a Body Area Network (BAN) and a smartphone that runs a software application. The former captures the information from a set of wearable sensors embedded in an ad hoc digital device, which is wore by the monitored person. Such information is sent to the software component running in the elderly smartphone, which is in charge of determining the current condition of the person (normal, with risk of falling, fell down). If the system detects a fall, it delivers alerts to the supporting people or healthcare organizations in order to obtain first aids as soon as possible.

L. Pecchia et al. (Eds.): IWAAL 2014, LNCS 8868, pp. 111–114, 2014.
© Springer International Publishing Switzerland 2014

2 Related Work

It has been shown that falls are one important cause of disability and also death in elderly people living alone [3]. Nevertheless, there is not a definite solution to this problem yet [4]. One possible approach to detect falls involves the use of wearable sensors (e.g. gyroscopes, accelerometers, or microphones) to collect data that helps identify falling situations [2]. These sensors can be used not only to detect falls, but also to identify periods with a high probability of falling; e.g. because the person periodically loses his stability when moving. In [1] the authors report a monitoring system to determine repetitive behavior patterns and falls in the elderly. In [4] a frail studio is presented. Frailty is a syndrome associated to the ederly that leads to falls. With the system proposed, a frailty coefficient is computed for instrumenting different prevention therapies. In [5] a mechanism based on the smartphone accelerometer is used to gather information that helps physicians to diagnose and treat cardiologic pathologies. In [6] it is proved that Bluetooth networks are useful for interconnecting wearable sensors, however these networks have not bandwidth enough for doing real-time monitoring of some pathologies; e.g. cardiovascular diseases. In fact, it is shown that most monitoring systems require performing a first processing of the collected data in order to reduce the information transmitted to the formal processing unit. In [7] the authors use NFC and RFID technologies to determine the localization of patients at a hospital, avoiding thus various patient identification problems. This type of technology has been successfully used for monitoring people activities. Clearly, there are several previous works related to the early detection of falls and monitoring diseases in elderly people. However, none of them present an integral, non-intrusive and self-trained system, able to be customized by a physician considering the patients features and also the situations to be detected.

3 System Architecture

The proposed system for detecting falls and vulnerable situations in elderly people has two main components: a BAN that interconnects a set of wearable sensors and a collaborative application that runs in the elderlys smartphone. This latter determines the current probability of fall risk in the older adult that is being monitored. It uses the data collected from the sensors, which is processed and transmitted to the smartphone through the BAN. This solution requires that the monitored person wears a digital device that implements the BAN and embeds most of the sensors.

This device can be attached to the people belt producing minimum disruption to the user. The system collaboratively balances the computational load, optimizing thus the energy consumption of the BAN and the smartphone application. Figures 1.a and 1.b show the architecture of both, the master wearable sensor (the digital device that represents the main component of the BAN) and the collaborative application running in the smartphone. The master wearable sensor (Fig. 1.a) embeds several small, lightweight and efficient (in terms of energy consumption) sensors, which usually have limited capability for data processing and exchange. This master sensor is implemented as an integrated circuit, designed to accomplish one or more activities. In this case, the component includes a pulse meter, a gyroscope, an accelerometer, a microphone, the

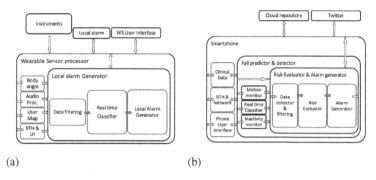

Fig. 1. (a) Architecture of the master wearable sensor, (b) Architecture of the smartphone software application

BAN-user-interface and a Bluetooth interface to keep a communication link with the smartphone. It also includes the logic to locally detect falls and instability patterns in the monitored people.

The wearable master sensor captures the body inclination and other clinically typified movements, which commonly precede a fall in impaired persons or people suffering certain pathologies. In order to do that, the data captured from the sensors is classified by the real-time classifier, which builds an inference table based on classical algorithms for decision making. Such a data is transmitted to the smartphone and processed accordingly. The software components monitoring the people motion and inactivity (Fig. 1.b) process this information trying to identify vulnerable or potentially vulnerable situations and alerting the person about the risky situation. Long periods of inactivity indicate potential problems and eventual falls. The application running at the smartphone periodically records the user status in a server that may be hosted in the Cloud. If the system detects a vulnerability situation or a fall, it notifies the relatives or healthcare emergency services about this situation. The target of these notifications and the channel used with that purpose can be set during the deployment of the system. The communication channels include sms, email and some social networks and instant messaging systems, like WhatApp. A detailed description of this system is available in [7].

In order to determine the level of vulnerability of a person in a certain time instant, the system uses an inference matrix that was filled using results of clinical studies. The columns of the matrix corresponds to clinical variables that contributes to identify instability of people; e.g. Orthostatic Hypotension. The rows of the matrix indicate four movements that also help identify the people instability; e.g. from-sit-to-stand. Therefore, each cell establishes (based on clinical studies) the level of risk that a from-sit-to-stand movement represents for a person having orthostatic hypotension for example.

The physician can configure the solution for a certain patient (i.e. an older adult) by instantiating the clinical variables according to the results of the tests performed to that person. The sensors identifies the movements done by the elderly and based on the recognized movement determine the current level of fall risk for that person. Computing the risk indicators, based on the elderlys movements and the clinical variables for such a person, it is possible to determine the instability level of that older adult. This value is used to determine the next action to be performed by the system.

Table 1. Inference Table

Motion	PHT	Incontinence	Medication	TSS>12s	Walker	Bath	Bedroom
Sit to Stand	H	H	H	H	H	H	M
Inctivity	H	M	L	L	L	L	L
Walking	L	H	M	L	M	H	L

4 Conclusions

This paper presents the architecture of a pervasive system designed to prevent and detect falls in elderly people. Based on empirical, clinical and inferred data, the system determines the level of fall risk of the monitored person, and eventually it delivers alerts to make the older adult aware of such a situation, preventing thus a possible accident. The system utilizes both, real-time and stored information, to accurately determine when delivering an alarm according to the elderly current activity and his clinical diagnostics. If the fall is not avoided, an alarm is delivered to supporting people and healthcare emergency services to reduce the latency in the medical attention of the elderly. The system implementation uses existing technology and it is currently in the first evaluation phase.

Acknowledgments. This work was partially supported by the European Community through the projects Community Networks Testbed for the Future Internet (CONFINE): FP7-288535, and A Community networking Cloud in a box (Clommunity): FP7-317879, and also by Spanish goverment under contract TIN2013-47245-C2-1-R, and also by the Generalitat de Catalunya as a Consolidated Research Group 2014-SGR-881.

References

1. Ryannen, O.P., Kivea, S.L., Honkanen, R., Laippala, P.: Falls and lying helpless in the elderly. Z Gerontol (25), 278–282
2. Ralhan, A.: A study on machine learning algorithms for fall detection and movement classification. Master's thesis, Department of Electrical and Computer Engineering, University of Saskatchewan (2009)
3. Dumitrache, M., Pasca, S.: Fall detection algorithm based on triaxial accelerometer data. In: E-Health and Bioengineering Conference (EHB), pp. 1–4 (November 2013)
4. Fontecha, J., Navarro, F., Hervás, R., Bravo, J.: Elderly frailty detection by using accelerometer-enabled smartphones and clinical information records. Personal and Ubiquitous Computing 17, 1073–1083 (2013)
5. Jara, A., Fernández, D., Lopez, P., Zamora, M., Ubeda, B., Skarmeta, A.: Evaluation of bluetooth low energy capabilities for continuous data transmission from a wearable electrocardiogram. In: 2012 Sixth International Conference on Innovative Mobile and Internet Services in Ubiquitous Computing (IMIS), pp. 912–917 (July 2012)
6. Martínez, M., Fontecha, J., Vizoso, J.R., Bravo, J., Cabrero-Canosa, M.J., Martín, I.: RFID and NFC in hospital environments: Reaching a sustainable approach. In: Bravo, J., López-de-Ipiña, D., Moya, F. (eds.) UCAmI 2012. LNCS, vol. 7656, pp. 125–128. Springer, Heidelberg (2012)
7. Orozco, J., Santos, R., Ochoa, S., Ordinez, L., Meseguer, R.: Collaborative systems for supporting autonomous life in elderly people. Technical report, Universidad Nacional del Sur (2014)

Moving Brain Computer Interfaces towards Home Based Systems for People with Acquired Brain Injury

Jean Daly [1], Elaine Armstrong [1], Eileen Thomson [1], and Suzanne Martin[2]

[1] Cedar Foundation, Belfast, BT100GW, UK
{j.daly,e.armstrong,e.thomson}@cedar-foundation.org}
[2] Faculty of life and Health Sciences, University of Ulster, BT370QB, UK
s.martin@ulster.ac.uk

Abstract. This paper presents the findings from an evaluation of a Brain Computer Interface (BCI) with a group of people without brain injury and end users with acquired brain injury. The system held a number of applications to enable communication, web browsing, smart home control and cognitive rehabilitation. Participants engaged in a three-session cycle of testing and completed usability questionnaires within the user centred design approach adopted. The average accuracy score for the people without brain injury was 82.6% (±4.7) with the cognitive rehabilitation reporting the highest response rate. End users recorded an average accuracy score of 74% (±11.5), with the speller logging the highest accuracy score. The findings outline the importance of engaging with end users to identify the current functionality and usability of such systems in order to move them closer towards a marketable product used in a domestic environment.

Keywords: Brain Computer Interface, User Centred Design, eHealth, Acquired Brain Injury.

1 Introduction

Brain Computer Interfaces (BCI) are complex hardware and software systems that can be controlled through brain signals. BCI harness brainwaves through non-invasive electrodes placed on the skull to enable users to interact with computer systems and their applications [1]. BCI offer the unique opportunity for people with complex disabilities to access services and applications that support inclusion, participation, enable independence and increase access to healthcare. The present challenge is to develop systems and services that are easy to use, reliable and accessible to people with disabilities and their caregivers. It is evident that BCI can now control a number of applications however little evidence of this is present beyond the laboratory [2]. Equally, limited evaluations have been undertaken with participants that would benefit from the use of such a system on a daily bases such as people with acquired brain injury (ABI) [3]. Post ABI a number of barriers can impact on a person's quality of life, including physical function, cognition and communication. Thus, BCI systems

L. Pecchia et al. (Eds.): IWAAL 2014, LNCS 8868, pp. 115–118, 2014.

have the potential to support this population through the trajectory of their rehabilitation and also on a more long-term basis.

The overall aim of this research is to develop and evaluate a platform operated by BCI that combines devices and applications like smart home control, social networking, online and offline entertainment applications, ambient intelligent systems, and eHealth through rehabilitation as well as telemonitoring and home support [3]. This ambitious project will identify user requirements and system usability within this population by adopting a user-centered approach. Therefore end-user evaluation and feedback will inform the technical developers throughout the lifecycle of the project. This paper will focus on the user centered evaluation of the second iteration of a BCI platform with applications for communication, rehabilitation, smart home control and web browsing.

2   Methodology

Ten people were recruited to evaluate the prototype. Five participants without an ABI (4 female/ 1 male, M= 36.6 years, ± 9.3) in the control group and five target end users (1 female/ 4 males, M= 37 years, ± 8.7) who are living with ABI (Post ABI M= 9.8 yrs, ±3.7) were recruited. All participants had evaluated the previous iteration of the BCI prototype. The testing phase required each participant to complete an extensive 40-step protocol on three occasions each on the P300 BCI platform using gel based non-invasive electrodes. The EEG was acquired using a non-invasive electrode cap with 8 active Ag/AgCl electrodes (g.Gamma, g.tec Austria), at electrode Fz, Cz, P3, POz, P4, PO7, Oz and PO8. Channels were referenced to the right earlobe and a ground electrode was placed at FPz and the signals were amplified by a g.USBamp (g.tec Austria). The protocol included spelling the word 'BRAINPOWER', completing two cognitive rehabilitation tasks, tweeting '#BCI #BACKHOME' and moving a camera application in three different directions, followed by the VAS (visual analogue scale) questionnaire to rate overall satisfaction between 0 and 10. After each final evaluation session participants completed the extended QUEST 2.0 (Quebec User Evaluation of Satisfaction with Assistive Technology: [4]), a customized usability questionnaire and the NASA-TLX (NASA-Task Load Index: [5]) to assess workload. Ethical approval was granted by the University of Ulster.

3   Results

The control group recorded an average accuracy of 82.6% (±4.7) following completion of the evaluation and end users achieved an overall average accuracy score of 74% (±11.5). End users stopped after each task was completed to facilitate a break and this also stabilised the systems in turn reducing its unreliability.

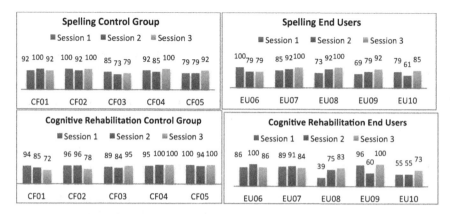

Fig. 1. Accuracies Percentages for Speller and Cognitive Rehabilitation Tasks

Figure 1 and Figure 2 illustrate the control group and end user group accuracy scores for the four applications. The cognitive rehabilitation task was the most responsive for the control group (91.87% ±8.6) and the Speller was the most accurate for the end user group (82.07% ±13.34). The camera task reported the lowest accuracy score for both groups. The difference in the camera task accuracy scores between groups could be attributed to a system stability issue as stopping and restarting the system between tasks for the end user group prevented the system crashing each time with this task as it had for the control group.

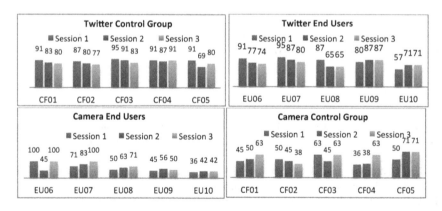

Fig. 2. Accuracies Percentages for Twitter and Camera Tasks

The end-users overall device satisfaction reported on the VAS was 7.64 out of 10 (±1.78) while the control group indicated a score of 6.57 (±1.2). The subjective work-load using the NASA TLX was reported as moderate to high workload (57.10 ±10.9) for the control group and moderate workload for end users (41.42 ± 23.5). The average QUEST score for the control group was 4.35 (out of 5: ±.5) and the QUEST Add-ed Items average was 4.24 (± .5). The average QUEST score for end users was 3.86 (±.6) and the QUEST Added Items average was 3.58 (± 1.1).

4   Discussion

The results presented are from the evaluation of a newly developed BCI prototype with a control group and end users with Acquired Brain Injury. All participants were satisfied with the overall improvements, applications and performance of the system since the evaluation of the first iteration of the prototype [3] however an increase in the response rate would still be required. The results indicated that end users reported an overall lower accuracy score, experienced fatigue and there was difficulty focusing on and dividing attention between two screens. It is possible this is due to the participant's residual cognitive impairment as a result of ABI such as difficultly concentrating for periods of time as well as decreased stamina, memory and attention.

The lessons learned from the present research have been disseminated to the developers so that the final platform will bring BCI closer to the ultimate goal of a commercial available system for home use. This included enhancing the aesthetic design of the electrode cap, enabling independent use of the system once the cap has been mounted and the training is complete, the applications and BCI matrix should be on one screen, and the ability to personalise the system to the unique needs of each user. Overall, the system is still too complex to be operated by a non-BCI expert with minimal support in a home environment although the findings can contribute to the knowledge base aimed at moving systems closer. The research aims to develop novel BCI systems to enhance the user's independence, increase access to services and ultimately enrich quality of life. The findings outline promising results for the functionality and usability of the system by people with ABI.

Acknowledgements. The research project BackHome is funded by the EU FP7/2007-2013 (grant agreement n° 288566).

References

1. Wolpaw, J.R., Birbaumer, N., Mcfarland, D.J., Pfurtscheller, G., Vaughan, T.M.: Brain-computer interfaces for communication   and control. Clinical Neurophysiology 113, 767–791 (2002)
2. Sellers, E.W., Vaughan, T.M., Wolpaw, J.R.: A brain computer interface for long-term independent home use. Amyotrophic Lateral Sclerosis, 1–7 (2010)
3. Daly, J., Armstrong, E., Wriessnegger, S.C., Müller-Putz, G.R., Hintermüller, C., Thomson, E., Martin, S.: The evaluation of a brain computer interface system with acquired brain injury end users. In: 6th International Brain Computer Interface Conference, Graz, Austria (2014)
4. Demers, L., Weiss-Lambrou, R., Ska, B.: Quebec user evaluation of satisfaction with assistive technology (QUEST 2. 0): An overview and recent progress. Technology and Disability 14, 101–105 (2002)
5. Sharek, D.: NASA-TLX Online Tool (Version 0.06) (Internet Application). Research Triangle, NC. (2009), http://www.nasatlx.com (retrieved)

Communication of Health Related Vital Sign- and Activity Data in the A²LICE Research Project

Sebastian Thiele and Anke Häber

University of Applied Sciences Zwickau,
Department of Computer Sciences
Dr. Friedrichs-Ring 2A, 08056 Zwickau, Germany
(sebastian.thiele,anke.haeber}@fh-zwickau.de

Abstract. From an organizational view the coordination of a trans-institutional process of patient treatment among different healthcare providers is difficult. If the care process includes home monitoring the problems like data dispatching and -usage by healthcare providers (HCP) increase.

Keywords: Ambient assisted Living, healthcare, it-architecture, monitoring, hl7.

1   Introduction

In the research project Ambient Assisted Living in Intelligent Controlled Environments (A²LICE) [1], apartments in a living quarter are upgraded with building automation sensors and medical devices. The main objective is to support elderly people with special care needs, in long-term living in their own home. To achieve this, functionalities such as activity detection and monitoring of health parameters are provided with options to communicate the resulting data to the HCP. In the home of the resident acquired data of medical parameters and recognized activities of daily living (ADL´s) must be forwarded to the appropriate target systems of HCP. Considerations include in particular the requirements of the healthcare partners regarding quality and coding of the data. This is why interface specifications must be observed, which have been defined by standardization initiatives such as 'Continua Health Alliance' (CHA) [2] or 'Integrating the Healthcare Enterprise' (IHE) [3]. Since the external service providers use very different application systems (AS), the exchange of data between apartments and these systems is complex. This paper presents communication architecture for data transmission between the domestic area of the residents and the providers of health care.

2   Domains of Interest

The consideration of a person´s apartment as a possible supplier of data is particularly interesting from the AAL perspective. This raises a number of new application scena-

L. Pecchia et al. (Eds.): IWAAL 2014, LNCS 8868, pp. 119–122, 2014.
© Springer International Publishing Switzerland 2014

rios in terms of safety and comfort which can offer an additional benefit especially for elderly persons. These scenarios include the electronic collection and transmission of health related and activity data to relatives and providers of health care.

A telemadical center is a facility for the telemedical care of particular chronically ill people. This facility provides besides technical resources to support as well as the expertise to monitor the health status of patients. The TMC usually uses a particular software system (TMC system TMCS), which assumes the data from domestic field of the inhabitants, process them and store it in databases by the means of an electronic case record or electronic medical record. The coupling of the TMCS with the AS of the HCP the monitoring of a person's health status can be optimally supported. For this purpose a number of standardized interfaces for service providers are offered. A broad introduction of telemedical centers is also complicated by the lack of a nation-wide central communication infrastructure.

The providers of health care in Germany are separated in the so-called ambulatory and inpatient sectors. The ambulatory care providers include physicians in private practice or nursing services whereas hospitals and nursing homes are part of the inpa-tient sector. Each of the service providers uses its own AS, which are available from different manufacturers. An electronic exchange of data between these systems is often not possible. To this end, appropriate interfaces must be obtained from the man-ufacturer which is in turn associated with increased cost.

3   Domain-Specific Processes

Once the data is collected in the home they are communicated either directly to the participating provider or (based on type of data, expected use and configurations) to a TMCS. In the direct scenario of data transmission to the systems of service providers, the collected data must be transformed into the correct data formats and distributed through various interfaces. This is associated with a high configuration overhead of the AS used in the home. In addition to the development of interfaces, target systems access credentials, data formats and necessary encodings need to be set up. By using various adapters, the above mentioned target systems of general practitioners, the nursing service and the hospital can be served with the collected data prototypically. A more consistent approach causing significantly lower development and configura-tion efforts (particularly in the home area) is the choice of coupling to a TMCS.

The TMCS acts as a central service instance for the domestic area and the provid-ers of the health care sector. Apart from the technical tasks such as acceptance of the data from home areas, processing, transformation and routing, organizational func-tions such as the steering of processes and the adherence of security policies are per-ceived. This process preceding rules sets, which react on the content of the message (measured values, situations, ADLs) are responsible for the pre-processing of the data in the TMCS. By maintaining a patient specific electronic health record a consistent record can be built. An alarm of the service provider (doctor, nurse, relatives) in case of health related problems based on event classification (threshold exceeded at measurement results) and intervention by them becomes possible. This requires that the TMCS has a current copy of the person specific threshold values of health related measurement data, which has to be provided by HCP.

Depending on the performance of the care provider's AS processing of the data received from the TMCS may be extensive. A general practitioner can import the received LDT-File directly into his AS and assign a patient reference. As a result, graphical analysis and time series comparisons for the (long-term) development of selected parameters are possible. A similar functionality can be provided for the AS of the ambulatory nursing service, where the data can be used directly from the applications database. In the clinical sector using the HL7 standard allows the transmission of additional information such as existing medication, allergies and diagnoses. However the programmatic extension of the appropriate clinical documentation and management system are required.

4   Communication Architecture

In the research project A²LICE a range of communication scenarios for health monitoring of patients between the domestic area and the HCP with and without the use of a central service instance (telemedical center application system TMCS) were defined. This includes the transmission of measured values, which were recorded by medical micro devices (blood pressure meter, weighting scales, etc.). In addition, activities of daily living and recognized situations are received from an independent software component installed in the home of the resident and have been classified as 'AAL incident'.

A communication between the participants within an IT infrastructure can only be successful if a common vocabulary and standardized communication schemes are used. The following communication standards are used in the health care sector and the A²LICE project. Health Level 7 (HL7) describes a standard that is used predominantly in the clinical sector and is currently available in version 3. A variety of scenarios in the AAL domain can be formulated by means of event-, message type (ETMT) combinations using HL7 v2, such as delivering unsolicited observation results without an existing order. In the general practitioner sector in Germany the Kassenärztliche Bundesvereinigung (KBV) started early to develop standards for data transmission between laboratories and the practitioner's office. A product of these standardization efforts is the Labordatenträger (LDT - laboratory test report) [5].

The developed communication architecture is modelled on the provisions of the Continua Health Alliance to build architecture for monitoring medical parameters. The communication network consists of home areas, a TMC and individual health care providers from different sectors utilizing various defined interfaces for data exchange. To fulfil the monitoring tasks in each area different application components are used. This means to use the same technical concepts for coupling the residential home AS to the TMCS via HL7 interface and web service. Through events raised in the home, communication is initiated. Different strategies to disseminate the data based on the classification schemas allow the preservation of privacy. In the case of a direct coupling, extensive configuration procedures in the AS of the residents are moved into the TMCS. In the present scenario, the communication relation aimed primarily from the domestic sector to the health care provider´s.

The HCP are responsible for defining and implementing robust interfaces or use (standardized) predefined ones from their AS manufacturer. CHA defines the usage of web services for the overall communication. The general practitioners AS ixx.concept and MediFox live (nursing service AS) in A²LICE do not support them. That's why other approaches such as the provision of a secure FTP server (S-FTP) or a proprietary database interface have been chosen. Only IS-H/ishmed (hospital AS) allows the implementation of own web services for the discussed scenario.

5   Discussion and Future Work

The developed communication architecture for residential areas benefits from the use of standardized interfaces. The components used within the architecture are operated on residential home level and exchange messages with the mentioned service providers of the health care sector. The data processing is carried out by means of different strategies for processing measurements of medical parametersADL´s and the energetic data of the flat. An exchange of data collected by sensors and medical technology is based on data usage guidelines, which are determined by the resident itself. The target system for collected data is a centralized software instance which refers to a telemedical center. This organization offers different services for the residents for monitoring the person's health status as well as energetic data. Within TMCS, the data is processed and distributed on the basis of person specific configurations to the health care.

Acknowledgement. The authors gratefully thank the European Social Fund (ESF) for supporting the junior research group and the doctoral scholarship at the University of Applied Sciences Zwickau.

References

1. Leonhard, S., et al.: ESF-Forschungsprojekt Ambient Assisted Living zur Schliessung der konzeptionellen Lücke in der medizinischen Versorgungskette zwischen stationärer Pflege und (kommunaler) Wohnungswirtschaft, Scientific Reports Ambient Assisted Living und neue Konzepte in der Pflege (2012)
2. Continua Health Alliance; Connected Health Vision (2014),
   http://www.continuaalliance.org/connected-health-vision
3. Integrating the Healthcare Enterprise. About IHE (2014),
   http://ihe.net/About_IHE/
4. Haas, P., Johner, C., et al.: Interoperabilität und Standards. In: Haas, P., Johner, C. (eds.) Praxishandbuch IT im Gesundheitswesen, Erfolgreich Einführen, Entwickeln, Anwenden und Betreiben, Carl Hanser Verlag, München (2008)

Automatic Summarization of Activities Depicted in Instructional Videos by Use of Speech Analysis

Joseph Rafferty[1], Chris D. Nugent[1], Jun Liu[1], and Liming Chen[2]

[1] School of Computing and Mathematics, University of Ulster, UK
rafferty-j@email.ulster.ac.uk, {cd.nugent,j.liu}@ulster.ac.uk
[2] School of Computer Science and Informatics, De Montfort University, UK
liming.chen@dmu.ac.uk

Abstract. Existing activity recognition based assistive living solutions have adopted a relatively rigid approach to modelling activities. To address the deficiencies of such approaches, a goal-oriented solution has been proposed that will offer a method of flexibly modelling activities. This approach does, however, have a disadvantage in that the performance of goals may vary hence requiring differing video clips to be associated with these variations. In order to address this shortcoming, the use of rich metadata to facilitate automatic sequencing and matching of appropriate video clips is necessary. This paper introduces a mechanism of automatically generating rich metadata which details the actions depicted in video files to facilitate matching and sequencing. This mechanism was evaluated with 14 video files, producing annotations with a high degree of accuracy.

Keywords: Annotation, Automated Speech Recognition, Parsing, Ontology, Assistive Living, Smart Environments, Video, Guidance.

1 Introduction

The global population is aging and as a result is developing an uneven demographic composition. It is expected that by 2050 over 20% of the population will be aged 65 or over [1]. Having such an aged population is expected to increase cases of age related illness subsequently increasing burden on healthcare provision [1].

Technology supporting independent living is one solution to alleviate a portion of these aging related problems [2]. This may come in the form of a Smart Home (SH), which is essentially a residential environment that is augmented with technology to promote independent living. Typically, SHs operate by embedding sensors throughout the environment. Signals generated by the sensors are processed with the goal of recognising the activities of the inhabitants of the SH. Based on the processing, support mechanisms, which are deployed throughout the SH, provide assistance as necessary [2, 3]. The assistance that current SHs provide is typically in the form of prompting systems, monitoring of behavioural trends and remote assessment of vital signs. Prompting systems within SHs provide guidance for inhabitants once specific criteria are encountered. Prompts may consist of video, audio or text or a combination of these media. Video prompts, which incorporate audio provide a promising method of providing instruction as it provides informative and relatable guidance [2, 4].

L. Pecchia et al. (Eds.): IWAAL 2014, LNCS 8868, pp. 123–130, 2014.

The research presented within this paper introduces a novel mechanism for profiling video clips to generate metadata to be used in support of the provision of dynamic instruction within a goal driven SH paradigm. This remainder of the paper is arranged as follows: Section 2 provides an overview of related work; Section 3 details the approach used in this study; Section 4 provides an evaluation of the approach and Section 5 concludes the paper.

2   Related Work

A number of SHs exist which provide assistance for inhabitants by offering guidance in the form of prompting [2, 3, 5, 6]. The prompting systems in these environments include video, audio or text instruction. In particular video based instruction provides detailed and relatable instruction for SH inhabitants.

Current SHs that offer video based guidance do so in a relatively static manner. This is due to the use of inflexible structures used to model activities [7]. For example, the COACH system [8] provided video based assistance to assist dementia sufferers with the task of washing their hands. This approach was based on Partially Observable Markov Decision Processes, where current interpretations of world states are associated with assistive policies. These policies in turn nominate specific video and audio clips to be supplied. Although this approach caters for some variation in activity performance it does not provide sufficiently flexible variation in performance. Additionally, the activity model cannot be modified without a large amount of effort. Also, the assistive policies have static associations with video clips and so provide rigid instruction.

In order to address the inflexibility of modelling activities, SHs focusing on inhabitant goals in place of activities have been proposed to support more variations of activities and flexibility with their performance [7].

To date video instruction provides assistance for activities in a relatively static manner. Such a static assignment is not compatible with a goal oriented approach. In the goal oriented approach, goals consist of flexible activity plans/fragments which can be sequenced in a multitude of ways covering variations in the activity itself. Video based guidance within a goal driven approach, therefore, requires a flexible mechanism to compile a number of video clips into relevant instructional sequences for a specific goal or to determine the most suitable candidate from a video repository. This repository will also be growing over time and so potentially providing better candidates for a particular goal variation. In order to create a sequence of video clips from a library or provide a suitable match from a repository metadata is required. The metadata can subsequently be used for sequencing within a planning mechanism or used with a selection mechanism to determine a suitable video clip. This type of metadata is usually provided through manual input which may lead to incorrect or incomplete records being provided in addition to taking a huge amount of effort [9].

Methods of automatically generating video annotations and metadata exist [10–13], however, do not provide a suitable method of producing activity annotations as they do not identify a set of goal actions in such video clips. In addition, the majority of these approaches require training with a dataset beforehand, resulting in a cold start problem [10–13].

3   Audio Based Profiling of Instructional Video

In order to automatically generate rich metadata for video clips an automated annotation method needs to be devised and implemented. In this work, an annotation method capable of generating rich metadata for video clips has been created and implemented within an evaluation platform called ABSEIL (Audio BaSEd Instruction profiLer). This annotation method is intended to work in conjunction with the video repository generated by the Personal IADL Assistant (PIA) project[1]. The goal of the PIA project is to assist older individuals by offering guidance with Instrumental Activities of Daily Living (IADL) [14]. In PIA, caregivers record videos which contain an accompanying, detailed, audio explanation of how to achieve a task associated with an IADL. Videos are then associated with NFC tags, which are affixed to items in an environment. Those in need of assistance can use an Android smart phone or tablet to interact with and read an ID from one of the NFC tags, which subsequently used to select a video to play. To offer effective support, the videos within the PIA repository should therefore be of assured quality and contain a useful audio explanation. Further information about the PIA project is available in [15].

In the proposed approach, videos are initially converted to audio clips. The audio clips are then sent to a black-box Automated Speech Recognition system (ASR) [16] which returns a transcription. This transcription is processed using actions from goals in the goal repository to determine if any are uttered by the explaining party. These goals and their actions are defined by caregivers. Variations of these actions are created using a semantic lexicon and homophone dictionary. A graphical depiction of this method is presented in Fig. 1.

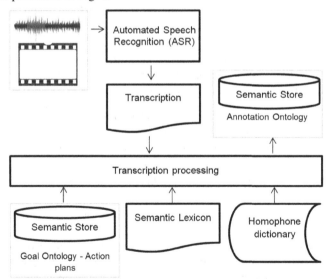

Fig. 1. An overview of the automatic metadata generation process

---

[1] Personal IADL Assistant, PIA – EU AAL Funded Research Project (AAL-2012-5-033), available at: http://www.pia-project.org/

When passed a video file, ABSEIL uses the FFMPEG suite to transcode it into a variety of audio files. These audio files vary in aspects such as channel count (mono or stereo), sample rates (e.g., 8000Hz) and CODECs (FLAC, MP3, or PCM). This range of files is created to allow interaction with a range of ASR systems.

Once the FLAC audio file has been transcoded from a video clip, it is then sent as a stream to the Google Speech API (GSAPI) service [17] which returns a transcription of the audio file. GSAPI was chosen over alternative ASR solutions (Apple, Dragon, Windows Speech) due to the high degree of accuracy that was obtained during evaluation of ASR systems for this application. The evaluation of these ASR systems was achieved by selecting 3 test videos from the PIA project, manually creating a transcription and comparing the accuracy of the manual transcription to those produced by ASR systems. The Dice coefficient was used as a string similarity metric [18], the equation for this metric is shown in (1).

$$S = \frac{2C}{A+B} = \frac{2|A \cap B|}{|A|+|B|} \tag{1}$$

The result of this comparison is presented in Table 1. ASR systems may be trained. Training increases accuracy of transcriptions, however, tailors the ASR mechanism towards recognising a specific voice. Given that video clips in the PIA repository would have multiple narrators, this training process would prove to be detrimental to ASR performance when trained to a specific voice. In addition, it does not reflect a realistic use scenario where training would not occur. As such, ASR systems were not trained in this evaluation (where possible).

The videos considered incorporated casual audio guidance containing English, Spanish and Norwegian accents reflecting the videos, which would be in the long term within the PIA repository.

Table 1. The accuracy of transcripts produced by ASR systems as compared to a manual transcription. N.B. Some systems produced no result, these are intended to produce transcripts from direct dictation and so are not tailored to transcribe narration as used in these videos.

Service provider	Accuracy of transcriptions			
	Video 1	Video 2	Video 3	Average
Apple[*]	0% - No Result	0% - No Result	0% - No Result	0%
Dragon[**]	0% - No Result	0% - No Result	0% - No Result	0%
Google (GSAPI)[*]	70.0%	57.142%	68.571%	65.238%
Windows Speech [**]	26.839%	22.377%	33.519%	27.587%

Online Systems are indicated by *, untrained systems are indicated by **

In this approach, a goal ontology exists which contains modelled goals for a SH. This ontology may contain inhabitant goals such as *MakeCoffee,* which may also reference other goals (sub-goals), such as *BoilWater*. These goals have an associated action plan which contains a number of atomic actions. These atomic actions represent the steps required to achieve the goal, such as *FillKettle, PourWaterInCup.* Once a transcription for a video clip has been created the atomic actions from all goals within the ontology are used as *seed terms* for a number of search sets that are used to process the transcription. Four search sets are generated: these are *direct, homophone substitution, synonym substitution* and *homophone/synonym substitution*. The generation of these sets and their uses are detailed in the proceeding paragraphs.

The evaluated ASR systems are black box systems and as such offer limited control over the transcription process. This can introduce issues when homophones are encountered. Homophones are words which may be phonetically confused, for example 'pour' and 'pore'. During evaluation, all of the ASR systems had issues with selecting the correct homophones for a transcription. As such some form of correction for these errors was introduced. Contemporary works within ASR correct for these homophones within the statistical/machine learning core of the ASR process [16, 19]. Due to the different use scenario of homophone correction required in this study an alternative method of substitution needs be used as there is no access to the internal working of the ASR systems. Instead, this correction needs to be applied to the produced transcriptions. In this approach simple substitution produces combinations of words from a pre-existing homophone dictionary [20] and stores them in a *homophone substitution* search set. For example the set generated from the atomic action *PourWater* is [*pore water, pour water, poor water*]. This provides some correction for ASR errors without requiring access to the internal operation of the ASR services.

The atomic actions provided by the goal plan provide a description of the task represented by that action, for example *PlaceCoffeeInCup*. The exact words used to depict these actions are specified by the person modelling the specific goal and are somewhat personalized. This introduces an issue when audio descriptions contained in illustrative videos use alternative and semantically compatible words. For example, the use of the phrase "Place coffee in mug" in an instructive video could be used to describe an action of a video which is semantically compatible with the *PlaceCoffeeInCup* atomic action. In place of the word cup some of its synonyms could semantically be used, these are [*beaker, cup, mug, teacup, tumbler*]. In order to cater for synonyms a lexicon that can identify and generate a listing of semantically similar words was used to produce the *synonym substitution* search set. In ABSEIL, the chosen semantic lexicon was Wordnet 3.1 [21] which was integrated using JAWS [22].

In order to correct for instances where both homophone errors and use of semantically compatible words occur it is necessary to create a search set that consists of synonyms of homophones of words. These combinations of terms are created and placed into the *homophone/synonym substitution* search set. An example of such a combination from the action *PourWaterInMug* could include [*poor water in cup, poor water in mug*]. The combinations in this set provide useful alternatives to atomic actions in addition to some nonsensical terms which are likely never to be uttered in the clear instruction provided in videos stored in the PIA repository.

Once the 4 search sets have been generated they are used to search the body of the transcription to determine if any terms from the search sets are uttered. During the search process, words within search terms are given a 4 word window between them. This allows atomic actions such as *OpenCupboard* to be found when more complex variations are uttered, for example "Open the top cupboard". In the evaluation implementation this search is performed by the Lucene text processing engine [23].

When matches from the 4 search sets are discovered they are placed in corresponding match arrays. The terms stored in these match arrays are placed in the video action annotation ontology. This ontology stores some metadata about videos; this consists of a unique identifier, an optional title for the video and an optional description. The unique identifier is a SHA512 hash of the original video file; this associates the metadata to the file in addition to allowing retrieval from the video storage repository. The ontology contains 4 classes to hold matched terms from the 4 search sets. These are the *DirectTerms, HomophoneTerms, SynonymTerms* and *HomophoneSynonymTerms* classes. All these classes contain the same set of data properties: *DepictedAction, TimeStamp and Duration*. In the evaluation using ABSEIL the *TimeStamp* and *Duration* properties are not used, their inclusion is to provide support for future variations of ABSEIL where the timestamp of each action is recorded. The video action annotation ontology is depicted in Fig. 3.

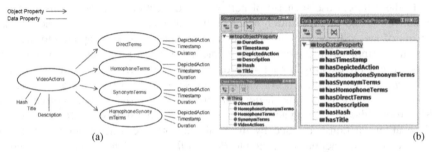

(a)   (b)

Fig. 2. The classes and object/data properties of the video action annotation ontology. As shown as a hierarchy of concepts (a) and in the Protégé ontology engineering tool (b).

4   Evaluations

In order to evaluate the performance of this automatic annotation generation method it was implemented in the form of the ABSEIL system. During testing 14 instructional videos were evaluated. 8 of which were from the PIA project and 6 were independently narrated PIA-Style videos. Both sets of videos detailed a number of IADLs. During evaluation these videos were manually annotated using a complete list of atomic actions that were extracted from a "Making Instant Coffee" goal and its 8 subgoals. The videos were analysed with the ABSEIL implementation and its accuracy was compared to the manually created annotations.

The PIA video set contained only 1 video that involved the steps of making coffee and so was used to evaluate incorrect profiling of video clips, where annotations would be generated without any relevant content.

The independently narrated videos covered a range of beverage making tasks and were used to determine the success of the method. The results of testing the implementation are presented in Table 2. In this evaluation each of the 4 search sets were assessed and averaged. Any erroneously identified actions are noted as false positives.

Table 2. The average accuracy of annotations produced by the automatic annotation method compared to the manual annotation, false positives are indicated in brackets

Video Source	Accuracy of generated annotation			
	DirectTerms	*HomophoneTerms*	*SynonymTerms*	*HomophoneSynonymTerms*
PIA	87.5 % (0)	87.5 % (0)	87.5 % (0)	87.5 % (0)
Independently Narrated	66.15% (0)	70.91 % (0)	81.41% (4.16)	84.32 % (3.83)

As shown in this evaluation, the devised method to automatically create annotations has proven to provide a promising approach to automatically generating the metadata required for provision of illustrative video based guidance for a goal driven SH. In all cases, false positives were phrases involving additional prepositions or combinations which formed nonsensical phrases. Such nonsensical phrases would not be present in videos intended to provide clear instruction, as would be the case for those in the PIA repository. On a number of occasions semantically compatible words were used in place of those specified in the action plan and were not discovered by the processing. In order to remedy this, additional sources of synonyms may be introduced. Additional issues were encountered when a narrator referred to a previous object as "it". Such utterances can be catered for by incorporating a more advanced natural language processing toolkit into the processing layer. In the case of the PIA videos, no actions were incorrectly assigned, however, in the single beverage video the system failed to profile any actions. These failures were due to the ASR system encountering strong regional accents; a manual transcription gained high accuracy.

5   Conclusion

This paper presented a method of automatically generating annotations for video files. These annotations are listed actions that are depicted within an instructional video file with the objective of providing the meta-data basis for offering assistance within a goal-driven SH. This method has been integrated into an evaluation platform and has shown promise as a way of automatically generating annotations. Future work will include evaluating this approach using a larger number of videos and producing assistance provisioning mechanisms which will leverage this rich metadata to automatically provide illustrative guidance which is best suited to each particular goal.

Acknowledgments. This work has been conducted in the context of the EU AAL PIA project (AAL-2012-5-033). The authors gratefully acknowledge the contributions from all members of the PIA consortium.

References

1. De Luca, d.E., Bonacci, S., Giraldi, G.: Aging populations: the health and quality of life of the elderly. Clin. Ter. 162, e13 (2011)
2. Acampora, G., Cook, D.J., Rashidi, P., Vasilakos, A.V.: A Survey on Ambient Intelligence in Health Care. Proc. IEEE. Inst. Electr. Electron. Eng. 101, 2470–2494 (2013)

3. Chen, L., Hoey, J., Nugent, C.D., Cook, D.J., Yu, Z.: Sensor-Based Activity Recognition. IEEE Trans. Syst. Man, Cybern. Part C (Applications Rev.), 1–19 (2012)
4. Lapointe, J., Bouchard, B., Bouchard, J.: Smart homes for people with Alzheimer's disease: adapting prompting strategies to the patient's cognitive profile. In: Proc. 5th Int. Conf. PErvasive Technol. Relat. to Assist. Environ., vol. 3 (2012)
5. Chan, M., Estève, D., Escriba, C., Campo, E.: A review of smart homes- present state and future challenges. Comput. Methods Programs Biomed. 91, 55–81 (2008)
6. Cook, D.J., Das, S.K.: How smart are our environments? An updated look at the state of the art. Pervasive Mob. Comput. 3, 53–73 (2007)
7. Rafferty, J., Chen, L., Nugent, C.: Ontological Goal Modelling for Proactive Assistive Living in Smart Environments. Ubiquitous Computing and Ambient Intelligence. In: Context-Awareness and Context-Driven Interaction, pp. 262–269 (2013)
8. Mihailidis, A., Boger, J.N., Craig, T., Hoey, J.: The COACH prompting system to assist older adults with dementia through handwashing: an efficacy study. BMC Geriatr 8, 28 (2008)
9. Filippova, K., Hall, K.: Improved video categorization from text metadata and user comments. In: Proc. 34th Int. ACM SIGIR Conf. Res. Dev. Inf. Retr., SIGIR 2011, pp. 835–842 (2011)
10. Papadopoulos, D.P., Kalogeiton, V.S., Chatzichristofis, S.A., Papamarkos, N.: Automatic summarization and annotation of videos with lack of metadata information. Expert Syst. Appl. 40, 5765–5778 (2013)
11. Ballan, L., Bertini, M., Bimbo, A., Seidenari, L., Serra, G.: Event detection and recognition for semantic annotation of video. Multimed. Tools Appl. 51, 279–302 (2010)
12. McCloskey, S., Davalos, P.: Activity detection in the wild using video metadata. Pattern Recognit, 3140–3143 (2012)
13. Perea-Ortega, J.M., Montejo-Ráez, A., Martín-Valdivia, M.T., Ureña-López, L.A.: Semantic tagging of video ASR transcripts using the web as a source of knowledge. Comput. Stand. Interfaces. 35, 519–528 (2013)
14. Lawton, M., Brody, E.: Instrumental Activities of Daily Living Scale, IADL (1988)
15. Rafferty, J., Nugent, C., Chen, L., Qi, J., Dutton, R., Zirk, A., Boye, L.T., Kohn, M., Hellman, R.: NFC based provisioning of instructional videos to assist with instrumental activities of daily living. Engineering in Medicine and Biology Society (2014)
16. Mehla, R., Aggarwal, R.: Automatic Speech Recognition: A Survey. Int. J. Adv. Res. Comput. Sci. Electron. Eng. 3, 45–53 (2014)
17. Google: Google Speech API, http://www.google.com/speech-api/v1/recognize
18. Dice, L.R.: Measures of the amount of ecologic association between species. Ecology 26, 297–302 (1945)
19. Chen, W., Ananthakrishnan, S.: ASR error detection in a conversational spoken language translation system. In: 2013 IEEE Int. Conf. Acoust. Speech Signal Process (ICASSP), pp. 7418–7422 (2013)
20. SIL: American English Homophones, http://www-01.sil.org/linguistics/wordlists/english/
21. Princeton University: About WordNet, http://wordnet.princeton.edu
22. Brett Spell: Java API for WordNet Searching (JAWS), http://lyle.smu.edu/~tspell/jaws/index.html
23. Apache: Lucene, http://lucene.apache.org

A New Feature Extraction Technique for Human Facial Expression Recognition Systems Using Depth Camera

Muhammad Hameed Siddiqi[1], Rahman Ali[1],
Byeong Ho Kang[2], and Sungyoung Lee[1,*]

[1] Department of Computer Engineering, Kyung Hee University
(Global Campus), Suwon, Korea
{siddiqi,rahmanali,sylee}@oslab.khu.ac.kr
[2] Department of Computing and Information Systems, University of Tasmania,
Australia
byeong.kang@utas.edu.au

Abstract. The analysis of facial expressions in telemedicine and health-care plays a significant role in providing sufficient information about patients like stroke and cardiac in monitoring their expressions for better management of their diseases. Due to some privacy concerns, depth camera is a good candidate in such domains over RGB camera for facial expression recognition (FER). The accuracy of such FER systems are completely reliant on the extraction of the informative features. In this work, we have tested and validated the accuracy of a new feature extraction method based on symlet wavelet transform. In this method, the human face is divided into number of regions and in each region the movement of pixels have been traced in order to create the feature vectors. Each expression frame is decomposed up to 4 levels. In each decomposition level, the distance between the two corresponding pixels is found by using the distance formula in order to extract the most informative coefficients. After feature vector creation, Linear Discriminant Analysis (LDA) has been employed to reduce the dimensions of the feature space. Lastly, Hidden Markov Model (HMM) has been exploited for expression recognition. Most of the previous FER systems used existing available standard datasets and all the datasets were pose-based datasets. Therefore, we have collected our own depth data of 15 subjects by employing the dept camera. For the whole experiments, 10-fold cross validation scheme was utilized for the experiments. The proposed technique showed a significant improvement in accuracy against the existing works.

Keywords: Facial Expressions, Depth Camera, Multilevel Wavelet Decomposition, Linear Discriminant Analysis, Hidden Markov Model.

* This work was supported by the National Research Foundation of Korea (NRF) grant funded by the Korea government (MSIP) (No. 2013-067321)). This research was also supported by the MSIP (Ministry of Science, ICT & Future Planning), Korea, under the ITRC (Information Technology Research Center) support program supervised by the NIPA (National IT Industry Promotion Agency) (NIPA-2014-(H0301-14-1003)).

L. Pecchia et al. (Eds.): IWAAL 2014, LNCS 8868, pp. 131–138, 2014.

1   Introduction

Telemedicine and healthcare applications that employ video technologies raise privacy concerns since it can lead to situations where subjects may not know that their private information is being shared and thus become exposed to a threat [13]. Unlike RGB-cameras, depth-cameras only capture the depth information and do not reveal the identity of the subject or other sensitive information, which makes them a superior choice over RGB-cameras. Therefore, we choose the depth-camera over RGB-cameras for the proposed FER system. To the best of our knowledge, no sufficient work has been done to study the expression recognition with depth camera.

There are three basic modules in a typical FER system: preprocessing, feature extraction and recognition. Much work has been done so far for preprocessing and recognition modules, and we also employed well-known method such as histogram equalization (HE) and hidden Markov model (HMM) for preprocessing and recognition modules respectively.

Regarding to the feature extraction, huge amount of methods have been proposed; however, most of them have their own limitations. These methods include global feature-based methods such as Nearest Features Line-based Subspace Analysis [12], Eigenfaces and Eigenvector [2, 8] and [7], Fisherfaces [1], global features [11], neural network, and Independent Component Analysis (ICA) [10]. However, these techniques are poor at handling data in which the classes do not follow the Gaussian distribution. Also, these techniques do not work well in case of a small sample size [5]. On the other hand, local feature-based methods have been proposed to compute the local descriptors from parts of the face and then integrate this information into one descriptor. These methods include Local Feature Analysis (LFA) [9], Gabor features [6], Non-negative Matrix Factorization (NMF), Local non-negative Matrix Factorization (LNMF) [4], and Local Binary Pattern (LBP) [15]. Among these methods, LBP is the most commonly employed feature extraction technique. However, LBP does not provide the directional information of the facial frame [16].

Accordingly, in this work, we have proposed a new feature extraction technique based on symlet wavelet transform. In this method, the human face is divided into number of regions and in each region the distance between the two pixels has been calculated by employing the distance formula. After that the average distance of each region is calculated and by this way the feature vector is calculated. Once the feature vectors have been created, the dimension of feature space is reduced by employing LDA, and finally, each expression is labeled by employing a well-known classifier like Hidden Markov Model (HMM).

We already described some related work about this field. The rest of the paper is organized as follows. Section 2 delivers an overview of the proposed feature extraction technique. Section 3 provides some experimental results along with some discussion on the results and a comparison with some of the widely used feature extraction methods. Finally, the paper will be concluded after some future direction in Section 4.

2   Material and Method

2.1   Symlet Wavelet Transform-based Feature Extraction

In real-life scenarios, some environmental parameters (such as lighting effects) may produce some noise in the expression frames that could reduce the recognition rate. The proposed method employs symlet wavelet to reduce such noise. Facial frames are converted to grey scale prior to applying this step. In the first feature extraction, the decomposition process has been applied, for which the facial frames were in grey scale. The wavelet decomposition could be interpreted as signal decomposition in a set of independent feature vector. Each vector consists of sub-vectors like

$$V_0^{2D} = V_0^{2D-1}, V_0^{2D-2}, V_0^{2D-3}, \ldots\ldots, V_0^{2D-n} \tag{1}$$

where V represents the 2D feature vector. If we have an expression frame X in the decomposition process, and it breaks up into the orthogonal sub images corresponding to different visualization. The following equation shows one level of decomposition.

$$X = A_1 + D_1 \tag{2}$$

where X indicates the decomposed image and A_1 and D_1 are called approximation and detail coefficient vectors respectively. If a facial frame is decomposed up to multiple levels, then Eq. 2 can be written as

$$X = A_j + D_j + D_{j-1} + D_{j-2} + \ldots. + D_2 + D_1 \tag{3}$$

where j represents the level of decomposition. The detail coefficients mostly consist of noise, so, for feature extraction only the approximation coefficients are used. In the proposed algorithm, each facial frame is decomposed up to two levels, i.e., the value of $j = 4$, because by exceeding the value of $j > 4$, the facial frame looses significant information, due to which the informative coefficients cannot be detected properly, which may cause misclassification. The detail coefficients further consist of three sub-coefficients, so the Eq. 3 can be written as

$$\begin{aligned}
X = A_4 &+ D_4 + D_3 + D_2 + D_1 \\
= A_4 &+ [(D_h)_4 + (D_v)_4 + (D_d)_4] \\
&+ [(D_h)_3 + (D_v)_3 + (D_d)_3] \\
&+ [(D_h)_2 + (D_v)_2 + (D_d)_2] \\
&+ [(D_h)_1 + (D_v)_1 + (D_d)_1]
\end{aligned} \tag{4}$$

where D_h, D_v and D_d are known as horizontal, vertical and diagonal coefficients respectively. Note that at each decomposition step, approximation and detail coefficient vectors are obtained by passing the signal through a low-pass filter and high-pass filter respectively. In each decomposition level, the distance between the pixels is found using the distance formula and by this way some of the informative coefficients are extracted and hence the feature vector has been created.

$$Dist = \sqrt{(x_2 - x_1)^2 + (y_2 - y_1)^2} \tag{5}$$

where (x_1, y_1) and (x_2, y_2) are the location of the two pixels respectively.

In a specified time window and frequency bandwidth wavelet transform, the frequency is estimated. The signal (i.e., facial frame) is analyzed by using the wavelet transform [17].

$$C(a_i, b_j) = \frac{1}{\sqrt{a_i}} \int_{-\infty}^{\infty} y(t) \Psi^*_{f.e} \left(\frac{t - b_j}{a_i} \right) dt \tag{6}$$

where a_i is the scale of the wavelet between lower and upper frequency bounds to get high decision for frequency estimation, and b_j is the position of the wavelet from the start to the end of the time window with the specified signal sampling period, t is the time, the wavelet function $\Psi_{f.e}$ is used for frequency estimation, and $C(a_i, b_i)$ are the wavelet coefficients with the specified scale and position parameters. Finally, the scale is converted to the mode frequency, f_m for each facial frame:

$$f_m = \frac{f_a(\Psi_{f.e})}{a_m(\Psi_{f.e}).\Delta} \tag{7}$$

where $f_a(\Psi_{f.e})$ is the average frequency of the wavelet function, and Δ is the signal sampling period. The feature vector is obtained by taking the average of the whole pixels distance for each facial frame that is given as:

$$f_{dist} = \frac{f_1 + f_2 + f_3 + ... + f_K}{N} \tag{8}$$

where f_{dist} indicates the average distance of each facial frame which is known as a feature vector of that expressions, f_1 f_2 f_3 .... f_K are the mode frequencies for each individual frame, K is the last frame of the current expression, and N represents the whole number of frames in each expression video.

In next step, the dimension of the feature space is reduced by employing a well-known technique Linear Discriminant Analysis (LDA) that maximizes the ratio of between-class variance to within-class variance in any particular data set, thereby guaranteeing maximal separability. For more details on LDA, please refer to [3]. At last, the expressions are recognized by employing HMM for which the parameters were 64, 4, and 4, respectively. For more details on HMM, please refer to [14].

3   Results and Discussion

In order to validate the performance of the proposed feature extraction technique, we have created our own data by utilizing Intel creative depth data. The dataset was collected from 15 subjects (university students) that displays frontal view of the face and each expression is composed of several sequences of expression frames. During each experiment, we reduced the size of each input image (expression frame) to 60×60, where the images were first converted to a zero-mean vector of size 1×3600 for feature extraction. All the experiments were performed in Matlab using an Intel® Pentium® Dual-Core^{TM} (2.5 GHz) with a RAM capacity of 3 GB. For all the experiments, a 10−fold cross-validation scheme (based on subjects) was used. In other words, out of 10 subjects data from a single subject was used as the validation data, whereas data for the remaining 9 subjects were used as the training data. This process was repeated 10 times with data from each subject used exactly once as the validation data. The total images utilized for the proposed system were 1,080 (6×15×12), where 6 represents the number of expressions, 15 indicates the number of subjects, and 12 shows the frames in each expression video.

The performance of the proposed feature extraction technique has been validated by comparing it with some of the previous widely used well-known techniques like: LBP, and LDP, and LTP. The experimental results of the proposed feature extraction technique are shown in Figure 1 and Table 1, while the results of the existing methods (LBP, and LDP) are described in Table 2. It is

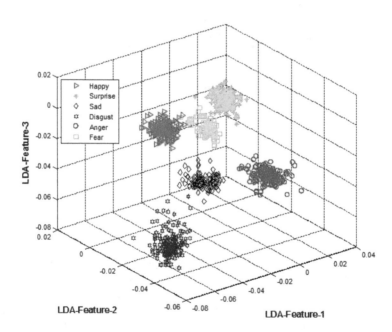

Fig. 1. 3D-feature plot for six different types of facial expressions. It is indicated that the proposed technique provides best classification rate on depth dataset of facial expression.

Table 1. Confusion matrix of the proposed method on Cohn-Kanade database of facial expressions (Unit: %)

	Happy	Sad	Anger	Disgust	Surprise	Fear
Happy	93	3	1	0	1	2
Sad	2	94	1	3	0	0
Anger	0	3	92	1	0	4
Disgust	2	1	1	94	2	0
Surprise	0	2	0	3	92	4
Fear	0	0	4	2	1	93
Average			93.00			

Table 2. Confusion matrix of (A) the LBP on our own dataset, and (B) the LDP on our own dataset of facial expression (Unit: %)

	Happy	Sad	Anger	Disgust	Surprise	Fear
Happy	87	3	2	2	3	3
Sad	4	85	3	3	3	2
Anger	2	2	88	2	4	2
Disgust	3	4	3	84	4	2
Surprise	3	2	5	4	80	6
Fear	1	2	5	3	2	87
Average			85.17			

(A)

	Happy	Sad	Anger	Disgust	Surprise	Fear
Happy	79	7	4	3	2	5
Sad	6	80	4	4	3	3
Anger	2	3	83	5	3	4
Disgust	0	2	4	90	1	3
Surprise	1	5	2	4	85	3
Fear	2	6	3	3	4	82
Average			83.10			

(B)

obvious from Figure 1 and Table 1 that the proposed technique achieved better recognition rate than that of the statistical methods as shown in Table 2. This is because symlet wavelet is a compactly supported wavelet on gray scale images with the least asymmetry and highest number of vanishing moments for a given support width. The symlet wavelet has the capability to support the characteristics of orthogonal, biorthogonal, and reverse biorthogonal of gray scale images, thats why it provides better classification results. The frequency-based assumption is supported in our experiments. We measure the statistical dependency of wavelet coefficients for all the facial frames of gray scale. Joint probability of a grey scale frame is computed by collecting geometrically aligned frames of the expression for each wavelet coefficient. Mutual information for the wavelet coefficients computed using these distributions is used to estimate the strength of statistical dependency between the two facial frames. Moreover, wavelet transform is capable to extract prominent features from gray scale images with the aid of locality in frequency, orientation and in space as well. Since wavelet is a multi-resolution that helps us to efficiently find the images in coarse-to-find way.

4   Conclusion

Facial Expressions Recognition (FER) has become an important research area for many applications over the last decade. Communication through facial expressions plays a significant role in telemedicine, and social interactions. In such applications, RGB cameras might not be used due some privacy concerns. A typical FER system consists of three basic modules such as preprocessing, feature extraction and recognition. Some very common methods such as histogram equalization (HE) and hidden Markov model (HMM) have been employed for preprocessing and recognition modules respectively. The facial features are very sensitive to noise and illumination, and quite merge with each other in the feature space, that's why in the feature space, it is very hard to separate these features. Therefore, very less amount of work can be found on the feature extraction module in literature; however, most of them have their own limitations. Accordingly, in this work, we utilized Intel creative depth camera in order to tackle the privacy issue in the proposed FER system. Moreover, we proposed a new and robust feature extraction technique based on symlet wavelet for feature extraction. In this technique, the human face is divided into number of regions and in each region the distance between the two pixels were calculated based on the distance formula. After that, the average distance was found for each region and hence by this way the feature vectors were created. To reduce the dimensions of the feature vectors in the feature space, LDA was exploited. Finally, the expressions were labeled by employing HMM. In order to validate the performance of the proposed technique, we have collected our own data from 15 subjects (university students) in the frontal view of the camera. For all the experiments, we applied 10-fold cross validation scheme. The proposed system produced a significant improvement in the recognition rate (93%) against the existing methods. The proposed FER system has been trained and tested in laboratory. The next step will be the implementation of the proposed feature extraction technique either in smarthomes or in smartphones.

References

1. Abidin, Z., Harjoko, A.: A neural network based facial expression recognition using fisherface. International Journal of Computer Applications 59(3) (2012)
2. Aguilar-Torres, G., Toscano-Medina, K., Sanchez-Perez, G., Nakano-Miyatake, M., Perez-Meana, H.: Eigenface-gabor algorithm for feature extraction in face recognition. International Journal of Computers 3(1), 20–30 (2009)

3. Belhumeur, P.N., Hespanha, J.P., Kriegman, D.J.: Eigenfaces vs. fisherfaces: Recognition using class specific linear projection. IEEE Transactions on Pattern Analysis and Machine Intelligence 19(7), 711–720 (1997)
4. Buciu, I., Pitas, I.: Application of non-negative and local non negative matrix factorization to facial expression recognition. In: Proceedings of the 17th International Conference on Pattern Recognition, ICPR 2004, vol. 1, pp. 288–291. IEEE (2004)
5. Chitra, S., Balakrishnan, D.G.: A survey of face recognition on feature extraction process of dimensionality reduction techniques. Journal of Theoretical and Applied Information Technology 36(1), 92–100 (2012)
6. Gu, W., Xiang, C., Venkatesh, Y.V., Huang, D., Lin, H.: Facial expression recognition using radial encoding of local gabor features and classifier synthesis. Pattern Recognition 45(1), 80–91 (2012)
7. Kalita, J., Das, K.: Recognition of facial expression using eigenvector based distributed features and euclidean distance based decision making technique. International Journal of Advanced Computer Science and Applications (IJACSA) 4(2), 196–202 (2013)
8. Kittusamy, S.R.V., Chakrapani, V.: Facial expressions recognition using eigenspaces. Journal of Computer Science 8(10), 1674–1679 (2012)
9. Li, S.Z., Hou, X.W., Zhang, H.J., Cheng, Q.S.: Learning spatially localized, parts-based representation. In: Proceedings of the 2001 IEEE Computer Society Conference on Computer Vision and Pattern Recognition, CVPR 2001, vol. 1, pp. 1–207. IEEE (2001)
10. Long, F., Wu, T., Movellan, J.R., Bartlett, M.S., Littlewort, G.: Learning spatiotemporal features by using independent component analysis with application to facial expression recognition. Neurocomputing 2(1), 126–132 (2012)
11. Mistry, V.J., Goyani, M.M.: A literature survey on facial expression recognition using global features. International Journal of Engineering and Advanced Technology 2(4), 653–657 (2013)
12. Pang, Y., Yuan, Y., Li, X.: Iterative subspace analysis based on feature line distance. IEEE Transactions on Image Processing 18(4), 903–907 (2009)
13. Ramli, R., Zakaria, N., Sumari, P.: Privacy issues in pervasive healthcare monitoring system: A review. World Acad. Sci. Eng. Technol. 72, 741–747 (2010)
14. Samaria, F.S.: Face recognition using hidden Markov models. PhD thesis, University of Cambridge (1994)
15. Shan, C., Gong, S., McOwan, P.W.: Facial expression recognition based on local binary patterns: A comprehensive study. Image and Vision Computing 27(6), 803–816 (2009)
16. Siddiqi, M.H., Farooq, F., Lee, S.: A robust feature extraction method for human facial expressions recognition systems. In: Proceedings of the 27th Conference on Image and Vision Computing New Zealand, pp. 464–468. ACM (2012)
17. Turunen, J., et al.: A wavelet-based method for estimating damping in power systems (2011)

Monitoring Moods in Elderly People through Voice Processing

Víctor Rojas[1], Sergio F. Ochoa[1], and Ramón Hervás[2]

[1] Computer Science Department, Universidad de Chile
Av. Blanco Encalada 2120, 3rd Floor, Santiago, Chile
{vrojas,sochoa}@dcc.uchile.cl
[2] Castilla-La Mancha University
Ciudad Real, Spain
ramon.hlucas@uclm.es

Abstract. Depression is a mental illness that is difficult to diagnose and treat. This mental disorder affects many older adults due several reasons, for instance because of their physical limitations and the natural reduction of their social circle. This article presents a system for monitoring the mood of the elderly through voice processing. The system is particularly focused on detecting sadness, which allows caregivers of family members to react on-time in supporting the person in need. The sadness recognition is done by classifying emotions in groups, according to the Circumflex Model of Affect. After evaluating the system using several emotion databases, the obtained results indicate that this solution is able to recognize 94% of the cases in men and 79% in women. This solution can be embedded in ubiquitous systems that monitor the mood of people in several scenarios.

Keywords: Emotion recognition, social isolation, older adults, voice processing, emotion monitoring, gender recognition.

1 Introduction

When people become older, physical and emotional problems affect them more and more. One of those problems is the depression, which can range from temporary episodes of sadness, to severe persistent depression. There are many factors that can cause a depressive status in elderly people, for instance the physical and cognitive limitations, emotional fragility and social isolation. Social isolation is affecting many older adults. The results of a recent study performed on 3858 random elders (> 75 years-old) indicate that 77% of them suffer social isolation, social inactivity or loneliness [1]. These psychological conditions make elders highly prone to suffer emotional disruptions or diseases, like the depression [2].

Frequently the relatives of elderly people suffering depression do not react because they are not aware of the real condition of an older adult. Detecting symptoms of depression and making family members aware of it must be a priority, as a first step to treat this mental illness. There is strong evidence indicating that the emotional condition of older adults suffering from depression improves, when they perceive

L. Pecchia et al. (Eds.): IWAAL 2014, LNCS 8868, pp. 139–146, 2014.

support from their social networks; e.g. from their relatives [3]. Therefore, making family members (or other supporting people) aware of these situations could contribute to address this problem.

The voice is an important instrument to get information about the emotional condition of a person [4]. Taking advantage of this situation, we developed a monitoring system able to detect negative emotions in elders through voice processing. The system runs, as a background process in a social application named *SocialConnector* [5], that elders have installed in their houses for interacting with other family members using (synchronous and asynchronous) voice messages. The SocialConnector runs on a slate that is fixed to a wall of a room where elders usually stay; for instance at the living room. The system that recognizes the negative emotions transforms the slate in a sensor able to identify when these people need external support. In these cases, the system delivers messages to caregivers or family members making them aware of this situation. The elderly people are not conscious of the sensing process or the actions taken by the system. This solution can be embedded in many other ubiquitous applications with similar purposes.

Next section reports the related work. Section 3 presents the strategy proposed to recognize negative emotions (particularly sadness) in elderly people. Section 4 shows the architecture of the monitoring system, which implements the strategy described in section 3. Section 5 presents the conclusions and further work.

2   Related Work

Dickerson et al. [6] created a real-time depression monitoring system for homes. The system involves several wireless sensors and devices that are used by the monitored people. In order to do a tracking of depression symptoms, the authors analyze the sleep, weight, speech and other factors. The results indicate that in speech analysis, the fundamental frequency and speech pause times are variables, which help predict affect in the voice.

Trying to detect mood in speech, Alghowinem et al. [7] recorded voice from several subjects with depression. The collected data was classified using Hidden Markov Models in order to evaluate different audio features in the mood detection process. The analysis of results indicated that the Mel-frequency cepstral coefficients, energy and intensity features allow high mood recognition rates when male and female audio samples are analyzed together.

The use of classification methods for detecting depression or mood using audio features is quite common. Several frameworks and tools are available to extract these audio features, for instance openSMILE [8] and Yaafe [9]. The first one is a toolbox developed specially for extracting audio features from voice and then processing this information in batch. This includes the use of audio descriptors (i.e. audio features) that allow extracting features from the voice, such as emotions, age range or sleepiness. The results can be returned in different formats; even in formats that eases the use of the support vector machine (SVM) classification technique [10].

Concerning Yaafe [9], it is focused only in the audio features extraction, and it can use any audio sample as input, including music and voice. The results are represented in CSV format, making easier the post processing of such information.

3   Emotions Recognition Strategy

Following the guidance of previous works in the area [4, 11], we used the SVM method to classify the emotions inferred from audio records. We utilized openSMILE for retrieving the audio features, and the LibSVM library [12] for the SVM modelling. The audio samples for evaluating the emotion detection proposal were taken from three emotion databases: SAVEE, Emo-DB and RekEmozio. SAVEE (Surrey Audio-Visual Expressed Emotion) [13] includes emotions in audio and video samples. The people in the samples use English language and the database includes seven emotions: anger, disgust, fear, happiness, neutral, sadness and surprise.

Concerning Emo-DB (Berlin Database of Emotional Speech) [14], it contains only audio samples in German language. The emotions included in the samples are: anger, boredom, disgust, fear, happiness, neutral and sadness. In case of RekEmozio [15], this database was built with samples in Basque and Spanish language. It includes audio and video samples, and the emotions considered in this database are the same as in the SAVEE database. All of the audio samples contained in these databases were recorded by professional actors, and all of them are adult people.

3.1   Strategies for Emotion Classification

In this section we describe the strategies used for classifying emotions and the obtained results.

3.1.1.   Individual classification of emotions

The first step was to classify the following seven emotions from the previously mentioned databases: anger, disgust, fear, happiness, neutral, sadness and surprise. For each emotion and database the samples were divided in two groups: *training* and *test*. The number of samples in both groups was similar. The tests were applied for every database in separated way. Two kinds of kernels were used in these tests, linear and polynomial, with different values for Gamma (G) and C parameters. For both kernels emobase2010 was chosen as the audio descriptor. This descriptor comes in openSMILE toolbox [16], and following the guidance of such an initiative we used degree 2 and 3 for a polynomial kernel, and different values for G and C: (G=1, C=1), (G=1, C=1000), (G=1000, C=1), (G=0.0001, C=1000), (G=1000, C=0.0001). After training data, generating the model and evaluating the strategy, the obtained results were the following quite poor. Using *linear kernel* the recognition rates for every emotion were below 30% in most cases. The results were even worst when using *polynomial kernel*, for degree 2 and 3. The differences in values of G and C did not make a difference. Moreover, using this classification strategy, sadness and neutral emotions tends to be in the same group.

3.1.2.   Classification Based on Two Groups

After bad results obtained with the first classification strategy, and taking advantage from the similarity found between some emotions, a new classification based in groups was evaluated. These groups were: anger-fear-happiness-surprise and disgust-neutral-sadness.

As expected, the results of classifying emotions in these two groups were better than in the previous case, since these two subsets are clearly differentiable. However, the emotion disgust was not expressed in the same way in the different databases; it was confused with anger in Emo-DB, and with neutral in SAVEE. Provided that disgust is not a frequent emotion in people, and given the problem for classify it, we decided to take it away from the second group. The new results were a bit better than the previous ones, but not good enough to be used in real scenarios. Therefore we evaluated a strategy that uses three groups of emotions.

3.1.3. Classification Based on Three Groups

The fear was put into a particular group, because sometimes it is confused with neutral and sadness. This leaves us three groups for classifying emotions: anger-happiness-surprise, neutral-sadness, and fear. Once again we used linear kernel with the emobase2010 descriptor for representing SVM model.

The classification using these groups improved considerably. Table 1 shows the classification rates (in terms of True Positives- TP) obtained for each group, using the average over all testing samples. However, the groups are still large and they do not allow isolate each emotion (particularly sadness); therefore they need extra processing to reach such a goal.

Table 1. Results in three groups' classification

Group	Average TP (%)
Anger-Happiness-Surprise	87.1
Neutral-Sadness	88.9
Fear	67.2

3.2   Detecting Sadness

Having emotions rightly classified in groups, the next step was to recognize each of them. From these six emotions, sadness is the one that is more related to depression. Therefore, next task was to recognize this emotion. Only neutral and sadness emotion samples were used in this test, because they are together in the same group.

We used a training-all-together strategy to improve classification rate. In this strategy all the training samples from all databases are joined in order to make the trained model more robust. This helps perform a better definition of the features that characterize each group.

The linear kernel and the emobase2010 and emo_large [16] descriptors were used for training the model. The emo_large descriptor was included because it helps obtain better results when using simple classes (e.g. a category with a single emotion).

The tests were done using both descriptors and the results showed that the emo_large descriptor was not useful for this task, having really low recognition rates. However, emobase2010 obtained a rate of TP close to 71% for sadness emotion. This result is good enough as to consider the use of this strategy in real scenarios.

3.3   Using Arousal and Valence

In 1980 the psychologist Russell designed a circular taxonomy of emotions known as the *circumflex model of affect* (Fig. 1), where an emotion represents an entity with two poles: *arousal* and *valence* [17]. Arousal means the intensity expressed through an emotion, and valence represents the pleasure that the people feel while expressing an emotion. Using these dimensions, we tried to improve the average TP recognition rate for sadness obtained with the previous strategies.

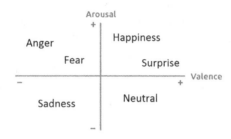

Fig. 1. Circumflex model of affect (from [17])

Four groups were created corresponding to every quadrant in Fig. 1. We used the emobase2010 descriptor with linear and polynomial kernel (degree=2, G=1, C=1). Although these kernels have a similar performance, the linear obtains more TP and less FP (False Positive). Using this classification strategy we reached an 81% of average of TP for sadness recognition. This represents a 10% higher than the last classification (see section 3.2).

The next step was to automate this classification process, by performing a first classification in three groups (see section 3.1.3), and then process the results using this strategy. The results of using this double filter process do not improve the rate of TP, but it allows us assuring that one sample belongs to the groups where it is classified.

3.4   Considering Gender in the Emotion Detection

Gender recognition was included in the double filter recognition process, because it provides additional information to identify the person that is talking. For instance, let us suppose that an elder female, who is being monitored, is visited by his neighbor. The system processing the voices captured from the physical environment will detect two people talking, and it can determine the mood of each of them. However it is required to determine the identify of these persons (when possible) to record properly such information and deliver notifications to relatives of a person when the system detects that such a person is in need of external support.

The use of contextual information about the gender of the people that is talking allows us performing a simple and accurate first filter to determine the people identity. In many cases, the use of this filter is enough to determine people identify; therefore we included it in the proposed strategy for emotion detection.

For gender recognition we used audio records of two minutes long for training the classifier. The audio records did not belong to the previously mentioned databases, and they included the five voice of woman and five of men.

After exploring several alternatives, we found a simple strategy that has high performance for gender recognition. It consists on classifying the training samples according to two criteria. First, we classify them according to the respective emotions (as shown in the previous section), and then we separated them considering the people gender. This gave us a training set that classifies the samples according to the emotion and gender.

Then, we used the linear kernel and the *IS_10paraling* descriptor [7]. This latter allows extracting the paralinguistic features of the voice, like age and gender. Using this solution we classified the samples stored in the three databases (i.e., SAVEE, Emo-DB and RekEmozio) according to the gender of the person that is talking. The results showed a 94% of TP in men and a 79% for women. This process was implemented in the mood monitoring system to classify and recognize sadness and gender. Next section describes the architecture of this system.

4   Architecture of System

The system uses two steps for processing the voice (Fig. 2): (1) recording the audio through the microphone of the slate that the older adults have at home and (2) recognizing emotion and gender using classification method described in section 3.4.

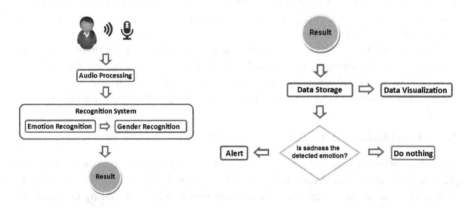

Fig. 2. Voice processing strategy   **Fig. 3.** Mood tracking process

These results are used as input for the mood tracking process. This process performs two activities (Fig. 3): (1) records the information about the mood of a person in a server, and (2) in case of detecting sadness, the system delivers a notification to a set of relatives whom provides support to the monitored person. The information stored in the server can be accessed on demand by these relatives (or caregiver or doctors). Several visual representations of this information are available to help them understand the whole situation.

The information stored in the server also indicates neutral emotions and happiness of the monitored people. These emotions were included in the records not only for their usefulness, but also because the recognition strategy showed high accuracy in the detection of these emotions (over 80% of TP). In a next step we will include as much emotions as we can; however it is important to keep in mind that the accuracy of the recognition process is (at least) as important as the detected emotion.

In order to tests the implemented system we replied the tests described in sections 3.3 and 3.4. The obtained results were the similar to those previously reported. This means that the implemented system can be embedded in an ubiquitous computing application, for monitoring of the people mood with a quite high accuracy (at least sadness, neutral emotion and happiness).

5   Conclusions and Future Work

In this work we focused on the detection of the sadness using voice processing. We have chosen this emotion because it is related to depressive states, particularly in elderly people. The detection of sadness was achieved using two group classifications strategies. During a first step the emotions were grouped according to similarities between them. In a second step these groups of emotions were processed considering arousal and valence (i.e. affective dimensions). This double filter process was eva-luated using three emotion databases, and the obtained results showed high rates of true positive for sadness recognition (94% in men and 79% in women). This process also recognizes neutral emotions and happiness of the monitored people with a high accuracy (over 80% of true positive). Although the emotion databases used in these tests had audio records in different languages, such an aspect does not seem to be relevant for the emotion detection. Something similar happened with the emotions detected in adults and elderly people. Therefore, the emotion detection performed in by the proposed solution seems to be transversal to various social contexts.

In a second stage we added gender recognition to such a solution as a way to ease the identification of people. This process was implemented as a mood monitoring service and embedded in the SocialConnector system [5]. The service keeps the pre-viously mentioned performance for sadness, neutral emotions and happiness.

After recording the voice, the system processes the audio record and stores in a server the information about the detected emotion. If that emotion is sadness, the system delivers a notification to relatives (according to a certain policy) in order to make them aware of such a situation.

The information stored in the server (about the mood of the monitored person) can be accessed on demand by the relatives, caregivers or doctors. Using visual representa-tions the system shows them the history of emotions detected in such a person. Such information can be used not only to monitor people suffering from depression, but also to perform early detection and diagnose of people vulnerable to these mental illness.

The next steps in this initiative considers to increase the number of emotions accu-rately detected using the monitoring system, and also to evaluate the proposal in a real scenario.

Acknowledgments. This work has been supported by Fondecyt (Chile), Grant N° 1120207, and by the UBIHEALTH project, FP7-PEOPLE-2012-IRSES, European Commission, Grant: 316337.

References

1. Tilvis, R.S., Routasalo, P., Karppinen, H., Strandberg, T.E., Kautiainen, H., Pitkala, K.H.: Social isolation, social activity and loneliness as survival indicators in old age: a nationwide survey with a 7-year follow-up. European Geriatric Medicine 3(1), 18–22 (2012)
2. Cornwell, E.Y., Wwaite, L.J.: Social Disconnectedness, Perceived Isolation, and Health among Older Adults. Journal of Health and Social Behavior 50(1), 31–48 (2009)
3. Cohen, S., Mermelstein, R., Kamarck, T., Hoberman, H.: Measuring the functional components of social support. In: Sarason, I.G., Sarason, B.R. (eds.) Social support: theory, research and application, Martinus Nijhoff Publishers, Dordrecht (1985)
4. Schuller, B.: The Computational Paralinguistics Challenge. IEEE Signal Processing Magazine 29(4), 97–101 (2012)
5. Muñoz, D., Gutierrez, F., Ochoa, S.F., Baloian, N.: Enhancing Social Interaction between Older Adults and Their Families. In: Nugent, C., Coronato, A., Bravo, J. (eds.) IWAAL 2013. LNCS, vol. 8277, pp. 47–54. Springer, Heidelberg (2013)
6. Dickerson, R., Gorlin, E., Stankovic, J.: Empath: a continuous remote emotional health monitoring system for depressive illness. In: Proc. of the Wireless Health 2011, San Diego, USA, pp. 5–14 (2011)
7. Alghowinem, S., Goecke, R., Wagner, M.: From joyous to clinically depressed: Mood detection using spontaneous speech. In: Proc. of the Int. Florida Artificial Intelligence Research Society Conference (FLAIRS 2012), pp. 141–146. AAAI Press, Marco Island (2012)
8. Eyben, F., Wöllmer, M., Schuller, B.: OpenSmile - The Munich Versatile and Fast Open-Source Audio Feature Extractor. In: Proc. of ACM Multimedia (MM), pp. 1459–1462. ACM Press, Florence (2010)
9. Yaafe, http://yaafe.sourceforge.net/ (last visit: June 12, 2014)
10. Cortes, C., Vapnik, V.: Support-vector networks. Machine Learning 20(3), 273–297 (1995)
11. Steidl, S.: Vocal Emotion Recognition: State-of-the-Art in Classification of Real-Life Emotions. International Computer Science Institute (ICSI). Berkeley, USA (2010), http://www.stanford.edu/class/linguist287/materials/steidl.pdf (last visit: June 17, 2014)
12. LibSVM, http://www.csie.ntu.edu.tw/~cjlin/libsvm/ (last visit: June 12, 2014)
13. Haq, S., Jackson, P.J., Edge, J.D.: Audio-Visual Feature Selection and Reduction for Emotion Classification. In: Proceedings of International Conference on Auditory-Visual Speech Processing, Tangalooma, Australia, pp. 185–190 (2008)
14. Burkhardt, F., Paeschke, A., Rolfes, M., Sendlmeier, W., Weiss, B.: A Database of German Emotional Speech. In: Proc. of Interspeech 2005, Lisbon, Portugal, pp. 1517–1520 (2005)
15. López, J.M., Cearreta, I., Garay, N., de López Ipiña, K., Beristain, A.: Creación de una base de datos emocional bilingüe y multimodal. In: Proc. of the 7th Spanish Human Computer Interaction Conference, Interaccion 2006, Puertollano, Spain, pp. 55–66 (2006)
16. Eyben, F., Wöllmer, M., Schuller, B.: OpenSMILE: the Munich open Speech and Music Interpretation by Large Space Extraction toolkit. OpenSMILE Book (2010), http://openSMILE book 2.0-rc1 (last visit: June 14, 2014)
17. Russell, J.A.: A circumflex model of affect. Journal of Personality and Social Psychology 39(6), 1161–1178 (1980)

Facial Expression Recognition from Webcam Based on Active Shape Models and Support Vector Machines

Elena Lozano-Monasor[1], María T. López[1,2], Antonio Fernández-Caballero[1,2], and Francisco Vigo-Bustos[2]

[1] Instituto de Investigación en Informática de Albacete (I3A), 02071-Albacete, Spain
[2] Universidad de Castilla-La Mancha, Departamento de Sistemas Informáticos, 02071-Albacete, Spain
Antonio.Fdez@uclm.es

Abstract. This paper introduces an application that uses a webcam and aims to recognize emotions of an elderly from his/her facial expression in real-time. Six basic emotions (Happiness, Sadness, Anger, Fear, Disgust and Surprise) as well as a Neutral state are distinguished. Active shape models are applied for feature extraction, the Cohn-Kanade, JAFFE and MMI databases are used for training, and support vector machines (ν-SVM) are employed for facial expression classification. In the future, the application is thought to be the starting point to enhance the mood of the elderly by external stimuli.

Keywords: Facial expressions, Emotions, Active shape model, Support vector machines.

1 Introduction

In recent years, there has been a growing interest in improving all aspects of interaction between humans and computers [1]. The emerging field of human-computer interaction has been of interest to researchers from a number of diverse fields, including Computer Science, Psychology, and Neuroscience. Gaining insight into the state of the user's mind via facial analysis can provide valuable information for affective sensing systems. Facial expressions reflect not only emotions, but also other mental activities, social interaction and physiological signals. For establishing emotional interactions between humans and computers, a system to recognize human emotion is of a high priority. An automated system that can determine the emotions of a person via his/her expressions provides the system with the opportunity to customize its response [2].

Now, emotion recognition using visual cues has been receiving a great deal of attention in the past decade. Most of the existing approaches do recognition on six universal basic emotions (Happiness, Sadness, Anger, Fear, Disgust and Surprise) because of their stability over culture, age and other identity related factors. For instance, an integrated system for emotion detection has

L. Pecchia et al. (Eds.): IWAAL 2014, LNCS 8868, pp. 147–154, 2014.

been presented, in which only eye and mouth expressions are used for detecting five emotions (all the above minus Disgust) [3]. Even, an approach to facial expression recognition for estimating patients' emotion is proposed with only two expressions (Happiness and Sadness) [4]. Applications that use these techniques are varied, ranging from software able to recognize and act according to the emotions of the user who is using it, systems capable of detecting lies, up to applications that allow knowing if a product is liked or not with only analyzing the emotional reaction of a user.

A facial expression recognition system is normally composed of four main steps: face detection/tracking, feature extraction, feature selection, and emotion classification. Choosing suitable feature extraction and selection algorithms plays the central roles in providing discriminative and robust information [5]. The selection of features employed for emotion recognition are classified into two main categories: geometric features and appearance features. In this paper, we are interested in geometric features, which are extracted from the shape or salient point locations of important facial components such as mouth and eyes. Moreover, this paper introduces the extraction of facial features to detect emotions represented by particular facial expressions. This involves a series of steps: (a) the study of techniques for detecting and extracting facial features, as well as the attainment of a model to operate in real-time, and, (b) the creation of an emotion detector through implementing the most suited classification techniques.

2   ASM and SVM for Facial Expression Recognition from Geometric Features

It has been demonstrated that the active shape model (ASM) is a good method for locating facial feature points [6]. Generally speaking, ASM fits the shape parameters using optimization techniques such as gradient descent. On the other hand, support vector machines (SVM) [7] exhibit good classification accuracy even when only a modest amount of training data is available, making them particularly suitable to a dynamic, interactive approach to expression recognition. This is why the tandem ASM-SVM is intensively being used for facial expression recognition.

For instance, 58 landmark points are used to construct an ASM for face expressions [8]. These are then tracked and give facial expressions recognition in a cooperative manner. Introducing a set of more refined features, facial characteristic points around the mouth, eyes, eyebrows, nose, and chin are utilized as geometric features for emotion recognition [9]. A quite recent approach [10] utilizes facial components to locate dynamic facial textures such as frown lines, nose wrinkle patterns, and nasolabial folds to classify facial expressions. Adaboost using Haar-like feature and ASM are adopted to accurately detect face and acquire important facial feature regions. Gabor filter and Laplacian of Gaussian are employed to extract texture information in the acquired feature regions. These texture feature vectors represent the changes of facial texture from one expression to another expression. Then, SVM is deployed to classify the six facial expression types including Neutral, Happiness, Surprise, Anger, Disgust and Fear. The Cohn-Kanade database is used to test the feasibility of the method.

Recently [11], an algorithm of face recognition based on ASM and Gabor features of key points has been proposed. Firstly, AdaBoost algorithm detects the face region in an image. Then, the ASM localizes the key feature points in the detected facial region. The Gabor features of these points are extracted. Finally, the features are classified using SVM. Preliminary experiments show promising results of the proposed algorithm on "The ORL Database of Faces" (see http:// www.cl.cam.ac.uk/research/dtg/attarchive/facedatabase.html). Another paper describes a method for recognition of continuous facial expression change in video sequences [12]. Again, ASM automatically localizes the facial feature points in the first frame and then tracks the feature points through the video frames. After that comes the selection of the 20 optimal key facial points, those which change the most with changes in expression. After building the feature space, SVM is trained for classification and results are tested. Another proposal for geometric feature extraction integrates the distances between face fiducial points and the center of gravity of the face's ASM shape with the FAU relative facial component deformation distances [13]. The approach also introduces a multiclass one-against-one ν-SVM for facial expression classification.

Another paper [14] empirically evaluates facial representation based on statistical local features, ASM and local binary patterns (LBP) for person-independent facial expression recognition. AdaBoost-LBP based ASM is used for emotion classification. Lastly, a work's system overview is explained next [15]. Face region of interest is detected with a boosted cascade of Haar-like features. Dynamic and static information are computed in separate pathways. Dynamic information is quantified with ASM; facial points detected with ASM are used for registration, and appearance features are developed from the registered images. Static information is obtained by estimating a static representation of the face and warping each face to minimize dynamics. Appearance features are generated from this representation. The two approaches are fused at the match-score level and emotion labels are classified with an SVM classifier.

3   Real-Time Recognition of Emotions from Face Expressions

This paper presents a real-time facial expression recognition system based on geometric features [16]. This method first uses ASM to track the fiducial points coarsely and then applies a method based on threshold segmentation and deformable model to correct the mouth fiducial points due to the incorrect locations in the presence of non-linear image variations such as those caused by large facial expression changes. The geometric features extracted from the fiducial points are classified in one of the six basic expressions plus Neutral by an SVM classifier.

3.1   Facial Expression Analysis

Today, less intrusive automatic emotion recognition is based on the facial expression of the subject. In recent years, several methods have been developed to extract and analyze facial features. To do this, a complete description of facial expressions is needed. The Facial Action Coding System (FACS) [17] is a system based on human observation to detect changes in facial features. This system encodes all possible facial expressions as action units (AUs) which take place individually or in combination.

Indeed, FACS considers 44 AUs, 30 anatomical which are contractions of certain facial muscles, and 14 miscellaneous ones that involve a change in expression but are not associated with a facial muscle. For each AU there are five levels of intensity, depending on the force you have to exert the muscle. Facial expressions associated with emotions are generally described as a set of AUs. The way to get the AUs of a subject is to locate a series of facial points and compare their distances to know what facial muscles are moving. This approach analyzes the changes that occur in facial expression and relate them to a specific emotion. Obviously, a reference database is used to associate the facial expressions observed.

3.2   Facial Emotion Detection

The approach described in this paper is divided into 4 steps:

1. **Detection of facial points.** Currently, the detection of emotions is based on the analysis of facial expression from different facial points. The first step is to generate points on a facial expression in the simplest possible way. At this early stage it is necessary to perform a series of tests to select the model of facial detection points that best fits the needs and provides better results.
2. **Feature extraction.** Once the facial points have been obtained, we study what are the most useful features which are obtained from these points for the detection of emotions. It is also detailed how to obtain each of the features.
3. **Training and classification.** The third step consists of the selection of images for training, the choice of the most appropriate SVM kernel function, and the generation of a classification model that operates in real-time.
4. **Detection of emotions.** At the last step, an emotion detection system is obtained. It is built from the models generated in the previous steps.

Detection of Facial Points and Features. ASMLibrary [18] is a library that easily creates an ASM from an image database and the images' corresponding log files. ASMLibrary is used in our case for generating ASMs that will later detect facial points. In order to construct a valid model, a series of face image files are needed along with an annotation file attached to each image. The coordinates of each of the image points of interest are annotated in the log file. On the other hand, several models are generated from databases prepared for this purpose.

This way, the advantages and disadvantages of each of them are studied before choosing the best model. The major database repositories are: (a) Informatics and Mathematical Modeling (IMM) [19], which contains the analysis of 37 images of frontal faces. The model is composed of 58 facial points; (b) BioID [20] is a database consisting of 1521 images of frontal faces. Each face is labeled with 20 facial points; (c) Extended Multi Modal Verification for Teleservices and Security (XM2VTS) [21] consists of 2360 images which have been marked-up 68 facial features.

Three ASMs are created with the images and log files that make up the above mentioned databases. The objective is to analyze new images and verify that the facial point detection is performed correctly. Each model is checked in terms of its performance for still images, recorded videos and real-time video input (webcam). The model of the XM2VTS database, with 68 facial points, is the most complete with respect to the other two models in terms of reliability of point detection. Furthermore, it allows a more accurate alignment of the face.

Training, Classification and Detection of Emotions. LibSVM [22] is a library for programming support vector machines (SVMs). The image features belonging to properly labeled emotion databases are extracted in order to generate the file that is used in training the SVM. The method used for classification is a multiclass SVM, because we aim at distinguishing among seven classes. We have chosen the one-vs-one method for multiclass SVM (see [23]) from the two possible alternative approaches. Although this method involves using more classifiers, the employed training time is much lower. It has been decided to use the RBF kernel as it is the one that offers best results in terms of accuracy and training time.

Furthermore, four different well-known image databases are selected to carry out the training of the SVM: (1) JAFFE (Japanese Female Facial Expression) database [24], (2) IMM facial expressions database [25], (3) Cohn-Kanade (CK) database [26], and, (4) Cohn-Kanade extended (CK+) database [27]. Finally, the ν-SVM algorithm is used due to the ease of adjustment of the ν parameter. The classification features and values used are shown in Table 1.

Table 1. Features of the ν-SVM model

Feature	Value
Type of SVM	ν-SVM
Type of kernel	RBF (Radial Basis Function)
Parameter ν	0.52
Parameter γ	0.12
Number of classes	7
Number of support vectors	237

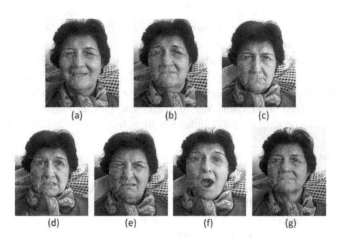

Fig. 1. Example of webcam capture where the detected emotion is (a) Joy. (b) Sadness. (c) Anger. (d) Fear. (e) Disgust. (f) Surprise. (g) Neutral.

4   Data and Results

In order to validate our proposal, we capture video in real-time from a webcam situated in front of older persons. The tests are performed by requesting each elderly to pretend the facial expression associated with a particular emotion. The user receives no other external stimulus. So, the tests are performed for each of the seven classes that the system has to distinguish, that is, Joy, Sadness, Anger, Fear, Disgust, Surprise and Neutral.

The emotions that offer better results are Surprise, Joy, Sadness and Anger (all of them with a hit rate over 0.95). The results are acceptable when the facial expression reflects Surprise and Fear (hit rate over 0.8). Emotion Disgust provides the most false positive results (around a hit rate of 0.5), probably because it contains features that can lead to confusion with other emotions, such as frowning (characteristic of emotion Anger) or lips down (characteristic of Sadness and Fear). The main reasons that probably explain the prediction errors are: (a) the ASM adjustment is incorrect, (b) the pretended emotion is clearly not representative of the expected emotion, (c) the features between two emotions are very similar, and, (d) the transition from one emotion to another causes troubles during a short interval of time.

5   Conclusions

This article has described the steps followed to study some facial feature extraction and detection techniques, as well as methods that allow the recognition of emotions in real-time. This has allowed choosing an appropriate face recognition system and establishing the most suitable features to discriminate emotions. We have implemented an emotion detector that uses the techniques studied. In this sense, we have studied models for automatic acquisition of facial features. We have decided to use an active shape model, due to its good performance in real-time. Tests have been performed with several models, and the best results were obtained with the 68 facial points model. Also, we have studied support vector machines for classification and used a ν-SVM with RBF kernel. Thus, we have obtained a suitable classification system to work with the six basic emotions, namely Happiness, Sadness, Anger, Fear, Disgust and Surprise, plus the Neutral emotion.

This has led to the construction of an application capable of distinguishing emotions of older people in real-time from their facial expressions captured by a webcam. It has been found that LibSVM and ASMLibrary libraries are adequate tools for programming such a system. The emotions that offer better results in terms of detection are Surprise, Joy, Sadness and Anger. The results are acceptable, especially when the facial expression reflects Surprise. For other emotions, such as Disgust and Fear, the system tends to get confused because emotions have very similar facial features. The work described in this paper is the first step in developing a system to improve mood in the elderly by external non-intrusive stimuli.

Acknowledgements. This work was partially supported by Spanish Ministerio de Economía y Competitividad / FEDER under TIN2013-47074-C2-1-R and TIN2010-20845-C03-01 grants.

References

1. Gascueña, J.M., Castillo, J.C., Navarro, E., Fernández-Caballero, A.: Engineering the development of systems for multisensory monitoring and activity interpretation. International Journal of Systems Science 45(4), 728–740 (2014)
2. Alugupally, N., Samal, A., Marx, D., Bhatia, S.: Analysis of landmarks in recognition of face expressions. Pattern Recognition and Image Analysis 21(4), 681–693 (2011)
3. Maglogiannis, I., Vouyioukas, D., Aggelopoulos, C.: Face detection and recognition of natural human emotion using Markov random fields. Personal and Ubiquitous Computing 13(1), 95–101 (2009)
4. Wang, L., Gu, X., Wang, Y., Zhang, L.: Happy-sad expression recognition using emotion geometry feature and support vector machine. In: Köppen, M., Kasabov, N., Coghill, G. (eds.) ICONIP 2008, Part II. LNCS, vol. 5507, pp. 535–542. Springer, Heidelberg (2009)
5. Zhang, L., Tjondronegoro, D.W., Chandran, V.: Discovering the best feature extraction and selection algorithms for spontaneous facial expression recognition. In: Proc. 2012 IEEE Conference on Multimedia and Expo, pp. 1027–1032 (2012)
6. Cootes, T.F., Taylor, C.J., Coper, D.H., Graham, J.: Active shape models - their training and application. Computer Vision and Image Understanding 61(1), 38–59 (1996)
7. Cortes, C., Vapnik, V.: Support-vector networks. Machine Learning 20(3), 273–297 (1995)
8. Chang, Y., Hu, C., Feris, R., Turk, M.: Manifold based analysis of facial expression. Image and Vision Computing 24(6), 605–614 (2006)

9. Pantic, M., Bartlett, M.: Machine analysis of facial expressions. In: Face Recognition, ch. 20, pp. 978–973 (2007) ISBN 978-3-902613-03-5
10. Hsieh, C.-C., Jiang, M.-K.: A facial expression classification system based on active shape model and support vector machine. In: Proc. 2011 International Symposium on Computer Science and Society, pp. 311–314 (2011)
11. Wu, J., Mei, L.: A face recognition algorithm based on ASM and Gabor features of key points. In: Proceedings of SPIE 8768, Article number 87686L (2013)
12. Wan, C., Tian, Y., Liu, S.: Facial expression recognition in video sequences. In: Proc. 10th World Congress on Intelligent Control and Automation, pp. 4766–4770 (2012)
13. Gang, L., Xiao-hua, L., Ji-liu, Z., Xiao-gang, G.: Geometric feature based facial expression recognition using multiclass support vector machines. In: Proc. 2009 IEEE International Conference on Granular Computing, pp. 318–321 (2009)
14. Zhao, X., Zhang, H., Xu, Z.: Expression recognition by extracting facial features of shapes and textures. Journal of Computational Information Systems 8(8), 3377–3384 (2012)
15. Cruz, A., Bhanu, B.: A biologically inspired approach for fusing facial expression and appearance for emotion recognition. In: Proc. 19th IEEE International Conference on Image Processing, pp. 2625–2628 (2012)
16. Zhou, Q., Wang, X.: Real-time facial expression recognition system based-on geometric features. Lecture Notes in Electrical Engineering, vol. 212, pp. 449–456 (2013)
17. Ekman, P., Friesen, W.V., Hager, J.C.: Facial Action Coding System (FACS) (2002), http://face-and-emotion.com/dataface/facs/new_version.jsp
18. Wei, Y.: Research on facial expression recognition and synthesis. Master Thesis. Department of Computer Science and Technology, Nanjing University (2009), http://code.google.com/p/asmlibrary
19. Stegmann, M.B.: Analysis and segmentation of face images using point annotations and linear subspace techniques. Technical Report IMM-REP-2002-22 (2002), http://www2.imm.dtu.dk/pubdb/views/publication_details.php?id=922
20. Cootes, T.F., Cristinacce, D., Babalola, K.: BioID face database (2005), http://www.bioid.com/index.php?q=downloads/software/bioid-face-database.html
21. Chan, C.H.: The XM2VTS Database (2000), http://www.ee.surrey.ac.uk/CVSSP/xm2vtsdb/
22. Chang, C.C., Lin, C.J.: LIBSVM: a library for support vector machines. ACM Transactions on Intelligent Systems and Technology 2(27), 1–27 (2011)
23. Wu, T.F., Lin, C.J., Wang, R.C.: Probability estimates for multi-class classification by pairwise coupling. Journal of Machine Learning Research 5, 975–1005 (2004)
24. Lyons, M.J., Kamachi, M., Gyoba, J.: Japanese Female Facial Expressions (JAFFE). Database of Digital Images (1997), http://www.kasrl.org/jaffe_info.html
25. Valstar, M.F., Pantic, M.: Induced disgust, happiness and surprise: an addition to the IMM facial expression database. In: Proc. International Conference on Language Resources and Evaluation, Workshop on Emotion, pp. 65–70 (2010)
26. Kanade, T., Cohn, J., Tian, Y.L.: Comprehensive database for facial expression analysis. In: Proc. 4th IEEE International Conference on Automatic Face and Gesture Recognition, pp. 46–53 (2000)
27. Lucey, P., Cohn, J.F., Kanade, T., Saragih, J., Ambadar, Z., Matthews, I.: The Extended Cohn-Kanade Dataset (CK+): A complete facial expression dataset for action unit and emotion-specified expression. In: Proc. 2010 IEEE Computer Society Conference on Computer Vision and Pattern Recognition Workshops, pp. 94–101 (2010)

Cloud-Based Remote Processing and Data-Mining Platform for Automatic Risk Assessment in Hypertensive Patients

Paolo Melillo[1,2], Paolo Scala[2], Filippo Crispino[2], and Leandro Pecchia[2,3]

[1] Multidisciplinary Department of Medical, Surgical and Dental Sciences,
Second University of Naples, Naples, Italy
paolo.melillo@unina2.it
[2] SHARE Project, Italian Ministry of Education, Research and University, Rome, Italy
[3] School of Engineering, University of Warwick, Coventry, UK

Abstract. The aim of this paper is to describe the design and the preliminary validation of a platform developed to collect and automatically analyze biomedical signals for risk assessment of cardiovascular events in hypertensive patients. This m-health platform, based on cloud computing, was designed to be flexible, extensible, and transparent, and to provide proactive remote monitoring via data-mining functionalities. Clinical trials were designed to test the system. The data of a retrospective study were adopted to train and test the platform. The developed system was able to predict a future vascular event within the next 12 months with an accuracy rate of 67%. In an ongoing prospective trial, almost all the recruited patients accepted favorably the system with a limited rate of inadherences causing of data losses (<20%). The developed platform supported clinical decision   by processing tele-monitored data and providing quick and accurate risk assessment of cardiovascular events.

Keywords: remote processing, data-mining, telemedicine, hypertension, Heart Rate Variability, cardiovascular risk.

1 Introduction

Several technological advances and new concepts, such as wearable medical devices, Body Area Networks (BANs), pervasive wireless broadband communications and Cloud computing, are enabling advanced mobile health-care services that benefit both patients and health professionals. In particular, they enable the development of several systems to perform remote real-time collection, dissemination and analysis of biomedical signal and data for the purpose of managing chronic disease and/or detecting health emergencies. [1-3]

Cardiology is one of the areas in which the new technology are showing major progress and several system for monitoring of electrocardiographic (ECG) signals have been proposed. Computer-based analysis of the ECG has been used during the last decades with significant success. Innovative signal processing and analysis techniques have been recently developed, resulting in more powerful clinical indexes.

L. Pecchia et al. (Eds.): IWAAL 2014, LNCS 8868, pp. 155–162, 2014.

Particularly, Heart Rate Variability (HRV), which is the variation over time of the period between consecutive heartbeats (RR intervals) [4], can be extracted from ECG. HRV is commonly used to assess the influence of the autonomic nervous system (ANS) on the heart [5]. The available technology and the encouraging findings of previous studies (for more details, see section 1.1) inspired the design of a telemedicine platform, based on HRV monitoring, for automatic identification of patients at higher risk of cardiovascular events. This paper describes the design and the preliminary validation of the platform, which was developed in the framework of the UE-funded research project "Smart health and artificial intelligence for Risk Estimation" (SHARE).

1.1   Related Works

Many studies demonstrated that HRV is an effective means for the risk assessment of mortality [6-11]. Recently, several studies proposed interesting results, by adopting data-mining approach to HRV measures [12-17]. Moreover, several telemedicine applications have been developed for home monitoring of patients at risk of cardiovascular events. However, very few of them included a decision support system or data-mining methods. Recently, Hervas et al.[18] proposed a mobile application on blood pressure monitoring and several related factors to determine the total cadiovascular risk. The authors [18]   adopted a reasoning engine based on Systematic Coronary Risk Evaluation Project chart hosted on a server with a Bluetooth mobile monitoring software

2   Materials and Methods

2.1   System Architecture

The general system architecture of the SHARE platform, integrating recording device and a Cloud infrastructure, consists of several basic services as shown in Figure 1. In the architecture design, the following requirements were considered:

- management of biomedical signal and data acquired in a highly seamless manner;
- set up a scalable framework to support the processing of multiple data streams for concurrent application services.
- persistent storage and exchange of data, their automatic analysis and availability everywhere to enable further decision making.

We aimed to provide a framework supporting data management, concurrent application execution, and data analysis. For that reason, we adopted a Cloud environment providing storage and Virtual Machine (VM)-based approach for computational process. In the next paragraphs, we detail on each component of the system.

The Bioharness™ (vers. 3 BH3, Zephyr Technology) is a state-of-art commercial wearable multi-sensing device, which enables long-term recordings of several biomedical signals and data. The BH3 is worn in epidermal contact with an elasticated strap at the chest (50 g, 50 mm width). The monitoring device (weight 35 g, 80x40x15mm) acts as a data logger or transmitter, has a memory of up to 480 hours and battery life of up to 24 hours. Particularly, it can record one-lead ECG, breathing signal and respiration rate, posture, temperature, accelerometer signals along the 3 orthogonal axes. We chose BH3, since it appeared a cheap and reliable device for health monitoring, useful both for cardiovascular issue and faller detection and since the manufacturer provided SDK.

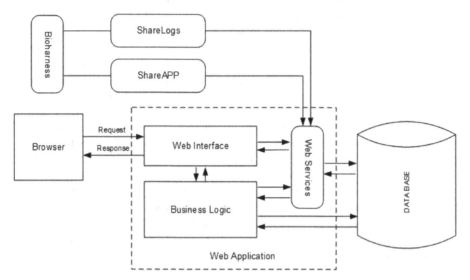

Fig. 1. The system architecture of the SHARE platform

ShareAPP (referred as Share Cardio Health in Google Play) is an Android application, which has been developed *ad hoc* to provide a user interface for the patients, who could transmit the data acquired by BH3 in real time though a smartphone. The App was designed in order to minimize the user interaction. Moreover, it enables the physician to submit a daily questionnaire to the patients.

ShareLogs is an *ad hoc* developed standalone application for Windows, which enables the upload of all the acquired signals by BH3 on the SHARE platform. It has been designed in order to follow the physician's usual workflow: at each planned visit, the physician upload all the data stored on the BH3. This avoid the risk of losing the data that were not stored in real-time (e.g., because the mobile device was offline or out of Bluetooth coverage area or network problems).

The Web Interface consists of a Content Management System (CMS) to show all the public information on the Project and a Restricted Area reserved to the system user, i.e. physician, researchers, patients. The CMS relies on Wordpress while the Restricted Area application was developed in ASP.NET (C#) by using Visual Studio 2013 and MySQL.

The Web Services represent the software interface to store the data, acquired by BH3 and transmitted though the ad hoc applications. Moreover, they provided the most advanced functionality of the system, i.e. remote processing and data mining.

2.2   Remote Processing and Data-Mining

The platform enabled the remote processing of ECG for HRV analysis. The ECG recording were analyzed concurrently in segments of user-specified length (default value: 30 minutes[19]). Standard linear HRV analysis according to International Guidelines was performed[5]. The frequency-domain HRV measures relied on the estimation of power spectral density (PSD), which was estimated with three different methods: by Welch periodogram, Auto-Regressive method and Lomb-Scamble periodogram. The frequency domain measures extracted from the PSD estimate for each frequency band included absolute and relative powers of VLF, LF, and HF bands, LF and HF band powers in normalized units, the LF/HF power ratio, and peak frequencies for each band. Moreover, nonlinear HRV properties were investigated by the following methods: Poincaré Plot[20], Approximate Entropy[21], Correlation Dimension[22], Detrended Fluctuation Analysis[23, 24], and Recurrence Plot [25-27]. More details about nonlinear HRV analysis were reported elsewhere[12, 28].

Moreover, the SHARE system provides an automatic assessment of cardiovascular risk, relying on data-mining approach applied to HRV measures. In order to train and test these algorithm, a retrospective study was designed and performed by enrolling patients with at least 24h nominal ECG with a one year clinical follow-up after recordings. Each subject was labelled as high risk if a vascular event occurred during the follow-up, otherwise the subject was labelled as low risk.

Different data-mining algorithms have been tested offline for risk assessment. In this paper, we present the results obtained with RUSBoost (RB), a new hybrid approach designed to handle class imbalance [29], since it is theoretically one of the state-of-art classifier for small and unbalanced dataset. RB relies on the Random Under-Sampling (RUS) technique and AdaBoost (AB) as boosting algorithm. RUS is one of the most common data sampling techniques, and simply removes examples from the majority class at random until a desired class distribution is achieved. AB is a well-known algorithm for boosting weak classifiers [30] and as base classifier, the CART, developed by Breiman[31], was adopted. Moreover, since HRV features have been shown to be correlated, there is the risk that some of the computed features might be redundant and could worsen the classifier performance by reducing its generalization ability. In order to find the optimal feature space, we adopted the Principal Component Analysis (PCA) method [32]. The remote processing was implemented in MATLAB and for Web integration the MATLAB scripts were compiled as .NET objects.

2.3   Validation Procedure

The platform validations was based on two clinical trials: the former, performed to develop and test the remote processing and data-mining modules, the latter, prospective, now ongoing to test the modules used by the patients.

To evaluate the performance of the data-mining methods, we computed the standard measurement for binary classifiers using the 10-fold-crossvalidation approach.

In order to assess the compliance of the patients, we computed the following measures: the ratio between the real length of the recordings and the expected length; the number of inadherences due to patients failing to use the device for the monitoring period (5-7 days); the number of calls from health operator to technical assistance and those from patients due to technical reasons.

3   Results

The SHARE platform for Remote Processing of Heart Rate Variability and Data-mining has been designed and deployed through a web portal.

The remote processing and data-mining modules have been trained, tested and validated thanks to a retrospective database of 139 hypertensive patients (including 50 female and 92 male, age 72 ± 7 years). The patients were enrolled at the Ambulatory Centre for Hypertension of University Hospital Federico II of Naples and had been follow up for at least one year: the subjects who experienced a major cardiovascular event or stroke during the follow-up were considered at high risk. No statistically significant differences .were assessed between the two groups (low and high risk subject) in terms of clinical and demographic parameters (i.e. gender 34% vs 47%, smoking habits 29% vs 29%, body mass index 27.6±3.9 vs 27.9±4.9). The performances of the best classifier are reported in Table 1 and compared with a clinical powerful predictor of vascular events, i.e. the intima media thickness.

Table 1. Performance of the automatic classification (Remote Processing and Data-mining)

Classification	Accuracy	Sensitivity	Specificity
HRV	67.0%	70.6%	66.4%
IMT	57.9	40.0	60.3

Moreover, a prospective clinical trial has been approved at the University Hospital of Naples Federico II in order to test the efficacy of the remote monitoring supported by the SHARE system in real environment. Up to now, 19 patients (aged 62 ± 4 yers; 7 women) have been enrolled at the Ambulatory Centre for Hypertension of University Hospital Federico II of Naples. They instructed to wear the wearable devices and invited to use them for a week. Moreover, as for clinically Holter recordings, they were asked to fill a brief report. The preliminary results of the patient compliance are reported in Table 2.

Table 2. Performance measurement of the SHARE platform (Patient and Physician Modules)

Measures	Value
Ratio between the real length of the recordings and the expected length;	82.5%
Inadherences due to patients failing to use the device for the monitoring period (5-7 days)	1
Calls from health operator to technical assistance	1
Calls from patients due to technical reasons	1

Only one patients failed to complete the expected monitoring period and performed a call to the health operator for technical reason. The other patients did not report any particular problem in using the provided devices, although 4 of them reported that the BH3 they received worked for a shorter time than expected. We checked and confirmed a shorter battery duration of these devices. The wearable device recorded the signals for about 82.5 of the expected time, meaning a data loss of 17.5%, mainly due to short battery duration of some devices.

4   Conclusions and Discussions

A platform for health remote monitoring with advanced remote processing and data-mining functionalities was described in the current paper. As regards signal acquisition, it relies on a commercial multi-sensing wearable device. The most advanced functionalities i.e. ECG processing and automatic classification, were provided by the centralized structure of the system, and the users, i.e. physician, needs only to have a Web browser running in a personal computer and a network connection to access these services. The technical programs can be updated and new tools can be easily added without interfering with the medical user. The addition or incorporation of a new technique in the GUI can be a quite simple task: a button is added which acts as a link to the function that runs under MATLAB and performs the corresponding processing. This fact makes the system into an open structure that can easily incorporate new tools as soon as they are developed, and therefore have an immediate presence in the support of clinical diagnosis. The proposed architecture overcome the system based on the discontinued MATLAB WEB SERVER toolbox[33]. Moreover, most system proposed in previous studies focused on ECG storage and processing[1-3], but they did not provide any automatic classification based on data-mining methods. The performance achieved by the classifiers suggest that a clinical decision support tool, processing tele-monitoring data, could contribute to a quicker and possibly more accurate clinical assessment of the patients. Moreover, the system appeared to be well accepted by almost all the patients (95%) with a limited amount of data lost (<20%). Finally, the results of the clinical trials could provide the scientific evidences needed for the CE marking of the system as a medical device.

Acknowledgements. The current study was partially supported by "the 2007-2013 NOP for Research and Competitiveness for the Convergence Regions (Calabria, Campania, Puglia and Sicilia)" with code PON04a3_00139 - Project Smart Health and Artificial intelligence for Risk Estimation.

References

1. Fortino, G., Pathan, M., Di Fatta, G.: BodyCloud: Integration of Cloud Computing and body sensor networks. In: 2012 IEEE 4th International Conference on Cloud Computing Technology and Science (CloudCom), pp. 851–856 (2012)

2. Hsieh, J.C., Hsu, M.W.: A cloud computing based 12-lead ECG telemedicine service. BMC Med. Inform. Decis. Mak. 12, 77 (2012)
3. Pandey, S., Voorsluys, W., Niu, S., Khandoker, A., Buyya, R.: An autonomic cloud environment for hosting ECG data analysis services. Future Generation Computer Systems 28, 147–154 (2012)
4. Rajendra Acharya, U., Paul Joseph, K., Kannathal, N., Lim, C.M., Suri, J.S.: Heart rate variability: a review. Med. Biol. Eng. Comput. 44, 1031–1051 (2006)
5. Malik, M., Bigger, J.T., Camm, A.J., Kleiger, R.E., Malliani, A., Moss, A.J., Schwartz, P.J.: Heart rate variability: Standards of measurement, physiological interpretation, and clinical use. Eur. Heart. J. 17, 354–381 (1996)
6. Guzzetti, S., Magatelli, R., Borroni, E., Mezzetti, S.: Heart rate variability in chronic heart failure. Autonomic Neuroscience-Basic & Clinical 90, 102–105 (2001)
7. Kruger, C., Lahm, T., Zugck, C., Kell, R., Schellberg, D., Schweizer, M.W.F., Kubler, W., Haass, A.: Heart rate variability enhances the prognostic value of established parameters in patients with congestive heart failure. Zeitschrift Fur Kardiologie 91, 1003–1012 (2002)
8. La Rovere, M.T., Pinna, G.D., Maestri, R., Mortara, A., Capomolla, S., Febo, O., Ferrari, R., Franchini, M., Gnemmi, M., Opasich, C., Riccardi, P.G., Traversi, E., Cobelli, F.: Short-term heart rate variability strongly predicts sudden cardiac death in chronic heart failure patients. Circulation 107, 565–570 (2003)
9. Aronson, D., Mittleman, M.A., Burger, A.J.: Measures of heart period variability as predictors of mortality in hospitalized patients with decompensated congestive heart failure. Am. J. Cardiol. 93, 59–63 (2004)
10. Hadase, M., Azuma, A., Zen, K., Asada, S., Kawasaki, T., Kamitani, T., Kawasaki, S., Sugihara, H., Matsubara, H.: Very low frequency power of heart rate variability is a powerful predictor of clinical prognosis in patients with congestive heart failure. Circulation Journal 68, 343–347 (2004)
11. Smilde, T.D.J., van Veldhuisen, D.J., van den Berg, M.P.: Prognostic value of heart rate variability and ventricular arrhythmias during 13-year follow-up in patients with mild to moderate heart failure. Clinical Research in Cardiology 98, 233–239 (2009)
12. Melillo, P., Bracale, M., Pecchia, L.: Nonlinear Heart Rate Variability features for real-life stress detection. Case study: students under stress due to university examination. Biomed. Eng. Online 10, 96 (2011)
13. Melillo, P., De Luca, N., Bracale, M., Pecchia, L.: Classification Tree for Risk Assessment in Patients Suffering From Congestive Heart Failure via Long-Term Heart Rate Variability. IEEE J. Biomed. Health Inform. 17, 727–733 (2013)
14. Melillo, P., Formisano, C., Bracale, U., Pecchia, L.: Classification tree for real-life stress detection using linear Heart Rate Variability analysis. Case study: students under stress due to university examination. In: Long, M. (ed.) World Congress on Medical Physics and Biomedical Engineering, Beijing, China, May 26-31, vol. 39, pp. 477–480. Springer, Heidelberg (2013)
15. Melillo, P., Fusco, R., Sansone, M., Bracale, M., Pecchia, L.: Discrimination power of long-term heart rate variability measures for chronic heart failure detection. Med. Biol. Eng. Comput. 49, 67–74 (2011)
16. Pecchia, L., Melillo, P., Bracale, M.: Remote health monitoring of heart failure with data mining via CART method on HRV features. IEEE Trans Bio. Med. Eng. 58, 800–804 (2011)
17. Pecchia, L., Melillo, P., Sansone, M., Bracale, M.: Discrimination power of short-term heart rate variability measures for CHF assessment. IEEE Trans. Inf. Technol. Biomed. 15, 40–46 (2011)

18. Hervás, R., Fontecha, J., Ausín, D., Castanedo, F., Bravo, J., López-de-Ipiña, D.: Mobile monitoring and reasoning methods to prevent cardiovascular diseases. Sensors-Basel 13, 6524–6541 (2013)

19. Hautala, A.J., Karjalainen, J., Kiviniemi, A.M., Kinnunen, H., Mäkikallio, T.H., Huikuri, H.V., Tulppo, M.P.: Physical activity and heart rate variability measured simultaneously during waking hours. Am J. Physiol.-Cell. Ph 298, H874 (2010)

20. Brennan, M., Palaniswami, M., Kamen, P.: Do existing measures of Poincare plot geometry reflect nonlinear features of heart rate variability? IEEE Trans. Bio. IEEE Trans. Bio. Med. Eng. 48, 1342–1347 (2001)

21. Richman, J.S., Moorman, J.R.: Physiological time-series analysis using approximate entropy and sample entropy. American Journal of Physiology-Heart and Circulatory Physiology 278, H2039–H2049 (2000)

22. Carvajal, R., Wessel, N., Vallverdú, M., Caminal, P., Voss, A.: Correlation dimension analysis of heart rate variability in patients with dilated cardiomyopathy. Computer Methods and Programs in Biomedicine 78, 133–140 (2005)

23. Peng, C.K., Havlin, S., Stanley, H.E., Goldberger, A.L.: Quantification of Scaling Exponents and Crossover Phenomena in Nonstationary Heartbeat Time-Series. Chaos 5, 82–87 (1995)

24. Penzel, T., Kantelhardt, J.W., Grote, L., Peter, J.H., Bunde, A.: Comparison of detrended fluctuation analysis and spectral analysis for heart rate variability in sleep and sleep apnea. IEEE Trans. Bio. Med. Eng. 50, 1143–1151 (2003)

25. Trulla, L.L., Giuliani, A., Zbilut, J.P., Webber, C.L.: Recurrence quantification analysis of the logistic equation with transients. Phys. Lett. A 223, 255–260 (1996)

26. Webber, C.L., Zbilut, J.P.: Dynamical Assessment of Physiological Systems and States Using Recurrence Plot Strategies. Journal of Applied Physiology 76, 965–973 (1994)

27. Zbilut, J.P., Thomasson, N., Webber, C.L.: Recurrence quantification analysis as a tool for nonlinear exploration of nonstationary cardiac signals. Medical Engineering & Physics 24, 53–60 (2002)

28. Melillo, P., Pecchia, L., Ursino, M.: Nonlinear analysis research in biomedical engineering. Focus on Nonlinear Analysis Research. Nova Science Publishers (2013)

29. Seiffert, C., Khoshgoftaar, T.M., Van Hulse, J., Napolitano, A.: RUSBoost: A hybrid approach to alleviating class imbalance. IEEE Transactions on Systems, Man and Cybernetics, Part A: Systems and Humans 40, 185–197 (2010)

30. Schapire, R.E., Freund, Y., Bartlett, P., Lee, W.S.: Boosting the margin: A new explanation for the effectiveness of voting methods. Annals of Statistics 26, 1651–1686 (1998)

31. Breiman, L., Friedman, J.H., Olshen, R.A., Stone, C.J.: Classification and regression trees. Wadsworth International Group, Belmont (1984)

32. Kuncheva, L.I., Rodríguez, J.J.: An experimental study on rotation forest ensembles. In: Haindl, M., Kittler, J., Roli, F. (eds.) MCS 2007. LNCS, vol. 4472, pp. 459–468. Springer, Heidelberg (2007)

33. Garcia, J., Martinez, I., Sornmo, L., Olmos, S., Mur, A., Laguna, P.: Remote processing server for ECG-based clinical diagnosis support. IEEE Trans. Inf. Technol. Biomed. 6, 277–284 (2002)

Predictability of Some Pregnancy Outcomes Based on SVM and Dichotomous Regression Techniques

Gabriele Guidi[1], Giulia Adembri[3], Silvia Vannuccini[2], and Ernesto Iadanza[1]

[1] Department of Information Engineering – University of Florence, 50039 - Florence, Italy
{gabriele.guidi,ernesto.iadanza}@unifi.it
[2] Department of Molecular and Developmental Medicine,
University of Siena, 53100 Siena - Italy
[3] ICON (International Center of Computational Neurophotonics) Foundation,
50019 Florence, Italy

Abstract. The objective of this study is developing a forecasting system for some childbirth outcomes, based on an input pattern of instrumental and anamnestic parameters detected at 37th week of pregnancy. The study stems from the need to be able to predict what to expect during labor and childbirth, while discovering new knowledge from the evidence of the data (data mining). Outcomes to predict concern: underweight newborn, post partum bleeding, need for artificially induced birth, necessity of cesarean birth. The predictors parameters are a total of 58 dichotomous inputs grouped into 4 categories: pre-conception risk factors, obstetric risk factors, risk factors associated with pregnancy, ultrasound parameters. The training database is populated with 420 patients, each with a single follow-up. Best leave one out cross-validation results were achieved in the estimation of underweight (ROC point chosen, sensitivity 0.69 - specificity 0.88).

Keywords: Pregnancy risk, Machine Learning, SVM, Regression.

1   Introduction

In this study we build predictive models to identify some birth outcomes with data mining operations, using machine learning techniques and logistic regression. The analytics was performed on a fully anonymized database of 420 patients, supplied by the Department of Development and Molecular Medicine - University of Siena, containing data related to the parametric situation at the thirty-seventh week of pregnancy. In the literature, studies on data mining in the field of pregnancy were mainly marked on establishing the risk of premature birth [1], [2], [3] or on detecting fetal parameters [4].

Outcomes to be found in this study are about clinical complications - such as the necessity of surgical cesarean birth or artificially induced birth, post-partum bleeding - as well as complications that affect the child such as risk of underweight. In particular, a newborn is considered clinically underweight if the birth weight is less than 2.5 kg; postpartum blood loss is considered as significant if greater than 500cc.

L. Pecchia et al. (Eds.): IWAAL 2014, LNCS 8868, pp. 163–166, 2014.

2   Material and Methods

2.1   Database

The database to be analyzed and used to build the model is populated with data consist of a series of 58 true/false conditions grouped into 4 categories: preconception risk factors, obstetric risk factors, risk factors associated with pregnancy, ultrasound parameters. Outcomes of childbirth that we are going to model and forecast are the following:

- Necessity of cesarean birth (Birth Type)
- Underweight newborn (Underweight infant)
- Post partum bleeding (Blood Loss)
- Need for artificially induced birth (Induction of Labor)

2.2   Analysis Techniques

Because of the database structure and of the presence of desired outputs, we decided to use supervised training techniques. To create the 4 models (one for each outcome to be investigated), we use and compare machine learning and regression techniques. As a representative for the machine learning we opted for the Support Vector Machine (SVM) [5] as we have already successfully tested it in our other studies in which the only SVM drawback was poor performances in the case of multiclass classification if compared to other techniques [6], [7], [8], [9]. In this case, each model has binary output (presence or absence of the considered outcome), so the SVM technique is in its best operation conditions. The chosen regression technique is a multiple logistic regression, because both the outcome and all the predictors are dichotomic.

2.3   Experiment Setup

We develop and test SVM and Regression in Matlab 7.11.0 (R2012b). We set the SVM with a linear kernel and, as a method to calculate the separation hyperplane, we chose the quadratic programming algorithm, included in the Matlab "Optimization Toolbox" . The function used for training is *svmtrain*. To realize the regression algorithm we have instead used the *glmfit* function (general linear model regression), setting its parameters so as to obtain a binomial distribution regression model with *logit* link function. In the use phase we obtained the output from the regression by using the beta coefficients generated in the train phase and combining it with the inverse of the *logit* function. As a method of performance evaluation we chose the leave-one-out cross-validation. Given that there are 420 patients in the database, this requires 420 training and testing operations. As a result from cross-validation we have an average sensitivity and specificity defined in formulas 1 and 2. All this is further cycled for 60 times by changing the internal thresholds of the two techniques to generate ROC curves at 60 points. Everything is repeated for four times, once for each outcome, and then for each model to generate.

Due to the very high number of inputs and the relatively low number of training examples (420 patients), we decided to perform a first selection of features to analyze the data from the SVM and logistic regression. Such operation of features selection was achieved by further operation of multivariate linear regression. As a selection criterion we used the standardized beta coefficients thus produced, and we have included in the analysis only the inputs having standardized beta coefficients above the average, if compared to other inputs.

3   Preliminary Results

In Table 1 are shown the performances of the SVM and of the Logistic Regression (LR) at the chosen work point in ROC Curves, in quantitative terms. Working point was chosen in agreement with our clinical partners, in order to find a good compromise between sensitivity and specificity, that are calculated with the following formulas, where TP = true positive, FP = false positive, TN = true negative, FN = false negative.

$$\text{Sensitivity} = TP/(TP+FN) \tag{1}$$

$$\text{Specificity} = TN/(TN+FP) \tag{2}$$

Are shown average values of these indicators, obtained by averaging the results of the various fold, of cross validation process.

Table 1.   Performances

Outcome	Method	Average Sensitivity	Average Specificity
Blood Loss	LR	0.64	0.72
Blood Loss	SVM	0.45	0.73
Birth Type	LR	0.59	0.74
Birth Type	SVM	0.42	0.88
Underweight infant	LR	0.69	0.88
Underweight infant	SVM	0.48	0.87
Induction of labor	LR	0.60	0.70
Induction of labor	SVM	0.50	0.72

4   Discussion and Conclusion

In this study we predict four pregnancy outcome using machine learning compared with a logistic regression method, combined with a regression-based feature selection. The results are validated with a standard method (cross-validation). Logistic Regression provide in general better results than SVM method.

Even though a system with these performances may still be useful as an aid to clinical decision-making, these performances are not as good as expected in sensitivity and specificity and suggest further effort to raise both. It is difficult to compare these results with others in the literature, because most of the outcomes considered in this study are never been treated. At this stage we consider that the only predictable outcomes, with a sufficient level of validation, using these methods and our database, are "Underweight infant" and "Blood loss".

Acknowledgments. The authors would like to thank Dr. F. Petraglia and Dr. F. M. Severi for their clinical contribution in this study.

References

1. Chen, H.-Y., Chuang, C.-H., Yang, Y.-J., Wu, T.-P.: Exploring the risk factors of preterm birth using data mining. Expert Systems with Applications 38(5), 5384–5387 (2011)
2. Goodwin, L.K., Iannacchione, M.A.: Data mining methods for improving birth outcomes prediction. Outcomes Management 6(2), 80–85 (2002)
3. Woolery, L.K., Grzymala-Busse, J.: Machine Learning for an Expert System to Predict Preterm Birth Risk Abstract Machine Learning. Journal of the American Medical Informatics Association 1(6) (1994)
4. Melillo, P., Santoro, D., Vadursi, M.: Detection and Compensation of Interchannel Time Offsets in Indirect Fetal ECG Sensing. IEEE Sensors Journal 14(7), 2327–2334 (2014)
5. Cortes, C., Vapnik, V.: Support-vector networks. Machine Learning 20(3), 273–297 (1995)
6. Guidi, G., Melillo, P., Pettenati, M., Milli, M., Iadanza, E.: Performance Assessment of a Clinical Decision Support System for analysis of Heart Failure. In: IFMBE Proceedings, vol. 41, pp. 1354–1357 (2014)
7. Guidi, G., Pettenati, M.C., Miniati, R., Iadanza, E.: Heart Failure analysis Dashboard for patient's remote monitoring combining multiple artificial intelligence technologies. In: Proceedings of Annual International Conference of the IEEE Engineering in Medicine and Biology Society, EMBS 2012, pp. 6346401, pp. 2210–2213 (2012)
8. Guidi, G., Pettenati, M.C., Miniati, R., Iadanza, E.: Random Forest for Automatic Assessment of Heart Failure Severity in A Telemonitoring Scenario. In: Proceedings of the Annual International Conference of the IEEE Engineering in Medicine and Biology Society, EMBS, pp. 3230–3233
9. Guidi, G., Iadanza, E., Pettenati, M.C., Milli, M., Pavone, F., Biffi Gentili, G.: Heart Failure Artificial Intelligence-Based Computer Aided Diagnosis Telecare System. In: Donnelly, M., Paggetti, C., Nugent, C., Mokhtari, M. (eds.) ICOST 2012. LNCS, vol. 7251, pp. 278–281. Springer, Heidelberg (2012)

To What Extent It Is Possible to Predict Falls due to Standing Hypotension by Using HRV and Wearable Devices? Study Design and Preliminary Results from a Proof-of-Concept Study

Giovanna Sannino[1], Paolo Melillo[2], Giuseppe De Pietro[1], Saverio Stranges[3], and Leandro Pecchia[3]

[1] Institute of High Performance Computing and Networking, CNR – Naples, Italy
[2] Dipt. Multidisciplinare Specialita Medico-Chirurgiche, Second Univ. of Naples
[3] School of Engineering, University of Warwick – Coventry, UK
{giovanna.sannino,giuseppe.depietro}@na.icar.cnr.it,
{paolo.melillo}@unina.it,
{s.stranges,l.pecchia}@warwick.ac.uk

Abstract. Falls are a major problem in later life reducing the well-being, mobility and quality of life. One of the main causes of falls is standing hypotension. This paper presents the design and the very preliminary results of a pilot study aiming to investigate if it is possible to predict standing hypotension and in projection those falls due to standing hypotension, using the HRV short term recording to estimate the blood pressure drop-down (ΔBP) due to fast rising up from a bed. The preliminary results shown that in the 79% of the experiment conducted, the HRV acquired with commercial wearable devices could predict ΔBP due to standing hypotension with an error below the sphigmomanoter measurement error.

Keywords: Standing Hypotension, Prediction of falls, HRV analysis, Blood Pressure drop-down Prediction.

1 Introduction

Standing Hypotension (SH) is a major drop-down in Blood Pressure (BP). Severe SH, referred as Orthostatic Hypotension (OH) [1], is defined as drop down (-20 mmHg) in systolic BP due to standing, has an incidence of 4% to 33% in elderly, and causes lightheadedness, cognitive impairment, blurred vision and vertigo. These symptoms, associated with exposure to extrinsic (environmental dependent) risk factors, causes up to the 30% of falls in later life, and consequently fractures and other major impairments [2]. Since 30% of elderly are expected to fall once per year and the mean cost of about £7k per fall, predicting falls due to SH would sabe million of pound per year. Nevertheless, the phenomena of an huge drop down in BP due to standing hypotension can be observed also in healthy young [3]. Therefore, this pilot study focused on healthy young subjects in order to acquire reliable priory knowledge to design in the next week a more reliable study involving elderly subjects. Heart Rate Variability (HRV) is one of most studied noninvasive markers of the Autonomic Nervous System (ANS) [4], which is

L. Pecchia et al. (Eds.): IWAAL 2014, LNCS 8868, pp. 167–170, 2014.
© Springer International Publishing Switzerland 2014

the controller of BP equilibrium. Therefore this study investigated the relationship between HRV and the BP drop-down (ΔBP) when a person stands up from a bed or couch. The study is a first attempt to understand the potential of HRV to predict the SH.

2   Method

According to [5], 10 healthy subjects were enrolled. Inclusion criteria were: no pathological cardiovascular conditions, neurological or psychiatric disorders or other severe diseases; not taking any medication at the moment of the study; not professional athletes or high-level sport participants; no caffeine or alcohol intake in the 12 hours prior to the measurements.

The protocol was defined to maximize repeatability and reproducibility of experiments and aiming to reproduce at best the real life standing from a couch. It was composed by three phases (seating, laying and standing) as described in figure 1. During the phase 1 the volunteers were invited to seat in a comfortable position for a baseline recording of the systolic BPs and ECG. In the phase 2, the volunteers were invited to lay down in supine position for 10 minutes. During the last 5 minutes, ECG was recorded continuously using commercial wearable devices and systolic BPs was recorded 4 times (once each 60 seconds). Finally, in the phase 3 the volunteers were invited to stand up actively and to stay in upright position for 5 minutes. Once standing, systolic BPs was recorded 4 times (once each 60 seconds) and ECG was recorded for 5 minutes. Phases 2 and 3 were repeated 4 times.

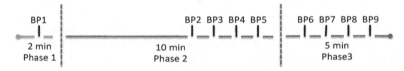

Fig. 1. The Experimental Protocol for the Pilot Study

ECG recordings from phase 2 were pre-processed by using Kubios [6] and associated with BP drop-down calculated as ΔBP=BP7-mean(BP2, BP3, BP4, BP5). 64 HRV features were extracted in linear [7] and non-linear domain [8, 9]. Details about HRV features extraction and convention can be seen in [10].

A model to predict ΔBP using the HRV registered in the 5 minutes before standing was developed using robust regression [11]. An exhaustive search was performed to select the best 5 HRV features to use the model. The employed model was validated with the leave-one-out cross-validation technique [12]. Particularly, the model was trained using the whole dataset except all the instances of one subject, which were then used to test the developed model. This process was repeated 10 times, leaving out in turn all the subjects.

3   Results

The best combination of features included was: the standard deviation of RR (NN) intervals (STDNN), the number of successive RR interval pairs that differ more than

50m divided by the total number of RR intervals (pNN50), the absolute powers of high frequency band (HF), the standard deviation of the Poincarè plot alond to the line of identity and the Deteminism (DET).

First numerical results show a correct prediction of 79.5%. This value percentage was calculated as the count of the prediction that differed from the measures ΔBP less than the measurement error ($\pm$4.5 mmHg). Results of the prediction are reported in Figure 2.

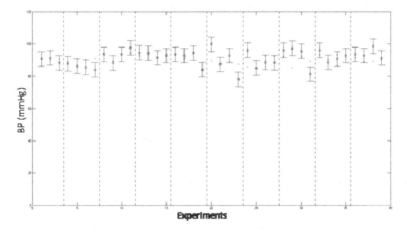

Fig. 2. Measured and predicted value of blood pressure after standing. The blue dots and the related error bars represent the measured values and their standard errors, respectively, while the red cross are the predicted value. Dashed vertical lines are plotted to distinghuish the repeated measurments of the different subjects: 3 repetitions the first and 4 the remaining 9 subjects. In about the 80% of cases, the predicted values are within the error bars.

4   Discussion

This paper presented the desing and the preliminary result of a prof-of-concept study investigating if it is possible to predict systolic ΔBP due to standing using short term HRV measures extracted from ECG recorded 5 minutes before the standing. The preliminary results show that ΔBP magnitude is predictable with the HRV features almost in the 80% of cases. Clearly this result is only obtained on healthy subjects, but it shows that it is theoretical possible to predict BP drop-down using HRV.

A recent retrospective study [13] demonstrated that there is a significant association between a depressed HRV and the risk of falling in elderly. The authors concluded that this was due to the fact that a depressed HRV reflects a reduced capability to react to risky situations. The preliminimary results presented in this paper could explain this association.

Other studies, [14] and [5], investigated the associations between SH and HRV. However, those papers focused on how HRV changes before and after standing, and mainly focusing on linear HRV measures. Differently, this pilot study aimed to understand how HRV changed before the BP drop-down and how it could be possible to predict the ΔBP from HRV measures.

This study had several limitations, as the small number and the young age of subjects involved, which require further investigations to extend those results to elderly.

References

1. Mukai, S., Lipsitz, L.A.: Orthostatic hypotension. Clinics in Geriatric Medicine 18, 253–268 (2002)
2. Rutan, G.H., Hermanson, B., Bild, D.E., Kittner, S.J., LaBaw, F., Tell, G.S.: Orthostatic hypotension in older adults. The Cardiovascular Health Study. CHS Collaborative Research Group. Hypertension 19, 508–519 (1992)
3. Streeten, D.H.: Orthostatic intolerance. A historical introduction to the pathophysiological mechanisms. The American Journal of the Medical Sciences 317, 78–87 (1999)
4. Dampney, R.A., Coleman, M.J., Fontes, M.A., Hirooka, Y., Horiuchi, J., Li, Y.W., Polson, J.W., Potts, P.D., Tagawa, T.: Central mechanisms underlying short- and long-term regulation of the cardiovascular system. Clinical and Experimental Pharmacology & Physiology 29, 261–268 (2002)
5. Kawaguchi, T., Uyama, O., Konishi, M., Nishiyama, T., Iida, T.: Orthostatic hypotension in elderly persons during passive standing: a comparison with young persons. The Journals of Gerontology. Series A, Biological Sciences and Medical Sciences 56, M273–M280 (2001)
6. Tarvainen, M.P., Ranta-Aho, P.O., Karjalainen, P.A.: An advanced detrending method with application to HRV analysis. IEEE Transactions on Bio-Medical Engineering 49, 172–175 (2002)
7. Electrophysiology, T.F.o.t.E.S.o.C.t.N.A.S.o.P.: Heart Rate Variability: Standards of Measurement. Physiological Interpretation, and Clinical Use. Circulation 93, 1043–1065 (1996)
8. Melillo, P., Bracale, M., Pecchia, L.: Nonlinear Heart Rate Variability features for real-life stress detection. Case study: students under stress due to university examination. Biomed. Eng. Online 10, 96 (2011)
9. Melillo, P., Pecchia, L., Ursino, M.: Nonlinear analysis research in biomedical engineering. Focus on Nonlinear Analysis Research. Nova Science Publishers (2013)
10. Melillo, P., Izzo, R., De Luca, N., Pecchia, L.: Heart rate variability and target organ damage in hypertensive patients. BMC Cardiovasc Disord 12, 105 (2012)
11. Huber, P.J.: Frontmatter. Robust Statistics, pp. i-xi. John Wiley & Sons, Inc. (1981)
12. Browne, M.W.: Cross-Validation Methods. Journal of mathematical psychology 44, 108–132 (2000)
13. Melillo, P., Jovic, A., De Luca, N., Morgan, S., Pecchia, L.: Automatic prediction of falls via Heart Rate Variability and data mining in hypertensive patients: the SHARE project experience. In: 6th European Conference of the International Federation for Medical and Biological Engineering, MBEC 2014 (2014)
14. Berntson, G.G., Cacioppo, J.T.: Heart Rate Variability: Stress and Psychiatric Conditions. In: Dynamic Electrocardiography, pp. 57–64. Blackwell Publishing (2007)

PChCT: A Tool to Monitor Child Whereabouts

Fernando Martínez-Reyes[1,*], Luis A. Castro[2], and Luis C. González-Gurrola[1]

[1] Facultad de Ingeniería, Universidad Autónoma de Chihuahua, Chihuahua, México
{fmartinez2004,gonzalezgurrola@gmail.com}@gmail.com
[2] Instituto Tecnológico de Sonora, Ciudad Obregón, Sonora, México
luis.castro@acm.org

Abstract. The commitment of time and effort that is necessary to the management of the household can be very significant, especially when nurturing activity has to be interwoven with other activities. It is necessary to understand the management of activities and spaces when a parent has to take care of a child while performing chores simultaneously. In this work, we present results of a field trial that monitored activity in a domestic setting. Information from the technology integrated in the living and the kitchen room allowed us to examine how the home spaces are used and some hints of the possible activity being done in these spaces. Through a careful analysis, we developed the "Parent-Child Companion Tool", a practical resource that parents can use to complement their awareness of the child whereabouts when he/she is not under direct supervision.

Keywords: pervasive technology, nurturing, domestic activity, intelligent spaces, activity aware tools.

1 Introduction

For a full- or part-time caregiver of young children, the home can be a demanding and stressful environment. The commitment of time and effort that is necessary both to keep a child safe and to help her/him develop is very significant, especially for the youngest children. The attendance of domestic work such as cleaning and cooking has to be traded off with nurturing activities, in particular, when the mother needs to look after a baby. As the child grows the mother would attend housework in episodes keeping always an eye on the child's behavior. Off the shelf surveillance technologies are commonly used to monitor children's whereabouts. There are, however, situations where such level of monitoring can be out of hand. Consider the situation when the mother's full focus of attention is for the cooking activity, the child is exploring near electrical sockets and the camera reports the child's back only, or an empty room.

This can be a good example where pervasive technologies could assist the parent with an alert-based tool that differentiates between children different levels of freedom to explore and experiment with their home environment, commensurate with their knowledge of the dangers that such environments present. That is, smart monitoring

---

[*] Corresponding author. E-mail: fmartine@uach.mx

L. Pecchia et al. (Eds.): IWAAL 2014, LNCS 8868, pp. 171–178, 2014.

technology can enhance nurturance experience for a young child while not putting her/him at risk, i.e., allowing exploration and learning of the home spaces while remotely supervised by means of alerts, video, and text sent to the mother if needed.

As a piece of work towards this goal, we have been investigating the challenges of sensing activity in real home scenarios, by installing a set of sensors, recording the data that they produce, and implementing techniques to analyse this data to extract relevant information.

The rest of this work is structured as follows. Section 2 shows the social motivation underlying the domestic study. Section 3, describes how the setting was prepared to carry out the field trial. Section 4, illustrates the data analysis used to identify location and activity. Section 5, introduces the PChCT tool that could be provided to support some level of parental awareness. Finally, section 6 offers conclusions and future work.

2   Social Motivation

When both parents have full-time jobs, and even in the case of single parenting, the attendance of domestic work and child rearing activity is considered hard to manage. Remarkably, in some social studies parents have expressed that home management regularly is stressful and time-consuming, and when involving nurturing activities children have to be kept occupied in a safe place [1,2]. Furthermore, there are some figures indicating that children under 5 years are the family members most subject to accidents within the home [3,4]. Off the shelf technology such as baby monitors, smoke alarms and fireplace guards is used to add up for the home safety. There are, however, spaces, artefacts and objects children may interact with from which we are not aware of potential risks; falls from stairs, drowning and poisoning lead statistics of children accidents.

In the domestic setting there is a strong need to maintain a daily awareness of home inhabitants, parents often need to be aware of their children's location, activity and status; information that individuals use to coordinate or to promote feelings of connectedness or comfort [5]. For instance, couples with children considered that there are potential applications of smart home technology to empower their everyday activities especially on busy days [6]. Technology augmented settings have been used to explore potential scenarios that can track children health and development [7]. For instance, data collected from the interaction of a child with technology-augmented toys helped get a better understanding of his/her developmental milestones [8]. A microphone-video camera based experiment was carried on to record audio-visual information available on the surrounding of a child in order to longitudinally study language development from birth to three years old [9], even more there is also particular interest in using technologies for the identification of speech related disorders [10]. Multimedia based tools have also been trialled in domestic spaces to allow families to capture emotional moments of their children [11], yet sharing these children achievements with other family members [12].

Our work seeks to contribute in this field by exploring what might support some of the important interactions that take place between parents and young children. We specifically consider the safety of babies and young children, as they are susceptible to accidents in the home while not been directly supervised. We focused on the particular case when the child is having an activity in the next room, different from where the parent actually is. We think that this scenario is rich in opportunities, since it is prone for the child to have an accident given the overconfidence of the parent who just relays on two assumptions: (1) the home is a safe place and (2) the feeling that he/she is not far away from his/her child, both of them being questionable.

 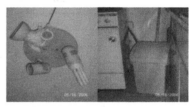

Fig. 1. Some of the objects and artifacts tagged with sensing technology

3 Experimental Setting: Pervasive Sensing in the Home Environment

Phidget-based sensor technology [13] was installed in the living and kitchen room of a semi-detached home. This includes proximity sensors, motion sensors and beam-break sensors. Beam break sensor attached along the doors' frames can offer a clue of whether a person enters or exits a room. Proximity sensors attached to the fridge, washing machine, and cabinets in the kitchen help identify when the mother is in this room and to some extent the moment in which she is using/interacting with the artifacts/appliances. For the living room we tagged the TV set, the central heating, the heater, and the toy box. Motion sensors were accommodated in the center of each of the rooms and help to support location information obtained from proximity sensors. We collected 15 days of sensor data. Figure 1 shows some of the tagged artifacts. A webcam was also installed in each of these rooms.

The family living in this house is composed by a young child aged 3 and a child aged 6, a full-time working father and a full time mom. During a typical family day, the father leaves home at around 8am and returns from work around 7pm. The daughter is at school from 8am to 3pm. Therefore, the daily activities are well suited for our analysis, where we will mainly focus on the interaction between the mother and the child.

4 Data Analysis

We obtained data from sensors installed in the kitchen and the living room. A total of 600,000 samples were obtained coming from the 14 sensors. Towards our first analysis we were able to track all the events that were detected by the set of sensors. We carefully checked the consistency of sensor readings. Firstly, we statistically characterized the base reading of each sensor, we used this as a reference of the moment when a person was nearby an artifact. Secondly, we filtered out unreasonable large sensors readings that were mainly caused by the presence of movable furniture, i.e., chairs, small tables. Through the complete and detailed log file of sensor readings of all days, we encountered very interesting findings that helped us understand the nature and needs of one mother and her child at home. This information is crucial to our understanding of how the home's spaces are used, what activities are carried on, and whether the child is not at the sight of the mother.

Table 1. Sensor events from door activity

Event	Event	Output	Time differences	User event
S_1	S_2	Entrée	$Ts_1 > Ts_2$	Adult entering the room
S_1	-	*	$Ts_1 \ll Ts_2$	Extraordinary event
-	S_2	Entrée/Exit	$Ts_1 \gg Ts_2$	Child crossing the door
S_2	S_1	Exit	$Ts_1 < Ts_2$	Adult exiting the room

">" = "greater than"; ">>" = "much greater than"

4.1   Rooms' Location and Activity

Events coming from sensors installed on doors are processed and used to infer the room being used and if it was the parent or the child who entered or left the living or the kitchen room. For this level of room location we apply a rule-based algorithm over consecutive time-based events. The order of how sensors are triggered and the time difference between two events determine, for example, if an adult enters or exits the room as shown in table 1. Activity data was obtained from the rest of the sensors. Motion sensors signal when a person is around the center of the room, and from proximity sensors we can draw whether the person is near an artifact.

Regarding activity, we observed that there are very well defined time periods within the home where activities are carried out. In our first analysis we were interested in tracking the activities on each particular home space. From this first analysis we wanted to know what would be a "normal" day for the house's inhabitants.

The exploration of collected data indicated that there is an average of 6 hours of activity within the kitchen and 4.5 hours within the living room, every day. Several questions were raised during this stage: What kinds of activities would be part of a normal-day? Are there behavioural patterns exhibited? How much consistency could we expect from these patterns? Are these patterns presented during specific time intervals?

We noticed that the mother has a very specific set of tasks to perform. Firstly, we associated these tasks to cooking and cleaning purposes, but as it is presented in the next section, the mother can alternate these activities with child nurturing. The kitchen experienced very busy time intervals, a tracking of these activities showed specifically that the mother interacts heavily and frequently with the cabinets and fridge whilst spending most of her time preparing food in the cooker and cupboard. Given the level of activity during these specific time intervals, we can infer that the mother had very low interaction with the activities that are being held in the living room. On the other hand, we were able to spot the spaces where the young child spends most of his time. With no surprise, these spaces are located near the TV set and the toy box, with minimum intervals near the heater or central heating system. At this point we identified normal situations, a single mother busy doing chores, mainly in the kitchen and a single young child playing and watching TV in the living room. In figure 2 we can observe moments at which the mother and the child share the room space and situations in which the child is left alone. The situation that is important here is the moment in which the parent would be unaware of what or how the child is behaving in a different room. For instance, when the mother is facing to the front side of the cooker is not possible to have a direct view of what is happening in the living room.

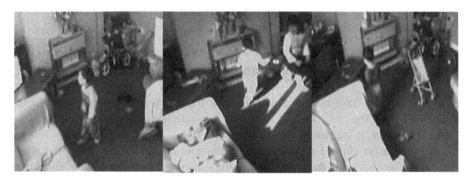

Fig. 2. Three moments of the child's activity. Cared by the mother (left), under his sister supervision (middle) and with no direct supervision (right)

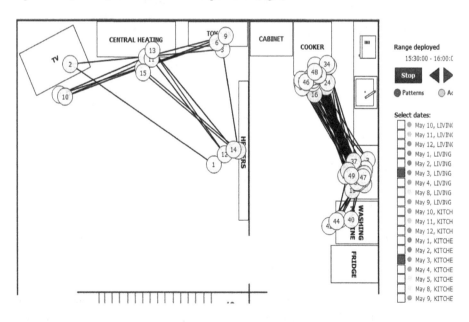

Fig. 3. There are moments where the mother might not be fully aware of the child's behaviour; here the child was detected six times near the central heating and in three occasions she/he was less than 10 centimetre apart from this artefact. This scenario might help illustrate the opportunity for supportive technology.

From the previous data analysis we inferred activities that simultaneously took place in different rooms. This analysis allowed us to detect sequences of activities, patterns and interactions between activities.

The activity analysis, shown in Figure 3, suggest that were the mother is doing something in the kitchen, the child passes several times near the central heating or the heather and it seemed the child is unaware of the kind of dangers around this type of objects/appliances. Although this is not the case, this type of scenario helps illustrate that the child may be exposed to potential risks while playing or exploring. Children like to play on sofas and sometimes they experiment falls. Couches are often located near windows, and fallouts are part of the statistics.

5   The Parent-Child Companion Tool (PChCT)

Previous sections have indicated that in order for the parent to attend some of the household work the child seemed to be left in a safe home space such as the living room. Moreover, it seemed that there are moments when the mother has not full supervision over her child. For such kinds of situations it may be helpful to offer a tool for the mother that could help her alleviate the situations where her child is in the next room apparently playing on safe places while she is busy.

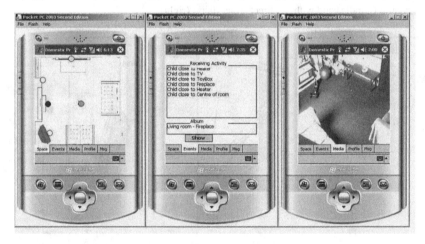

Fig. 4. PChCT's interfaces. Space interface (left); Events interface (centre); Media interface (right)

The PChCT is a tool aiming to provide notifications whenever the child is playing nearby potentially risky artifacts, see figure 4. The PChCT provides a notification system to keep the mother informed of the child whereabouts, especially, when a potentially risky activity is identified. Notifications are drawn from the events provided by the sensing layer. The PChCT offers three interfaces for the delivering of notifications. The Space interface uses a visual plain view to represent the child's whereabouts; the Events interface uses text-messages to provide a short history of the most recent child activity; and the Media interface, available from any of the other interfaces, shows the image of the living room that corresponds to the most recent activity event. For any of these interfaces it is possible to configure whether sound alarms can be part of the notifications. The parent can also define the level of sensitivity for the triggering of notifications. The sensitivity is a function of the distance of the child to tagged artifacts. More configuration options include the possibility to let the tool working in the background to record a digital album of the child activity, or to update information of the child whereabouts by the parent explicit request. In general, the configuration of the PChCT, see figure 5, allows reducing interruptions to the parent's everyday activities.

Fig. 5. Parents can configure the level and source of notifications

6   Conclusions and Future Work

In this work we analyzed data from a home setting that allowed us to explore the concept of pervasive spaces that would aim supporting parents in the home. Particularly, we focused on the case when a mother and her child are at home, each one on different room. Data collected from the pervasive technology installed in the kitchen and the living room helped with the identification of what kind of activities are carried on simultaneously. We noticed that the mother has very busy time intervals where her attention is focus on daily chores. This situation is relevant since we detected that in a completely different room her young child is having his own activity indirectly supervised. Given the hectic routines of these days, most of us would consider the home environment as a relatively safe place, this overconfidence can play against us, since it decreases the level of attention paid to our children and the locations they play at. In some cases, parents assume that there is no risk in the living room for the child so that she/he could leave him alone for a moment.

Following our results, it was possible to identify technology that can offer support to parenting within the home setting. The PChCT tool was envisioned to empower parenting awareness on busy days. Through this tool, one can pinpoint periods of time in which the mother and son are in different rooms, and an alarm is sent to her mobile device if the child is playing close to risky artefacts. One of the main features of this tool is that it takes into account social issues such as avoiding interruptions. For instance, if the mother or the daughter is looking after the young child, or if the young child is not that close to risky artefacts, the tool will not send any notification. Parents can also configure the level and type notifications that meet their needs. As a future work, we would like to explore other methodology for the analysis of the data. We would like to apply data mining techniques to deeply explore the nature and relationships of the sensor readings and the correspondent representation of the home activity.

References

1. Baxter, J., Hewitt, B., Haynes, M.: Life course transitions and housework: Marriage, parenthood, and time on housework. Journal of Marriage and Family 70(2), 259–272 (2008)
2. Yun-Suk, L., Waite, L.J.: Husbands and wives time spent on housework: a comparison of measures. Journal of Marriage and Family 67, 328–336 (2005)
3. Fauth, R., Ellis, A.: Reducing Unintentional Injuries in Childhood, National Children's Bureau (2010)
4. Currie, J., Hotz, V.J.: Accidents will happen?: Unintentional childhood injuries and the effects of child care regulations. Journal of Health Economics 23(1), 25–59 (2004)
5. Neustaedter, C., Elliot, K., Greenberg, S.: Interpersonal awareness in the domestic realm. In: Proc. Conference of the Computer-Human interaction Special interest Group (Chisig), Sydney, Australia, November 20-24 (2006)
6. Green, W., Gyi, D., Kalawsky, R., Atkins, D.: Capturing user requirements for an integrated home environment. In: Proceedings of the Nordic conference on Human-Computer Interaction, NordiCHI 2004, Tampere, Finland, October 23-27 (2004)
7. Kientz, J.A., IArriaga, R., Chetty, M., Hayes, G.R., Richardson, J., Patel, S.N., Abowd, G.D.: Grow and know: understanding record-keeping needs for tracking the development of young children. In: Proc. CHI 2007, pp. 1351–1360. ACM Press (2007)
8. Westeyn, T.L.: Designing toys with automatic play characterization for supporting the assessment of a child's development. In: Workshop at IDC 2008 (2008)
9. Roy, D.: The Human Speechome Project. Cognitive Science, 192-196 (2006)
10. Fell, H., Cress, C., MacAuslan, J., Ferrier, L.: Visibabble for reinforcement of early vocalization. In: Proc. of Accessibility and Computing (2004)
11. Kientz, J.A., Abowd, G.D.: KidCam: toward an effective technology for the capture of children's moments of interest. Pervasive 115–132 (2009)
12. Foucault, B.E.: Designing technology for growing families, in:Technology@Intel Magazine (2005)
13. http://www.phidget.com

A Low-Cost ZigBee-Based Gateway System
for Indoor Localization and Identification of a Person

Claudio Guerra, Francesco Montalto, Valentina Bianchi, Ilaria De Munari,
and Paolo Ciampolini

Dip. di Ingegneria dell'Informazione, Parco Area delle Scienze 181/A, 43124 Parma, Italy
{claudio.guerra,francesco.montalto}@studenti.unipr.it,
{valentina.bianchi,ilaria.demunari,paolo.ciampolini}@unipr.it

Abstract. The European population is becoming older and older, causing AT (Assistive Technology) and AAL (Ambient Assisted Living) topics to become increasingly important. A ZigBee based low-cost home automation system named CARDEA has been developed at the University of Parma, with the aim to allow elderly people to live their lives autonomously and independently. In this paper a new feature is presented, named CARDEAGate: a gateway monitoring system which allows to detect crossing of a doorway or a predefined gateway and, if the person is carrying a wearable ZigBee sensor, to identify he/she. This technology is very useful to supervise the habits of a not completely self-sufficient person monitoring the access to particular locations or tracking he/she in order to execute a long term behavioral analysis.

Keywords: ZigBee, Indoor localization, Identification, AAL, AT.

1 Introduction

During the last 30 years a steady increase of the life expectancy and a decrease of the birth rate has been recorded in Europe [1]. The combination of these two factors have led to a strong increase of the population average age, that is expected to become more and more marked in the near future: in the next 20 years the number of people over 80 years old is in fact estimated to raise by 50% or more [2]. Consequently, our social structure is expected to change, with older adults becoming the majority class. Increasing needs of care is therefore to be faced, to allow elderly people to remain independent and autonomous as long as possible, also allowing them to actively contribute to the community life. In this context, support is expected from AT (Assistive Technology) and AAL (Ambient Assisted Living) research in fostering the "ageing at home" paradigm, according to which the living environment itself plays an active role in preserving autonomy and independency. ICT technologies can be exploited to this purpose, having large relevance in both economic and social aspects of our society.

At DoTALab, the Domotics and Assistive Technology Laboratory at the Department of Information Engineering (University of Parma, Italy) an Ambient Assisted Living system named CARDEA [3] has been developed, merging in the same framework environmental, control functions and personal and health monitoring features.

L. Pecchia et al. (Eds.): IWAAL 2014, LNCS 8868, pp. 179–186, 2014.

The system is based on the Ethernet standard for the wired part while the wireless part is based on ZigBee protocol [4], due to its low cost, versatility and low power consumption. CARDEA handles the usual features of a home automation system (lights, windows and temperature control) and deals with safety and security (floods or gas leaks, intrusions). A small wearable device, called MuSA (Multi-Sensor Assistant [5]) can be interfaced to CARDEA to monitor vital signs of the home residents (body temperature, heart and breath rates) and to detect falls. An important feature of such system is the localization capability of the people inside the house. Localization information can be exploited to discriminate, in a multi-user environment, if the user is actually interacting with the system at a given touch-point, in order to personalize system response and adaption. In specific situations, tracking location can be used to provide accurate alarm information (for instance, within an assisted-living facility, fall alarm can include precise location of the fallen person) or to prevent hazards (e.g. wandering of a cognitive-impaired person toward dangerous areas). Besides such primary purposes, the aim is to exploit localization information for behavioral analysis (BA) i.e. the extraction of behavioral patterns from AAL systems activity logs, to provide an indirect monitoring of the health status [6]. Changes in user's habits can be meaningful to many respects (functional decline, adherence and effectiveness of medical therapies, need of specific support, etc.) making available to the healthcare systems a new tool for health assessment, based on a long-term, objective observation perspective, complementary and supporting to the caregiver in day-by-day evaluation. Other wearable devices are being studied to improve the system capabilities in terms of BA [7]. Behavioral analysis is inherently based on the fusion of data coming from multiple sensors: within this framework, localization information is relevant in itself (as an inherent behavioral component) and as a complement of other data sources (again allowing for attributing an action detected by any environmental sensor to a specific user).

In this paper, we discuss a novel approach to user localization and identification, particularly suited for behavioral analysis purposes. In general, indoor location is a complex and multi-faceted issue and the scientific community is still actively debating on it, looking for a way to implement reliable and low cost solutions [8,9]. It is worth to be emphasized, though, that the behavioral analysis application we are aiming at does not require high accuracy and spatial resolution in user localization, and may inherently rely on cooperation among different system components. The MuSA platform, in particular, includes an accelerometer, a gyroscope and a compass, this making possible to implement an inertial navigation system. Inertial navigation is based on double integration of acceleration components to obtain actual position, starting from a known reference position. This solution is cheap and accurate in the short term, but integration errors tend to stockpile over time, causing progressive drift of the solution and thus needing a periodic recalibration: the drift can be zeroed whenever the trajectory touches any known location [10]. To provide the MuSA inertial navigation system with such a feature, in this paper a new component of the CARDEA system is introduced, consisting of a low-cost gateway monitoring system. CARDEAGate allows to detect crossing of a doorway or a predefined gateway, and, interacting with MuSA, the identification of him/her.

It has the basic functionality of any "sight-line" sensor (e.g., infrared barriers), detecting any person crossing the gateway line (regardless of wearing a MuSA device), however posing much less stringent constraints in terms of placement, alignment, maintenance. Wearing a MuSA further "active" interaction modes with the passing user are enabled: user's identification and zeroing the drift error in inertial navigation. CARDEAGate features low cost and is completely ZigBee based, so that it can be straightforwardly integrated (not needing ad-hoc hardware solutions) not only with MuSA and CARDEA, but with any ZigBee-based system.

2   The Gateway System

The CARDEAGate structure is sketched in Fig. 1: it is composed by a couple of Zig-Bee transceivers, named Ga and Gb, continuously communicating with each other and mounted on the two sides of a door or wherever there is a monitoring need.

Unlike optical-based sensors, CARDEAGate does not need line-of-sight visibility, so it can easily be embedded into doorframes, home furniture or stand behind curtains and thin (and non-metallic) walls. This makes the system also less intrusive, and allows for smooth integration into most home environments. The gateway system exploits the absorption of a part of radio signal power caused by the body of the person crossing it [11]. To identify a person, the MuSA device has to be worn. Ga and Gb exchange a message every 200ms and monitor the RSSI (Received Signal Strength Index [12]): if a sudden loss is observed, a walking across the gateway is detected. When this happens the identification procedure is started: Ga and Gb transmit an identification request to the MuSAs in the network and send the RSSI of the replies to the ZigBee network coordinator connected to a PC, which finds out the MuSA crossed the gateway and shows it on a friendly UI (User Interface, Fig. 2). It is possible to load a picture of a map in the UI, to easily monitor the movements of the MuSAs in the network (in the picture the map represents a part of the Information Engineering Department in which DoTALab is located).

The tables and the Logger contain the information about the devices in the network, the detections and the identifications. The dots on the map represent the location of the gateways: once a passage is detected, the corresponding gateway is highlighted.

Fig. 1. The CARDEAGate structure

As already mentioned, indoor location is a very complex topic and reliable solutions are still to be found. Lots of studies have been made involving RSSI [13,14] or tomography [15,16] to locate a person, but, to the best of our knowledge, no study so far has been presented based on the absorption of the human body and the RSSI evaluation between the nodes.

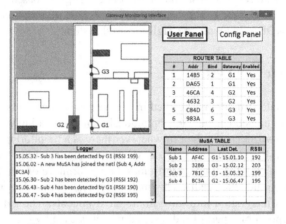

Fig. 2. The gateway monitoring user interface

3   Detection Experiments

The detection capability of the system was tested and some important features were evaluated: a) the variation of the detection rate with the distance between Ga and Gb, b) the influence of the crossing position (in the middle of the gate or closer to one of the two devices) on the detection rate c) the incidence of the presence of a person close to the gateway causing false positives. Six different distances between Ga and Gb were considered (from 0.5m to 3m with 0.5m steps), and for each distance four tests were made: crossing the gateway in the middle (Test 1), crossing it close to Ga or Gb (Test 2), walking parallel to the gateway and perpendicular to the normal pathway (Test 3) and walking on the outer side of the gateway and parallel to the normal pathway (at a distance of about 0.5m) (Test 4). In Fig 3, a sketch of the tests is depicted: the arrows represent the direction in which the person was walking. The first two tests were conceived to check the detection rate, while the other two were made to evaluate the percentage of false positives. For each test, 50 tries were made. The gateway was placed in the middle of an empty room in order to avoid interference with furniture or other objects that could interact with the waves (only metal objects should have a major impact on the propagation of the waves, but any solid object in general can contribute to create some reflections and\or refractions of the signals), at a high of 1m.

In the first and second test, the 100% of the passages was correctly detected in each of the six different distances between Ga and Gb. It is important to underline that when the distance between the devices was small, the passage was always detected

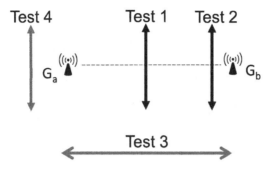

Fig. 3. A sketch explaining the tests performed

while the person was actually crossing the imaginary optical line between the antennas, while as the distance increased, the passage was detected also when the person was a little bit behind or a little bit above the line-of-sight. As expected, the distance between Ga and Gb affects the signal path, but not the detection rate, at least in the range used in these tests.

The aim of the third test was to find the lower distance from the gateway that could give false positives. This resulted to be pretty hard to find accurately, since the human body doesn't have a regular shape , and it is difficult, for a person, to walk on a perfect straight line. However, a rough evaluation has been attempted: the limit range grows with the distance between Ga and Gb, at 0.5m it is between 15-20cm, while at 3.0m it is above 60cm. This is consistent with the changes in the signal path observed during the first two tests.

The results of the fourth test show that walking in the outer side of the gateway does not lead to false positive independently from the distance of the two devices.

After that, a gateway was installed on an actual door (110cm wide) to see if the success rate was affected by the real scenario, and also on this case the 100% of the passages were correctly detected. Subsequently, the third test was replied in the real scenario and the limit distance to have a false positive resulted to be about 0.3m. These experiments proved that the system is efficiently capable of recognize the crossing of the gateway without generating many false positives, and that the interferences caused by walls and furniture don't impact the detection rate. Consequently, the following step was to test the identification algorithm.

4 Identification Experiments

As mentioned before, a person has to carry a MuSA device in order to be identified. Since MuSA is a battery-operated device using a sleep-awake cycle to reduce power consumption (as specified in the ZigBee protocol [17]), it can receive messages only when it is awake (every 1s from the last message): its messages are stored in a ZigBee router until MuSA is ready to receive them. For this reason it is impossible to communicate with a MuSA device using a 1-hop message, necessary to evaluate the correct RSSI value. Taking into account this, the following procedure has been implemented:

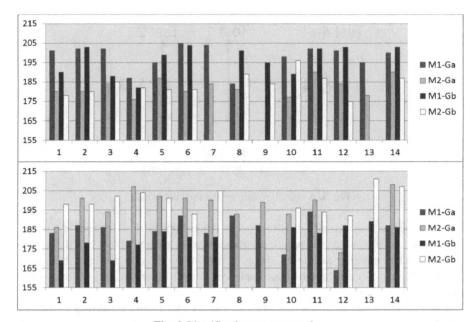

Fig. 4. Identification process results

once a passage is detected by a gateway, G_a and G_b send to each MuSA in the network a message, to which they reply in 1-hop mode. Then G_a and G_b send the RSSIs of the replies and the ID of the MuSA who replied to the coordinator, who passes the information to a PC which finally finds the gateway who detected the passage and identifies the MuSA.

A first test has been executed, in which a person was walking across the gateway (placed on an actual door) wearing a MuSA (M_1) and another person, with a second MuSA (M_2), was standing at a distance of about 3m. The same test was repeated inverting the roles, so that M_2 was the device crossing the gateway and M_1 was the one standing at some distance. For each situation, 14 tries were made. Fig. 4 shows the results, showing the RSSI of G_a and G_b from M_1 and M_2 for each of the 28 tries.

Seeing the results a simple decider has been implemented, which selects the MuSA replying with the greatest RSSI as the one who crossed the gateway.

The previous experiment was then repeated to test the decider. A rate of success above 97% has been obtained, since only one error (i.e. choosing the wrong MuSA) has been made on 44 tries.

5   Multiple Gateways Experiments

A test of the system has been conducted in a more realistic and complex situation. Three different gateways (G1, G2, G3) were placed on three actual doors and four subjects were involved, each one of them wearing a different MuSA (the number of the gateways and of the MuSAs in this test were not chosen because of a limit of the system but just not to have huge differences from the previous situation): they had to walk through a path in which they had to enter and exit from each room where the gateways were placed, so that for each person six passages should have been detected, two for every gateway. In Fig. 5 a map with gateway placement and one with the itinerary are shown. The other three people that were waiting for their turn about two meters inside the room where G1 was placed (crosses on the map): this was made to monitor the possible interferences between different MuSAs. A success rate of 87.5% has been obtained, that is a positive result considering the setup conditions, the simplicity of the decider and that this system is conceived to be used in a behavioral analysis context. Integrating it with a tracking system based on inertial sensors and using a more accurate decider, taking into account the user position history, will probably improve overall performances.

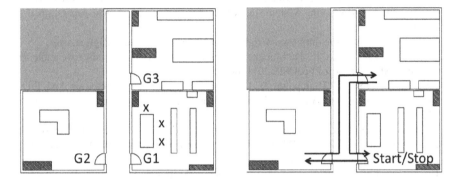

Fig. 5. Gateway placement and itinerary of the experiments

6   Conclusions

In this paper a ZigBee-based gateway system has been presented, which allows to detect the passage of a person across a predefined gateway and to identify that person if he is carrying a ZigBee device (MuSA). This system is highly innovative since it allows the detection and the identification using the same technology used by the devices adopted for home automation purposes, without the need of ad-hoc hardware, leading to a very low cost maintaining high reliability. A gateway system may be very helpful in a assistive context, for example to detect when a not self-sufficient person reaches a place where he/she needs help or should not go for his/her safety, or to improve a behavioral analysis system.

In this paper a first implementation of the gateway system is shown, that is yet reliable since a success rate above 97% is obtained, in terms of detecting a passage and identifying the correct person between two of them.

Future works will lead to improve the decider (the algorithm to identify the correct person) and the signal transmission process between the devices, in order to improve the reliability even in crowded or more complex areas. The final goal to be achieved is to merge this system to a tracking system based on inertial sensors to create an accurate low-cost indoor positioning system, or to use it as a standalone monitoring system for sensitive areas. Both this uses are helpful in order to execute a behavioral analysis of a person.

References

1. European Commission, Active ageing and solidarity between generations (2012), http://epp.eurostat.ec.europa.eu/cache/ITY_OFFPUB/KS-EP-11-001/EN/KS-EP-11-001-EN.PDF
2. European Commission, Population statistics at regional level (2013), http://epp.eurostat.ec.europa.eu/statistics_explained/index.php/Population_statistics_at_regional_level
3. Ciampolini, P., De Munari, I., Bianchi, V., Matrella, G., Grossi, F.: An Assistive Home Automation and Monitoring System. In: ICCE 2008 Digest of technical papers, pp. 1–2 (2008)
4. ZigBee Alliance website, http://www.zigbee.org/About/UnderstandingZigBee.aspx
5. Bianchi, V., Ciampolini, P., De Munari, I., Grossi, F.: MuSA: a multisensor wearable device for AAL. In: Proc. of FedCSIS 2011, pp. 375–380 (2011)
6. Losardo, A., Grossi, F., Ciampolini, P., De Munari, I., Matrella, G.: Exploiting AAL Environment for Behavioral Analysis. Assistive technologies: from research to practice 33, 1121–1125 (2013)
7. Affanni, A., Chiorboli, G.: Wearable Instrument for Skin Potential Response Analysis in AAL Applications. In: 20th IMEKO TC-4 International Symposium, Measurement of Electrical Quantities, 418-904-1-DR
8. Gu, Y., Lo, A., Niemegeers, I.: A Survey of Indoor Positioning Systems for Wireless Personal Networks. IEEE Communications Surveys & Tutorials 11(1), 13–32 (2009)
9. Kundra, I., Ekler, P.: The Summary of Indoor Navigation Possibilities Considering Mobile Environment. In: 3rd Eastern European Regional Conference on the Engineering of Computer Based Systems, pp. 165–166 (2013)
10. O. J. Woodman.: An introduction to inertial navigation. University of Cambridge technical report, 696 (2007)
11. Wilson, J., Patwari, N.: Radio Tomographic Imaging with Wireless Networks. IEEE Transactions on Mobile Computing 9(10), 621–632 (2010)
12. Parker, S.J., Hal, J., Kim, W.: Adaptive Filtering for Indoor Localization using ZIGBEE RSSI and LQI Measurement. Adaptive Filtering Applications 14, 305–324 (2007)
13. Honkavirta, V., Perala, T., Ali-Loytty, S., Piché, R.: A Comparative Survey of WLAN Location Fingerprinting Methods. In: 6th Workshop on Positioning, Navigation and Communication, pp. 243–251 (2009)
14. Chan, C.L., Baciu, G., Mak, S.C.: Using Wi-Fi Signal Strength to Localize in Wireless Sensor Networks. In: International Conference on Communications and Mobile Computing, pp. 538–542 (2009)
15. Wilson, J., Patwari, N.: A Fade-Level Skew-Laplace Signal Strength Model for Device-Free Localization with Wireless Networks. IEEE Transactions on Mobile Computing 11(6), 947–958 (2012)
16. Wagner, B., Patwari, N., Timmermann, D.: Passive RFID Tomographic Imaging for Device-Free User Localization. In: 9th Workshop on Positioning, Navigation and Communication, pp. 120–125 (2012)
17. http://www.zigbee.org/Standards/Downloads.aspx

Method, Design and Implementation
of a Self-checking Indoor Localization System

Fabio Veronese, Daniel Soleimani Pour, Sara Comai, Matteo Matteucci,
and Fabio Salice

Politecnico di Milano Department of Electronics, Informatics and Bioengineering
- Polo Regionale di Como - Via Anzani 42, 22100, Como, Italy
{name.surname}@polimi.it

Abstract. RF-based localization systems have been deeply investigated
due to their flexibility and limited costs. These systems, when designed
to support the independent life, are generally mission critical and they
should be designed to be dependable. In this paper, we present a method
to provide human localization systems with concurrent fault detection. We
focus on two possible sources of faults: natural hardware (e.g., empty battery, faulty components) and human-made (e.g., device not worn). The
adopted strategy relies on two independent measurement systems and on
a fault detection apparatus. We present an implemented case-study, were
the collected data are temporally annotated, processed, compared and, in
case of anomalies, the system activates a notification, eventually to trigger
an intervention.

Keywords: Indoor Human Localization, Home Automation, Assistive
Technology, Smart Home, Dependability, Fault Detection, Human-made
Faults.

1 Introduction

The widespread and well-studied localization systems are the basis for context-
aware services, but they are being widely used also as assistive aids: a tool
able to share the position of a fragile person with his/her relatives, can play
a significant role to satisfy the need for security. This need is certainly one of
the most important needs, standing at the second level of Maslow's hierarchy
[1]. This applies both to fragile people (such as elderly, people suffering from
small impairments), who need their family to be watching over them, and to
their families, who want to be sure that their loved ones are in safe conditions.
When systems are designed for some crucial purposes, they are often referred to
as Critical Systems: their failure can result in significant losses, physical damage
or even threats of human life. In particular a Mission Critical Systems, is a
system where a failure can degrade or prevent the successful completion of an
intended operation [2]. In our assistive system for human indoor localization, we
need dependability features. While most of the design effort is often devoted to
manage natural faults, i.e. those generated by components of the system (e.g.,
Hardware or Software), we will focus also on those generated by the users.

L. Pecchia et al. (Eds.): IWAAL 2014, LNCS 8868, pp. 187–194, 2014.

2   Related Work

Nowadays several technologies for Indoor Human Localization (IHL), based on various physical principles, are available [3,4,5]. Radio Frequency (RF) waves are widely used, in cost-effective and flexible localization systems, by leveraging several different methods. Looking at different technologies inside the RF category, system can leverage Radio Frequency Identification (RFID), Wireless Local Area Network (WLAN), Bluetooth, Wireless Sensor Netwok (WSN), Ultra Wide Band (UWB), TV broadcasts (UHF) or mobile phone communications (UMTS, GPRS, etc.) [4].

Wireless RF technologies rely on an uncontrolled and highly shared medium: many possible happenings (e.g., interference, shadowing, multipath) inevitably lead to inaccuracies and errors. The most diffused approach to increase the accuracy of localization, is to leverage two or more physical quantities and combine them to obtain improvements both in precision and reliability [4].

A dense literature has been developed about methods to exclude wrong measurements thanks to redundancy, when dealing with localization and lateration. Sturza developed a method in 1988 [6], and since then several techniques improved or leveraged those principles, but mainly in GPS (Global Positioning System) applications and outdoor environments. Three conventional versions of receiver autonomous integrity monitoring (RAIM) methods are the chi-square test, the horizontal protection level test (HPL) and the multi-hypothesis solution separation test (MHSS) [7]. Do et Al. [7] used these techniques within an hybrid TV-GPS-WLAN localization system, facing multi-faults conditions. In indoor settings, anyway, there are few examples of works explicitly devoted to dependability. YunFei et Al. [8] use the same principle (of redundancy) to identify faulty measurements. This is used not to exclude the measure from the estimation procedure, but to warn the user that the measurements are not reliable.

3   System Architecture

When designing and implementing such systems, costs are considered extremely important, as well as installation effort and maintenance. A very precise and extensive system, with a price too high to be affordable by the user is useless. Furthermore the system must be accepted by the host person, especially in terms of not feeling invaded by unpleasant devices. This can be respected by preferring wireless technology, non visual sensors, small and/or not visible devices. This philosophy drove our decisions, keeping our aim to build best effort useful system. Its subsystems are an RF localization system for healthcare indoor environment named LAURA, an off-the-shelf modular wireless Home Automation (HA) system, Z-wave, and a Fault Detection apparatus based on Esper.

3.1   The Indoor RF Localization Subsystem

LAURA [9,10] is a localization system designed for people tracking in indoor environments, based on a 2.4GHz WSN. Originally developed by Lim et AL. [11], the localization method relies on the RSSI between a mobile node of the WSN and the other location-known fixed nodes (anchors). It takes advantage of an adaptative calibration by considering the RSS measurements also among fixed anchors. These features make the LAURA system an ideal candidate for our settings: it is a critical mission assistive system, wireless, battery powered and no configuration is needed, making it particularly suitable for home environment. In the setting presented by Redondi et Al. [9,10], it still lacks any method to provide dependability.

3.2   The Home Automation Subsystem

Ambient Assisted Living (AAL) and Home Automation (HA) technologies are nowadays spreading in our cities, bringing comfort and the services of a pervasive home control. Though they also provides a great opportunity to monitor and assist fragile people in their homes. The market of such products is highly competitive: Saidinejad et Al. [12] present an iterative method for the choice of suitable HA technology, given a set of constraints, considering also financial aspects. The application of their approach to a more general setting of a reliable system, providing not-invasive AAL and home monitoring, identified Z-wave and 6LowPAN as good candidates for our case study. Between them we adopted Z-wave, for the lower costs and its orientation toward home environments.

Z-wave [13] has a very large set of different functional devices. Two sensor types were selected: PIR (Passive InfraRed) sensors and Door/Window contact sensors. The first detects the human motion (with a persistence of 10s) in a range up to 5m, with a view angle of 360°, when ceiling mounted, or 10m and 110°, when wall mounted. The Door/Window contact sensor (or simply DWS), has a very common design: the presence of a person can be inferred when the sensor status toggles (opening or closing).

3.3   Fault Detection Apparatus

The information collected from the two subsystems is numerical and has a strong temporal connotation. This kind of *data stream* is not extremely complex, and has not the gigantic size that usually characterizes Streams of Complex Event [14], still the processing engine needs a certain flexibility to implement the introduced model. Furthermore, we want our approach to be potentially applied to more complex settings (e.g., higher sampling frequencies, devices and/or subsystems number, problem complexity). Among the available Complex Event Processing (CEP) Systems we identified Esper [15] as a candidate for our study. Esper is an open source *event series analysis and event correlation engine (CEP)* [15], able to recognize rich situations in event series and to trigger custom actions. It is designed for high volume event processing, where millions of events coming in would be impossible to record using classical database architectures. In our setting, we have adopted Esper's Java background to represent the system model and EPL queries to implement the Fault Detection apparatus.

4 System and Fault Modeling

Aiming for dependability and, in particular, to the identification of system miss-behaviors, it is crucial to analyze the possible faults. In the following we work under the assumptions that firmware and software are flawless and only a single fault can affect the system.

4.1 Faults Scenarios (FS)

We can define separately Human-made Faults Scenarios (HFS) and Natural Fault Scenarios (NFS). The most important HFS are: (a) the inhabitant is not wearing the localization device; (b) the inhabitant damages the device.

NFS are related to devices and components wearing, etc., we can report few examples such as: (c) A device (HA or IHL) is not reachable (e.g., out of the WSN range); (d) A sensor (HA or IHL) is defective or malicious; (e) The localization mobile device cannot reach enough anchors to perform a valid localization; (f) A device (HA or IHL) runs out of power.

Furthermore both the IHL and the HA subsystems are able to provide specific information used to detect simpler fault conditions:

E_{L1} - An anchor device is not reachable anymore.

E_{L2} - Not enough anchors are detected.

E_{L3} - The user device is not reachable.

E_{Z1} - Device has run out of power.

E_{Z2} - Device is not reachable.

These more common (and simpler) errors are managed by the systems in a different and more traditional way, and, being not related to the model based methodology introduced with this work, they will not be further tested.

4.2 System Modeling

To approach the fault scenarios hereby presented we decided to apply a model based method. As stated by Isermann [16] it is possible to detect a fault *by using the dependencies between different measurable signals*; to this aim it is necessary to build a model of the dependency itself. Given the measured real-world quantities and a model, reproducing the expected system behavior, it is possible to generate features (e.g., states, parameters or residuals coming from the system model). If their values do not comply with the nominal characteristics of the system, a fault is detected [16]. In the presented settings we have two subsystems (LAURA localization and Zwave HA): in the following we will model the relation linking their (shared) input and their measurable quantities.

If we consider the Localization problem, an IHL subsystem is able to return the estimation of the person's position. Knowing the precision of this estimation, we can fix a threshold value δ_{th} (maximum acceptable error): we can represent the output of the system as a circular area, centered around the estimation itself, with radius identified by the maximum acceptable error. Anyway areas not reachable (e.g., behind walls) should be rejected even if in the acceptable range. It is immediate to state that the IHL system is working properly if the real position of the target person falls inside this area.

Concerning the HA system, we have that activations of sensors are caused by the person's presence, according to its position and interaction with the environment. To model this behavior, we can identify a sensor-specific activation area: given the position of the sensor, its orientation, its maximum interaction angle and distance, we can define a precise region of space (excluding again not reachable areas). In fault-free conditions the sensor activates only if the person is inside this area, and he/she interacts properly with the sensor. This do not exclude that the person is inside that area, without activating the sensor. Finally, considering the PIR sensors dynamics (blind to still person, 10s persistence), it is opportune to consider that the person must be inside the last active PIR sensor's area. This holds true even if none of these sensor is active: in case the person stops in a sensor's area, letting the device turn off, to exit that area he/she must necessarily move, activating again the sensor.

During the usage it is not possible to obtain the real position of the person, but the systems are independently providing information about the position of the person. In particular he/she must stand into the area identified by the localization, but also into the last active PIR sensor and the active DWSs ones. This comparison is performed by the Fault Detection Apparatus, by checking that the areas admit a not empty intersection. As this condition is not respected a fault can be detected.

5   Experiments

The tests were held in some rooms of a Politecnico di Milano building in Como. As illustrated in Figure 1, nineteen fixed LAURA anchors and 7 Z-wave devices were distributed along the walls of a portion of one floor. One device was worn by a tester simulating the inhabitant, to track his movements.

To detect the human presence, four PIRs were mounted in three rooms and one corridor. Three DWSs were mounted on top of doors to monitor their states. Data gathered through these sensors were transmitted to the HA system. The activation, which were stored on the Z-wave controller, were fetched via an ad hoc developed module.

The model described in the previous sections can be adapted to the subsystem by tuning a specific set of parameters. In our settings the localization error of LAURA was studied, determining the value of δ_{th}=3m, which is respected in the 84% of the estimations. Concerning HA sensors, the values of maximum range provided by the producers of each device were reduced to the 80%: wall mounted PIRs had a maximum detection distance of 10m, thus r_{pw}=8m, similarly ceiling mounted ones had a reported range of 5m, which were reduced to r_{pc}=4m. While for DWS, activation areas were assumed to be identified by the human arm length, thus by a radius r_d=1.5m.

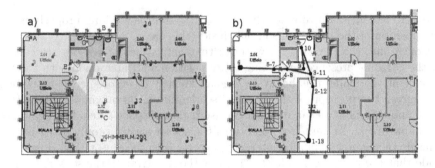

Fig. 1. Testing environment and deployed sensors. In the map a) are visible the test areas and rooms (colored ones), LAURA fixed devices (blue numbered dots) and Z-wave devices (labeled with capital letters). PIRs (A-D) have corresponding colored activation areas. In the map b) the path followed by the testers during experimental acquisitions. The gray areas represent the not sensorized space.

5.1   Test Protocol

As illustrated in Figure 1, the trajectory for the path was polygonal: the inhabitant walked along the predefined path (designed to trigger the available sensors), with a constant speed. Since PIRs have time limitations, as mentioned previously in (*Sensor Types*), two lingering zones were added, where the tester remained still for a while in order to be undetected by the PIRs, highlighted in Figure 1 by greater dots (identified by numbers 1-13 and 6). The average test duration was about 3min, the overall duration of the tests was approximately 18min.

In order to model faults in the environment, two different policies were applied: *Forgotten Device* - the worn device is left in a predefined location, while the tester continues its trajectory; *Blinded PIR* - A PIR sensor is blinded in order not to detect the user, but being fully operative.

6   Results

The first run of experiments were in fault-free conditions. The collected data revealed no significant fault detection. As reported in Figure 2, an initial error

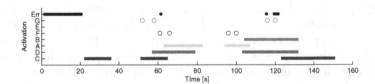

Fig. 2. Experiment in fault-free conditions. The brief and instantaneous fault activations are due to IHL system inaccuracies, which is concordant to the 84% precision threshold imposed. Letters refer to sensors as in Figure 1.

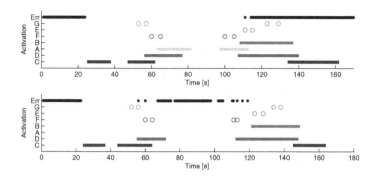

Fig. 3. Experiment in faulty conditions. Testing the Forgotten Device (top), the device is left in position 6 (Figure 1) along the trajectory. While, with Blind PIR sensor A (bottom), as the tester enters the room (point 5-7 in Figure 1) the Error is risen. The sensor's A green activation, present in the other figures, here is missing.

condition is risen and few short-duration error are visible (see first line in the figure). The initial fault is detected since no sensor has been activated yet. While the brief fault detections (e.g., around $t=120$s) are due to localization inaccuracies. Since we accepted $p=84\%$ when defining δ_{th}, it is possible that the actual position of the person is outside of the estimated area. In those cases, the fault has punctual duration (up to 5s) and can be neglected.

When we emulated the forgotten device condition, the system result was an expected fault detection. As visible in Figure 3 as the inhabitant moves away from the device, left in position 6 (Figure 1) and activates other sensors, the fault detection response is sharp and stable.

If we blind a sensor, the system result is again an evident fault condition. As visible in Figure 3 we blinded PIR A (Figure 1): as the inhabitant enters the room (path from 5 to 7 in Figure 1), the fault is detected. In this conditions the fault detection is less sharp due to the same inaccuracies in localization, as already explained for fault-free conditions.

7   Conclusions

In this work we presented the method, design and implementation of a dependable best-effort IHL system. The system relies on two independent subsystems, whose result data are jointly checked by a fault detection apparatus. The proposed method is based on the definition of a model representing each of the two subsystems, defining a joint consistency condition.

The obtained experimental results showed the validity of our approach, correctly reporting errors in fault injected conditions. Thus, even under some limitations due to localization system inaccuracies, our approach enables the dependable localization of a person inside an instrumented house, recognizing both hardware and human-made faults.

8   Future Work

More tests will be performed in controlled environments, but it will be interesting to investigate the system behavior also in an actual home environment.

Further work will include the dependable IHL for many persons, and investigate the possibility of locate the fault on the system.

References

1. Maslow, A.: Motivation and personality (1954)
2. Fowler, K.: Mission-critical and safety-critical development. IEEE Instrumentation & Measurement Magazine 7(4), 52–59 (2004)
3. Torres-Solis, J., Falk, T., Chau, T.: A review of indoor localization technologies: towards navigational assistance for topographical disorientation. Ambient Intelligence, 51–84 (2010)
4. Deak, G., Curran, K., Condell, J.: A survey of active and passive indoor localisation systems. Computer Communications (2012)
5. Franceschini, F., Galetto, M., Maisano, D., Mastrogiacomo, L.: A review of localization algorithms for distributed wireless sensor networks in manufacturing. International Journal of Computer Integrated Manufacturing 22(7), 698–716 (2009)
6. Sturza, M.A.: Navigation system integrity monitoring using redundant measurements. Navigation 35(4), 1988–1989 (1988)
7. Do, J.-Y., Rabinowitz, M., Enge, P.: Multi-fault tolerant raim algorithm for hybrid gps/tv positioning. In: Proc. ION Institute of Navigation National Technical Meeting (2001)
8. Park, J., Choi, M., Zu, Y., Lee, J.: Indoor localization system in a multi-block workspace. Robotica 28(3), 397–403 (2010)
9. Redondi, A., Chirico, M., Borsani, L., Cesana, M., Tagliasacchi, M.: An integrated system based on wireless sensor networks for patient monitoring, localization and tracking. Ad Hoc Networks 11(1), 39–53 (2013)
10. Redondi, A., Tagliasacchi, M., Cesana, M., Borsani, L., Tarrio, P., Salice, F.: Laura - localization and ubiquitous monitoring of patients for health care support. In: 2010 IEEE 21st International Symposium on Personal, indoor and mobile radio communications workshops (PIMRC Workshops), pp. 218–222. IEEE (2010)
11. Lim, H., Kung, L.C., Hou, J.C., Luo, H.: Zero-configuration indoor localization over ieee 802.11 wireless infrastructure. Wireless Networks 16(2), 405–420 (2010)
12. Saidinejad, H., Radaelli, J., Veronese, F., Salice, F.: Mixed Technical and Market Evaluation of Home Automation Networks for AAL Solutions. Assistive Technology: From Research to Practice of Assistive Technology Research Series, vol. 33, pp. 865–870 (2013)
13. Z-Wave Alliance: Official website (2013), http://www.z-wavealliance.org/
14. Stuckenschmidt, H., Ceri, S., Della Valle, E., van Harmelen, F.: Towards expressive stream reasoning. In: Proceedings of the Dagstuhl Seminar on Semantic Aspects of Sensor Networks, p. 241 (2010)
15. EsperTech: Official website (2013), http://www.espertech.com
16. Isermann, R.: Model-based fault-detection and diagnosis–status and applications. Annual Reviews in control 29(1), 71–85 (2005)

Wearable Computing to Support Activities of Daily Living

Colin Shewell, Chris D. Nugent, Mark Donnelly, and Haiying Wang

University of Ulster, Computer Science Research Institute
and School of Computing and Mathematics, University of Ulster,
Newtownabbey, Co. Antrim, BT37 0QB, UK
{shewell-c}@email.ulster.ac.uk,
{cd.nugent,mp.donnelly,hy.wang}@ulster.ac.uk

Abstract. This paper proposes an approach to determining an occupant's indoor location through the use of machine vision techniques combined with wearable computing. Based on "off-the-shelf" machine vision tools a system is introduced to obtain a user's indoor location through the detection of "reference" objects in their immediate environment. This information is subsequently cross-referenced with a knowledge base containing details of which rooms reference markers are located in. Details of the architecture required to realize the solution are presented which also accommodates for the fusion of information sources overcoming the heterogeneous nature of data gathered from multiple sources within the environment. The solution can be used to provide context aware assistance with Activities of Daily Living to those who may normally require assistance in their day-to-day life hence allowing them to live independently at home for longer.

1   Introduction

One of the most important achievements of the 20th century has been the remarkable increase in life expectancy throughout the world. This has, however, resulted in the oldest group of society (aged 65 plus) being the most rapidly expanding segment of society [3]. The burden being placed on health care systems to address health problems associated with an aging society will continue to increase as this segment of the population continues to grow [3]. One potential solution to ease this is postulated to be through the use of an automated "smart environment" which affords occupants who would normally require the assistance of carers, to be supported within their own home through the use of technology based solutions and gain a larger degree of independence. A smart environment can be defined as being one that is "able to acquire and apply knowledge about the environment and its inhabitants in order to improve their experience in that environment" [4]. It is in the purest sense an example of ubiquitous and pervasive computing which represents the idea of "computing everywhere", in other words, making computing and communication effectively transparent.

L. Pecchia et al. (Eds.): IWAAL 2014, LNCS 8868, pp. 195–202, 2014.

Wearable technology offers new opportunities within pervasive computing, allowing data to be continuously collected from a user and their immediate environment. Such a solution is particularly useful to support intelligent applications within smart environments where contextual information is required. Contextual information includes the "user's physical, social, emotional or informational state" [5]. This information allows an applications behavior to be altered to the users current situation to provide task relevant information to the user and cannot be gleaned by any other means. This paper proposes a solution to facilitate indoor localization through the use of a single "always on" wearable camera. Location is determined using machine vision techniques that identify "reference" objects within an environment and cross references these against a knowledge base that indicates which rooms these reference markers are located in.

The current work also aims to address one of the main challenges faced within smart environments; namely the heterogeneous nature of the data. Each sensing device within the environment generates data in a different format. This can create difficulties when data is being exchanged and processed between different system in addition to limiting the opportunity for data to be reused and compared [10]. This challenge is further compounded given that there is no single common standard being used [10]. HomeML, an XML based open format, offers significant potential for solving the problems caused by the heterogeneous nature of data generated within a smart environment [11]. In Section 2 a review of the related work is presented prior to discussing the proposed system architecture in Section 3. A discussion of the current limitations and what the system hopes to achieve will be presented in Section 4.

2   Related Work

Gómez-Romero *et al.* developed a system that used multiple fixed cameras placed within a smart environment which allowed them to detect objects, including people, in the camera's field of view [6]. As the system was able to determine between people and objects it also allowed simple scene recognition using simple rules such as touch or enclosing (determined by overlapping boundary boxes) to establish which object the occupant was interacting with [6]. Whilst this technique was effective there were limitations with this approach. Due to the static nature of the cameras occlusion was an issue and, while they tried to overcome this problem by reassigning the size and position of the boundary box when a size variation over 80% was detected, this did not solve the problem of total occlusion [6]. One further problem with static systems in general is due to the static nature of the cameras multiple cameras are required in each room to attempt to cover all angles, which still may not be possible, driving up the cost in terms of retro-fitting the users environment. Multiple occupancy is also an issue as cameras can only detect if a person is present or not and cannot distinguish between multiple occupants.

Kurze and Roselius proposed an open architecture and runtime environment for mobile augmented reality applications that would allow the monitoring of environmental information to provide context aware support [9]. They also provided an example system consisting of wearable smart glasses along with a facial recognition application. Their proposed architecture did not, however, take account of other external sensors that may be placed within a smart environment.

Kang et al. proposed an approach to identify and segment objects from scenes that are commonly encountered when completing Activities of Daily Living (ADLs). They used a bottom-up segmentation approach and extracted object candidates as groups of mutually consistent segments [8]. Whilst this work could detect objects in the scene it could not determine what activity the occupant was performing. The approach has been built on by Pirsiavash and Ramanan in order to determine what ADL the occupant was performing [12]. Pirsiavash and Ramanan were able to achieve a 77% accuracy rate in determining the correct activity with higher accuracy being limited due to genuine ambiguities in the data, in addition to difficulties in annotation (annotations consist of an action label, bounding box, identity, and human-object interaction). Examples of such actions involve interactions with the same object or objects which are small and often occluded and so may not be fully annotated [12]. While both these techniques could detect objects in a scene and determine ADLs they could not use this information in order to determine context or provide contextual information.

The challenges involved include determining the occupant's indoor location along with inferring contextual information from their location and activity. There is also the challenge of the heterogeneous nature of the data gathered being from multiple sources. It is hypothesized that using a single wearable camera to determine a users location will provide improved contextual information through the use of machine vision techniques along with a sensorised environment [6]. It will also lower the impact, in terms of equipment installation, to the users environment when compared with fixed vision or dense sensing based technologies. Also offering the potential to "follow" a user within an environment and provide enhanced contextual information based on location based information, along with the use of a common data storage format.

This research proposes a concept to facilitate indoor localization through the use of a single "always on" wearable camera. Location is determined using a wearable camera that identifies objects within the scene and cross-references these to determine the users location within the environment. For example, if a cooker and fridge are detected by the machine vision processing then it can be inferred that the user is in the kitchen. The approach proposes to use "off the shelf" machine vision tools, more specifically an OpenCV Haar Feature-based Cascade Classifier for rapid object detection [2]. This method involves training a classifier using a series of positive images, positive images being images that contain the object of focus, which are subsequently compared with a set of negative images in order to "train" the algorithm to discriminate between environmental objects observed within a given video stream. In an ideal scenario the negative images would be identical to the positive images minus the object of focus. The approach uses AdaBoost to combine several "weak" classifiers to form one "strong" classifier [2].

3   System Architecture

The architecture of the system is presented in Figure 1. It consists of five main layers — the physical, data, service, knowledge, context and presentation. What follows is a brief description of each layer.

Physical layer — this layer consists of the numerous objects that the occupant will come into contact with in their day-to-day life, such as their bed, cookers, to name but a few.These objects will be used to determine which room the occupant is currently in through the use of a wearable camera that will be on their person at all times. Other objects of note in this layer are the various sensors that will be placed throughout the environment such as contact and pressure sensors. This layer will also provide accelerometry data which will support determining if the occupant is active in addition to more urgent information such as if they have fallen. One problem from this stage that will have to be addressed is the heterogeneous nature of that data as all these sensors will be returning data in their own specific format which will need to be addressed and converted into a common format for use throughout the system.

Data layer — due to the real-world scenario this system will be used in, i.e. a patient's own home, it will not be possible to take account of every object that may be introduced or that over time more occupants may inhabit the environment. The Apache Felix framework [1] is a potential solution to mitigate this risk. It is a community effort to implement the OSGi (Open Service Gateway Initiative) framework under the Apache license. This allows new devices to be added on the fly with new services being registered if a new device is detected and like-wise services de-registered if a device is removed. It also allows communication with a wide variety of devices, sensors and applications in a uniform way, this ensures openness and allows new technology to be introduced as it becomes available.

Service layer — this layer contains agents and composite services along with the Apache Felix framework which maintains the current active sensors. Once powered, a sensor registers itself with the service layer by sending its service bundle definition. This layer will also contain agents which will be responsible for a certain task within the environment, for example there may be a *"grooming"* agent that will be responsible for detecting if the occupant is grooming as well as relevant reminders *etc.* about that task.

Knowledge layer — this layer contains all the information pertaining to the smart environment in an XML format, using the homeML schema. It contains information such as rooms, sensors in each room, and the classifiers for each object that can be detected within each room. This layer will also contain a user profile which will contain personalized information about the occupant such as their personal schedule. This layer also contains the rules within homeRuleML (a model for the exchange of decision support rules within smart environments [7]) that specifies the conditions that need to be met to determine if an activity is being carried out, *e.g.* if the sink tap is turned on and the razor contact sensor has been activated then the conditions of the grooming rule will have been met.

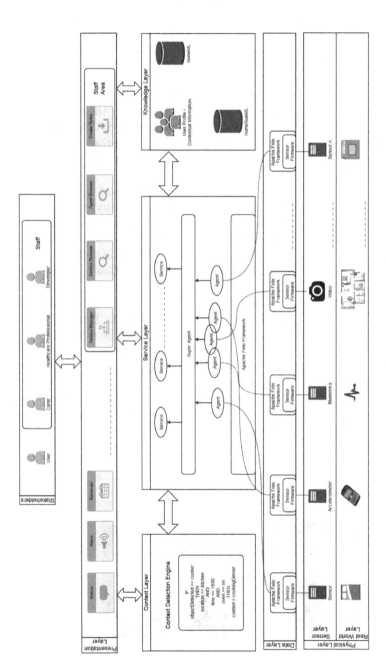

Fig. 1. proposed system architecture showing each layer along with example layer components. The physical layer representing real world objects and sensors, the data layer representing the data/rule collection, the service layer showing agents and composite services, the knowledge layer showing data storage, the context layer's *"detection engine"* for determining context, and the presentation layer the user interacts with.

Context layer — the context layer will contain a *"context detection engine"* which will be responsible for detecting the current user's context with the environment, if we take a simple scenario of a dementia patient using this system to assist in ADL, with the activity being cooking dinner. The system will show that the cooker has been turned on, that the fridge/cupboards are being opened/closed along with high activity levels from the user and if the time is in a pre-defined evening range then the detection engine can determine that the occupant is making dinner. Opposed to if the cooker is being turned on and fridge/cupboards are being opened/closed at 0400 then the detection engine could determine that the occupant has become confused. Or if the user is in a room with multiple people with a moderate activity level then the detection engine can infer that the user is in a meeting and would not interrupt the user with low priority reminders/alerts.

Presentation layer — this is the layer where the user would receive any notices or reminders that are determined to be relevant in addition to a developer area which contains tools such as the Service Manager and Service Browser. The Service Manager allows the developer to activate or deactivate services throughout the environment through a graphical interface, whilst the Service Browser allows the developer to browse and discover services in addition to register new services.

To contextualize the real world application of the architecture, consider the following scenario description. John is a patient who suffers from Dementia. John performs his normal morning grooming routine, when he gets up his bed pressure sensor registers that there is no longer anyone on the bed. John puts on the wearable camera and powers it on; the camera then registers itself as a new service with the system. John moves towards the bathroom; once he opens the door a sensor event is triggered that has the ID of the bathroom door. The system then loads the classifiers contained with the "bathroom" tag within homeML to detect bathroom objects, as shown in Figure 2, as that was the last sensor event logged.

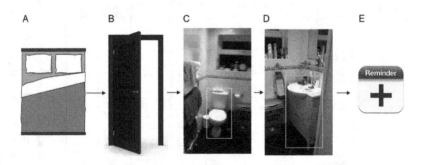

Fig. 2. Image A – pressure sensor on bed deactivated, Image B – door sensor activated, Image C – toilet detected, Image D – sink detected, Image E – reminder issued

In this scenario if John becomes confused or forgets what he is supposed to be doing then the system can infer the task from the users personal profile as well as other environmental variables such as the object recognition. For example if the camera detects that John is staring at the sink for a prolonged period of time (Figure 3) and it detects the time and that the razor contact sensor status has not changed since John has gotten out of bed then it could infer that John still needs to shave. A reminder will then be issued giving to John about the task he should be completing along with any instructions should they be needed.

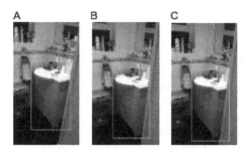

Fig. 3. Images A, B and C showing the same image being detected over a period of time, suggesting the occupant has forgot or become confused with the task, which would result in a reminder being issued to the occupant

4   Discussion

Due to being early stage work there are some limitations. There has only been partial implementation of the architecture, with the machine vision aspect being able to return the names of objects that have been detected along with the ability to append new sensor event data to a homeML file in order to record sensor events. The proposed solution will hopefully address the issues previously discussed in the Related Work section. It should hope to mitigate the multiple occupancy problems encountered with static vision systems, such as [6], due to each occupant having a wearable camera to determine their location from their immediate surroundings. The proposed solution will also expand on the limitations faced by Kurze and Roselius by combining the machine vision aspect with information gleaned from other external sensors situated within the environment, along with building on the work of Kang *et al.* by applying context to the information that is acquired from the machine vision aspect of the system.

5   Conclusion

This research aims to develop a context aware application through the use of wearable technology. In doing so, the research will advance the utility of wearable vision based systems through improved location based services based on vision processing of environmental objects. An effective data storage and inferencing system will also be developed to enable sensor integration of video based data along with other environmental and biometric sensors. Future work will focus on collecting and analyzing data from real smart environments and extending homeML to accommodate video data. Consequently, the adoption of homeRuleML will be investigated as a method to manage rules through a multi-agent based system.

References

1. Apache: Apache Felix (2013)
2. Bradski, G., Kaehler, A.: Learning OpenCV, 1st edn. O'Reilly (2008)
3. Christensen, K., Doblhammer, G., Rau, R., Vaupel, J.W.: Ageing populations: the challenges ahead. Lancet 374(9696), 1196–1208 (2009), http://www.pubmedcentral.nih.gov/articlerender.fcgi?artid=2810516&tool=pmcentrez&rendertype=abstract
4. Cook, D.J., Das, S.K.: How smart are our environments? An updated look at the state of the art. Pervasive and Mobile Computing 3(2), 53–73 (2007), http://linkinghub.elsevier.com/retrieve/pii/S1574119206000642
5. Dey, A.K., Abowd, G.D.: Towards a Better Understanding of Context and Context-Awareness. In: What, Who, Where, When, Why and How of Context-Awareness, Rotterdam, pp. 304–307 (2000)
6. Gómez-Romero, J., Serrano, M.a., Patricio, M.a., García, J., Molina, J.M.: Context-based scene recognition from visual data in smart homes: an Information Fusion approach. Personal and Ubiquitous Computing 16(7), 835–857 (2011), http://link.springer.com/10.1007/s00779-011-0450-9
7. Hallberg, J., Nugent, C.D., Davies, R.J., Synnes, K.R., Donnelly, M.P., Member, S., Finlay, D., Mulvenna, M.: HomeRuleML - A Model for the Exchange of Decision Support Rules Within Smart Environments. In: IEEE Automation Science and Engineering, Scottsdale, pp. 513–520 (2007)
8. Hebert, M., Kanade, T.: Discovering object instances from scenes of Daily Living. In: International Conference on Computer Vision, pp. 762–769. IEEE (November 2011), http://ieeexplore.ieee.org/lpdocs/epic03/wrapper.htm?arnumber=6126314
9. Kurze, M., Roselius, A.: Smart Glasses: An open environment for AR apps. In: Mixed and Augmented Reality ISMAR 2010 9th IEEE International Symposium. pp. 313–313. IEEE (2010), http://ieeexplore.ieee.org/lpdocs/epic03/wrapper.htm?arnumber=5643622
10. McDonald, H., Nugent, C., Hallberg, J., Finlay, D., Moore, G., Synnes, K.R.: The homeML suite: shareable datasets for smart home environments. Health and Technology 3(2), 177–193 (2013), http://link.springer.com/10.1007/s12553-013-0046-7
11. Nugent, C.D., Finlay, D.D., Davies, R.J., Wang, H.Y., Zheng, H.: homeML - An Open Standard for the Exchange of Data Within Smart Environments. In: ICOST, pp. 121–129 (2007)
12. Pirsiavash, H., Ramanan, D.: Detecting activities of daily living in first-person camera views. In: 2012 IEEE Conference on Computer Vision and Pattern Recognition, pp. 2847–2854. IEEE, Providence (2012), http://ieeexplore.ieee.org/lpdocs/epic03/wrapper.htm?arnumber=6248010

Revisiting the User Experience of a Virtual Rehabilitation Tool for the Physical Activation and Cognitive Stimulation of Elders

Alberto L. Morán[1], Victoria Meza[1], Cristina Ramírez–Fernández[1],
Ana I. Grimaldo[1], Eloísa García-Canseco[1],
and Felipe Orihuela-Espina[2], and Luis Enrique Sucar[2]

[1] Facultad de Ciencias, UABC, Ensenada, B.C., México
[2] Instituto Nacional de Astrofísica, Óptica y Electrónica, Tontanzintla,
Puebla, México
{alberto.moran,mmeza,a302126,ana.grimaldo}@uabc.edu.mx,
{eloisa.garcia}@uabc.edu.mx,{f.orihuela-espina,esucar}@ccc.inaoe.mx

Abstract. We report the results of an indirect observation usability and user experience (UX) study on the use of the Gesture Therapy (GT) rehabilitation platform, as a physical activation and cognitive stimulation tool for the elderly. The results from this study complement those of a former self-report study [8]. Elders perceived the system with high usefulness, usability, and UX, as well as generating low anxiety in both studies. Also, the results allowed us to analyze and evaluate the impact of elders' previous experience on computer use on specific aspects. Interestingly, the significance of the effect of previous computer use experience on perceived anxiety and perceived enjoyment aspects of UX was different in both studies, although there is an important overlap for ease of use factors. These results, although not conclusive yet on the causes for the difference, provides us with further evidence to establish that elders' previous experience (or not) on computer use affects their user experience on the use of the GT platform.

Keywords: Rehabilitation, user experience, cognitive stimulation, evaluation.

1 Introduction

The increasing incidence of age-related diseases on a larger elderly population have led to a quest for alternative non-pharmacological treatments to address them in a preventive manner. Examples of these technologies are those aimed at supporting cognitive and physical fitness, seeking to maintain cognitive and physical state in the elderly through cognitive stimulation and physical activation activities [4,5,6,8]. However, the characteristics of the elderly user group, caused by a decline in their physical and cognitive abilities, make necessary to evaluate which is their perception regarding its use, so that a greater acceptance and adoption by this population could be achieved.

In the literature various types of usability and user experience (UX) evaluations have been reported to assess the perceptions of older adults regarding

L. Pecchia et al. (Eds.): IWAAL 2014, LNCS 8868, pp. 203–210, 2014.
© Springer International Publishing Switzerland 2014

the use of technology [3,7]. Achieving this type of evaluations can be difficult given their reported inherent limitations. A common effect in techniques based on subjective information provided by users (i.e. self-report), participants tend to answer what they think the researcher wants to listen, or tend to be insincere and "improve" the perception of their results because they feel evaluated, or because they have forgotten the details of their experience [1].

Also, in techniques based on subjective information provided by an external observer (i.e. indirect observation), the observers may introduce a bias due to subjectivity associated to views and prejudices given their prior experience. For these reasons, it is desirable to conduct evaluations of both types to complement their results, and make them more reliable and comprehensive.

In this work we report the results of an indirect-observation UX evaluation of Gesture Therapy (GT) [10,11], a virtual rehabilitation tool, as an alternative interface for the cognitive stimulation and physical activation of the elderly. Also, we compare the results of this evaluation to those of a previous one based on a self-report approach [8]. As mentioned above, the results of each evaluation provide complementary information and allow establishing more clearly the contribution and specific usability problems of the proposed tool, which would not be possible if we had only used one technique.

2 Background

We are interested in evaluating the UX of the elderly regarding their use of the GT platform for their cognitive stimulation and physical activation. In a first exercise, we conducted a usability and UX evaluation using a self-report technique [8]. The main features of the tool, and the study and its main results are briefly described next.

2.1 Self-report UX Evaluation Study

Apparatus. Gesture Therapy (GT) is a low cost virtual rehabilitation platform for the upper limb [10,11]. It uses a gripper to control a user avatar by tracking a color ball as well as monitoring gripping forces using a pressure sensor (see Figure 1). It incorporates serious games that encourage repetitive exercises beneficial for the motor rehabilitation of patients. The games are based on activities of daily living (e.g. cooking a steak, cleaning a window, or killing a mosquito).

Participants. 32 elderly (age mean±std: 64.96±6.31 years) were recruited from a local municipal third age support group, who live an independent life and have no apparent cognitive problems.

Procedure. Participants were exposed to three games of the rehabilitation platform (Steak cooking, Window cleaning and Fly killer), and asked to evaluate them in terms of perceived usefulness, ease of use and UX. The subjects played the games for 15 minutes each, and the order in which the games were played was randomized. Participants filled a 29-element extended TAM-based questionnaire [12], addressing perception of usefulness, ease of use, intention of use (should the system be available), anxiety experienced, and UX.

Fig. 1. The Gesture Therapy platform. The user interacts with the games by means of the gripper.

Main Results. The elderly perceived the use of the evaluated tool as useful (93.75/100), easy to use (93.75/100) and as generating a high UX (91.66/100). Additionally, we identified that previous experience on the use of computers by the participants did not significantly impacted their usability perception for usefulness, ease of use, intention of use, and UX. However, we found a significant effect of previous experience on the perception of anxiety [8].

3 Usability Evaluation from the Observer's Perspective

In order to perform an additional validation of the borrowed use of the GT platform for the cognitive stimulation and physical activation of the elderly, as well as to gather additional evidence regarding their perceived usability and UX of the platform, we conducted an additional indirect observation usability and UX evaluation from the perspective of an expert observer.

3.1 Procedure

Two researchers analyzed the videos of the sessions of 16 of the 32 participants from the previous self-report usability study (8 experienced and 8 inexperienced subjects). As mentioned above, each session lasted about 15 minutes, which resulted in a total of approximately 218 minutes of video recordings.

The researchers used indirect observation analysis techniques to obtain data, and encoded actions, gestures, body language and verbal interactions of the elderly with the devices, the application and the facilitator as a rich source of data [9]. This allowed us identifying the form and function of these interactions and behaviors, and use them as additional evidence to explain and support the results from the evaluation conducted. To be able to compare the results from this evaluation with those obtained from the previous self-report evaluation, observers were asked to analyze the videos based on a custom observation guide.

This guide considered aspects such as Usefulness, Ease of use, UX, and Low Anxiety. After criteria unification and training, inter-observer agreement was 78% (Kappa = 0.557).

3.2 Evaluation Results, Observers' Perspective

Overall Usability Perception. To evaluate the overall perception, we scored the seven Likert scale items reported by observers on ease of use, UX and anxiety following the approach used for the previous self-report evaluation, that is, in a similar way as the SUS [2]. Considering that the usefulness of the games will be based on the observers' own perception, this factor will be analyzed apart from the overall usability perception of the elderly, and thus, not taken into account in this part of the study.

Table 1. Evaluation results concerning the overall usability perception of subjects (according to the observers' opinion) per groups using the seven Likert scale items only

Overall Usability of the observed participants (alpha = 0.05, p = 0.033)*			
Experienced Subjects (ES)		Inexperienced Subjects (NES)	
Median	82.93	Median	92.86
IQR	4.46	IQR	7.14
Mean Rank	6.3	Mean Rank	10.8

Table 1 presents a summary of the results categorized according to the observed participants having or not experience on the use of the computer. Contrary to hypothesized, observers granted higher notes for inexperienced subjects (median = 92.86 (Inter-Quartile Range (IQR) = 7.14)) than for experienced subjects (median = 82.93 (IQR = 4.46)); and the effect was found to be significant at the 0.05 level (Mann-Whitney U: p=0.033). As for the previous self-report evaluation with older adults, this result suggests that the application provides or promotes each of the evaluated factors (i.e. ease of use, user experience, etc.). However, contrary to the result of the previous auto-report evaluation, we found that previous experience on computer or game console use does have an effect on the subjects' overall usability perception of the virtual rehabilitation platform.

3.3 Perceived Ease of Use, User Experience and Anxiety

To further scrutinize usability aspects, and aiming at explaining the possible causes that lead to the overall usability contradictory result, we further analyzed the results on the perception of ease of use, user experience and anxiety of elders (see Table 2). As can be seen in Table 2, both groups of participants perceived high values for the aspects considered in this section of the study.

Table 2. Summary of Mann-Whitney U Test results on the perception of ease of use, user experience and anxiety by category

Experienced Subjects (ES)		Inexperienced Subjects (NES)	
Perceived Ease of Use (alpha = 0.05, p = 0.281)			
Median	95.83	Median	100
IQR	8.33	IQR	4.17
Mean Rank	7.8	Mean Rank	9.3
Perceived User Experience (alpha = 0.05, p = 0.016)*			
Median	75	Median	87.5
IQR	4.69	IQR	9.38
Mean Rank	5.9	Mean Rank	11.1
Perceived Anxiety (alpha = 0.05, p = 0.456)			
Median	100	Median	100
IQR	25	IQR	25
Mean Rank	8.7	Mean Rank	8.3

Once again, observers granted higher notes for subjects in the inexperienced group (NES) than for subjects in the experienced group (ES) on the perceived ease of use (NES: Median = 100 (IQR = 4.17), ES: Median = 95.83 (IQR = 8.33)), and on the perceived user experience (NES: Median = 87.5 (IQR = 9.37), ES: Median = 75 (IQR = 4.69)). Additionally, observers granted very similar notes for subjects on both groups on the perceived (low) anxiety (NES: Median = 100 (IQR = 25), ES: Median = 100 (IQR = 25)).

Given the perceived differences on the ease of use and user experience results, we conducted Mann-Whitney U tests to determine whether they were significantly different. The first test showed no significant difference at the 0.05 level for perceived ease of use ($p=0.281$). However, the difference was found to be significant for the perceived user experience ($p<0.05$). These results suggest that although the experience on computer or game console use does not have an effect on the perceived ease of use or anxiety of older adults interacting with the GT platform, it does have an effect on the perceived user experience, which could be the reason for the contradictory overall usability result in this indirect observation evaluation vs. the self-report evaluation. A further analysis on the UX and Anxiety factors is provided in the next section.

4   Detailed Analyses on User Experience and Anxiety

By contrasting the results of this indirect observation evaluation with those of the previous self-report evaluation (see Table 3), it can be seen that although there is an overlap in the findings of both evaluations for the ease of use aspect; and that it is not possible to compare the usefulness and intention of use results as these are not available for the second evaluation; it is necessary to perform a further analysis on the findings of the perceived user experience and anxiety aspects, which are contradictory. A discussion on these follows.

Table 3. Summary of the significance of results of the conducted evaluation. N_i: (group) sample size.

		Significance of difference		
Perceived factor	Self-report evaluation	Effect size $N_1 = 17$ $N_2 = 15$	Indirect observation evaluation	Effect size $N_1 = 8$ $N_2 = 8$
Usefulness	Not significant	$r^2 = 0.06$	N/A[*]	N/A
Ease of use	Not significant	$r^2 = 0.02$	Not significant	$r^2 = 0.04$
Intention of use	Not significant	$r^2 = 0.05$	N/A	N/A
User experience	Not significant	$r^2 = 0.001$	Significant	$r^2 = 0.58$
Low anxiety	Significant	$r^2 = 0.25$	Not significant	$r^2 = 0.001$

[*]Observers' perspective only

4.1 Detailed Analysis on Perceived User Experience

In order to identify which of the aspects considered in the user experience factor contributed to the contradictory user experience result, we looked at the three 5-point Likert scale items regarding excitement, immersion and enjoyment. Firstly, observers reported that inexperienced older adults looked more excited (NES: Median = 75, IQR = 6.25) than experienced older adults (ES: Median = 50, IQR = 25) while performing the tasks. However, a Mann-Whitney U test later showed that this difference is not significant at the 0.05 level (p = 0.113). This means that although observers agreed that inexperienced participants looked more excited than experienced participants, whom looked neutral, the difference was not significant. Secondly, observers reported having perceived the participants in both groups with an equally high level of immersion during task execution (NES: Median = 100, IQR = 0) and (ES : Median = 100, IQR = 0). Finally, observers perceived inexperienced older adults having more fun (NES: Median = 75, IQR = 12.5) than experienced older adults (ES: Median = 50, IQR = 6.25) while performing the task. A Mann-Whitney U test later showed that this difference is significant at the 0.05 level (p = 0.033). With these results, from the perspective of an observer, we can identify that previous experience on using the computer or video game console has a significant effect on the observed enjoyment in older adults during the platform use; however, this is not the case for the level of excitement and immersion of users during the execution of the task.

4.2 Detailed Analysis of Perceived Anxiety

Regarding anxiety levels, observers reported that only two participants (from the experienced group) presented significant anxiety behaviors while performing one of the tasks. These participants were those who obtained the first and second best scores on the other tasks in which they participated (ES16 and ES14, respectively). In the case of participant ES14, he had problems with the Fly killer game. The problems arose because he was so immersed in the game, and wanting to achieve the most points, that he consistently moved in very close to the screen, which put the gripper out of the camera's scope, and therefore did not worked to control the application. This also reflected a usability problem in the design of the system, as the mechanism used to notify this, a change in color and lack of motion of the gripper's cursor in the video tracker window, was not salient enough as the make the user aware of this problem. In the case of participant ES16, she had problems in the Clean window game. The problems arose because for this activity she located her hand (i.e. the gripper) next to a part of her blouse that was of the same color of the gripper's distinctive ball. This tricked the tracking feature of the application, and resulted in a very poor tracking performance for the application and a low score for the participant. Thus, in both cases, a usability problem with the gripper affected the performance of the participants, and in turn, turned them anxious during the execution of the particular task. It should be highlighted that for the additional tasks, the two participants placed their hands (i.e. the gripper) in positions that were more adequate, so that they did not have the same problems for those other tasks. This means that participant ES14 kept the gripper within the scope of the camera and participant ES16 kept her hand up from the position of her blouse that was of the same color as the gripper.

5   Discussion and Conclusions

We have reported the results of an indirect observation usability and UX study on the use of the GT platform, a rehabilitation tool, that was "borrowed" from the rehabilitation domain to be used as a physical activation and cognitive stimulation tool for the elderly. The results from this study complement those of a first self-report usability and UX study with older adult participants. In both studies, elders perceived the system with high usefulness, usability, and UX, as well as generating low anxiety for the proposed tasks. Additionally, the results allowed us to analyze and evaluate the impact of elders' previous computer use experience on specific usability and user experience aspects on the evaluated tasks. Interestingly, and not unexpectedly as observed in the literature, the significance of the effect of previous computer or game console use experience on the different evaluated factors was different in both studies, although there is an important overlap for ease of use factors. On the one hand, in the self-report evaluation, we found that for the perceived anxiety factor, which was slightly higher for the participants of the inexperienced user group, the effect of previous experience on computer use was found to be significant, although it was not the case for the indirect-observation evaluation. On the other hand, in the indirect-observation evaluation, we found that for the perceived enjoyment factor, which also was higher for participants from the group of inexperienced users, the effect of previous experience was found to be significant, although this was not the case for the self-report evaluation. Thus, even though there is an overlap in the findings of both evaluations for the ease of use aspect; it is necessary to perform a more in-depth analysis regarding the contradictory findings for the perceived anxiety and perceived enjoyment aspects of UX in order to clarify the meaning and causes of these results. This latter aspect represents our line of future work.

Acknowledgments. This work was partially funded by CONACYT under grant 218709 of the "Programa de Estímulos a la Innovación 2014; and by UABC under grant 0212 of the Convocatoria de Proyectos de Servicio Social 2014.

References

1. Arhippainen, L., Tähti, M.: Empirical evaluation of user experience in two adaptive mobile application prototypes. In: Proceedings of the 2nd International Conference on Mobile and Ubiquitous Multimedia (January 2003)
2. Brooke, J.: SUS-A quick and dirty usability scale. Usability Evaluation in Industry 189, 194 (1996)
3. Consolvo, S., Roessler, P., Shelton, B.E.: The CareNet display: Lessons learned from an in home evaluation of an ambient display. In: Mynatt, E.D., Siio, I. (eds.) UbiComp 2004. LNCS, vol. 3205, pp. 1–17. Springer, Heidelberg (2004)
4. Gamberini, L., Raya, M.A., Barresi, G., Fabregat, M., Ibanez, F., Prontu, L.: Cognition, technology and games for the elderly: An introduction to ELDERGAMES project. PsychNology Journal 4(3), 285–308 (2006)
5. Hollmann, W., Strüder, H.K., Tagarakis, C.V.M., King, G.: Physical activity and the elderly. European Journal of Cardiovascular Prevention & Rehabilitation 14(6), 730–739 (2007)
6. Meza-Kubo, V., Morán, A.L.: UCSA: a design framework for usable cognitive systems for the worried-well. Personal and ubiquitous computing 17(6), 1135–1145 (2013)
7. Morán, A.L., Meza-Kubo, V.: User experience of elders and relatives in a collaborative cognitive stimulation tool. In: Bravo, J., Hervás, R., Rodríguez, M. (eds.) IWAAL 2012. LNCS, vol. 7657, pp. 287–294. Springer, Heidelberg (2012)
8. Morán, A.L., Orihuela-Espina, F., Meza-Kubo, V., Grimaldo, A.I., Ramírez-Fernández, C., García-Canseco, E., Oropeza-Salas, J.M., Sucar, L.E.: Borrowing a virtual rehabilitation tool for the physical activation and cognitive stimulation of elders. In: Collazos, C., Liborio, A., Rusu, C. (eds.) CLIHC 2013. LNCS, vol. 8278, pp. 95–102. Springer, Heidelberg (2013)
9. Sanderson, P.M., Fisher, C.: Exploratory sequential data analysis: Foundations. Hum.-Comput. Interact. 9(4), 251–317 (1994)
10. Sucar, E., Luis, R., Leder, R., Hernández, J., Sánchez, I.: Gesture therapy: a vision-based system for upper extremity stroke rehabilitation. In: Engineering in Medicine and Biology Society (EMBC), 2010 Annual International Conference of the IEEE, pp. 3690–3693. IEEE (2010)
11. Enrique Sucar, L., Orihuela-Espina, F., Velazquez, R., Reinkensmeyer, D., Leder, R., Franco, J.H.: Gesture therapy: An upper limb virtual reality-based motor rehabilitation platform. IEEE Transactions on Neural Systems and Rehabilitation Engineering 22(3), 634–643 (2014)
12. Venkatesh, V., Davis, F.D.: A theoretical extension of the technology acceptance model: four longitudinal field studies. Management science 46(2), 186–204 (2000)

Decision Modeling in Smart Home Design

The Importance of Lifestyle in an Individual's Design Decision

Mohammadali Heidari[1,*], Erfaneh Allameh[1,*], Bauke De Vries[1],
Harry Timmermans[1], and Farhang Mozaffar[2]

[1] Department of Built Environment, Eindhoven University of Technology,
Eindhoven, The Netherlands.
{m.heidari.jozam,e.allameh,b.d.vries,h.j.p.timmermans}@tue.nl
[2] Department of Architecture and Urban Design, Art University of Isfahan, Isfahan, Iran
F.mozaffar@aui.ac.ir

Abstract. In this paper, we propose a framework for decision modeling of users in smart home design. Individual's preferences that derived from both of his/her "Current Lifestyle" and "Future Lifestyle" are considered as the main factors that influence the final decision, Such that the compatibility of the choice alternatives with these preferences sets up the final decision for the individual.

We tested this framework with a virtual experiment. The experiment was conducted among 250 respondents, who were asked to explore a smart home in a virtual environment and then to make a decision among design alternatives for different parts of a smart home. Choices and the underlying effective factors were evaluated by MultiNomial Logit model. The outcomes adequately ascertained the proposed framework. Understanding of the effective factors on the user's design decisions for a smart home helps designers to incorporate design alternatives with users' demands in the real world.

Keywords: Smart Home Design, Decision Modeling, User Preference, Lifestyle, Virtual Experiment.

1 Introduction

The ultimate goal of this paper is to improve the smart home design process in such a way that smart homes become as one the important house type's in future housing industry. But smart homes are still faced with the lack of success to be widely accepted by the public. Many people overview smart homes just as luxury homes or as assisted-living homes, which are suitable only for elderly and disabled people. Whereas smart homes have the capability to benefit different target groups such as middle income families, busy lifestyle people, Teleworkers, dual income families and etc. Hence, eliciting user preferences of different target groups seems essential in smart home design. Reviewing the literature [1] shows that most of the research centers try to make smart homes technically possible with little attention to the acceptability issues in the real world. In this paper, we try to bring user perspectives to the design

---

* These authors contributed equally to this work.

L. Pecchia et al. (Eds.): IWAAL 2014, LNCS 8868, pp. 211–218, 2014.

process of smart homes. If we would be able to evaluate individuals' decisions in a smart home design, we could understand the effective factors on users' satisfaction of a smart home. Knowing the underlying reasons of users' satisfaction can help designers and technology developers to match their design alternatives to what users really need and prefer. Accordingly, user acceptance of smart homes is expected to increase.

2   Smart Home Definition

Smart home is a multidisciplinary notion. An increasing number of research groups are working in this domain [1]. Each of these research centers is focusing on the smart home from a distinctive perspective. The different names, such as Automatic home, Adaptive home, Com home, Aware Home, Internet Home, Independent Living Home and Smart Home, show their different perspectives. But what unifies all types of smart homes in a joint domain is their final goal. According to the "smart home association" in the Netherlands, smart homes integrate technology and services through home environments for higher comfort and quality of living at home [2].

Several smart technologies are involved in a smart home such as "smart, flexible partitions", "smart boundaries with adjustable transparency", "smart kitchen table with flexible cook top, wireless power system and wireless data network", "smart wall with intelligent and interactive system", "smart furniture with programmable context and sensor network", "smart floor", etc. All of these devices help users to do their daily activities (both inside and outside of the house) in a more flexible, interactive, natural and comfortable way.

3   An Individual's Decision Model in Smart Home Design

There are several important factors that influence decisions of an individual. In a design context, knowing the influential factors of a decision helps designers to adapt the design alternatives with users' latent preferences. Investigating the effects of prior experiences on individuals' decisions is not a new topic in behavioral and psychological researches. In 1998, Aaarts and et al.[3] discussed about repeated behaviors and decisions of people based on the actions they had in the Past; Jullisson and et al.[4] Also discussed the effects of prior experiences on the decisions of people for a business investment. In a house design, prior experiences refer to the lifestyle of people. Meaning that the decision which an individual make can be influenced by the types of lifestyle he/she follows in current daily routines. As an example, the extent that an individual work at home, has e-meetings or need privacy for working in his/her current lifestyle can affect the decision of choosing a specific design alternative for a working area at a smart house; In a way that the "Current Lifestyle" forms different preferences for the individual (e.g. Preference for the level of flexibility or privacy and the layout of public-private). These preferences affect the final decision made by the individual. (see Fig. 1)

Technological changes in the home environment will affect the way people live in the house and accordingly the upcoming lifestyle forms new preferences for them [5].

Hence, when an individual wants to make a decision among the design alternatives of a smart home, the decision can also be influenced by the preferences resulted from his /her "Future Lifestyle" in a smart home. For instance, preference for the kitchen layout can be affected by applying a smart kitchen table in the kitchen area. In such a way that, an individual who generally prefer to have a separated kitchen may change his/her preference to have a more open space kitchen area if he/she has a smart kitchen table. Because the smart kitchen table lets him/her do also other activities such as Tele-working, Tele-shopping, Telecommunication and family-gathering in the kitchen area. Hence, we propose that an individual evaluates the "Choice Alternatives" based on not only the preferences come from his/her "Current Lifestyle" but also the preferences, which come from his/her "Future Lifestyle" (see Fig.1).

Another important issue which needs to be considered in the decision model is the individual differences. Preferences vary among people according to their age, gender, working status, nationality, household type and etc. For instance, it is expected that an individual from a dual-income family with children who prefer a high level of privacy for working at home and high level of flexibility for managing child related activities, choose a different alternative for the bedroom layout of a smart home than an elderly who is retired and lives alone at home (see Fig. 1).

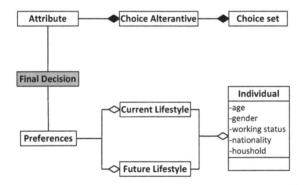

Fig. 1. The decision Model for an individual in the context of smart home design

It is obvious that the Choice Alternatives are different in their Attributes. As Fig. 1 shows, an individual evaluates the Attributes with his/her Preferences for arriving at a Final Decision. As soon as, the individual feels that the Attributes of an Alternative are compatible with his/her Preferences and adequately cover the major part of them, he/she will choose the Alternative from the Choice set.

4   Virtual Experiment

In order to test the proposed framework (Fig. 1), we design an experiment which simulates a smart home in a virtual environment. The virtual smart home consists of several smart technologies, namely, smart walls, smart kitchen table, smart private zone and smart furniture [6]. During the experiment, each respondent performs four tasks:

Task1 contains a questionnaire with two main sections. The first section is composed of multiple questions about socio-demographic characteristics, while the second section is more about the types of living (e.g. To what extent a respondent works at home, does Tele activities, has a busy lifestyle, needs privacy). The outputs of this task give us information about the current lifestyle of respondents.

Task 2 provides a virtual environment for representing a smart home in which respondents can take a virtual tour though the environment and watch several movies about smart technologies and their functionalities. This task helps respondents to gain a general overview toward the smart home (Fig. 2-a).

Task 3 is exploring daily living in the smart home, in which respondents are asked to imagine if they have a smart home, how they would like to live inside it. This task consists of two scenarios: "weekday" and "weekend". Respondents are able to virtually explore different spaces and technologies in the smart home using the navigation bar and arrange their activities in the time blocks and space zones. There are several hot zones near the smart kitchen table, smart wall, smart work space and smart private zone. By clicking on each hot zone, the camera goes there and a blank schedule appears on the screen in which the respondent can report the activities he/she would like to perform in that zone (Fig. 2-b). For instance, the respondent can report the types of activities, the duration of activities, possible interactions or conflicts during the activities. At the end of the task, a complete daily schedule for each respondent is created which give us information about the Future Lifestyle of respondents in a smart home. The outputs can be used for further analysis such as preference elicitation.

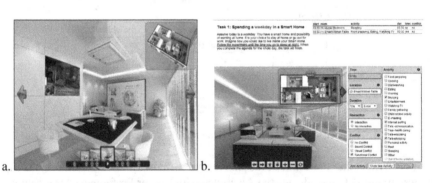

Fig. 2. a. Virtual tour, b. Daily living in a smart home.

Task 4 is the final task, in which respondents are asked to make multiple choices for different parts of a smart home and make their preferred home layout. For each part, respondents explore multiple design alternatives and then choose one of them. In this paper, we discuss only one of the choice tasks in which respondents choose their preferred private layout of the smart home among three available alternatives: Small-Flexible private zone, Medium-Semi-Flexible private zone and large-Not Fixed private zone (Fig. 3). Selecting this choice task as a sample for testing is only because of simplifying the paper's structure and no other reasons is involved in its selection.

a.   b.   c.

Fig. 3. Three design alternatives for private layout of the smart home; a. Small, Flexible Private, b. Medium, Semi-Flexible Private, c. Large, Fixed Private

5   Model Specification

The experiment was conducted with the sample size of 250 respondents. As for the sample composition, 57 percent were males, while 43 percent were females. From all of the respondents, 57 percent lived in apartments, 21.7 percent lived in middle-scale houses, while the remainder lived in large-scale houses. 7.9 percent of the respondents were Dutch, 67.7 percent were Iranian and the remainder had other nationalities. This sample contains more young people with high education.

Choice modeling attempts to model the decision of an individual with its underlying rationale [7]. The typical discrete choice models capture statistical relationships between a dependent and a set of independent variables. The models statistically relate the choice made by each person to the attributes of the person and the attributes of the alternatives available to the person. The models estimate the probability that a person chooses a particular alternative. They are often used to forecast how people's choices will change under changes in demographics and/or attributes of the alternatives [8].

To test the proposed framework (Figure1) and to analyze the influence of users' preferences on their decisions, a multinomial logit model was estimated. The independent variables consisted of appropriately "effect coded" variables related to personal characteristics, variables related to Current Lifestyle and variables related to Future Lifestyle. The dependent variable in the multinomial logit model was the choice for private layout of the smart home. As depicted in Figure3, this dependent variable had three different choice alternatives: a. Small, Flexible Private, b. Medium, Semi-Flexible Private and c. Large, Fixed Private.

The multinomial logit or MNL model form is commonly used in choice modeling as it is a good approximation to the economic principle of utility maximization. That is, human beings strive to maximize their total utility. In fact, the utility function, U, has the property that an alternative is chosen if its utility is greater than the utility of all other alternatives in the individual's choice set [8]. The utility that an individual n associates with alternative i is written as:

$$U_{ni} = V_{ni} + \varepsilon_{ni} \tag{1}$$

$$V_{ni} = \beta_0 + \beta_1 . X_{i1} + \beta_2 . X_{i2} + ... \tag{2}$$

Where $\beta 0$ is the constant and β k is the set of estimated parameters of variables X, and X i is the set of independent variables. In fact, $\beta 0$ represents the mean utility of 'alternative i' and the 'βk parameters' measure deviations from this mean utility.

6   Results

The multinomial logit model for the private layout choice was estimated using LIMDEP (Econometric Software). The Table 1 shows the Estimated Parameters of Variables X. According to the results, the decision for private layout of a smart home depends on both of the Current Lifestyle and the Future Lifestyle. The influential factors (variables X) are Gender, Nationality, Current housing types and the Level of doing Tele activities in Current Lifestyle. In addition, some other factors such as the Activity types that people would like to do in the semi- private zone of a smart home and the most time-spending zone in the smart home have significant effects on the decision for private layout of a smart home. These factors are based on the Future Lifestyle of people in a smart home. Some interpretations of the results are as follows:

– Males appear to have a higher preference for choosing the two alternatives of Small- Flexible Private and Medium-Semi-Flexible Private than females. In other words, females prefer the third alternative (Large- Fixed Private) more than males.
– Nationality of Iranian reduces the probability of choosing Small-Flexible Private. In contrast, Dutch respondents have the highest preferences for Small-Flexible Private. Meaning that they prefer to have several small private areas with flexible boundaries rather than having two large bedrooms with fixed boundaries.
– Respondents who currently do Tele activities in a medium level appear to have the highest preference for the alternative of Medium-Semi-Flexible Private comparing to the two other groups (people who rarely do Tele activities or people who are fans of doing Tele activities). One of the underlying logic is that people who rarely do Tele activities generally like to do their daily activities in ordinary ways. They are not interested in the flexible opportunities that a smart home provides for e-activities. According to the Table 1, this group of respondents has high preferences for the third alternative which is closer to the ordinary homes with the Large, Fixed Private. The second logic refers to the choice behavior of the respondents who are fans of doing Tele activities. They mostly prefer Small-Flexible Private, since this alternative gives them the opportunity to have more flexibility for doing Tele activities and also a large public area. Therefore, they can have more space around the smart wall and the smart kitchen table as the main hubs of Tele activities.
– In general, the probability of choosing Small-Flexible Private is much lower than choosing the two other alternatives, according to the value of Constant presented in Table1; but spending most of the time in private zones of the virtual smart home is one of the factors that increases the probability of choosing this alternative. This interesting result can be based on the reason that this alternative provides different privacy levels thanks to several flexible boundaries while the other alternatives have limited opportunities for providing different levels of privacy. Therefore,

respondents who spent most of their time in private zones have higher preferences for choosing this alternative (see Fig.3 and Table 1). In all of the interpretations, alternative of Large-Fixed Private is considered as the reference. Meaning that, the two other alternatives are compared to this alternative.

Table 1. Estimated Parameters of Variables X (Multinomial Logit Model). The bold numbers represent the significant coefficients (***, **, * ==> Significance at 1%, 5%, 10% level.)

Main Category	Independent Variables	Small Flexible Private	Medium Semi-Flexible Private
	Constant	-2.93***	0.15
Current Lifestyle: socio- demo and current daily living	Male	0.05	0.17*
	Female	-0.05	-0.17
	Nationality (Netherlands)	1.16**	0.13
	Nationality (Iranian)	-1.39***	0.04
	Nationality (Other)	0.23	-0.17
	Housing Type (Apartment)	0.62	-0.23*
	Housing Type (Middle-scale House)	0.14	0.20
	Housing Type (Large-scale House)	-0.76	0.03
	Doing Tele activities at current lifestyle (Low)	-0.61	-0.16
	Doing Tele activities at current lifestyle (Medium)	0.49	0.55***
	Doing Tele activities at current lifestyle (High)	0.12	-0.39
Future Lifestyle	Activity Type in semi- private zone of smart home (None)	0.29	0.40***
	Activity Type in semi- private zone of smart home (1 type)	-0.92	-0.37**
	Activity Type in semi- private zone of smart home (2 types)	0.63	-0.03
	Most time-spending zone in smart home (kitchen)	-0.46	0.13
	Most time-spending zone in smart home (public)	0.05	-0.23
	Most time-spending zone in smart home (private)	1.23**	-0.30
	Most time-spending zone in smart home (semi- private zone)	-0.82	0.40

7   Conclusion

In this paper, we reported the results of a decision modeling in the context of smart home design. We aimed at providing evidence that users' satisfaction of a smart home is based on the evaluation users made for the extent of meeting their preferences through the design alternatives. We tried to advocate that these latent preferences come from both current and future lifestyles which differ among different individuals.

In the experiment and analysis part, we focused only on one choice task in which we asked respondents to choose their most preferred private layout of a smart home. Accordingly, the estimated parameters of the multinomial logit model adequately fit in the described decision model. Such that gender, nationality, current housing types of the respondents, the level of doing Tele activities in their current lifestyle, also the activity types and the time spending patterns they would like to have in a smart home had significant effects on their decision of choosing a specific alternative for the private layout in a smart home. This provides evidence for the hypothesis that for being satisfied of a design, an individual looks for an alternative which is more compatible with the preferences derived from his/her lifestyle. Hence, taking into account user' preferences in smart home design can increase users' satisfaction and consequently users' acceptance of smart homes. Such a user centered approach for smart homes helps designers to match smart home development with users' real need and future demands and to broaden the domain of smart homes to the future housing industry.

References

1.

Living tomorrow lab, Brussels, Belgium	http://www.livingtomorrow.com/#/en
The Smartest Home, Eindhoven, The Netherland	http://www.smart-homes.nl/
Australia's first Smart Home, Sydney, Australia	http://www.ausgrid.com.au/smarthome
Com HOME, Madrid, Spain	http://www.leal-junestrand-arquitectos.com/?page_id=212
Easy Living, Microsoft, United States	http://www.cs.washington.edu/mssi/tic/intros/Shafer/index.htm
House of the Future , MIT, United States	http://architecture.mit.edu/house_n/
Smart Home, Siemens, Munich, Germany	http://www.siemens.com/innovation/en/publikationen/publicati ons_pof/pof_fall_2008/gebaeude/vernetzung.htm
ENER-G Controls, Sussex, England	http://www.chessclubs.webspace.virginmedia.com/smarthomec ontrols/index.htm
Intel Architecture Labs, Santa Clara, United States	http://techresearch.intel.com/ProjectDetails.aspx?Id=84
Panasonic Smart Home V.2, Tokyo, Japan	http://wn.com/panasonic_prototype_ecohouse_in_tokyo,_japan
Aware Home, Georgia Tech, United States	http://awarehome.imtc.gatech.edu/

2. Bierhoff, I., Van Berlo, A., Abascal, J., Allen, B., Civit, A.: Smart Home environment. In: Roe, P.R.W. (ed.) Towards an inclusive future, Impact and wider poten-tial of information and communication technologies, COST, Brussels, pp. 110–156 (2007)
3. Aarts, H.,, Verplanken, B., Knippenber, A.: Predicting Behavior From Actions in the Past: Repeated Decision Making or a Matter of Habit? Journal of Applied Social Psychology 28(15), 1355–1374 (1998)
4. Jullisson, E.A., Karlsson, N., Garling, T.: Weighing the past and the future in de-cision making. Journal of Cognitive Psychology 17, 561–575 (2005)
5. Allameh, E., Heidari Jozam, M., Vries, B., de Timmermans, H.J.P., Masoud, M.: Smart Homes from vision to reality: eliciting users' preferences of Smart Homes by a virtual experimental method. In: The Fist International Conference on Civil and Building Engineering Informatics, pp. 297–305. ICCBEI Organizing Committee, Tokyo (2013)
6. Heidari, M., Allameh, E., De Vries., B., Timmermans,; Jessurun, J., Mozaffar, F.: Smart-BIM virtual prototype implementation. Automation in Construction 39, 134–144 (2014)
7. Wang, Y., Ruhe, G.: The Cognitive Process of Decision Making. Journal of Cognitive Informatics & Natural Intelligence 1(2), 73–85 (2007)
8. Koppelman, F., Bhat, C.: A Self Instructing Course in Mode Choice Modeling: Multinomial and Nested Logit Models, Prepared For Department of Transportation, U.S (2006)

Garment Design for an Ambulatory Pregnancy Monitoring System

Monica Perusquía-Hernández, Wei Chen, and Loe Feijs

Industrial Design, Eindhoven University of Technology, Eindhoven, The Netherlands
{m.perusquia.hernandez,w.chen,l.m.g.Feijs}@tue.nl

Abstract. Constant pregnancy monitoring is a promising alternative to reduce the number of stillbirths and preterm delivery due to false alarms. Tele-monitoring systems can provide regular, accurate and timely monitoring to reduce risks, costs and the time the mothers-to-be spend at hospitals. A smart garment integrated with sensors and a flexible printed circuit board for ambulatory pregnancy monitoring is proposed. A study was conducted to gather user requirements to ensure comfort during long registrations of Fetal Heart Rate (FHR) and Electrohysterogram (EHG). Based on those requirements, several garment alternatives for the monitoring system are proposed and evaluated.

Keywords: Pregnancy monitoring, user research, body area networks.

1   Introduction

Assessing fetal well-being during pregnancy and labor is a priority to reduce the number of stillbirths and preterm deliveries due to false alarms. Around 3 million annual third-trimester stillbirths occur around the world [1]. Moreover, the counts might be underestimated, as stillbirths are often not counted nor included in the Global Burden of Disease. Most of these stillbirths occur in low-income countries where interventions in the maternity care are not enough. In high-income countries the rates of stillbirths have been reduced in since 1940, but the improvements have decreased in recent years [2]. To effectively identify fetal distress and to ensure timely interventions, screening tools for fetal well-being can be used. These tools include fetal movement, heart rate, fetal growth, among others. Currently, pre-existing or pregnancy related medical conditions are predictors of high-risk pregnancies [1]. In the Netherlands, obstetric care differs for low- and high-risk mothers. Low-risk pregnancies are handled by the primary care system, with the help of midwives. As soon as a high-risk situation is identified, mothers-to-be are referred to the secondary care. Most pregnant women are scheduled for regular screenings, regardless of their status. If complications arise, they are referred to secondary care for additional checkups. Within this system, women at low-risk in the primary care have a greater risk of prenatal dead than those at high-risk who deliver in the secondary care. Furthermore, mortality increases with transfers between primary and secondary care. A potential explanation is that fetal distress is not detected on time [1], [3]. Hence, tele-monitoring might prove to be a good solution to provide a

L. Pecchia et al. (Eds.): IWAAL 2014, LNCS 8868, pp. 219–227, 2014.

timely alert of fetal distress by letting future mothers monitor the progress of their babies at home, without increased risk or discomfort.

Previous work has proven the feasibility of such tele-monitoring systems. First, tele-monitoring of pregnancies at risk would imply a considerable cost-reduction per year [4]. Second, patient-directed FHR monitoring and transmission is successful with high level of satisfaction from the patients [5]. There are even some commercial wireless pregnancy monitors, such as the Avalon CTS Cordless Fetal Transducer System [6], the Monica AN24 monitor [7], and the Remote Fetal Monitor [8]. From these, only the last two aim at home usage. They consist of a big and cumbersome-to-carry handheld device to which the sensing electrodes are attached using wires. Ideally, the monitoring device is not only to provide accurate monitoring and timely identification of possible complications, but also, to ensure the comfort of the mother while doing so. In this sense, the Telefetalcare monitor [9] improved the user experience by using a textile belt with eight ECG leads attached to the fabric. However, its battery life is still limited and the garment is prone to motion artifacts. Therefore, there is still room for improvement in the development of a portable monitoring system.

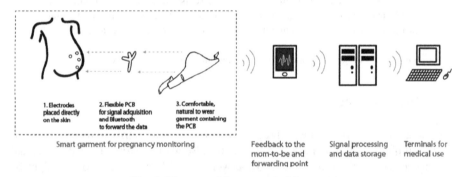

Fig. 1. Diagram of the system architecture

2   System Concept

Smart Energy Body Area Sensor Network (SEBAN) is an ongoing project. Its goal is to create a wearable with an integrated fully wireless electronic system (Figure 1) which continuously monitors the progress of pregnancy at home. Its safety will be ensured by keeping the wireless communication within the recommended Specific Absorption Rate (SAR) levels[10], and using it only on battery power. It will use an energy efficient amplifier as described by [11]. The data gathered will be sent to the mobile phone of the users with low-power Bluetooth 4.0. On the phone, moms-to-be will get information about the status of the unborn baby. Furthermore, the phone will be used as forwarding point for the data. The data will be transferred to a back-end server where additional signal processing will be performed. The outcome of the monitoring will be accessible by terminals at the hospital, so that caregivers can assess it and take the necessary actions in case of an emergency. Moreover, five electrodes placed directly on the pregnant belly skin will be used. Solid-gel sticky electrodes are chosen to have a good electrode-skin contact, and thus, reduce motion artifacts. They will be optimally arranged [12] for measurement of FECG and EHG during the last weeks of pregnancy. With this, the system aims to have an increased robustness against signal loss due to constant changes in the fetal position.

3   User Requirements

Several user needs were identified by user research. The main goals were to (1) identify opportunities of improvement in the current monitoring process; and (2) elicit the experiences they have with garments for pregnancy such as support belts. Finally, it was also asked (3) feedback about initial prototypes, and the (4) type of wearable they would like to have. This information led to several user requirements.

3.1   Methods

Participants
Six pregnant women (average gestational age = 31.8 weeks, SD = 5.17) and two women who recently had a child (less than 3 months after delivery) were interviewed. The average age of the participants was 31 years (SD = 3.4).

Procedure and Analysis
To help participants elicit their previous experiences and better imagine the possible use of the monitoring system at home, in contrast with the hospital, a semi-structured contextual inquiry was conducted. Five women were interviewed at their home, and three were interviewed at the hospital, where they were admitted for diverse reasons. Hospitalized women had Cardiotocographs (CTG) at least once a day, and the interviews took place during this monitoring time. Techniques proposed by the co-constructing-stories method were also used. In the sensitization part of the interviews, the questions addressed goals 1 to 3. In the elaboration phase, the concept of the ambulatory monitoring system was introduced and illustrated with paper and fabric prototypes. The questions encouraged participants to provide feedback on the concept and to propose desired solutions. The analysis was done with affinity diagrams.

3.2   Results

The results indicate that the current monitoring system is satisfactory for low-risk pregnant women. They go to their scheduled checkups, which include Ultrasound and FHR monitoring. In case of an unusual event, they are referred to the hospital, where CTGs are more common. The monitoring devices are, in general, comfortable. Women appreciate the information provided by their caregiver and the opportunity to make questions. Also, they expressed that looking at the baby through the ultrasound is pleasant, and it is always reassuring to know that the baby is healthy.

> *"It is a long time between the 8, 12 and 20 weeks ultrasound. For me it would be more comforting if I had this visual image [of the baby]more often." - Participant 3*

On the other hand, they dislike the coldness of the gel used to improve conductivity; the tightness of the CTG bands; difficulty to find a moving baby with the CTG; and the long time it takes to make a good registration.

> *"The CTG would be better if the monitoring times were shorter. I do not like to lie down without moving. If I want to go to the toilet I have to call the nurse to unplug me." - Participant 7*

Most of the participants experience uncertainty about what is happening to their body. They constantly seek more information with relatives, caregivers, online or in books. Women, who had complications in this or previous pregnancies, also expressed that they would like to have extensive checkups more regularly to be sure the baby is alright. However, the low-risk mothers-to-be were also aware that excessive information can cause more worries than needed.

Required characteristic for the monitoring system were that it should: prevent uncertainty; provide a sense of safety and control; increase the bond between mother and baby; and reduce time at the hospital for monitoring. The system feedback should include information about: correct position of the sensors; auditory feedback with the sound of the FHR; a visual image of the baby and his/her status; differences between sensors in case of twins; fetal movement levels; the correct registration of the measurements and their transmission to the hospital; and have timely, noticeable alarms in case of fetal distress. Finally, the wearable should be: unnoticeable to other people; easy to combine with other clothes; a shirt or a belt; soft, elastic, not warm or "sweaty", non-sticky, and not heavy. The wearable also should: allow movement of the mother; provide clear instructions for use; allow to easily find a moving baby; have non-sticky electrodes; and have the ability to grow with the belly.

4   Garment Design, Prototyping and Evaluation

The garment consists of two parts: the soft-fabric wearable and a flexible Printed Circuit Board (PCB). The PCB contains five female Anorak snaps to plug the electrodes without wires; and the electronic system to filter, amplify and transmit the data to a mobile device. The fabric wearable aims at providing a comfortable, natural wear whilst ensuring that the sensors are firmly in place, therefore reducing possible motion artifacts. The integration between the PCB and the garment should reduce movement in the sensor-skin contact and let the user remove the PCB during washing.

4.1   Printed Circuit Board

The PCB was designed to meet the sensor distribution requirements [12]. Its substrate (DuPont Kapton polyimide film) is flexible only in one direction, which makes it difficult to adapt a squared PCB to the round pregnant belly shape. Therefore, a star-like shape was designed (Figure 2a). Its advantages are that (1) the shape can be bent to follow a round surface; (2) it is less uncomfortable and noticeable to third persons; (3) the electrodes connect directly to the PCB with the correct distribution; (4) the filters/amplifiers can be placed near to each electrode to reduce environment noise; and (5) there is enough area to place all the required electronic components.

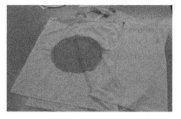

Fig. 2. (a) The PCB shape in a Kapton polyimide film, attached to fabric using Anorak snaps. (b) Double layer with mesh fabric to adjust the PCB in the Wrap top.

4.2   Garment

Based on the requirements, four prototypes were developed and evaluated (Figure 3).

Fig. 3. Garments, from left to right: Belly band, Belly belt, Wrap top and Shirt

Table 1. Garment description

Garment	Garment type	Adjustment type	Material	Color
Belly band	Band	Closed garment	Cotton span	White
Belly belt	Band	Open garment with wrapped closure secured by a knot	Lycra	Black
Shirt	Shirt	Closed garment	Knitted cotton structure	White
Wrap top	Shirt	Open garment with wrapped closure secured by hooks	Lycra	White

The type of garment and the type of adjustment for different sizes were varied among shirt, band, open, and closed, to test which one was preferred (Table 1). Shirts are more natural to wear, whereas bands are easier to fit different belly sizes. In contrast, open garments allow tightness adjustment according to the gestational age, while closed garments are easier to put on. Another advantage of open, wrapped garments is that they provide multiple layers of fabric. Thus, the PCB can be placed in between them to prevent its contact with the skin. A mesh fabric was used in the inner layer to let the electrodes be placed directly on the skin, followed by the mesh fabric layer, the PCB, and finally, by a layer of regular fabric. This was also implemented in closed garments using bags (Figure 2b).

4.3   Evaluation

The aforementioned prototypes were evaluated to select the best features of each one, their comfort and their usability.

Methods

Participants
Five pregnant women (average gestational age = 27.8 weeks, SD=2.38, average age = 32.2, SD=2.78) participated in the evaluation. Four of them evaluated the prototypes at the hospital (high-risk), and one of them (low-risk) did the evaluation at home.

Procedure and analysis
The low-risk participant was considered as a pilot, and therefore she tested only one prototype: the shirt. The rest tried three prototypes (i.e., Belly band, Belly belt, and Wrap Top). Each prototype was provided with a set of instructions (Figure 4) on how to wear it. They were asked to wear the garment without help from the facilitator, and to think aloud during the process. After the task, a semi structured interview was conducted. It covered questions about wearable features (fabric, color, type of wearable, PCB – garment integration, usability, and desired frequency of use).

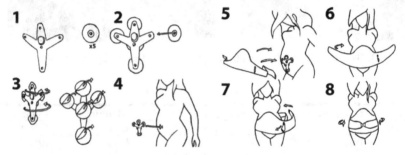

Fig. 4. Example of the instructions followed by the participants (Wrap top)

Results

In general, electrode placement was easily understood by the participants. The PCB is light and after its placement, most women did not feel it anymore. However, they did not appreciate the metallic look and the sharp edges of the PCB.

The instructions to wear the garments were quickly understood. Yet it did not mean that the garments were easy to use. The main difficulty was that the size of the garment was inappropriate for most women, i.e., it was either too big or too small. Especially the Wrap was not easy to close. The hooks were not easy to see or reach. Furthermore, only two participants understood the concept of using the mesh fabric in between the PCB and the electrodes. However, this was not their first interpretation of the instructions. In the case of the Belly band, the mesh pocket was rather confusing.

The preferred type of garment was the Belly band because it was the easiest to put on and the prototype size fitted better most of the women. Nevertheless, several participants mentioned that if the shirt fitted them better, they would prefer it. As for the fabric, participants preferred cotton than Lycra, as the latter is perceived as a "sweaty" material. The preferred color was black, as white was often called "hospital white".

Four participants would recommend the system. They liked that it is user friendly and that they can move around while wearing it. However, they would miss the contact with the doctor and they suggested providing different sizes of the garment.

5   Discussion and Conclusions

A novel concept for a wearable for pregnancy monitoring was presented and developed through user research. In general, it was liked by all participants, especially if their baby would benefit from it. The proposed garments and the PCB shape have been rated as comfortable, and relatively easy to use. However, features such as the mesh fabric layer have to be revised and improved.

None of the participants complained about the possibilities to combine the garments with other clothes. In this evaluation, the most preferred garment was the Belly band, but this outcome has to be considered carefully. This result might be because the Belly band fitted best most of the participants and not because it is their preferred garment type. Future versions of the garment should address the fitting issue more carefully, either by providing different garment sizes, improving the fitting technique in open garments or by designing a one-size-fits-all closed garment.

Table 2.   Summary of the advantages and disadvantages of each garment type. + means good, and – bad

Feature	Band	Belt	Shirt	Wrap-top
Combination with PCB	-	+	-	+
Preference for wear	+	-	+	-
Easiness to understand (affordances)	+	-	+	-
Easy to adjust PCB	+	+	-	-
Tightness	+	++	+	++
Less Movement Artifacts	++	++	+	+
Natural to wear	-	-	+	+
Unnoticeable	+	+	+	+
Total positive scores	**7**	**7**	**6**	**6**

Table 2 provides an overview of the advantages and disadvantages of each garment type. The scores for the types of garment are very close to each other. The main cause is that they have complementary advantages. To make a decision, an extra weight factor was given to those aspects related to tightness and less movement artifacts. These were considered most important as they might influence the accuracy of the measurements. Thus, they are critical to keep the core functionality of the system.

The PCB shape was rated as comfortable. However, the current prototype was tested only with the substrate. Adding the electronic components might change how comfortable it is. Even though it is a technical requirement for improved registrations, the size of the PCB is still big. Women tend to shrink or fold the fabric-metal integration region when they do not see the metal part, which can eventually lead to breaking of the PCB. In contrast, when the PCB is visible, women are afraid of getting cut by the sharp edges. Future work should improve the PCB-Garment integration.

Finally, the SEBAN pregnancy monitor differs from other systems because it improves energy management to provide long-term usage; the data acquisition garment is optimized for robust data acquisition (i.e., optimal arrangement of electrodes, no wires, sensors next to the amplifier); it is completely wireless; it uses a common device as a mobile phone to give feedback and forward the data; and the wearable design considers comfort and usability. Nevertheless, it still uses sticky electrodes to ensure good electrode-skin contact, which might cause skin irritation.

The garment design can be further improved: first, by considering several options for the garment-PCB integration; a complete evaluation of the garment and the performance of the monitoring; and the design of other elements of the system architecture, such as the App to provide feedback to mothers-to-be, and the software for the caregivers. Furthermore, as technology advances, regular electrodes could be replaced with textile electrodes to improve even more the comfort of the mother.

Acknowledgements. This work was supported by the STW SEBAN project, E. Cantatore, M. Rooijakkers, S. Song and G. Kraak.

References

[1] Haws, R., Yakoob, M.Y., Soomro, T., Menezes, E., Darmstadt, G., Bhutta, Z.: Reducing stillbirths: screening and monitoring during pregnancy and labour. BMC Pregnancy Childbirth 9 (January 2009)

[2] Flenady, V., Middleton, P., Smith, G.C., Duke, W., Erwich, J.J., Khong, T.Y., Neilson, J., Ezzati, M., Koopmans, L., Ellwood, D., Fretts, R., Frøen, J.F.: Stillbirths: the way forward in high-income countries. Lancet 377(9778), 1703–1717 (2011)

[3] Evers, A., Brouwers, H.: Perinatal mortality and severe morbidity in low and high risk term pregnancies in the Netherlands: prospective cohort study. BMJ 341, 1–8 (2010)

[4] Buysse, H., De Moor, G., Van Maele, G., Baert, E., Thienpont, G., Temmerman, M.: Cost-effectiveness of telemonitoring for high-risk pregnant women. Int. J. Med. Inform. 77(7), 470–476 (2008)

[5] Kerner, R., Yogev, Y., Belkin, A., Ben-Haroush, A., Zeevi, B., Hod, M.: Maternal self-administered fetal heart rate monitoring and transmission from home in high-risk pregnancies. Int. J. Gynecol. Obstet. 84(1), 33–39 (2004)

[6] Philips, "Avalon CTS",
http://www.healthcare.philips.com/nl_nl/products/
patient_monitoring/products/avalon/
(accessed: September 5, 2014)

[7] MonicaHealthcare, "Monica AN24",
http://www.monicahealthcare.com/products/index.php
(accessed: September 5, 2014)

[8] CIDESI, "Monitor Fetal Remoto"
http://www.conacyt.mx/agencia/index.php/innovacion/
103-cidesi-desarrolla-monitor-fetal-remoto-tecnologia-para-
el-cuidado-de-la-salud-prenatal (accessed: September 5, 2014)

[9] Fanelli, A., Signorini, M.G., Ferrario, M., Perego, P., Piccini, L., Andreoni, G., Magenes, G.: Telefetalcare: a first prototype of a wearable fetal electrocardiograph. In: IEEE Engineering in Medicine and Biology Society. Annual Conference, vol. 2011, pp. 6899–6902 (2011)

[10] Std, I., Standards, I., Committee, C., Hazards, N.R., Board, I.S.: IEEE Standard for Safety Levels with Respect to Human Exposure to Radio Frequency Electromagnetic Fields, 3 kHz to 300 GHz (1999)

[11] Song, S., Rooijakkers, M.J., Rabotti, C., Mischi, M.: a. H. M. van Roermund, and E. Cantatore.: A low-power noise scalable instrumentation amplifier for fetal monitoring applications. In: 2013 IEEE Int. Symp. Circuits Syst., pp. 1926–1929 (May 2013)

[12] Rooijakkers, M.J., Song, S., Rabotti, C., Oei, S.G., Bergmans, J.W.M., Cantatore, E., Mischi, M.: Influence of electrode placement on signal quality for ambulatory pregnancy monitoring. Comput. Math. Methods Med. 2014, 960–980 (2014)

Acceptance of Selected Applications of Ambient Assisted Living in the Project A²LICE

Anne Randow, Christian Poßögel, Sebastian Thiele, and Martin Grünendahl

University of Applied Sciences Zwickau,
Gesundheits- und Pflegewissenschaften, Physikalische Technik/Informatik
Dr. Friedrichs-Ring 2A, 08056 Zwickau, Germany
(anne.randow,christian.possoegel,sebastian.thiele,
martin.gruenendahl}@fh-zwickau.de

Abstract. Germany, in particular the state of Saxony, has one of the oldest average populations in the world. The impact of demographic and social changes has led to large challenges. The process of population aging combined with changing family structures has led to a large increase of needy and dependent people and this trend is likely to continue. Germany is strenuously seeking to find suitable solutions to manage this problem. The financial viability and future quality of healthcare will continue to play a crucial role. This paper is intended to present an overview of the project A²LICE (Ambient Assisted Living in Intelligent Controlled Environments) and depicts the first results of acceptance research with elderly people.

Keywords: Ambient assisted Living, technology, acceptance, elderly.

1   Introduction – The A²LICE Research Project

Germany, among other western industrialized nations, is severely affected by socio-demographic changes of an aging population. Of the 16 states of Germany, Saxony has the highest proportion of seniors (people 65 years or older (24.7%)). [1] The costs of healthcare have increased dramatically due to this demographic development and the associated growing need for the medical and nursing care of people with chronic and age-related diseases. The resulting higher costs and the growing lack of qualified staff in the healthcare sector urgently require new solutions and concepts. Thus, technical support systems, which increase the independence of older people, support them in everyday activities or improve their commitment and adherence to medical programmes are gaining in importance. Intensive research is being carried out in the context of Ambient Assisted Living (AAL) for the development of technical welfare and assistance systems as well as provision and support systems. The research project A²LICE develops concepts for technically assisted homes for the elderly with a focus on single-person households for people with isolation tendencies. A²LICE is a cross-disciplinary project combining the expertise of the Departments of Health and Nursing Sciences, Computer Sciences and Economics from the University of Applied Sciences Zwickau (WHZ) and the Chair of Factory Planning and Factory

L. Pecchia et al. (Eds.): IWAAL 2014, LNCS 8868, pp. 228–235, 2014.

Management of Chemnitz University of Technology. In addition, a housing society and an outpatient care service are integrated as regional partners. A²LICE benefits from previous research projects of the WHZ in the field of energy efficiency through home automation and is based on a KNX-infrastructure. Light and heating can be controlled automatically and per room, energy consumption can be visualized and power sockets can be turned off with a single button push. To improve safety, the system generates alarm signals such as "poor air quality"; "open windows" when leaving the apartment and can automatically turn off a forgotten oven hot-plate. In the apartment, a variety of manual emergency call devices are installed. These are, for example, touch sensors in each room, a pull cord in the bathroom or a mobile alarm button for the classic home emergency call phone.

The main objective of the project is to observe human behavior by sensors installed in an apartment. The goal is to detect deviations in behavior and inform relatives or medical providers if necessary. On the one hand, recognizing and responding to inactivity is possible and on the other hand, the monitoring of basal and instrumental activities of daily living is also feasible. Analyzing the previous day's profiles allows the detection of undesirable trends. Therefore, the specially developed middleware software component evaluates the sensor events of smart meters, presence detectors, contact sensors, pressure sensors, water meters and others. The activity monitoring exposures short- and long-term changes in health or self-sufficiency of the resident. Normal everyday activities such as meal preparation, personal hygiene, toilet use, or sleep patterns are considered significant indicators, especially for the long-, and medium-term deterioration of general health. [2, 3] Various projects and studies have shown, that targeted questions on the occurrence of warnings from evaluated sensor data can reveal physical and mental health problems that would not have been detected without the support of a technical system. [4, 5, 6] A²LICE also takes health-related values into account such as weight, blood pressure and blood sugar level. Data is collected by certified medical equipment and analyzed by the above-mentioned middleware, stored and displayed graphically to the end-user. For comfort and safety, various lighting scenarios and a calendar with reminders for appointments or medication are integrated into the A²LICE concept.

2   Methods

At the beginning of the project a detailed analysis of literature and project-internal workshops on appropriate scenarios and target groups, as well as a market analysis of existing technologies, products and applications in the field of AAL had been carried out. The target groups are people in need of care with a risk for falls or cognitive disorders and those with hypertension and diabetes mellitus. A questionnaire was developed to explore needs, desires and acceptance of selected AAL applications. It includes questions for socio-demographics, housing conditions, health, support services and use of technology. To determine the acceptance of different AAL applications was of particular interest for the assessments taken.

3   Results

This section summarizes the results of the study gathered by questionnaires. People, who were acquired through the care service, received assistance in completing the questionnaire by an interviewer. This approach was important for the participants over 80 years, because comprehension problems could be counteracted. Results of the interview protocols are also integrated in this section. Because of the direct speech of subjects, the sample is selective and not representative.

The mean age of the 46 in the evaluation included respondents was 75.5 years (median 78 years) with a range from 48-90 years. 44% of the participants are between 80 and 90 years old. 39.1% of the respondents are male and 60.9% female. 67.4% of the participants live alone in their household, 23.9% in two-person households. Overall, 45.7% have a care classification, but in the sample nobody has care level 3. The subjects were asked to classify their physical limitations on a scale of 0-10, with the means of 10 being maximum impaired. The average for the limitations of the respondents is 5.09 (median 5). A hearing aid or utilities to support personal mobility (i.e. wheelchair or cane) is used by 41.3%. 21.7% of the respondents were fallen in their own home within the last year. 67.4% of respondents receive support services provided by persons not living in the household. Overall, 60.9% receive assistance with housework and in the home, 58.7% for errands or shopping, 50% assistance with administrative matters, 47.8% get delivered lunch or eat in assisted living. Other 41.3% receive assistance in setting or oral medication and 41.3% with personal hygiene. Based on the description of the detected features it is clear that there is a selective sample with special assistance and support requirements.

Considering a telemedical scenario, it was of particular interest how many people measuring health values by their own and how often this takes place. Half of the respondents measure the body weight independently, therefrom approximately 1/3 daily and the half once per week. Approximately a quarter (26.1%) of the sample measures blood pressure independently, the incidence varied of several times a day; weekly or when they are feeling bad. The blood sugar level is measured independently of one fifth (19.6%) of the respondents, mostly daily. All 46 participants regularly use a telephone, 32 a flat screen, 24 a cell phone, 16 a DVD player, 12 a digital camera, 9 a laptop, 8 a computer, 6 an emergency telephone, 3 a smartphone and 2 a tablet PC. The internet is used by 12 people, ostensibly for social networking and to inform about products, services, travel and health related questions.

The question for the acceptance of AAL application(s) and assistance functions was: "How important are the following ways of support by a technically assisted apartment for you?" The examinees were able to evaluate every application and assistance function on a four-point scale (from "not important" to "very important"). The participants should indicate their interest (attitude) for selected AAL applications now and with increased impairment. There were a total of 33 different applications and assistance functions. In summary, it was confirmed like in other research projects, that especially assistance functions in terms of safety had the most positive ratings given [7], followed by those in the field of health. Assistance functions in the context of support for daily activities were evaluated restrained, which could be associated with the suspected operation and interaction effort. Overall, the assistance functions are evaluated with increasing impairment as "more important". A not inconsiderable proportion of respondents often answered with "not important". The respondents attached great importance to the improvement of barrier-free housing and living environment design. Be criticized as current deficiencies: lack of walk-in shower, the exit to the balcony (not infinitely / missing grab rails), uneven footpaths and lack of seat options.

Especially subjects who live in the countryside (52.2%) also find fault with missing shopping possibilities. Figure 1 depicts the current rating of AAL applications in the field of safety. Figure 2 gives an overview of the assessment of the safety assistance functions with increasing impairment.

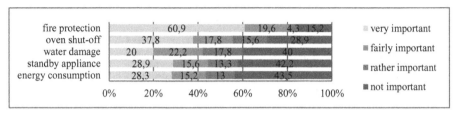

Fig. 1. Current rating of AAL applications regarding to safety

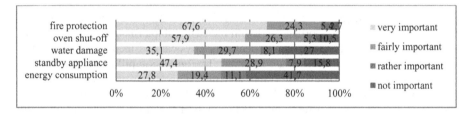

Fig. 2. Rating of AAL applications reg. to safety with increased personal-impairment

The comparison of the current rating to the valuation by increase of impairment makes clear that the first four assistance functions, in particular oven shut-off/ stove shutdown, technique against water damage & standby appliance[1], especially in the rating categories "very important" and "fairly important" show considerably shifts in the acceptance and the proportion of negative attitude is reduced. The automatic shutdown function for forgotten hobs is evaluated "very important" by 37.8% of the participants, with increasing impairment even 57.9%. A fifth classified technology against water damage now as "very important", with increasing impairment there are 35.1%. Especially expected decline in cognitive functions and increase of forgetfulness in age were called as reasons. Figure 3 represents the current rating of assistance functions of the overlapping area of safety/ health while figure 4 illustrates the evaluation of the assistance functions safety/ health with increasing impairment.

A comparison of the assistance functions of the overlapping areas of safety / health show strong changes in the evaluations, especially in the first four support options: classic emergency call, sensor based emergency call system with inactivity detection, fall detection[2] and medication reminder. With an increase of the impairment-level,

---

[1] Automatic shutdown of the devices when leaving the apartment by pushing a single button.

[2] Fall bracelet / fall detector (a body-worn sensor automatically detects immobility and fall).

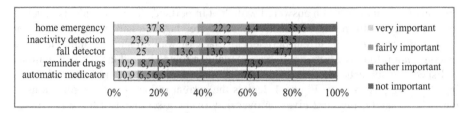

Fig. 3. Current rating of AAL applications regarding to safety/ health

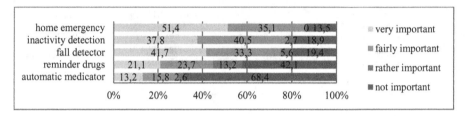

Fig. 4. Rating of AAL applications reg. to safety/ health with increased personal-impairment

higher acceptance ratings are given. 23.9% of the respondents rate sensor based inactivity detection as "very important" and with increasing impairment 37.8%. As justification for the reviews here, especially declining physical and mental abilities due to the expected increase of diseases are attached. The automatic pill dispenser is considered too modern for some participants and the subjects see problems with liquid medications, syringes, and the reliability / functionality of the device itself. Figure 5 gives an overview of the current rating of the support functions in the field of health and figure 6 summarizes the evaluation with increasing restriction on health.

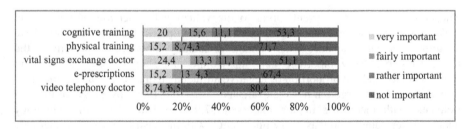

Fig. 5. Current rating of AAL applications regarding to health

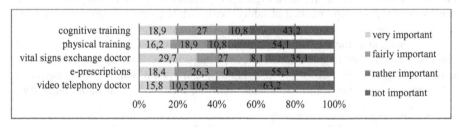

Fig. 6. Rating of AAL applications reg. to health with increased personal-impairment

With health related assistance functions the depreciation "fairly important" recorded a growth with increasing impairment. Currently only 8.7% of the subjects evaluate physical exercise supported by a computer as "fairly important", with increasing impairment 18.9%. A treatment or diagnostic consultation with the doctor from home through video telephony is difficult to imagine, especially for the oldest age classes. They rarely see a need because the doctors usually perform home visits and the participants prefer personal treatment conversations. The older respondents indicate a lack of technical competencies. In e-prescriptions and video telephony with the doctor, the actual implementation and establishment in the standard care is difficult to imagine. As conditions for the implementation simplicity / ease of use, reliability and accuracy of the technique are mentioned.

Figure 7 depicts the current rating of the assistance functions in supporting daily activities while Figure 8 illustrates the evaluation of the assistance functions in the field of daily activities with increase of personal impairment.

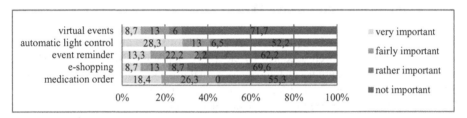

Fig. 7. Current rating of AAL applications regarding to daily activities

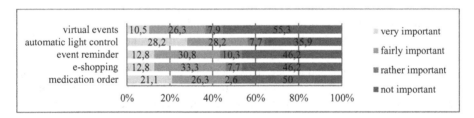

Fig. 8. Rating of AAL applications reg. to daily activity with increased personal-impairment

Again, the greatest gain in the valuation category "fairly important" recorded with increase of impairment. In particular, the electronically-assisted purchase of products and services (e-shopping) will increase with the impairment (current rating "fairly important" 13%, rating with increasing impairment 33.3%). In contrast, the evaluation of electronic medication ordering from home changed only slightly.

In the case of a potential emergency situation, 37.8% of the participants wish to inform the family first, 24.4% the care service and 17.8% a rescue ambulance service or the local hospital. Approximately a quarter of the respondents (24.4%) had previously heard of technically assisted apartments. It is particularly interesting to say that a half of the participants (45.5%) could imagine moving to a technically equipped apartment. This decision is ostensibly linked to conditions such as age, health status, affordability and privacy.

The pros and cons for a move to a technically assisted housing are consistent with the overall objectives and obstacles of AAL. People who can imagine to move to a technically assisted apartment gave the following reasons: helpful, useful, relief; support for existing limitations (mobility, autonomy, cognitive ability); security aspects, protection; increase in comfort, convenience, quality; increased quality of life. The people who would not move to a technically assisted apartment reasoned: no willingness to move; currently working support and care networks; high level of satisfaction with the current housing situation; to old; usability / low technology experience / competence; lack of funding, distrust in modern technology, fear of technology; fear of surveillance. The subjects were asked: Who should pay for the financing technically assisted apartments. Where 34.1% suggested a cost-sharing between end-users and health care funds, 18.2% see only health care funds in duty and 13.6% in favor of a cost-sharing between end-users, health care funds and housing associations.

4   Conclusion and Future Work

The results show that AAL-applications in the fields of safety and health/ safety have already been relatively well accepted by elderly respondents. But as practice shows, acceptance and interest are no guarantees for actual use and willingness to pay. It was established, as in other research projects too, that persons who could really benefit from AAL often see no need of it for themselves because of aspects like subjective evaluation of their own health status or lack of technical expertise and therefore they are often unwilling to adopt it. On the other hand, "younger" people around 60/70 years of age expect they might need AAL-applications later, but only in 15 to 20 years' time, or upon the occurrence of some physical impairment. Interviews with the patient care service and the elderly showed that too little is known about technical support and its applications for the elderly yet, but that there is a growing interest in gaining more information and advice. This should be improved through more training for and by carers, awareness programmes in the media or trade fairs. Much discussed were the affordability of AAL and the financial situation of older people, especially when they are in need of care. Because of the need for private co-funding for care and aid-utilities, as well as low pensions there are little or no resources for other expenses such as AAL. It is still unclear whether and how AAL will be funded in Germany. Viable business models are rare in this area and are mostly based on special forms of compensation such as the concept of integrated care according to §140 a-d SGB V, programs for chronically ill people like Disease-Management-Programs (DMPs), models of self-payment or franchise models. [8] Unfortunately, most research projects in the field of AAL do not find market recognition and many projects ebb after the end of the financial support.

This is primarily due to legal and financial hurdles as well as the fact that the actual users default, or lag behind the presumed utilization. From the point of view of funding, social security institutions say there is a lack of evidence-based results that AAL actually achieves the quality of life, safety, independence and well-being it purports to. Also, it has not yet been convincingly proved that it helps elderly people to stay longer in their own apartment and so reduce care expenditures for inpatients. [9] It is also still unclear what benefits and effects, the activity monitoring actually has to offer for patients in need of care. [4] In the experimental apartment, workshops, focus groups and usability tests with potential end-users such as nurses and doctors are planned to evaluate the A²LICE prototype.

Acknowledgement. The authors gratefully thank the European Social Fund (ESF) for supporting the junior research group and the doctoral scholarship at the University of Applied Sciences Zwickau.

References

1 Statistisches Bundesamt, Im Blickpunkt: Ältere Menschen in Deutschland und der EU, Wiesbaden (2011)

2 Kleinberger, T., Jedlitschka, A., Storf, H., et al.: Evaluation of ADL Detection in the EMERGE project, 3. Deutscher AAL-Kongress, VDE VERLAG GMBH, Berlin und Offenbach (2010)

3 Storf, H., Kleinberger, T., Becker, M., et al.: Modelle und Reasoning-Ansätze für die ambiente Notfallerkennung im eigenen Heim, 3. Deutscher AAL-Kongress, VDE VERLAG GMBH, Berlin und Offenbach (2009)

4 VDI/ VDE Innovation + Technik GmbH (C. Weiß, M. Lutze, D. Compagna), IEGUS (G. Braeske, T. Richter, M. Merda), Abschlussbericht zur Studie: Unterstützung Pflegebedürftiger durch technische Assistenzsysteme (2013)

5 Glascock, A., Kutzik, D.: The impact of behavioral monitoring technology on the provision of health care in the home. JUCS 12(1), 59–79 (2006)

6 Rantz, M.J., Skubic, M., Miller, S.J., et al.: Sensor Technology to Support Aging in Place. JAMDA 14, 386–391 (2013)

7 Grauel, J., Spellerberg, A.: Akzeptanz neuer Wohntechniken für ein selbstständiges Leben im Alter – Erklärung anhand sozialstruktureller Merkmale, Technikkompetenz und Technikeinstellungen. ZSR (2), 191–215 (2007)

8 Zähringer, S., Kicherer, F.: (IAO) Lifescience.BIZ, Geschäftsmodelle für kommerzielle Angebote zur Gesundheitsprävention, Fallstudien zu Geschäftsmodellen für Angebote zur Gesundheitsförderung und Prävention im deutschen Gesundheitsmarkt, Fraunhofer Verlag,Stuttgart (2011)

9 Gast, R.: Der Unsichtbare Pfleger. Die Zeit (02), 27–28 (2013)

Informal Carer Role in the Personalisation of Assistive Solutions Connected to Aspirations of People with Dementia

Maria Laura De Filippis[1,3], Michael P. Craven[2,3], and Tom Dening[1,3]

[1] The University of Nottingham, Division of Psychiatry and Applied Psychology,
The Institute of Mental Health, Jubilee Campus, Nottingham, NG7 2TU, UK
[2] The University of Nottingham, Electrical Systems and Optics Research Division,
Faculty of Engineering, University Park, Nottingham NG7 2RD, UK
[3] NIHR MindTech Healthcare Technology Co-operative, The Institute of Mental Health,
Jubilee Campus, Nottingham, NG7 2TU, UK
{maria.de_filippis,michael.craven,tom.dening}@nottingham.ac.uk

Abstract. The increase in the elderly population over the last thirty years with consequent increase in the number of people living with dementia (PwD) has resulted in a research focus on improving quality-of-life and well-being beyond basic needs, to address psychosocial needs and to provide technological support for these. As part of a UK industry-led, publically supported, project Connecting Assistive Solutions to Aspirations (CASA), research is being conducted to inform the design of assistive technology packages that are aspiration-led. Focus groups were conducted with informal carers (family relatives) of persons with dementia to elicit views on technology use for increasing independence of PwD (with a carer living at home). The focus groups were analysed through thematic analysis and the results have been used to produce personas and scenarios for creation of demonstrator assisted living packages.

Keywords: Assistive Technologies, Telecare, Ambient Assisted Living, User experience, Dementia.

1   Background

The ageing global population has led to increased prevalence of chronic diseases that cause functional impairment and consequent disability. Dementia, *a syndrome of progressive decline of the brain and its abilities,* including memory and cognitive functions, can greatly impact on independence and autonomy. At present, the number of people with dementia is doubling every 20 years, and in 2013 among there were overall 44.4 million people with dementia (PwD) in the world (62% living in developing countries)[1]. As part of the 'Dementia Challenge', the UK government has committed increasing funding for research and several new feasibility projects have been funded by the Technology Strategy Board (TSB) via the industry-led Small Business Research Initiative (SBRI), through a funding competition 'Long-term care revolution'. The TSB projects include CASA (Connecting Assistive Solutions to Aspirations),

L. Pecchia et al. (Eds.): IWAAL 2014, LNCS 8868, pp. 236–243, 2014.
© Springer International Publishing Switzerland 2014

a commercial/academic partnership which will develop an aspiration-led approach and produce assistive technological solutions to support increased independence and autonomy in two populations: older people (including PwD and their carers) and young adults (school leavers) with complex learning difficulties, emotional, behavioural and communication difficulties, and autism spectrum disorders. The authors' contribution to CASA is primarily in relation to carers of PwD.

A focus on technological solutions for PwD in particular has developed within the more general area of assistive technologies and telecare for older people. A review of assistive technologies (AT) and services for PwD in the UK by Gibson et al. produced a useful taxonomy with three types: AT used 'by', 'with' and 'on' PwD [2]. Technology used 'by' PwD includes clocks and signage, reminders, communication aids, furniture and daily living aids, and alerts/alarms. Technology used 'with' PwD includes reminiscence devices, games/puzzles and communications aids (such as books and cards). Technologies used 'on' PwD are telecare monitoring systems and devices such as fall detectors. This typology of AT is helpful in portraying a spectrum of autonomy for PwD in relation to technology. Much of the AT used 'by' and 'on' PwD is also found in the generational taxonomy of telecare whereby 1st generation is typified by alarms, 2nd generation by home sensors and monitors, and 3rd generation telecare, much less prevalent in current provision, by contemporary information and communication technologies (ICT) on a variety of digital platforms.

Much of traditional AT addresses physiological need and safety. However, in our approach to design and evaluation of AT connected to aspirations in gerontology we and others have found the Maslow Hierarchy of Needs to be useful [3]. According to Maslow different levels of needs are motivational drivers of decision-making processes. Lower level functional drivers include physiological needs (e.g., need to eat, drink etc.) but the higher levels of social needs, self-esteem and self-actualisation are more closely linked to aspirations. Aspirations are also described as personal goals in life that push people to achieve one or more needs in different ways in tune with a person's knowledge and beliefs [4], are strongly associated to personal well-being [5], [6] and can be fully achieved only when the need of autonomy, intended as self-determination, independence, freedom of choice and action are satisfied [7].

Federici *et al.* have drawn on a 'biopsychosocial' approach to the design and evaluation of AT aimed at addressing psychological and social as well as biological or medical needs [8]. Evidence already suggests that for older people including PwD, identity, stigma and choice are important factors in the acceptance of AT (such as telecare) [9]. This work has concluded that since telecare can both create stigma and protect identities, there may be a trade-off between how a product looks and how it makes people feel versus how it can enable them to live independently. Future telecare devices therefore need to be redesigned or repackaged to make them desirable.

In a world of ubiquitous computing that we are increasingly exposed to, more people are becoming more competent in choosing and operating technology packages that include mobile, PC or entertainment systems in and outside the home environment. While PwD may have difficulty installing or using them, carers may usefully employ non-traditional AT e.g. a tablet PC with apps that provide digital versions of traditional AT e.g., calendars, notes and lists, alerts etc. This can then support remote telecare (including telepresence) through networking and multimedia capability [10]. One vision of future AT packages as conceived by the CASA project is thus much closer to the provision of personalised consumer product packages, with a stronger link to lifestyle and a flexible modular configuration that adapts to requirements over time, for both PwD and their carer(s).

2   Methods and Study Design

In line with Human Computer Interaction (HCI) research in the area [11] the best way to appropriately design or modify and integrate technologies for people with disabilities or difficulties is to deeply understand the person's motivations, how they currently use technological tools, and how they will use future technologies. Tools to support design and evaluation include scenarios and personas and these are particularly useful when linked to a participatory design approach where users are involved in the process at early stage and preferably throughout the design process [12], [13], [14]. Personas can be used to rarify individual aspirations that new technology packages could support and scenario-based tools support designers with reliable examples of use during their development. Figure 1 shows a model for informing aspiration-led selection of technologies according to a user-centred approach.

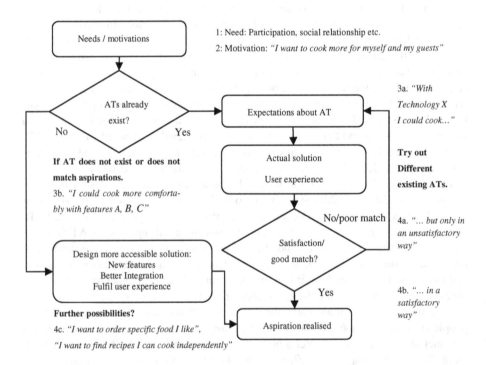

Fig. 1. Model of aspiration-led evaluation and design

The main focus of the study was to elicit informal carer opinion about household technologies and AT to build plausible personas and scenarios to be used in later work involving creation of technology packages aimed at supporting PwD in daily living activities. Focus groups were arranged with a convenience sample of carers recruited through the Alzheimer's Society, Nottingham branch. For a short feasibility project (9 months funding), primarily due to ethical approval time constraints, it was decided not to involve PwD directly, with the caveat that PwD and carers may provide different and potentially conflicting perspectives so care must be taken to guide respondents so they consider desires of the PwD as well as the problems faced by the PwD and carer(s), and also encourage them to think more broadly about existing and potential technology support beyond that of traditional AT so as to avoid concentrating only on safety.

Ethical approval was obtained from the University of Nottingham Medical School Ethics Committee and an Alzheimer's Society Research Partnership form was completed with the Nottingham branch who agreed to recruit volunteer carers from the local community. Carers were given project information and completed a consent form, and reimbursement was offered for travel expenses and sitting allowances. The carer focus groups were audio recorded and field notes taken for thematic analysis.

Two focus groups were run involving three male (L., F., Z.) and three female (W., H., T.) informal carers participating overall who were all family relatives including: spouses (carer for their husband or wife at home); a son (secondary carer to his mother who was caring for her husband in their home); a brother (carer for his younger brother in the same home); a mother caring for her daughter at home, with secondary care from the daughter's sister-in-law. The carers were aged from 52 to 83 and the PwD from 55 to 86 having a variety of dementia types.

3   Results

Three main themes emerged during the discussion with the carers: i) Their feelings about dementia in relation to aspirations and technology; ii) PwD and carer stigma-related issues; iii) Technology and dementia - how technology could improve a PwD's independence, and the carers' opinions about the current and possible future technologies. Results within each theme are presented either as quotes or the gist of responses from several respondents.

3.1   Carer Feelings about Dementia, Associated with Technologies

Informal carers were strongly aware of their role in the decisions of PwD to use or disuse ATs. Carers in the groups had sometimes suggested new tools to PwD (e.g. picture cards to prompt self-care) and on other occasions had prevented or discouraged the use of ATs or other tools due to safety concerns or because the tool was too complicated to use by the PwD, the carer, or both. Also a generational issue was perceived in the use of technologies: *people with dementia and their relatives/carers (especially elderly people) do not accept using advanced technologies, or to ask for external support to help them use them.*

All of the interviewed carers believed that human prompting is more important than the technologies used. As H. suggested: *"We are the main AT ..."* Associated with that, carers underlined that the more an individual loses their autonomy with disease progression, the more carers also lose their independence and their social life. As Z. said, *"[it] can cause frustration and tiredness."*

As the carers underlined, a major consequence of dementia is the loss of independence perceived by their relative. As H. underlined, *"The diagnosis of dementia causes frustrations and depression ... In some cases the person is well-aware of they own status, and they can have suicidal thoughts... In particular, these feelings are caused by the awareness that they are not able to take care of themselves."*

In discussion with the carers, examples of aspirations of the PwD in their care were to maintain or recover the ability to take their own decisions, cook for themselves or others (or select food items from the fridge), to answer and talk on the phone, to continue their hobbies or leisure activities (e.g. swimming) and maintain their relationships with friends. In tune with this result, any technology or set of integrated tools that could avoid or reduce the social isolation of PwD and support them in self-care, would be seen by carers as a very useful solution.

3.2   Stigma

The carers in this study underlined several issues associated to stigma, reporting that their relatives refused to use wearable technologies (such as a fall alarm). As T. suggested PwD *"... do not want that others to identify them as persons with a disease. However, sometimes they need other people to know that they have an issue, for instance when they behave in unexpected ways."* All the carers also agreed that stigma is one of the causes of self-imposed social isolation in PwD, due to a feeling of shame about their situation, or their being afraid of derision, or to be seen as dangerous people. Carers reported a reluctance to identify dementia as a disability on benefits forms or job applications. As F. (and also L.) indicated, *"if asked to tick the option I prefer to not say."* All the carers agreed stigma could an important barrier to PwD using ATs and only an AT with good appearance, or with a design that looks similar to known (non-AT) technologies, would accepted and used.

3.3   Technology for Independence

All the carers reported that PwD were familiar with lo- and hi-tech tools in everyday use. The most commonly used artefacts – by PwD autonomously or with the help of a carer – were found to be: telephone, TV, kitchen appliances, watches and alarms, paper and digital calendars, whiteboards, PCs and tablets. All the carers underlined that PwD would experience a rapid descent in individual functioning and gradually lose their previous capability to use existing artefacts. For example, all the carers reported that their relatives have had several issues in the use of telephone or mobile phones, such as problems in dialing or remembering how to unlock a mobile phone. Five of six carers said the PwD would appreciate tools such as *"a phone dialer system with pre-memorised numbers"* that could be used to make a quick call in a stressful situation. Carers also reported experience of communication problems during telephone conversations. As W. said, *"People with advanced stages of dementia can experience problems putting sentences together when they speak over the phone."*

When PCs or tablets were available in the home environment, carers reported that these kind of advanced tools were rarely by the PwD but some carer found them useful to manage and organise daily routines for them e.g., appointments. As T. suggested tablets and apps could, in principle, be useful to *"manage daily routine with reduced text and powerful graphical presentations [...], for instance to organise a menu for the day or a shopping list."* However, at present these kind of apps were not considered smart enough by the carers and suggested that PwD would forget to open the app, and would therefore need human prompting to use these systems effectively.

Entertainment tools, and in particular TV and radio were considered useful technologies to help PwD to exercise memory. Nevertheless, a decrease in the ability of PwD to focus attention was considered to lead to a reduction of use of media devices.

Among the common domestic technologies, all the carers agreed that the use of kitchen appliances was the most problematic for PwD for several reasons, including safety associated with the use of water boiling tools and the use of gas hobs. As W. suggested, *"The use of a gas hob could be dangerous"* since the PwD could forget the appliance was hot or to turn off the gas after cooking. Carers therefore usually cook for PwD, or with them. All the carers agreed that when PwD strongly express the aspiration to cook for themselves, microwaves to cook pre-assembled food was the most effective and safe solution. Overall, though, the opinion of carers was that PwD cannot easily cook autonomously. As T. suggested, *"they could experience issues with following instructions or they may not be fully aware of cooking time. Often they eat raw or overcooked meals. In the light of that, devices that can help them to handle the cooking procedure could be very useful."*

Carers reported that for PwD the most effective domestic tools were simple artefacts such as calendars and message boards. These tools were placed in the house to help the PwD to remember routines and appointments and meal times. As H. suggested, *"it is useful to write notes in different colours. Colours assist people with dementia to easily discriminate and remind them the things to do."* All the carers suggested use of coloured indications and pictures in the house to help PwD to recognise spaces and to oriente themselves. Outside the home, all carers agreed about the usefulness of identification systems, such as bracelets containing personal data and carer contacts. Door opening systems (one with RFID keyfob, although with a nightoperating PIN code reported as problematic) and an outdoor key-safe system (for carer access) were reported as being used.

In addition to domestic appliances and lo-tech technologies, several hi-tech systems and existing ATs were reported being used or suggested by carers: fall alarms, door sensors, a centrally control alert system, heat and smoke detectors and medication devices. As Z. said, *"hi-tech pill dispensers with an alarm which starts when a person has to take medications and stops when the medication is taken are amazing tools [...] after a while if they have not taken the pills, the central control can send a message."* In general ATs and control systems were considered by informal carers to be important tools, especially when they were not present. In particular carers underlined that central control and remote control monitoring systems with an alarm and cameras could be useful when the main carer is a worker, or when PwD lives alone or with an elderly carer (assumed to be less capable with technologies). Global Positioning System (GPS) devices were consider to be potentially useful for tracking movement when the PwD was out of the house or at work, although concern was expressed about the visibility of such devices to others. As H. explained, *"Tracking technologies could be a reassurance, both for the carers and for people with dementia, especially if these technologies are well designed and wearable. Maybe the best thing is that these tools are invisible to other people."*

Carers reported that any kind of ATs or tools that could help PwD to avoid the social isolation and prompt their independence in daily tasks could be considered a *"real life changer."* Carers suggested smart tools, equipment and appliances that could identify if the user has a particular difficulty and react in personalised manner. One example was a 'smart hob' that could identify an individual and then support them in making their own meals, with the opinion that something like this could really change the life of both PwD and carers. Having recently purchased a Smart TV with voice control and camera, one carer speculated how it might be used for the individual in their care e.g. the PwD could control the TV better, and the carer could remotely check if they are safe, and communicate with them.

4   Conclusions

From a small convenience sample one must be wary about generalising but, as might be expected from carer groups, there was great focus on safety in and outside of the home and on things the PwD was not able to do. On the other hand a desire was expressed to help the individual in their care perform tasks more independently (that would also reduce effort for the carer) and to continue their hobbies and leisure activities or maintain social relationships. Carers stressed their role as a vital adjunct to assistive technologies. Carers revealed the use of a number of mainly lo-tech technologies in their households used as AT but were aware of or saw the potential for hi-tech devices that could be used as AT including some recently acquired e.g. Smart TV, and also had ideas for technologies not currently available.

Personas of informal carers were produced using the information and the opinions gathered, taking into account varying exposure to existing technologies and different roles in the care of PwD. The results are now being used to define scenarios. The idea of 'enabler packs', that was conceived jointly by the CASA partnership, is leading to the design of customisable technology packages aimed at carers to assist PwD with minimal support. Meal-making and leisure activity technology packages are being considered initially. The plausibility of scenarios and packages will first be explored using brochures prior to the production of actual packages, thus introducing a degree of co-production into the final package designs.

Acknowledgements. The research reported in this paper was conducted by the National Institute for Health Research MindTech Healthcare Technology Co-operative (NIHR MindTech HTC). The views expressed are those of the author(s) and not necessarily those of the NHS, the NIHR or the Department of Health. The authors acknowledge funding support for the research through the Connecting Assistive Solutions to Aspirations (CASA) project, provided by the Technology Strategy Board Long Term Care Revolution initiative by means of a Small Business Research Initiative grant. The CASA project is a collaborative venture led by commercial partner Leone Services Ltd., in partnership with Sensixa Ltd., The University of Nottingham, University of the West of England, Bristol and Swiss Cottage School, Development & Research Centre. The authors would also like to thank the Nottingham branch of the Alzheimer's Society, for organising the recruitment of carers and for hosting the focus groups, and all of the carer volunteers.

References

1. Alzheimer's Disease International, Dementia Statistics (accessed June 2, 2014), http://www.alz.co.uk/research/statistics
2. Gibson, G., Newton, L., Pritchard, G., Finch, T., Brittain, K., Robinson, L.: The provision of assistive technology products and services for people with dementia in the United Kingdom, Dementia (London) (May 5, 2014) (Epub ahead of print)
3. Brink, M., van Bronswijk, J.E.M.H.: Addressing Maslow's deficiency needs in smart homes. Gerontechnology 11(3), 445–451 (2013)
4. Deci, E.L., Ryan, R.M.: The "What" and "Why" of Goal Pursuits: Human Needs and the Self-Determination of Behavior. Psychological Inquiry 11(4), 227–268 (2000)
5. Katz, J., Holland, C., Peace, S., Taylor, E.: A better life- what older people with high support needs value. Joseph Rowntree Foundation (November 2011), http://www.jrf.org.uk/ (accessed April 2, 2014)
6. Peace, S., Werner-Wahl, H., Oswald, F., Mollenkoph, H.: Environment and ageing. In: Bond, J., Peace, S. Dittmarr-Kohli, F., Westerhof, G. (eds.) Ageing in Society: European Perspectives on Gerontology, pp. 209-234. Sage Publications, London (2007)
7. Collopy, B.J.: Autonomy in long-term care. Generations: Journal of the American Society on Aging 14(Suppl), 9–12 (1990)
8. Federici, S., Scherer, M.: Assistive technology assessment handbook. CRC Press (2012)
9. Hamblin, K.: Lifestyles in Later Life: identity, choice and stigma, AKTIVE Research Report, vol. 5, CIRCLE (2014), http://www.aktive.org.uk (accessed June 2, 2014)
10. Borsci, S., Kurosu, M., Federici, S., Mele, M.L.: Computer systems experiences of users with and without disabilities: an evaluation guide for professionals. CRC Press (2013)
11. Consolvo, S., Roessler, P., Shelton, B.E., LaMarca, A., Schilit, B., Bly, S.: Technology for Care Networks of Elders. IEEE Pervasive Computing 3(2), 22–29 (2004)
12. Lindsay, S., Jackson, D., Ladha, C., Ladha, K., Brittain, K., Olivier, P.: Empathy, participatory design and people with dementia. In: Proceedings of the SIGCHI Conference on Human Factors in Computing Systems, pp. 521–530. ACM Press (2012)
13. Carroll, J.M.: Making use: scenario-based design of human-computer interactions. MIT Press (2000)
14. Vincent, C.J., Blandford, A.: The challenges of delivering validated personas for medical equipment design. Applied Ergonomics 45(4), 1097–1105 (2014)

Designing ICT for Health and Wellbeing

An Allostatic, Behavioral-Change Approach to a Monitoring and Coaching App

Anders Hedman[1,*], Niklas Karvonen[2], Josef Hallberg[2], and Juho Merilahti[3]

[1]Royal Institute of Technology, Sweden
ahedman@kth.se
[2]Luleå University of Technology, Sweden
{niklas.karvonen,josef.hallberg}@ltu.se
[3]VTT Technical Research Centre of Finland
juho.merilahti@vtt.fi

Abstract. We are developing a monitoring and coaching app for health and wellbeing based on (1) an allostatic model of adaption combined with (2) behavioural change theory and (3) user-oriented design. The (1) allostatic model comes from stress research and was introduced to explain how human health and wellbeing can be maintained. It suggests that human health and wellbeing is a complex multidimensional phenomenon that needs to be understood holistically. We have used this model to incorporate the dimensions of human health and wellbeing that are key for stress reduction: physical and social activity and sleep. The allostatic model can allow us to understand human health and wellbeing but it does not tell us how to support the behavioural changes needed in order to reach a healthy state of allostasis. For this we rely on (2) theory of behavioural change. This article describes how we have integrated (1-3) into the system design and reports from an initial workshop with users.

Keywords: Health and Wellbeing, allostasis, allostatic design, interaction design, design, monitoring, coaching.

1 Introduction

In westernized societies diseases related to sedentary life styles and stress constitute a major health and wellbeing challenge. We present a mobile application designed to motivate people to engage in physical and social activities. The application design is an attempt to go beyond the state of the art in apps for health and wellbeing through a combination of an allostatic model of human adaption [1, 2, 3] and the Transtheoretical model of Behaviour change developed by Dr. Prochaska. Although effects of the latter has been debated, we believe it is a good fit for this application. To measure progress, the system uses external sensors (heart rate monitor, accelerometer and microphone) to monitor the user's physical activity, stress level, social interactions

---

* Corresponding author.

L. Pecchia et al. (Eds.): IWAAL 2014, LNCS 8868, pp. 244–251, 2014.

and quality of sleep. The user's activities are then compared over time with challenges defined by both the system and by the user. Challenges are based on achieving a certain amount of units in activities, for example "Walk 10.000 steps" or "Spend 30 minutes talking to a friend". When a challenge is completed, the user gets positive visual and audio feedback to reinforce the behaviour. The user also gets "health points" for completed challenges and these can be used to get discounts at 3rd party partners (e.g., local gyms, sports retailers), further motivating the use of the application.

1.1   The Allostatic Model in Health and Wellbeing

Health and wellbeing depends on maintaining physiological and psychological balance. Much of our understanding of how to maintain such balance comes from the research on stress. The stress research began with a focus on homeostasis [4]. Stress was thought of in terms of a generalized stress response [4]. Today the field of stress research has moved from a generalized model of stress to one based on allostasis [1,2,3]. We have chosen an allostatic model because it is more realistic for modelling stress than older homeostatic models. According to the allostatic model, a human being's stress tolerance depends on many factors, such as genetic disposition, individual biology, and developmental history. Thus, the tolerance is affected by multiple interactive systems that can become unbalanced. According to the allostatic model of stress, how well a person can deal with the stressors of life and thus maintain health and wellbeing, depends on:

    a. Genetic factors
    b. Social activity patterns
    c. Sleep and resting patterns
    d. Physical activity patterns
    e. Stress coping techniques
    f. Diet and nutrition habits

We have chosen to look more closely at (b-e) and to a limited extent on (f). Genetic factors (a) are important for understanding health and wellbeing. We can expect that much work will be done in the future on genetic screening. In the not so distant future, preventive genetic screening for health and wellbeing may become common. (b) Our social life is important for understanding stress. Too little social interaction can be a source of stress and the wrong forms of social interaction can lead to immense stress while nurturing social relationships can have the opposite effect. (c) Sleep and activity patters modulate our stress levels. If we get insufficient sleep our bodies respond with increasing levels of stress hormones. Increasing levels of stress hormones make us sleep less and we can find ourselves in a stress spiral. (d) Physical activity can make us more stress resilient. Someone who is physically fit typically has a greater ability to rebound from stressful situations. The levels of stress hormones go back to normal faster than for someone who is less fit. (e) Stress reduction techniques such as deep breathing and somatic quieting can help to bring down stress levels. Someone who practices these techniques may cope better with stressors than one who doesn't. (f) Diet and nutrition can be important factors in determining how well we cope with stress. E.g., it has been shown that strict vegetarians become less likely to suffer from cardiovascular disease. Our allostatic model for health and wellbeing takes into account all dimensions above apart from genetic factors. It could be extended to such factors in the future but at present we have chosen to leave it out until genetic screening techniques become more commonplace. According to our allostatic model how well a person can maintain health and wellbeing depends on how well the person is doing on b-f. More concretely this means that we have systematically attempted to construct a health and wellbeing monitoring and coaching platform and app that allows the user to do better in areas b-f.

1.2   Transtheoretical Model of Behavioral Change

The Transtheoretical Model of behavioural change developed by Dr. Prochaska is based on more than 25 years of research measuring behaviour change for a variety of health behaviours. This model serves as a blueprint for effecting self-change in health behaviours and can be readily applied in health, fitness and wellness coaching [5, 6]. The model consists of five stages of change:

(I)   **Pre-contemplation**
(II)   **Contemplation**
(III) **Preparation**
(IV)   **Action**
(V)   **Maintenance**

These stages sequentially approach behaviour change with the first stage being furthest from change and the fifth stage being maintaining an already achieved behaviour. We now present these 5 stages further together with our suggested solutions for how our application could influence the user to progress through the stages.

Pre-contemplation (Stage I) The subject is not yet thinking about changing behaviour. The person may not admit they have a problem or think that change is possible [5]. It is unlikely that a person in this stage would engage with our application on their own, but this stage is still important since application users in higher stages might fall back into this stage during their behaviour change process. Persons in the pre-contemplation stage may get the application out of curiosity or through recommendation. To move the subject to the next stage, a simple challenge is presented to the user at the first use of the application. The challenge consists of answering simple questions about themselves, their health and goals. Between each question there are brief assertions of how better health can be attained with little effort. Upon completing the first challenge the user receives rewarding feedback of having taken a step in changing behaviour and becoming healthier. This feedback can hopefully help the user move to the contemplation stage.

Contemplation (Stage II) Subjects in this stage are thinking about changing behaviour and are considering taking action. They are generally aware of the positive effects a behaviour change could yield but may perceive making the change as difficult. Moore et al. [5] suggests that increasing awareness of compelling reasons to change and getting people to connect with others that have successfully changed is important. This is done in our application by showing information splash screens from other successful users (that have agreed to this). Seeing others completing challenges and reaching results could motivate the user to take action and reach the preparation stage.

Preparation (Stage III) Subjects have overcome most negative feelings about the change process, strengthened their motivation and are planning to take action. Subjects also experiment with possible solutions [5]. Moore et al. suggest assisting subjects with their plans and encouraging them to write down a statement of what they are committed to do. They also suggest identifying small steps to put into action. By allowing the user to choose or even create his/her own challenges our suggested application helps the subject through the preparation stage. The premade challenges in our application are simple to complete so the majority of users can finish them in a day. After the challenges are chosen, the application monitors progress and notifies the user with positive feedback as challenges are completed. This hopefully keeps the subject motivated to make positive behaviour changes, and if motivated enough move to the action stage.

Action (Stage IV) Subjects are consistently working towards their goals through practicing new behaviours including building new relationships [5]. Moore et al. state that assisting subjects in developing new relationships with people who share their interests and goals can make a significant difference. In our application this is addressed by enabling chatting with other users. Users can also add their custom challenges to the public challenge database to further encourage user-to-user involvement. It is also possible for users to add real-life events such as meet-ups and competitions. If the user is active in the action stage for a longer period of time (6 months [5]) he/she is considered to have changed and is considered to be in the maintenance stage.

Maintenance (Stage V) This stage begins when the new behaviour has turned into a habit. Coaching in this stage is focused on retaining the positive habit and preventing lapses. A lapse occurs when the subject temporarily abandons the new behaviour. When this happens, the subject may need assistance to set new goals and refocus [5]. By detecting changes in habits, our suggested application could recommend the user to enter a competition, challenge a friend or participate in an event to get the user back on track. The application will also periodically encourage the user to share his/her results with others since this has a positive effect on motivation [5].

2   The Monitoring and Coaching Platform

The monitoring and coaching platform is being built in modules, parallel to the design of the interfaces. The primary focus has been on monitoring the four dimensions of our allostatic model: social activity, sleep and resting, physical activity, and stress levels. The architecture is easily extendable with new sensors and devices, and improved measurement techniques as they become available. A number of quantifiable *DataUnits* have been defined for the four dimensions. These *DataUnits* allow aggregation and fusion of data to vary as long as the quantified value is produced as a result. This also allows for many different devices to be used, given that a sensor module is developed to capture the data and that the *DataUnits* support the data type being captured. Social interactions are manually input by the user, but the user can also choose to have them automatically detected using the mobile phone microphone and voice activity detection algorithms. It should be noted that the accuracy of this feature is highly dependent on the placement of the device.

Sleep and resting is sensed through heart rate and accelerometer-data from the wrist-worn device. The algorithm detects movement in the night, coupled with the heart-rate variability to detect quality of sleep, such as resting, sleep and deep sleep.

Physical activity is calculated from movement and heart rate. Movement is sensed using Laban Movement analysis of data from the wrist-worn accelerometer, which has been shown as the best placement of a single accelerometer to detect movement intensity [7]. This analysis is complemented with heart-rate data for complementary detection of activity intensity.

Stress levels are detected through heart-rate variability and accelerometer-data from a wrist-worn device. The wrist-worn device uses an optical sensor for detecting heart rate, which yields the accurate heart-rate detection required for heart-rate variability calculations. It has been shown that heart rate variability can be used to determine stress during a number of different activities, such as while sitting, standing, and walking [8].

The sensing modules are currently under development and will soon be integrated into a working prototype together with the interfaces that are evaluated in this paper. Furthermore, the detected aspects will be used by the coaching application to provide automatic and helpful advice and information to motivate users to perform healthy behavioural changes. For example, the application can provide information on the positive effects of an active physical life, and offer suggestions on activities to improve quality of life, such as what to do to improve the quality of sleep. These advices will be developed in collaboration with healthcare professionals and mined from common- and best practices.

3   Evaluation

Two monitoring prototypes and one coaching prototype (see fig. 1.) were evaluated in a user workshop. The monitoring prototypes contained the proposed main monitoring interface related to activity tracking, and the coaching prototype contained the proposed user interface for a coaching component. 12 users participated in the test and their ages ranged from 20-60. The test participants were first briefed about the project. A short demonstration was then given of the prototypes. The participants were then asked to explore the prototypes for themselves in groups of four people. The two monitoring prototypes were web-based and were presented on iPod touch devices. The coaching prototype was presented on a laptop. Each group had one iPod and one laptop. The coaching prototype was in PowerPoint format and lent itself better for a laptop device. As the users explored the prototypes they were also asked to fill in a questionnaire. The users were also given post-it notes to jot down notes and any reflections they might have about the prototypes. These notes were then saved along with each questionnaire to aid in the analysis. All prototypes had many pages that are not shown here.

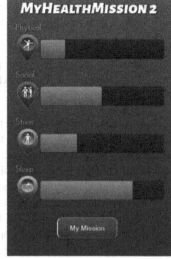

| Monitoring prototype 1 | Monitoring prototype 2 | Coaching protoype |

Fig. 1. Prototypes tested in the first user workshop

3.1   Initial Findings

We found the following in our evaluation of the first prototypes.

1. The second monitoring prototype was the one we should choose for further development. It was perceived as easier to navigate and allowed the users to get a better sense of what the capabilities were of the app and how it could be used. From the responses to the questionnaire we saw that the first monitoring prototype was received slightly negatively with respect to how easy it was for the users to understand what could be done with the application. The same was true for how the information was presented. Monitoring prototype two fared better and was, on the whole evaluated in positive regard. When asked which prototype they preferred most users said monitoring prototype two. Some of the reasons given were that it was: "simpler, better with horizontal bars", "clearer—if you target a group around 40 years old prototype one might be difficult to handle" and that "the information is easier to understand". It was clear that the prototype to continue development with was the second monitoring prototype.
2. The users thought that the coaching component ought to be included in the app and that it was important. The users held the coaching prototype in positive regard.
3. The monitoring parts of the app were also perceived favourably.
4. Our users were not in favour of having a social sharing component. They did not want to share their results with other users through the app.
5. They wanted the coaching feedback to be personalized—not just general advice.
6. Most users preferred to be coached via the app and not via interaction with peers.
7. Most users believed that people are likely to use a health and wellbeing app for a long period of time.

These findings are based on our questionnaire and also supported by the user's notes and our discussions with them. From reading the notes and discussing with the users we also found that:

8. User opinions diverged greatly. Some users in the test wrote largely negative comments and reviewed the apps unfavourably while others were highly positive and reviewed the prototypes favourably.

Here it is interesting to note that the users revealed a preference for having a coaching component in the application. They also thought that the coaching should be personalized. However, the users neither wanted to share the information within the coaching app with their friends nor to be coached through social peer-to-peer coaching. Lastly, it is interesting to note that they believed that a health and wellbeing app is something that people would be likely to use on a more permanent basis. Our initial evaluation of the prototype was only meant to provide rapid initial feedback for guiding system design. We plan to conduct further studies once we have a working system. To understand how the system would work in the real world it would be best to perform our future evaluation in everyday life situations, i.e., having users use the system as intended.

4   Discussion

From our user study it became evident that some users were highly critical of our prototypes while others were highly positive. Most users fell somewhere in between those extremes. What made some users so critical? Some raised concerns about the validity of the monitoring measures and soundness of coaching suggestions. Perhaps these users would be more satisfied with an improved coaching and monitoring app. However, there might be a group of users who would not be satisfied with any monitoring and coaching app. After all, a human coach can offer things that a computational system cannot such as the presence of a caring and empathic professional.

The users did not object to our multi-dimensional model of health and wellbeing. Indeed they seem to support such a model. If they had not supported it, then they would have objected to the inclusion of one or more dimensions of monitoring and coaching. Implicitly then, one could argue that the allostatic model was supported. It was natural for the users to think of wellbeing as the result of interplay of social activity, sleep and physical activity patterns. In the future we might extend this model with a nutritional model in order to strengthen the allostatic model further. Another possibility would also be to include lessons or other content on the allostatic model within the coaching module. It would also be possible to include content on the behavioural-change model. Whether we do this or not in the future could be decided after our next user workshop. According to the behavioural change model it is important that users want to understand the mechanisms of change. It is a model that involves changing behaviour, but it is also one that can be further strengthened through understanding. To some extent this could be said about the allostatic model as well. Once users understand how it works it allows them to change their behaviour more easily. If a user sees that he or she is not doing so well in one category (such as sleep or physical activity) then this can be a strong incentive to change behaviour within that category.

5   Conclusions and Future Work

We learned from our first user study how to proceed with the development of our health and wellbeing app. We will continue with the second monitoring prototype and we will include the coaching component. The fact that the users preferred to have a coaching component included supported our underlying allostatic, behavioural-change model. If the users had not preferred to have a coaching model it would be unclear how the behavioural-change model could be included. As it is we will continue to work with the coaching component. We will continue to work with the allostatic model as well. It is a model that fits well with the results from the first user workshop. Moreover, it is also compatible with the behavioural-change model. Indeed the two models can work as mutually supporting. The allostatic model gives support from a fundamental bio-psycho-social perspective while the behavioural-change model works at a higher psychological level to motivate change. In the next user workshop we plan to explore whether or not learning about these underlying models is something that the users would want.

Acknowledgements. This work has been supported by the European Institute of Innovation & Technology (EU EIT ICT Labs) within the HWB Cognitive Endurance activity.

References

1. Sterling, P., Eyer, J.: Allostasis A new paradigm to explain arousal pathology. In: Fisher, S., Reason, J. (eds.) Handbook of Life Stress, Cognition, and Health. John Wiley & Sons, New York (1988)
2. Schulkin, J.: Rethinking homeostasis: Allostatic regulation in physiology and pathophysiology. MIT Press, Cambridge (2003)
3. Schulkin, J.: Allostasis, homeostasis and the costs of physiological adaptation. Cambridge University Press, New York (2004)
4. Cannon, W.B.: The Wisdom of the Body. WW Norton & Co, Inc. Publishers, New York (1932)
5. Moore, M., Tschannen-Moran, B.: Coaching Psychology Manual, pp. 33-51. Libbincott Williams and Wilkins (2009) ISBN: 0781772621
6. Prochaska, J.O., Velicer, W.F.: The Transtheoretical Model of Health Behavior Change. the American Journal of Health Promotion 12(1) (1997)
7. Kikhia, B., Simón, M.G., Jimenez, L.L., Hallberg, J., Karvonen, N., Synnes, K.: Analysing Body Movements within the Laban Effort Framework using a Single Accelerometer. The Journal of Sensors 14(3) (2014)
8. Sun, F., Kuo, C., Cheng, H., Buthpitiya, S., Collins, P., Griss, M.: Activity-Aware Mental Stress Detection Uisng Physiological Sensors. In: Mobile Computing, Applications, and Services. Lecture Notes of the Institute for Computer Sciences, vol. 76, pp. 211–230 (2012)

Usability Evaluation Method for Mobile Applications for the Elderly: A Methodological Proposal

Doris Cáliz and Xavier Alamán

Autonomous University of Madrid, Department of Computer Engineering
C/ Francisco Tomás y Valiente, 11, 28049 Madrid. Spain
Doris.Caliz@estudiante.uam.es, Xavier.Alammán@uam.es

Abstract. This study aims to propose a practical methodology to measure and evaluate the usability of mHealth mobile applications, focusing on elderly users and their primary limitations. The study starts with an analysis of existing methodologies and tools to evaluate usability and integrates concepts related to inspection and inquiry methods into a proposal. The proposal includes the opinions of experts and representative users; their limitations; their profiles; the types of applications and their domains; the type of devices used; the applicability during the development process; and the accessibility. To facilitate the application of the methodology and integrate concepts found in different tools into one application, the creation of a software tool that automates the evaluation process is proposed. The applicability of the methodology and tools is evaluated and finally the results, conclusions and recommendations for future work are presented.

Keywords: Usability, Usability Evaluation, Mobile Applications, Older Adults, Elderly, Human -Computer Interaction CHI, Mobile Devices.

1   Introduction

The main objective of this research is to study and propose a methodology to determine the degree of usability of mHealth applications running on mobile devices with a focus on elderly users. Additionally, this paper proposes to build a tool to determine the degree of usability of the applications running on mobile devices in order to adapt and improve its use. It is estimated that by 2051, 71% of the worldwide population will be elderly (CCHS, 2014). Almost 30 million people in the United States are accessing health information via smartphones. By 2015, 500 million are projected to use a health app (Burnay E 2013).

From a social inclusion standpoint, it is important to consider the limitations of older adults when creating applications so as to not discriminate against these users. While the research related to usability and human-computer interaction has been the subject of extensive study, more focus should be placed on the use of mobile applications by the elderly population. It is essential to consider the needs of this important and growing population in order to create useful mobile applications that can best facilitate their daily lives.

L. Pecchia et al. (Eds.): IWAAL 2014, LNCS 8868, pp. 252–260, 2014.
© Springer International Publishing Switzerland 2014

2   Background

Software quality can be defined as the set of properties that give the software the ability to satisfy the explicit and implicit requirements of the user who uses it. The quality model ISO/IEC 9126 ISO/ IEC 9126 defines the quality of a software product in terms of six main features: functionality, reliability, usability, efficiency, maintainability and portability. Additionally, usability has the sub-characteristics of: understandability, learnability, operability, attractiveness, and compliance (ISO IEC 9126-1 2001). The following are also mentioned as usability attributes: effectiveness, efficiency, security, utility, ease of learning, remembering in the moment, and satisfaction. It is also important to remember the functional diversity of older adults: sensory (sight, hearing touch), motor (dexterity, mobility), and cognitive (understanding, language, learning) (Martínez L 2014). Furthermore, ISO IEC 25062 proposes Software product Quality Requirements and Evaluation (SQuaRE) as the Common Industry Format (CIF) for usability test reports (2006). The Health IT Usability Evaluation Model (Health-ITUEM) was developed as an integrated model of multiple theories as a comprehensive usability evaluation framework (William 2013). The Technology Acceptance Model (TAM) helps determine if a technology will be optimally used (F Davis 1989). The standard of Human-Centered Design for Interactive Systems provides guidance on human-centered design activities throughout the development life cycle of interactive computer-based systems (ISO 9241-210 2010).

2.1   Research Related to Usability and Mobile Devices

Alshehri and Freeman developed an outline of usability evaluation methods and mobile devices which aims to improve the usability of touch screen mobile devices. This study provides background information about different methods for usability evaluations of mobile devices that can be used in this project (2012).

A study published by Balakrishnan on the effect of thumb sizes of participants in relation to the experience of using mobile phone keypads to send text messages is one way to consider user satisfaction for text entry. Analysis found that varying thumb sizes have significant effects on the satisfaction of text messaging users (2008).

Lee, Kozar (2012). investigated the common dimensions of website usability by considering previous studies on the subject and then analyzing focus groups of web usability experts

2.2   Research Related to People with Special Needs

Ehmen, Haesnera and Steinkeb(2012). presented a study comparing four different mobile devices for measuring heart rate and ECG. The data suggests that there was a high acceptance by older adults; however, none of the devices were completely usable

Hoggan, Brewster and Johnston(2008).performed a study on text input with fingers for mobile devices with touchscreens. They concluded that demand and effort is significantly higher when a touchscreen keyboard is used instead of a physical keyboard

A practical case of applying usability in geriatric research can be found in the paper of Gonzalez, Millan and Balo(2010).. The research found that the application of computerized assessment and cognitive stimulation will have widespread use among elderly populations (2010).

2.3   Usability Evaluation Tools

The tools for usability evaluation vary widely in their capabilities and costs. Some tools only allow for entry and processing surveys. For example, Feedback Army creates questionnaires and collects user feedback (2014). Datalogger and SUM Calculator present Excel templates for collecting and analyzing usability attributes (2014).

Other tools, like Google Analytics (2014), Usabilia (2014), Seevolution (2014) and FiveSecondTest (2014), analyze user acceptance and behavior. They create heat maps by looking at user behavior upon entering a website and determine areas where the user clicks most frequently. Similarly, Click Density (2014) provides a map of clicks, ranking the top 20 regions where the total number of clicks is most concentrated over a period of time. ClickTale (2014) provides information about which forms are more complicated to complete and why. DejaClick (2014) can record user activity and generate reports on their use. ConceptFeedback (2014) records application usage and combines it with opinion forums with feedback on user experience provided by the users. Tools like Morae (2014), Noldus (2014) and Clixpy (2014) record both user activities and the gestures made by the user while using an application. Google Website Optimizer (2014) or Google Analytics (2014) are most oriented towards website optimization and can perform an A/B test, i.e., compare various designs of the same page and analyze the behavior of visitors in order to decide which design is the most effective.

2.4   Conclusion

While there is a great quantity of material and research related to usability of web applications, there is far less devoted to evaluate usability of mHealth applications for the elderly. The selection of a method depends on several factors, such as: software development methodology, economic capacity and available time. As a hypothesis, though most software development companies know the importance of usability in the development of quality software, the usability practices might not have been incorporated into most of their development processes.

Lack of attention to health IT evaluation may result in an inability to achieve system efficiency, effectiveness, and satisfaction (ISO 9241- 11, 1998). Consequences may include frustrated users, decreased efficiency coupled with increased cost, disruptions in workflow and increases in healthcare errors (Kaufman, Roberts, Merrill, Lai, &Bakken, 2006). Based on the analyzed studies, there is not an Evaluative Methodology of Usability for mHealth specifically for elderly people.

3   Proposal

After studying the primary usability evaluation methodologies, this research proposes a practical methodology to determine the degree of usability of mHealth applications running on mobile devices, focusing on older adult users.

To complement this research, the construction of a tool to determine the degree of usability of mobile device applications is proposed to adapt and improve usage performance. The innovative value of this project lies in the methodology that will allow quantitative identification of the degree of usability of mobile applications, including relevant aspects to be considered when this software is used by elderly people.

3.1   Scope Definition

The usability evaluation methodology raised should cover the aspects in Table 1:

Table 1. The scope of the proposal

Aspect	Scope
Representative users	The objectives of this study are those users identified as elderly. From the National Statistical Institute of Spain, elderly people are defined as those who are 65 years and older.

Aspect	Scope
Limitations of users	This research project will incorporate aspects to mitigate the problems and facilitate the use of mobile applications while considering the limitations that are most related to the usability of mobile applications by the elderly: vision, hearing, psychomotor and cognitive problems.
Application domain	For this project, we have selected applications conducted using mobile devices for health-related behaviors.
Types of applications	There are three types of mobile applications: native, web and hybrid applications. Applications will be evaluated with mHealth technology.
Types of devices	The present study is limited to analyzing the applicability of the methodology for applications running on smartphones and tablets with the Apple iOS and Android operating systems.

3.2   Proposal Requirements

The usability evaluation methodology proposed will have the requirements in Table No. 2:

Table 2. Requirements for the proposed method

Requirement	Description
Consider expert	Considering experts is essential for assessing the compliance of design standards focusing on elderly users and the application type and domain evaluated.
relation to the application development life cycle	The proposed methodology can be applied to prototypes during the design stage, the test stage, and also to applications that are already running in order to improve usability. Both the research results in the previous section and the specific aspects added to the proposed methodology will provide a clear understanding of the requirements needed to develop a tool that supports usability evaluation for elderly users.

Requirement	Description
Evaluation of user profiles	According to the educational level of the elderly population in Spain, 30.7% of people ages 65 to 74 years old have used a computer and 25.2% of the elderly population has used the Internet. However, 76.8% of the elderly have used a mobile phone in the past 3 months. (CSIC and CCHS, 2014). This indicates a need to create a methodology that allows elderly users to classify themselves as novice, intermediate, or advanced users. Chadwick et al. have shown a correlation between a user's level of computer experience and their success rate in using applications (2004).
Accessibility	From a geographical standpoint, the methodology and its tool are remotely accessible. This is a cost-saving benefit because the physical presence of an expert or a laboratory is not necessary. Evaluations via web system will allow both experts and users to report their suggestions as well as the user experience evaluations.

3.3   Methodological Proposal

The methodology will be applied within the standard ISO 9241-210 (2010).   in phase requirements to evaluate the designs against the requirements For older adults, the methodology is used to improve the user experience for those who participate in the Usability Evaluation to use the application. For the developers, the methodology will be useful to evaluate the usability of mHealth, keeping in mind the elderly users.

This project has considered the following aspects:

3.3.1   Research

This includes the research on mobile device usability; existing methods and techniques for usability evaluation; a comparative analysis of the studied methods; an elderly user profile analysis and the analysis of existing tools for usability evaluation. The goal is to integrate these concepts and incorporate additional aspects according to the scope and requirements.

3.3.2   The Proposed Method

The proposed method will include:

- Usability attributes selection – Some usability attributes will be selected according to their importance: effectiveness, efficiency, satisfaction, learnability, accessibility, operability, memorability, acceptability, and flexibility.
- Selection of goals per attribute – Specific goals will be determined depending on the attribute.
- Usability aspects for the elderly must be included – Recognizing vision, hearing, psychomotor, and cognitive problems.
- Considering the importance of the expert evaluation as well as the criteria of users, this methodology will combine two methods of evaluation: *Inspection methods* and *Methods of inquiry* and include the evaluation according to the ISO standards.
- Tools can lead to a practical methodology, which helps choose the priority of the attributes, like an automated questionnaire.
- A new measurement scale will be created the using Health IT Usability Evaluation Scale (Health-ITUES) to evaluate the mHealth application, giving a certain value to the scale with specific attributes of elderly people and their limitations. The Health IT Usability Evaluation Model (Health-ITUEM) is based on the TAM Model.
- Different answers in questionnaires will be mapped in order to calculate different metrics.
- The proposed weighting model combines the different metrics based on their importance and consolidates a global usability metric.
- The results, recommendations, and feedback will be presented.

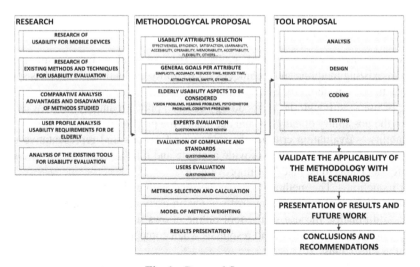

Fig. 1. Proposal Summary

3.4   Tool Proposal

To facilitate the methodology application and integrate several concepts from various tools into one single application, we propose a software tool. This tool will help measure the satisfaction scale, which is already a function of the limitations of the elderly population and should provide as a result a quantitative value. The tool will calculate this value.

The software tool will include the following functionality: User Management (managers, experts, and users), Application Management to be evaluated, Release Management, Standards Management, Indicators Management, Expert Heuristic Criteria, Management of Questionnaires (Perception Survey Generator, Form Evaluator), and Report Generator of Results and Recommendations Management.

4   Conclusions, Results and Future Work

Currently there is a lack of literature on the usability of mHealth technology. There are a number of studies focused on mHealth applications and others focused on the usability of the devices. However, usability evaluations of mHealth technology have not yet reached the level of rigor of web-based electronic health application evaluations with a focus on elderly users (Amith et al, 2012) Luxton D (2012), Burnay E (2013) ,Sheehan B (2012) Sparkes (2012). The proposed methodology presents a practical model for evaluating hybrid and web applications on mobile devices. Additionally, once we understand the limitations of the elderly, we see that, in many cases, these applications have barriers that exclude this important and growing part of the population. The proposal incorporates elements that maximize their level of use of these applications.

4.1   Expected Results

New comprehensive and integrated model – This proposal includes some aspects present in existing methods and techniques for usability evaluation. It also has specific criteria to be considered for elderly users.

Ease of use – Although the methodology can be applied manually, a software tool provides the possibility of easy use and automates the process.

Reliability – Evaluation criteria, the selection of experts and representative users are critical in the methodology to provide accurate and reliable results. This accuracy allows for decisions to be made for improvements.

Cost reduction – The methodology can be used with a simple prototype of an application, which creates significant cost savings in early stages of usability improvements. Additionally, the use of the tool online allows users and experts to connect with significant savings in time and resources when compared to other options such as physical usability labs.

Efficiency – The methodology achieves the goal of evaluating a mobile application and its usability with a focus on the elderly, who have minimal resources.

4.2   Future Work

Based on this research, future work may be done in the following areas:

Incorporating smart elements on mobile applications what can react with tutorials or modify the appearance of the application. This would allow the application to be used by different types of users, including the elderly.

Expanding the scope of the study to other domains or types of applications and for other types of devices.

Applying artificial intelligence elements where the tool is able to understand and learn the user behavior in order to formulate the criteria for improvement.

Incorporation of audiovisual tools into the assessment tool to better enable user interaction.

This work has been funded by the Spanish Ministerio de Ciencia e Innovación through the e-Integra project (TIN2013-44586-R).

References

1. Alshehri, F., Freeman, M.: Methods of usability evaluations of mobile devices. In: Lamp, J.W. (ed.) Paper presented at 23rd Australian Conference on Information Systems, pp. 1–10. Deakin University, Geelong (2012)
2. Amith, M., et al.: Optimization of an HER mobile application using the UFuRT conceptual framework. Paper presented at AMIA Annual Symposium Proceedings, pp. 209-217 (2012)
3. Balakrishnan, Y.: A Study of the Effect of Thumb Sizes on Mobile Phone Texting Satisfaction. Journal of Usability Studies 3(3), 118–128 (2008)
4. Chadwick, A., et al.: Older Adults and Web Usability: Is Web Experience the Same as Web Expertise? In: CHI 2004 Extended Abstracts on Human Factors in Computing Systems, Paper presented at Conference on Human Factors in Computing Systems, Vienna, Austria, pp. 1391–1394 (2004)
5. Abellán García, A., Vilches Fuentes, J., Rodríguez, R.P.: Centro de Ciencias Humanas y Sociales/Consejo Superior de Investigaciones Científicas (2013), Un perfil de las personas mayores en España, 2014: Indicadores estadísticos básicos. (Informes Envejecimiento en red 6), Madrid
6. Ehmen, Haesner: Steinke Comparison of four different mobile devices for measuring heart rate and ECG with respect to aspects of usability and acceptance by older people. SciVerse Science Direct Applied Ergonomics 43(3), 582–587 (2012)
7. Davis, F.: Perceived usefulness, perceived ease of use, and user acceptance of information technology. MIS Quart. 13(3), 319–340 (1989)
8. Gonzalez, Millan: Balo Accessibility and usability of computer-based cognitive stimulation. Balo Accessibility and usability of computer-based cognitive stimulation 45(1), 26–29 (2010)
9. Hoggan, Brewster: Johnston Investigating the effectiveness of tactile feedback for mobile touchscreens. In: Proceedings of the SIGCHI Conference on Human Factors in Computing Systems, vol. 1, pp. 5–10 (2008) ISBN: 978-1-60558-011-1
10. Imserso. Informe 2004. Las Personas Mayores en España. Madrid: IMSERSO. Observatorio de las Personas Mayores, 938 p. (2004)

11. ISO IEC .- 9126-1, International Organization for Standardization. Software Engineering – Product Quality – Part 1: Quality model. June 2001. 95.99 (September 13, 2012), pp 13- 14 (2001)
12. ISO 9241-210:2010 Ergonomics of human-system interaction – Part 210: Human-centered design for interactive 60.60 (2010-03-03), p. 32 (2010)
13. Kumin, Lazar, Feng: A Usability Evaluation of Workplace-Related Tasks on a Multi-Touch Tablet Computer by Adults with Down Syndrome. Journal of Usability Studies 7(4), 118–142 (2012)
14. Lee, Kozar: Understanding of website usability: Specifying and measuring constructs and their relationships. SciVerse ScienceDirect. Decision Support Systems 52(2), 450–463 (2012)
15. Normand, L.M.: Usabilidad y Accesibilidad (2014),
    https://nube.cesvima.upm.es/public.php?service=
    files&t=99339ab034b204a3a0421519232c851a
16. Kaufman, D., Roberts, W.D., Merrill, J., et al.: Applying an evaluation framework for health information system design, development, and implementation. Nurs. Res. 55(2 Suppl), S37–S42 (2006)
17. M.de Lara, R. Los Mayores en la Sociedad de la Información: situación actual y retos de futuro. *Fundación Auna*. Madrid (2004) ,
    http://www.fundacionauna.com/documentos/analisis/cuadernos/C
    uadernos_04.pdf (Consulta: May 4, 2014)
18. Brown III, W., Yen, P.-Y., Rojas, M., Schnall, R.: Assessment of the Health IT Usability Evaluation Model (Health-ITUEM) for evaluating mobile health (mHealth) technology. Journal of Biomedical Informatics 46(6), 1080–1087 (2013)

GeoFencing on a Mobile Platform with Alert Escalation

Natalie Carr and Paul McCullagh

School of Computing and Mathematics, University of Ulster, UK
carr-n@email.ulster.ac.uk, pj.mccullagh@ulster.ac.uk

Abstract. GPS-enabled mobile devices can utilize location information to potentially provide a safer tracked environment allowing vulnerable people to continue with their daily activities, as much as possible. This paper presents the options for alert escalation. The aim is to provide a safety net, without triggering unnecessary alarms. The escalation procedure involves initial speech alert to the user, then a speech and vibrate alert to the user as a reminder; this is followed by a text message to an identified carer if the user has not re-entered the designated safe zone. Parameters for alert escalation can be tuned to individual circumstances. The user can seek help by getting directions from the current position to home or by calling a carer. We report on a small user evaluation (n=6), an essential pre-requisite to testing with the intended cohort.

Keywords: geofence, alerts, escalation, interface, evaluation.

1 Geofencing and Dementia

The 21st century has brought an era of global population ageing. This will inevitably lead to an increase in the number of older people with dementia, with escalating costs for long term care. In 2010 it was estimated that worldwide cost of dementia care was US$604 billion [1]. Due to problems with memory and orientation, older people and people with early stage dementia can easily get disorientated when away from their home [2]. The increasing availability of GPS-enabled mobile devices can utilize location information to provide a safer tracked environment allowing users to continue with their daily activities, as much as possible, and providing some reassurance to their carers. Of course, 'the people versus technology' debate continues [3]. This paper investigates the technology options for 'geo-fencing' with alert escalation. The aim is to provide a 'safety net', without triggering unnecessary alarms. It does not address user acceptance or usability with the intended cohort, but is a necessary pre-requisite technical validation.

Mobile phones have become progressively more important in healthcare and are becoming a method of encouraging better communication between a vulnerable person and their carer [4]. We are becoming more aware of the desires of the older population to remain in their own living environment, and for example if they have been diagnosed with early stage dementia. Dementia is the decline of cognitive functioning such as the ability to think, remember and reason; it adversely affects a person's daily life and quickly excludes them from society. With advances in

L. Pecchia et al. (Eds.): IWAAL 2014, LNCS 8868, pp. 261–265, 2014.

medicine and technology the proportion of elderly people along with life expectancy is increasing; thus the number of people with dementia is predicted to almost double every twenty years [5]. Management of dementia increases the burden on the carer. Carers need to assist with activities of daily living whilst promoting some independence. Being a carer may also have a negative impact on health, employment and financial security. About one third of family carers showed signs of depression, while half reported effects caused by caring to be their major health problem [6].

One of the most demanding behaviours to cope with is that of wandering. Wandering occurs because many dementia sufferers have hypertension and feel an urge to walk; roughly 40% get lost [7]. Using mobile phone technology, it is technically possible to provide a safer environment for the person and to assist their carers by contacting them if the person gets lost. By helping caregivers to form a better understanding of when, where and how to intervene, GPS could extend the time that a vulnerable person can perform unsupervised outdoor activities [8].

Apps that use tracking were compared for functionality. Some provided useful geofencing functionality with alerting functionality; the escalation of alerts was not considered, see Table 1.

Table 1. A comparison of existing alerts approach for 'Geofence' apps

Application	Alerts	Predetermined safe area
Geofence (Android)	Alert family, not user	Yes, but no route given
Garmin Tracker (iOS)	Alerts family and user	Yes, but no route given
GPS Tracker (iOS)	Alert user, not family	Yes, and route given
Vismo (iOS)	Alert family, not user	No
Trax (iOS)	No alerts	Yes
GPS tracking Pro (Android)	No alerts	No
Real Time GPS Tracker (Android)	No alerts	Route given

Alert escalation will impact significantly upon the usability and hence uptake of geofencing applications. The 'GeoCare' application described in section 2 attempts to address these limitations.

2   Geocare Design

The GeoCare app uses Android version 4.0 [9] or higher and was developed using Java. Additional development tools included Google maps Application Programmer Interface (API), Google directions API, Android Preference API, and Android Plot API. It uses `LocationClient`, part of the Google Play Services, and the environment must provide both GPS and WiFi connectivity. QR functionality should also be installed to potentially supplement functionality and complement GPS data. Communication via the Internet utilizes RESTful API. The performance is dependent on the strength and coverage of the GPS signals. The Geofence (series of concentric circles) size varies appropriate to individual circumstances and preferences and is entered by the carer in a 'settings' file. The app locates the user every 30 seconds (provides a trade of between time resolution and battery life) and determines if the user has breached the geofence. The escalation process is as follows. It uses speech alerts if user has not returned to safe area after the first alert within the time_1 specified in settings. It escalates by using speech alerts and additional vibrate alerts if user has not returned to safe area after the second alert within the time_2 specified in settings. The system sends a text message to the mobile number in settings if user has not returned to safe area after the third alert within the time_3 specified in settings. Diameter of the fence(s) can be set. A number of options are available should a user get lost. The user can click a button to determine directions from the current location back to their starting location and display them on map. If the environment is enriched with QR codes which provide location, these can be scanned to provide information. A further 'SOS' button allows the user to call a designated emergency contact if they get lost or disoriented.

Of course the app will also perform in benign fashion when the user has not got into any difficulty. For example, it allows the user to share activity on social networks and via email. This can provide reassurance to the carer.

Fig. 1. User interfaces to promote user interaction; start of activity, geo-fence perimeters, QR scanner and 'SOS' button; feedback and options for sharing activity

3   Discussion

In order to gauge the functionality, usability and overall rating of the application six users tested the app. The users were final year Computer Science students (age range 22-25) and hence not representative of the intended user demographic. Thus this is an initial evaluation of the technology and user interface. Each user was provided with an evaluation questionnaire and informed of the purpose and functionality. Evaluation results from the returned questionnaires are shown in Fig 2.

First impressions, navigation rating, appearance rating and overall application rating were recorded on a scale of 1-6; 6 being excellent and 1 being very poor. On the metrics an overall score of 132 out of 144 was achieved. As well as the ratings, five participants stated they would use the application and all participants stated they would recommend it to a friend. Of the feedback received, one participant stated that "it was easy to program different settings for different types of patients". One participant encountered a technical problem whereby the application crashed; this was due to the website used to retrieve the weather data which had temporarily gone down. Another participant stated that an icon to ensure the user knew their location on the map would be useful.

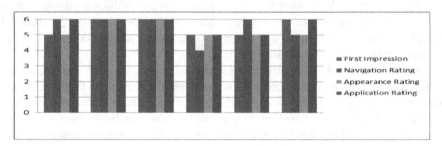

Fig. 2. Evaluation (scale 1-6): impression, navigation, and appearance, overall rating

Recommendations include the use of a database to allow the users to query and visualize data; functionality to forecast weather. Of course further evaluation on the intended population of users (older and vulnerable people and their carers) is fundamental to both the acceptance of the technology and addition of useful features. Clear information on how to react to an alert should be provided. A study with intended users is necessary to validate the effectiveness of our escalation strategy. Such studies are beginning to emerge [10]. There are ethical issues to the deployment of such technology, which must be addressed to pursue this. Further work can also be undertaken on a more intelligent approach to escalation, which determines actual street topography, and if the user is moving towards home.

References

1. Wimo, A., Prince, M.: The Globab Economic Impact of Dementia, World Alzheimer report (2010), http://www.alz.co.uk/research/world-report-2010 (accessed on September 15, 2014)
2. Dunk, B., Longman, B., Newton, L.G.: technologies in managing the risks associated with safer walking in people with dementia- a practical perspective. J. Assistive Technologies 4(3), 4–8 (2010)
3. McShane, R., Skelt, L.G.: tracking for people with dementia. Working with Older People 13(3), 34–37 (2009)
4. Armstrong, N., Nugent, C., Moore, G., Finlay, D.: Smartphone Application Design and Knowledge Management for People with Dementia. Pervasive Health Knowledge Management Healthcare Delivery in the Information Age, 135–153 (2013)
5. Rose, D.: Number of dementia suffers 'will double every 20 years', The Times (2009), http://www.thetimes.co.uk/tto/health/article1965177.ece (accessed February 12, 2014)
6. Alzheimer's Association. Alzheimer's disease Facts and Figures, Alzheimer's& Dementia, vol. 6 (2010)
7. Stratton, A.: Charity backs tagging for dementia suffers, The Guardian, http://www.theguardian.com/society/2007/dec/27/longtermcare.socialcare (accessed February 12, 2014)

8. Essén, A.: The two facets of electronic care surveillance: an exploration of the views of older people who live with monitoring devices. Social Science & Medicine 67(1), 128–136 (2008)
9. Android-App-Market. Android Architecture – The Key Concepts of Android OS, http://www.android-app-market.com/android-architecture.html (accessed January 13, 2014)
10. Milne, H., van der Pol, M., McCloughan, L., Hanley, J., Mead, G., Starr, J., Sheikh, A., McKinstry, B.: The use of global positional satellite location in dementia: a feasibility study for a randomised controlled trial. BMC Psychiatry 14, 160 (2014)

Predicting Technology Adoption in People with Dementia; Initial Results from the TAUT Project

Ian Cleland[1], Chris D. Nugent[1], Sally I. McClean[2], Phillip J. Hartin[1], Chelsea Sanders[3], Mark Donnelly[1], Shuai Zhang[1], Bryan Scotney[2], Ken Smith[4], Maria C. Norton[3], and JoAnn T. Tschanz[3].

[1] Computer Science Research Institute and School of Computing and Mathematics, University of Ulster, Newtownabbey, Co. Antrim, BT37 0QB, UK
{i.cleland,cd.nugent,mp.donnelly,s.zhang}@ulster.ac.uk,
{hartin-p1}@email.ulster.ac.uk
[2] Computer Science Research Institute and School of Computing and Information Engineering, University of Ulster, Coleraine, BT52 1SA, UK
{si.mcclean,bw.scotney}@ulster.ac.uk
[3] Department of Phycology, Utah State University, Logan, UT 84322-4440, USA
{joann.tschanz,chelsea.saunders,maria.norton}@usu.edu
[4] Population Sciences, Huntsman Cancer Institute, University of Utah, Salt Lake City, UT 84112, USA
{ken.smith}@fcs.utah.edu

Abstract. The acceptance of technology is a crucial factor in successfully deploying technology solutions in healthcare. Our previous research has highlighted the potential of modelling user adoption from a range of environmental, social and physical parameters. This current work aims to build on the notion of predicting technology adoption through a study investigating the usage of a reminding application deployed through a mobile phone. The TAUT project is currently recruiting participants from the Cache County Study on Memory in Aging (CCSMA) and will monitor participants over a period of 12 months. Information relating to participants' compliance with usage of the reminding application, details of cognitive assessments from the CCSMA and medical and genealogical related details from the Utah Population Database (UPDB) will be used as inputs to the development of a new adoption model. Initial results show, that with an unscreened dataset, it is possible to predict refusers and adopters with an F-measure of 0.79.

Keywords: Technology adoption, Assistive technology, dementia, Reminding Technology.

1   Introduction

People with mild dementia generally exhibit impairments of memory, reasoning and thought. As a result, they require varying levels of support to complete everyday activities and to maintain a level of independence. Yet for many, a live in carer is neither practical nor affordable. Around one-third of people with dementia currently live

L. Pecchia et al. (Eds.): IWAAL 2014, LNCS 8868, pp. 266–274, 2014.
© Springer International Publishing Switzerland 2014

alone without this caring presence [1]. Furthermore, the cost of providing such care is often unsustainable. Assistive technologies may provide an opportunity to alleviate the burden faced by Persons with dementia (PwD) and their carers, however, even with such a technology based solution a one size fits all solution remains elusive. Not everyone will be capable or willing to use the technology. Consequently, there is merit in considering a user's characteristics and specific needs when determining whether or not to recommend a form of assistive technology. Efforts to date have largely focused on the issues surrounding the technology and its perceived utility [2] whilst largely overlooking the challenges associated with people with dementia and their carers.

In this current work we aim to build upon our previous research to investigate the usage and adoption of a reminding application deployed through a mobile phone. This paper provides details of the methodology and initial results from the Technology Adoption and Usage Tool (TAUT) project which aims to model adoption and usage of assistive reminding technology for people with dementia. In section 2, a review of relevant research is provided prior to discussing the development and implementation of a smartphone app in section 3. The study protocol and initial results from the mid-term analysis will then be presented in sections 4 and 5 respectively. This will include details of the profile of users who preferred not to engage with the evaluation and those who are currently using the application.

2   Background

The acceptance of technology is a crucial factor in successfully deploying technology solutions in healthcare and cannot be taken for granted [3]. A number of attempts been made to develop models aimed at predicting technology adoption [4, 5, 6, 7]. Originally, these models focused on the concept of perceived usefulness and ease of use [6]. Nevertheless, with increasingly diverse user backgrounds, a variety of technical solutions and use context, additional aspects may be of relevance in understanding the reasons for adopting a technology or not [7]. A common approach is to separate factors that impact upon technology adoption into external environmental factors, such as social structures, the use environment and infrastructure in addition to internal personal factors such as perceived utility, expectations and self-esteem [8]. These types of models have, however, been criticized in terms of their theoretical assumptions and practical effectiveness [2].

It is clear that there is growing academic research and societal interest in understanding factors that determine acceptance of assistive technologies for older people [9, 10, 11]. Specifically, there is demand to gain deeper insights into technology adoption through additional research. This is evidenced by the evaluations of the Whole Systems Demonstrator, which aims to build upon its existing qualitative evaluation in order to identify predictors of early removal of telehealth [12].

Our previous research in the area of technology adoption models aimed to characterize individuals with dementia and identify features that may be relevant to the adoption of assistive technology [13]. Features were collected through an iterative design process, involving evaluations with 40 participants with dementia. Features included age, gender, Mini mental state exam (MMSE) score, profession, technology experience and environmental conditions such as access to broadband, mobile reception and living arrangement. Based on these features, an optimal predictive model was developed. Overall, the model trained using kNN classification algorithm on data collected from 7 features performed the best over the four evaluation criteria of model evaluation. The model was found to maximise the opportunity of using assistive technology to allow people to stay in their home for longer and can minimize the risk of negatively impacting of mood and quality of life of the PwD and minimizing the financial risk associated with investing in assistive technology for those who do not adopt. It was noted, however, that the prediction models may have been limited by the small amount of data used for training. Given the positive results from our previous work, the current project aims to increase the amount of data available to train and test the models through engagement with a larger cohort of individuals over a longer period of time. Furthermore, through collaborations with the University of Utah and Utah State University it is possible to evaluate the use of more types of features, which we can use to develop the models. Data from the Cache County Study on Memory in Aging (CCSMA) and the Utah Population Database (UPDB) will provide further information for each participant relating to genealogical, medical, vital signs, environmental factors and demographic records.

3   Reminder Application

The TAUT reminder application benefits from 10 years of experience in the design, implementation and evaluation of assistive cognitive prosthetics. This system has been designed by a multidisciplinary team through an iterative design process and have been previously evaluated on a small scale with a representative cohort [14]. The current version of the app, described in [15], has been developed for the android platform and is designed to provide the user with an interface to schedule and acknowledged reminders for a range of daily activities including, medication, meals, appointments and bathing. The reminders can be set by the PwD, or by a caregiver or family member and are delivered at the time specified and presented as a popup dialog box on screen accompanied by a picture indicating the type of ADL, a textual description and a melodic tone. The user has a time window of 60 seconds in which to acknowledge the reminder, after which, the popup closes, the tone stops playing and the reminder is logged as 'missed'. If acknowledged within the 60 seconds the reminder is logged as being 'acknowledged' and the popup closes. To provide additional functionality, the ability to record audio messages has also been included.

In addition to providing reminders, the TAUT application records details of the user's interactions. The app records information such as when the reminders are scheduled, when reminders are acknowledged, the type of reminder and how many reminders the person has missed. These details are then used to assess how well the user is adopting or engaging with the application in addition to providing insight into how the application is used; i.e. which activities the user requires the greatest assistance with, the most common times to receive reminders and in what form they prefer the reminder (text or voice). This data will facilitate the assessment of how users have been using the app and to what extent. Research by Hartin *et al.* [17] is investigating the context around missed reminders with the aim of providing an insight into why reminders were missed and the possibility of improving acknowledgement rates through context aware scheduling and delivery of reminders.

4   Methods

In order to collect the data with which to build the adoption models the project is actively recruiting participants from the CCSMA. The CCSMA is an ongoing longitudinal, population-based study of Alzheimer's disease (AD) and other dementias, which has followed over 5,000 elderly residents of Cache County, Utah (USA) since 1995. In addition, this database has been linked to the Utah Population Database (UPDB) at the University of Utah, which contains genealogical, medical, vital signs and demographic records for each of the participants, with updates made annually and with full coverage of medical information for the past 20 years. Participants have been recruited from the CCSMA to participate within the current study. At least 125 people are being recruited to partake in the study, with at least 30 participants undertaking a 12 month evaluation of the TAUT app. Some of the 125 participants will adopt the technology; others will be categorized into 3 types of non-adopter, as described in Fig. 1. In order to profile all types of non-adopter it is important to profile the users at two stages. Non-adopter (1); those who are willing to try the technology, however, for some reason are unable to use it are, profiled along with adopters using insights gained from the evaluation process. Whereas non-adopters (2) and (3) are profiled using insights gained through questionnaires delivered when the participant refuses to partake in the evaluation during the recruitment phase.

Mapping of adoption with two factors of capability and willingness to use technology		Capable of using the technology	
		Yes (can use it)	No (cannot use it)
Willingness to use the technology	Yes (want to use it)	Adopter	Non-Adopter (1)
	No (don't want to use it)	Non-Adopter (2)	Non-Adopter (3)

Fig. 1. User adoption matrix showing the various types of adopter and non-adopter

A summary of the recruitment process to date is shown in Fig. 2. Initially 335 participants were contacted by mail. 51 of these participants refused to engage at that stage of the process (non-adopter 2) and 55 where deceased. The remaining 227 were contacted by the research team by telephone; this resulted in 98 people being unreachable, 90 refusing (non-adopter 2) and 41 people agreeing to participate. Following a telephone assessment of the 41 participants who agreed, 12 are currently enrolled, 9 have agreed to participate but are currently being screened and 18 have been successfully enrolled with two participants dropping out subsequent to beginning the evaluation. Sixteen where deemed ineligible (non-adopter 3) due to cognitive status or currently or planning to move out of the local area in next 18 months.

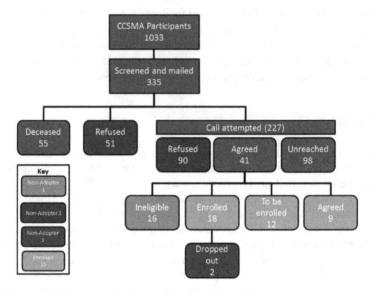

Fig. 2. The recruitment process that has been undertaken and the various routes where adopters and non-adopters are obtained from

5   Results

Using information gathered from participants who are currently enrolled within the study it was possible to analyze the results in a number of ways. First we considered the difference between participants who chose to be involved in the evaluation of the reminder app, following screening for eligibility, and those who refused to participate. To date, forty one people have agreed to participate in the study, although some may be ineligible due to health related factors, such as substantial memory loss. Those who agreed to partake are referred to as adopters, although they may later drop out or not engage with the technology throughout the course of the study. One hundred and forty one participants have refused to participate in the evaluation. These participants can, however, still be profiled using information from the CCSMA and the UPDB; at this stage these participants will be referred to as refusers. The following Sections will first profile each of these groups, followed by presenting the initial results from the process of modelling adoption or refusers.

5.1   Profile of Adopters and Non-adopters

Of the 335 (male=153, female=182) participants who screened as eligible for the study, the average age was 89 years. Forty one (male=23, female=18) participants agreed to participate in the study (Average age: 89). Two males have subsequently dropped out. One hundred and forty one (male=66, female=75) participants refused to participate in the study (average age:89). There is no statistical difference in the age of the two groups ($p=0.28$).

5.2 Modelling Adoption and Refusal

In contrast to our previous work, we assessed the ability to classify whether or not a person was likely to agree or refuse to participate within this research study. In order to develop the most suitable model for prediction, we assessed a range of popular data mining algorithms. We also assessed the effect of feature selection on each of these algorithms, using features extracted from the CCSMA dataset only. These features focus on health and genealogy in contrast to features in previous works, which focused more on perceived utility, usefulness and experience. Data from 141 refusers and 41 adopters was used to build and test the models. Initially, 31 features (Table 1) were extracted from the CCSMA. These covered a range of areas including, age, gender, MMSE score, employment and details of a range of health conditions. Information gain (IG) was used for the purposes of feature selection. Features were ranked from highest to lowest based on IG, where a higher IG value indicates that the feature provides a better discriminative power for classification. Results showed that only 5 features had an IG greater than 0 (Last CCSMA observation IG=0.18, APOE Genotype IG=0.156, Any APOE4 IG=0.145, Dementia code AD any IG=0.132 and Dementia code AD pure IG=0.120). APEO features describe the presence and type of the APEO/APEO4 gene. Features describing Dementia codes relate to the presence of AD or other forms of dementia.

Table 1. The 31 features extracted from the CCSMA database. These features where used to train the classification models.

1	Gender	12	3MS score	23	Stroke first observ.
2	Age (Years)	13	3Ms sensory adjusted (1)	24	Stroke Age
3	Ethnicity	14	3Ms sensory adjusted (2)	25	Hypertension self-endorsed
4	APOE Genotype	15	3Ms sensory adjusted (3)	26	Hypertension first observ.
5	APEO4 copy number	16	Diabetes self-endorsed	27	Hypertension age onset
6	Any variant of APOE4	17	Diabetes first observ.	28	High Cholesterol self-endorsed
7	Education level	18	Diabetes age onset	29	High Cholesterol first observ.
8	Dementia code AD pure	19	Heart attack self-endorsed	30	High Cholesterol age onset
9	Dementia code Any	20	Heart attack first observ.	31	Job category
10	Last CCSMA observ.	21	Heart attack age		
11	CCSMA observ. date	22	Stroke self-endorsed		

In order to investigate the correlation between the number of features and classifier accuracy a 10-fold cross validation with 10 iterations was performed within Weka Experimenter (University of Waikato, Version 3.6.10). Using datasets containing subsets of 1, 2, 3, 4, 5, 10, 15, 20 and 31 ranked features. Features with the highest IG value were selected first. A range of recognized data mining algorithms for classification were selected for evaluation, namely C4.5 decision tree (DT), K-nearest neighbor (kNN) and Naïve Bayes (NB). To handle the data imbalance between the two classes, SMOTE was applied. The proportion of the data distribution was approximately 70% refusers and 30% adopters. The adopter minority class was boosted by 100%. A conventional p-value of 0.05 was used for the threshold of significance for a paired T-test. The F-measure was used as a performance index to evaluate the performance of each of the classifiers.

Results from the analysis are presented in Fig. 3. The NB algorithm performed statistically worse than both the C4.5 and kNN algorithm. There was, however, no statistical difference between the C4.5 and the kNN. The DT achieved the highest F-measure with an average of 0.79 when using all 31 features and 85 when using 4 features, Last CCMS observation, APOE Genotype, Any variant of APOE4 and Dementia including AD any.

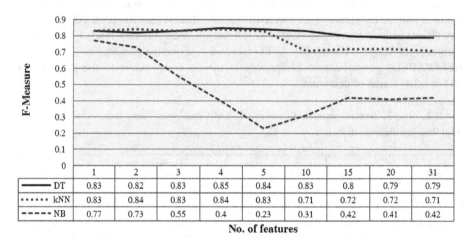

	1	2	3	4	5	10	15	20	31
——— DT	0.83	0.82	0.83	0.85	0.84	0.83	0.8	0.79	0.79
•••••• kNN	0.83	0.84	0.83	0.84	0.83	0.71	0.72	0.72	0.71
----- NB	0.77	0.73	0.55	0.4	0.23	0.31	0.42	0.41	0.42

No. of features

Fig. 3. Graph showing the average classification F-measure for a 10 fold cross validation with 10 iterations for the C4.5 decision tree (DT), K-nearest neighbor (kNN) and Naïve Bayes (NB). Results for datasets containing 1, 2, 3, 4, 5, 10, 15, 20 and 31 features are shown.

6   Conclusions

Methods of predicting whether or not a user is likely to adopt an assistive technology may prove to be a powerful tool in successfully deploying technology solutions in healthcare, by reducing unnecessary costs and improving acceptance rates. This current work builds upon our previous research which has highlighted the potential of modelling user adoption from a range of environmental, social and physical parameters. Based on an initial analysis of an unscreened dataset, it was possible to predict adopters vs non-adopters with an F-measure of 0.79 using a C4.5 DT. The dataset was unbalanced, with 70% refusers to 30% adopters, this was in line with previous work [16] and the SMOTE algorithm was used to correct for this imbalance. Future work, will involve an in depth analysis of variables which can maximize the discrimination between the two classes of refusers and adopters. In addition, a closer examination will be made between the adopters and those who dropout. Furthermore, data from the CCSMA will be combined with data from the UPDB, observations from the evaluation and questionnaires to assess the variability in user's perceptions, to provide a further insight into the situation.

Acknowledgment. The Alzheimer's Association is acknowledged for supporting the TAUT project under the research grant ETAC-12-242841.

References

1. Kane, M., Cook, L.: Dementia 2013: The hidden voice of loneliness. Alzheimer's Society, London (2013)
2. Chuttur, M.: Overview of the Technology Acceptance Model: Origins, Developments and Future Directions. Sprouts: Working Papers on Information Systems 9, Article 37 (2009)
3. Wilkowska, W., Gaul, S., Ziefle, M.: A Small but Significant Difference – The Role of Gender on Acceptance of Medical Assistive Technologies. In: Leitner, G., Hitz, M., Holzinger, A. (eds.) USAB 2010. LNCS, vol. 6389, pp. 82–100. Springer, Heidelberg (2010)
4. Day, H., Jutai, J.: Measuring the Psychosocial Impact of Assistive Devices: the PIADS. Canadian Journal of Rehabilitation 9(2), 159–168 (1996)
5. Yen, D.C., Wu, C., Cheng, F., Huang, Y.: Determinants of users' intention to adopt wireless technology: An empirical study by integrating TTF with TAM. Comput. Hum. Behav. 26, 906–915 (2010)
6. Davis, F.D., Bagozzi, R.P., Warshaw, P.R.: User Acceptance of Computer Technology: A Comparison of Two Theoretical Models. Management Science 35(8), 982–1003 (1989)
7. Kowalewski, S., Wilkowska, W., Ziefle, M.: Accounting for User Diversity in the Acceptance of Medical Assistive Technologies. In: Szomszor, M., Kostkova, P. (eds.) e-Health. LNICST, vol. 69, pp. 175–183. Springer, Heidelberg (2011)
8. Scherer, M.J., Jutai, J., Fuhrer, M., Demers, L., Deruyter, F.: A framework for modelling the selection of assistive technology devices (ATDs). Disab. & Rehab.: Assis. Tech. 2, 1–8 (2007)
9. Stronge, A.J., Rogers, W.A., Fisk, A.D.J.: Human factors considerations in implementing telemedicine systems to accommodate older adults. Telemed Telecare 13, 1–3 (2007)
10. Ziefle, M.: Age perspectives on the usefulness on e-health applications. In: International Conference on Health Care Systems, Ergonomics, and Patient Safety (HEPS), Straßbourg, France (2008)
11. Arning, K., Ziefle, M.: Different Perspectives on Technology Acceptance: The Role of Technology Type and Age. In: Holzinger, A., Miesenberger, K. (eds.) USAB 2009. LNCS, vol. 5889, pp. 20–41. Springer, Heidelberg (2009)
12. Cartwright, M., Hirani, S.P., Rixon, L., Beynon, M., Doll, H., Bower, P., et al.: Effect of telehealth on quality of life and psychological outcomes over 12 months (Whole Systems Demonstrator telehealth questionnaire study): nested study of patient reported outcomes in a pragmatic, cluster randomized controlled trial. BMJ 346, 653 (2013)

13. Zhang, S., McClean, S.I., Nugent, C.D., et al.: A predictive model for assistive technology adoption for people with dementia. IEEE Journal of Biomedical and Health Informatics 18(1), 375 (2014)
14. O'Neill, S.A., Parente, G., Donnelly, et al.: Assessing task compliance following mobile phone-based video reminders. In: Proceedings of the IEEE EMBC 2011, pp. 5295–5298 (2011)
15. Hartin, P.J., Nugent, C.D., McClean, S.I., et al.: A smartphone application to evaluate technology adoption and usage in persons with dementia. In: 2014 Annual International Conference of the IEEE Engineering in Medicine and Biology Society, EMBC, Chicago, pp. 5389–5392 (2014)

Ergonomic-Monitoring of Office Workplaces Using Kinect

Lukas G. Wiedemann[1], Rainer Planinc[2], and Martin Kampel[2]

[1] University Of Applied Sciences Technikum Wien, Vienna, Austria
[2] Vienna University of Technology, Vienna, Austria

Abstract. Prolonged sitting is an aggravating factor in low back and neck pain. Increased use of computers at workplaces could therefore cause health risks. This paper evaluates the application of the Microsoft Kinect in order to investigate the ergonomics at the place of employment. The Kinect is a cheap device and commercially available which enables the user to record 3D data of the human body. Within this paper, guidelines for the 'ideal' placement of the Kinect are provided in order to enhance the robustness of the skeleton recog-nition algorithm. An evaluation of 35 sequences (7 different positions in com-bination with 5 different sitting postures) showed that placing the Kinect sen-sor slantingly forward at an angle of 20° (in front of the subject) the joint rec-ognition rate achieved 89.62%. According to these results, the device should be positioned between 20° to 45° in order to robustly track a sitting person.

Keywords: Ergonomics, Kinect, sitting, workplace.

1 Introduction

About 75% of employees in industrializes countries perform their work seated [1]. Most of the working time is spent in front of a computer which results in sedentary activity of 597 ± 122min/day [2]. In this process sitting is considered to be an aggra-vating factor in lumbal back and neck pain [3, 4]. Moreover, it is not quite clear which sitting posture is 'ideal' [5]. However, a number of international standards are devel-oped to provide ergonomic guidelines for workplaces (EN ISO 9241). The goal of this article is to evaluate the suitability of the Microsoft Kinect to investigate ergonomic parameters of workplaces. The Kinect is a markerless and low-cost motion capture system which enables the user to investigate the joints of the human body without the need for additional sensors or markers. A free Software Development Kit (SDK) pro-vided by Microsoft is used to access sensor data which makes it intelligibly to apply own code within the scope of proposed research questions [6]. In this paper different Kinect positions are compared to each other in order to provide guidelines for the 'optimal' positioning of the device.

2 Methodology

The Kinect sensor contains a depth sensor, allowing to record 3D data of human joints with 30 frames per second (fps). Thus ergonomic parameters like the viewing distance

L. Pecchia et al. (Eds.): IWAAL 2014, LNCS 8868, pp. 275–278, 2014.
© Springer International Publishing Switzerland 2014

to the screen, tilting of the head, spine curvature, hip and knee angle can be analyzed. Within the framework of this paper seven positions of the Kinect sensor are compared to each other (tab. 1). Additionally, five sitting postures are defined for each measurement: an "upright" (upright upper body, knee angle is 90°), "supporting" (head supported by the hands, right leg stretched), "slumped" (leaning backwards, both legs stretched), "lordosis" (strong lumbar lordosis, right leg bent) and "tired" (head resting on the arms, both legs bent) sitting position. These postures were chosen to analyze different angles in the upper and lower extremity.

Table 1. Definition of the Kinect placements with the corresponding angles and distance to the hip centre

Kinect placement	Angle [°]	Distance [m]
1. "lateral"	90	2
2. "inclined 45°"	45	2.5
3. "inclined 20°"	20	2.5
4. "inclined 20° with armrest"	20	2.5
5. "frontal"	0	2.3
6. "upper body only"	45	1.7
7. "inclined 110°"	110	1.8

The angle is formed by the points of the middle of the computer screen, the hip center and the middle of the depth sensor of the Microsoft Kinect. The distance from the device to the subject is as low as possible while the whole body can be viewed. Each trial is recorded for 60s and therefore 1800 frames are captured. A total of 35 measurements are recorded (7 Kinect placements with 5 sitting postures each). 3D-coordinate data and the "Tracking States" of each joint are analysed using Matlab. The relative tracking rates are examined through the number of frames where each joint is stated "tracked" divided by the total number of frames. Joints, which are identified "tracked" but seem to be tracked incorrectly because they contain jitter, are defined as "not-tracked" by defining a velocity threshold. While a joint's velocity exceeds this limit, it is recognized as jitter and thus not tracked. This threshold is calculated using the joint with the minimum mean velocity plus three times of its standard deviation.

3   Results

3.1   Tracking Rates Depending on the Kinect Placement

On average the tracking rate of the whole-body joints (WB) using all sitting postures is 86.03%. The rates of each position range from 80.95% (position 1) to 89.62% (position 3). Further, the mean tracking rate of the lower body equals 78.37% and the joints of the upper body are tracked 76.23% of the whole time (tab. 2). The head-joint has the lowest mean velocity of 0.05m/s ± 0.36m/s (0.17km/h ± 1.30km/h). The velocity limit for jitter is set to 1.13m/s (4.06km/h).

Table 2. Relative joint-rates (Mean ± Standard Deviation in %) for each Kinect placement (joints of the whole-body - WB; lower body - LB; upper body - UB)

Kinect placement	WB [%]	LB [%]	UB [%]
1. "lateral"	80.95 ± 6.92	69.84 ± 10.16	74.53 ± 4.07
2. "inclined 45°"	88.22 ± 7.69	73.69 ± 17.33	80.69 ± 8.45
3. "inclined 20°"	89.62 ± 12.85	84.70 ± 18.90	78.63 ± 9.67
4. "inclined 20° armrest"	87.28 ± 8.61	79.36 ± 18.36	79.69 ± 9.95
5. "frontal"	85.78 ± 4.57	82.16 ± 3.78	71.19 ± 8.75
6. "upper body only"	-	-	80.68 ± 11.88
7. "inclined 110°"	84.32 ± 11.49	80.45 ± 18.10	67.11 ± 18.90

3.2 Tracking Rates Depending on the Sitting Posture

The tracking rates depending on the posture range between 82.23% (1. sitting posture) and 90.17% (2. sitting posture) of the WB joints (tab. 3).

Table 3. Relative joint-rates (Mean ± Standard Deviation in %) for each sitting posture (joints of the whole-body - WB; lower body - LB; upper body - UB)

Sitting posture	WB [%]	LB [%]	UB [%]
1. "upright"	82.23 ± 6.94	71.02 ± 9.52	78.60 ± 8.28
2. "supporting"	90.17 ± 8.37	77.48 ± 18.08	81.41 ± 7.17
3. "slumped"	87.82 ± 12.31	85.69 ± 17.09	74.67 ± 17.01
4. "lordosis"	84.22 ± 10.73	74.57 ± 20.17	75.93 ± 12.27
5. "tired"	85.69 ± 4.10	83.08 ± 4.02	70.55 ± 8.02

4   Discussion

The third Kinect position and the sitting posture "supporting" show the highest tracking rates with 89.62% and 90.17% respectively. The joints in Kinect position 3 contain 3.24% jitter of the whole measurement time. Hence, an inclined Kinect placement of 20° results in robust tracking of body joints. The rather small difference of 2.34% between Kinect-placement "inclined 20°" and "inclined 20° with armrest" indicate the possibility to gain 3D-coordinate information via Kinect even if the worker sits in a chair with armrests. When only analyzing the upper body joints, the Kinect is placed 45° relative to the line of sight of the subject and the results of this paper indicate a joint tracking rate of 80.68% while using this Kinect placement. Based on the results of this work, it is recommended to locate the Kinect sensor between 20° and 45° relative to the line of sight and about 5cm above the table height. Its distance to the subject should be as low as possible - to minimize measuring errors due to the distance - ensuring that the whole body is within the field of view.

References

1. McCrady, S., Levine, J.: Sedentariness at work; how much do we really sit? Obesity 17(11), 2103–2105 (2010)
2. Zemp, R., Taylor, W.R., Lorenzetti, S.: In vivo spinal posture during upright and reclined sitting in an office chair. BioMed Research International (2013)
3. O'Sullivan, K., O'Sullivan, P., O'Sullivan, L., Dankaerts, W.: What do physiotherapists consider to be the best sitting spinal posture? Manual Therapy 17(5), 432–437 (2012)
4. Caneiro, J.P., O'Sullivan, P., Burnett, A., Barach, A., O'Neil, D., Tveit, O., Olafsdottir, K.: The influence of different sitting postures on head/neck posture and muscle activity. Manual Therapy 15(1), 54–60 (2010)
5. O'Sullivan, K., O'Dea, P., Dankaerts, W., O'Sullivan, P., Clifford, A., O'Sullivan, L.: Neutral lumbar spine sitting posture in pain-free subjects. Manual Therapy 15(6), 557–561 (2010)
6. Diego-Mas, J.A., Alcaide-Marzal, J.: Using Kinect sensor in observational methods for assessing postures at work. Applied Ergonomics 45(4), 976–985 (2014)

Affectively Aligned Cognitive Assistance Using Bayesian Affect Control Theory

Luyuan Lin[1], Stephen Czarnuch[2], Aarti Malhotra[1], Lifei Yu[1],
Tobias Schröder[3], and Jesse Hoey[1]

[1] School of Computer Science, University of Waterloo,
Waterloo, N2L3G1, ON, Canada
[2] Institute of Biomaterials and Biomedical Engineering,
University of Toronto, 500 University Ave., Toronto, M5G1V7, ON, Canada
[3] Potsdam University of Applied Sciences, 14469 Potsdam, Germany

Abstract. This paper describes a novel emotionally intelligent cognitive assistant to engage and help older adults with Alzheimer's disease (AD) to complete activities of daily living (ADL) more independently. Our new system combines two research streams. First, the development of cognitive assistants with artificially intelligent controllers using partially observable Markov decision processes (POMDPs). Second, a model of the dynamics of emotion and identity called *Affect Control Theory* that arises from the sociological literature on culturally shared sentiments. We present background material on both of these research streams, and then demonstrate a prototype assistive technology that combines the two. We discuss the affective reasoning, the probabilistic and decision-theoretic reasoning, the computer-vision based activity monitoring, the embodied prompting, and we show results in proof-of-concept tests.

1 Introduction

Persons with dementia (PwD, e.g. Alzheimer's disease) have difficulty completing activities of daily living, such as handwashing, preparing food and dressing. The short-term memory impairment that is a hallmark of Alzheimer's disease leaves sufferers unable to recall what step to do next, or what important objects look like, for example. We have been developing a smart home system called the *COACH* to assist older adults with dementia to carry out basic ADL (e.g. handwashing) through step-by-step audiovisual prompts [2,7,14]. The *COACH* is effective at monitoring and making decisions about when/what to prompt [14], and works well for some persons, but not as well for others. Considering the heterogeneity in socio-cultural and personal affective identities, a primary reason for lack of effectiveness may be the static, non-adaptive nature of the "canned" (pre-recorded) prompts. While we have made significant effort to design prompts founded on the methods and styles of human caregivers [19], a simple "one size fits all" style of prompting may be limiting. For example, one person might find our prompts to be too imperious, and would respond better to a more servile approach. However, this will not be the case with every person, and some may

L. Pecchia et al. (Eds.): IWAAL 2014, LNCS 8868, pp. 279–287, 2014.

prefer the more imperative prompting style. Each person comes from a different background, has a different sense of "self", and has different emotional responses to prompts, whether given by human or machine. Affective identity is believed to be a powerful tool for reasoning about illness in general [11]. In particular, studies of identity in Alzheimer's disease have found that identity changes dramatically over the course of the disease [15], and that persons with AD have more vague or abstract notions of their identity [17].

In this paper, we build explicit models of emotional identity and personality into a cognitive assistant, and we give ideas about how this can improve the overall (cross-individual) effectiveness and potential uptake of such systems. Our system use a RGB-D camera to detect the body postures of a person while handwashing, and infers both the functional meaning (e.g. does the person have soap on their hands or not, or, is the water running?), and the affective meaning (e.g. is the person feeling powerless, in control, angry, or depressed?) of the observed behaviours. The observed functional and affective behaviours are then fed into a reasoning engine that uses a partially observable Markov decision process (POMDP), a probabilistic and decision theoretic model of both the handwashing task and the affective identity of the person using the system. The affective component is based upon a sociological theory called *Affect Control Theory* [5], which models the dynamic affective identities and behaviours of the person and the handwashing assistant. The POMDP policy produces an approximately optimal action for the system to take, again on both functional (e.g. what step is next) and affective (e.g. imperious vs. servile delivery of the prompt) dimensions. This prompt is delivered as a video of an embodied caregiver acting in a style that is consistent with the recommended affective action.

2   Background

2.1   Affect Control Theory

Affect Control Theory (ACT) arises from work on the sociology of human interaction [5]. ACT proposes that social perceptions, behaviours, and emotions are guided by a psychological need to minimize the differences between culturally shared fundamental affective sentiments about social situations and the transient impressions resulting from the interactions between elements within those situations. Fundamental sentiments, $\mathbf{f}$, are representations of social objects, such as interactants' identities and behaviours or environmental settings, as vectors in a three-dimensional affective space. The basis vectors of the affective space are called Evaluation/valence, Potency/control, and Activity/arousal (EPA). The EPA space is hypothesized to be a universal organizing principle of human socio-emotional experience, based on the discovery that these dimensions structure the semantic relations of linguistic concepts across languages and cultures [16]. They also emerged from statistical analyses of the co-occurrence of a large variety of physiological, facial, gestural, and cognitive features of emotional experience [4], relate to the universal dimensionality of personality, non-verbal behaviour, and social cognition [18], and are believed to correspond to the fundamental logic of social exchange and group coordination [18].

EPA profiles of concepts can be measured with the *semantic differential*, a survey technique where respondents rate affective meanings of concepts on numerical scales. In general, within-cultural agreement about EPA meanings of social concepts is high even across subgroups of society, and cultural-average EPA ratings from as little as a few dozen survey participants are extremely stable over extended periods of time [6]. For example, the EPA for the identity of "nurse" is [1.65, 0.93, 0.34], meaning that nurses are seen as quite good (E), a bit powerful (P), and a bit active (A) [1]. Comparatively a "patient" is seen as [0.9, −0.69, −1.05], less powerful and less active than a "nurse". Social events cause transient impressions, τ, of identities and behaviours that deviate from their corresponding fundamental sentiments, $\mathbf{f}$. ACT models this formation of impressions from events with a minimalist grammar of the form agent-behaviour-client. Consider, for example, a nurse (agent) who ignores (behaviour) a patient (client). Observers agree, and ACT predicts, that this nurse appears (τ) less nice (E), and less potent (P), than the cultural average ($\mathbf{f}$) of a nurse. The Euclidean distance between τ and $\mathbf{f}$ is called the *deflection* (D), and is hypothesized to correspond to an aversive state of mind that humans seek to avoid (the *affect control principle*). For example, the nurse who "ignores" a patient has a deflection of over 15 (very high), whereas if the nurse "comforts" the patient, the deflection is 1.5 (very low). The *affect control principle* also allows ACT to compute *normative* actions for artifical agents: those that minimize deflection. ACT has been shown to be a powerful predictor of human behaviour [12].

2.2 Partially Observable Markov Decision Processes

A partially observable Markov decision process (POMDP) [1] is a general model of stochastic control that has been extensively studied in operations research and in artificial intelligence. A POMDP consists of a finite set S of states; a finite set $\mathcal{A}$ of actions; a stochastic transition model $\Pr : S \times A \to \Delta(S)$, with $\Pr(s'|s,a)$ denoting the probability of moving from state s to s' when action a is taken[2], and $\Delta(S)$ is a distribution over S; a finite observation set Ω; a stochastic observation model with $\Pr(\omega|s)$ denoting the probability of making observation ω while the system is in state s; and a reward assigning $R(a, s')$ to a transition to s' induced by action a. A *policy* maps *belief states* (i.e., distributions over S) into choices of actions, such that the expected discounted sum of rewards is (approximately) maximised. In this paper, we will be dealing with *factored* POMDPs in which the state is represented by the cross-product of a set of variables or features. Assignment of a value to each variable thus constitutes a state. POMDPs have been used as models for many human-interactive domains, including intelligent tutoring systems, and human assistance systems [7].

---

[1] EPA values range from −4.3 to 4.3 by convention.

[2] primes indicate post-event variables, unprimed are pre-event variables.

2.3 *BayesAct*

Recently, we have developed a probabilistic and decision-theoretic generalization of ACT, and have demonstrated how it can be leveraged to build affectively intelligent artificial agents [9]. The new model, called *BayesAct*, can maintain multiple hypotheses about sentiments simultaneously as a probability distribution, and can make use of an explicit utility function to make value-directed action choices. This allows the model to generate affectively intelligent interactions with people by learning about their identity, predicting their behaviours using the affect control principle, and taking actions that are simultaneously goal-directed and affect-sensitive.

A *BayesAct* POMDP models an interaction between two agents (human or machine) denoted *agent* and *client*. The state is the product of six 3-dimensional continuous random variables corresponding to fundamental and transient sentiments about the *agent*'s identity $(\mathbf{F}_a, \mathbf{T}_a)$, behaviour $(\mathbf{F}_b, \mathbf{T}_b)$ and *client*'s identity $(\mathbf{F}_c, \mathbf{T}_c)$. The transient impressions, $\mathbf{T} = \{\mathbf{T}_a, \mathbf{T}_b, \mathbf{T}_c\}$, evolve according to the deterministic impression-formation operator in ACT. Fundamental sentiments, $\mathbf{F} = \{\mathbf{F}_a, \mathbf{F}_b, \mathbf{F}_c\}$, are expected to stay approximately constant over time, but are subject to random drift (with noise Σ_f) and are expected to also remain close to the transient impressions because of the *affect control principle*. This allows us to estimate the posterior probability distribution over sentiments, $Pr(\mathbf{f}', \boldsymbol{\tau}'|\mathbf{f}, \boldsymbol{\tau})$, which gives the normative (expected) action as $\mathbf{f}'_b$. Thus, by integrating over $\mathbf{f}'_a, \mathbf{f}'_c, \boldsymbol{\tau}'$ and the previous state, we obtain a probability distribution over $\mathbf{f}'_b$ that acts as a *normative action prediction*: it tells the agent what to expect from other agents, and what action is expected from it. This normative action is used as the POMDP policy directly.

BayesAct includes an application-specific set of random variables $\mathbf{X}$ that are interpreted as the remainder of the state space, including *non-affective* elements of the domain (e.g. steps of the handwashing task). The dynamics of $\mathbf{X}$ are application specific, but depend in general on the *deflection*, and on the propositional component of the action, a (which complements the affective component, $\mathbf{b_a}$, a 3D EPA vector). Finally, *BayesAct* has a two observation variables, Ω_x and Ω_f, that give evidence for the variables, $\mathbf{X}$ and $\mathbf{F}_b$, respectively, through observation functions $Pr(\Omega_x|\mathbf{X})$ and $Pr(\Omega_f|\mathbf{F}_b)$.

3 System Description

3.1 Handwashing POMDP with Affective Reasoning

We use a model of the handwashing system with 8 *plansteps* corresponding to the different steps of handwashing, desribing the state of the tap (on/off), and hands (dirty/soapy/clean and wet/dry). An eight-valued variable PS describes the current planstep. The client's behaviour is modeled with a six-valued variable BEH dscribing his/her actions: turn on/off water, use soap, use towel, rinse and null (do nothing). There are probabilistic transitions between plansteps described in a probabilistic plan-graph (e.g. a PwD sometimes uses soap first, but sometimes turns on the tap first). We also use a binary variable AW describing if the PwD is *aware* or not. In [14], we also had a variable describing how *responsive* a person is to a prompt. Here, we replace that with the current deflection in the interaction. Thus, $\mathbf{X} = \{PS, BEH, AW\}$ and the dynamics of the PS are

- If the client is aware, then if there is no prompt from the agent, the client will advance stochastically to the next planstep with a probability that is dependent on the current observation of client behaviour and the deflection, D. If the client does not advance, she loses awareness.
- If the client is aware and is prompted, and D is high, then the prompt will likely confuse the client and (stochastically) cause him/her to lose awareness.
- If the client is not aware, then if there is a prompt from the agent, and D is low, the client will likely follow the prompt and gain awareness. Otherwise (i.e. there is no prompt, or the deflection D is high), the client will not do anything (or do something other than the one prompted) with high probability.

We have found that a fixed affective policy may work well for some affective identities, but not for others, whereas the actions suggested by *BayesAct* work well across the different identities that the client may have [8].

3.2 Functional Motion Classification

Caregivers of older adults with dementia have indicated that any assistive technologies must integrate into the environment to reduce the likelihood of stigmatization, but be out of reach [2]. The tracker we use classifies individual body parts from a single overhead depth image on a per-frame basis [3]. The tracker first uses a random decision forest with a simple depth feature to provide intermediate multiclass probability density functions (PDF) for each sampled image pixel. The tracker then proposes final body part positions by aggregating the information contained in the underlying PDF. The tracker is trained on a set of images that are manually annotated to optimize key parameters. The optimal parameters are then used to train a final decision forest resulting in a new depth-based hand tracker. The tracker outputs the locations of the two hands and the head, and has been independently evaluated [3].

The hand locations are mapped to a set of pre-defined spatial regions (soap, tap, sink, water, towel). If multiple areas are detected, then a set of rules, based on the distances from the region centers and current hand-locations, are applied to decide the "winner" region that is used as the observation $\boldsymbol{\omega_x}$ (of variable $\mathbf{x}$) in the POMDP. Further details are found in [10].

3.3 Affective Motion Classification

Hands' coordinates obtained from the hand tracker are used to extract EPA values as follows. Evaluation ("E") stays neutral for all situations as it is the most difficult one to measure (e.g. facial expressions or vocal tone could be used in future). The mean of the distances between the user's two hands within a set of $n = 10$ frames is an indication of the "open-ness" of a body posture, known to be a good indication of feelings of dominance or power. A piecewise linear function maps from this average inter-hand distance to potency, $P \in [-4.3, 4.3]$.

The activity (A) is based on the speed of movement of the user's hands. In each pair of successive frames, the maximum difference between any two hand positions is computed. These differences are averaged over $n = 10$ frames, and a second linear interpolation function is used to map these differences to activity, $A \in [-4.3, 4.3]$. The linear interpolants for P and A are learned from experimental data. Further details and precise settings can be found in [10].

The EPA vector that results from the calculations above is used as the observation ω_f (of $\mathbf{f}_b$) in *BayesAct*. We set the covariance in the observation function $Pr(\omega_f|\mathbf{f}_b)$ to be such that the "E" dimension is ignored (infinite variance), and the "P" and "A" dimensions have relatively small effects on the agent's estimate of $\mathbf{f}_b$. That is, we set the covariance to be a diagonal with entries $(10000, 1.0, 0.5)$. The variance in "P" is set to be larger than that in "A" since the distance between user's hands is a much weaker indication of potency than the speed of user's hands is an indication of activity. If other measures were used for EPA observations, these variances could be adjusted accordingly.

3.4 Affective Prompting

We created a set of audio-visual prompts using a virtual human developed with the USC Virtual Human Toolkit (VHT)[3]. We built a set of six audio-visual prompts with five different emotional deliveries (e.g. "bossy", "motherly" or "bored" - see screenshots in Table 1). An online survey was then conducted in which participants were asked to watch the 30 videos and rate them based on Evaluation, Potency, and Activity dimensions (on a discrete scale of -4 to +4 with increments of 1 for a total of 9 options). Following [6], we showed sets of concepts at either end of the scales: bad/awful to good/nice (Evaluation); impotent/powerless/little to potent/powerful/big (Potency); inactive/slow/quiet to active/fast/noisy (Activity). The questions were presented in randomized order. There were total of 27 respondents.

To determine consensus amongst participants, we followed the culture-as-consensus model measuring the shared knowledge of the culture within the respondents [6]. The method computes the Eigenvalues of the covariance matrix of all responses for each of E,P,A separately. These eigenvalues indicate the extent to which respondents agree in their ratings across all items. If the ratio of the first to second Eigenvalue is large, this reflects cultural commonality in the respondent's ratings and provides evidence of one dominant factor governing respondent's judgement [6]. The Eigenvalue ratios for E were 8.518, that for P was 1.523 and that for A was 1.914, indicating that the respondents agreed most on the evaluation dimension, with reasonable agreement on potency and evaluation (see details in [13]).

---

[3] https://vhtoolkit.ict.usc.edu

For use in the handwashing assistant, we compute the mean value across all respondents (ignoring missing values). Given the propositional and emotional descriptions of desired prompts (obtained from the *BayesAct* POMDP), our system selects the video prompt that matches the propositional label and whose mean value (from the survey results) is closest in the EPA space.

4   Experiments and Results

The system operates with server-stubs and client-stubs, and Google's protocol buffer mechanism were used as the way to define the request and response messages shared by the two communicating parties. Open source libraries, such as zeromq and libVLC for prompts, were utilized as well. The experiments were conducted on a PC running 64-bit Ubuntu 12.04 LTS, with AMD FX(tm)-6300 Six-Core Processor 6 and Gallium 0.4 on llvmpipe (LLVM 0x300) Graphics. A kinect camera was mounted above the sink area and was the only sensor. Further details on the experiments can be found in [10].

Table 1 shows the first four steps of an example run with the system, along with the tracked hand locations, the prompts given and the various beliefs the system has about the user. We can see that the behaviours of the user are monitored correctly, and the system responds with appropriate prompts.

We did two tests with an actor washing her hands while the system observes and assists her in real time. The actor acted more powerfully (with her hands more "open") and more actively (with her hands moving more quickly) in the first test than in the second one. $\mathbf{f}_c^0$ was set to $[1.61, 0.84, -0.87]$ in test #1, and was set to $[-0.64, -0.43, -1.81]$ in test #2[4]. Recall that $\mathbf{f}_c$ denotes the agent's belief of the client's identity, and $\mathbf{f}_c^0$ denotes the initial value of this belief. Throughout the tests, the user behaviours in the first test generally had larger P and larger A values than those in the second test. The P and A values computed for user behaviours in test #1 reached an average of $[1.32, -1.3]$, while that in the second test was $[0.77, -1.74]$. Further, the f_c's in the first test generally had larger P and larger A values than those in the second test, and the system prompts in the first test generally had smaller P and higher A values. The mean of the EPA values of f_c's in the two tests were $[2.8, 1.03, -0.73]$ and $[1.13, -0.43, -1.47]$, respectively. And the mean of the EPA values of system prompts in the two tests were $[1.62, 0.32, 0.75]$ and $[1.53, 0.66, 0.08]$. Prompts with lower P values and higher A values are produced for identities with higher P values and higher A values. This correlation makes sense, since people who think of themselves as powerful persons tend to expect respect from others in interactions (i.e. prompts should be expressed to them with low potency levels), and that active people are likely to interact better with persons who are active as well — these "intuitions" are born out with *BayesAct* simulations, and thus are in accord with the predictions of Affect Control Theory.

---

[4] These EPAs are close to the identities of "elder" and "lonesome elder", resp.

Table 1. First 4 steps of an experimental test run with acted behaviours. f_c: system's estimate of the user's affective identity. f_b: user's affective behaviour. b_a: affective delivery of prompt. Plansteps are tap/hands/wet = [off/dirty/dry, on/dirty/dry, off/soapy/dry, on/soapy/dry, on/clean/wet, off/clean/wet, on/clean/dry, off/clean/dry]. Propositional prompts (prop) are 0:none, 1:water on, 2: soap.

time (sec)	f_c (E,P,A)	behaviour video/value	f_b	planstep belief/value	prop	b_a	avatar
0	$\begin{bmatrix} 1.70 \\ 1.40 \\ -1.39 \end{bmatrix}$	*TOWEL*	$\begin{bmatrix} 0 \\ 1.86 \\ -1.7 \end{bmatrix}$	[1 0 0 0... 0 0 0 0] most likely: 0	1	$\begin{bmatrix} 1.82 \\ 0.22 \\ 0.47 \end{bmatrix}$	*"Hello I am so glad to have you here. Please turn on the water"*
4	$\begin{bmatrix} 2.73 \\ 1.14 \\ -1.03 \end{bmatrix}$	*TAP*	$\begin{bmatrix} 0 \\ 1.68 \\ -0.58 \end{bmatrix}$	[.26 .74 0 0... 0 0 0 0] most likely: 1	0	$\begin{bmatrix} - \\ - \\ - \end{bmatrix}$	
6	$\begin{bmatrix} 2.67 \\ 1.21 \\ -0.72 \end{bmatrix}$	*RINSE*	$\begin{bmatrix} 0 \\ 1.49 \\ -0.16 \end{bmatrix}$	[.27 .73 0 0... 0 0 0 0] most likely: 1	2	$\begin{bmatrix} 1.51 \\ 0.12 \\ 0.52 \end{bmatrix}$	*"You are washing your hands. Please use the soap."*
10	$\begin{bmatrix} 2.57 \\ 0.69 \\ -0.66 \end{bmatrix}$	*SOAP*	$\begin{bmatrix} 0 \\ 0.73 \\ -1.52 \end{bmatrix}$	[0 .01 .35 .64... 0 0 0 0] most likely: 3	0	$\begin{bmatrix} - \\ - \\ - \end{bmatrix}$	

5 Conclusion

We have presented a prototype of an assistance system that reasons about affective identities. Our hypothesis is that older adults with AD will be more engaged with, and will adhere to more prompts by, the prompting system that uses affective reasoning. This will result in an increase in the number of ADL steps completed independently. In future, we plan to investigate notions of identity in Alzheimer's disease, to work on measurement of EPA from verbal and non-verbal behaviours, and to develop dynamic (continuous) video prompts.

References

1. Åström, K.J.: Optimal control of Markov decision processes with incomplete state estimation. J. Math. Anal. App. 10 (1965)
2. Czarnuch, S., Mihailidis, A.: The design of intelligent in-home assistive technologies: Assessing the needs of older adults with dementia and their caregivers. Gerontechnology 10, 165–178 (2011)
3. Czarnuch, S., Mihailidis, A.: Depth image hand tracking from an overhead perspective using partially labeled, unbalanced data: Development and real-world testing (2014), http://arxiv.org/abs/1409.2050v1
4. Fontaine, J.R.J., Scherer, K.R., Roesch, E.B., Ellsworth, P.C.: The world of emotions is not two-dimensional. Psychological Science 18, 1050–1057 (2007)
5. Heise, D.R.: Expressive Order: Confirming Sentiments in Social Actions. Springer (2007)
6. Heise, D.R.: Surveying Cultures: Discovering Shared Conceptions and Sentiments. Wiley (2010)
7. Hoey, J., Boutilier, C., Poupart, P., Olivier, P., Monk, A., Mihailidis, A.: People, sensors, decisions: Customizable and adaptive technologies for assistance in healthcare. ACM Trans. IIS 2(4) (2012)
8. Hoey, J., Schröder, T., Alhothali, A.: Affect control processes: Intelligent affective interaction using a POMDP (2013), http://arxiv.org/abs/1306.5279v2
9. Hoey, J., Schröder, T., Alhothali, A.: Bayesian affect control theory. In: Proc. Conf. on Affective Computing and Intelligent Interaction, ACII (2013)
10. Lin, L.: An Assistive Handwashing System with Emotional Intelligence. Master's thesis, University of Waterloo (2014)
11. Lively, K.J., Smith, C.L.: Identity and illness. In: Handbook of the Sociology of Health, Illness, and Healing, pp. 505–525. Springer, New York (2011)
12. MacKinnnon, N.J., Robinson, D.T.: 25 years of research in affect control theory. Advances in Group Processing 31 (2014)
13. Malhotra, A., Yu, C., Schröder, T., Hoey, J.: An exploratory study into the use of an emotionally aware cognitive assistant. TR# CS-2014-15, U. of Waterloo (2014)
14. Mihailidis, A., Boger, J., Candido, M., Hoey, J.: The coach prompting system to assist older adults with dementia through handwashing: An efficacy study. BMC Geriatrics 8(28) (2008)
15. Orona, C.J.: Temporality and identity loss due to Alzheimer's disease. Social Science & Medicine 30(11), 1247–1256 (1990)
16. Osgood, C.E., May, W.H., Miron, M.S.: Cross-Cultural Universals of Affective Meaning. University of Illinois Press (1975)
17. Rose Addis, D., Tippett, L.: Memory of myself: Autobiographical memory and identity in Alzheimer's disease. Memory 12(1), 56–74 (2004)
18. Scholl, W.: The socio-emotional basis of human interaction and communication: How we construct our social world. Social Science Information 52, 3–33 (2013)
19. Wilson, R., et al.: Quantitative analysis of formal caregivers' use of communication strategies while assisting individuals with moderate and severe alzheimer's disease during oral care. Journal of Communication Disorders 46(3), 249–263 (2013)

Stay in Touch: An in Context Evaluation of a Smartphone Interface Designed for People with Dementia

Rens Brankaert[1,*], Liselore Snaphaan[2], and Elke den Ouden[1]

[1] University of Technology Eindhoven, Department of Industrial Design and Department of Industrial Engineering and Innovation Sciences, Den Dolech 2, 5612 AZ, Eindhoven, The Netherlands
[2] Geestelijke Gezondheidszorg Eindhoven, Doctor Poletlaan 40, 5626 ND Eindhoven, The Netherlands
{R.G.A.Brankaert,E.d.Ouden}@tue.nl, LJAE.snaphaan@ggze.nl

Abstract. Assistive technology can play an important role in supporting people with dementia and their caregivers. For this study a smartphone interface with new functionalities is evaluated in context. This evaluation aimed at how elderly affected by dementia and their caregivers used it and how they experienced using such a device.

In this study ten couples participated, in which both received a smartphone. They were free to use the phone over a period of three weeks as they desired. During this period objective and subjective data was logged. After this period, the smartphones were discussed with the users.

The results showed everybody tried actively to use the phone but only few maintained using it. The main difficulties occurred with the smartphone itself, forgetting to take it along and/or with charging the battery. Most functionality seemed to be desired by the participants, also by those that could not properly use them via the smartphone. This suggests a need for the improvement of the design of assistive technology for this particular group.

Keywords: Living Lab, Interaction Design, User centered design, Dementia.

1 Introduction

The number of people affected by dementia is growing rapidly, posing numerous societal challenges. Research estimates that the number of people with dementia will double by 2040 [5]. Because there is no cure available to date, the treatment focuses on long-term care. Currently this is the most costly disease to treat for the healthcare system. Because of this continues growth of the populations, the costs will rise further. At some point professional care for this group will become too, and as a result, people with dementia will need to live longer in their home environment, relying on informal caregivers and social care services. This increases the risk of becoming

---

* The study is part of the Innovate Dementia project, funded by the Interreg IVB NWE program.

L. Pecchia et al. (Eds.): IWAAL 2014, LNCS 8868, pp. 288–295, 2014.

overburdened for these informal caregivers, often spouses of older age [5]. Moreover, it reduces the quality of life for both people with dementia and these caregivers, as the home environment is simply not designed to provide such extensive care.

Developing assistive technology is proposed to support these people in living independently. Cahill and colleagues [3] argue that, since there is no cure for dementia, innovative solutions such as assistive technology need to be developed to improve the quality of life for people with dementia. Several challenges caused by the disease can be addressed with such technology, for example, coping with the disease, providing support for daily activities and improving safety.

Literature describes some attempts to develop assistive technology for people affected by dementia, and poses several challenges for this. Topo [7] puts forward that in the development of such assistive technology personal aspects of those with dementia are often neglected. Instead, assistive technology is often evaluated or discussed with the informal caregiver rather than with the person affected by dementia directly [2]. Moreover, studies that evaluate assistive technology are often conducted in a clinical setting, not including people in a natural environment directly. In addition, Wallace and colleagues [8] suggest that the person is often forgotten in the design for people with dementia, and argue for greater personalization in such assistive solutions.

Therefore, to develop suitable assistive technology, we need to include both the person diagnosed with dementia and their caregivers in their natural context. Additionally characteristics of the disease, and of elderly in general need to be considered.

In this research project we focus on assistive technology that people with dementia can use throughout the early stages of the disease. A smartphone interface was designed with additional functionalities aimed at this target group, with a focus on simplicity and personalization [8].

2   Methods

The main goal of this study is to explore the potential benefit of the smartphone interface and accompanied new functionalities. We would like to see how such devices could support elderly with dementia and their caregivers, and make them more independent. The smartphone interface was designed for elderly with dementia, offering three main functionalities: (1) communicating with caregivers and family, (2) providing support when lost in public space by personal navigation and (3) sending out an emergency signal to caregivers. The latter two are new functions.

In this study we aim to answer the following question: How should we design smartphone interfaces, and novel functionalities, so they are usable by people with dementia and their caregivers and promote independence?

This question is explorative, and therefore we evaluated the smartphone interface design on itself rather than comparing it with other assistive technologies. The evaluation is in the field as research suggests this is necessary for stronger insights. The participants were instructed to use the smartphone as they desired.

Because of the involvement of people affected by dementia, being cognitively impaired, ethics are an important factor. As such we cooperated with a mental healthcare organization in this study. They, together with the spouse, functioned as gatekeepers. These gatekeepers monitored the research and the participant with dementia continuously and evaluated whether the person with dementia could participate. In this process, the informed consent has to be seen as a continuous conversation rather than a one-time agreement at the start of the process [4]. The perspective of the users must be respected continuously and this overrules the research protocol.

2.1 Smartphone Interface Design

The smart phone interface is specifically designed for older adults, and now evaluated if it could be interesting for elderly with dementia, for more information please visit the website (http://www.gociety.eu/en/golivephone/). Design features are sizable icons, high contrast, no scrolling and a simple menu (figure 1).

The new functionalities are a 'bring me home' function (E) and a help button. The 'guide me home' function guides users home step by step. The help button (A) is designed to alarm direct caregivers. When it is pressed a push message (email and text message) is sent to these caregivers. Regular functionality of a phone is available as well, such as contacts (B), Calling (C) and messages (D). Furthermore a settings button (F) was present to adjust advanced settings, this could only be reached by pressing OK three times. Additionally the overview (figure 1) shows the number of interactions was kept minimal.

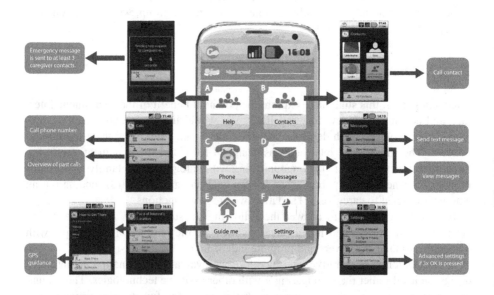

Fig. 1. The smartphone interface used for this study. The menu options are A) Help. B) Contacts. C) Phone/calling. D) Messages. E) Guide me home function and F) Settings.

2.2   Subjective Evaluation

To evaluate the experience and perspective of the users during the study we issued a bi-daily questionnaire for both caregiver and person with dementia (Table 1).

Table 1. The questions and goals for these questions in the bi-daily questionnaire

Questions	Goal:
Open questions:	
What functionality did you use most?	To find out what the users used most.
How long did you use the phone?	To get an indication of the estimated use time.
Which function gave trouble?	To find out what was most difficult to use.
Closed questions:	**Fully Agree to Fully Disagree on a 5 point scale**
Today the device was useful	Perceived benefit
Today there were no problems	Perceived issues
Battery was satisfactory	Perspective on the battery
With this I feel more safe	If it contributed to the feeling of safety
It increases my communication	If it let to more communication with fami-
Additional comments:	ly/friends
	Capture additional comments users want to make

2.3   Objective Evaluation

Concerning the objective data we monitored two aspects, the main goal for these data logs are to make a comparison with the subjective data, and potentially spot deviations. The following aspects were collected from the smartphone directly:

- GPS data, to find the reach of the users.
- The activity levels measured by the accelerometer translated in calories, to see how often and how intensively the phone was used.

3   Results

In this section the results of the objective and subjective data collected are presented. Of all participants (n=10) one dropped out after seven days, because both the caregiver and the person with dementia had trouble using the Smartphone. For the other participants (n=9) an average length of 17,9 days (with a min. of 13 and a max. of 21 days) was registered.

3.1   Objective Data

The accelerometer was used to measure the activity of the participants over the test period; the application presents this data in terms of calories burned by the user. The participants joined the study voluntary, and were instructed to use the smartphone as they desired. The following graphs show the average results, with standard deviations, for each day, for the persons with dementia (Figure 2). The data of the informal care-givers is not presented as it showed significant lower use of the phone, mainly be-cause they often already had phones and did not want to change.

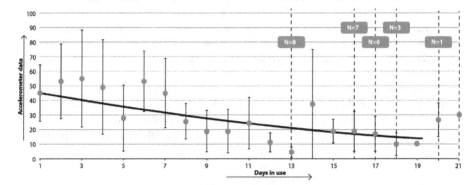

Fig. 3. The average accelerometer data of participants with Dementia, and

In general we can see that the participants used the phone over the test period yet very irregular. The data shows that almost all users enthusiastically started using the smart-phone when they received it. However, after the first week (from day 7, figure 3) we see a drop in average use. Some users continued to use it after this first period and these users also indicated they experienced the smartphone as beneficial. From the day 13 participants started to drop (orange box, figure 3), and the data is no longer repre-sentative from day 18 when there were only 3 participants left.

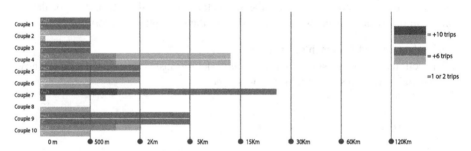

Fig. 4. The GPS reach from PwD (Person with Dementia) and IC (Informal Caregiver)

The GPS data (Figure 4) shows for each couple their distance from home, the upper bar represents the person with Dementia (PwD) and the lower bar the Informal Care-giver (IC). It shows that almost all participants tried the phone around their house in an area of 500 meters. Moreover, some users took the phone on larger trips (ie. Couples 9 – both). Additionally, some users took it almost everywhere they went showing intensive use. Couple 7 – PwD – took it almost everywhere everyday, Couple 9 – both – experimented a lot on near, mid and far trips almost daily, Couple 5 – both – showing near to mid distance trips uses and Couple 10 – PwD – showing near and mid distance trips.

3.2   Subjective Data

The bi-daily questionnaires were generally not well adhered to during the study. We aimed at 7 questionnaires per person, yet an average of 3,3 questionnaires were completed per couple (with a minimum of 0 and a maximum of 7). Nevertheless some of these users provided additional input by putting their experience in a separate text file. Table 2 shows the results of the questionnaires.

Table 2. The results of the the bi-daily questionnaire

Questions	Goal:
Open questions:	
Most used functionality	Calling each other (N=7), Navigation (N=4),
Average time phone used (that day):	0 – 10 min (N=5), 10 – 30 (N=3), 30 – 60 (N=2)
Which function gave most trouble?	General use (N=5), Help (N=3), Navigation (N=2)
Most common issues:	
Battery	The battery empties too quickly (N=8)
Forgetfulness	Users often forgot their phone, difficult to integrate in routine of dementia patients, use menu (N=5)
New functionality: HELP	help button is difficult (N=4), or not used (N=6), although caregivers think this is nice (N=3)
Guide me home application	Very positive (N=3), and Ok (N=2)

In general we saw that about half of the participants could use the phone decently. Two of them were very active users of the phone; the other three felt they didn't need the phone yet. The other five participants experienced many difficulties with the system, and indicated they could not use it and did not want to use it. The battery was indicated to be a major problem for almost all (N=8), and needs to be dealt with. Furthermore the navigation app was the most interesting new functionality, which was used a lot by three users and a couple of times by two users.

4   Discussion

In this study we examined a smartphone interface used by people with dementia and their caregivers, in their natural home context. From the objective activity data we found that all participants actively started using the smartphone, but only few maintained to use it. Also, based on the GPS reach data, we found that only few participants took the phone with them on their trips.

From the subjective data we learned interacting with the system, and integrating it in their daily routine proved most difficult. Even basic functionalities like calling somebody were often mentioned to be challenging. However, some users were capable of using the smartphone to its full extent and actually very happy with it. Especially the guide me home application was appreciated and used often by some. On the contrary, the other new feature, a help button was received less positive. Participants often pressed it by accident, causing moments of distress. Nevertheless, some caregivers felt more secure knowing that for example their spouse had access to such a feature.

Additionally the evaluation showed that for some users some usability improvements could already enhance their experience. This includes minor improvements like consistency in the interface, avoiding non-native language, improving the battery life and avoiding deep menu structures. However, for some users this technology was not suitable at all. This was for example apparent for the couple that dropped out after 7 days because the healthy caregiver could not use the device. This shows that the disease might not be the only factor to determine usability with assistive technology.

Fortunately, some people with dementia could interact with the device very well. These users tended to be the younger elderly (age<80) and those within an earlier stage of dementia. They could often use the smartphones independently, but some also felt they did not need it yet. More research is needed to find out if such successful use cases are disease-related, age-related or both.

Furthermore, we experienced a low adherence to the bi-daily questionnaire. However, some users took up a very active role and provided all kinds of suggestions for new functionalities and interaction approaches. This shows the importance of active involvement, even for this target group [6].

Most interestingly we also found that the participants desired most of the functionality. This opens up the design space, and challenges researchers and designers to come up with alternative, more radical solutions for assistive technology. We also recommend for future studies to put these new design features in the wild as soon as possible, as this generates many insights you would not get from incremental testing.

4.1   Limitations

In the current study a number of limitations were present, which need to be considered for future studies involving people with dementia. First considering the evaluation method, a questionnaire was not very suitable for this explorative study. The informal caregiver provided most answers, and it was up to them to involve people with dementia. However we recommend keeping a subjective component, as this inspired us most for new directions. Also, the questionnaire was not adhered to very well. This confirms the method is not suitable; nevertheless it is positive our participants felt free to not fulfill them. Eventually most participants only filled out three to four copies on average. So for future studies, the method needs to be improved so that it includes both participants as well as be more attractive with perhaps more variance in the questions over the testing period to keep it interesting. Second, the objective data collection should be improved as well. Some conclusions could be connected to the accelerometer and GPS data, but for very specific answers more data was needed. For example, to find out whether the functionalities that user preferred were actually used most could easily be logged in a smartphone.

4.2   Future Ambitions

Based on this study our future ambitions are twofold. Firstly, we need to develop a new evaluation method that allows us to capture experiences in situ. Such method should focus more on involving the person with dementia directly, and be more attractive to motivate users to contribute to the study more regularly. Also a stronger link with objective data might be interesting.

Secondly, the smartphone interface needs a major design iteration in which insights from this study are integrated. Examples are a more consistent interface, adaptations in the new features and an improved battery life. Taking this even further, as some users couldn't use the device at all, new design directions should be explored. This could for example allow similar functionality to be provided via a different 'interface' than a smartphone. For the users who could use the device, or could partly use it, we need to improve the design and re-evaluate the smartphone interface. By aiming at various approaches for different levels of dementia we contributed to the quality of lives of people with dementia and their caregivers, and aid in solving the societal challenge.

References

1. Armstrong, N., Nugent, C.D., Moore, G., Finlay, D.D.: Developing smartphone applications for people with Alzheimer's disease. In: Proceeding of 10th IEEE International Conference on Information Technology and Applications in Biomedicine, Corfu, Greece, pp. 1–5 (2010)
2. Astell, A.J., Ellis, M.P., Bernardi, L., Alm, N., Dye, R., Gowans, G., Campbell, J.: Using a touch screen computer to support relationships between people with dementia and caregivers. Interacting with Computers 22(4), 267–275 (2010)
3. Cahill, S., Macijauskiene, J., Nygård, A.M., Faulkner, J.P., Hagen, I.: Technology in dementia care. Technology and Disability 19(2), 55–60 (2007)
4. Coughlan, T., Leder Mackley, K., Brown, M., Martindale, S., Schlögl, S., Mallaband, B., Arnott, J., Hoonhout, J., Szostak, D., Brewer, R., Poole, E., Pirhonen, A., Mitchell, V., Pink, S., Hine, N.: Current Issues and Future Directions in Methods for Studying Technolgy in the Home. Psychology Journal 11(2), 159–184 (2013)
5. Kinsella, K., He, W.: An Ageing World: 2008. International Population reports, US Census Bureau, Published June 2009 (2009)
6. Sanders, E.B.-N., Stappers, P.J.: Co-creation and the new landscapes of design. CoDesign 4(1), 5–18 (2008)
7. Topo, P.: Technology studies to meet the needs of people with dementia and their caregivers a literature review. Journal of Applied Gerontology 28(1), 5–37 (2009)
8. Wallace, J., Wright, P.C., McCarthy, J., Green, D.P., Thomas, J., Olivier, P.: A design-led inquiry into personhood in dementia. In: CHI 2013 Extended Abstracts on Human Factors in Computing Systems on - CHI EA 2013, p. 2883 (2013)

A Case Study on the Analysis of Behavior Patterns and Pattern Changes in Smart Environments

Paula Lago[1], Claudia Jiménez-Guarín[1], and Claudia Roncancio[2]

[1]Systems and Computing Engineering Department, School of Engineering,
Universidad de los Andes, Colombia
{pa.lago52,cjimenez}@uniandes.edu.co
[2] Univ. Grenoble Alpes, LIG, France
claudia.roncancio@imag.fr

Abstract. Societies need to devise mechanisms of caring for the well aging of the increasing number of seniors, as it is very important for elderly people to maintain their independence. Smart environments are being devised as a form of care in what has been called ambient assisted living. A smart environment should be able to respond in case of emergency or risk and inform any abnormal behavior. Still, not much research is done to understand behavior patterns, temporal changes and other particularities that can affect the effectiveness of smart environments in ambient assisted living. We explored the behavior of two adults in a smart environment in order to reveal temporal, spatial and sequential relations among the activities as well as the changes that these relations undergo overtime and across individuals. This paper presents an analysis of three human behavior patterns: temporal, location and frequency. These patterns are mined on two experimental subjects using the dataset provided by the CASAS project.

Our analysis evidences how temporal, spatial and sequential patterns differ from person to person, day to day and after some time. Learning personalized behaviors and identifying and adapting to changes is a crucial aspect for smart environments since one-fit-all solutions are not suitable.

Keywords: behavior analysis, patterns, activities of daily living, elder care.

1 Introduction

Socio-economic development around the world has led to improvements in life-expectancy which, together with lower fertility rates, are changing the demographic structure of countries. Population is now older than ever before and people over 60 years represented in 2010 8% of the total world population [1]. These numbers are expected to grow even more in the years to come, posing challenges to societies in order to help elders maintain their autonomy and independent living for as long as possible. Assisted Living based on ambient intelligence (Ambient Assisted Living, AAL) is proposed as a way to enable independent living while still giving elders the proper support in cases of disease, disability or emergency [2].

There are many commercial [3, 4] and academic [5, 6] projects working towards AAL that will enable elders to live independently and safe at their own home. These

L. Pecchia et al. (Eds.): IWAAL 2014, LNCS 8868, pp. 296–303, 2014.
© Springer International Publishing Switzerland 2014

systems monitor activities of daily living in order to tell routine compliance, or detect some early signs of disease and/or risk situations that should be watched over.

It is agreed that AAL solutions could benefit from a better understanding of activity dynamics, behavior patterns and routines [7] and that changes in behavior trends could reveal a decline in health. In the field of gerontology, some studies have been made to understand activity patterns of seniors. Pruchno and Rose [8] study single day activities for a large population. This study shows variations as a function of personal characteristics, social context and environmental context. A similar study [9] concludes that obligatory activities are done in the morning while leisure activities are more common during the evenings. However, these studies don't consider long-term patterns of single individuals or frequent activity sequences or days' correlation or behavior evolution.

In this work, we present a case study for analyzing patterns of behavior of two subjects in a real-life setting with respect to some contextual variables: time, day of the week and location. We analyze the frequency of each activity and frequent sets of activities at the light of changes in each of these variables. This allows us to visualize and reinforce three hypotheses that result from intuition:

1. People have different routines and behavior patterns. Consequently we require personalized classifiers for activity recognition. For each person we can learn what features better describe an activity,
2. People behave differently on different days of the week. This means that day to day differences may not be abnormal and that classifiers can base their knowledge on a weekly correlation,
3. Routines change overtime, thus, one-fit-all solutions are not suitable for this problem.

This paper is organized as follows: Section 2 provides considerations for the analysis in our work. It also presents the datasets used for this analysis. Section 3 presents the analysis performed together with the results and findings. Section 4 summarizes the findings, presents some conclusions and future work to be done.

2   Behavior Analysis in Smart Environments

In this section we present the considerations made prior to the behavior analysis and the data used for the case study.

2.1   Considerations for Behavior Analysis to Discover and Understand Routines

A first step when creating a smart environment for ambient assisted living is to understand the activities and routines of its inhabitants.

In our approach, an activity is the fundamental semantically described unit, and it is why we used activities and not sensor data to analyze patterns. An activity is defined by its context: start time, duration and location, and by a goal, which defines its label. When activities occur in similar contexts, i.e. at the same times, on the same locations or followed by the same activities, we can infer patterns. Recurrent patterns lead to routines, allowing us to infer usual or unusual situations.

Inferred patterns can change over time. Health conditions, new doings, new friends, new interests can happen on any time, making the learned routines and patterns obsolete. The models describing the individual daily life must be adaptable to the evolving situations, considering new patterns as normal when they arise.

We want to analyze these patterns and their changes to construct a semantically enriched context that can be used to create recommendations, alerts or notifications, both to the individual and to her care-givers, respecting the individual's privacy.

2.2   Data Description

For this study we used the Aruba (1ˢᵗ subject in the paper) and Cairo (2ⁿᵈ subject in the paper) CASAS Dataset which are made public by the CASAS project [5] through their repository (http://ailab.wsu.edu/casas/datasets.html). Both datasets consist of sensor data that was collected in the home of a volunteer adult with annotated activities. We used these datasets because they have data for long periods of time, are collected in real-life settings, and share similar activities that enable comparison. We used only two persons since it is hard to find other datasets with the same features.

The first dataset contains data from 2010-11-04 to 2011-06-11 (193 days) and the second dataset contains data from 2009-06-10 to 2009-08-05 (56 days). The annotated activities are[1]: meal preparation, sleeping, relax, wash dishes, work, bed to toilet, enter and leave home, housekeeping and resperate[2]. The last activity is not considered in this work. Also, enter and leave home activities are re-labeled as not at home.

Each record in the dataset contains a timestamp, a sensor id, a sensor reading and a label, if an activity is starting or ending (see Fig. 1 (a)). Since we are concerned with studying spatial, temporal and sequence patterns of the activities and not with the sensor activations, we first transformed the dataset in order to have records that contain the start and end time of the activity, the location and the label (see Fig. 2(b)).

```
2010-11-04 00:03:50.209589 M003 ON Sleeping begin
2010-11-04 00:03:57.399391 M003 OFF
2010-11-04 00:15:08.984841 T002 21.5
2010-11-04 05:40:40.482626 M003 OFF
2010-11-04 05:40:40.844463 M003 ON
2010-11-04 05:40:43.642664 M003 OFF Sleeping end
```

```
Bedroom 2010-11-04 00:03:50.20  2010-11-04 05:40:42.45  Sleeping
Bedroom 2010-11-04 05:40:44.22  2010-11-04 05:40:46.31  Other
Bedroom 2010-11-04 05:40:52.34  2010-11-04 05:43:29.71  Bed to toilet
Bedroom 2010-11-04 05:43:34.26  2010-11-04 05:43:40.82  Other
Bedroom 2010-11-04 05:43:45.61  2010-11-04 05:43:45.61  Other
Bedroom 2010-11-04 05:43:53.18  2010-11-04 08:01:09.83  Sleeping
Living  2010-11-04 08:01:16.51  2010-11-04 08:10:51.2   Other
```

(a)   (b)

Fig. 1. (a) Original dataset and, (b). transformation done for this paper We used data that defines the location, start time and end time for each activity.

The location of each activity was defined as the room with the more sensor events during the time of the activity. The distribution of the sensors is available with each dataset.

---

[1]   Meal preparation, relax and wash dishes are not annotated for the second subject. Also, housekeeping refers to only laundry in the second subject.

[2]   Resperate is a device used to lower blood pressure.

3   Analysis of Behavioral Patterns Based on Time and Location

This section presents the method and results for the analysis of three kinds of patterns that emerge from the data used: temporal patterns by days and hours, location patterns and activity sets, that is, activities that often occur one after the other.

3.1   Temporal Patterns

To study how activity probabilities correlate with temporal characteristics, we performed in a first step a qualitative analysis of the data the usual start times of each monitored activity. Figure 2 shows, for subject 2, the hour at which each of the activities started activity for different days of the week. Figure 3 shows, for subject 1, the same information for different months of the years.

On one hand, the analysis of the data of subject 2 showed that while some activities exhibit similar start times for every day, others show clear differences depending on the day of the week they are done. For instance (Fig. 2), the first meal of the day is taken earlier on Wednesdays than on Sundays. Also, laundry is done earlier on Sundays. Clearly, the day of the week can change the start time of some activities.

On the other hand, the analysis of the data of subject 1 showed that routines, in the sense of start times for activities, change during the course of the year. When studied in two different periods of the year, housekeeping and washing dishes are almost non-existent for the second period (Fig. 3). Also, during the second period eating is only done in the mornings. These changes could be alerted to a care-giver or, if they correspond to a new routine, they should be learned by the system

We also compared quantitatively the differences in the start times for each activity depending on the day of the week with two-proportion z- tests. For the test we calculated the probability of doing each activity at each hour of the day for each day.

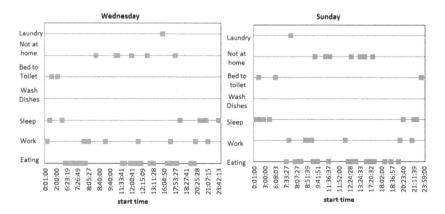

Fig. 2. Start times of the different activities for a period of two months on three different days of the week for subject 2. Different days show different probable activities for similar hours

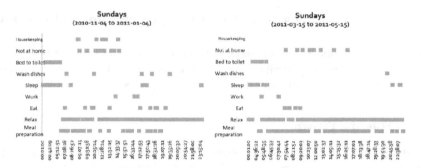

Fig. 3. Start times of the different activities on Wednesdays (top) and Sundays (bottom) for different two-month periods. Routines change from one period (right) to the other

The tests compared the probabilities for weekdays to weekends and for each day against every other day. The z-value for the test is calculated as in eq. (1), where $\hat{p}_1$ is the proportion of the activity being tested at day 1, $\hat{p}_2$ is the proportion of the activity at day 2 and p is the combined proportion of the activity at both days and is calculated as in eq. (2). n_1 is the total number of activities on day 1 and n_2 is the total number of activities of day two for the hour being tested.

$$z = \frac{\hat{p}_1 - \hat{p}_2}{\sqrt{p(1-p)(1/n_1 + 1/n_2)}} \tag{1}$$

$$p = \frac{x_1 + x_2}{n_1 + n_2} \tag{2}$$

The results of the test show that although most of the days are very similar, for some activities there are significant differences (using p-value<0.05). For example, when comparing proportions of the week with those of the weekend, the activities at 7am where found to be different. When comparing Wednesdays and Sundays (as in fig. 2), a difference was found for the activities eating at 6am and 1pm (p-value =0.041) and not at home at 8am (p-value= 0.043) and 13pm and (p-value=0.041). Also, when comparing Mondays with Sundays there are differences at 8am for eating (p-value=0.01) and for the activity not at home at 8pm (p-value=0.004) and at 5pm (p-value=0.02). These experiments allow us to detect temporal patterns and to measure daily and long-term differences in the monitored activities. Nevertheless, a more profound study needs to be done in order to determine if the changes correspond to different routines, alert signs, anomalies or some other factor.

3.2   Location Patterns

To study how activities correlate to a location in the house and how this varies for different persons, we explored the frequency each activity happened at the different locations at home. For the first subject, most activities occur mainly at one location, while for the second subject most activities take place at different locations around the house (Fig.4). This means that location could be a good feature for a classifier for the first subject but not for the second subject.

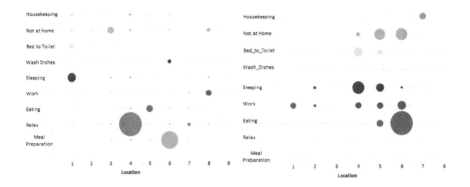

Fig. 4. Frequency (bubble area) of each activity per room in the house (x-axis) for subject 1 (left) and subject 2 (right). Not for every person location is a good feature for classification.

3.3 Frequent Activity Sets

To analyze frequent activity sequences, we treated the sequence of activities as a string and collected 5-grams[3]. We then found frequent item set using the FP-growth algorithm available at the mahout[4] library with 5-grams used as sets. We analyzed patterns for each day of the week for the 2nd subject and for the 1st subject we studied patterns for two periods of two months each separated by 4 months between them.

Visibly, behavior patterns on different days of the week differ even for the same person (Fig. 5) and so do behavior patterns across the year (Fig. 6). In the first case (Fig. 5), the eating activity is not always paired with the not-at-home activity, and it is mostly paired with it on Mondays, Saturdays and Sundays. Also, on Wednesdays and Fridays, eating is not paired with Working, but it is on every other day. Perhaps, the most remarkable example is that eating was only paired with housekeeping on Wednesdays, possibly because that is the day designated for this last activity.

In the second case, most patterns appear in both time periods; however, there is a frequency change from one period to the other (Fig. 6). Some patterns even disappear, for example, the ones that include housekeeping. Classifiers need to adapt to these changes in routines. One challenge that arises from this is identifying when a routine change has occurred instead of an abnormal event.

Finally, to evaluate how pattern changes affect classifiers over time, we trained a hidden Markov Model (HMM) to classify activities of subject .1. Then we evaluate its performance with data 1, 2, 3 and 4 months older than the data the model was trained with. The F-measure for most activities dropped after 4 months compared to the evaluation made with data 1-month after (Fig. 7).

---

[3] For the graphics on this subsection, the following acronyms are used: M: Meal preparation, R: relax, E: eating, W: work, S: sleep, D: Washing Dishes, T: bed to toilet, H: housekeeping N: Not at home.

[4] https://mahout.apache.org/

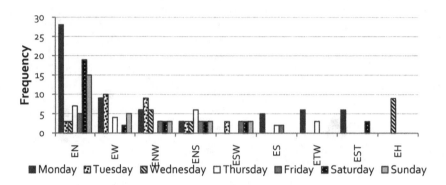

Fig. 5. Frequent activity sets (and frequency per day of the week) for subject 2. The frequency of each pattern changes according to the day of the week.

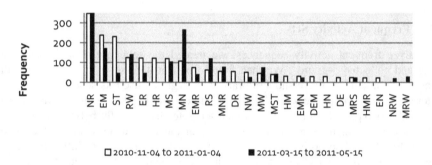

Fig. 6. Frequent activity sets for different two-month periods for the 1st subject. There are differences in the patterns and in the frequencies of the patterns that appear in both periods.

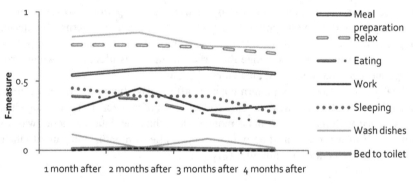

Fig. 7. F-measure for each activity obtained with a HMM trained with 2-month data. For most activities there is a decrease in the f-measure from the first month to the fourth month

4 Conclusions and Future Work

In this paper, we analyzed three behavior patterns: temporal, location and frequent activity sets for two persons in a smart environment. We were able to measure how routines change when analyzed under different contextual variables. We also measured how the fact that patterns change over time, affect the performance of a static model. This implies that static models do not fit well to human activity recognition. Moreover, we evidenced the need for personalized services as different people behave differently. Future work will focus on the use of an algorithm to improve the accuracy of activity recognition. This should help in the creation of better elder care solutions.

Acknowledgement. The authors would like to thank the Google Research Grant that partially financed the presentation of this article.

References

1. National Institute on Aging: Global Health and Aging (2011)
2. European Commission: Ambient Assisted Living Joint Programme (2008), http://www.aal-europe.eu/
3. Lively Inc.: MyLively (2014), http://www.mylively.com/
4. Hanson, M.A., Barth, A.T., Silverman, C.: In home assessment and management of health and wellness with BeClose™ ambient, artificial intelligence. In: Proceedings of the 2nd Conference on Wireless Health, pp. 25:1–25:2. ACM, San Diego (2011)
5. Cook, D.J., Crandall, A.S., Thomas, B.L., Krishnan, N.C.: CASAS: A Smart Home in a Box. IEEE Comput. 46, 62–69 (2013)
6. Munguia Tapia, E.: Activity Recognition in the Home Setting Using Simple and Ubiquitous Sensors (2003)
7. Brush, A.J., Krumm, J., Scott, J.: Activity Recognition Research: The Good, the Bad, and the Future. In: Pervasive 2010 Workshop: How to do Good Research in Activity Recognition, pp. 1–3 (2010)
8. Pruchno, R.A., Rose, M.S.: Time Use by Frail Older People in Different Care Settings. J. Appl. Gerontol. 21, 5–23 (2002)
9. Baltes, M.M., Wahl, H., Schmid-Furstoss, U.: The daily life of elderly Germans: activity patterns, personal control, and functional health. J. Gerontol. 45, 173–179 (1990)

The Caregiver Perspective: An Assistive AAL Platform

Angelo Costa[1,*], Paula Magalhães[2,3], José Ferreira-Alves[2], Tito Peixoto[4],
Ricardo Simoes[3,5,6], and Paulo Novais[1]

[1] CCTC-Computer Science and Technology Center, University of Minho, Braga, Portugal
{acosta, pjon}@di.uminho.pt
[2]School of Psychology, University of Minho, 4710-057 Braga, Portugal
{pmagalhaes,alves}@psi.uminho.pt
[3]Institute for Polymers and Composites IPC/I3N, University of Minho, Guimarães, Portugal
rsimoes@dep.uminho.pt
[4]Santa Casa da Misericórdia de Vieira do Minho, Portugal
[5]Life and Health Sciences Research Institute (ICVS), School of Health Sciences,
University of Minho, Campus de Gualtar, 4710-057 Braga, Portugal
[6]Polytechnic Institute of Cavado and Ave, Campus do IPCA, 4750-810 Barcelos, Portugal
rsimoes@ipca.pt

Abstract. The Ambient Assisted Living area has spawned several projects that aim to help the user on his/her daily activities. The AAL4ALL (ambient assisted living for all) project aims to develop a unified ecosystem using fully compatible devices and services. The UserAccess platform is part of the AAL4ALL and has as a goal to provide assistance to a type of actor that is commonly forgotten in the Ambient Assisted Living area, the caregiver. This paper presents the architecture, implementation, and interfaces, along with a brief analysis of caregiver's needs and work related issues.

Keywords: Ambient Assisted Living; Ambient Intelligence; Intelligent Environments; AAL4ALL; e-Health; Active Ageing; Artificial Intelligence.

1   Introduction

In a not so distant future, it is expected a complete inverse of the population's pyramid [1]. Specifically, estimates are that by 2050 people aged 65 or older will represent about 21% of the world's population, and 25% in places such as the European Union [2, 3]. This fact creates profound challenges to each nation worldwide: who will take care of the people who need assistance in one or more activities of daily living, and, importantly, who will pay for the solutions?

The challenge itself suggests that one cannot solely rely on people as a solution, as people in working-age will become a scarce asset, and thus an expensive one. Therefore, the act of caring itself needs to be reinvented. This reinvention can be achieved to some degree with the help of a technological approach, although some challenges of the caring process already have technological solutions [4]. The key idea is to create technological solutions that allow to postpone, or completely eliminate the need for full time caring that many individuals request and require nowadays. If techno-

L. Pecchia et al. (Eds.): IWAAL 2014, LNCS 8868, pp. 304–311, 2014.
© Springer International Publishing Switzerland 2014

logical solutions could lessen the physical contact-time of the caregiver without diminishing the individualized and effective care, it would certainly have a great impact on the lives of caregivers and care receivers. Another central idea is to allow for a complete monitoring of the elderly through digital means, and digital contact between the old person and the caregiver, that is, without the need of commuting.

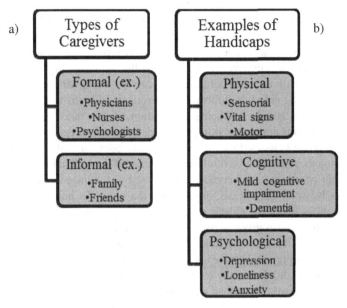

Fig. 1. Types of caregivers (a) and Examples of Handicaps of the care receivers (b)

Caring, however, can assume many forms, and be performed by many different actors; it can occur in a variety of settings, and be more or less formal. Specifically, in a primary care setting, or hospital setting, we can find different formal carers: physicians, nurses, psychologists, medical auxiliaries, among others (Figure 1a). Each of these professionals will have different needs regarding technological solutions, and different expectations about what technology can do for them. Additionally, the care receiver can present a variety of handicaps that pose different challenges to the caregivers and ultimately to those developing technological solutions (Figure 1b). Because of this, the technology that will be developed has to be flexible to adapt to the different profiles of carers, and affordable and intuitive so that it can reach the maximum number of users. Considering the diversity of people who provide care, as well as the diversity of possible settings of intervention, we consider that, overall, the pattern of usage of the new technologies will differ between informal and formal carers, and also within the variety of formal carers. Finally, we consider that *communication* is a key requirement that needs to be addressed by future solutions.

This document is constituted by the following sections: section 2 presents the caregiver's perspective of an AAL platform; section 3 presents the AAL4ALL project, its architecture and structure; section 4 shows the UserAccess project; and finally, section 5 presents the conclusions and the future work.

2   Caregiver's Perspective

To be a caregiver of a family member is a role that has plenty potential for facing multiple demands that disrupt the individual's wellbeing [5]. On the one hand, there are challenges that every individual faces in their lifetime to maintain wellbeing and health: self-care, nurture of relationships with family and friends, keep engagement with the community, practice prevention, among others. On the other hand, there are demands associated with and specific to the caregiver's role: being effective in the care provided; receive support and adequate supervision, mainly when the caring tasks are new and challenging; being available to the person being cared for; and, conciliate own needs with the needs of the care-receiver, among others [6].

We can conceive that elderly's informal caregivers could be particularly concerned about the parent or relative's wellbeing or location, if has taken the prescription, whether he/she is feeling lonely, or in urgent need. Informal caregivers could also be concerned whether the house's doors and windows are open, or if the oven and lights are on. Technology's role could be of alleviating some of these demands and concerns raised by the act of caring. This could be achieved by, for instance, facilitating the communication between individuals; monitoring the elderly's house conditions; or creating notifications about the elderly's activities and appointments. For instance, an agenda shared with the caregiver, a list of to-do tasks, or a list of medicine that the elderly has to take, which could be ticked when performed, among other information that the caregiver could remotely have access to. Having an easy access to information related to the elderly could drastically reduce the amount of stress and overload associated with caring. Caregiver's overload can result from the actual number of hours devoted to caring – which could be reduced by technological solutions - or from the special characteristics of the person being cared. Additionally, overload can manifest in several ways, such as: difficulties in sleeping, changes in mood, or eating patterns; struggling to balance all aspects of his/ her life; through physical pain and complaints, or exhaustion. These symptoms clearly lessen the ability caregiver's have to look after others. Therefore, to develop a set of solutions that have the potential to alleviate the stress associated with caring would greatly reduce the strain caregiver's face, improve their quality of live, and ultimately improve the quality of care provided.

Regarding formal caregivers, one can conceive that they have different needs and expectations regarding the role that new technologies can assume in their profession when compared with informal caregivers, but also when comparing different professionals. Physicians and nurses, for instance, could greatly benefit of monitoring of vital signs, teleappointments, and telediagnostics technologies, whereas medical auxiliaries will hardly benefit with these technologies. However, medical auxiliaries could greatly benefit with systems that allow them to monitor the elderlies' performance of the activities of daily living, or to monitor the environment in which the elderly is living in. A practical example could be that of a medical auxiliary in a nursing home. In Portuguese nursing homes, this person is responsible for several aspects of the elderly's wellbeing, namely, bathing, checking and caring after the skin condition, accompanying the elderly to the lunch room, among others. All these tasks should be registered and, in case there is a problem, communicate it to the person responsible for addressing that particular issue. For instance, if the elderly is not eating well, the auxiliary should record that information and notify the nursing home's nutritionist. However, there are several obstacles to successfully accomplish these goals. The process of recording is complex and takes time that should be devoted to taking care of the patient. Moreover, there is not a reliable vehicle to communicate the information about and the needs of the elderly to the appropriate professional. That is, sometimes the communication between the auxiliary and the other professionals is not effective and is prone to errors as does not rely in a notifications system. Another obstacle relates to the fact that medical auxiliaries tend to be less educated than other professionals. Finally, it is important to understand that although an individual completes every required task, it does not necessarily imply that the final result is the expected or desired one.

All considered, there is the need for platforms promoting and facilitating communication between the different actors involved in caring. The solutions will need to be simple and of easy interaction so that users from all educational backgrounds can learn how to use them effectively. The solution should allow for the creation of notifications, and ideally this system should be able to differentiate between different degrees of urgency of the different kinds of notification. A system with these characteristics would reduce stress and anxiety inherent to caregiving, and would increase the caregiver's feelings of control, self-worth and accomplishment in his/her work, and within the colleagues. This would not only increase satisfaction in the workplace, but also prevent potential negligence and abuse.

3   AAL4ALL

The AAL4ALL project is a Portuguese consortium whose goal is to provide its users with smart care. Being composed of hardware and software companies and universities this project is developing technological geriatric solutions. Some solutions are directed to the elderly and disabled people, which will help on their daily tasks, whereas other solutions focus on the informal and formal caregivers. This approach leads to an innovative AAL ecosystem, that not only focus on the elderly and disabled users, but also in those directly connected to them, increasing what is known as the users sphere and incorporating all actors directly and indirectly involved .

In terms of technological advances, AAL4ALL aims for two main features: integration and certification. As demonstrated in [7] there are a great number of projects that do not provide enough resources or are simply uninterested in integrating with other solutions, which can be a major problem. Specifically, in [8] it is clearly demonstrated that there are many projects that are overlapping their efforts to provide solutions in the same ambit, whereas other domains, such as the caregiver assistance, remain poor in technological platforms. Most of the current projects direct their efforts to the final user, leading to an unbalanced distribution of the AAL ecosystem distribution. Additionally, this becomes a problem to the user, as typically a combination of devices and services must be used and, without integration, the full potential of each product is not achieved. In addition, features such as machine learning and artificial intelligence cannot be implemented due to the lack of combined information and individual data processing [9].

The certification is crucial to the correct deployment of the devices and services to the market. As evidenced in [10–12], projects developed without a plan to a possible commercialization end with obsolete products, belonging only to the academic realm. Importantly, there is the need for certification as most of the AAL solutions are imminently (and some really are) medical products. Even software can be considered a medical product, due to the use of private and medical information, by being able to control medical devices, and to generate reports that will be used by medical personnel.

The AAL4ALL solutions range from body and home sensors to virtual actors that interact with the users, enlarging the monitoring and actuation sphere that usually AAL projects are bounded to. This tactic complies with the integration and certification goals, by keeping all solutions under the same umbrella and providing them with modular abilities. Being a complete ecosystem means that all people involved in the task of aiding the care-receiver, such as relatives and professionals, must be considered when developing solutions that ease their interaction with the care-receiver. That is the case of the UserAccess platform, a solution with the goal of integrating all users and connect them with each other.

4   UserAccess

The UserAccess platform aims to offer an assistive platform to the formal and informal caregiver [13, 14]. It provides automatized warnings, user environment monitoring, and events managing. Currently, the work of the formal caregiver is stressful and requires long hours. This means a decline in terms of efficiency and attention, and the UserAccess platform aims to alleviate the workload and allow more users to be monitored. Several studies [15–17] relate long hours, exigency and attention to a decrease in attention and increasing stress. Therefore, the user cannot benefit from a good service, and most importantly, in critical situations the response of the caregivers may not be the appropriate and put the care-receiver in great risk. Hence, the UserAccess provides a technological solution to create a more harmonious environment and ultimately provide additional security to the care-receiver and the caregiver.

The UserAccess is built to be used by every AAL4ALL user (caregiver and care-receiver), but tuned to the caregivers. For instance, the informal caregiver, including relatives and friends, can access to comprehensible information about the user and schedule events with him/her. In terms of architecture, the UserAccess platform is currently available in mobile (resorting to Android operating system) and web page formats. It is structured by a server that connects to the AAL4ALL platform, sustaining a modular structure based in multi-agent systems. Figure 2 shows the overview of the architecture, in which the AAL4ALL and the UserAccess platforms are highlighted.

In terms of operation, the UserAccess receives high-level information, such as "user exited home" or "lights are on", through the *UserAccess MQ Node*, which saves information in a queue and performs a verification of the incoming data, checking the validity and restructuring it according to the internal communication method. Furthermore, the messages form the other users and external services arrive and go through this module, serving as the gateway to all information entering and exiting.

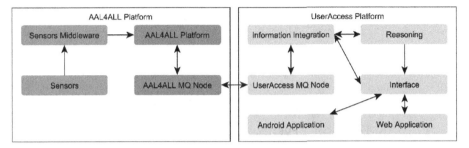

Fig. 2. UserAccess platform overview

The information is sent to the *Information integration,* being sorted according to the context it possesses. For instance, whether it is a warning coming from a sensor or a calendar update. The information can then be directly sent to the interfaces or further processed in the *Reasoning* module. The *Reasoning* module is the most complex module of the platform, being in fact composed of several logical agents. These agents are responsible for the complex processing of information, for instance, if an event is received, it must fetch all calendars, verify the collisions, and, if possible, schedule or find another suitable time frame. The use of several agents was adopted to benefit from the heterogeneity they present, easy upgradability, and communication flow flexibility that makes the addition of new agents easy to perform and integrate with the rest of the agents. Finally, a set of actions is devised and transformed into information or notifications to send to the caregiver mobile platform.

The interfaces are of the uttermost importance, being the tangible element to all users. Thus, it is imperative that interfaces appeal and can conjugate with the users. Figure 3 displays the interfaces developed. Currently, they are able to display the most important messages and the overall information, as well as receive events and display them directly on the interface. Furthermore, an SOS and shortcuts have been placed to ease the task of calling to predefined people or services.

The calendar module is one of the most important features of the platform. As stated before, freeing the caregiver of constant attention is crucial, and, in our perspective, the calendar can serve to micromanage some aspects of each care-receiver's life. The UserAccess android application is built to manage several care-receiver's that the caregiver is responsible for, as it can be seen in Figure 3 a), and, resorting to the calendar, to monitor each aspect of the care-receiver's life (even warnings).

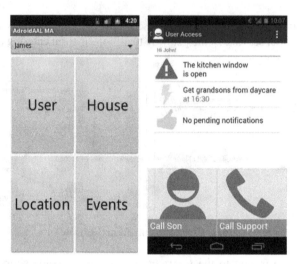

Fig. 3. a) The Android application home interface, **b)** Alpha stage caregiver interface (warnings and activities)

5   Conclusions and Future Work

In this paper was presented the UserAccess project. The AAL4ALL project allows the heavy data processing to be done on the cloud, where the UserAccess is expected to work. The UserAccess is currently focusing on three features: the agenda management, automatic profiling, and user interfaces. The agenda management is currently the core of the platform, being the profiling essential to determine the preferred activities and peers of the users. The users' interfaces are being rebuilt to better accommodate information and improve in style.

Currently, we can state that the UserAccess is close to completion, most of it having already been implemented. The Reasoning module is undergoing several developments and is expected to be fully operational during the current year.

Acknowledgments. Project "AAL4ALL", co-financed by the European Community Fund FEDER, through COMPETE - Programa Operacional Factores de Competitividade (POFC). Foundation for Science and Technology (FCT), Lisbon, Portugal, through   Project   PEst-C/CTM/LA0025/2013   and   the   project   PEst-OE/EEI/UI0752/2014.

Project CAMCoF - Context-aware Multimodal Communication Framework funded by ERDF -European Regional Development Fund through the COMPETE Programme (operational programme for competitiveness) and by National Funds through the FCT - Fundação para a Ciência e a Tecnologia (Portuguese Foundation for Science and Technology) within project FCOMP-01-0124-FEDER-028980.

References

1. United Nations: Population estimates and projections section (2012)
2. United Nations, Department of Economic and Social Affairs, P.D.: World Population Ageing 2013 (2013)
3. Grauel, J., Spellerberg, A.: Attitudes and requirements of elderly people towards assisted living solutions. In: Mühlhäuser, M., Ferscha, A., Aitenbichler, E. (eds.) AmI 2011. CCIS, vol. 11, pp. 197–206. Springer, Heidelberg (2008)
4. Rashidi, P., Mihailidis, A.: A survey on ambient-assisted living tools for older adults. IEEE Journal of Biomedical and Health Informatics 17, 579–590 (2013)
5. Hirst, M.: Carer distress: a prospective, population-based study. Social Science & Medicine 61, 697–708 (2005)
6. Nolan, M.R., Grant, G.: Addressing the needs of informal carers: a neglected area of nursing practice. Journal of Advanced Nursing 14, 950–961 (1989)
7. Norgall, T., Wichert, R.: Towards Interoperability and Integration of Personal Health AAL Ecosystems. In: Studies in Health Technology and Informatics, pp. 272–282. IOS Press (2012)
8. Antonino, P.O., Schneider, D., Hofmann, C., Nakagawa, E.Y.: Evaluation of AAL platforms according to architecture-based quality attributes. In: Keyson, D.V., et al. (eds.) AmI 2011. LNCS, vol. 7040, pp. 264–274. Springer, Heidelberg (2011)
9. Fagerberg, G., et al.: Platforms for AAL applications. In: Lukowicz, P., Kunze, K., Kortuem, G. (eds.) EuroSSC 2010. LNCS, vol. 6446, pp. 177–201. Springer, Heidelberg (2010)
10. Kung, A., Jean-Bart, B.: Making AAL Platforms a Reality. In: de Ruyter, B., Wichert, R., Keyson, D.V., Markopoulos, P., Streitz, N., Divitini, M., Georgantas, N., Mana Gomez, A. (eds.) AmI 2010. LNCS, vol. 6439, pp. 187–196. Springer, Heidelberg (2010)
11. Hanke, S., Mayer, C., Hoeftberger, O., Boos, H., Wichert, R., Tazari, M.-R., Wolf, P., Furfari, F.: universAAL - An Open and Consolidated AAL Platform. In: Wichert, R., Eberhardt, B. (eds.) Ambient Assited Living 4 Deutscher AAL Kongress, pp. 127–140. Springer (2011)
12. Walderhaug, S., Mikalsen, M., Salvi, D., Svagård, I., Ausen, D., Kofod-Petersen, A.: Towards quality assurance of AAL services. Stud. Health Technol. Inform. 177, 296–303 (2012)
13. Costa, A., Novais, P., Simoes, R.: A caregiver support platform within the scope of an ambient assisted living ecosystem. Sensors (Basel) 14, 5654–5676 (2014)
14. Costa, A., Gama, O., Novais, P., Simoes, R.: A Different Approach in an AAL Ecosystem: A Mobile Assistant for the Caregiver. In: Highlights of Practical Applications of Heterogeneous Multi-Agent Systems. The PAAMS Collection, pp. 101–110. Springer International Publishing, Salamanca (2014)
15. Robinson-Whelen, S., Tada, Y., MacCallum, R.C., McGuire, L., Kiecolt-Glaser, J.K.: Long-term caregiving: What happens when it ends? J. Abnorm. Psychol. 110, 573–584 (2001)
16. Schulz, R., Mendelsohn, A.B., Haley, W.E., Mahoney, D., Allen, R.S., Zhang, S., Thompson, L., Belle, S.H.: End-of-life care and the effects of bereavement on family caregivers of persons with dementia. N. Engl. J. Med. 349, 1936–1942 (2003)
17. Sherwood, P.R., Donovan, H.S., Given, C.W., Lu, X., Given, B.A., Hricik, A., Bradley, S.: Predictors of employment and lost hours from work in cancer caregivers. Psychooncology 17, 598–605 (2008)

Towards Holistic Support of Active Aging through Cognitive Stimulation, Exercise and Assisted Nutrition

Vanesa Espín, María Visitación Hurtado, and Manuel Noguera

Departamento de Lenguajes y Sistemas Informáticos, University of Granada
E.T.S.I.I.T., c/Daniel Saucedo Aranda s/n 18071, Granada, Spain
rebel@correo.ugr.es, {mhurtado,mnoguera}@ugr.es

Abstract. The incorporation of new technologies in elder care is becoming more and more usual over time. This is largely due to a great extent to the awareness and familiarity that this sector of population has acquired with the use of technology in their daily lives. In this paper, we present a nutritional recommender system, NutElCare (Nutrition for Elder Care), intended to help elderly users to draw up their own healthy diet plans following, at the same time, the nutritional experts guidelines. This recommender system is currently being integrated into VIRTRA-EL (VIRtual TRAining in ELderly people), a platform that provides support to active aging.

1 Introduction

Continued physical activity and good nutritional status are important determinants of physical and cognitive function in the elderly [17]. Several changes in body composition associated with aging, as lean body mass loss caused by the wastage of muscle mass and increase of body fat, are the main causes of malnutrition risk in elderly [8]. However, various studies demonstrate that many of the elderly do not feed well. This is due to somatic, psychic or social problems such as decreased sense of taste or appetite, cardiac insufficiency, chewing or swallowing disorders, depression, social deprivation and loneliness [16].

To prevent and even address these problems, experts work to develop healthy nutritional and physical activity plans for elderly along with cognitive stimulation programs. New technologies have much to contribute in this task. Elderly are becoming increasingly familiar and willing with technology. Thanks to the Internet, users can access to a big amount of data to help them in many tasks. But, this big volume of data may often hinder users to know what information they find is reliable or complete. Also, handling the large volume of data and extracting the information correctly to suit their needs efficiently is not an easy task.

Recommender systems are capable of storing the information provided by experts and offer it in the form of recommendations to users. However, traditional recommendation systems suffer from some limitations, where one of the most important is the heterogeneity of information representation, preventing the communication and sharing between agents and systems. To alleviate this problem, some proposals have

L. Pecchia et al. (Eds.): IWAAL 2014, LNCS 8868, pp. 312–319, 2014.

adopted Semantic Web technologies in the system development [14], [21], [4]. Ontologies are one of the main components of the Semantic Web. They provide universal semantics, easing knowledge sharing and its unambiguous interpretation. Ontologies can be represented by means of the OWL Web Ontology Language [23], a formal language based on Description Logics [2] that allows ontologies to support reasoning to infer new knowledge.

In the nutritional context, several recommender systems have been proposed [20], [9], [22]. Most of them are focused on obtaining recipes that appeal to users, but there are very few oriented to health care. Finally, the fact that intended users belong to sensitive areas of the population is taken into account in an even smaller number of them.

NutElCare (Nutrition for Elder care) [7] is a recommender system which allows elderly to make their own healthy diet plans according their needs due to aging. The system considers not only the healthy requirements, but also the user taste preferences, hence contributing to a better motivation on the use of the system caused by the more appealing and satisfactory diets for the users. It retrieves reliable and complete nutritional information from expert sources, either humans (e.g. nutritionists and gerontologists) or computerized (e.g. information systems, nutritional databases from World Health Organization WHO - and Spanish Society of Parenteral and Enteral Nutrition SENPE - recommendations). It assists older people to benefit of these tips, following the daily and weekly healthy nutritional requirements of the users and keeping track of the food ingested previously during the week. Although the system can be used with the help of a caregiver, its main purpose is that the elderly could use it on their own at home, so that, elderly self-sufficiency is boosted, giving a major value to the system.

VIRTRA-EL is a platform that provides support to active ageing [19]. In this paper, we address the inclusion of NutElCare into VIRTRA-EL so as to intend to supply as holistic as possible support to different dimensions of active aging.

The remaining of this paper is organised as follows. Section 2 introduces some work related to active aging support and nutritional recommender systems. In Section 3, it is explained NutElCare, its architecture and its integration into VIRTRA-EL. Finally, in Section 4, conclusions and future work are presented.

2   Related Work

Many research efforts in the field of technology devoted to elder care are focused on assisted living. Most of them are based on passive assistance which user participation is not required and the work rests mainly on technology, as pervasive computing or robotics. Talking about active aging assistance, the major part of research relies on usability of devices and interfaces. The lack of tools that help elderly to deal age effects actively by development of different aspects which promote self-sufficiency is substantial. Nevertheless, there are some works that aim the support of one of the different dimensions of active aging.

[15] propose a system to deliver step training to users, measuring, at the same time, the parameters of stepping performance that are shown to predict falls in older people.

In [1], authors affirm that an adaptive version of NeuroRacer game, in multitasking training mode, help older people to enhance multitask capacity and to improve cognitive abilities. FoodManager [11] is an assistive system to support the elderly in eating and cooking activities. It requires special domestic appliance and sensors to its operation.

3   NutElCare

NutElCare is a semantic recommender system which provides healthy diet plans for the elderly making use of semantic technologies in its development, as ontologies, to improve the information representation.

Regarding the way to obtain recommendations, it can be considered as a hybrid recommender system [3] that carries out two different techniques:

— Knowledge-based techniques, which use knowledge about users and items to generate a recommendation, reasoning about what items meet the user's requirements.
— Content-based techniques, where the recommendation process consists in learning from the user's behavior and recommending items that are similar to the items rated by them in the past.

The first recommendation carried out by NutElCare is a knowledge-based recommendation in which a healthy plan is obtained having into account the ontological user profile that contains the relevant features of the users in the nutritional context.

After that, the content-based recommendation starts, allowing the users to make variations on the selected diet to fit their taste preferences, or availability of ingredients. The recommendations must be flexible and take into account, the user preferences, their allergenic contraindications and what food has been taken during the week, offering alternatives to the original diet plan based on these factors. These recommendations are always nutrient guided, providing alternative suggestions of similar conditions, to continue meeting the original healthy requirements of the diet. The system learns from the user selections to improve further recommendations.

3.1   Nutritional Requirements and User Profiles

To offer a model diet, in addition to typical demographic data (such as name, gender, age, and address), the following information of the user is required:

Physical properties.

— The weight and height of the user in order to calculate the body mass index (BMI). Regarding the classification of the nutritional state in terms of the BMI of the elderly in the consensus document created by SENPE, NutElCare will classify the nutritional state of the users as: malnutrition, under-weight, normal-weight, over-weight or obesity.
— Swallowing and chewing level, to distinguish whether the user needs normal, soft, semi-liquid, or easily digested diets.

Environmental factors.
It contains the season and geographical area in which recommendations are made.

Activity factors.
It represents the amount of exercise that the user carries out a week (active, standard or sedentary life). Next, the system collects the explicit interests of the user by means of questions about allergies and taste preferences. If one of these food elements or nutrients, considered as "no-interesting", appears on the diet model to recommend, the system must reason which aliment from the knowledge base is the most similar and offer it instead.

This information about the users is represented into ontological user profiles. These profiles are composed of two different kinds of information: explicit, that is obtained from the initial form that the users fulfil in the registration process and implicit that is collected from users' selections in the recommendations.

3.2 Nutritional Ontology

The knowledge base of NutElCare is represented as an OWL ontology, to which, the nutritional expert knowledge has been transferred from the expert sources. The ontology contains that information which the system reasons with, in order to obtain proper recommendations and it is mainly formed by a food taxonomy enriched with nutritional properties and the alimentary factors that combine in the recommendation process.

One of the major motivations in the use of ontologies is the reusability of a domain knowledge possibility, for this reason the nutritional ontology is built from the AGROVOC FAO Thesaurus [5] of the United Nations. To fit the requirements of a nutritional recommender system, only the relevant nutritional information was extracted from the AGROVOC Thesaurus and nutritional properties of food were added to the ontology.

3.3 NutElCare in VIRTRA-EL Architecture

NutElCare is introduced into VIRTRA-EL architecture as a module, which is accessible to users and nutritionists (or caregivers) after authentication (Fig. 1).

To a better comprehension of the NutElCare module, we proceed to the explanation of its own architecture, which is based on the main elements of the semantic recommender systems, namely:

— Knowledge base and items representation.
— User profiling and learning techniques of user interests.
— Obtaining and providing recommendations about items in the knowledge base through semantic similarity measures.

We can thus represent the architecture of the system as shown in Fig. 1.

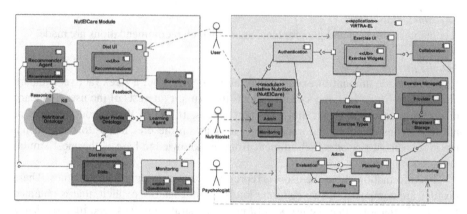

Fig. 1. NutElCare module basic architecture and its inclusion into VIRTRA-EL

The following describes a summary of the NutElCare basic components.

1. *User Interface.* One of the main success factors of the system is to be easy to use, almost as a game, while motivating the users to its correct and serious utilization. As a consequence of both functional limitations and a simple lack of technological experience, seniors suffer more by usability problems than younger users [12]. For this reason, the design of the user interface is carried out taking special care of these particular needs. Non-functional properties (as adaptability, anticipatory interaction and heterogeneity) of Ambient Home Care Systems (AHCS) have a major impact on the overall acceptance of the system and at the same time, ethical, social, medical, and technological constraints must be considered [13].

2. *User Profile Ontology.* It contains the user model, which is composed by the explicit information, obtained at the initial contact with a new user, and the implicit information, built with the help of the learning agent which studies the behaviour of the user in the system.

3. *Learning Agent.* It analyses the user behaviour in the system interaction. It uses learning techniques to extract behaviour patterns and communicates them to the user profile in order to building the dynamic part of the model (composed of the implicit information collected).

4. *Diet Manager.* It is responsible for retrieving the suitable diet models for a user profile. Once a diet model is selected, it builds a personalized diet for the current user and sends it to the user interface.

5. *Recommender Agent.* It computes the nutritional recommendations from the knowledge base through semantic similarity techniques and recommendation strategies.

6. *Knowledge Base (Ontology).* It stores all the nutritional information needed. It is modelled through the NutElCare food ontology, where food items are represented with instances in order to allow reasoning over them. A small sample can be found in Fig. 2.

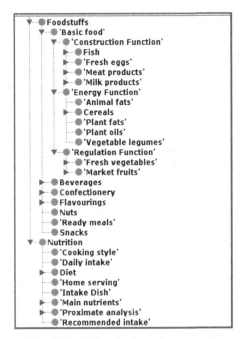

Fig. 2. NutElCare food ontology sample

7. *Screening.* Although this component is accessible through the user interface, is represented as an external element due to its importance, special treatment and different frequency of use. The screening strategy used is the Mini Nutritional Assessment (MNA) [10] in its short form (MNA-SF) [18]. MNA is considered the most worldwide used methodology for the brief evaluation of older persons' nutritional status [6]. MNA-SF is able to identify malnourished persons or at risk of malnutrition. It consists in a short questionnaire that users fill in each 3 months (this value can change but is the recommended one by the MNA) via the user interface.

8. *Monitoring.* This component contains all the MNA results of the users and whether he has followed the daily recommendations or not, including, in this case, why not and what has been ingested instead. In this way, the nutritionist, and the system itself, are aware of the impact that the use of the system causes to the user and the real daily food ingestion. It can be accessed by the nutritionist at any time for consulting a specific user or obtaining different informs of the results. Essential elements of the monitoring component are the *Alarms*. When the monitoring detects possible symptoms of malnutrition or its risk in a specific user, it sends an alarm notification to the caregiver and the user itself. At this moment, the state of the system changes to *awaiting* until it is notified to resume and continue with its normal operation.

4   Conclusions and Future Work

Recent awareness and familiarity of the elderly with new technologies is boosting the development of tools which they can use in their own benefit. However, many of current proposals are intended for telemonitoring purposes without intervention of the users or are focused in one single aspect of aging. The lack of systems that help elderly users to deal age effects actively by development different aspects which promote self-sufficiency of the elderly, has been one of the main motivations of this work. VIRTRA-EL platform was created with the aim of providing support to active aging by means of cognitive stimulation.

In this work, we have presented NutElCare, a recommender system that provides healthy and appealing diet plans to the elderly following the expert guidelines. The integration of NutElCare into VIRTRA-EL has been addressed in order to contribute to the holistic active aging support through three main dimensions: cognitive stimulation, exercise and assisted nutrition.

As future work we plan full integration of NutElCare into VIRTRA-EL architecture to achieve a complete homogeneous user interaction. Relevant steps for this goal are the unification of users and users profiles of both systems as well as their ontological representation as well as the homogenization of user interfaces so as to provide a compacted and uniform displaying.

One of the main values of VIRTRA-EL is its support for collaborative engagement. For this reason, it is expected to include collaborative assistance functionalities in the nutritional recommender system.

Acknowledgements. This research work has been funded by the Innovation Office from the Andalusian Government under project TIN-6600.

References

1. Anguera, J.A., Boccanfuso, J., Rintoul, J.L., Al-Hashimi, O., Faraji, F., Janowich, J., Gazzaley, A.: Video game training enhances cognitive control in older adults. Nature 501(7465), 97–101 (2013)
2. Baader, F., Horrocks, I., Sattler, U.: Description logics as ontology languages for the semantic web. In: Hutter, D., Stephan, W. (eds.) Mechanizing Mathematical Reasoning. LNCS (LNAI), vol. 2605, pp. 228–248. Springer, Heidelberg (2005)
3. Burke, R.: Hybrid web recommender systems. In: Brusilovsky, P., Kobsa, A., Nejdl, W. (eds.) Adaptive Web 2007. LNCS, vol. 4321, pp. 377–408. Springer, Heidelberg (2007)
4. Cantador, I.: An Enhanced Semantic Layer for Hybrid Recommender Systems. Semantic Web: Ontology and Knowledge Base Enabled Tools, Services, and Applications, 235 (2013)
5. Caracciolo, C., Stellato, A., Morshed, A., Johannsen, G., Rajbhandari, S., Jaques, Y., Keizer, J.: The agrovoc linked dataset. Semantic Web 4(3), 341–348 (2013)
6. Delacorte, R.R., Moriguti, J.C., Matos, F.D., Pfrimer, K., Marchina, L., Ferriolli, E.: Mini-Nutritional Assessment score and the risk for undernutrition in free-living older persons. The Journal of Nutrition 8(6) (2004)
7. Espín, V., Hurtado, M.V., Noguera, M., Benghazi, K.: Semantic-Based Recommendation of Nutrition Diets for the Elderly from Agroalimentary Thesauri. In: Larsen, H.L., Martin-Bautista, M.J., Vila, M.A., Andreasen, T., Christiansen, H. (eds.) FQAS 2013. LNCS, vol. 8132, pp. 471–482. Springer, Heidelberg (2013)

8. Evans, W.J., Cyr-Campbell, D.: Nutrition, exercise and healthy aging. Journal of the American Dietetic Association 97(6), 632–638 (1997)
9. Freyne, J., Berkovsky, S., Smith, G.: Recipe recommendation: Accuracy and reasoning. In: Konstan, J.A., Conejo, R., Marzo, J.L., Oliver, N. (eds.) UMAP 2011. LNCS, vol. 6787, pp. 99–110. Springer, Heidelberg (2011)
10. Guigoz, Y., Vellas, B., Garry, P.J., Vellas, B.J., Albarede, J.L.: Mini Nutritional Assessment: a practical assessment tool for grading the nutritional state of elderly patients. The Mini Nutritional Assessment: MNA. Nutrition in the Elderly, 15–60 (1997)
11. Iglesias, R., Ibarguren, I., de Segura, N.G., Ugalde, J., Coello, L., Iturburu, M.: FoodManager: a cooking, eating and appliance controlling support system for the elderly. In: Proceedings of the 3rd International Conference on Pervasive Technologies Related to Assistive Environments, p. 38. ACM (2010)
12. Ijsselsteijn, W., Nap, H.H., de Kort, Y., Poels, K.: Digital game design for elderly users. In: Proceedings of the 2007 Conference on Future Play, pp. 17–22. ACM (2007)
13. Kleinberger, T., Becker, M., Ras, E., Holzinger, A., Müller, P.: Ambient intelligence in assisted living: Enable elderly people to handle future interfaces. In: Stephanidis, C. (ed.) UAHCI 2007 (Part II). LNCS, vol. 4555, pp. 103–112. Springer, Heidelberg (2007)
14. Loizou, A., Dasmahapatra, S.: Recommender systems for the semantic web (2006)
15. Obdrzalek, S., Kurillo, G., Ofli, F., Bajcsy, R., Seto, E., Jimison, H., Pavel, M.: Accuracy and robustness of Kinect pose estimation in the context of coaching of elderly population. In: 2012 Annual International Conference of the IEEE Engineering in Medicine and Biology Society (EMBC), pp. 1188–1193. IEEE (2012)
16. Pirlich, M., Lochs, H.: Nutrition in the elderly. Best Practice & Research Clinical Gastroenterology 15(6), 869–884 (2001)
17. Rosenberg, I.H., Miller, J.W.: Nutritional factors in physical and cognitive functions of elderly people. The American Journal of Clinical Nutrition 55(6), 1237S–1243S (1992)
18. Rubenstein, L.Z., Harker, J.O., Salvà, A., Guigoz, Y., Vellas, B.: Screening for undernutrition in geriatric practice developing the short-form mini-nutritional assessment (MNA-SF). The Journals of Gerontology Series A: Biological Sciences and Medical Sciences 56(6), M366–M372 (2001)
19. Rute-Pérez, S., Santiago-Ramajo, S., Hurtado, M.V., Rodríguez-Fórtiz, M.J., Caracuel, A.: Challenges in software applications for the cognitive evaluation and stimulation of the elderly. Journal of NeuroEngineering and Rehabilitation 11(1), 88 (2014)
20. Snae, C., Bruckner, M.: FOODS: a food-oriented ontology-driven system. In: 2nd IEEE International Conference on Digital Ecosystems and Technologies, DEST 2008, pp. 168–176. IEEE (2008)
21. Szomszor, M., Cattuto, C., Alani, H., O'Hara, K., Baldassarri, A., Loreto, V., Servedio, V.D.: Folksonomies, the semantic web, and movie recommendation (2007)
22. van Pinxteren, Y., Geleijnse, G., Kamsteeg, P.: Deriving a recipe similarity measure for recommending healthful meals. In: Proceedings of the 16th International Conference on Intelligent User Interfaces, pp. 105–114. ACM (2011)
23. W3C: OWL web ontology language overview, http://www.w3.org/TR/owl-features/

A Framework for Recognizing
and Regulating Emotions in the Elderly

José Carlos Castillo[1], Antonio Fernández-Caballero[2], Álvaro Castro-González[1],
Miguel A. Salichs[1], and María T. López[2]

[1] Universidad Carlos III de Madrid, Robotics Lab, 28911-Madrid, Spain
{jocastil,acgonzal,salichs}@ing.uc3m.es
[2] Universidad de Castilla-La Mancha, Instituto de Investigación en Informática de
Albacete, 02071-Albacete, Spain
{Antonio.Fdez,Maria.LBonal}@uclm.es

Abstract. This paper introduces a gerontechnological framework which
enables real-time and continuous monitoring of the elderly and provides
the best-tailored reactions of a social robot and the proper ambience in
order to regulate the older person's emotions towards a positive emotion.
After describing the benefits of the framework for emotion recognition
and regulation in the elderly, the eight levels that compose the framework are described. The framework recognizes emotions through studying physiological signals, facial expression and voice. Emotion regulation
is enabled by tuning music, color and light to the specific need of the
elderly.

Keywords: Gerontechnological Framework, Emotion Regulation, Emotion Recognition, Elderly Monitoring, Social robotics.

1 Introduction

Developed countries are dealing with the effects of population ageing, generally due to lower birth rates and higher life expectancy. Population ageing is
defined as a shift in the distribution of a country's population towards greater
ages [1]. Elderly frequently have special needs and require a close and personalized monitoring, specifically at home and mainly due to health-related issues
[2], [3]. Indeed, there is a growing trend towards ambient assisted living approaches which provide support to the older people in a personalized way. Also,
the inclusion of companion robots in the intelligent habitat of the older person
is a solution towards quality of life of the elderly living alone [4], [5]. In recent
years, the robotics community has seen a gradual increase in social robots, that
is, robots that exist primarily to interact with people [6]. We believe that perceiving / enhancing the quality of life of the elderly living at home is possible
through automatic emotion recognition and regulation (from now on ERR). Indeed, it has been largely studied that positive emotional states promote healthy
perceptions, beliefs, and physical well-being [7].

L. Pecchia et al. (Eds.): IWAAL 2014, LNCS 8868, pp. 320–327, 2014.
© Springer International Publishing Switzerland 2014

Existing emotion recognition technologies are divided into three major categories depending on what kind of data is analyzed: physiological signals, facial expressions, or voice [8]. Physiological emotion recognition shows acceptable performance but has some critical weaknesses that prevent its widespread use; they are obtrusive to users and need special equipment or devices [9]. Facial analysis includes a number of processing steps which attempt to detect or track the face, to locate characteristic facial regions such as eyes, mouth and nose on it, to extract and follow the movement of facial features. Most of the proposed works are based on the Facial Action Coding System (FACS), based on the definition of "action units" of a face that cause facial movements [10]. Lastly, the speech signal conveys a large amount of information. Two main problems are addressed: (1) finding the set of features in the speech signal that are most significant in conveying emotions and (2) finding the best classification algorithm that can indicate emotional expression, based on the above features [11].

Now, emotion regulation refers to a set of processes that either stop the emotion from emerging or prevent it from being expressed once it is triggered [12]. Bottom-up emotion generation refers to the elicitation of emotion by the presentation of a stimulus that is thought to have simple physical properties that are inherently emotional [13]. Antecedent emotion regulation strategies apply while the emotion is still unfolding and has not reached its peak. In our case, we are interested in response-focused emotion regulation, which tries to aim at altering and controlling the experiential, behavioral and physiological response to the fully established emotion. There is a great deal of work based on the use of music [14], color [15] and lighting [16] in emotion regulation.

This paper discusses the need of frameworks capable of accepting any sensor and actuator dealing with the problem of detecting and regulating emotions through ambient intelligence and social robotics. In this sense, we introduce a gerontechnological framework that enables continuously monitoring the elderly and provides the best-tailored reactions of a social robot and the proper ambience in order to regulate their emotions towards a positive emotional state.

2   Why a Framework?

Nowadays, frameworks are playing a critical role in complex software systems development. A software framework is a set of software blocks that programmers can use, extend or modify to fit specific applications. This mechanism allows the decomposition of an application into a set of independent modules describing a set of interfaces to ease communications. Therefore, frameworks constitute a flexible approach that enables the quick creation and deployment of applications. Under this scheme, components are defined as reusable and independent blocks that are combined to other components in order to build a specific system. From a developer perspective, building an application consists of assembling some existing components and a few of their own.

Among the number of advantages, the biggest one is that a software framework reduces the time in developing any software as it provides a set of blocks users can directly use or improve. This means that users can be abstracted from the lower level implementation and focus the effort on programming their required module. Another important feature provided by frameworks is the use of design patterns, which makes code cleaner and more extensible for future requirements.

The main disadvantage of frameworks is the development complexity. For small projects, it is faster to code directly rather than implement a whole framework infrastructure. In contrast, for big projects, like the one proposed in this paper, a framework is an appropriated option.

Real time ERR involves a wide diversity of technologies. This will result in a complex system which will require a powerful, flexible framework. Designing a new framework presents crucial challenges:

Deciding the purpose of the framework. This simple decision involves several issues related to the scope of the problem to be solved. For instance, a framework for web development has nothing to do with the one presented in this paper, so the requirements of each must be carefully analyzed before taking further steps.

Assessing the levels. After having confirmed the purpose of the framework, it is necessary to establish a division to allow a structured development. Finding an optimal decomposition involves both a deep analysis of the problem as well as subject matter experts.

Determining the grain size. This problem is related to the levels one. At an early design stage, the functionalities included in each level have to be clearly defined at design time.

Avoiding being restrictive. Finally, a framework must be adaptable to a growing problem, but not too wide to loose its purpose. This is an important trade-off that must also be considered at the design stage.

3   Other Frameworks in ERR

Frameworks are widely spread for web-based environments or user-oriented applications. Some examples are *Grails* or *Springs* to develop Java-based applications, or *ASP.NET* for Windows-based ones. The academic community has adopted such paradigm for research projects related to ERR.

Affect sensing by machines has been argued as an essential part of next-generation human-computer interaction (HCI). To this end, in the recent years a large number of studies have been conducted, which report automatic recognition of emotion as a difficult, but feasible task. However most effort has been put towards off-line analysis, whereas to date only few applications exist able to react to a user's emotion in real-time. The framework called Smart Sensor Integration considerably boosted the development of multimodal on-line emotion recognition systems [17]. Furthermore, Gehrig and Ekenel presented a common framework for real-time action unit detection and emotion recognition [18]. For these tasks, they employed a local appearance-based face representation approach using discrete cosine transform. Santos et al. came up with a proposal that performed

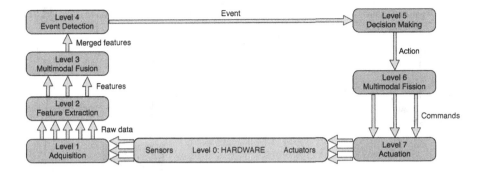

Fig. 1. The levels of the proposed framework

real-time stress detection based only in two physiological signals: heart rate and galvanic skin response [19].

In relation to the emotion regulation, the literature does not offer many software frameworks. The emotion regulation will be inspired by works from the area of psychology. Psychologists have explored traditional frameworks (defined as a set of concepts, practices, and criteria to deal with a particular kind of problem) for diagnosis and treatment of deceases. An example is the work presented by Werner and Gross provides a framework for researchers and clinicians interested in understanding the role of emotion regulation processes in psychopathology [20]. We will use these works to provide the proper reaction of the social robot and the ambience.

4   A New Framework for ERR

The proposed framework is intended to deal with the problems that can be found in real environments (hardware abstraction, noise in the data, or real-time processing). In this section we provide a high level description of the framework and the functions performed in each level. An overview of the framework we propose is shown in Fig. 1.

Each level is defined by the information that it consumes (receives), how this incoming data is transformed, and the resulting data it provides (sends) to the next level. Therefore these data flows are detailed for each level in the next subsections. Fig. 2 shows the outstanding elements to be considered in the proposed framework for ERR.

Level 0: Hardware - Sensors and Actuators. Frameworks are formed by software elements located at different levels. However, when dealing with data coming from the real world, also referred as the environment, we need to place the hardware elements at some level. In our case, this is Level 0. This layer represents the hardware components in charge of perceiving the environment

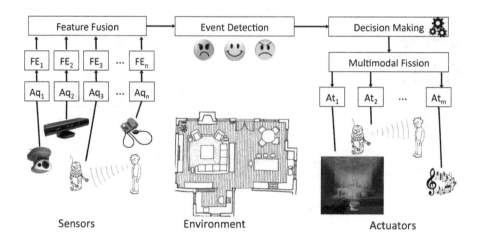

Fig. 2. Outstanding elements that are described in the proposed framework

and performing actions. No software module is considered here although the software from other levels directly interacts with it.

Sensors are devices that sense the environment and convert the information into electronic format. They can be roughly classified according to the information they provide, among others, visual data (RGB cameras, IR cameras, or depth sensors), audio (microphones), biometric data (blood pressure, perspiration, breathing rate, and so on). Actuators are devices able to alter the environment by receiving instructions and transforming them into actions. Some actuators considered in this project can be: projectors, lights, a robot, a sound system, or a heating system.

Level 1: Acquisition. Software at this level handles the communication with the sensors. For each sensor, there is a module in this level that understands the data received. Since this is the lowest processing level, it does not consume data from other levels. It reads the low-level, raw data from the sensors and provides it the next levels.

Level 2: Feature Extraction. This is one of the key levels. Here the raw data provided by the sensors is interpreted by different algorithms. This means that the input data is transformed into more informative, numerical features that summarize the raw data. Each feature represents an important characteristic of the data that is of special interest.

From a computer vision perspective, this level is in charge of detecting, recognizing and tracking those objects of interest contained in the scene. In this sense, features may be understood as the track and shape of the object, as well as the kind of object detected. Other example, some features coming from the elder's utterances can be extracted, such as the sentiment (positive, negative, neutral), the gender of the speaker, or the topics involved within the speech. So, this level consumes raw data and provides features to the upper level that will have to interpret them.

Level 3: Multimodal Fusion. As the system will not be able to completely rely on the separate sources (noise, false positives, or occlusions), a fusion step is crucial in order to reduce the uncertainty associated to the extracted features. Indeed, feature extraction can be performed over data coming from very different sources. In our scenario, we have information coming from cameras, wearable sensors sending biometric data, microphones, and others. For each kind of data, different features are extracted. All these heterogeneous features are combined in order to provide higher level abstraction of information. This is known as the multimodal fusion.

In our particular problem, the recognition of the elder's emotion in the scenario is crucial. For this task, our framework uses features related to the user's speech, their blood pressure, and their face. The fusion of all these features results on richer information at the time of assessing the elder's emotion. This level consumes the features extracted in Level 2, and provides a combination of feature in a time window. It is important to consider the time constrains in order to determine how often the fusion process is performed. For example, if it is detected that the elder is talking about a sad event, how long do we have to consider this feature? Therefore, the frequency of the fusion process will determine the lifespan of the features. The fusion process gives temporal coherence to the features.

Level 4: Event Detection. This level receives a set of features and processes them. The result is a high-level description of the situation (e.g. the elder is happy). In our problem, the emotion analysis logic is in this level. Its inputs are the array of features sent by the multimodal fusion. The output is the events related to the emotion of the elder. This means that the emotion recognition algorithm corresponds here. Moreover, our framework is not limited to detect user's emotion. The algorithms intended to detect other events have to be implemented at this level and the inputs would be the same.

Level 5: Decision Making. Here is where the *intelligence* of the system lies: considering the events published by the Level 4, the system reacts and decides the action to execute. For example, considering that our system reacts to the elder's mood, once this is detected, the system can vary the illumination, move the shutters, change the music, as well as the robot can interact with them in a proper way. This level consumes events and provides actions to be executed by the different actuators in the scenario.

Level 6: Multimodal Fission. This level defines the particular result of an action. A multimodal fission component accepts actions and split it into several commands. Each command is directed to a different actuator in the environment. For instance, if the action is to create a relaxing environment, the multimodal fission will publish commands addressed to dim the lights, project warm colors, play pleasant music, and the robot will have a conversation about the weather. The fission process is tuned according to the user's likes. Hence, some information associated to the user is welcomed. Knowing some of their preferences some environmental conditions, such as the background music and the projections, can be selected accordingly. This results in a faster achievement of the desired effect. This level consumes actions from the decision making level, and provides commands to the proper actuators.

Level 7: Actuation. This level is the counterpart of Level 1. Here the modules communicating with the actuators send the proper commands. There is one module in charge of managing each actuator. The modules at this level consume commands published by the Fission level. Meanwhile, there is not information sent to other levels but they write low level instructions, or primitives, to hardware components. As an example, the text-to-speech module receives the command *say hello* that is transformed into low level instructions that synthesize "hello" through the speakers.

5 Conclusions

This paper has justified the need of a specific framework for emotion recognition and regulation tasks. Beside, we have introduced a new gerontechnological framework for monitoring the elderly at home. In first place, the framework is aimed at detecting the elder's emotions by analyzing their physiological signals, facial expression and voice. Then, the framework provides the best-tailored reactions of a social robot and the ambience to regulate the elder's emotions towards a positive emotion. The current state of the art in emotion regulation through music, color and light is used by the framework with the final goal of enhancing the quality of life of elder people living alone at their homes. After describing the benefits of a framework for ERR in the elderly, the eight levels that compose the proposed framework have been described.

Acknowledgements. This work was partially supported by Spanish Ministerio de Economía y Competitividad / FEDER under TIN2013-47074-C2-1-R and TIN2010-20845-C03-01 grants. José Carlos Castillo was partially supported by a grant from Iceland, Liechtenstein and Norway through the EEA Financial Mechanism, operated by Universidad Complutense de Madrid.

References

1. Castillo, J.C., Carneiro, D., Serrano-Cuerda, J., Novais, P., Fernández-Caballero, A., Neves, J.: A multi-modal approach for activity classification and fall detection. International Journal of Systems Science 45(4), 810–824 (2014)
2. Costa, Â., Castillo, J.C., Novais, P., Fernández-Caballero, A., Simoes, R.: Sensor-driven agenda for intelligent home care of the elderly. Expert Systems with Applications 39(15), 12192–12204 (2012)

3. Dosi, G.: Sources, procedures and microeconomics effects of innovation. Economic Literature 26, 1120–1171 (1998)
4. Gascueña, J.M., Garijo, F.J., Fernández-Caballero, A., Gleizes, M.P., Machonin, A.: Deliberative control components for eldercare robot team cooperation. Journal of Intelligent and Fuzzy Systems (2014), doi:10.3233/IFS-141199
5. Martínez-Gómez, J., Fernández-Caballero, A., García-Varea, I., Rodríguez, L., Romero-González, C.: A taxonomy of vision systems for ground mobile robots. International Journal of Advanced Robotic Systems 11, 111 (2014), doi:10.5772/58900
6. Kirby, R., Forlizzi, J., Simmons, R.: Affective social robots. Robotics and Autonomous Systems 58, 322–332 (2010)
7. Salovey, P., Rothman, A.J., Detweiler, J.B., Steward, W.T.: Emotional states and physical health. American Psychologist 55(1), 110–121 (2000)
8. Lee, H., Choi, Y.S., Lee, S., Park, I.P.: Towards unobtrusive emotion recognition for affective social communication. In: IEEE Consumer Communications and Networking Conference, pp. 260–264 (2012)
9. Picard, R.W., Vyzas, E., Healey, J.: Toward machine emotional intelligence: analysis of affective physiological state. IEEE Transactions on Patterns Analysis and Machine Intelligence 23, 1175–1191 (2001)
10. Ekman, P., Friesen, W.: The Facial Action Coding System. Consulting Psychologists Press, San Francisco (1978)
11. Devillers, L., Vasilescu, I., Lamel, L.: Emotion detection in a task-oriented dialog corpus. In: IEEE International Confererence on Multimedia & Expo (2003)
12. Gross, J.J., Barrett, L.F.: Emotion generation and emotion regulation: one or two depends on your point of view. Emotion Review 3(1), 8–16 (2011)
13. McRae, K., Misra, S., Prasad, A.K., Pereira, S.C., Gross, J.J.: Bottom-up and top-down emotion generation: implications for emotion regulation. Social Cognitive & Affective Neuroscience 7(3), 253–262 (2012)
14. Bachorik, J.P., Bangert, M., Loui, P., Larke, K., Berger, J., Roew, R., Schlaug, G.: Emotion in motion: investigating the time-course of emotional judgments of musical stimuli. Music Perception 26(4), 355–364 (2009)
15. Elliot, A.J., Maier, M.A.: Color and psychological functioning. Current Directions in Psychological Science 16(5), 250–254 (2007)
16. Pail, G., Huf, W., Pjrek, E., Winkler, D., Willeit, M., Praschak-Rieder, N., Kasper, S.: Bright-light therapy in the treatment of mood disorders. Neuropsychobiology 64, 152–162 (2011)
17. Wagner, J., Andre, E., Jung, F.: Smart sensor integration: a framework for multimodal emotion recognition in real-time. In: 3rd International Conference on Affective Computing and Intelligent Interaction and Workshops, pp. 1–8 (2009)
18. Gehrig, T., Ekenel, H.K.: A common framework for real-time emotion recognition and facial action unit detection. In: IEEE Computer Society Conference on Computer Vision and Pattern Recognition Workshops, pp. 1–6 (2011)
19. de Santos, A., Sánchez, C., Guerra, J., Bailador, G.: A stress-detection system based on physiological signals and fuzzy logic. IEEE Transactions on Industrial Electronics 58(10), 4857–4865 (2011)
20. Werner, K., Gross, J.J.: Emotion regulation and psychopathology: a conceptual framework. In: Emotion Regulation and Psychopathology, pp. 13–37. Guilford Press (2010)

Applying the Gerontechnology Matrix for Research Involving Ageing Adults

Helianthe S.M. Kort[1,2], Ryan Woolrych[3], and Johanna E.M.H. van Bronswijk[2]

[1] Faculty of Healthcare, Utrecht University of Applied Sciences,
Utrecht, The Netherlands
helianthe.kort@hu.nl

[2] Department of the Built Environment, Eindhoven University of Technology,
Eindhoven, The Netherlands
{h.s.m.kort,J.e.m.h.v.Bronswijk}@tue.nl

[3] School of the Built Environment, Heriot Watt University, Edinburgh, UK
r.d.woolrych@hw.ac.uk

Abstract. The world population is ageing rapidly, during which technology innovation has become increasingly advanced. Ageing adults are expected to meet the demands of new technologies which offer potential to support independence and social participation. To facilitate this developers and designers need to better design technology around the opportunities, capacities and learning strategies of older adults. The Gerontechnology Matrix, which is based on Maslow's Hierarchy of Needs, provides a framework to guide researchers, designers and engineers in their effort to seek solutions which support older adults to age graciously. The Gerontechnology Matrix comprises the following live domains: Housing & Daily activities, Communication & Governance, Health & Self-esteem, Mobility & Transportation and Work & Leisure. All live domains will at some point provide challenges to the everyday life of ageing adults. Technology interventions, to reach the goals set in these live domains, might be designed for enhancement and satisfaction, prevention and engagement, compensation and assistance or for care and organization. This paper will be organized as a round table to discuss the pros and cons of the Gerontechnology Matrix with the participants.

Keywords: User perspective, Active ageing, Technology literacy.

1 Introduction

Gerontechnology, a combination of the words gerontology and technology, is an interdisciplinary academic and professional research field dedicated to helping ageing adults fulfill their life goals [1]. Gerontechnology is concerned with providing technology to better support the health, housing, mobility, communication, leisure and work needs of older people [2].

The concept of gerontechnology was first described in 1989 at the Human Factors Society meeting in Denver, Colorado, USA. After this meeting, the term gerontechnology was used in 1991 in the title of a major conference in the Netherlands.

L. Pecchia et al. (Eds.): IWAAL 2014, LNCS 8868, pp. 328–331, 2014.

Gerontechnology was created to address the technology needs of all age cohorts across the life course and not just the needs of today's older people. This is achieved by establishing a framework for setting goals for technology for the different age cohorts across the life course in five domains. At first a framework was used which combines the disciplinary groups of the aging process with innovative technologies [3]. In the currently used matrix the five life domains are the columns in Table 1. Integrated technological purposes are, displayed as the rows in Table 1, supporting the concept of quality of life as defined by Maslow's theory Hierarchy of Needs. Needs start from the basic necessities (water, food and air) and rise to self-esteem, and then further to self-actualization, such as seeking personal growth. Technology purposes are based on these needs and may comprise: Enhancement & Satisfaction, Prevention & Engagement, Compensation & Assistance and Care & Organization (see Table 1). The main goal of ageing adults is to reach enhancement and satisfaction of life, creating the conditions for older adults to be autonomous and independent whilst achieving self-fulfillment [4].

Table 1. Gerontechnology cross-fertilization matrix

Goal	Life Domain				
	Health & Self-esteem	Housing & Daily Living	Mobility & Transport	Communication & Governance	Work & Leisure
Enhancement & Satisfaction					
Prevention & Engagement					
Compensation & Assistance					
Care support & Organization					

2   Organization of ISG

The educational activities of gerontechnology began in the Netherlands with the formation of the International Society for Gerontechnology (ISG) in 1993, and were further supported by the establishment of the journal Gerontechnology in 2001. In 2011 the ISG also became a standing committee of IAGG (International Association of Gerontology and Geriatrics). The ISG mission is to encourage and promote technological innovations in products and services that address older peoples' ambitions and needs on the basis of scientific knowledge about ageing processes including cultural and individual differences [1].

ISG has a board consisting of an executive board and all presidents of the regional chapters. Currently ISG has 6 regional chapters namely; the Dutch-Flemish chapter, the Francophone chapter, the Japanese chapter, the Sinophone chapter, the North-American chapter and recently the German-Austrian chapter was formed. In addition to the regional chapters, there is a student chapter, for those PhD students who want to be educated and trained in gerontechnology. Each chapter has to consist of a minimum of 25 members. All individuals working in any field of ageing and technology can be member of the ISG and can be linked to the chapter they wish to belong to.

3   Conferences and Master Classes

The ISG has organized special Master Classes for PhD students since 2006. Master classes can be seen as the 4th pillar in the mission of the ISG, after biannual conferences, the journal, and the chapters [5]. Master Classes have been organized in the Netherlands, Canada, France and in Taiwan. Between 2006 and 2012 ISG Master Classes have been organized by Eindhoven University of Technology (The Netherlands) and Nankai University of Technology (Taiwan). Other universities that have supported Master Classes were in Vancouver in 2010, Utrecht in 2010, Nice in 2014 and Taipei in 2014.

The Master Classes have an interdisciplinary approach and are a combination of lectures, coaching and individual guidance. Master Classes are open for PhD students working in any field of ageing and technology.

In the Master Classes PhD students are learning to apply the gerontechnology matrix to determine the focus of their PhD thesis. Across 2-3 days, students are lectured by (grand) masters in gerontechnology. The title 'ISG-Grandmaster' is given to those teachers and members who have authored a long list of publications addressing both technology and gerontology [5]. In the Master Classes students are questioned and examined via their submitted poster about their work in gerontechnology principles. Furthermore, (grand)masters not only give feedback and coaching but they also encourage that students give each other feedback.

In the Master classes students will learn how to apply the gerontechnology cross fertilization matrix on their work. Students need to reason, reflect and choose the life domain for the technology the student is using or is developing. In addition, they must be very clear about the goal they which to reach for ageing adults by applying the technology. Usually students need to attend more than one Master class before they have gained insight into aging and the challenges of old age. Furthermore, they learn to focus on ageing adults goals and ambitions when developing a technology application, instead of limiting themselves to technological requirements only.

In general, Master Classes will be scheduled prior the start of an international conference. Occasionally Master Classes can be organized by a regional chapter. Currently there have been nine international conferences and the tenth conference will be held in Nice in 2016 (see Table 2).

Table 2. Overview of all ISG conferences, with the year the congress took place, the location and titles which were addressed

Year	Moto	Location
1991	Gerontechnology, the study on technology and aging	Eindhoven, The Netherlands
1996	Gerontechnology, a sustainable investment in the future	Helsinki, Finland
1999	Technology and aging, starting into the third millennium	Munich, Germany
2002	Creative use of technology for better aging	Miami, USA
2005	Challenges in aging and work from Asia to Eastern Europe	Nagoya, Japan
2008	Smart technology for active longevity	Pisa, Italy
2010	Technologies for health, quality of life, and aging-in-place	Vancouver, Canada
2012	Who's afraid of aging? Work, leisure, care robotics and construction for aging	Eindhoven, The Netherlands
2014	Cultural and social diversity in Gerontechnology	Taipei, Taiwan
2016	*Not yet decided*	Nice, France

4 To End

Gerontechnology evolved from the scientific world, addressing issues about technologies for older people into a society with individuals with various expertise cognising the need for a multidisciplinary approach to best meet the needs of older adults. Master Classes are needed to educate technology or gerontology students the complexity of gerontechnology. Contact ISG: info@gerontechnology.org.

Acknowledgements. We would like to thank all grandmasters and other ISG members for their contribution to the growth of gerontechnology.

References

1. International Society for Gerontechnology (2014), http://gerontechnology.info
2. Taipale, V.T.: Global, trends, policies and gerontechnology. In: The 9th World Conference of Gerontechnology, Keynote (2014)
3. Bouma, H., Fozard, J.L., Bouwhuis, D.G., Taipale, V.T.: Gerontechnology in perspective. Gerontechnology 6(4), 190–216 (2007)
4. Bouma, H., Fozard, J.L., van Bronswijk, J.E.M.H.: Gerontechnology as a field of endeavour. Gerontechnology 8(2), 68–75 (2009)
5. van Bronswijk, J.E.M.H.: Master class: The 4th pilar under gerontechnology. Gerontechnology 12(2), 63–67 (2014)

Automatic Emotion Recognition from Cochlear Implant-Like Spectrally Reduced Speech

Md Jahangir Alam [1], Yazid Attabi[1,2], Patrick Kenny [1], Pierre Dumouchel[2],
and Douglas O'Shaughnessy [3]

[1] CRIM, Montreal (QC) Canada
[2] ETS, Montreal (QC) Canada
[3] INRS-EMT, University of Quebec, Montreal (QC) Canada
{jahangir.alam,yazid.attabi,patrick.kenny}@crim.ca

Abstract. In this paper we present a robust feature extractor that includes the In this paper we study the performance of emotion recognition from cochlear implant-like spectrally reduced speech (SRS) using the conventional Mel-frequency cepstral coefficients and a Gaussian mixture model (GMM)-based classifier. Cochlear-implant-like SRS of each utterance from the emotional speech corpus is obtained only from low-bandwidth subband temporal envelopes of the corresponding original utterance. The resulting utterances have less spectral information than the original utterances but contain the most relevant information for emotion recognition. The emotion classes are trained on the Mel-frequency cepstral coefficient (MFCC) features extracted from the SRS signals and classification is performed using MFCC features computed from the test SRS signals. In order to evaluate to the performance of the SRS-MFCC features, emotion recognition experiments are conducted on the FAU AIBO spontaneous emotion corpus. Conventional MFCC, Mel-warped DFT (discrete Fourier transform) spectrum-based cepstral coefficients (MWDCC), PLP (perceptual linear prediction), and amplitude modulation cepstral coefficient (AMCC) features extracted from the original signals are used for comparison purpose. Experimental results depict that the SRS-MFCC features outperformed all other features in terms of emotion recognition accuracy. Average relative improvements obtained over all baseline systems are 1.5% and 11.6% in terms of unweighted average recall and weighted average recall, respectively.

Keywords: Automatic emotion recognition, cochlear implant, spectrally reduced speech, MFCC, AMCC, GMM.

1   Introduction

The aim of automatic emotion recognition (AER) from speech is to recognize the underlying emotional state of a speaker from his or her voice. Motivated by a broad range of commercially promising applications, speech emotion recognition has gained rapidly increasing research attention over the past few years [1]. In recent years a great deal of research has been done to automatically recognize emotions from human speech [1-10]. Some of this research has been further applied to call centers, multi-agent systems and other areas [11-15].

L. Pecchia et al. (Eds.): IWAAL 2014, LNCS 8868, pp. 332–340, 2014.
© Springer International Publishing Switzerland 2014

Extraction of features from a speech signal that efficiently characterize the emotional content of speech and at the same time do not depend on the speaker or lexical content is an important issue in speech emotion recognition [2, 16]. Speech signals may contain linguistic and paralinguistic features indicating emotional states. The paralinguistic features can be classified to one of three categories: Prosodic such as pitch (F0), intensity, and duration, Voice Quality such as jitter and shimmer, and Spectral such as MFCC (Mel-frequency cepstral coefficients) or LPCC (linear prediction cepstral coefficients) [6, 7, 16]. Among the features mentioned in the literature as being relevant for characterizing the manifestations of speech emotions, the most widely used are prosodic features. This is because the earliest studies of emotion detection were carried out using acted speech, where the linguistic content was controlled [16]. The spectral features, when used in combination with other categories of features (or even as a stand-alone feature vector), have been found to improve (or to achieve good) performance [6-7, 10, 17]. MFCC [18] and Perceptual Linear Prediction (PLP, with or without RASTA filtering) [19] are examples of spectral features that achieve good results not only on speech processing in general but also on emotion recognition [6-7, 9]. Reduction of speech variability due speech production or environment is important to achieve robust emotion recognition performances. Therefore, in an AER system, the aim of speech analysis module is to reduce signal variability and extract relevant acoustic features for emotion recognition. In spite of speech variability reduction achieved by the standard MFCC and PLP features AER performance is still affected by the sources of speech variability. As most of the emotion recognition features are extracted by analyzing speech in the spectral domain it is natural to seek the relevant spectral information from the speech signal that is sufficient for AER [20]. One technique to estimate relevant speech spectral information for a GMM (gaussian mixture model)-based AER system is to train GMM models for emotion classes and evaluate emotion recognition performance on the cochlear implant-like spectrally reduced speech (SRS) signals. The acoustic simulation of a cochlear implant is a spectrally reduced transform of original speech and it has been shown in [24] that normal hearing listeners could achieve a nearly perfect recognition score when listening to these SRS signals.

MFCC and PLP front-end, which mimic the speech processing performed by the human auditory system, are basically aimed at reducing the acoustic variability while putting emphasis on the most relevant spectral information for recognition. Therefore, cochlear implant-like SRS should contain sufficient information for AER based on conventional MFCC or PLP features. Inspired from the algorithm, introduced in [24], to synthesize acoustic simulation of a cochlear implant, spectrally reduced speech has already been applied in HMM-based automatic speech recognition [20-22], and GMM-UBM -based speaker verification [23] tasks. In this work, our objective is to find out whether cochlear implant-like SRS contains sufficient spectral information for AER based on the conventional MFCC features.

In order to evaluate the performance of SRS-MFCC features and make a comparison with the original speech-based cepstral features MFCC, PLP, MWDCC (Mel-warped DFT spectrum-based cepstral coefficients), AMCC (amplitude modulation cepstral coefficient), and SRS-MFCC features are used in experiments on the FAU AIBO corpus, a well-known spontaneous emotion speech corpus. The extracted features are used as short-term information (analysis frame length is 25 ms with a frame shift of 10 ms) and modeled using GMM models. Experimental results show the effectiveness of the SRS-MFCC features in terms of emotion recognition accuracy.

2   Cepstral Features from Spectrally Reduced Speech

This section describes the procedure to obtain spectrally reduced speech (SRS) from the original speech and compute mel-frequency cepstral coefficients (MFCC) features from it. Here, we denote this as SRS-MFCC features. Fig. 1 presents a complete block diagram for the SRS-MFCC feature extraction process and Fig. 2 shows the various steps to compute MFCC features from the SRS signal.

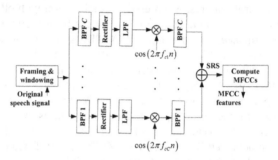

Fig. 1. Block diagram showing various steps to obtain spectrally reduced speech (SRS) from a original speech signal and then computation of mel-frequency cepstral coefficients (MFCC) features from that SRS signal. BPF and LPF stands for bandpass filter and low-pass filter, respectively.

Original speech signal is first framed (frame length is 20 ms with a frame shift of 10 ms) and windowed using a Hamming window. The windowed speech signal is then decomposed into C channel (or subband) signals $x_{c'}(t), c' = 1, 2, ..., C$ by applying a perceptually motivated analysis filterbank and overlap-add technique. The analysis filterbank consists of C non-uniform bandwidth bandpass filters (BPFs) which are linearly spaced on the Bark scale in order to approximate the nonlinear characteristics of the human auditory system. Each bandpass filter (BPF) in the filterbank is a 2nd order elliptic BPF having a minimum stopband attenuation of 50 dB and a 2 dB peak-to-peak ripple in the passband [20, 23]. The lower, upper, and central frequencies of the BPFs are computed in the same way as described in [27]. Fig. 3 presents the frequency response of an analysis filterbank comprised of $C = 16$ second order BPFs that are linearly spaced on the Bark scale.

The c'-th channel amplitude modulation $a_{c'}(t)$ (or temporal envelope) of the c'-th signal $x_{c'}(t), c' = 1, 2, ..., C$ is then obtained by applying a low pass filter followed by full-wave rectification of the output signal of the c'-th channel bandpass filter. The purpose of using a low-pass filter, a fourth order elliptic LPF with 2 dB of peak-to-peak ripple and a minimum stopband attenuation of 50 dB, is to limit the bandwidth of the subband temporal envelopes.

The c'-th channel amplitude modulation $a_{c'}(t)$ is then used to modulate a sinusoid whose frequency f equals the centre frequency $f_{cc'}$ of the BPF of that channel.

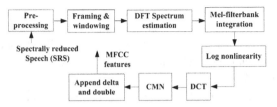

Fig. 2. Various steps for the MFCC feature extraction process from the spectrally reduced speech signals

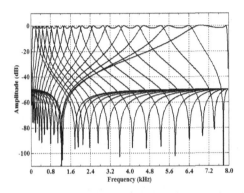

Fig. 3. Frequency response of an analysis filterbank consisting of sixteen 2nd order elliptic bandpass filters (BPFs) that are linearly spaced on the Bark scale. Sampling frequency is 16 kHz.

The modulated signal of c'-th channel $\hat{x}_{c'}(t) = a_{c'}(t)\cos(2\pi f_{cc'}t)$ is again bandpass filtered using the same BPF used for the original analysis subband. If $\mathbb{F}_{BPF}^{c'}(\cdot)$ denotes the c'-th channel bandpass filtering operation then the spectrally reduced signal (SRS) $\hat{x}(t)$ of the original signal can be expressed as:

$$\hat{x}(t) = \sum_{c'=1}^{C} \mathbb{F}_{BPF}^{c'}\left(\hat{x}_{c'}(t)\right)$$

$$= \sum_{c'=1}^{C} \mathbb{F}_{BPF}^{c'}\left(a_{c'}(t)\cos(2\pi f_{cc'}t)\right). \tag{1}$$

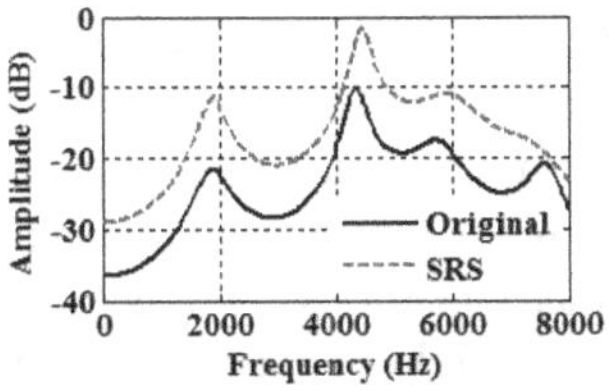

Fig. 4. All-pole spectral envelopes (using linear prediction with a model order of 20) of a frame of original speech and the corresponding spectrally reduced speech (SRS). Sampling frequency of the speech signal is 16 kHz. Number of subbands in the analysis filterbank is 16 and the cut-off frequency of the LPF (low-pass filter) is 50 Hz.

Fig. 4 shows short-term spectral envelopes of a frame of original speech (taken from the emotion corpus) and the corresponding SRS signals. Linear prediction with a model order of $p = 20$ is used to estimate the short-term all-pole spectral envelopes. Fig. 4 demonstrates that the global shapes of the all-pole spectral envelope of the SRS signal, obtained with $C = 16$, and $f_c = 50$ Hz, frame is rather similar (specifically, up to 6 kHz) with that of the all-pole spectral envelope of that frame of original speech. By increasing the number of subbands C and the cut off frequency f_c it is possible to obtain SRS spectral envelopes that are more similar to the original speech spectral envelopes [23].

The SRS signal it is then passed through the feature extraction process to compute cepstral features. MFCC processing begins with pre-emphasis, typically using a first-order high-pass filter. Short-time Fourier Transform (STFT) analysis is performed using a hamming window, and triangular-shaped Mel-frequency integration is performed for auditory spectral analysis. The logarithmic nonlinearity stage follows, and the 13-dimensional static features are obtained through the use of a Discrete Cosine Transform (DCT). After normalizing the static features using a cepstral mean normalization (CMN) technique, first and second derivatives are appended with the static features, making a final set of 39-dimensional MFCC features.

3   Emotion Recognition Experiments

The effectiveness of the spectrally reduced speech-mel-frequency cepstral coefficients (SRS-MFCC) features on an emotion recognition task is tested using the FAU AIBO [28, 17] emotional speech corpus. For comparison the following features computed from the original signal are chosen: conventional MFCC [18], Mel-warped DFT (discrete Fourier transform) spectrum-based cepstral coefficients (MWDCC) [7], and amplitude modulation cepstral coefficients (AMCC) [7] features. The dimension of features for each system is $d = 39$ and all systems use the cepstral mean normalization method as a post-processing scheme to normalize the static features.

3.1   Emotion Recognition Corpus

The FAU AIBO dataset consists of spontaneous recordings of German children interacting with a pet robot. The corpus is composed of 9959 chunks for training and 8257 chunks for testing. A chunk is an intermediate unit of analysis between the word and the turn, which is manually defined based on syntactic-prosodic criteria. The chunks are labeled into five emotion categories: Anger (A), Emphatic (E), Neutral (N), Positive (P, composed of motherese and joyful) and Rest (R, consisting of emotions not belonging to the other categories such as bored, helpless, and so on). The distribution of the five classes is highly unbalanced. For example, the percentage of training data of each class is as follows: A(8.8%), E(21%), N(56.1%), P(6.8%), R(7.2%).

3.2   Gaussian Mixture Models (GMMs)

Cepstral feature vectors are modeled using a GMM model. GMM is a generative model widely used in the field of speech processing. It is a semi-parametric probabilistic method that offers the advantage of adequately representing speech signal variability. Given a GMM modeling a d-dimensional vector, the probability of observing a feature vector given the model $M = \{w_i, \mu_i, \Sigma_i\}$ is computed as follows:

$$P(\mathbf{x}|M) = \sum_{i=1}^{m} w_i N(\mathbf{x}; \mu_i, \Sigma_i),$$ (2)

where m, w_i, μ_i, and Σ_i correspond to the number of Gaussians, weight, mean vector and diagonal covariance matrix of the i-th Gaussian, respectively.

GMM parameters are estimated using a Maximum Likelihood (ML) approach based on the Expectation Maximization (EM) algorithm [26]. The classification of a test sequence of T frames $\mathbf{X} = \{\mathbf{x}_1, \mathbf{x}_2, ..., \mathbf{x}_T\}$ is based on the Bayes decision. Using an equal prior probability for all classes, the classification is achieved by computing the log-likelihood of the test utterance against the GMM of each emotion class. The test recording is classified as the emotion class label that maximizes the log-likelihood value over all class models [7].

3.3   Experimental setup

The training of GMM models has been made with different numbers of mixtures taken from the set {2,4,8,16,32,64,128,256,512,1024}. The best parameter is tuned separately for each system based on the training data using a 9-fold cross validation protocol. Each fold contains a separate group of speakers to ensure speaker independent evaluation. After optimization, the selected numbers of Gaussians used for test data are as follows: 128 for the baseline MFCC, 128 for MWDCC, 128 for PLP, 256 for the AMCC, and 256 for SRS-MFCC systems. The metrics used for the evaluation of automatic speech emotion recognition performances are: unweighted average recall (UAR) and weighted average recall (WAR). The results are optimized to maximize the UAR measure and secondly the WAR (namely accuracy) given that FAU AIBO emotion classes are highly unbalanced (i.e., one class is disproportionately more represented than the others).

3.4   Results and Discussion

Similar to [20-23, 24], in order to evaluate the effect of reducing the bandwidth of the temporal envelope information we did emotion recognition experiments by varying the cut-off frequency f_c of the low-pass filter (LPF) from 16 Hz to 500 Hz. The value of f_c was chosen optimal that provided highest emotion recognition accuracy. To find the optimal number of subbands, we synthesized spectrally reduced speech (SRS) from the original speech by varying the number of subbands (or channels) C from 16 to 50 and found that $C = 16$ with $f_c = 50$ Hz provided highest accuracy. Here, we report emotion recognition results on the eval (or test) data for $C = 16$ & $f_c = 50$ Hz.

Table 1 presents the results obtained using the baseline systems and the SRS-MFCC system. It is observed from this table that the SRS-MFCC system outperformed the baseline MFCC, PLP and MWDCC systems in terms of both UAR and WAR measures. Although the performance of SRS-MFCC is close to that of AMCC in terms of the UAR metric SRS-MFCC outperformed AMCC in WAR metric. It has been shown in [7] that the MFCC obtained via the direct warping of the DFT (discrete Fourier transform) spectrum, denoted as MWDCC, achieved better recognition accuracy, in terms of the WAR scoring metric, than the conventional MFCC. The performance of MWDCC was almost the same as the MFCC in UAR scoring metric. Relative improvements obtained by the SRS-MFCC, in UAR metric, over the baseline MFCC, PLP, MWDCC, and AMCC are approximately 1.3%, 3.9%, 1.9% and -1.3%, respectively. With the WAR metric, the relative improvements are approximately 14.9% and 11.4%, 11.5%, and 8.6%, over the MFCC, PLP, MWDCC, and AMCC, respectively. Presented results demonstrate that the cochlear implant-like SRS is a relevant speech model for using in AER. Our future work is to compute PLP and AMCC features from SRS signals and compare their performances with the PLP and AMCC features computed from the original speech signals.

Table 1. Emotion recognition results achieved on FAU AIBO test data for the baseline MFCC, PLP, MWDCC (Mel-warped DFT spectrum-based MFCC), AMCC and SRS-MFCC systems in terms of the UAR and WAR scoring metrics

	UAR (%)	WAR (%)
MFCC	43.37	40.26
PLP	42.30	41.50
MWDCC	43.11	41.48
AMCC	**44.50**	42.58
SRS-MFCC	43.94	**46.24**

4   Conclusion

In this paper, we present spectrally reduced speech (SRS) -based Mel-frequency cepstral coefficients (SRS-MFCC) features for emotion recognition. Inspired from speech signal processing algorithms in standard cochlear implants, the SRS signals are obtained by applying cochlear implant-like synthesis algorithm to the original emotion corpus. Although SRS has reduced spectral information than the original one it is observed, experimentally, that SRS-MFCC features carry relevant information for emotion recognition. Performance of the SRS-MFCC features is compared, in the context of speech emotion recognition task on the FAU AIBO emotion corpus, with the conventional MFCC, PLP, MWDCC, and AMCC systems. SRS-MFCC features are shown to outperform the baseline features in terms of emotion recognition accuracy measured using UAR and WAR scoring metrics. Average relative improvements obtained over all baseline systems are 1.5% and 11.6% in terms of UAR and WAR, respectively.

References

[1] Wu, S., Falk, T.H., Chan, W.-Y.: Automatic speech emotion recognition using modulation spectral features. Speech Comm. 53(5), 768–785 (2011)

[2] Chen, L., Mao, X., Xue, Y., Cheng, L.L.: Speech emotion recognition: Features and classification models. Digital Signal Processing 22, 1154–1160 (2012)

[3] Ververidis, D., Kotropoulos, C.: Emotional speech recognition – resources features and methods. Speech Commun. 48, 1162–1181 (2006)

[4] Scherer, K.: Vocal communication of emotion: A review of research paradigms. Speech Commun. 40, 227–256 (2003)

[5] Sobol-Shikler, T., Robinson, P.: Classification of complex information: Inference of co-occurring affective states from their expressions in speech. IEEE Trans. Pattern Anal. Mach. Intell. 32(7), 1284–1297 (2010)

[6] Dumouchel, P., Dehak, N., Attabi, Y., Dehak, R., Boufaden, N.: Cepstral and long-term features for emotion recognition. In: Proc. INTERSPEECH, pp. 344–347 (2009)

[7] Alam, M.J., Attabi, Y., Dumouchel, P., Kenny, P., O'Shaughnessy, D.: Amplitude Modulation Features for Emotion Recognition from Speech. In: Proc. INTERSPEECH, Lyon, France (2013)

[8] Georgogiannis, A., Digalakis, V.: Speech emotion recognition using nonlinear Teager energy based features in noisy environments. In: Proc. EUSIPCO, Bucharest, Romania (August 2012)

[9] Sato, N., Obuchi, Y.: Emotion recognition using Mel-frequency cepstral coefficients. Journal of Natural Language Processing 14(4), 83–96 (2007)

[10] Neiberg, D., Elenius, K., Laskowski, K.: Emotion recognition in spontaneous speech using GMMs. In: Proc. of INTERSPEECH Conference, pp. 809–812 (2006)

[11] Peter, C., Beale, R. (eds.): Affect and Emotion in Human-Computer Interaction. LNCS, vol. 4868. Springer, Heidelberg (2008)

[12] Yoon, W.-J., Park, K.-S.: A study of emotion recognition and its applications. In: Torra, V., Narukawa, Y., Yoshida, Y. (eds.) MDAI 2007. LNCS (LNAI), vol. 4617, pp. 455–462. Springer, Heidelberg (2007)

[13] Schuller, B., Müller, R., Eyben, F., Gast, J., Hörnler, B., Wöllmer, M., Rigoll, G., Höthker, A., Konosu, H.: Being bored? Recognizing natural interest by extensive audiovisual integration for real-life application. Image Vis. Comput. 27(12), 1760–1774 (2009)

[14] Van Deemter, K., Krenn, B., Piwek, P., Klesen, M., Schröder, M., Baumann, S.: Fully generated scripted dialogue for embodied agents. Artificial Intelligence 172(10), 1219–1244 (2008)

[15] Lorini, E., Schwarzentruber, F.: A logic for reasoning about counterfactual emotions. Artificial Intelligence 175(3), 814–847 (2011)

[16] Scherer, K.R., Bänziger, T., Roesch, E.B. (eds.): Blueprint for Affective Computing - A Sourcebook. Oxford University Press, Oxford (2010)

[17] Schuller, B., Steidl, S., Batliner, A.: The INTERSPEECH 2009 Emotion Challenge. In: Interspeech, ISCA, Brighton (2009)

[18] Davis, S., Mermelstein, P.: Comparison of parametric representations for monosyllabic word recognition in continuously spoken sentences. IEEE Trans. Acoustics, Speech, and Signal Processing 28(4), 357–366 (1980)

[19] Hermansky, H.: Perceptual linear predictive (PLP) analysis of speech. Journal of the Acoustical Society of America 87(4), 1738–1752 (1990)

[20] Do, C.-T., Pastor, D., Goalic, A.: A novel framework for noise robust ASR using cochlear implant-like spectrally reduced speech. Speech Communication 54(1), 119–133 (2012)

[21] Do, C.-T., Pastor, D., Le Lan, G., Goalic, A.: Recognizing cochlear implant-like spectrally reduced speech with HMM-based ASR: experiments with MFCCs and PLP coefficients. In: Proc. of INTERSPEECH 2010, pp. 2634–2637 (September 2010)

[22] Do, C.-T., Taghizadeh, M.J., Garner, P.N.: Combining cepstral normalization and cochlear implant-like speech processing for microphone array-based speech recognition. In: Proc. SLT 2012 - IEEE Workshop on Spoken Language Technology, pp. 137–142 (December 2012)

[23] Do, C.-T., Barras, C.: Cochlear implant-like processing of speech signal for speaker verification. In: Proc. SAPA 2012 Conference - Statistical and Perceptual Audition (Satellite Workshop of Interspeech 2012), pp. 17–21 (September 2012)

[24] Shannon, R.V., Zeng, F.-G., Kamath, V., Wygonski, J., Ekelid, M.: Speech recognition with primarily temporal cues. Science 270(5234), 303–304 (1995)

[25] Zeng, F.-G., Nie, K., Stickney, G., Kong, Y.-Y., Vongphoe, M., Bhargave, A., Wei, C., Cao, K.: Speech recognition with amplitude and frequency modulations. Proceedings of National Academy of Sciences 102(7), 2293–2298 (2005)

[26] Dempster, A.P., Laird, N.M., Robin, D.B.: Maximum Likelihood from Incomplete Data via the EM Algorithm. Journal of the Royel Stastical Society B, 1–38 (1997)

[27] Gunawan, T.S., Ambikairajah, E.: Speech enhancement using temporal masking and fractional Bark gammatone filters. In: Proc. 10th Australian Int. Conf. Speech Sci. Technol., Sydney, Australia, December 08-10, pp. 420–425 (2004)

[28] Steidl, S.: Automatic Classification of Emotion-Related User States in Spontaneous Children's Speech. Logos Verlag, Berlin (2009)

First Contribution to Complex Emotion Recognition in Patients with Alzheimer's Disease

Susana A. Arias Tapia[1], Sylvie Ratté[2], Héctor F. Gómez A.[1],
Alexandra González Eras[1], José Barbosa[1], Juan Carlos Torres[1], Ruth Reátegui Rojas[1],
Priscila Valdiviezo Díaz[1], Franco Guamán Bastidas[1],
Guido Eduardo Riofrío Calderon[1], and Juan Manuel García Samaniego[3]

[1] Departament of Computer Science, Universidad Técnica Particular de Loja, Ecuador
`{saarias,hfgomez,acgonzalez,jbarbosa,jctorres,rmreategui,`
`pmvaldiviezo,foguaman,geriofrio,mgarcia}@utpl.edu.ec`
[2] Département de génie logiciel et des TI, École de Technologie Supérieure, Canada
`sylvieratte@etsmtl.ca`
[3] Departament of Natural Science, Universidad Técnica Particular de Loja, Ecuador
`mgarcia@utpl.edu.ec`

Abstract. The analysis of emotions in patients with Alzheimer's disease is a field that has been extensively studied in recent years with the purpose of tracking the progress of the disease. This study shows a first idea to contribute with a method to retrieve not only simple but complex emotions from patients, which we will call emotion pattern. Preliminary results showed that it is possible to identify the emotions of depression and guilt, which are typical in this kind of patients. Our work is in development, and aims to identify not only basic emotions but complex emotions through semantic tools, in order to identify complex patterns which facilitate the tasks of caregivers of Alzheimer's patients.

Keywords: Alzheimer's disease, ontologies, emotions, GSP.

1   Introduction

Recently, there were 35.6 million people in the world with Alzheimer's disease (AD) and other dementias; and the forecasts are not good since they predict that this amount will increase to 65.7 million by 2030, and 115.4 million by 2050. According to the World Health Organization (WHO), there is a new case of dementia every four seconds (1). In addition, little is known about emotions in patients with AD, so an understanding of the way in which the brain processes and integrates emotions is essential to determine an appropriate treatment for these patients. The human brain is made up of millions of nerve cells. These cells are connected to each other through a process called synapsis. When people "live" more experiences, nerve cells generate more patterns. These patterns are related to thoughts, memories and abilities, and they change when AD at-tacks the brain, altering nerve cells and their connections (2) (3). Alzheimer's disease is progressive and has no cure. In its final stages, the person

L. Pecchia et al. (Eds.): IWAAL 2014, LNCS 8868, pp. 341–347, 2014.

cannot control their emotions, recognize mistakes and patterns, or coordinate movements. This disease will bring about with it negative implications for the well-being, especially of elders (4). Likewise, patients with AD in its early stages show a lower capacity to differentiate emotional patterns. This happens because the disease causes damage to the temporal lobe, which impedes the recognition of expressions of joy, sadness, fear and other normal expressions. The effect is such that the mechanisms responsible for processing face identity can be suppressed to such an extent that patients can identify human faces but not facial expressions (5). However, patients with AD, even in advanced stages, are capable of feeling emotions in these situations, and, in a way, recall or form memories (6).

Emotions refer especially to the volitional faculties. Its attribution to this faculties is that they can stimulate the desire to take control of a situation and emotionally affective encourage creativity or they may hinder or suppress the desire when emotions are depressed character, or they lead to exaggeration or distortion when are aggressive character[1]. One of them proposes the combination of basic emotions with the purpose of obtaining complex emotions; as seen in Table 1.

Table 1. Composition of complex emotions (7)

Complex emotion	Primary emotions
Guilt	Fear + Anger
Envy	Sadness + Anger
Shame	Sadness + Anger (at self) + Fear
Depression	Sadness + Anger (at self)

There are previous studies related to recognition of basic emotions from text, video footage, body devices, audio and a combination of different types. But, there are no studies that recognize compound emotions from basic emotions. Compound (secondary) emotions are also called complex or derived emotions and they do not have characteristic facial features or a particular tendency to action. In this study, we attempt to contribute to the recognition of complex emotions in patients with Alzheimer's disease. These complex emotions are identified through the combination of basic emotions retrieved by processing video footage. The focus here is facial expressions, but our proposal can also work with software that recognizes emotions by analyzing body movements (8). The hypothesis is that, by proposing an intelligent system for emotion recognition, it is possible to model and recognize complex emotions in patients with Alzheimer's disease through a) basic emotions, which are based on an a priori model (qualitative-deterministic model); and, b) basic emotions, which are automatically retrieved by using the knowledge obtained from a case database to train probabilistic learning algorithms (qualitative-non-deterministic model). This study

---

[1]   Rielo F. Concepción genética del método. Sección III. Función Experiencial.

facilitates the design of a prototype for experimental use, the reuse of concepts of semantic tools, and the elimination of ambiguity of emotions for each study context.

2   State of the Art

The difficulties in recognizing emotions are associated with interpersonal prob-lems, reducing the development of psychopathologies (9). This situation could be misinterpreted as a symptom of depression (10); however, in Alzheimer's patients there is a reduction in the capacity to experience emotions. A study published in the Journal of Neuropsychiatry & Clinical Neurosciences shows how patients with Alz-heimer's disease, who were asked to associate an emotional value to certain images, see pleasant images as less pleas-ant, and the negative images as less negative, in comparison to a control group of normal elders.

Studies on facial expression recognition have shown that older people have selective deficiencies in identifying simple emotions, compared to young people, for instance, to detect negative emotions such as sadness (11) (12); anger (11), and fear (11), (13). We can also say that fear is the most difficult emotion to recognize on the face unlike joy because not all facial stimuli are equally complex (11). Disgust and fear are more complex emotions that need at least five facial movements (2). The possible causes of these results are the emotion of complexity (the amount of facial movements required to demonstrate emotion) and the ability to show emotion, which in older people, is gradually lost as people get older. Based on research described in this literature review, Fig. 1 shows the proposal of this study:

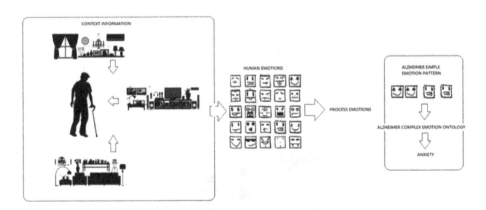

Fig. 1. Complex emotions in patients with Alzheimer's disease

Fig. 1 will be useful to describe our proposal. Simple emotions that are expressed in the face of patients, with the influence of the context (considering that even emo-tional working memory remains in patients (3)), can be analyzed by semantic algo-rithms that, based on an ontology, can be executed to obtain a complex emotion as a result. In order to retrieve emotional patterns, the Generalized Sequential Patterns

(GSP) algorithm will be used due to its successful results when identifying patterns of human situations in scenarios related to sports and human coexistence (14) (15). The objective here is to retrieve common complex emotions in the patients studied. For this purpose, the following method has been established.

3   Method

In order to retrieve emotional patterns, we will use the Generalized Sequential Patterns (GSP) algorithm because it has yielded successful results when identifying patterns of human situations in scenarios related to sports and human coexistence. (14) (15). The GSP algorithm works as follows (16):

- All individual activities with the highest frequency are taken (1- sequences).
- During the second stage, a set of candidate 2 –sequences is formed by considering the most frequent (1– sequences). The frequent 2- sequences (subsequences) are used to generate the candidate of 3- sequences. This process is repeated until no more frequent sequences are found.
- Candidates generation is done considering the set of frequent (k-1) – frequent sequences of F (k-1). The candidates for the next pass are generated by joining F(k-1) with itself. A pruning phase eliminates any sequence; that is, at least one of those frequencies is not considered frequent because it exceeds a threshold value known as minimum support threshold (min_support).

In order to obtain the training file for the GSP algorithm, two techniques were used: a) a tagger who watched videos on which patients are interviewed, and b) an automatic tagging system that was developed by our group[2] Fig. 2. We took an image of video per second in order to eliminate errors as was done in (17), so in each image of the video we recorded a basic emotion, and the time window (timeout to combine the basic emotions) was 20 seconds. This resulted in 20 emotions per row in the file of training, emulating at (18). We worked with 54 videos of youtube where the emotions of a patient are recorded. The results of both techniques were compared to establish a unique training file.

Fig. 2. An emotion recognition system on youtube

---

[2] http://200.0.29.83:8080/hse2/

Fig. 2 shows that the system recognizes an emotion and makes recommendations about what type of emotions are identified. This is verified by manual tagging in order to ensure the quality of the process. The results of GSP are the input for an ontology that is used to identify emotions with high level semantics. Here, we make use of the semantic proposal by (19) in which they go from a low level (simple emotions) to a middle and high level semantics (complex emotions). In this study, the proposal is the use of the HEO ontology, developed in (20) as a base. The emotion pat-terns recognized by GSP are the input for HEO so this ontology can be used to infer emotions of high-level semantics. However, due to the phase of development of this study that pretends to ensure the accurate recognition of simple emotions (this is the base for the rest of the semantic testing), the focus is to establish the appropriate method and testing, which are the base of our research. For the moment, we will only show the results of the emotion patterns, and after that, we will work with HEO ontology.

4   Testing

The focus of this study is youtube [3] videos about interviews with patients. In order to obtain the training file two techniques were used: a) a tagger who watched videos and recorded emotions by using a temporal window of 20 seconds. This time is based on a study by (21) in which it is demonstrated that temporal signals related to thoughts and emotions last between 10 and 20 seconds; and b) an automatic video tagging software, which was developed by our group, was used. Afterwards, the results obtained through both techniques were compared with the purpose of establishing one final training file. The GSP algorithm was used to identify "emotional patterns" in order to conclude if this algorithm is capable of automatically obtaining emotions that are typical of people with Alzheimer's disease. The minimum support used in this study was 0.7%, similar to how it was done in (22) for emotion recognition. The results were the following:

Table 2. Results of applying GSP in order to recognize complex emotions

Number of videos	Emotions recognized by GSP	Complex emotions
16	Sadness and anger	Depression
16	Fear and anger	Guilt
40	Normal	--
50	Sadness and anger	Depression
50	Fear	--

---

[3] Examples of these videos are: http://www.youtube.com/watch?list=PLF78FD59D33B3495E&v=MZ_NKWBoVC8 and http://www.youtube.com/watch?v=SXmXj2sra20

Table 2 shows that the complex emotions of Depression and Guilt have been detected. These emotions are typical of patients (6); therefore, there are indications that it is possible for intelligent algorithms to automatically detect "emotion patterns" in patients with Alzheimer's disease, which can help predict changes in the disease when emotional findings are not present in the patients analyzed.

5   Conclusions and Future Work

This study is a first contribution to automatic recognition of human emotions in patients with Alzheimer's disease. We start with the premise that when there are emotional changes in patients, the disease is progressing, thus, our proposal is that the techniques for identification of patterns and semantics can help recognize simple and complex emotions in patients, and also, help to verify changes or increase in such emotions in the patients studied. This research is still being developed since we are trying to adjust computer algorithms in order to obtain patients' emotional patterns with a high accuracy, and then, through semantic inference, obtain complex emotions. For this, we used GSP to obtain emotions – pattern, Fear, Joy, and Surprise, which indicates the right path for this study. The combinations of these emotions are the complex emotions of Depression and Guilt that are typical of patients with Alzheimer's disease (6). The next step is to consolidate computer algorithms such as GSP, and work with ontologies such as HEO in order to test semantic inference. In conclusion, we believe that we have the opportunity to demonstrate that it is possible to recognize emotions in patients with Alzheimer's disease and check the progress of the disease based on emotional changes. For this reason, we will continue working on this area of research.

References

1. World Health Organization. Dementia a public health priority (2012),
   http://whqlibdoc.who.int/publications/2012/9789241564458_eng.
   pdf (cited: August 20, 2014)
2. García-Rodriguez, B., Fusari, A., Ellgring, H.: Procesamiento emocional de las expresiones faciales en el envejecimiento normal y patológico. Neurol. 46, 609–617 (2008)
3. Mammarella, N.: Is Emotional Working Memory Training a New Avenue of AD Treatment? A review. Aging and Disease 5(1), 35–40 (2013)
4. Seeman, T.E., Lusignolo, T.M., Albert, B.L.: Social relationships, social support, and patterns of cognitive aging in healthy, high-functioning older adults: MacArthur studies of successful aging. Health Psychology 20(4), 243–255 (2001)
5. Roudier, M., et al.: Discrimination of facial identity and of emotions in Alzheimer's disease. J. Neyrol. Sci. 154(2), 151–158 (1998)
6. Almagro Antúnez, C.: Congreso Internacional de Intervencion Psicosocial arte Social y Arteterapia. Arte, emociones y alzheimer. s.n., Murcia (2012)
7. Izard, C.E., Kagan, J., Zajonc, R.B.: Emotion, Cognition, and Behavior, 1st edn. Cambridge University Press, New York (1988)

8. Burgoon, J., et al.: Augmenting Human Identification of Emotional States in Video. In: Intelligence Analysis Conference. s.n., VA (2005)
9. Surcinelli, P., et al.: Facial emotion recognition in trait anxiety. Journal of Anxiety Disorders 20(1), 110–117 (2006)
10. Neurologia.com, et al.: Emotional Indifference in Alzheimer's Disease. The Journal of Neuropsychiatry & Clinical Neurosciences 22, 236–242 (2010)
11. Calder, A.J., et al.: Facial expression recognition across the adult life span. Neuropsychologia 41(2), 195–202
12. Keightley, M.L., et al.: Age effects on social cognition: faces tell a different story. Psychology and Aging 21(3), 558–572 (2006)
13. Isaacowitz, D.M., et al.: Age Differences in Recognition of Emotion in Lexical Stimuli and Facial Expressions. Psychology and Aging 22(1), 147–159 (2007)
14. Karikrishna, N.: Temporal Classification of events in cricket videos. In: National Conference Communications, pp. 1–5 (2011)
15. Chikhaoui, B., Wang, S., Pigot, H.: A new Algorithm Based on Sequential Pattern for person identification in ubiquitous environments. In: Proceedings of the Fourth International Workshop on Knowledge Discovery from Sensor Data, pp. 20–28 (2010)
16. Srikant, R., Agrawal, R.: Mining sequential patterns: Generalizations and performance improvements. In: Apers, P.M.G., Bouzeghoub, M., Gardarin, G. (eds.) EDBT 1996. LNCS, vol. 1057, pp. 3–17. Springer, Heidelberg (1996)
17. Wimmer, M., MacDonald, B.A., Jayamuni, D., Yadav, A.: Facial Expression Recognition for Human - Robot Interaction - A Prototype. In: Sommer, G., Klette, R., et al. (eds.) RobVis 2008. LNCS, vol. 4931, pp. 139–152. Springer, Heidelberg (2008)
18. Gunes, H., Vallverdú, J.: Automatic, Dimensional and Continuous emotion Recognition. International Journal of Synthetic Emotions 1 (2010)
19. Martínez-Tomas, R., et al.: On the correspondence between objects and events for the diagnosis of situations in visual surveillance task. Pattern Recognition Letters 29(8), 1117–1135 (2008)
20. Grassi, M.: Developing HEO Human Emotions Ontology. In: Fierrez, J., Ortega-Garcia, J., Esposito, A., Drygajlo, A., Faundez-Zanuy, M. (eds.) BioID MultiComm2009. LNCS, vol. 5707, pp. 244–251. Springer, Heidelberg (2009)
21. NewScientist (November 2008), http://axxon.com.ar/not/191/c-1911080.htm
22. MacPherson, S.E., Phillips, L.H., Della Sala, S.: Age-related differences in the ability to perceive sad facial expressions. Aging Clinical and Experimental Research 18(5), 418–424

Improvement of the Elderly Quality of Life and Care through Smart Emotion Regulation

Antonio Fernández-Caballero[1], José Miguel Latorre[2], José Manuel Pastor[3], and Alicia Fernández-Sotos[4]

[1] Universidad de Castilla-La Mancha, Instituto de Investigación en Informática de Albacete, 02071-Albacete, Spain
Antonio.Fdez@uclm.es
[2] Universidad de Castilla-La Mancha, Instituto de Investigación en Discapacidades Neurológicas, 02071-Albacete, Spain
[3] Universidad de Castilla-La Mancha, Instituto de Tecnologías Audiovisuales, 16071-Cuenca, Spain
[4] Universidad de Castilla-La Mancha, Facultad de Educación de Albacete, 02071-Albacete, Spain & Conservatorio Profesional de Música Maestro Gómez Villa, 30530-Cieza (Murcia), Spain

Abstract. This paper introduces a project named "Improvement of the Elderly Quality of Life and Care through Smart Emotion Regulation". The objective of the project is to find solutions for improving the quality of life and care of the elderly who can or wants to continue living at home by using emotion regulation techniques. Cameras and body sensors are used for monitoring the elderlies' facial and gestural expression, activity and behaviour, as well as relevant physiological data. This way the older people's emotions are inferred and recognized. Music, colour and light are the simulating means to regulate their emotions towards a positive and pleasant mood.

Keywords: Emotion recognition, Emotion regulation, Ambient intelligence, Gerontechnology.

1 Introduction

Quality of life is the perceived quality of the daily life of an individual, the appreciation of being of a person. It includes emotional, social and physical aspects in a person's life. Now, quality of life and care (QL&C) assesses how welfare is affected due to illness or disability. In order to appreciate QL&C an adequate monitoring of the individual is essential. It is widely recognized that elderly people generally prefer to live in their own homes over other options. But it is difficult to provide the necessary security and home care without monitoring, especially when the old person encounters some trouble. In this sense, Information Technology and Communications (ICT) may be part of the solution to the most common problems that the elderly faces at home.

The "Improvement of the Elderly Quality of Life and Care through Smart Emotion Regulation" project addresses a challenge related to "Economy and

L. Pecchia et al. (Eds.): IWAAL 2014, LNCS 8868, pp. 348–355, 2014.

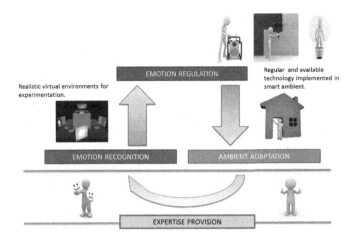

Fig. 1. General layout of the smart emotion regulation project

Digital Society", linked to the Spanish Strategy for Science, Technology and Innovation. Specifically, the purpose of the project is to find solutions for improving the quality of life and care of the elderly who can or wants to continue living at home, by using advanced tools and techniques of Information Technology supplemented with expert knowledge based on experimental techniques from Psychology, Neurobiology and Music about the regulation of emotions.

Computer tools and techniques used in this project are directly linked to the concepts of Ambient Intelligence (AmI). Indeed, we are convinced that AmI is a well-suited area for the design, implementation and deployment of global systems that seek to provide effective solutions to real problems in our society. The general objective results in some specific goals, such as: (1) to analyse the emotional states and the regulation techniques based on the expert knowledge, (2) to monitor and recognize emotions in Ambient Intelligence environments, (3) to regulate emotions through adapting the environment, (4) to construct an intelligent emotion regulation system, and, (5) to validate the emotion regulation system based on the expert knowledge. The project expected outcome is an intelligent emotion regulation system where the elderly can raise his/her sense of quality of life and care. Fig. 1 shows the general layout of the proposed system.

2   Fundamentals of Smart Emotion Recognition and Regulation

Automatic monitoring of emotional states is a valuable tool in the areas of Health Sciences and Rehabilitation, Clinical Psychology, Psychiatry and Gerontology. Current research in wireless area networks (WSNs) [1] and body area networks [2] has enabled the inclusion of advanced monitoring devices. Energy efficiency and small size devices are being dedicated to body feature measurements. It is important to consider the multisensory approach, which combines multiple sources of information presented by various sensors to generate a more accurate and robust interpretation of the environment [3]. Ultimately, we are talking about semantic interpretation from multi-sensed and video-controlled environments [4], which is the need to recognize situations, activities and interactions between different actors involved [5]. In our case, the goal is to apply smart techniques to the recognition of the activity and mood of older people living alone in their homes [6]. Indeed, we believe that the ability to monitor changes in the emotional state of a person in his/her own context allows implementing regulatory strategies for reducing negative affect. Emotion interpretation in humans has traditionally been an area of interest in disciplines such as Psychology and Sociology. However, there is a lack of applications that relate emotion with human behaviour.

Currently, the less intrusive process of automatic emotion recognition is based on the study of facial expression. The Facial Action Coding System [7] encodes all possible facial expressions as unitary actions (AUs) which may occur individually or in combination. In fact, facial expressions associated with emotions are generally described as a set of AUs [8]. Also, the analysis of physiological data is used for emotion recognition. The capture of physiological data is increasingly done through body sensor networks. These allow continuous measurement of physiological parameters such as heart rate, muscle tension, skin conductance, breathing rate, and so on, in the daily life of a person. When combined with contextual information extracted from the environment through WSNs, these parameters are used to infer emotions [9].

However, different innovative strategies have been developed to improve mood through external stimulation. In the field of gerontology, some techniques have been used to aid reminiscence and life review that claim to help the elderly to remember in organized manner autobiographical events using auditory stimuli such as music and visual stimuli such as photographs or videos. Specifically, "Life Review Based on Specific Positive Events" (ReVISEP) [10] is a technique aimed at the recovery of especially positive memories occurred throughout life. The main effect of this technique is improved mood and increased life satisfaction, both in older people with and without major depression. The power of music for modulating mood has also been proved [11].

Since the apparition of a pioneering work [12], renewed interest in the study of the relationship between cognition and emotion has led to the development of a wide range of techniques that allow temporary induction of different mood, both positive and negative. The first modern technique is the Velten mood induction procedure [13]. Other developed techniques are induction through music [14], film sequences [15] and autobiographical memory [16]. It is considered more useful to combine two or more induction techniques simultaneously, since multiple inductions contribute additively to mood [17]. The most studied field is the induction of positive emotional states through music, which has been tested with some success in various mental health conditions like depression [18]. Emotional responses to music are born of different musical features, including mode, harmonic complexity, tempo and intensity [19]. On the other hand, one of the most used set of stimuli in experimental research on emotions is the International Affective Picture System (IAPS) The IAPS is a collection of more than 1000 colour photographs that represent objects, people, landscapes and everyday situations. It allows accurate selection of the stimuli according to their position in the affective space defined by the dimensions of valence, arousal and dominance.

For emotion interpretation and regulation we heavily bet on Ambient Intelligence (AmI) [20] which proposes the creation of intelligent environments to suit the needs, tastes and interests of people that live in them. Moreover, the relationship between emotions and AmI is called "emotion-aware AmI" (AmE), which could be defined as emotion conscious AmI. AmE exploits concepts from Psychology and Social Sciences to adequately analyse the state of the individual and enrich the contextual information. AmE achieves this objective by extending the AmI devices through a collection of improved sensors able to recognize human emotions from facial expressions [21] and human behaviours, such as hand gestures, body movements and speech [22], [23].

3   Smart Ambient for the Elderly Emotion Recognition and Regulation

As depicted in Fig. 1, the four main modules of the smart ambient are "Emotion Recognition", "Emotion Regulation", "Ambient Adaptation" and "Expertise Provision".

3.1   Emotion Recognition

The "Emotion Recognition" module is dedicated to two tasks as shown in Fig. 2. The first one is aimed at stimulating the elderly in accordance with the actual emotion and the emotion that should be reached. The monitored elderly is being stimulated by means of music, colour and light in the so-called "Emotion-Oriented Perceptual Stimulation" task. These simultaneously provided stimuli should force a change in the mood of the elderly.

Obviously, it is necessary to capture the change through different sensors which are used in the "Emotion Monitoring and Recognition" task. Emotion monitoring as such is performed through the following sensors: camera(s) to capture the elder's face and gestures; camera(s) to follow the elder's behaviour; and, body sensors to get the elder's most important physiological data. Now, all these sensors work jointly to recognize emotions. It is our desire to use as less intrusive sensors as possible. At least a great effort will be put to miniaturize the needed body sensors. Face and gesture detection is the first step towards obtaining (positive / negative) emotion interpretation, the user's behaviours are aimed at (normal / abnormal) activity recognition, and affect recognition is gotten from the analysis of the physiological data.

3.2   Emotion Regulation

The next module is "Emotion Regulation", which input are the detected emotions, as shown in Fig. 3. Its objective is to provide the best-suited conditions

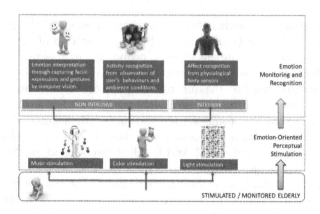

Fig. 2. Emotion Recognition subsystem

of music performance, and colour and light to attain the desired emotion in the elderly. The "Data Fusion and Mining" task is a fundamental one in this proposal. Indeed, a big deal of work is foreseen in data fusion, as emotion detection and regulation is only viable if all the data recorded from all the sensors provides enough evidence. Although there will be redundant information obtained from some sensors, some contradictory information will appear. The data to be fused comes from face and gesture recognition, activity detection and physiological data interpretation. Data mining is required to look for the most relevant information from all the data captured in order to get a correct knowledge on emotion regulation. As EEG and fMRI based techniques provide relevant previous knowledge on emotions as studied by psychologists and neuroscientists, some ground-truth data is used to validate the approach after crossing with the data obtained in our experimentation.

The other task present in this module is "Emotion Interpretation and Regulation", which obtains the emotion-tailored music, colour and lighting conditions for each situation.

3.3   Ambient Adaptation

"Ambient Adaptation" uses the emotion-tailored music, colour and lighting conditions as an input to build up an AmI system which integrates the whole process (see Fig. 4). "Ambient Intelligence" creates an intelligent system capable of adapting the ambience towards regulating emotions. It is important to highlight that this no private / sensitive information is sent out of the proper system. The only information transmitted consists of alarms to the foreseen stakeholders, that is, physicians, care providers and relatives. Secondly, "Smart Ambient Assessment" is a lifelong task aimed at assessing the system after each modification in the emotion recognition and regulation process.

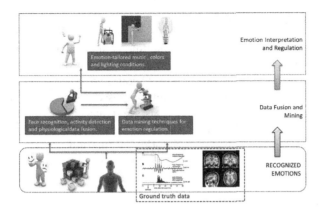

Fig. 3. Emotion Regulation subsystem

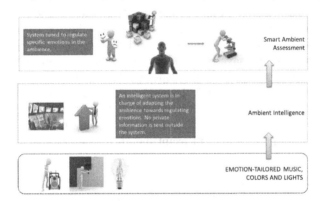

Fig. 4. Ambient Adaptation subsystem

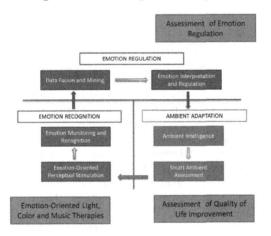

Fig. 5. Expertise Provision subsystem

3.4   Expertise Provision

The "Expertise Provision" (see Fig. 5) module is mandatory in introducing the current expert knowledge on the emotion detection and regulation issue though the task named "Emotion-Oriented Light, Colour and Music Therapies". We are happy to count on a multidisciplinary team composed of computer scientists, electrical engineers, psychologists, neurobiologists and musicians. The module is compulsory as well for technically and scientifically assessing both the emotion regulation smart system ("Assessment of Emotion Regulation" task) and the quality of life improvement wager ("Assessment of Quality of Life Improvement" task).

4   Conclusions

This paper has described a project named "Improvement of the Elderly Quality of Life and Care through Smart Emotion Regulation". The objective of the project is to find solutions for improving the quality of life and care of the elderly who can or wants to continue living at home by using emotion regulation techniques. For this sake, we have introduced the four main modules that make up the smart ambient system. These are "Emotion Recognition", "Emotion Regulation", "Ambient Adaptation" and "Expertise Provision". Heterogeneous vision and body sensors are used for monitoring the elderly and detecting his/her emotions, whilst music, colour and light are the simulating means to regulate the emotions towards a positive and pleasant mood.

Acknowledgements. This work was partially supported by Spanish Ministerio de Economía y Competitividad / FEDER under TIN2013-47074-C2-1-R and TIN2010-20845-C03-01 grants.

References

1. Chen, M., Gonzalez, S., Vasilakos, A., Cao, H., Leung, V.C.M.: Body area networks: a survey. Mobile Networks and Applications 16, 171–193 (2011)
2. Jovanov, E., Milenkovic, A.: Body area networks for ubiquitous healthcare applications: opportunities and challenges. Journal of Medical Systems 35, 1245–1254 (2011)
3. Pavón, J., Gómez-Sanz, J.J., Fernández-Caballero, A., Valencia-Jiménez, J.J.: Development of intelligent multi-sensor surveillance systems with agents. Robotics and Autonomous Systems 55, 892–903 (2008)
4. Gascueña, J.M., Fernández-Caballero, A.: On the use of agent technology in intelligent, multi-sensory and distributed surveillance. The Knowledge Engineering Review 26, 191–208 (2011)
5. Fernández-Caballero, A., Castillo, J.C., López, M.T., Serrano-Cuerda, J., Sokolova, M.V.: INT3–Horus framework for multispectrum activity interpretation in intelligent environments. Expert Systems with Applications 40, 6715–6727 (2013)

6. Bartholmai, M., Koeppe, E., Neumann, P.P.: Monitoring of hazardous scenarios using multi–sensor devices. In: The Fourth International Conference on Sensor Device Technologies and Applications, pp. 9–13 (2013)
7. Ekman, P., Friesen, W.V., Hager, J.C.: The new Facial Action Coding System (2002)
8. Soleymani, M., Lichtenauer, J., Pun, T., Pantic, M.: A multi–modal affective database for affect recognition and implicit tagging. IEEE Transactions on Affective Computing 3, 42–55 (2012)
9. Medjahed, H., Istrate, D., Boudy, J., Baldinger, J.-L.: A pervasive multi-sensor data fusion for smart home healthcare monitoring. In: IEEE International Conference in Fuzzy Systems, pp. 1466–1473 (2011)
10. Serrano, J.P., Latorre, J.M., Montanes, J.: Life review therapy using autobiographical retrieval practice for older adults with depressive symptomatology. Psychology and Aging 19, 272–277 (2004)
11. Kim, J., André, E.: Emotion recognition based on physiological changes in music listening. IEEE Transactions on Pattern Analysis and Machine Intelligence 30, 2067–2083 (2008)
12. Schachter, S., Singer, J.E.: Cognitive, social and physiological determinants of emotional state. Psychological Review 69, 379–399 (1962)
13. Velten, E.: A laboratory task for induction of mood states. Behaviour Research and Therapy 6, 473–482 (1968)
14. Niedenthal, P.M., Halberstadt, J.B., Setterlund, M.C.: Being happy and seing happy: Emotional state mediates visual word recognition. Cognition & Emotion 11, 403–432 (1997)
15. Gross, J.J., Levenson, R.W.: Emotion ilicitation using films. Cognition & Emotion 9, 87–108 (1995)
16. Brewer, D., Doughtie, E.B.: Induction of mood and mood shift. Journal of Clinical Psychology 36, 215–226 (1980)
17. Bower, G.H.: Mood and memory. American Psychologist 36, 129–148 (1981)
18. Livingstone, S.R., Palmer, C., Schubert, E.: Emotion response to musical repetition. Emotion 12, 552–567 (2012)
19. Livingstone, R.S., Thompson, W.F.: The emergence of music from the theory of mind. Musicae Scientiae 17, 83–115 (2009)
20. Acampora, G., Vitiello, A.: Interoperable neuro–fuzzy services for emotion–aware ambient intelligence. Neurocomputing 122, 3–12 (2013)
21. Susskind, J.M., Littlewort, G., Bartlett, M.S., Movellan, J., Anderson, A.K.: Human and computer recognition of facial expressions of emotion. Neuropsychologia 45, 152–162 (2007)
22. Vogt, T., André, E., Wagner, J.: Automatic recognition of emotions from speech: A review of the literature and recommendations for practical realisation. In: Peter, C., Beale, R. (eds.) Affect and Emotion in HCI. LNCS, vol. 4868, pp. 75–91. Springer, Heidelberg (2008)
23. Silva, P.R.D., Osano, M., Marasinghe, A., Madurapperuma, A.P.: Towards recognizing emotion with affective dimensions through body gestures. In: Seventh IEEE International Conference on Automatic Face and Gesture Recognition, pp. 269–274 (2006)

Detecting Disruptive Vocalizations
for Ambient Assisted Interventions for Dementia

Jessica Beltrán[1], René Navarro[2], Edgar Chávez[1], Jesús Favela[1],
Valeria Soto-Mendoza[1], and Catalina Ibarra[1]

[1] CICESE Research Center, México
{jbeltran,vsoto}@cicese.edu.mx, {elchavez,favela}@cicese.mx,
catalina.ibarra@uabc.edu.mx
[2] Universidad de Sonora, México
rnavarro@industrial.uson.mx

Abstract. People suffering from dementia exhibit abnormal behaviors
that can put them at risk or burden their relatives and caregivers. Many
of these behaviors have acoustic manifestations, such as shouting, mumbling, cursing or making repetitive tapping. In this paper we propose
an approach for detecting disruptive behavior manifested through audio. The solution proposed is an specialized speech, verbal and ambient
sound detector and classifier, using speech and CASA techniques. We
illustrate how the detection of these symptoms can be used to enact
non-pharmacological interventions aimed at stopping such behavior or
mitigating its negative impact.

1 Introduction

People who suffer from dementia exhibit abnormal behaviors that can put them
at risk or burden their relatives and caregivers. Traditionally, cognitive problems
have been the main focus of interest in the treatment of people with dementia
(PwD). However, a number of common non-cognitive symptoms are challenging
not only for the person, but also for their caregivers. Behavioral and psychological
symptoms of dementia (BPSD) are defined as symptoms of disturbed perception,
thought content, mood, behavior frequently occurring in patients with dementia [1]. Psychological symptoms of dementia relate to anxiety, depression, and
psychosis whereas behavioral symptoms include aggression, apathy, agitation,
disinhibited behaviors, wandering, nocturnal disruption, and vocally disruptive
behaviors. Such behaviors are typically identified by observation of the PwD and
only considered challenging when they affect other people or cause self-injury.
Approximately 90 percent of patients with dementia of the Alzheimer's type
exhibit these problematic behaviors turning their care a complex and challenging task. For instance, vocally disruptive behavior (VBD), such as screaming,
shouting, abusive language, perseveration and repetitive inappropriate requests,
have been found to cause severe emotional distress for caregivers and other residents in nursing homes. Moreover, nursing staff expressed significantly more
frustration, anxiety and anger towards patients with VDB and even distanced
themselves from them [4].

L. Pecchia et al. (Eds.): IWAAL 2014, LNCS 8868, pp. 356–363, 2014.
© Springer International Publishing Switzerland 2014

There is a growing agreement that dementia treatment should include non-pharmacological interventions (NPI) to ameliorate challenging behaviors such as those aforementioned [11]. Heterogeneity in the manifestations of dementia stems from three sources: predisposing characteristics, life events, and the person's current condition. Each of these sources occurs in several domains: a genetic-biological-medical domain, a psychosocial domain, and an environmental domain. This is why recommendations for caring for a PwD include simplifying the physical environment, avoiding unfamiliar settings, and maintaining a relatively fixed routine.

We propose to leverage on pervasive technologies to detect problematic behaviors in PwDs in order to enact interventions in an overly-disruptive environment, suggest interventions to the caregiver, or prompt the PwD to carry out comforting activities. These interventions aim at reducing the frequency of incidences of BPSD, and ultimately stimulating definite changes in behavioral patterns in the PwD and the caregiver. Therefore, making it less troublesome for the caregiver and providing the PwD with a better quality of life. We refer to such an environment as an Ambient-assisted Intervention System (AaIS).

Several BPSD have audible manifestations, such as yelling or mumbling. In this paper we describe an approach that can be used to detect these types of behaviors. In the next section we describe the general approach we have called Ambient Assisted Interventions for Dementia. Section 3 presents a case study conducted in a geriatric residence from which we derived use scenarios and gathered data to evaluate the feasibility of our approach. The approach proposed is discussed in Section 4, with some preliminary results. Finally, Section 5 presents our conclusions and proposes future work.

2   AAID: Ambient Assisted interventions for Dementia

Figure 1 depicts the general approach of an Ambient-assisted Intervention system (AaIS). The approach focuses on suggesting or enacting strategies aimed at addressing problematic behaviors, rather than assisting the user to complete a specific task or monitor the PwD for safety. An AaIS uses ambient intelligence to improve PwDs quality of life by identifying the presence of BPSDs, deciding on an appropriate intervention and either modifying the environment or persuading the PwD or their caregiver to act on the system's advice. Both, inappropriate environments and upsetting personal interactions combine with unmet needs to trigger problematic behaviors. For instance, a PwD might exhibit apathy after being scolded by her caregiver or might undergo wandering triggered initially by her need to move after a long period of rest. These BPSDs can be observed and reported by the caregiver or, alternatively, BPSDs can be inferred from information obtained from sensors located in the environment or worn by the PwD. Agitation, for instance, is manifested via repetitive movement and verbal expressions such as shouting or continuous talk. These behaviors can be inferred from data obtained from accelerometers and microphones. Finally, once there is evidence that the PwD is exhibiting a BPSD, a decision model is used to decide on an intervention, which will be enacted in one of these three ways: a) Intervene directly to change the configuration of the physical environment; b) Communicate with the caregiver to recommend an action to perform; or, c) Communicate with the PwD to suggest an activity or provide her with information that could change her current behavior. The decision model is tailored to a PwD from an assessment of BPSD, scientific evidence of the efficacy of behavioral interventions, and feedback provided by the caregiver about the efficacy of specific interventions experienced by the PwD.

By detecting problematic behaviors and inferring probable causes, behavior-aware applications could provide tailored and more opportune interventions, notifying caregivers, offering assurances to the patient, or directly modifying the physical environment. For example, as daylight decreases at nightfall, a person with dementia might experience confusion and anxiety and not recognize his or her surroundings. This could lead to a desire to wander a phenomena known as sundowning syndrome. If this behavior is detected, increasing the lighting conditions could eliminate the problematic behavior.

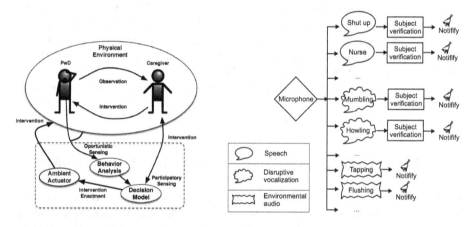

Fig. 1. (left) An ambient-assisted intervention system monitors a person with dementia and the physical and social environment for problematic behaviors to select an appropriate intervention. (right) System proposed. The system detects in parallel all the trigger sounds.

3   Field Study and Case Studies

In collaboration with the staff of an assisted living facility, five residents suffering from dementia (Females=4, Males=1, ranging from 81 to 94 years old) were selected to participate in an observation study of BPSDs. During four weeks, participants were closely observed for five hours a day for three days each week to document agitation manifestations according the Cohen-Mansfield Agitation Inventory (CMAI)[6,2]. Precise signs exhibited by the PwD, along with the duration of the episode were recorded for each incident. Additionally, we kept track of social interactions with the residence staff and other residents. Participants wore a mobile phone running an opportunistic sensing application. The application collected accelerometer data to monitor activity intensity. Additionally, participants wore a small clip-on audio recorder during the observation sessions. We present two scenarios derived from observations and interviews with caregivers to illustrate the diversity of problematic behaviors that concern the caregivers, and the need to personalize the interventions to their background and context.

3.1 Scenario A

Rose is a 94 years old lady living in a nursing home. She suffers from moderate dementia of the Alzheimer type. Her behavioral and neuropsychiatric symptoms that include disorientation, agitation, and outbursts of unpremeditated aggression are a common cause of distress for other home residents, and require constant attention from the staff. It is lunchtime and all the residents are gathered in the dining area enjoying soft background music. The table seating arrangement is challenging since Rose is particularly susceptible to loud noises and table manners of other residents. Today Doris, a fellow resident, has been suffering from severe verbally disruptive behavior like yelling and mumbling. Because of her disorientation, Rose is unable to go to a quieter place, like her bedroom, since she does not know how to get there. Doris disruptive behavior usually would trigger verbal aggression from Rose repeatedly shouting Shut up! and slamming the table with her hand. The sound that may trigger Rose aggression is detected by the AaIS microphones, and in anticipation the background music is changed according to Roses preferences to soothe her mood. If the problem arises, the AaIS would enable voice guidance and visual stimuli to simulate caregiver's presence. The set of stimuli will provide orientation clues to guide Rose to her bedroom or a quieter place inside the residence, as well as to take her away from discomfort. At the same time, caregivers are informed about the situation and receive a message when Rose gets in her room.

3.2 Scenario B

Frank suffers from moderate dementia. He is 90 years old and lives in a nursing home and is one of the most attention demanding residents. He yells nurse! nurse! whenever he needs to go to the restroom, wants something to drink, or needs to find something. If he is not attended promptly, he starts crying bothering other residents. Moreover, a bigger cause of concern for the nursing staff is his misbelief of being held captive by them. Even though he depends on his wheelchair to move around the nursing home, he is always trying to get away and requesting to be taken to the bank to reclaim his savings. Today he is hanging around the nursing home main entrance waiting for an opportunity to run away. As time goes by he starts getting agitated. A repetitive handling of the brake lever in the wheelchair or a repetitive tapping on the wheelchair armrest are frequent manifestations of this behavior. The sound scene generated by his behavior is detected by the AaIS sensors and along with Frank's current location, is interpreted as a wandering

behavior. In response, the system turns on the LCD screen in the nearby area
and plays back a previously recorded soccer match, which is his favorite, in order
to distract his attention from the door.

Figure 2 depicts an interaction between the PwD in Scenario A and another
resident, showing how these audible behaviors become problematic. We now
illustrate how this VBD can be automatically detected to suggest or enact appropriate interventions.

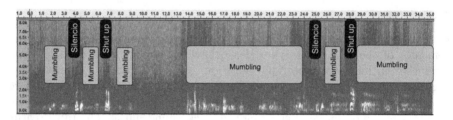

Fig. 2. Spectrogram on a 35 second stream of audio and annotations of VBD

4 Detecting Verbal Manifestations of Problematic Behaviors

As suggested in [9], the AaIS should be able to automatically detect specific type
of sounds. We propose the system depicted in Figure 1. We generate models for
identifying sounds from an inventory of disruptive sounds from all residents.
They can be either verbal or environmental. The input audio is available to all
the models in parallel. If one model detects a keyword, e.g. *Shut up, Silencio(in
spanish)* and *nurse*, the system verifies the volume and the identity of the person making the utterance, it will only act if the keyword is said by the right
person and will report the loudness of the utterance. The disruptive vocalization
component recognizes mumbling and other utterances like the one exhibited by
Doris. The component for environmental sound recognition detects sounds like
the tapping in a wheelchair produced by Frank when he is agitated or the sound
of flushing the toilet.

We use techniques developed for speech [5] and environmental sound recognition [10] to detect disruptive audible manifestations. The typical procedure
for sound recognition, consist in representing the audio as a vector of features
obtained trough a feature extraction. This is followed by a classification step,
which indicates if the audio corresponds to a sound type in a previously trained
model. The choice of the proper features and classifiers for recognizing each type
of sound is obtained through an initial analysis of the properties from the specific
type of sound, the features and the classifier are refined following some rounds
of performance evaluation.

Estimating Keywords: Each keyword model is constructed using examples
of the word to be identified. Those examples will come from a stream of sounds
recorded from the residents suffering from dementia. We have decided to use

Mel Frequency Cepstrum Coeficientes (MFCC) as audio features, since its the state of the art feature set for speech processing. In addition, Hidden Markov Models (HMM) have been found to be appropriate to handle the regularity in patterns proper of human speech. We plan to use the Hidden Markov Model Toolkit (HTK) [12]; a research toolkit widely used for speech recognition. A nice feature of HTK is that it provides the flexibility of training models with the speech of the specific users, improving the efficiency of the system. With this personalized approach it is possible to detect utterances by the same speaker in several languages (which is an important scenario for our purposes). From the data captured from Rose in the field study, we have found 19 examples of the keyword *shut up*, 12 examples of *silence*, 9 examples of *chicken shit* and 3 examples of *stop it*. From the total 60 hours recorded from Rose, indicates that she says 0.7 of these keywords per hour. We generate models for the keywords *shut up*, *silence* and *chicken shit*. Then, we evaluate using 3-fold cross validation.

Estimating Mumbling: The second type of models shown in Figure 1 are VBD. The closest work reported in the literature aims at detecting babble from babies [7] but neither for VBD nor with elders. In a subset of 113 hours, from 203 hours recording, we found 198 examples of VBD, this indicates a rate of 1.4 VBD instances per hour.

In this work, we obtained preliminary results from a experiment for classifying mumbling. The database is formed by manually segmenting 43 instances of mumbling recorded from Doris in the field study. We used additionally 43 manually cut examples of random environmental data also captured in the field study. On average, the length of each instance is 2.25 seconds. The features extraction techniques used for represent each sound are: MFCC, spectral roll off, spectral flux, spectral flatness and spectral Centroid. The classifier used for this experiment is a continuos ergodic HMM with one gaussian and 3 states. We evaluated the classification using 10-fold cross validation. The confusion matrix obtained is depicted in table 1. More sounds would permit re-training and refine the models. Given a speech as an input, the system will recognize a keyword and verify if the the word was said by the subject of interest and will also report the volume.

Table 1. Confusion matrix for mumbling and other sounds

	Mumbling	Other
Mumbling	81.24	18.75
Other	38.28	61.71

This experiment gives a hint of the feasibility of our approach. More experimentation must be conducted using other types of disruptive vocalization. Also it is necessary to perform classification on streams of audio without manual segmentation. By classifying over long periods of time we can improve the effectiveness of the approach by choosing strategies. For example, we can reduce false positives by adding extra information to the representation of the sounds by indicating if the previous segment of audio had a high probability of being a mumbling.

Environmental Sound Recognition: This includes detection of sounds like tapping or flushing. An approach based on entropy signatures as we have proposed [8] detects environmental sounds like washing hands o tooth brushing seems to fit our needs. Some adjustments in the feature selection will be needed to detect tapping in the wheelchair, or the sound of flushing a toilet.

We acknowledge the importance of avoiding false positives, i.e. reporting that a specific sound was detected when actually it did not happen (type I error). Since the system is designed for helping the caregiver it is important to page them only when an event actually happened, and avoid disturbances from false positives or misleading information. False positives (type I errors) and false negatives (type II errors) can be tuned to avoid one of them at the expense of increasing the other.

5   Discusion

Several problematic behaviors exhibited by PwDs have audible manifestations. We have proposed an approach to detect these utterances in order to mitigate the impact of these behaviors trough ambient-assisted interventions. Initial results attest to the feasibility of the approach. We plan to conduct additional tests with the data we have gathered in the nursing home.

A key issue in managing behaviors of PwD is to document their actions, the circumstances, and the impact of these actions on them and others. Additional applications of our approach include the documentation of problematic behaviors. Frequently, nursing home residents are affected by inadequacies in staffing and training. As a result, clinical data often consists of brief observations of residents over relatively short periods of time, filtered through the lens of an overburdened staff member. In the absence of objective, reliable assessment and outcomes measurement, effectiveness of interventions is challenging. To overcome the above scenarios, the AaIS may use a log of sounds for each resident which contains historical sound records: the frequency and duration of shouting, mumbling, yelling and crying. These long-term tagged records when analyzed by the AaIS may find correlations of the PwD behavior and the therapeutic actions (pharmacological and non pharmacological interventions) of the caregivers. This way, the AaIS may suggest a suitable intervention to the caregivers. For instance, crying spells are symptoms of clinical depression. However, depending on the context and characteristics of the manifestation, crying spells might be attributable to an involuntary emotional expression disorder (IEED), which requires a different treatment [3].

References

1. Burns, K., Jayasinha, R., Tsang, R., Brodaty, H.: Behaviour Management: A Guide to Good Practice. Dementia Collaborative Research Centre – Assessment and Better Care, pp. 1–190 (May 2012)
2. Cohen-Mansfield, J.: Conceptualization of agitation: Results based on the cohen-mansfield agitation inventory and the agitation behavior mapping instrument. International Psychogeriatrics 8, 309–315 (1997)
3. Cummings, J., Arciniegas, D., Brooks, B., Herndon, R., Lauterbach, E., Pioro, E., Robinson, R., Scharre, D., Schiffer, R., Weintraub, D.: Defining and diagnosing involuntary emotional expression disorder. CNS spectrums 11(6), 1–7 (2006)
4. Fick, W.F., van der Borgh, J.P., Jansen, S., Koopmans, R.T.C.M.: The effect of a lollipop on vocally disruptive behavior in a patient with frontotemporal dementia: a case-study. International Psychogeriatrics FirstView, 1–4 (June 2014)
5. Huang, X., Baker, J., Reddy, R.: A historical perspective of speech recognition. Commun. ACM 57(1), 94–103 (2014), http://doi.acm.org/10.1145/2500887
6. Cohen-Mansfield, J.: Assessment of agitation in older adults. In: Handbook of Clinical Gerontology Assessment. John Wiley & Sons, New York (1999)
7. Krishnamurthy, N., Hansen, J.: Babble noise: Modeling, analysis, and applications. IEEE Transactions on Audio, Speech, and Language Processing 17(7), 1394–1407 (2009)
8. Márquez, J.B.: Activity recognition using a spectral entropy signature. In: Proceedings of the 2012 ACM Conference on Ubiquitous Computing, UbiComp 2012, pp. 576–579. ACM, New York (2012), http://doi.acm.org/10.1145/2370216.2370313
9. Navarro, R.F., Rodríguez, M.D., Favela, J.: Intervention tailoring in augmented cognition systems for elders with dementia. IEEE J. Biomedical and Health Informatics 18(1), 361–367 (2014)
10. Potamitis, I., Ganchev, T.: Generalized recognition of sound events: Approaches and applications, pp. 41–79 (2008)
11. Sadowsky, C.H., Galvin, J.E.: Guidelines for the Management of Cognitive and Behavioral Problems in Dementia. The Journal of the American Board of Family Medicine 25(3), 350–366 (2012)
12. Young, S.J.: The htk hidden markov model toolkit: Design and philosophy. Entropic Cambridge Research Laboratory, Ltd. 2, 2–44 (1994)

Adaptive Training for Older Adults Based on Dynamic Diagnosis of Mild Cognitive Impairments and Dementia

Anna Kötteritzsch[1], Michael Koch[1], and Fritjof Lemân[2]

[1] Universität der Bundeswehr, Werner-Heisenberg-Weg 39, 85577 Neubiberg, Germany
[2] FamilyVision, Trademark of VirtuoSys GmbH, Grainwinkel 8a, 82057 Icking, Germany
anna@koetteritzsch.net

Abstract. An increasing number of older adults with neurodegenerative diseases and a growing gap in healthcare services lead to a higher need of suitable means of prevention and intervention in order to support the maintenance of an autonomous life. Software for cognitive and psycho-motoric training has the potential to provide an adapted training that challenges without producing cognitive overload. To achieve this goal, the status of a person's cognitive and motoric abilities must be assessed. We propose a system that provides adapted training for older adults based on dynamic diagnosis of mild cognitive impairment and dementia. Within this contribution, a concept of content adaptation on the individual needs of a user and actual stage of development, a training application prototype as well as first results of user studies in a geriatric day clinic are presented.

1 Introduction

Neurodegenerative diseases, including Parkinson's and Alzheimer's disease, affect an increasing number of older adults in Germany. Symptoms of dementia, e.g. poor concentration, rapid exhaustion, and mental overload, restrain autonomy and quality of life. Continuous cognitive and psycho-motoric training in combination with social interaction increase the chances to delay mild cognitive impairments (MCI) and dementia as well as slow down the progression of dementia by addressing risk factors. However, care facilities cannot cope with the increasing need of means to prevent and intervene with cognitive and motor impairments and diseases.

Technologies in the area of Ambient Assisted Living (AAL) aim at supporting the autonomy of older adults in their home environment. Interactive systems have the potential to support people with age-related impairments by offering digital trainings and prevention activities. Furthermore, they may track a person's status and adapt to it based on the results. Considering rapidly changing and varying abilities in older adults with neurodegenerative diseases, it is important to provide dynamic adaptation of preventive measurements. By those means, mental overload can be avoided despite a challenging training. We present an approach to provide automatic adaptive cognitive and psycho-motoric training based on information entered by the user and information gathered from user interaction. The additional value of this approach is the

L. Pecchia et al. (Eds.): IWAAL 2014, LNCS 8868, pp. 364–368, 2014.

design of a complete user model based on the application domain and its usage in assistive technologies. In this contribution, we present first results of an adaptive training application for older adults based on measurements for dynamic diagnosis of MCI and dementia within the scope of the project FamilyVision.

2   Digital Therapy and Diagnosis of Dementia

Several assistive technologies offer cognitive and psycho-motoric training and the long-term diagnosis of abilities. Products include therapy applications as well as cognitive or motoric training games which adjust the level of difficulty based on limited user information. However, when not considering the cognitive or motoric state, a training effect may be decreased [2]. Research projects draw an increasing focus on adaptation of applications for older adults, providing an adaptation based on specific user requirements. Yet, these must me manually adapted [3] or consider single aspects of the user's abilities [4]. When focusing on older adults, all available information on context, abilities and impairments of the user might influence the user state. Some research projects track the usage context for adapting the system, yet do not take into account the user state [5]. Pielawa et al. [6] present a management system for long-term tracking of multi-morbid patients, providing modelling techniques that might be useful for training systems. Assistive technology for older adults with MCI and dementia must be adaptive in order to react to the rapidly changing needs and difficulties of the user [7]. Brouillette et al. show that a digital dynamic diagnosis application is feasible, reliable and valid when assessing levels of cognitive functioning [8]. Integrating dynamic diagnosis, advanced user modeling and adaptation techniques into the development of cognitive and psycho-motoric trainings may address the challenge of providing a suitable training for people with different abilities and requirements.

3   Dynamic Diagnosis and Adaptive Training

The aim of FamilyVision is to track and analyze short- and long-term user and usage information in order to adapt applications for prevention and intervention of MCI and dementia in its early stages. We developed a mobile software application combining dynamic diagnosis and an automatically adapted training for older adults with varying abilities.

3.1   Concept

Our approach supports older adults living in their own home environment by providing a tablet-based application for MCI and dementia prevention. Measurements addressing risk factors of dementia are automatically adapted, based on information about the user and his cognitive status.

Training of cognitive and psycho-motoric abilities requires an engaging training avoiding mental overload. Thus, training applications must be adapted to the abilities and impairments of the user. In order to adapt reliable diagnosis measurements into our system, we compared the items of existing screenings for MCI and dementia (e.g. the Mini Mental State Test) and general geriatric instruments. We extracted seven categories of cognitive and psycho-motoric abilities that are analyzed by the screening instruments: 1. Orientation ability, 2. short-term memory, 3. attention, 4. calculation ability, 5. long-term memory, 6. executive functioning, and 7. logic / abstraction. These categories were integrated into our user model in addition to demographic information, areas of interest, preferences and past results of cognitive assessments. One to four items that diagnose the different abilities and are suitable for digital implementation were extracted for each category to be included in our prototype.

We conducted a preliminary qualitative study evaluating tablet applications in terms of usability and topics of interest with 12 patients (70 to 92 years; 8 f, 4 m) in a geriatric day clinic. The results showed common areas of interest of older adults concerning training applications and pointed out that different gestures are ineffective for older adults. The participants rated their enjoyment higher and challenge more adequate for contents that focused on the surrounding location, nature, and areas of interest (e.g. sports). Very difficult and very easy tasks were generally rated lower on the enjoyment scale then tasks with an adequate difficulty. These results stress the importance of adaptive technologies to engage older adults in training activities. We also analyzed and categorized existing trainings from research and practice. These trainings could supported one or more of the following user abilities: 1. Concentration and situation interpretation, 2. response, 3. short-term memory, 4. procedural long-term memory, 5. episodic long-term memory, 6. attention, 7. calculation ability, 8. Logical reasoning, 9. executive functioning, 10. abstraction and spacial imagination, and 11. fine motor skills. Based on existing literature and exercises, we developed one to eight training concepts for each of the training categories, taking into account design guidelines and requirements of the user group.

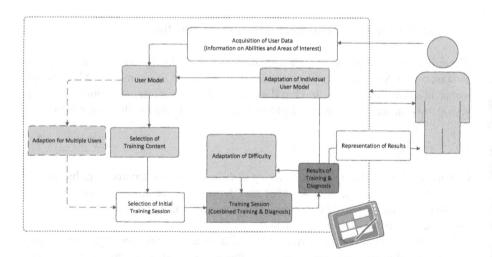

Fig. 1. Adaptation of cognitive and motoric training based on user and usage data

The diagnosis items and trainings were combined in an overall adaptive training concept. Using a playful approach, the users are guided through a 20 minute daily training session including all training and diagnosis categories. The results of the diagnosis and trainings are used to achieve a better adaption and selection of trainings as well as the customization of difficulty and help functions (e.g. repetition or highlight of items). Figure 1 shows the adaptation process of the self-adaptive training concept.

3.2   Prototype and Evaluation

In order to evaluate the concept with the user group, we developed a prototype of the proposed application. The prototype includes at least two items for each of the seven suggested diagnosis categories and five trainings that address eight of the eleven user abilities. A randomized training sequence consists of all trainings and one question of each diagnosis category. Figure 2 shows different screens of the diagnosis and training. When a user profile is created, difficulties are initially set. Based on the actual and former results of the trainings and diagnosis items, a value for each of the user abilities is calculated with every training reset. According to the values of user abilities, one of five levels of difficulty is set for the individual trainings.

Fig. 2. Prototype of an adaptive training based on dynamic diagnosis (First row: Video quiz, sequence training, reaction game. Second row: Memory task, two dynamic diagnosis items)

The evaluation in a geriatric day clinic in cologne started in April 2014. Each patient is tested in three recorded sessions, including an interview, a training session and a standardized geriatric assessment. The results of the sessions give an insight into the validity of the diagnosis as well as the usability of the application. Furthermore, we evaluate the mental adequacy of the trainings in order to improve adaptation of the difficulties based on user abilities. First results indicate that heterogeneous users with varying abilities are likewise able to interact with the application. However, with declining cognitive abilities, the complexity of the proposed training is still too high.

4   Conclusion and Future Work

When developing prevention and intervention trainings for older adults, varying and changing abilities and impairments of the user must be considered. In order to provide challenge and avoid mental overload, we proposed an adaptation of trainings based on dynamic diagnosis of abilities on different scales. However, the developed prototype provides a limited adaptation mechanism and is based on a static calculation. A learning system will dynamically react to long-term changes as well as to the daily form. Thus, an advanced adaptation algorithm will be implemented into the prototype and tested in comparison to the simple adaptation. Furthermore, social interaction contributes in maintaining cognitive abilities. Therefore, we will face the challenge of implementing an adaptive multi-user training in our further research. In our future work, we will investigate how adaptation for multiple users with different abilities and impairments can be achieved. By means of providing adapted training based on dynamic diagnosis for older adults with varying abilities, our goal is to contribute to maintaining a long and autonomous life.

Acknowledgements. The research presented in this contribution is conducted as part of the FamilyVision project, which is funded by the EXIST program of the German Ministry of Economics (BMWi) and the European Social Fund (ESF) and by the FLÜGGE program of the Bavarian State Ministry of Education, Science & Art.

References

1. Garcia Marin, J.A., Lawrence, E., Felix Navarro, K., Sax, C.: Heuristic Evaluation for Interactive Games within Elderly Users. In: Proceedings of eTELEMED 2011, pp. 130–133 (February 2011)
2. Alcañiz, M., Botella, C., Rey, B., Baños, R.M., Lozano, J.A., de la Vega, N.L., Castilla, D., Montesa, J., Hospitaler, A.: EMMA: An adaptive display for virtual therapy. In: Schmorrow, D.D., Reeves, L.M. (eds.) Augmented Cognition, HCII 2007. LNCS (LNAI), vol. 4565, pp. 258–265. Springer, Heidelberg (2007)
3. Ma, M., McNeill, M., Charles, D., McDonough, S., Crosbie, J., Oliver, L., McGoldrick, C.: Adaptive virtual reality games for rehabilitation of motor disorders. In: Stephanidis, C. (ed.) UAHCI 2007 (Part II). LNCS, vol. 4555, pp. 681–690. Springer, Heidelberg (2007)
4. Vogt, J., Luyten, K., Van den Bergh, J., Coninx, K., Meier, A.: Putting Dementia into Context. In: Winckler, M., Forbrig, P., Bernhaupt, R. (eds.) HCSE 2012. LNCS, vol. 7623, pp. 181–198. Springer, Heidelberg (2012)
5. Pielawa, L., Helmer, A., Brell, M., Hein, A.: Intelligent environments supporting the care of multi-morbid patients: a concept for patient-centered information management and therapy. In: Proceedings of ISABEL 2011(15). ACM (2011)
6. Wolf, P., Schmidt, A., Otte, J.P., Klein, M., Rollwage, S., König-Ries, B., Dettborn, T., Gabdulkhakova, A.: openAAL - the open source middleware for ambient-assisted living (AAL). In: AALIANCE Conference, March 11-12, Malaga, Spain (2010)
7. Brouilette, R.M., Foil, H., Fontenot, S., Correro, A., Allen, R., Martin, C.K., Bruce-Keller, A.J., Kxeller, J.N.: Feasibility, Reliability, and Validity of a Smartphone Based Application for the Assessment of Cognitive Function in the Elderly. PloS One 8(6), e65925 (2013)

Identification of Ideal Contexts to Issue Reminders for Persons with Dementia

Phillip J. Hartin[1], Chris D. Nugent[1], Sally I. McClean[2], Ian Cleland[1], Maria C. Norton[3], Chelsea Sanders[3], and JoAnn T. Tschanz[3]

[1] School of Computing and Mathematics, University of Ulster, Jordanstown Campus, BT370QB, UK
{pj.hartin,cd.nugent,i.cleland}@ulster.ac.uk
[2] School of Computing and Information Engineering, University of Ulster, Coleraine Campus, BT521SA, UK
si.mclean@ulster.ac.uk
[3] Department of Psychology, Utah State University, Logan, UT 84322-4440, USA
{maria.norton,joann.tschanz}@usu.edu,
chelsea.sanders@aggiemail.usu.edu

Abstract. Dementia is a global health concern that primarily effects cognitive functioning, leading to forgetfulness and reducing the capacity for independent living. In this paper, we present an app designed as a reminding aid for persons with dementia as part of a 12-month randomised control trial with 125 participants who have shown a decline in cognition, evaluated by a Modified Mini-Mental State Exam (TC cohort). The app was also evaluated by healthy adults from the University of Ulster (HC cohort). In addition to reminding, the app also acts as a sensor data collection tool, which records selective data from a range of sensors around the time a reminder is delivered in an effort to gain an insight into relevant contextual information. To date, over 3000 sensor recordings from both cohorts have been collected and analysed. The recordings have been used to develop and validate a model that can identify in which contexts a reminder is typically acknowledged or missed, allowing for context-aware delivery of reminders or notifications at a time when the individual is mostly likely to receive the prompt. Using data from both cohorts weakened the accuracy of the model for the TC cohort, signifying that the TC cohort require their own non-generalised model. Future work will involve implementing the models developed into the app based on the existing TC data, so that the reminder delivery can be altered in real-time for this cohort.

Keywords: context-aware reminding, personalised computing, assistive technology, mobile computing, dementia.

1   Introduction

There is at present over 44 million persons with dementia (PwD) globally, which is projected to increase to over 135 million by 2050 [1]. Whilst pharmaceutical treatments for the condition continue to improve, the symptoms that stem from cognitive

L. Pecchia et al. (Eds.): IWAAL 2014, LNCS 8868, pp. 369–376, 2014.
© Springer International Publishing Switzerland 2014

decline, such as forgetfulness, difficulty performing familiar tasks and disorientation regarding time and place, still place a large burden on the PwD and also their carer. Whilst in the early stages of the condition a PwD may not require physical assistance from a carer to perform a task, they may benefit from mental assistance to complete a task due to the loss of cognitive functioning. This increased reliance on others, results in a loss of their independence. PwD experience their condition as a state of forgetfulness accompanied by cognitive losses and increased dependency on others [2]. It has been long thought that this dependency on others due to forgetfulness can be negated by reminding solutions [3]. Reminding solutions have evolved from simple paper based reminders placed around the home, to ubiquitous technological solutions that can facilitate multimedia playback, in the form of audio-visual reminders [4]. Most of these reminding solutions are purely time-specific, nevertheless, recently in the wider literature base of reminding technology, an interest has emerged in creating reminding solutions that are context-aware [5]. Time-specific reminders are often delivered during inconvenient situations, such as when the user is eating, working or in a different location from the reminding device. These types of reminders can cause a person to experience stress and increased frustration, given that they feel obliged to address the alerts [6]. Consequently, context-aware reminders aim to observe these types of situations and reschedule the delivery of reminders to a more suitable time based on observed contexts.

1.1   Context Aware Reminders

Reminder systems to aid scheduling can be classified into 4 main groups, based on the type of information used to issue the reminder: (1) time-based, (2) location-based, (3) activity-based and (4) complex context-based reminder systems [5]. For PwD time-based scheduling is the most rudimentary and the most commonly implemented. NeuroPage [7] is one such example. It was designed to be used by persons with memory impairments as a result of brain injury, however, could also be used by those with progressive conditions, such as dementia. iReminder [8] is a location based reminder system that predicts a user's future location based on previous routes and issues a location specific reminder before they arrive. Activity-based reminders use detected inferred activities to trigger a reminder. Autominder [9] is an activity-based reminder robot that uses artificial intelligence techniques and quantitative temporal Bayesian networks to observe and reason about ADLs which have been performed to develop a model of an elder's typical daily plan. It then maintains and uses this model to schedule future reminders. A limitation identified from this approach is that once a given schedule is learned, it cannot be altered manually. Complex context-based reminder systems combine various other context types as part of a larger model. The COGKNOW project [10] proposed a complex context-aware system for persons with mild dementia. The architecture incorporated time, location and user activity as contexts, along with the time that the to-be-prompted activity was typically performed. The full feature set of the system was, however, not realised upon the project's close.

　　None of the aforementioned studies considered how delivery of the reminder may interrupt the user, nor did they alter the delivery based on past acknowledgment rates.

There is therefore an opportunity to develop and evaluate these missing elements with PwD who are in need of better reminding solutions. In this paper initial data collected from PwD using a context-aware reminder app is presented and considered within the context of the Technology Adoption and Usage Tool (TAUT) project [11].

2   Methods

The TAUT project is a collaborative project between Utah State University (USA), the University of Utah (USA) and the University of Ulster (UK), that is specifically focused on developing a predictive model for assistive technology adoption, specifically for PwD. To appropriately assess technology adoption a smartphone app, dubbed 'TAUT Reminders"[1], was developed for the study cohort to use. The app acts as an assistive reminder tool for activities of daily living (ADL), whilst simultaneously recording usage data for the purpose of the study [12]. The TAUT project integrates data from two large databases, the Cache County Study on Memory in Aging (CCSMA) and the Utah Population Database (UPDB) in an effort to build a user profile. The CCSMA is a longitudinal, population based study of Alzheimer's disease (AD) and other dementias, which has followed over 5,000 elderly residents of the Cache County, Utah (USA) over a period of twelve years (1995-2007) [13]. The UPDB contains genealogical, medical and demographic records, with full coverage of medical information for the past 20 years. From this integrated dataset, a subset of people showing the greatest decline in cognition, evaluated by a Modified Mini-Mental State Exam (3MS) [14], have been selected for the purpose of evaluating the predictive model for technology adoption in a pilot study for a period of 12 months. To date 28 PwD are using the TAUT Reminders app, and will be hereafter be referred to as the TAUT study cohort (TC).

2.1   Assistive Reminders

When using the app reminders can be set by the PwD, or by a proxy, such as a caregiver or family member. The reminders are time and date specific and can be configured to repeat in a daily, weekly, monthly or custom pattern. Living and caring arrangements affect each individual's use of the app. A typical use case is a PwD living independently and having their carer set an array of reminders based on their understanding of the PwD's daily routine and needs. Each reminder is delivered at the time specified and presented to the user as a popup dialog box accompanied by a picture indicating the type of ADL (6 types: Meal, Drink, Medication, Hygiene, Appointment, Other), a textual description of the ADL and a melodic tone. The user has a time window of 60 seconds in which to acknowledge the reminder, after which, the popup closes, the tone stops playing and the reminder is logged as 'missed'. If acknowledged within the 60 seconds, the reminder is logged as being 'acknowledged'

---

[1] The TAUT Reminders app is available on the Google Play store via https://play. google.com/store/apps/details?id=com.phorloop.tautreminders

and the popup closes. To provide additional functionality the ability to record audio messages has also been included. This acknowledgement data is stored locally on the device, and synchronised to a central server when internet connectivity is available

Although for the PwD the app's role is simply an assistive reminder aid, the current research aims to observe if the PwD adopts the technology, how they interact with it and if their interactions can be more meaningful and effective. A key component of this approach is to observe the contexts around the time of interaction with the device, specifically around the point in time when reminders are acknowledged or missed.

2.2   Observing Contextual Information

The app has been developed for android smartphones, and as such can utilise a variety of on-board sensors to observe and record contextual information.

Sensors. The android platform categorises its on-board sensors into 3 main categories: Motion, Positional and Environmental. The motion sensors comprise an accelerometer and gyroscope, positional sensors include a magnetic field sensor and also a proximity sensor and the environmental sensors include light, pressure and temperature sensors. Nevertheless, not all android handsets have the full range of available sensors, due to increased cost per handset. Given that identical handsets were required to be purchased for the study, taking into consideration the cost to sensor ratio, it was decided that the Motorola Moto G smartphone was an appropriate choice for the study. The Moto G is equipped with an accelerometer, magnetic field sensor, proximity sensor, light sensor and a GPS receiver chip. These sensors cover the 3 main sensor categories of the android platform and are consistent with the sensors used in similar studies [15].

Observation Window. The time period in which the reminders are scheduled to be delivered presents an opportunity to observe contextual information in a controlled window. By observing the contexts around this window it may be possible to associate certain sensor states with acknowledged or missed reminders. This study aims to utilise this association to build a model that can be used to regulate the delivery of the reminders, specifically targeting past contexts that have a high rate of acknowledgment. In this study the TAUT Reminder app has been configured to record the outputs of all available sensors 3 minutes prior to a reminder being delivered, and continues to record for 3 minutes after it has been delivered, creating a total recording time of 6 minutes. It was found that during initial beta testing of the app, that a 6 minutes window provided a good balance of contextual information, whilst keeping file size relatively low. A typical 6 minute recording from the Moto G, using all available sensors, records at approximately 130KB/min. Each sensor logs to an individual csv file, using millisecond Unix timestamps to enable synchronicity.

2.3   Study Cohorts

In addition to the TC (Median age: 91), an internal testing and evaluation cohort was formed from 6 members of the Smart Environments Research Group at the University of Ulster[2] (Median age: 27). These 6 members will hereafter be referred to as the healthy control cohort (HC). The HC installed and used the app on their personal smartphones for seven days to assist them with scheduling meals, appointments and other general ADLs. Ethical approval from the University of Ulster Research Ethics Committee (HARTIN001) and the University of Utah Institutional Review Board (FWA#00003308) was granted to engage with the HC and TC studies, respectively. The HC cohort had continual internet connectivity, via Wi-Fi or mobile data, to enable uploading of the collected data, which resulted in a complete dataset of adherence and sensor data for each user. The TC cohort, however, had extremely limited internet connectivity. Data collection was therefore performed manually via home visits. At present, 3 users from the TC cohort had a validated adherence and sensor dataset. Participants from both cohorts (HC:6, TC:3) are presented in this study.

2.4   Sensor Data Pre-processing

Each sensor recording was windowed to contain only the data prior to the reminder delivery point (approx. 3mins). For each sensor, across the entire window, 6 descriptive statistics were calculated: mean, minimum, maximum, variance, standard deviation and root square mean. For the accelerometer and magnetometer data, the signal vector magnitude (SVM) of the 3 axis signal was calculated and the descriptive statistics were extracted from this measure. In addition to the descriptive statistics, frequency analysis using the Fast Fourier Transform (FFT) algorithm was performed on the accelerometer data to glean the energy content of the signal. In total, 32 features were generated for each reminder instance. The selected features are typically used for context recognition from acceleration data as previously outlined in similar studies [16]. Using the acknowledgment data on the central server, the extracted features are labelled as acknowledged or missed for the purposes of supervised machine learning techniques.

3   Results

After pre-processing, the data produced 3 core datasets: (1) TC, (2) HC and (3) Generalised. The TC and HC datasets contain only their cohort's data respectively, and the generalised (G) dataset consolidated the data processed from both cohorts. In datasets where the class attributes (Acknowledged, Missed) were significantly imbalanced, the Synthetic Minority Oversampling TEchnique (SMOTE) was used to balance the data (Oversampling factor: TC=78.8%, HC=381%, G=98.7%). Using the 32 features calculated from the sensor data (labelled as acknowledged or missed), it was possible to train a predictive model capable of identifying if a reminder issued during certain sensor contexts will be missed or acknowledged. For each dataset a 10-fold cross validation procedure was employed for classifier training on a variety of commonly used supervised machine learning techniques. The results are presented in Table 1.

---

[2]   The Smart Environments Research Group's website is available at:
       http://scm.ulster.ac.uk/~scmresearch/SERG/

Table 1. Accuracy, precision and recall results for each classifier using data trained and tested on each dataset using 10-fold cross validation (highest is bolded). TC is TAUT study cohort dataset, HC is healthy control cohort dataset and G is the generalised dataset (TC+HC).

Classifier		G	TC	HC
C4.5 Decision Tree	Accuracy (Precision/Recall)	74.19% (0.74/0.74)	73.75% (0.74/0.74)	80.72% (0.81/0.81)
Bayesian Network	Accuracy (Precision/Recall)	73.98% (0.75/0.74)	**76.38%** (0.78/0.76)	81.93% (0.82/0.82)
Random Forrest	Accuracy (Precision/Recall)	**76.24%** (0.77/0.76)	74.67% (0.75/0.75)	**86.75%** (0.88/0.87)
K*	Accuracy (Precision/Recall)	74.41% (0.75/0.74)	72.44% (0.73/0.72)	80.12% (0.80/0.80)

The results demonstrate that Random Forest has the highest overall accuracy across the HC and G datasets, with the Bayesian network having the highest accuracy for the TC. To gain a further insight into the results, each dataset was trained and validated using the remaining datasets as test sets (refer to Table 2).

Table 2. Accuracy results for each classifier when validated across all 3 datasets (highest in bold). TC is TAUT study cohort dataset, HC is healthy control cohort dataset and G is the generalised dataset (TC+HC).

Classifier	Training	Test		
		G	TC	HC
C4.5 Decision Tree	G	82.69%	80.58%	**84.94%**
	TC	79.25%	85.56%	60.84%
	HC	53.01%	47.64%	95.78%
Bayesian Network	G	75.59%	75.07%	73.49%
	TC	**75.48%**	77.95%	65.66%
	HC	64.84%	61.42%	84.94%
Random Forrest	G	98.17%	96.98%	**96.99%**
	TC	92.47%	98.69%	69.88%
	HC	60.86%	55.77%	98.80%
K*	G	99.25%	**95.93%**	93.98%
	TC	92.80%	99.21%	71.69%
	HC	57.63%	51.31%	100.00%

It is clear that when trained on the G data the remaining datasets perform well during validation. In this case, the top 3 classifiers are: C4.5, Random Forest and K*. It is also clear that when trained using the HC dataset, the overall accuracy for the TC data is low and vice-versa. There are two possible compounding reasons for this: (1) a disparity in the number of samples, due to having only 1 week's worth of data for the HC opposed to 12 weeks for the TC, (2) a discernible difference in how the HC and TC use the smartphone device. Table 3 presents the results from testing the G trained models on individual participant's datasets, without applying SMOTE to balance their data. During individual classification, K* performs exceptionally well for all participants.

Table 3. Classifier accuracy results from unbalanced individual participant data using the generalised dataset as training set

	Classifier		
Participant	**C4.5**	**Random Forrest**	**K***
P01 (TC)	73.9%	97.6%	98.7%
P02 (TC)	98.3%	94.8%	100.0%
P03 (TC)	66.7%	66.7%	100.0%
P04 (HC)	80.0%	100.0%	100.0%
P05 (HC)	77.8%	100.0%	100.0%
P06 (HC)	100.0%	100.0%	100.0%
P07 (HC)	94.7%	100.0%	100.0%
P08 (HC)	100.0%	100.0%	100.0%
P09 (HC)	91.4%	100.0%	100.0%

4   Conclusions

From offline analysis of the data collected in the study thus far, it is apparent that it is possible to create a model to detect contexts in which reminders are typically acknowledged or missed. Using data from both cohorts weakened the accuracy of the model for the TC cohort, signifying that the TC cohort require their own non-generalised model. Future work will involve implementing the models developed from the TC data into the app, so that the reminder delivery can be altered in real-time for this cohort. Due to the TAUT app's time-sensitive properties, a context-observation window of 10 minutes, will be used prior to the scheduled reminder time to escalate or postpone reminders if the observed contexts have a strong correlation to the model. This will hopefully improve the efficacy of each reminder that is issued by improving adherence to the reminders, which should ultimately improve, even if only marginally, the quality of life for its users.

Acknowledgements. The Alzheimer's Association is acknowledged for supporting the TAUT project under the research grant ETAC-12-242841. The authors also wish to acknowledge the funding support from the Department of Education and Learning, Northern Ireland.

References

1. Guerchet, M., Prina, M., Prince, M.: Policy Brief for Heads of Government: The Global Impact of Dementia 2013–2050 (2013), http://www.alz.co.uk/research/G8-policy-brief
2. Mazaheri, M., Eriksson, L.E., Heikkilä, K., Nasrabadi, A.N., Ekman, S.-L., Sunvisson, H.: Experiences of living with dementia: qualitative content analysis of semi-structured interviews. J. Clin. Nurs. 22, 3032–3041 (2013)
3. Mason, S., Craig, D., O'Neill, S., Donnelly, M., Nugent, C.: Electronic reminding technology for cognitive impairment. Br. J. Nurs. 21, 855–861

4. O'Neill, S., Mason, S., Parente, G., Donnelly, M., Nugent, C., McClean, S., Scotney, B., Craig, D.: Video Reminders as Cognitive Prosthetics for People with Dementia. Ageing Int. 36, 267–282 (2011)
5. Zhou, S., Chu, C.-H., Yu, Z., Kim, J.: A context-aware reminder system for elders based on fuzzy linguistic approach. Expert Syst. Appl. 39, 9411–9419 (2012)
6. Mark, G., Gudith, D., Klocke, U.: The cost of interrupted work: more speed and stress. In: Proc. SIGCHI Conf. ..., pp. 8–11 (2008)
7. Hersh, N., Treadgold, L.: Neuropage: The rehabilitation of memory dysfunction by prosthetic memory and cueing. NeuroRehabilitation 4, 187–197 (1994)
8. Tu, Y., Chen, L., Lv, M., Ye, Y., Huang, W., Chen, G.: iReminder: An Intuitive Location-Based Reminder That Knows Where You Are Going. Int. J. Hum. Comput. Interact. 29, 838–850 (2013)
9. Pollack, M., Brown, L., Colbry, D.: Autominder: An intelligent cognitive orthotic system for people with memory impairment. Rob. Auton. Syst., 1–10 (2003)
10. Zhang, D., Hariz, M., Mokhtari, M.: Assisting Elders with Mild Dementia Staying at Home. In: 2008 Sixth Annu. IEEE Int. Conf. Pervasive Comput. Commun., pp. 692–697 (2008)
11. Zhang, S., McClean, S.I., Nugent, C.D., Donnelly, M.P., Galway, L., Scotney, B.W., Cleland, I.: A predictive model for assistive technology adoption for people with dementia. IEEE J. Biomed. Heal. informatics 18, 375–383 (2014)
12. Hartin, P.J., Nugent, C.D., McClean, S.I., Cleland, I., Norton, M.C., Sanders, C., Tschanz, J.T.: A smartphone application to evaluate technology adoption and usage in persons with dementia. In: Conference proceedings: Annual International Conference of the IEEE Engineering in Medicine and Biology Society, Chicago, pp. 5389–5392 (2014)
13. Tschanz, J.T., Norton, M.C., Zandi, P.P., Lyketsos, C.G.: The Cache County Study on Memory in Aging: factors affecting risk of Alzheimer's disease and its progression after onset. Int. Rev. Psychiatry. 25, 673–685 (2013)
14. Tschanz, J.T., Welsh-Bohmer, K.A., Plassman, B.L., Norton, M.C., Wyse, B.W., Breitner, J.C.S., Group, T.C.C.S.: An Adaptation of the Modified Mini-Mental State Examination: Analysis of Demographic Influences and Normative Data: The Cache County Study. Cogn. Behav. Neurol. 15 (2002)
15. Poppinga, B., Heuten, W., Boll, S.: Sensor-Based Identification of Opportune Moments for Triggering Notifications. IEEE Pervasive Comput. 13, 22–29 (2014)
16. Figo, D., Diniz, P.C., Ferreira, D.R., Cardoso, J.M.P.: Preprocessing techniques for context recognition from accelerometer data. Pers. Ubiquitous Comput. 14, 645–662 (2010)

A Collaborative System for Designing Tele-Therapies

Arturo C. Rodríguez[1], Cristina Roda[1],
Francisco Montero[2], Pascual González[2], and Elena Navarro[2]

[1] Instituto de Investigación en Informática de Albacete (I3A), Albacete, Spain
{art.c.rodriguez,cristinarodasanchez}@gmail.es
[2] Computing Systems Department, University of Castilla-La Mancha, Albacete, Spain
{fmontero,pgonzalez,enavarro}@dsi.uclm.es

Abstract. Nowadays, the progressive aging of the population in developed countries is becoming a problem for health systems, which must invest more and more money to care their citizens. One of the most important issues are those derived of the physical and cognitive problems associated to the elderly. In order to reduce the effect of these problems, therapists have to design therapies that should be adapted to each person. To assist therapists in this design process, we have created a new system that allows them to create and manage specific therapies in a collaborative and efficiency way. In addition, the elderly can use this system to carry out their treatment at home thanks to the developed intelligent system that can control the effectiveness of their treatment.

Keywords: Gerontechnology, telerehabilitation, intelligent system, collaborative system.

1 Introduction

Nowadays, the progressive aging of the population in developed countries is becoming a problem for health systems, which must invest more and more money to care their citizens [1]. Moreover, the European Commission Information Society and Media [2] suggests that, "the way healthcare is presently delivered has to be deeply reformed. The situation is becoming unsustainable and will only worsen in the future as chronic diseases and the demographic change place additional strains on healthcare systems around Europe." the European Commission calls for a "new healthcare delivery model based on preventative and person-centered health systems. This new model can only be achieved through proper use of Information and Telecommunication Technologies (ICT), in combination with appropriate organizational changes and skills".

Gerontechnology [3] is an interdisciplinary field of scientific research in which technology is directed towards the aspirations and opportunities of the elderly. This field of science aims at good health, full social participation and independent living up to a high age. In order to achieve it, research, developments as well as design of products and services are being defined to increase the quality of life of the elderly.

L. Pecchia et al. (Eds.): IWAAL 2014, LNCS 8868, pp. 377–385, 2014.

In the area of rehabilitation, there are two different strategies for developing geron-technology-based support systems. The first one makes use of specialized hardware to aid the elderly in their recovery [4]. Although these proposals could be designed to solve each concrete problem more efficiently, they are not designed for general proposals, but they are used by final user directly and their cost is usually higher. The other strategy makes use of general purposed devices, mainly depth sensors like Microsoft Kinect [5][6], to control the rehabilitation therapies. In general, there are two alternatives to carry out the rehabilitation task: (i) in a controlled space with the assistance of the therapist or (ii) at home so that the elderly work on their own. The second alternative can be called *telerehabilitation* because of the need of using ICT [710]. These telerehabilitation systems should use general purposes devices that can be easily installed and managed directly by a user that could have some cognitive problems derived from his/her age.

Therefore, in order to design these telerehabilitation systems, it is necessary to take into account that they are to be managed (i) by the elderly that may have some physical and/or cognitive problems and (ii) without the direct presence of therapists. The first restriction imposes the use of usability and accessibility guidance in its design. The second restriction enforces the development of some kind of automatic system during the execution of the therapies. In addition, this system should allow the therapists to define the rules that control the therapies execution. To address these needs, we have created a new collaborative design system that assists the therapists with the design of the therapies as well as a self-control system for managing and organizing the therapies execution.

The rest of the paper is structured as follows. After this introduction, in Section 2, some of the most relevant works in the area of assistive technology are analyzed. Then, in Section 3 the developed system is presented. Finally, the conclusions and future work are described in Section 4.

2   Assistive Technologies for Tele-Therapy

Many elderly people' motor impairment problems improve with a rehabilitation program specifically designed and monitored by therapists. Although the use of specific devices to control the patient's movements is not necessary when the therapist assists in the rehabilitation session, their use can help him/her to control such movements.

The telerehabilitation systems are not new. As Brennan et al. stated [8] the first systems were created as a proof of concept. They tried to demonstrate that patients, physically located in remote locations, could be provided with some rehabilitation assessment and treatment techniques by using just the telephone for their monitoring [9]. As communication technologies advanced, new video-conference capabilities were included [10]. These advances are also facilitating the development of more complex functions. The great majority of published work focuses on the clinical application of a specific technology to offer a remote rehabilitation service [11]. Winters [12] have identified four different categories of remote rehabilitation services:

- *Teleconsultation* is a standard "face-to-face" telemedicine model that uses interactive videoconference between a local provider (patient) and a remote rehabilitation expert.
- *Telehomecare* is defined as service delivery that allows a clinician (usually a nurse or technician) to coordinate services with a low-to-moderate bandwidth interactive connection.
- *Telemonitoring* is the clinical application wherein the rehabilitation provider sets up unobtrusive monitoring or assessment technology for the client (patient).
- *Teletherapy* is defined as a model of telerehabilitation service delivery wherein the client conducts therapeutic activities (such as exercise) at home using a therapy remotely managed by a therapist.

Recently, the field of physical therapy design has achieved a great relevance because new devices, like Wii or Microsoft Kinect, facilitate the control of complex user gestures. Moreover, some studies have shown that these devices have results similar other devices, like OptiTrack [13], much more expensive. There are several works [14][15][16] that use MS Kinect to manage teletherapy tasks related to physical rehabilitation. Although it is not usual that these systems provide therapists with the possibility of creating their own therapies, we can find some exceptions. For instance, Oliver et al. [6] propose a system that allows the therapist to define concrete tasks related to physical exercises that are controlled by MS Kinect. However, these elemental tasks cannot be easily linked with others to create therapies that are more complex. Another example is the system presented by Pirovano et al. [17] that allows the therapist to adapt several parameters of the game to the specific user needs. In addition, the therapist can define the criteria of success and failure depending on the patient. Unfortunately, this system does not allow defining activities not related to previously created games. HABITAT [18] and APADYT [19] are also telerehabilitation systems that enable therapists to create new types of physical and cognitive therapies but the customization parameters are prefixed.

As can be noticed, there are a high number of systems for controlling the execution of motor rehabilitation tele-therapies. However, these systems do not offer a flexible system that provides therapist with support to design new therapies or to adapt them to each specific person. Moreover, despite providing facilities to control the execution of one exercise, these systems do not control the execution of more complex therapy as those applied usually by the therapists in their daily work [20]. This work was developed to address these shortcomings.

3   A Collaborative and Natural System to Design and Monitor Complex Tele-Therapies

In order to address the shortcomings detected in the current systems, we have created a system that has a collaborative environment where several therapists can work together to define complex therapies. This environment has been designed to interact in a natural way and therapies can be visualized, documented, specified and developed by a group of therapist. For these goals, collaboration and natural interaction, Microsoft PixelSense is used to define therapies and MS Kinect to define concrete physical rehabilitation tasks that the therapies can use. In the following sections a description of the main design features and a detail of the collaborative design environment are presented.

Fig. 1. Therapy and treatment metamodel

3.1 Therapies and Treatments Design

One of the main goals of our proposal is to define a metamodel that allows therapists to design therapies for specific patients in order to provide them with an individualized treatment (see Fig. 1). Therefore, this metamodel must be flexible enough to define complex relationships between the different activities and tasks that involve a therapy.

Some of the most important concepts included in this metamodel are the following. *Therapy* entity is defined as a set of activities or exercises to rehabilitate a specific physical impairment. Each *Activity* can be divided into elemental tasks, *Task*, which are those tasks that can be either controlled by the MS Kinect or informative. In addition, sometimes it is useful to define some task aggregation (*TaskGroup*) in order to manage situations more general such as the initial phase of a concrete activity.

Fig. 2 shows a concrete description of a specific *Activity* of a *Therapy*. As can be observed, it is important to define some conditions (*TransitionGuard*) to control the transition between different *Task*, *TaskGroup*, *Activity* or *Therapy*. In order to manage all these elements, we have used compound states state-machine diagrams to control the transition between each type of element.

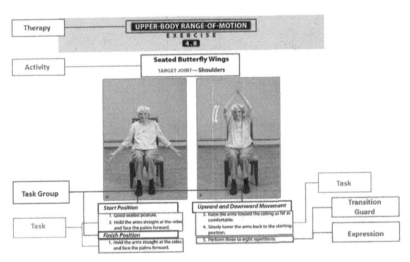

Fig. 2. Example of a physical activity (adapted from [20])

Fig. 3 presents the model associated to the therapy shown in Fig. 2. Finally, therapists assign a *Treatment* to a *Patient* and this treatment contains several therapies. Our model also allows defining specific rules to control the transition between therapies that compound the treatment.

3.2 Supporting Collaboration in the Specification of Therapies

As aforementioned, the collaborative system presented in this work has been developed for its use with MS PixelSense. This environment allows therapists to create a treatment from scratch using *tagged objects*, that is, physical objects marked with a dot pattern called *tag*. For instance, Figure 4 shows one of these objects placed on the MS PixelSense to create a task. Currently, four different types of tags can be used to design a treatment each one associated to one of the main elements of the metamodel described in Fig. 1, that is, there are tags for *Therapy*, *Activity*, *TaskGroup* and *Task*. In this manner, the therapist is able to create as many elements as needed only by dropping the specific tag on the MS PixelSense. In addition, therapists can define transitions between two elements just by tapping and holding the source element, and doing a drag and drop movement towards the target one. These transitions include conditions that the therapist can customize in order to establish when a transition from one element to another can be done.

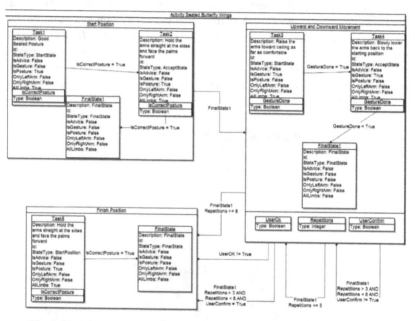

Fig. 3. Model of the Exercise 4.8 of the upper body range of motion therapy

Fig. 4. Snapshot of the user interface to define a therapy

The *Treatment* is defined as a compound state (see Fig. 3) where the outermost level is the patient doing the treatment, followed by the scenarios associated with the therapies that compound such treatment, later the scenarios associated with the activities within a concrete therapy, then the groups of tasks within a particular activity, and finally, the tasks belonging to a group of tasks. Notice that every element is created with a size proportional to the elements that it contains. If its size is too small, the application will allow user to zoom in to improve its visualization and see its nested structure in a suitable manner. This zoom can be done in a natural way by means of a pinch movement, such as in most touch devices.

Furthermore, every element considered in the metamodel (*Therapy*, *Activity*, *TaskGroup* and *Task*) has its own control variables, such as number of repetitions, percentage of success or time that can be used to establish under what conditions a transition to another element must be done. On the other hand, the system also uses MS Kinect to define concrete physical rehabilitation tasks, such as the ones associated with positions, gestures and suggestions/comments. Specifically, during the definition of a treatment, therapists can create tasks by capturing their own position and/or gestures in front of the MS Kinect device. In this way, they are able to specify, control and assess how these tasks should be performed by patients and the precision level of them.

4 Conclusions and Future Works

In this paper, a new system for creating therapies using a collaborative and natural user interface has been presented. This system allows therapists to visualize, specify, document and create their own therapies from scratch, by defining the concrete tasks, group of tasks and activities that each patient should carry out for his/her specific treatment.

By using this system, therapies are defined as a composition of several interrelated scenarios where the patient is doing physical rehabilitation postures and gestures, with a specific flow among them. In addition, these elemental rehabilitation tasks (positions and gestures), are identified by using a MS Kinect device. Finally, thanks to its user interface of this system, therapists can define treatments in an efficient way by using tagged objects, multimodal (voice and tactile) interaction and direct manipulation of specific rehabilitation elements.

Acknowledgements. This work was partially supported by Spanish Ministerio de Economía y Competitividad / FEDER under TIN2012-34003 grant and through the FPU scholarship (FPU12/04962) from the Spanish Government.

References

1. Costa, A., Castillo, J.C., Novais, P., Fernández-Caballero, A., Simoes, R.: Sensor-driven agenda for intelligent home care of the elderly. Situations 39(15), 12192–12204 (2012)
2. European Commission Information Society and Media, ICT for Health and i2010: Transforming the European healthcare landscape towards a strategy for ICT for Health, Luxembourg, 10, ISBN 92-894-7060-7 (2006)

3. Harrington, T.L., Harrington, M.K.: Gerontechnology: Why and How. Shaker Publishing BV (2000)
4. Schónauer, C., Pintaric, T., Kaufmann, H., Jansen-Kosterink, S., Vollenbroek-Hutten, M.: Chronic pain rehabilitation with a serious game using multimodal input. In: International Conference on Virtual Rehabilitation, pp. 1–8 (2011)
5. Chang, Y., Chen, S., Huang, J.: A Kinect-based system for physical rehabilitation: A pilot study for young adults with motor disabilities. Research in Developmental Disabilities 32(6), 2566–2570 (2011)
6. Oliver, M., Molina, J.P., Montero, F., González, P., Fernández-Caballero, A.: Wireless multisensory interaction in an intelligent rehabilitation environment. In: Ramos, C., Novais, P., Nihan, C.E., Corchado Rodríguez, J.M. (eds.) Advances in Intelligent Systems and Computing. AISC, vol. 291, pp. 193–200. Springer, Heidelberg (2014)
7. Brennan, D., Tindall, L., Theodoros, D., Brown, J., Campbell, M., Christiana, D., Smith, D., Cason, J., Lee, A.: A blueprint for telerehabilitation guidelines. International Journal of telerehabilitation 2, 31–34 (2010)
8. Brennan, D.M., Mawson, S., Brownsell, S.: Telerehabilitation: enabling the remote delivery of healthcare, rehabilitation, and self-management. Stud. Health. Technol. Inform. 145, 231–248 (2009)
9. Vaughn, G.R.: Tel-communicology: health-care delivery system for persons with communicative disorders. ASHA 18(1), 13–17 (1976)
10. Brennan, D., Georgeadis, A., Baron, C., Barker, L.: The effect of videoconference-based telerehab on story retelling performance by brain injured subjects and its implications for remote speech-language therapy. Telemedicine Journal and e-Health 10(2), 147–154 (2004)
11. Parmanto, B., Saptono, A.: Telerehabilitation: state-of-the-art from an informatics perspective. International Journal of Telerehabilitation 1(1), 73–84 (2009)
12. Winters, J.M.: Telerehabilitation research: Emerging opportunities. Annual Review of Biomedical Engineering 4, 287–320 (2002)
13. Chang, C., Lange, B., Zhang, M., Koenig, S., Requejo, P., Somboon, N., Sawchuk, A., Rizzo, A.: Towards pervasive physical rehabilitation using Microsoft Kinect. In: 6th International Conference on Pervasive Computing Technologies for Healthcare, pp. 1–4 (2012)
14. Chang, Y.J., Chen, S.F., Huang, J.D.: A Kinect-based system for physical rehabilitation: A pilot study for young adults with motor disabilities. Research in developmental disabilities 32(6), 2566–2570 (2011)
15. Davaasambuu, E., Chiang, C., Chiang, J., Chen, Y., Bilgee, S.: A Microsoft Kinect based virtual rehabilitation system. In: 5th International Conference on Frontiersof Information Technology, Applications and Tools, pp. 44–50 (2012)
16. Da Gama, A., Chaves, T., Figueiredo, L., Teichrieb, V.: Improving motor rehabilitation process through a natural interaction based system using Kinect sensor. In: 2012 IEEE Symposium on 3D User Interfaces, pp. 145–146 (2012)
17. Pirovano, M., Mainetti, R., Baud-Bovy, G., Lanzi, P., Borghese, N.: Self-adaptive games for rehabilitation at home. In: IEEE Conference on Computational Intelligence and Games, pp. 179–186 (2012)
18. Rubio, G., Navarro, E., Montero, F.: APADYT: a multimedia application for SEN learners. Multimed. Tools Appl. 71, 1771–1802 (2014)

19. Montero, F., López-Jaquero, V., Navarro, E., Sánchez, E.: Computer-aided relearning activity patterns for people with acquired brain injury. Comput. Educ. 57, 1149–1159 (2011)
20. Best-Martini, E., Jones-DiGenova, K.: Exercise for Frail Elders. Human Kinetics (2014) ISBN: 9781450416092
21. Microsoft PixelSense. Welcome to Microsoft PixelSense (2012), http://www.microsoft.com/en-us/pixelsense/default.aspx

A High-Level Model for a Healthy Smart City

Gabriel Urzaiz[1], Ramón Hervás[2], Jesús Fontecha[2], and José Bravo[2]

[1] Universidad Anahuac Mayab, Merida, Yucatan, Mexico
gabriel.urzaiz@anahuac.mx
[2] Universidad de Castilla-La Mancha, Ciudad Real, Spain
{ramon.hlucas,jesus.fontecha,jose.bravo}@uclm.es

Abstract. This short paper presents a high-level model aimed to obtain uniform functionality and performance of the services provided within a healthy smart city. The model is based on a three-layer architecture and uses an overlay network to provide enhanced network and semantic functionality. This is a novel approach that incorporates the use of health-related data coming from different information sources to provide smart health services along the city.

Keywords: healthy smart cities, Internet of Things, IoT.

1 Introduction

A smart city is a place in which modern Information and Communication Technology (ICT) is used to support economic development and a high quality of life with a wise management of natural resources. Cities need to evolve towards intelligent dynamic infrastructures that serve citizens fulfilling the criteria of energy efficiency and sustainability [1].

Smart cities can be ranked along six axes or dimensions [2]: regional competitiveness, transport and ICT economics, natural resources, human and social capital, quality of life, and participation of citizens in the governance of cities. Health services in a city contribute to several of these dimensions, especially to quality of life and regional competitiveness.

Wireless Sensor Networks (WSN) is commonly used to implement a smart city, by helping to create a distributed network of intelligent sensor nodes which can measure many parameters of the city.

There are also more complicated approaches to validate and complement the information coming from the city sensors. Those solutions are based on Online Collaborative Sensor Data Management (OCSDM) platforms, such as the Wikisensing platform [4]. The main idea here is to use on-line database services that allow sensor owners to register and connect their devices to feed data into an online database for storage and to connect to the database and build their own applications based on that data.

There is a wide range of current solutions monitoring a wide variety of city parameters, such as vehicle traffic, road surface temperature and noise, CO_2 emissions [5] among others. However, it is not common to find a solution which includes biometric or other parameters related to a health smart city service.

L. Pecchia et al. (Eds.): IWAAL 2014, LNCS 8868, pp. 386–389, 2014.

Health also involves several participants, such as the patient, the caregiver, the physician, the hospital, the drugstore, the ambulances, etc. We've been working to provide a comprehensive solution [3] to integrate all these participants into a single platform to collaborate, and we are now focused on taking advantage of the smart city concept in order to consistently extend the solution to urban dimensions.

The Mexican state of Yucatan has a strategic location and high quality services, which have allowed Merida, the capital city, to be positioned as the hub for medical services in the Yucatan Peninsula [6], generating a huge window of opportunities for the provision of services and manufacturing of products related to the health sector.

Yucatán currently has health institutions, both public and private, using the best technologies and offer the highest quality care services, whose services are much cheaper than similar services offered in the United States, Canada and Europe. The Yucatan government is currently promoting a project of medical tourism [7], where foreign patients can benefit not only from recognized professional medical services at moderate cost, but also can see benefit of warm weather, the natural beauty, cultural wealth and high quality of life, taking advantage of the same benefits of the status and growth in demand for services by older adults, it is driving the housing industry, care and services for 50 years old people and older, already an attractive destination for retirees segment Canadians and Americans.

2   Model Description

The primary objective of the proposed model is to provide a structure for a healthy smart city to enhance the quality of life of patients and caregivers, and to achieve a regional competitive advantage by allowing that any patient who is within the city limits is continuously monitored and supported by all the people and services that he or she needs at any time.

Quality of services in different parts of the city can vary significantly. Our strategy to assess the proposed model is based on the effectiveness to provide the same functionality and performance regardless of the physical location where the user is located, provided that it is within the smart city boundaries.

The model is based on a three-layer architecture (Fig. 1), and includes an input side and a user side. The input side is located at the bottom of the model. It considers several types of information sources. One of the most important inputs is the patient real-time data sent by biometric and specialized sensors (such as the alarms of an automatic medication dispenser, location, etc.). Other important input is the real-time data from services mobile sensors (such as the location or availability of an ambulance, caregivers or physicians). It is also considered the real-time input from services fixed sensors (hospitals availability, drugstore inventory, etc.). It is important to say that input may include several forms of information, such as data-streams, images, audio or video, coming from different sensors and devices which are probably connected using different communication standards and technologies through a city-wide heterogeneous network. The input is finally complemented by the information coming from a historical and statistical information database.

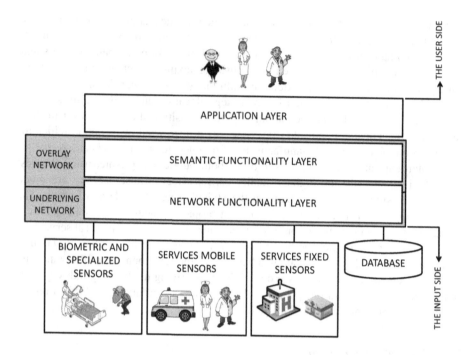

Fig. 1. The model architecture

The user side is located at the top of the model and it is designed to provide a front end interface to all the people that need information of the system, such as the caregiver and the patient relatives, the physicians, the hospitals, etc.

The network functionality layer is mainly used to provide enhanced connectivity services. This layer is capable to find the best communication path based on Quality-of-Service (QoS) specifications, and to determine dynamic alternate routes when needed. These features are not commonly part of the underlying layer, but they must be included in the model due to the fact that human life is involved. The way to do so is by using an overlay network to provide the needed additional functionality.

The overlay network is also used to implement the semantic functionality layer, which is responsible for providing other important features such as the automatic responses or actions in case of routine decisions that do not need any human intervention (automatic call to an ambulance, automatic drug reorder, etc.), online user collaboration, data analysis foundation, etc.

The application layer provides a user interface, and it is also responsible for the control and the management of the information and the users. This layer provides a number of Application Program Interface (API) web services to be used by external applications to get relevant information coming from one or more inputs, and/or to perform actions and responses as needed.

3   Conclusions and Work in Progress

A high-level model has been proposed to be used as a guide for the Mexican city of Mérida to become a healthy smart city. This model could also be adapted for other cities in the world.

We are currently working on the development of all the model components.

References

1. Pellicer, S., Santa, G., Bleda, A.L., Maestre, R., Jara, A.J., Skarmeta, G.: A Global Perspective of Smart Cities: A Survey. In: 2013 Seventh International Conference on Innovative Mobile and Internet Services in Ubiquitous Computing (IMIS), pp. 439–444 (2013), doi:10.1109/IMIS.2013.79
2. Smart cities. Ranking of European medium-sized cities. Final report. Edited by the Centre of Regional Science, Vienna UT, http://www.smart-cities.eu/download/ smart_cities_final_report.pdf (Date consulted: June 9, 2014) (retrieved)
3. Urzaiz, G., Murillo, E., Arjona, S., Hervas, R., Fontecha, J., Bravo, J.: An Integral Medicine Taking Solution for Mild and Moderate Alzheimer Patients. In: Nugent, C., Coronato, A., Bravo, J. (eds.) IWAAL 2013. LNCS, vol. 8277, pp. 104–111. Springer, Heidelberg (2013)
4. Silva, D., Ghanem, M., Guo, Y.: WikiSensing: An Online Collaborative Approach for Sensor Data Management. Sensors 12(12), 13295 (2012), doi:10.3390/s121013295
5. Butgereit, L., Nickless, A.: Capturing, Calculating, and Disseminating Real-Time CO2 Emissions and CO2 Flux Measurements via Twitter in a Smart City. In: Green Computing and Communications (GreenCom), 2013 IEEE and Internet of Things (iThings/CPSCom), IEEE International Conference on and IEEE Cyber, Physical and Social Computing, pp. 2013–2017 (2013), doi:10.1109/GreenCom-iThings-CPSCom.2013.377
6. OECD. Estudios territoriales de la OCDE: Yucatán, México 2007, Fundación Plan Estratégico de Mérida, A.C., Mexico (2008) ISBN 9789264062122, doi:10.1787/ 9789264062122-es
7. http://www.sefoe.yucatan.gob.mx/esp/oportunidades/medicodescr ipcion.php (Date consulted June 4, 2014)

Analytic Hierarchy Process for Determining the Most Important Factors to Empower Elderly People in Taking an Active Role in Their Health: Study Design

Giuseppe Fico[1], Maria Teresa Arredondo[1], Estibaliz Gamboa Moreno[2],
Lourdes Ochoa de Retana García[2], Manuel Serrano-Gil[3], Nicola Cornally[4],
and William Molloy[4]

[1] Life Supporting Technologies Group, Universidad Politécnica de Madrid, Spain
[2] Department of Health of the Basque Country, Basque Country, Spain
[3] Global Alliance for Self Management Support, Murcia, Spain
[4] Centre of Gerontology and Rehabilitation, University College Cork, Ireland
*Members of the European Innovation Partnership on Active and Healthy Aging,
Adherence to Treatment, Action group A1*
{gfico,mta}@lst.tfo.upm.es,
{estibaliz.gamboamoreno,
lourdes.ochoaderetanagarcia}@osakidetza.net,
manuel.serrano@globalalliancesms.org,
{n.cornally,w.molloy}@ucc.ie

Abstract. Adherence to treatment in elderly citizens is influenced by multiple factors. In order to achieve effective results, a patient-centred approach is needed, focused on empowering citizens to take an active role in their care. Despite the information available in literature, gathering the experience of relevant healthcare stakeholders that are active in this field could be useful for understanding which are the most important factors to take into account for having an activated patient that adheres to a treatment agreed and produced together with a proactive and prepared care team. This paper presents the preliminary results of a study aiming to use the Analytic Hierarchy Process (AHP) to elicit user needs and to identify these factors.

Keywords: Elderly People, Patient Activation, Empowerment, Analytic Hierarchy Process, User Requirements.

1   Introduction

Adherence can be defined as "the extent to which a person's behaviour - taking medication, following a diet, and/or executing lifestyle changes, - corresponds with agreed recommendations from a health care provider" (World of Health Organization, 2003) 1. Adherence behaviour is influenced by a wide array of factors, such as social/economic factors, factors related to the health system, condition-related factors, therapy-related factors and patient related factors 1. The primary challenge in treating chronically ill patients is to improve adherence to the treatment, a worldwide issue of striking magnitude. This is especially true for the ageing population where multi-morbidity is a common condition. The presence of multiple chronic conditions also

L. Pecchia et al. (Eds.): IWAAL 2014, LNCS 8868, pp. 390–393, 2014.
© Springer International Publishing Switzerland 2014

makes it more challenging for patients to participate effectively in their own care. Few strategies exist that proved effectiveness across all disease, patients and situations 1. **A patient-centred approach**, which tailors interventions to the specific characteristics of a patient, seems a more promising strategy to improve adherence behaviour. The lack of patients' information and skills to self-manage their problems with motivation and the difficulties to adopt and maintain behavioural changes, appear to be among the main barriers to adherence reported in the literature. Different methodologies, techniques and technologies exist to empower +65 citizens and patients to be responsible for their health and improve their adherence to plans. Literature in the field can provide useful systematic reviews and insights, but this information [...] could be complemented by collecting experiences resulting from in situ experiences that healthcare stakeholders that are not always active in the scientific dissemination of their daily activities can transmit. The European Innovation Partnership on Active and Healthy Ageing (EIP-AHA, 2) initiative represent an opportunity to carry out such kind of activity. The study described in this paper delineates the work done by a group of healthcare actors, working together in the EIP-AHA, to identify the most important elements to take into account, when empowering elderly users, in different diseases and situations, to be "activated" and establish "productive interactions with a proactive and prepared care team". For this study, we identified outcomes and then created an initial hierarchy of needs that can be used by developers and human computer interaction experts in the system design.

2   Materials and Methods

2.1   The EIP-AHA

The EIP-AHA is the first pilot of the European Innovation Public-Private Partnerships (PPP), proposed in the Europe 2020 Strategy, to tackle innovation barriers for major societal issues. The EIP-AHA aims to identify and remove persisting barriers to innovation for active and healthy ageing, through interdisciplinary and cross-sectorial approaches. The work is structured in three pillars, A: Prevention, screening and early diagnosis; B: Care and cure and C: active ageing and independent living. Under pillar A, Action on "Prescription and adherence action at regional level", the Action Group A1 on "Adherence to treatment" brings together partners representing more than 60 multi-stakeholder commitments from national, regional and local authorities, research centres, academia, industry, enterprises and existing consortiums across the EU. This group is currently working in four thematic areas: adherence, polypharmacy, research methodologies and user empowerment. One of the collaborative works currently carried out, in the user empowerment area, is called "ICT Empowerer Toolkit": the aim is to collect information about the most important elements to take into account to create an activated patient, establishing productive interactions with a proactive and prepared care team. Information will be collected for healthy citizens, dependent and independent patients. The final result will be a matrix of technological interventions that can be used to support whoever is working in the creation of tools to activate (empower)elderly population in their living environments.

2.2   The AHP, the concepts of Patient Activation and Proactive Interactions

The Chronic Care Model 3 (CCM) emphasizes patient-oriented care with proactive management of health and collaboration, with patients and families integrated as members of the care team. There are two critical elements of this model: 1) "An activated patient is a person who has the confidence and skills to engage in a process of shared decision making and take a proactive role in the management of his/her own health" 3. 2) "Productive Interactions aim at improving patient outcomes by a) reviewing data related with patients' perspectives and critical information about the management of the condition; b) help patients to set goals and solve problems for improved self-management; c) apply clinical and behavioural interventions; d) ensure continuous follow-up" 3. We are using the Analytic Hierarchy Process (AHP) 4 to elicit requirements about the most important needs and interventions to take into account to create an ACTIVATED PATIENT and a PROACTIVE and PREPARED CARE TEAM. The AHP provides a framework for structuring a decision problem, for representing and quantifying its elements, for relating those elements to overall goals. Users of the AHP first decompose their decision problem into a hierarchy of more easily comprehended sub-problems. Once the hierarchy is built, the decision makers evaluate its elements by performing pairwise comparisons. This method has proven to be effective in medical decision-making and in user requirements 6 7. In the Case of ACTIVATION we took, as a starting point, the Patient Activation Measure instrument 5, to create a hierarchy around the concepts of: 1) Belief, 2) Knowledge and Confidence, 3) Taking Action and 4) Maintaining Behaviours. In the case of PROACTIVE and PREPARED CARE TEAM, the tree of needs has been created by the experts, starting from the definition given by the CCM. The trees have been analyzed and completed by three couple of experts (from primary care, regional public health authority and geriatric secondary care units), analyzing them separately for 1) Healthy Subjects, 2) Independent Patients and 3) Dependent Patients.

3   Results

The resulting trees are presented in Table 1 and Table 2. For space limitation, we present only the main categories and some example for each subcategory. Questionnaires have been developed and will be piloted within the user empowerment team members (n>=30).

4   Discussion

This paper proposed a method to extract requirements in a comprehensive way, to design interventions for older population basing on available scientific evidence and pragmatic experiences, through the AHP. This information will be validated by members of the EIP-AHA to define a matrix of technological interventions to support those who are creating tools to activate elderly people.

Table 1. Categories and Subcategories to Activate elderly people

Goal	CATEGORIES	SUBCATEGORIES
ACTIVATING ELDERLY PEOPLE	*BELIEF*	Being responsible for managing health condition
		Taking an active role to determine health
	CONFIDENCE AND KNOWLEDGE TO TAKE ACTIONS	Ability to tell concerns to the healthcare provider
		How emotions influence one own condition.
	TAKING ACTION	Ability to maintain lifestyles changes
		How preventing problems with one condition
	STAYING THE COURSE UNDER STRESS	maintain lifestyle changes during times of stress
		handle problems on one's health condition at home

Table 2. Categories and Subcategories to have a proactive and prepared care team

Goal	CATEGORIES	SUBCATEGORIES
PROACTIVE AND PREPARED CARE TEAM	*REVIEW DATA AND MANAGE CONDITION*	Access to an integrated view of the clinical data
	APPLY CLINICAL AND BEHAVIOURAL INTERVENTION	Knowledge of clinical guidelines and EBP
		Incentives are given to health professionals.
	CONTINUOUS FOLLOW-UP	Explore remote monitoring actions
		To establish different pathways within the HCS.

Acknowledgement. This work is partially funded by the European Commission under the MOSAIC project (Grant Agreement 600914). The authors wish to thank the EIP-AHA members for their contributions.

References

1. WHO. Adherence to Long-Term Therapies. Evidence for Action. Geneva: WHO 2003, http://who.int (accessed June 17, 2014)
2. EIP-AHA, official web page, http://ec.europa.eu/research/innovation-union/index_en.cfm?section=active-healthy-ageing (accessed June 27, 2014)
3. Wagner, E., et al.: The Milbank Quarterly. Organizing Care for Patients with Chronic Illness 74(4), 511–544 (1996)
4. Saaty, T.L.: A scaling method for priorities in hierarchical structures. Journal of Mathematical Psychology 15(8) (1977)
5. Hibbard, J.H., Stockard, J., et al.: Development of the Patient Activation Measure (PAM): Conceptualizing and Measuring Activation in Patients and Consumers. Health Serv. Res. 39(4 pt 1), 1005–1026 (2000), doi:10.1111/j.1475-6773.2004.00269.x
6. Pecchia, L., et al.: User needs elicitation via analytic hierarchy process (AHP). A case study on a Computed Tomography (CT) scanner. BMC Med. Inform. Decis. Mak. 13, 2 (2013)
7. Pecchia, L., et al.: Analytic Hierarchy Process (AHP) for Examining Healthcare Professionals' Assessments of Risk Factors The Relative Importance of Risk Factors for Falls in Community-dwelling Older People. Methods Inf. Med. 50(5), 435–444 (2011)

Quality of Life Tools to Inform Co-design in the Development of Assistive Technologies for People with Dementia and Their Carers

Michael P. Craven[1,3], Maria Laura De Filippis[2,3], and Tom Dening[2,3]

[1] The University of Nottingham, Electrical Systems & Optics Research Division,
Faculty of Engineering, University Park, Nottingham NG7 2RD, UK
[2] The University of Nottingham, Division of Psychiatry and Applied Psychology,
The Institute of Mental Health, Jubilee Campus, Nottingham, NG7 2TU, UK
[3] NIHR MindTech Healthcare Technology Co-operative, The Institute of Mental Health,
Jubilee Campus, Nottingham, NG7 2TU, UK
{michael.craven,maria.de_filippis,tom.dening}@nottingham.ac.uk

Abstract. A number of tools exist to measure quality of life (QoL) for people with dementia (PwD). A selection of existing measures are summarised, obtained from an online literature survey, comprising of scales administered either by healthcare professionals with the PwD (self-report) and/or their carers (proxy report) or from observation. It is suggested that a combination of such tools with user satisfaction questionnaires may provide a way to approach the problem of evaluating Assistive Technology (AT) solutions or inform co-design of technological solutions with PwD and their carers.

Keywords: Assistive Technologies, Telecare, Ambient Assisted Living, User experience, Dementia, Quality of Life measures, Health Technology Assessment.

1 Introduction

A major goal of designers during preliminary phases of development of new technology products is to investigate user expectations, needs and desires, in recognition of the distance between mental model(s) of designers and those of users. In particular this distance needs to be reduced when the designed product is an Assistive Technologies (AT) for people with dementia (PwD), in order prevent non-use or abandonment [1]. In the field of interaction design there is a long tradition of user involvement in early design stages which and such methods are being applied to technology support for PwD and carers [2]. One approach to eliciting user needs is to investigate dimensions of quality-of-life (QoL)[3],[4], [5].

As Peterson et al. have noted [6], tools in use are mainly derived from the constructs of Lawton. There are two main ways to determine QoL of patients with dementia: i) Questionnaires and interviews (self-report by the PwD and/or proxy-report by the carer) and ii) direct observation of behaviours assumed to be related to QoL. The selection of the most appropriate tool will depend on the setting (home or care

L. Pecchia et al. (Eds.): IWAAL 2014, LNCS 8868, pp. 394–397, 2014.
© Springer International Publishing Switzerland 2014

institution), the severity of dementia and the nature of the technology being considered. The advantage of using disease specific tools in pre-design and post–use phases are: i) to understand which are the needs and aspirations of PwD on the basis of reported or observable aspects of their daily life, ii) an indirect measure of the potential impact of ATs in their life, based on the improvement in their QoL that the technology could provide.

2   Quality of Life (QoL) Tools

In the following section, in Table 1, a summary of tools to measure QoL for PwD are presented. The search was performed on Google Scholar with free text search terms: {dementia}AND{quality-of-life, QoL, scales} for English language papers (including reviews) published in the last 20 years. The tools selected were those intended to be administered by healthcare professionals with the PwD (self-report) and/or their carers (proxy report) or from observation. Papers solely about staging were excluded.

Table 1. QoL tools for people with dementia

Name	Description
Cornell-Brown Scale for Quality of Life in Dementia (CBS)[7]	Clinician rated scale administered jointly with the PwD and carer using 19 bipolar items (-2,+2) in a semi-structured interview format, to provide a single score (-38,+38). High QoL is indicated by the presence of positive affect, physical and psychological satisfactions, self-esteem and the relative absence of negative affect and experience. Adapted from the Cornell Scale for Depression in Dementia. Can be used for mild, moderate and severe dementia although for severe the validity and reliability may be affected by lack of patient self-observations.
Dementia Quality of Life Instrument (DQoL)[8]	Administered to PwD with mild to moderate dementia. 5-point visual scale used to present multiple choice questions. Each point on the scale is associated with a verbal description. 29-item scale to measures 5 domains of QoL: Positive Affect (6 items), Negative Affect (11 items), Feelings of Belonging (3 items), Self-esteem (4 items), and Sense of Aesthetics (5 items) plus one global item (Overall, how would rate your quality of life?). Subscale scores are not summed.
Quality of Life-Alzheimer's Disease (QoL-AD)[9]	Questionnaire of 13 items designed to provide seperate PwD and carer reports of the patient's QoL with a 4 point rating (1 = poor, 4 = excellent). Measures domains of physical condition, mood, memory, functional abilities, interpersonal relationships, ability to participate in meaningful activities, financial situation, and global assessments of self-as-a-whole and QoL-as-a-whole. Response options are 4-point multiple choice options (1 = poor, 4 = excellent). Overall score range (13, 52). Composite scores that combine reports from patients and caregivers are weighted to favour patient self-reporting. Can be used for mild, mod-
Quality of Life Assessment Schedule (QOLAS)[10]	Interview and rating scale where PwD and carers (may include care home staff) are interviewed separately to identify 2 QoL issues for each of 5 domains: Physical, Psychological, Social/family, Usual activities, and Cognitive functioning. PwD and carers rate each issue they have identified 6-point scale (0 = no problem, 5 = it could not be worse). Overall score range (0,50) with higher score for poorer QoL.

DEMQOL[11]	Health professional administered questionnaires to assess health related quality of life for PwD and/or carer as proxy. There are two versions: 28-item DEMQOL for people with mild/moderate dementia and 31 item DEMQOL-proxy for carers of people with mild/moderate dementia or with severe dementia. 4 point scale.
OPQOL-35[12]	35-item questionnaire. Not a dementia-specific tool but can be applicable to people with mild to moderate dementia. 5 point scale.
Alzheimer Disease Related Quality of Life (ADRQL)[13]	Binary (Agree, Disagree) questions administered to the carer as proxy to the PwD in a structured interview format. The ADRQL evaluates 5 QoL domains: social interaction, awareness of self, feelings and mood, enjoyment of activities, response to surroundings. There are two versions of ADRQL , the original composed of 47 items and a revised version with 40 items, the majority of items in both versions measuring actions and observable behaviours. Each item has a specific numerical score provided in the ADRQL manual.
Quality of Life in Late-Stage Dementia (QUALID)[14]	Carer (proxy report) instrument that measures 11 observable behaviours of PwD over 7 days, indicating activity and emotional states, administered by nursing home personnel. 5-point Likert scale. Designed for quick administration (5 minutes).
Dementia Care Mapping (DMC)[15]	Structured observational tool for assessing PwD well-being in residential care who are unable to provide their own report. Health professional administered. Covers all stages of dementia (mild, middle or severe). Well-being and activities are recorded every 5 minutes over a period of 6 hours. 24 activity categories and indicators of social withdrawal are measured in terms of ill-being/well-being (-5,

3   Conclusions

Although a number of valid and consistent QoL scales are in use there is presently no one tool to directly assess the impact of AT for dementia in terms of QoL improvement [6]. Consequently there is a lack of a standard approach to formative evaluation and user-centred design of new AT for PwD and their carers. However, some tools exist to evaluate user satisfaction and usability after a use of an AT prototype e.g., Psychosocial Impact of Assistive Devices Scale (PIADS)[16], Quebec User Evaluation of Satisfaction with Assistive Technology (QUEST)[17] which may be used in formative evaluation. For people with mild or moderate dementia a combination of QoL tools with satisfaction questionnaires may provide a solution which therefore warrants further investigation e.g. to determine which tools to combine. There is unmet need of a tool for severe dementia related to AT evaluation with respect to QoL, although the proxy version of PIADS may be applicable.

Acknowledgements. The research reported in this paper was conducted by the National Institute for Health Research MindTech Healthcare Technology Co-operative (NIHR MindTech HTC). The views expressed are those of the author(s) and not necessarily those of the NHS, the NIHR or the Department of Health. The authors acknowledge funding support for the research through the Connecting Assistive Solutions to Aspirations (CASA) project, provided by the Technology Strategy Board Long Term Care Revolution initiative by means of a Small Business Research Initiative grant. The CASA project is a collaborative venture led by commercial partner Leone Services Ltd., in partnership with Sensixa Ltd., The University of Nottingham, University of the West of England, Bristol and Swiss Cottage School, Development & Research Centre.

References

1. Scherer, M.J.: Outcomes of assistive technology use on quality of life. Disability & Rehabilitation 18(9), 439–448 (1996)
2. Lindsay, S., et al.: Empathy, participatory design and people with dementia. In: Proceedings of the SIGCHI Conference on Human Factors in Computing Systems, pp. 521–530. ACM Press (2012)
3. Ettema, T.P., et al.: A review of quality of life instruments used in dementia. Quality of Life Research 14(3), 675–686 (2005)
4. Ready, R.E., Ott, B.R.: Quality of life measures for dementia. Health and Quality of Life Outcomes 1(11), 1–9 (2003)
5. Orpwood, R., et al.: Designing technology to support quality of life of people with dementia. Technology and Disability 19(2), 103–112 (2007)
6. Peterson, C.B., Prasad, N.R., Prasad, R.: Assessing assistive technology outcomes with dementia. Gerontechnology 11(2), 259–268 (2012)
7. Ready, R.E., et al.: The Cornell-Brown scale for quality of life in dementia. Alzheimer Disease & Associated Disorders 16(2), 109–115 (2002)
8. Brod, M., et al.: Conceptualization and measurement of quality of life in dementia: The dementia quality of life instrument (DQoL). The Gerontologist 39(1), 25–36 (1999)
9. Hoe, J., et al.: Use of the QOL-AD for measuring quality of life in people with severe dementia—the LASER-AD study. Age and Ageing 34(2), 130–135 (2005)
10. Selai, C.E., et al.: Assessing quality of life in dementia: Preliminary psychometric testing of the Quality of Life Assessment Schedule (QOLAS). Neuropsychological Rehabilitation 11(3-4), 219–243 (2001)
11. Smith, S., et al.: Measurement of health-related quality of life for people with dementia: development of a new instrument (DEMQOL) and an evaluation of current methodology. Health Technology Assessment 9(10), 1–93 (2005)
12. Bilotta, C., et al.: Quality of life in older outpatients living alone in the community in Italy. Health & Social Care in the Community 20(1), 32–41 (2012)
13. Rabins, P.V., et al.: Concepts and methods in the development of the ADRQL: An instrument for assessing health-related quality of life in persons with Alzheimer's disease. Journal of Mental Health and Aging 5(1), 33–48 (1999)
14. Weiner, M.F., et al.: The quality of life in late-stage dementia (QUALID) scale. Journal of the American Medical Directors Association 1(3), 114–116 (1999)
15. Fossey, J., Lee, L., Ballard, C.: Dementia Care Mapping as a research tool for measuring quality of life in care settings: Psychometric pROPERTIES. International Journal of Geriatric Psychiatry 17(11), 1064–1070 (2002)
16. Jutai, J., Day, H.: Psychosocial impact of assistive devices scale (PIADS). Technology and Disability 14(3), 107–111 (2002)
17. Demers, L., Weiss-Lambrou, R., Ska, B.: The Quebec User Evaluation of Satisfaction with Assistive Technology (QUEST 2. 0): an overview and recent progress. Technology and Disability 14(3), 101–105 (2002)

Critical Success Factors for e-Healthcare: Integrated Set of Performance Indicators System (ISPIS)

Fabio De Felice[1] and Antonella Petrillo[2]

[1] University of Cassino and Southern Lazio, Cassino, Italy
[2] University of Naples "Parthenope", Napoli, Italy

Abstract. Healthcare information technology (health IT) is a critical factor of healthcare system worldwide. The aim of this paper is to propose an integrated performance measurement system to evaluate access to healthcare and healthcare cost reduction is proposed. This paper presents the use of the Analytic Hierarchy Process (AHP) to prioritize all of the measures and strategies in a Balanced Scorecard framework (BSC). Results show that the methodological approach is very flexible and useful in several scenarios.

Keywords: e-healthcare, telemedicine, performance, service innovation, AHP, BSC.

1   Introduction

Over the last few decades, innovation in healthcare services and services in healthcare innovation has become a topic of growing importance. The result is that today's hospitals are particularly interested in increasing the quality and efficiency of patient identification and monitoring procedures. From this point of view healthcare information technology is a *key factor* useful to improve quality and reducing cost in healthcare, and yet, the successful implementation of health IT varies greatly among healthcare systems [1]. According to a recent literature review [2] the implementation of electronic health records (EHRs) and health IT systems is considered as one of the highest priorities of modern healthcare systems modernization. This implementation brings to increase *efficiency*, *quality of care* and *reducing medical error*, and open the way to the development of new services on top of it such as telemedicine and internet-based chronic disease management. Recognized barriers preventing the adoption and effective use of IT in healthcare are: (1) *Financial and business barriers*, (2) *Structural barriers*, (3) *Cultural barriers* and (4) *Technical and professional barriers*. When a decision has to be taken in healthcare management, evidence is a fundamental component but not always the available evidence is adequate and needs to be compensated and supported by experience [3], [4]. Thus, the aim of the present paper is to propose an integrated performance *measurement system* in order to increase access to healthcare and reducing its cost. This paper proposed the use of the *Analytic Hierarchy Process* (AHP) model to analyze strategic performance of e-healthcare system, and proposes the use of the AHP to prioritize all of the measures and strategies in a *Balanced Scorecard* framework.

L. Pecchia et al. (Eds.): IWAAL 2014, LNCS 8868, pp. 398–401, 2014.
© Springer International Publishing Switzerland 2014

2   Materials and Methods

The purpose of this paper is to design a framework to provide health care management with an overarching view of the performance of their overall organization. The consideration underlying the model is to ensure *"innovative management"* through an organizational process for implementation and monitoring achievement of objectives. In order to develop our model we tried to answer the following research questions: How can management select the best strategy? What can we do? Thus, we proposed a balanced scorecard hierarchy. First devised by Kaplan and Norton in 1992, the balanced scorecard approach consists of four perspectives: *Financial Perspective*; *Customer Perspective*; *Internal Business Perspective* and *Innovation Perspective* [5]. BSC is a strategic approach and performance management system which organizations can use for vision and strategy implementation [6]. It represents a translation of business unit strategy into a linked set of measures that define both long-term strategic objectives and the mechanisms for achieving/obtaining feedbacks regarding those objectives [7]. On the other hand, the AHP is a powerful and flexible decision making process which helps people to set priorities and make the best decision when both qualitative and quantitative aspects of a decision need to be considered [8], [9]. In Figure 1 is shown conceptual model with AHP approach and BSC Perspectives and critical enabling factors for e-healthcare.

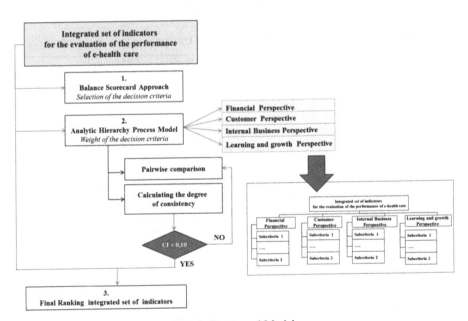

Fig. 1. Conceptual Model

The AHP is based on the following principles: (1) decomposition of the decision problem, (2) comparative judgment of the elements using the evaluation scale recommended by Saaty [10]. This scale consists of importance scales that are defined from1 to 9, (3) calculation the degree of consistency (CI) = $(\lambda - n)/(n- 1)$, λ is the average consistency measure for all alternatives, n = the number of alternatives, and (4) synthesis of the priorities. In order to define an integrated set of indicators for the evaluation of the performance of e-health care we identified two main activities. The first is the selection of the decision criteria according the Balance Scorecard approach. The second is the weight of the decision criteria according the Analytic Hierarchy Process Model. A questionnaire was designed for this purpose. A sample of the questionnaire is *"From your point of view, which criterion is more important to assess the effectiveness of e-healthcare services?"* The result is the definition of the final ranking of the integrated set indicators. Additionally, the study checks convergent validity by comparing the rankings derived from AHP with the opinion of a team of experts (managers, clinicians, patients).

3   Discussion and Results

This paper has established a framework and process for the implementation of a performance measurement system. The development of a performance measurement system cannot be regarded as static and must therefore be kept under review. In summary the implementation process requires initial impetus, commitment, training and co-ordination in order to overcome cultural and organizational barriers. The final selection of the performance measures is shown Table 1.

Table 1. Performance measures: Integrated Set of Performance Indicators System

Indicator	Sample Performance Measures
Financial Perspective (31%)	Increased number of e-healthcare services (29 %)
	Cost per projects(40%)
	Number of project milestones and budget reviews (31%)
Customer Perspective (35%)	Increased user satisfaction with the effectiveness and efficiency of the e-healthcare system (42%)
	Increased user confidence in the e-services (25%)
	% of stakeholder participation in projects (33%)
Internal Business Perspective (19%)	Reduced average time to resolve problems (45%)
	Number of enquiries (23%)
	RD expense/total revenues (32%)
Learning and growth Perspective (15%)	Number of IT training programmes attended by staff (55%)
	Employee satisfaction (%) (45%)

For instance the importance level of scorecard sizes is identified as 35% for customer perspective, 31% for financial perspective, 19% for internal business perspective and 15% for learning and growth perspective. Additional indexes can be applied if they are needed, and if there are adequate data. In our opinion it is useful to compare costs (Ch) and effectiveness (Eh) of e-healthcare services with costs (Ct) and effectiveness (Et) of traditional services. If Ch≤Ct and Eh>Et then it is convenient adopt e-healthcare services. Otherwise it is necessary to estimate the incremental cost-effectiveness ratio (R), or in other words R= (Ch-Ct)/(Eh-Et). The adoption of the proposed measurement system could provide the following benefits: (1) Alignment of the organization around its mission and strategies; (2) Facilitation, monitoring, and assessment of strategy implementation; (3) Assignment of accountability for performance at all levels of the organization; and (4) Continual feedback on the strategy and opportunities for adjustment. The strength of the proposed approach is that the method is very flexible and it can be use in different scenarios in different countries. Furthermore the proposed method provided an useful framework for the decision process, which is essential in the public sector. Future work will address different scenarios in order to compare them.

References

1. Kaye, R., Kokia, E., Shalev, V., Idar, D., Chinitz, D.: Barriers and success factors in health information technology: A practitioner's perspective. J. of Management & Marketing in Healthcare 3, 163–175 (2010)
2. De Felice, F., Petrillo, A.: Key success factors for organizational innovation in the fashion industry. International J. of Engineering Business Management 5, 47–57 (2013)
3. Poveda-Bautista, R., Baptista, D.C., García-Melón, M.: Setting competitiveness indicators using BSC and ANP. International J. of Production Research 50, 4738–4752 (2012)
4. De Felice, F.: Editorial Research and applications of AHP/ANP and MCDA for decision making in manufacturing. International J. of Production Research 50, 4735–4737 (2012)
5. Kaplan, R.S., Norton, D.P.: The balance scorecard. Measures that drive performance. Harvard Business Review. 70, 71–79 (1992)
6. Atkinson, M.: Measuring the Performance of the IT Function in the UK Health Service Using a Balanced Scorecard Approach. Electronic J. of Information Systems Evaluation 7, 1–10 (2004)
7. Kloot, L., Martin, J.: Strategic performance management: A balanced approach to performance management issues in local government. Management Accounting Research 11, 231–251 (2000)
8. Saaty, T.L.: The Analytic Hierarchy Process. McGraw-Hill, New York (1980)
9. Pecchia, L., Martin, J.L., Ragozzino, A., Vanzanella, C., Scognamiglio, A., Mirarchi, L., Morgan, S.P.: User needs elicitation via analytic hierarchy process (AHP). A case study on a Computed Tomography (CT) scanner. BMC Medical Informatics and Decision Making 13, 1–11 (2013)
10. Saaty, T.L.: Fundamentals of Decision Making and Priority Theory with the Analytic Hierarchy Process. RWS Publications, Pittsburgh (1994)

Exergames as Tools Used on Interventions to Cope with the Effects of Ageing: A Systematic Review

Amado Velazquez[1,*], Wilfrido Campos-Francisco[2], Juan Pablo García-Vázquez[3], Hussein López-Nava[4], Marcela Deyanira Rodríguez[3], Alberto Isaac Pérez-San Pablo[5], Alicia Martínez-Rebollar[2], Hugo Estrada-Esquivel[6], Ana Martinez-García[1], Angélica Muñoz-Meléndez[4], and Jesús Favela[1]

[1] CICESE, Ensenada, Mexico
montalvo@cicese.edu.mx, {martinea,favela}@cicese.mx,
[2] CENIDET, Cuernavaca, Mexico
{mcwilfrido11c,amartinez}@cenidet.edu.mx
[3] Engineering School, UABC, Mexicali, Mexico
{pablo.garcia,marcerod}@uabc.edu.mx
[4] INAOE, Puebla, Mexico
hussein@ccc.inaoep.mx, munoz@inaoep.mx
[5] INR, Mexico City, Mexico
albperez@inr.gob.mx
[6] Industry Information and Documentation Fund, INFOTEC, Mexico City
hugo.estrada@infotec.com.mx

Abstract. Exergames are currently used as a new tool for medical purposes. In this context, this paper presents an overview of the approaches used to gather evidence about the use and impact of exergames-based interventions on elderly. In total, 2306 abstracts were returned from a database search, yielding 52 relevant papers. Our analysis found a group of papers mostly published in engineering forums with emphasis on evaluating novel technologies and an evaluation providing low-evidence, another group of studies, published mostly in medical journals, use more conventional technologies, but conduct more comprehensive evaluations from which stronger evidence is obtained.

Keywords: Systematic Review, Exergames, Older Adults, Health Condition.

1   Introduction

With the development of new gaming platforms that support full-body motion interaction there has been increasing interest in the development and evaluation of exergames for ageing. Studies have been conducted to assess or improve health conditions such as depression, balance, or assist in rehabilitation (see studies 42, 37 and 53 listed in [5]). The type of studies conducted and the evidence strength level gathered varies considerably. In addition, some research efforts have focused on developing new exergames aimed at producing certain health outcomes, while others have evaluated the use of commercial games. Systematic reviews have been conducted in the area of exergames for older adults, mostly focused on making a meta-analysis of Randomized

L. Pecchia et al. (Eds.): IWAAL 2014, LNCS 8868, pp. 402–405, 2014.
© Springer International Publishing Switzerland 2014

Control Trial studies for a specific health outcome, for instance, to study their effect on the older adult balance [1], or on their cognitive decline [2]. In contrast, our study focuses on evaluating the use of exergames in interventions to cope with the effects of ageing, as novel technologies at an early stage of development (engineering approach) as well as conventional technologies in clinical context (medical approach).

To provide an analysis of the scope of existing studies, the evidence strength level on their impact on the elderly wellbeing, and the technological approaches used for their deployment, we conducted a rapid Literature Systematic Review (LSR). Which is a "streamlined approach to synthesizing evidence in a timely manner" [3]. Our LSR was led by the following research question: *What are the approaches used to gather evidence about the impact of exergames-based interventions on elderly?*

2   Search and Selection Process

We conducted searches on five databases to retrieve high quality literature in medicine and life science (*i.e.* PubMed), engineering and technology (*i.e.* ACM and IEEE Xplore), and all-science databases (*i.e.* Web of Science and Scopus). Fig. 1a presents the search strings with keywords associated with the main terms representing our domain of interest: 1) "exergames-based interventions" for 2) "elderly".

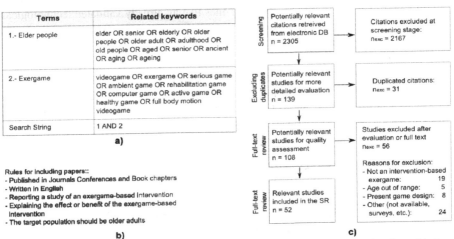

Fig. 1. Literature search and selection strategy was determined by: a) the search strings; b) the criteria used during the selection process; and c) the stages of the literature selection process

To select relevant papers, we defined the inclusion criteria described in Fig. 1b, to focus our study on exergame-based interventions reported in English. These criteria were used in a peer-review manner during the first and third stages (Fig 1c). The first selection stage was based upon screening and rating of abstracts (0: exclude; 1: consider for inclusion). The second stage consisted in eliminating duplicate papers. Afterwards, a review and assessment was carried out on full papers by extracting some characteristics of the studies, such as the aim of the exergame-intervention and the target population age, which were not easily identified by reading abstracts.

3   Quality Assessment

A quality assessment procedure was defined by three of the authors to produce a taxonomy of characteristics that determine the studies quality:

Technology in health care could be used (*intervention aim*) either to find or evaluate a health condition (*diagnostic tool*), or to modify it (*therapeutic tool*). Health is a very broad concept, therefore, a complete framework that analyzes all *health components* considering individual's function and structure with his perceptual and mobility capabilities (SMBF/*Sensory-Motor Body Function*), and his interaction with and within his world (AP/*activity and participation*) is needed[11]. *Evidence strength level* (*ESL*) and the quality of a study are closely related to its methodological design (*study type*). Best evidence is provided by systematic reviews based on experimental randomized controlled studies (*High ESL*), followed by controlled studies (*Medium ESL*). However in some cases observational studies like cohort studies, cross-sectional studies, case series or case reports (*Low ESL*) give better evidence when they report dramatic effects, or when systematic reviews are unavailable [4]. Consequently, an easy to understand and apply scale was used to classify ESL by reviewers based on the study type. Another quality aspect for diagnostic and therapeutic studies is the inclusion of a reference standard to compare results between evaluation methods, or before and after a treatment respectively (*comparison with a clinical standard*). Clinical reference standards could be objective ones like an already validated technological instrument; or subjective ones like clinical scales or physical examination which depends on examiner's expertise.

Each paper was assigned to two reviewers, who agreed on how to categorize it based on the defined criteria. They completed a format with each paper's descriptive information such as journal title, publication year, results, etc. Finally, each paper was classified according to the subject area as provided by the Journal[2] and Conferences[3] Rankings. Grouping expertise was requested on any difference of opinion.

4   Results and Discussion

As depicted in Fig. 1c, 2,306 papers were retrieved from the five databases, which were reduced to 139 papers after the abstract-based screening and to 108 by eliminating duplicates. Full-text of these papers was reviewed by using the inclusion and quality assessment criteria resulting in 52 papers published from 2008 to 2014.

Table I summarizes our results. Twenty-nine (29) were studies published in Journals and 23 in Conference Proceedings. Most of the Journal papers (25/29) pertain to the medical & biological (*Med/Bio*) subject area, whilst most of the Conference papers (21/23) pertain to Engineering and Computer Science (*Eng/CSc*). Two works were published in media classified as both *Eng* and *CSc-Med/Bio*.

---

[1] http://www.who.int/classifications/icf/en/

[2] http://www.scimagojr.com/index.php

[3] http://thomsonreuters.com/conference-proceedings-citation-index/

There are more studies on the Med/Bio area (20/26), reporting the use of exergames as a diagnostic tool, than on Eng/CSc (10/24). Not surprisingly, more Med/Bio papers (22/26) reported the use of a clinical standard to compare and assess their results, than Eng/CSc papers (9/24). Therefore, studies using a clinical approach for assessing the health benefits of exergames-based interventions tend to be published in Med/Bio journals and conferences (20/52). Additional 16 papers (mostly in Eng/Cs) report usability evaluations. Most of these are formative evaluations of exergames developed by the authors, that is, these evaluations aim at informing a design process.

Table 1. Studies classification based on the criteria used to assess study quality

Subject area	Intervention Aim			Health benefit		Evidence strength level			Comparison with a clinical standard		Aspects evaluated			A self development?		
	Therapeutic tool	Diagnostic tool	N/A	AP	SMBF	Low	Medium	High	No	Yes	Clinical	Functionality	Usability	No	Yes	N/A
Eng/CSc	10	10	4	11	13	19	4	1	15	9	13		11	6	18	
Med/Bio	6	20		5	21	7	14	5	4	22	20	1	5	16	9	1
Eng/CSc-Med/Bio	1	1	4		2		1	1	1	1	2				2	
TOTAL	17	31	4	16	36	26	19	7	20	32	35	1	16	22	29	1

5   Conclusions

Our results showed that though the big potential of exergames to become a therapeutic tool, they remain mostly as a diagnostic one in the SMBF component, perhaps because of stringent requirements of research and product development in the medical field. But even as a diagnostic tool, stronger evidence that compares presumed health outcomes with clinical standardized assessment methods is needed, before this technology can be trusted for common clinical applications. The results could also help researchers to find further applications and to propose new research questions. It has been noticed also a lack of collaboration between the clinical and engineering field, as evidenced by the struggle of clinicians to fit off-the-shelf technology to fulfill their needs instead of self-developing more suitable solutions in collaboration with technology professionals. Finally we conclude that more developments taking advantages of pervasive capabilities of exergames in all health components with more collaboration between health professionals and technology experts are needed.

References

1. Larsen, L.H., Schou, L., Lund, H.H., Langberg, H.: The Physical Effect of Exergames in Healthy Elderly—A Systematic Review. Games for Health J. 2(4), 205–212 (2013)
2. Kueider, A.M., Parisi, J.M., Gross, A.L., Rebok, G.W.: Computerized cognitive training with older adults: A systematic review. PLoS ONE 7(7), e40588 (2012)
3. Khangura, S., et al.: Evidence summaries: the evolution of a rapid review approach. Systematic reviews 1(1), 1–9 (2012)
4. Howick, J., et al.: Explanation of the 2011 Oxford Centre for Evidence-Based Medicine (OCEBM) Levels of Evidence (Background Document), OCEBM, Oxford (2011)
5. References to the 52 studies reported on this Systematic Review (2014), http://1drv.ms/1mO2L3i

A Preliminary Model to Choose the Most Appropriate Target Population for Home Monitoring Telemedicine Interventions Basing on the Best Available Evidence

Paolo Melillo[1] and Leandro Pecchia[2]

[1] School of Medicine, Second University of Naples, Naples, Italy
paolo.melillo@unina2.it
[2] School of Engineering, University of Warwick, Coventry, UK
l.pecchia@warwick.ac.uk

Abstract. Evaluating new telemedicine interventions for chronic disease is not easy and it remains unclear how to use the existing evidence to inform the design of new telemedicine programs. In particular, there are not structured methods to define relevant aspects of a new home monitoring intervention as frequency of monitoring (daily vs weekly), complexity of monitoring (symptoms vs bio-potentials) and the severity of target population (age, pathology severity). This paper describes a second order polynomial model that has been used to define the target population for the clinical protocol of the UE-funded research project titled "Smart health and artificial intelligence for Risk Estimation" (SHARE).

Keywords: home monitoring design, heart failure, telemedicine, early stage Health Technology Assessment (HTA).

1 Introduction

Congestive Heart Failure (CHF) is a complex clinical syndrome in which the heart's pump function is inadequate to deliver oxygen-rich blood to the body, representing a challenge to national health services because of its mortality and morbidity, burden and impact on quality of life[1]. Usual Care (UC) for CHF consists of ambulatory follow up, with frequency depending on CHF severity. Limited funding pushes NHSs to search for new modes of service delivery that will provide high-quality care in non-hospital settings. Telemedicine and particularly, Home Monitoring (HM), have been widely explored in recent years because, compared to UC, can provide specialized home care services to a larger number of patients, reducing hospital admissions, mortality and readmissions [2]. However, it remains unclear how to use the existing evidence to inform the design of new telemedicine interventions for chronic cardiovascular disease as CHF. Particularly, there are no models to choose the target populations, which can maximally benefit from HM intervention. In [3], a linear model was proposed to investigate the relation between HM design and clinical efficacy of monitoring intervention. The current paper presents a model to identify the best target population according to the available evidence.

L. Pecchia et al. (Eds.): IWAAL 2014, LNCS 8868, pp. 406–408, 2014.

2   Materials and Methods

2.1   Systematic Literature Review with Meta-analysis

As described in [3], 314 journal papers published before December 2012 were identified, of which 32 met the inclusion criteria and only 8 were eligible for this study, being RCTs comparing HM versus UC. Six outcomes were meta-analyzed: mortality, bed days and, readmissions for both CHF and all causes.

2.2   HM Study Classification: Patient Severity

As described in [3], each RCT was classified according to the severity of the enrolled patients. Severity was defined as a function of: mean NYHA class, which is a symptomatic scale widely used to measure CHF severity; reduction of ejection fraction, which is a measure of the blood flow ejected from the heart to the body at each heart beat; mean patient age.

2.3   HM Designing Curves: Severity vs Efficacy

The association between target patient severity and HM efficacy was modelled fitting the effect sizes of the outcomes with polynomials, using the patient severity as independent variable. In order to minimize the over fitting, the order of the polynomials was fixed at 2, given the limited number of realizations: only 8 RCT comparing HM versus UC and not all reporting the 6 outcomes. As shown in Figure 1, three planes were defined (one for each outcome), where the abscissa reported the severity and the ordinate reported the effect size. For each RCT, the CHF-related and all-causes outcomes were represented on these plans, respectively as red and blue asterisks. The asterisks were fitted with 2 curves: one representing the association between patient severity and CHF-related outcomes (red line) and the other (blue line) representing the relation between patient severity and all-causes outcomes. This was repeated for mortality, re-hospitalization, and bed-days of care. The severity minimizing the curves was chosen as ideal target population.

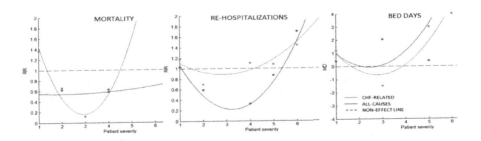

Fig. 1. HM designing curve

3   Results

The results (Figure 1) suggested that the population that would maximally benefit from the HM intervention was the one scored with severity 3, which equated to CHF in NYHA 2 or 3, ejection fraction<40 and mean age of 68 years old. According to this analysis, more severe patients would not benefit from an HM program, generating an unsustainable number of re-hospitalization and bed days. For less severe patients, the HM would be as effective as the UC in terms of re-hospitalization, as suggested by the convergence of both red and blue lines to the non-effect line (black dot line in Figure 1). Regarding bed days, it seems that for target population in severity 3 the HM would give similar effect than UC, while for all the other patients, the HM would cause more bed days. Some authors justify this by saying that the number of bed-days increased but the complexity (and therefore the associated costs) reduced.

4   Discussion

This paper proposed a method to select the best target population for a home monitoring interventions basing on available scientific evidence. This method consisted in analyzing design and outcomes of RCTs that assessed home monitoring interventions for CHF and fitting this evidence with a second order polynomial model. The main preliminary result achieved was to demonstrate that not all the patients had the same benefit from HM. There are groups of patients that apparently had a better benefit from telemedicine. However, future works are needed to provide further insights.

It is not easy to compare the model proposed with existing ones, because as far as author knowledge, there are not similar attempts in literature. However, similar models are needed as demonstrated by the results of the systematic review performed, which demonstrated that the heterogeneity among different HM interventions is massively huge. This model is now under validation investigating its predictive value when applied to RCT published after December 2012.

Acknowledgment. The current study was partially supported by "the 2007-2013 NOP for Research and Competitiveness for the Convergence Regions (Calabria, Campania, Puglia and Sicilia)" with code PON04a3_00139 - Project Smart Health and Artificial intelligence for Risk Estimation.

References

1. Faller, H., Steinbuchel, T., Stork, S., Schowalter, M., Ertl, G., Angermann, C.: Impact of depression on quality of life assessment in heart failure. Int. J. Cardiol. 142(2), 133–137 (2008), doi:S0167-5273(08)01497-6[pii]10.1016/j.ijcard.2008.12.093
2. Inglis, S.C., Clark, R.A., McAlister, F.A., Ball, J., Lewinter, C., Cullington, D., et al.: Structured telephone support or telemonitoring programmes for patients with chronic heart failure. Cochrane Database Syst Rev. (8) (2010)
3. Pecchia, L., Melillo, P., Attanasio, M., Orrico, A., Pacifici, E., Iadanza, E.: Health technology assessment of home monitoring for patients suffering from heart failure. In: Roa Romero, L.M. (ed.) XIII Mediterranean Conference on Medical and Biological Engineering and Computing 2013. IFMBE Proceedings, vol. 41, pp. 1132–1135. Springer, Heidelberg (2014)

E-Smart Real-Time Blood Sugar Administration

Mwaffaq Otoom[1], Hussam Alshraideh[2], Hisham M. Almasaeid[1],
Diego López-de-Ipiña[3], and José Bravo[4]

[1]Yarmouk University, Jordan
[2]Jordan University of Science and Technology, Jordan
[3]University of Deusto, Spain
[4]Castilla-La Mancha University, Spain

Abstract. We develop a prototype for real-time blood sugar control
based on the hypothesis that there is a medical challenge in determining
the exact, real-time insulin dose. Our system controls blood sugar by
observing the blood sugar level and automatically determining the appropriate insulin dose based on patient's historical data, all in real time.
At the heart of our system is an algorithm that determines the appropriate insulin dose. Our algorithm consists of two phases. In the first phase,
the algorithm identifies the insulin dose offline using a Markov Process
based model. In the other phase, it recursively trains the web hosted
Markov model to adapt to different human bodies responsiveness.

Keywords: Diabetes, Insulin Management, Markov Processes.

1 Introduction

Three hundred forty seven million people worldwide have diabetes. The World
Health Organization predicts that diabetes will be the seventh leading cause
of death in 2030 [6]. Blood sugar control is the major impeding challenge to
overcome the devastating effects of this disease.

Blood sugar level for an individual is a function of multiple factors including demographics, diet, exercises, and medications. Medically, determining the
proper insulin dose, for insulin-dependent diabetics, is done in an ad-hoc manner
by a diabetes consultant [3]. Since most of the aforementioned factors are varying over time, the determination of insulin dose becomes a continuous process
that needs medical supervision and intervention, on almost a daily basis. Significantly, the responsiveness to the same dose of insulin may vary among patients,
even with same factors. One key solution to stop the negative effects of diabetes
is the continuous administration of insulin. While it is inconvenient to consult a
diabetes consultant on a daily basis especially for elderly, inexperienced people,
there is also a medical challenge to determine the exact insulin dose required [7].

In this paper we develop, for insulin-dependent diabetics, a prototype for
real-time blood sugar control. At real time, our system controls blood sugar by
observing the blood sugar level and automatically determining the appropriate
insulin dose based on patient's historical data. A number of proposals which

L. Pecchia et al. (Eds.): IWAAL 2014, LNCS 8868, pp. 409–412, 2014.

tackled the same problem have appeared in literature over the past few years [2], [1], [5]. Our proposed system is different in two aspects. First, we use an on-line estimation algorithm based on a Markov model that continuously updates itself with the observed historical data. Second, we incorporate the use of modern technology to facilitate the use of the system for patients. In our system, the collected historical data is automatically transferred to an online server for processing without external intervention (beyond initial setup). The estimated next dose is also calculated automatically by a mobile application installed on a patients smart phone, and the pump is activated without user intervention.

2   Markov Processes for Modeling Blood Sugar Level

In statistics, the collection of a random variable X over an index set T is called a stochastic process [4]. In most applications, T is the time spots at which the random variable of interest is being observed. A stochastic process that satisfies the Markovian property, that is:

$$P(X_{t+1} = j \mid X_0 = x_0, X_1 = x_1, \cdots, X_t = i) = P(X_{t+1} = j \mid X_t = i) \quad (1)$$

is called a Markov Process. This property implies that the future value of the random variable depends on its history only through the current observation [4]. The right hand side of (1) reads as the probability that the process will move to state j given that the process is currently at state i. This probability is usually abbreviated as p_{ij} and is called the transition probability. For a Markov process with n possible states, the transition probabilities p_{ij} can be concatenated in a matrix form called the transition matrix [4]. The transition probability p_{ij} is estimated using the frequentist approach as the ratio of the number of transitions from state i to state j to the total number of transitions from state i.

Let the random variable SL represent the blood sugar level and assume that SL is observed at several time spots. The set of observations of SL form a stochastic process. Furthermore, assume that the next value of SL depends on previous history through its current value, then this is a Markov Process.

An experiment for blood sugar profiles generation was conducted at one of the Jordanian hospitals. The experiment consisted of four factors. These were the body weight, the amount of carbohydrates intake at breakfast, the amount of carbohydrates intake at lunch and the amount of carbohydrates intake at dinner. Three levels for the body weight factor were considered, 100 lb, 200 lb and 300 lb. One patient of each body weight category was volunteered for the study. The amount of carbohydrates intake at breakfast and dinner was changed at three levels of 30, 60 and 90 grams, while the amount of carbohydrates intake at lunch was changed at three levels of 60, 120 and 180 grams. Assuming a factorial design, each of the three patients was under study for 27 days resulting in 81 sugar profiles. These sugar profiles were used to estimate the transition probabilities for the Markov Process assumed.

For validation, the built Markov chain model was used to estimate several blood sugar profiles. The estimated versus the actual data of one sugar profiles

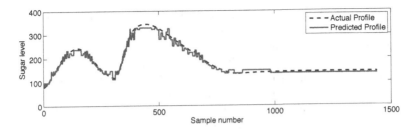

Fig. 1. Actual versus estimated sugar profiles used for model validation

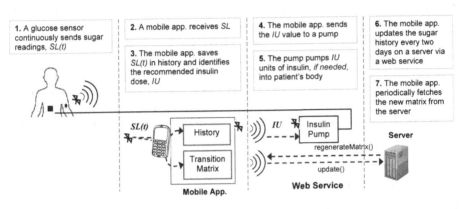

Fig. 2. The E-Smart Real-Time Insulin Injection System

is shown in Figure 1. This plot shows that the model is capable of providing acceptable blood sugar estimates.

3   System Architecture

Our overall goal is to precisely determine the required insulin dose for a specific patient, taking into consideration that different diabetics respond to insulin differently. Existing approaches rely mainly on specialist consultation [8]. Other automated approaches consider only giving notifications on oncoming highs and lows without real time insulin dose determination and injection [8]. Up to our knowledge, none of existing approaches has considered sharing patients sugar history online for tracking and monitoring. Our solution to achieve this goal is by using a web based framework that enables the patient's data to be communicated via web with specialists, research institutes, and more significantly with an automated system that computes the required insulin dose based on the sugar levels history of the patient. Figure 2 depicts our suggested system and illustrates its functionality step by step.

Our system consists of three hardware components: glucose sensor, mobile phone, and pump, all are Bluetooth enabled. The glucose sensor continuously sends sugar readings, SL(t), via Bluetooth. The mobile phone which hosts the injection application receives SL readings via Bluetooth, as well. The mobile application saves each reading in history and processes it using our algorithm. Using the estimated transition matrix, for a given sugar reading the application predicts the next reading using the expected value method. We define the required insulin dose, IU, as the insulin units required to dispose the difference sugar between the expected value and the current value. Once the IU is identified, the mobile application sends this value to the pump that is connected to the patient's body. The pump, in turn, pumps IU units of insulin into patient's body. The mobile application also communicates the patient's data with the server via a web service. The mobile application updates the database via the `update()` web method with patient's sugar levels periodically with period T_u which can be configured at the mobile application. Upon receiving new updates, the server runs our suggested algorithm to regenerate the transition matrix. The mobile application can then fetch the updated matrix by calling the `getUpdatedMatrix()` web method at the server. Again, this call is made every period T_u. We choose to update the history on server every two days to make sure that the given insulin is precise as well as to clear the history from the limited size memory of the cell phone. Note that all data is stored in the database and viewed via our web dashboard by both the specialist and the patient.

4   Conclusions

Diabetes is one of the fastest growing diseases. At the same time, technology is increasingly engaging in human health systems. The intersection of these two trends has inspired us to come up with a novel approach that integrates mobile phone, web, and sensor technologies to help a diabetic to automatically administer insulin injection; something is considered a burden in Diabetes medication. While our approach is effective, it is also simple. Simplicity comes from the fact that we utilize the ubiquity of mobile, sensor, and internet technologies, and that our proposed algorithm is computationally inexpensive.

References

1. Andrianasy, F., Milgram, M.: Applying neural networks to adjust insulin-pump doses. In: IEEE Workshop Neural Networks for Signal Processing (1997)
2. Campos-Cornejo, F., Campos-Delgado, D.U.: Self-Tuning Insulin Dosing Algorithm for Glucose Regulation in Type 1 Diabetic Patients. PAHCE (2009)
3. Rizza, R.A., Mandarino, L.J., Gerich, J.E.: Dose-response characteristics for effects of insulin on production and utilization of glucose in man. In: AJPEM (1981)
4. Ross, S.M.: Introduction to Probability Models, 10th edn. Elsevier, AP (2010)
5. Shimauchi, T., et al.: Microcomputer-aided insulin dose determination in intensified conventional insulin therapy. In: IEEE TBE (2013)
6. http://who.int/mediacentre/factsheets/fs312/en/index.html
7. Wallace, T.M., Matthews, D.R.: The assessment of insulin resistance in man. Diabetic Medicine 19(7), 527–534 (2002)
8. King, A.B., et al.: How much do I give? Endocrine Practice (2012)

Comparative Analysis between ANP and ANP- DEMATEL for Six Sigma Project Selection Process in a Healthcare Provider

Miguel Ortiz Barrios[1], Heriberto Felizzola Jiménez[2], and Santiago Nieto Isaza[1]

[1] Universidad del Norte, Department of Industrial Engineering, Puerto Colombia, Colombia
mortiz1@cuc.edu.co, nietos@uninorte.edu.co
[2] Universidad de la Salle, Department of Industrial Engineering, Bogotá, Colombia
healfelizzola@unisalle.edu.co

Abstract. This paper presents an ANP technique applied to identify and prioritize Six Sigma projects for healthcare providers whose results allow selecting the project that ensures the maximum financial benefits for the healthcare company. First, the Six Sigma evaluation model is determined, then the criteria weights are established by ANP (Analytic Network Process) and finally, results from ANP and ANP- DEMATEL (Decision Making Trial and Evaluation Laboratory) are compared. The results show a better decision making performance for ANP-DEMATEL. An empirical case from healthcare sector is presented, showing the effectiveness of the proposed technique.

Keywords: Six Sigma, Evaluation model, ANP, Healthcare provider.

1 Introduction

Recently, multicriteria decision making methods have played a very important role in complex decision making processes due to their effectiveness at the moment of finding the best solution. One of these methods is Analytic Network Process (ANP), which allows to evaluate the linear relationships among criteria, subcriterias and alternatives. Additionally, it analyses interdependence and feedback relationships, giving the most suitable decision [1].

ANP has been used for the selection of improvement projects, specially Six Sigma, area in which it is required to make a right decision with the purpose of choosing the project that provides maximum benefits at a low risk; which permits the optimal utilization of the available resources. In this sense, the present study describes the application of ANP technique for Six Sigma project selection in a healthcare provider. In addition, a comparative analysis is done, between ANP and ANP-DEMATEL with the goal of evaluating the effectiveness of the combined technique. This is an important aspect when it is required to have a decision making process that gives much more information at the moment of selecting a solution alternative that is subject to a complex analysis and a process with high sensitivity to mistake [2].

L. Pecchia et al. (Eds.): IWAAL 2014, LNCS 8868, pp. 413–416, 2014.

2   Literature Review

Several researchers have published some studies related to the use of ANP and its combination with other Six Sigma project selection techniques. For instance, Boran, Resit y Goztepe [3] use a fuzzy ANP approach for Six Sigma project prioritization in a company from automotive industry.

Büyüközkan and Öztürkan [4] present a combined ANP and DEMATEL technique for Six Sigma project selection and prioritization in a logistics Enterprise. In this case, DEMATEL detects interrelations among criteria.

Wang, Hsu and Tzeng [5] use a hybrid model that combines ANP, DEMATEL and VIKOR for Six Sigma project prioritization in film printing industry from Taiwan. This model includes the VIKOR method that allows to evaluate the performance gaps in each criteria and dimension.

3   Methodology

The selection process is started with the creation of a Six Sigma project portfolio in a hospital, with which healthcare processes are optimized. Then, each project is evaluated; that is why goals, strategies, factors and subfactors should be previously defined taking into account quality, cost, efficiency and processing time criterias. As next step, pairwise comparisons are made and computed by the hospital´s Six Sigma team in Superdecisions software to solve the evaluation model. For decision making process, ANP and ANP-DEMATEL were used to select the most effective Six Sigma project with respect to the hospital goals. Finally, a comparative analysis is done between ANP and ANP-DEMATEL to evaluate the decision making performance in each technique.

4   Six Sigma Project Selection Process

In this study, the project portfolio was composed by six projects alternatives called as P1 (Improving of patient care opportunity in Obstetric Outpatient), P2 (Improving of patient care opportunity in Internal Medicine), P3 (Improving of User Information System), P4 (Improving of information system opportunity), P5 (Improving of patient care opportunity in Emergency Department) and P6 (Optimization of Drug Inventory System). The evaluation model was designed according to the different criterias that should be taken into account by healthcare providers at the moment of caring their patients (See Fig. 1). After having defined the evaluation model, ANP is applied with the aid of Superdecisions to identifiy the most suitable six sigma project for the healthcare provider without taking into account possible inner dependencies among the elements of each cluster. The project ranking obtained through this technique is shown in Table 1.

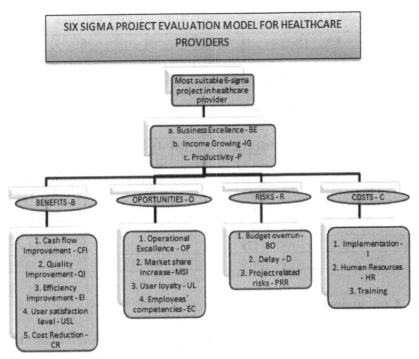

Fig. 1. Evaluation model for Six Sigma project portfolio in healthcare providers (Source: Author´s own)

Table 1. Project ranking according to ANP technique.

Ranking	1	2	3	4	5	6
Project	P1	P2	P3	P5	P4	P6
Score	0.16208	0.1029	0.08294	0.07728	0.05604	0.01875

As next step, ANP is combined with DEMATEL in order to evaluate the interactions among elements and identify causal relationships that could exist in a complex and conected structure where these kind of interrelations define the effectiveness of the decision making process. The project ranking obtained through this method is shown in Table 2. Upon doing the comparison between ANP and ANP-DEMATEL techniques (See Table 3), it is observed that there are some gaps between the scores, showing the presence of inner interactions in each cluster of the evaluation model. Even though, the gaps are not significant, there are causal relationships that affect the decision making, reason by which, they should be taken into account in order to guarantee a better and reliable choice upon reducing the error probability by interactions.

Table 2. Project ranking according to ANP-DEMATEL technique

Ranking	1	2	3	4	5	6
Project	P1	P2	P5	P3	P4	P6
Score	0.1168	0.09166	0.08920	0.08530	0.06366	0.01919

Table 3. Comparative Analysis between ANP and ANP-DEMATEL for six sigma project selection in a healthcare provider

PROJECT	ANP SCORE	ANP-DEMATEL SCORE	GAP
P1	0.16208	0.1168	0.04528
P2	0.1029	0.09166	0.01124
P3	0.08294	0.08530	-0.00236
P4	0.05604	0.06366	-0.00762
P5	0.07728	0.08920	-0.01192
P6	0.01875	0.01919	-0.00044

5   Conclusions

ANP and ANP-DEMATEL results were compared in order to choose the best MCDM tool at the moment of selecting the most suitable Six Sigma project in a healthcare provider. ANP-DEMATEL showed a better decision making performance upon reducing the error probability subject to the existing interactions and dependencies among criterias from evaluation model. This method led the healthcare provider towards an optimal use of its financial resources in the improvement of its obstetric outpatient process (Project P1), which represents the best contribution for organizational goal achievement with 11.68%.

References

1. Saaty, T.L.: Analytic network process. In: Encyclopedia of Operations Research and Management Science, pp. 28–35. Springer, US (2001)
2. Banuelas, R., Tennant, C., Tuersley, I., Tang, S.: Selection of Six Sigma projects in the UK. The TQM Magazine 18(5), 514–527 (2006)
3. Boran, S., Yazgan, H.R., Goztepe, K.: A fuzzy ANP-based approach for prioritising projects: a Six Sigma case study. International Journal of Six Sigma and Competitive Advantage 6(3), 133–155 (2011)
4. Büyüközkan, G., Öztürkcan, D.: An integrated analytic approach for Six Sigma project selection. Expert Systems with Applications 37(8), 5835–5847 (2010)
5. Wang, F.-K., Hsu, C.-H., Tzeng, G.-H.: Applying a Hybrid MCDM Model for Six Sigma Project Selection. Mathematical Problems in Engineering 2014, e730934 (2014)

A Framework to Design Parameterized and Personalized m-health Applications according to the Patient's Diseases

Vladimir Villarreal[1], Ramón Hervás[2], José Bravo[2], and Jesús Fontecha[2]

[1] GITCE Research Lab, Technological University of Panamá, David, Chiriquí, Panamá
vladimir.villarreal@utp.ac.pa
[2] MAmI Research Lab, University of Castilla-La Mancha, Ciudad Real, Spain
{ramon.hlucas,jose.bravo,jesus.fontecha}@uclm.es

Abstract. The development of personalized mobile applications is a complex work. Currently, the most of applications for patients monitoring through mobile devices, is not developed considering the particular characteristics of each patient, but these applications have been developed taking into account a general behavior depending on the diseases instead of the own patients. The diseases manifest different symptoms depending on the patient situation. Mary and John (hypothetic patients) have diabetes, but the same measurement of glucose for each one affects their health in a different way. This paper describes a framework that allows the development of mobile applications, personalized for each patient, in such a way that even if they have the same disease, the application will respond to the individual needs of each patient.

Keywords: mobile monitoring, m-health, chronic diseases, adaptive framework.

1 Introduction

Evolution of technological devices has allowed the integration of new technologies for the treatment and follow-up of diseases in which patients find support through the device use. The increasing integration of new technical features in mobile devices, and the communication capabilities allows the deployment of multiple services.

The solutions developed provide a "specific" solution to health care issues. Health Buddy System [1] is a system that provides health monitoring of patients by reducing the possibilities of hospitalization. Everyday, patients respond to a set of questions about their health and well being using the simple Health Buddy appliance. AirStrip Patient Monitoring [2] is a software platform for providing monitoring information about critical patient aspects and ensuring the transmission of date between hospital devices and clinical records. WellDoc [3] is an application designed to be a service of monitoring for diabetics that allows monitoring the current condition of a patient through the manual introduction of food and glucose parameters. METABO [4] is a system for monitoring and handling of diabetes that aims the recording and interpretation of the context of the patient, as well as the decision support for the patient and the physician. However these applications have been developed for monitoring of patients regardless of their individual peculiarities, which are not configurable or customizable

L. Pecchia et al. (Eds.): IWAAL 2014, LNCS 8868, pp. 417–420, 2014.

to each patient. This paper presents a solution to these problems, developing a customizable application which can be adapted to each patient according to the particular disease. We present a framework that allows the development of parameterized and personalized mobile applications and medical monitoring through mobile devices. This leads to a medical follow up through mobile devices, which are used day to day by the patient, and biometric devices that currently provide high technological capabilities.

2   Parameterized and Personalized m-health Application

2.1   The Design Goals of the Architecture

The vital signal is sent via wireless communication from the biometric device, suitable for each case (glucometer, blood pressure monitor, ECG, etc.), to the mobile device without any intervention by the patient. This signal will be analyzed taking into account some important aspects such as the requirements of the physician about situations of risk and maintenance, considering the clinical record and the profile of the patient, etc. Once the analysis is complete, the mobile device will warn with an alarm or reminder according to the situation. Thus, the mobile device can warn of an injection of insulin or a notification to relatives or medical staff, in case of a possible fall or a rise sudden blood sugar, in the case of diabetes.

The framework enables meta-definitions according to a set of clinical areas previously determined, subsequently, the physician, complete the profile of each patient and can provide a suitable group of recommendations to facilitate the self-control. This architecture must allow a correspondence between physician definitions and mobile software services for self-control according to each patient profile and disease to be monitored.

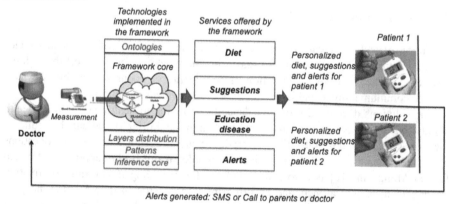

Fig. 1. Parameterized and adaptive functionality of the m-health application

In Figure 1, a doctor can have more than one patient with the same disease. The doctor recommends to each patient the use of the application for monitoring of glucose in blood, with a set of parameters and ranges initially defined. The doctor can adapt the new settings depending on each patient. Otherwise, the application, according the use and the glucose new values, adapts every range taking into account the last measures obtained from the patient. The framework provides services such as diet, suggestions, basic information about the disease and alerts according to the last five ranges obtained from the patient. Predictive inference engine, adapted to these values of the patient can be proposed, providing new suggestions, diets and alerts for each patient.

2.2   Technological Elements Defined in the Framework

The final application generated by the framework consists of different elements related to the following: communication platform, interfaces design, data processing and human interaction. The elements defined in the development of the framework, and which establish the functionalities of the mobile applications are: definition of an ontological model [5], oriented to the definition of the domain in the study and description of each of its elements; development of a reference architecture for the development of modules that allows mobile monitoring of patients, independently of the technology, as well as the dynamic integration of new elements in the environment; patterns for the definition and creation of modules associated with each disease and the patient's individual profile [6]; the structure of the relationship between each of the modules generated by the architecture, defining the architecture of communication between mobile and biometric devices and the predictive inference engine that facilitates the deployment of self-control, assessing past situations that may arise in the future associated with the user [7]. This is the point of the framework, since it is that allows each user the adaptation and customization of the final application.

3   Results: Some Patients Experiences

It is very important to assess the impact the system has on patients using a mobile application that allows them to store, manage, handle information and also provides appropriate suggestions to the patient.

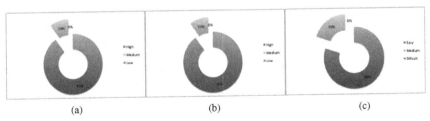

Fig. 2. User evaluation of the application generated by the framework: a. response time, b. efficiency of generated suggestions and c. applications interaction

The application was evaluated in ten patients with diabetes, considering aspects such as the application response time, accuracy of the generated recommendation, assessment of the patient record stored in mobile device, and ease of interaction with the mobile device. The results are shown in Figure 2, where we can see that the response time of the application to the patient is high (90% of answers present a high score and 10% medium score). In the accuracy of the generated recommendation 90% of patients responded with high score and 10% medium, which show that the application responds according to the patient needs. Other aspect evaluated was the interaction of the patient with the mobile application obtaining high score in 80% of cases.

4   Conclusions

This paper presents a framework that allows the generation of mobile applications for the monitoring of patient diseases. The difference between our architecture and other systems is based on the development of a personalized and parameterized application for each patient. Our application is able to be adapted to patient requirements providing different modules for diet, suggestions, education and alerts depending on the last measures obtained through the communication between biometric devices and mobiles devices. This module sends the measurement to predictive inference engine for the interpretation and adaptation of the new modules. The evaluation related to the time of response, suggestions generated and the application interaction presented a high score for the evaluated patients.

References

1. BOSCH, Health Buddy System. (2011), http://www.bosch-telehealth.com (last access 2012)
2. AirStrip, T.: AirStrip Patient Monitoring (2011), http://www.airstriptech.com/ (last access 2011)
3. WellDoc. WellDoc Health Platform (2011), http://www.welldoc.com/ Products-and-Services/Our-Products.aspx (last access 2012)
4. Georga, E., Protopappas, V., et al.: Data mining for blood glucose prediction and knowledge discovery in diabetic patients: The METABO diabetes modeling and management system. In: Annual International Conference of the IEEE Engineering in Medicine and Biology Society (2009)
5. Villarreal, V., Hervás, R., Fdez, A.D., Bravo, J.: Applying ontologies in the development of patient mobile monitoring framework. In: 2nd International Conference on e-Health and Bioengineering - EHB 2009, IEEE, Constata (2009)
6. Villarreal, V., Laguna, J., López, S., Fontecha, J., Fuentes, C., Hervás, R., de Ipiña, D.L., Bravo, J.: A Proposal for Mobile Diabetes Self-control: Towards a Patient Monitoring Framework. In: Omatu, S., Rocha, M.P., Bravo, J., Fernández, F., Corchado, E., Bustillo, A., Corchado, J.M. (eds.) IWANN 2009, Part II. LNCS, vol. 5518, pp. 870–877. Springer, Heidelberg (2009)
7. Villarreal, V., et al.: Diabetes Patients' Care based on Mobile Monitoring. In: IADIS International Conference, Applied Computing 2009, Rome, Italy (2009)

Author Index